Praise for the Reformation Commentary on Scripture

"Protestant reformers were fundamentally exegetes as much as theologians, yet (except for figures like Luther and Calvin) their commentaries and sermons have been neglected because these writings are not available in modern editions or languages. That makes this new series of Reformation Commentary on Scripture most welcome as a way to provide access to some of the wealth of biblical exposition of the sixteenth and seventeenth centuries. The editor's introduction explains the nature of the sources and the selection process; the intended audience of modern pastors and students of the Bible has led to a focus on theological and practical comments. Although it will be of use to students of the Reformation, this series is far from being an esoteric study of largely forgotten voices; this collection of reforming comments, comprehending every verse and provided with topical headings, will serve contemporary pastors and preachers very well."

Elsie Anne McKee, *Archibald Alexander Professor of Reformation Studies and the History of Worship, Princeton Theological Seminary*

"This series provides an excellent introduction to the history of biblical exegesis in the Reformation period. The introductions are accurate, clear and informative, and the passages intelligently chosen to give the reader a good idea of methods deployed and issues at stake. It puts precritical exegesis in its context and so presents it in its correct light. Highly recommended as reference book, course book and general reading for students and all interested lay and clerical readers."

Irena Backus, *Professeure Ordinaire, Institut d'histoire de la Réformation, Université de Genève*

"The Reformation Commentary on Scripture is a major publishing event—for those with historical interest in the founding convictions of Protestantism, but even more for those who care about understanding the Bible. As with IVP Academic's earlier Ancient Christian Commentary on Scripture, this effort brings flesh and blood to 'the communion of saints' by letting believers of our day look over the shoulders of giants from the past. By connecting the past with the present, and by doing so with the Bible at the center, the editors of this series perform a great service for the church. The series deserves the widest possible support."

Mark A. Noll, *Francis A. McAnaney Professor of History, University of Notre Dame*

"For those who preach and teach Scripture in the church, the Reformation Commentary on Scripture is a significant publishing event. Pastors and other church leaders will find delightful surprises, challenging enigmas and edifying insights in this series, as many Reformational voices are newly translated into English. The lively conversation in these pages can ignite today's pastoral imagination for fresh and faithful expositions of Scripture."

J. Todd Billings, *Gordon H. Girod Research Professor of Reformed Theology, Western Theological Seminary*

"The reformers discerned rightly what the church desperately needed in the sixteenth century—the bold proclamation of the Word based on careful study of the sacred Scriptures. We need not only to hear that same call again for our own day but also to learn from the Reformation how to do it. This commentary series is a godsend!"

Richard J. Mouw, *President Emeritus, Fuller Theological Seminary*

"Like the Ancient Christian Commentary on Scripture, the Reformation Commentary on Scripture does a masterful job of offering excellent selections from well-known and not-so-well-known exegetes. The editor's introductory survey is, by itself, worth the price of the book. It is easy to forget that there were more hands, hearts and minds involved in the Reformation than Luther and Calvin. Furthermore, encounters even with these figures are often limited to familiar quotes on familiar topics. However, the Reformation Commentary helps us to recognize the breadth and depth of exegetical interests and skill that fueled and continue to fuel faithful meditation on God's Word. I heartily recommend this series as a tremendous resource not only for ministry but for personal edification."

Michael S. Horton, *J. G. Machen Professor of Systematic Theology and Apologetics,*
Westminster Seminary, California

"The Reformation was ignited by a fresh reading of Scripture. In this series of commentaries, we contemporary interpreters are allowed to feel some of the excitement, surprise and wonder of our spiritual forebears. Luther, Calvin and their fellow revolutionaries were masterful interpreters of the Word. Now, in this remarkable series, some of our very best Reformation scholars open up the riches of the Reformation's reading of the Scripture."

William H. Willimon, *Professor of the Practice of Christian Ministry, Duke Divinity School*

"The Reformation Scripture principle set the entirety of Christian life and thought under the governance of the divine Word, and pressed the church to renew its exegetical labors. This series promises to place before the contemporary church the fruit of those labors, and so to exemplify life under the Word."

John Webster, *Professor of Divinity, University of St. Andrews*[†]

"Since Gerhard Ebeling's pioneering work on Luther's exegesis seventy years ago, the history of biblical interpretation has occupied many Reformation scholars and become a vital part of study of the period. The Reformation Commentary on Scripture provides fresh materials for students of Reformation-era biblical interpretation and for twenty-first-century preachers to mine the rich stores of insights from leading reformers of the sixteenth century into both the text of Scripture itself and its application in sixteenth-century contexts. This series will strengthen our understanding of the period of the Reformation and enable us to apply its insights to our own days and its challenges to the church."

Robert Kolb, *Professor Emeritus, Concordia Theological Seminary*

"The multivolume Ancient Christian Commentary on Scripture is a valuable resource for those who wish to know how the Fathers interpreted a passage of Scripture but who lack the time or the opportunity to search through the many individual works. This new Reformation Commentary on Scripture will do the same for the reformers and is to be warmly welcomed. It will provide much easier access to the exegetical treasures of the Reformation and will hopefully encourage readers to go back to some of the original works themselves."

Anthony N. S. Lane, *Professor of Historical Theology and Director of Research, London School of Theology*

"This volume of the RCS project is an invaluable source for pastors and the historically/biblically interested that provides unparalleled access not only to commentaries of the leading Protestant reformers but also to a host of nowadays unknown commentaters on Galatians and Ephesians. The RCS is sure to enhance and enliven contemporary exegesis. With its wide scope, the collection will enrich our understanding of the variety of Reformation thought and biblical exegesis."

Sigrun Haude, *Associate Professor of Reformation and Early Modern European History, University of Cincinnati*

"The Reformation Commentary on Scripture series promises to be an 'open sesame' to the biblical exegesis, exposition and application of the Bible that was the hallmark of the Reformation. While comparisons can be odious, the difference between Reformation commentary and exposition and much that both preceded and followed it is laid bare in these pages: whereas others write about the Bible from the outside, Reformation exposition carries with it the atmosphere of men who spoke and wrote from inside the Bible, experiencing the power of biblical teaching even as they expounded it. . . . This grand project sets before scholars, pastors, teachers, students and growing Christians an experience that can only be likened to stumbling into a group Bible study only to discover that your fellow participants include some of the most significant Christians of the Reformation and post-Reformation (for that matter, of any) era. Here the Word of God is explained in a variety of accents: German, Swiss, French, Dutch, English, Scottish and more. Each one vibrates with a thrilling sense of the living nature of God's Word and its power to transform individuals, churches and even whole communities. Here is a series to anticipate, enjoy and treasure."

Sinclair Ferguson, *Senior Minister, First Presbyterian Church, Columbia, South Carolina*

"I strongly endorse the Reformation Commentary on Scripture. Introducing how the Bible was interpreted during the age of the Reformation, these volumes will not only renew contemporary preaching, but they will also help us understand more fully how reading and meditating on Scripture can, in fact, change our lives!"

Lois Malcolm, *Associate Professor of Systematic Theology, Luther Seminary*

"Discerning the true significance of movements in theology requires acquaintance with their biblical exegesis. This is supremely so with the Reformation, which was essentially a biblical revival. The Reformation Commentary on Scripture will fill a yawning gap, just as the Ancient Christian Commentary did before it, and the first volume gets the series off to a fine start, whetting the appetite for more. Most heartily do I welcome and commend this long overdue project."

J. I. Packer, *Retired Board of Governors Professor of Theology, Regent College*

"There is no telling the benefits to emerge from the publication of this magnificent Reformation Commentary on Scripture series! Now exegetical and theological treasures from Reformation era commentators will be at our fingertips, providing new insights from old sources to give light for the present and future. This series is a gift to scholars and to the church; a wonderful resource to enhance our study of the written Word of God for generations to come!"

Donald K. McKim, *Executive Editor of Theology and Reference, Westminster John Knox Press*

"Why was this not done before? The publication of the Reformation Commentary on Scripture should be greeted with enthusiasm by every believing Christian—but especially by those who will preach and teach the Word of God. This commentary series brings the very best of the Reformation heritage to the task of exegesis and exposition, and each volume in this series represents a veritable feast that takes us back to the sixteenth century to enrich the preaching and teaching of God's Word in our own time."

R. Albert Mohler Jr., *President, The Southern Baptist Theological Seminary*

"Today more than ever, the Christian past is the church's future. InterVarsity Press has already brought the voice of the ancients to our ears. Now, in the Reformation Commentary on Scripture, we hear a timely word from the first Protestants as well."

Bryan Litfin, *Professor of Theology, Moody Bible Institute*

"I am delighted to see the Reformation Commentary on Scripture. The editors of this series have done us all a service by gleaning from these rich fields of biblical reflection. May God use this new life for these old words to give him glory and to build his church."

Mark Dever, *Senior Pastor, Capitol Hill Baptist Church, and President of 9Marks.org Ministries*

"Monumental and magisterial, the Reformation Commentary on Scripture, edited by Timothy George, is a remarkably bold and visionary undertaking. Bringing together a wealth of resources, these volumes will provide historians, theologians, biblical scholars, pastors and students with a fresh look at the exegetical insights of those who shaped and influenced the sixteenth-century Reformation. With this marvelous publication, InterVarsity Press has reached yet another plateau of excellence. We pray that this superb series will be used of God to strengthen both church and academy."

David S. Dockery, *President, Trinity International University*

"Detached from her roots, the church cannot reach the world as God intends. While every generation must steward the scriptural insights God grants it, only arrogance or ignorance causes leaders to ignore the contributions of those faithful leaders before us. The Reformation Commentary on Scripture roots our thought in great insights of faithful leaders of the Reformation to further biblical preaching and teaching in this generation."

Bryan Chapell, *Chancellor and Professor of Practical Theology, Covenant Theological Seminary*

"After reading several volumes of the Reformation Commentary on Scripture, I exclaimed, 'Hey, this is just what the doctor ordered—I mean Doctor Martinus Lutherus!' The church of today bearing his name needs a strong dose of the medicine this doctor prescribed for the ailing church of the sixteenth century. The reforming fire of Christ-centered preaching that Luther ignited is the only hope to reclaim the impact of the gospel to keep the Reformation going, not for its own sake but to further the renewal of the worldwide church of Christ today. This series of commentaries will equip preachers to step into their pulpits with confidence in the same living Word that inspired the witness of Luther and Calvin and many other lesser-known Reformers."

Carl E. Braaten, *Cofounder of the Center for Catholic and Evangelical Theology*

REFORMATION COMMENTARY ON SCRIPTURE

NEW TESTAMENT
VIII

ROMANS 9–16

EDITED BY
PHILIP D. W. KREY AND PETER D. S. KREY

GENERAL EDITOR
TIMOTHY GEORGE

ASSOCIATE GENERAL EDITOR
SCOTT M. MANETSCH

IVP Academic
An imprint of InterVarsity Press
Downers Grove, Illinois

InterVarsity Press
P.O. Box 1400, Downers Grove, IL 60515-1426
www.ivpress.com
email@ivpress.com

InterVarsity Press® is the book-publishing division of InterVarsity Christian Fellowship/USA®, a movement of students and faculty active on campus at hundreds of universities, colleges and schools of nursing in the United States of America, and a member movement of the International Fellowship of Evangelical Students. For information about local and regional activities, visit intervarsity.org.

Excerpts from John Calvin, Institutes of the Christian Religion (1559), *edited by John T. McNeill, translated by Ford Lewis Battles, Library of Christian Classics 20-21, are ©Westminster Press, Philadelphia, 1960. Used by permission.*

Excerpts from Desiderius Erasmus, Annotations on Romans, *edited by Robert D. Sider, translated by John B. Payne et al., CWE 56, are ©University of Toronto Press, Toronto, 1994. Reprinted with permission of the publisher.*

Excerpts from Desiderius Erasmus, Paraphrases on Romans and Galatians, *edited by Robert D. Sider, translated by John B. Payne, Albert Rabil Jr., and Warren S. Smith Jr., CWE 42, are ©University of Toronto Press, Toronto, 1984. Reprinted with permission of the publisher.*

Excerpts from Desiderius Erasmus and Martin Luther, Luther and Erasmus: Free Will and Salvation, *edited and translated by Gordon E. Rupp and Philip S. Watson, Library of Christian Classics 17, are ©Westminster Press, Philadelphia, 1969. Used by permission.*

Excerpts from Balthasar Hubmaier: Theologian of Anabaptism, *translated and edited by H. W. Pipkin and J. H. Yoder, are ©1989 Herald Press, Scottdale, PA 15683. Used with permission.*

Excerpts from Philipp Melanchthon, Commentary on Romans, *translated by Fred Kramer, are ©Concordia Publishing House, St. Louis, 1992. Used by permission. All rights reserved.*

Excerpts from The Writings of Dirk Philips, 1504–1568, *trans. and ed. C. J. Dyck, W. E. Keeney, and A. J. Beachy, are ©1992 Herald Press, Scottdale, PA 15683. Used with permission.*

Design: Cindy Kiple
Images: Wooden cross: iStockphoto
The Protestant Church in Lyon: The Protestant Church in Lyon, called "The Paradise" at Bibliotheque Publique et Universitaire, Geneva, Switzerland, Erich Lessing/Art Resource, NY.

ISBN 978-0-8308-2971-2 (print)
ISBN 978-0-8308-9912-8 (digital)

Printed in the United States of America ∞

Library of Congress Cataloging-in-Publication Data

A catalog record for this book is available from the Library of Congress.

P	26	25	24	23	22	21	20	19	18	17	16	15	14	13	12	11	10	9	8	7	6	5	4	3	2	1
Y	39	38	37	36	35	34	33	32	31	30	29	28	27	26	25	24	23	22	21	20	19	18	17	16		

Dedicated to our father, the Rev. Rudolf E. M. Krey

Reformation Commentary on Scripture
Project Staff

Project Editor
David W. McNutt

---

*Managing Editor and
Production Manager*
Benjamin M. McCoy

Copyeditor
Jeffrey A. Reimer

Assistant Project Editors
Andre A. Gazal
Todd R. Hains

Editorial and Research Assistants
David J. Hooper
Ethan McCarthy

Assistants to the General Editors
Le-Ann Little
Jason Odom

Design
Cindy Kiple

Design Assistant
Beth McGill

Content Production
Richard M. Chung
Maureen G. Tobey
Daniel van Loon
Jeanna L. Wiggins

Proofreader
Travis Ables

Print Coordinator
Jim Erhart

InterVarsity Press

Publisher
Jeff Crosby

Associate Publisher, Director of Editorial
Cindy Bunch

Associate Publisher, Director of IVP Academic
Daniel G. Reid

CONTENTS

ACKNOWLEDGMENTS

The apostle Paul wrote, "What do you have that you did not receive?" (1 Cor 4:7). And again: "For whatever was written in former days was written for our instruction, so that by steadfastness and by the encouragement of the Scriptures we might have hope" (Rom 15:4). We owe a debt of thanks to the insights of the host of Reformation commentators whose works have been included in this volume. As we are only partly responsible for this book, we wish to thank many people, beginning with the general editors of the Reformation Commentary on Scripture project, Timothy George and Scott M. Manetsch, for their confidence in us.

We owe special thanks to our project editor, David McNutt, and the assistant project editors, Todd Hains and Andre Gazal, whose attention and determination have helped to shape this volume. Since this has been a long project, we would also like to thank Mike Gibson and Brannon Ellis, who served as project editors along the way.

In addition, we would like to thank other editorial staff and assistants on this project, including David Hooper and Ethan McCarthy, as well as James Kellerman and Caroline Kelly, who helped us with translation.

We thank God for the patience and support of our spouses Nora and René, who allowed us to bring all our books and often camp in each other's homes as we traveled from Oakland to Philadelphia to work on the volume together.

Finally, we wish to dedicate this book to our father, the Rev. Rudolf E. M. Krey, who had the vision and determination to teach us Greek, Hebrew and German while we were young and teachable. He insisted that we learn Latin and other foreign languages in school and with our mother, Gertrude E. Krey, he took his responsibilities to teach us the Scriptures and the catechism faithfully.

"May the God of steadfastness and encouragement grant you to live in harmony with one another, in accordance with Christ Jesus, so that together you may with one voice glorify the God and Father of our Lord Jesus Christ" (Rom 15:5-6).

Philip D. W. Krey
Peter D. S. Krey
The Festival of Pentecost 2016

ABBREVIATIONS

ANF   The Ante-Nicene Fathers. 10 vols. Edited by Alexander Roberts and James Donaldson. Buffalo, NY: Christian Literature, 1885–1896. Available online at www.ccel.org.

ACCS   Ancient Christian Commentary on Scripture. 29 vols. Edited by Thomas C. Oden. Downers Grove, IL: InterVarsity Press, 1998–2009.

BoC   *The Book of Concord: The Confessions of the Evangelical Lutheran Church.* Edited by Robert Kolb and Timothy J. Wengert. Translated by Charles Arand et al. Minneapolis: Fortress, 2000.

BNP   *Brill's New Pauly: Encyclopedia of the Ancient World.* Edited by Hubert Cancik and Helmuth Schneider. 20 vols. Leiden: Brill, 2002–2011.

BRN   Bibliotheca Reformatoria Neederlandica. 10 vols. Edited by S. Cramer and F. Pijper. The Hague: Martinus Nijhoff, 1903–1914. Digital copy online at babel.hathitrust.org.

BSLK   *Die Bekenntnisschriften der evangelisch-lutherischen Kirche.* 12th ed. Göttingen: Vandenhoeck & Ruprecht, 1998.

CHB   *Cambridge History of the Bible.* 3 vols. Cambridge: Cambridge University Press, 1963–1970.

CNTC   *Calvin's New Testament Commentaries.* 12 vols. Edited by D. W. Torrance and T. F. Torrance. Grand Rapids: Eerdmans, 1959–1972.

CO   *Ioannis Calvini Opera quae supersunt omnia.* 59 vols. Corpus Reformatorum 29–88. Edited by G. Baum, E. Cunitz and E. Reuss. Brunswick and Berlin: C. A. Schwetschke, 1863–1900. Digital copy online at archive-ouverte.unige.ch/Calvin.

Creeds   Philip Schaff. *The Creeds of Christendom: With a Critical History and Notes.* 3 vols. New York: Harper & Row, 1877. Reprint, Grand Rapids: Baker Books, 1977.

CRR   Classics of the Radical Reformation. 12 vols. Waterloo, ON, and Scottdale, PA: Herald Press, 1973–2010.

CTS   Calvin Translation Society edition of Calvin's commentaries. 46 vols. Edinburgh, 1843–1855. Several reprints, but variously bound; volume numbers (when cited) are relative to specific commentaries and not to the entire set.

CWE   *Collected Works of Erasmus.* 86 vols. planned. Toronto: University of Toronto Press, 1969–.

DMBI   *Dictionary of Major Biblical Interpreters.* Edited by Donald K. McKim. Downers Grove, IL: IVP Academic, 2007.

DNB	*Dictionary of National Biography*. Edited by Leslie Stephen and Sidney Lee. 63 vols. London: Smith, Elder, 1885–1900. Digital copy online at en.wikisource.org.
E²	*Dr. Martin Luther's sämmtliche Werke*. 2nd ed. 26 vols. Frankfurt and Erlangen: Heyder & Zimmer, 1862–1885. Digital copies online at babel.hathitrust.org.
EEBO	Early English Books Online. Subscription database, eebo.chadwyck.com.
FC	Fathers of the Church: A New Translation. Washington, DC: Catholic University of America Press, 1947–.
LB	*Desiderii Erasmi Roterodami Opera Omnia*. 10 vols. Edited by Jean LeClerc. Leiden: Van der Aa, 1704–1706. Reprint, Hildesheim: Georg Olms, 1961–1962. Digital copy online at babel.hathitrust.org.
LCC	Library of Christian Classics. 26 vols. Edited by John Baillie et al. Philadelphia: Westminster, 1953–1966.
LCL	Loeb Classical Library. Edited by Jeffrey Henderson. Cambridge, MA: Harvard University Press, 1911–. Digital copy online at www.loebclassics.com.
LW	*Luther's Works [American Edition]*. 82 vols. planned. St. Louis: Concordia; Philadelphia: Fortress, 1955–1986; 2009–.
MO	*Philippi Melanthonis Opera quae supersunt omnia*. 28 vols. Corpus Reformatorum 1–28. Edited by C. G. Bretschneider. Halle: C. A. Schwetschke, 1834–1860. Digital copy online at archive.org and books.google.com
NDB	*Neue Deutsche Biographie*. 28 vols. projected. Berlin: Duncker & Humblot, 1953–.
NPNF	A Select Library of the Nicene and Post-Nicene Fathers of the Christian Church. 28 vols. in two series, denoted as NPNF and NPNF². Edited by Philip Schaff et al. Buffalo, NY: Christian Literature, 1887–1894. Several reprints; also available online at www.ccel.org.
OER	*Oxford Encyclopedia of the Reformation*. 4 vols. Edited by Hans J. Hillerbrand. New York: Oxford University Press, 1996.
PG	Patrologia cursus completus. Series Graeca. 161 vols. Edited by J.-P. Migne. Paris: Migne, 1857–1866. Digital copies online at books.google.com.
PL	Patrologia cursus completus. Series Latina. 221 vols. Edited by J.-P. Migne. Paris: Migne, 1844–1864. Digital copies online at books.google.com.
QGT	Quellen zur Geschichte der Täufer. 18 vols. Leipzig: M. Heinsius; Gütersloh: Gerd Mohn, 1930–. The first two volumes are under the series title Quellen zur Geschichte der Wiedertäufer.
RCS	Reformation Commentary on Scripture. 28 vols. projected. Edited by Timothy George and Scott M. Manetsch. Downers Grove, IL: IVP Academic, 2011–.
r, v	Some early books are numbered not by page but by folio (leaf). Front and back sides (pages) of a numbered folio are indicated by *recto* (r) and *verso* (v), respectively.
SCal	*Supplementa Calviniana: Sermon inédits*. 11 vols. planned. Neukirchen-Vluyn: Neukirchener Verlag; Geneva: Droz, 1961–.

WA   *D. Martin Luthers Werke, Kritische Gesamtausgabe: [Schriften].* 73 vols. Weimar: Hermann Böhlaus Nachfolger, 1883–2009. Digital copy online at archive.org.

WABr   *D. Martin Luthers Werke, Kritische Gesamtausgabe: Briefwechsel.* 18 vols. Weimar: Hermann Böhlaus Nachfolger, 1930–1983. Digital copy online at archive.org.

WADB   *D. Martin Luthers Werke, Kritische Gesamtausgabe: Deutsche Bibel.* 12 vols. Weimar: Böhlaus Nachfolger, 1906–1961. Digital copy online at archive.org

WATR   *D. Martin Luthers Werke, Kritische Gesamtausgabe: Tischreden.* 6 vols. Weimar: Hermann Böhlaus Nachfolger, 1912–1921. Digital copy online at archive.org.

ZSW   *Huldreich Zwinglis Sämtliche Werke.* 14 vols. Corpus Reformatorum 88–101. Edited by E. Egli et al. Berlin: C. A. Schwetschke, 1905–1959. Reprint, Zürich: Theologischer Verlag Zürich, 1983. Digital copy online at www.irg.uzh.ch.

BIBLE TRANSLATIONS

BCP   Book of Common Prayer (1979)

CEB   Common English Bible

ESV   English Standard Version

KJV   King James Version

LXX   Septuagint

NASB   New American Standard Bible

NIV   New International Version

NKJV   New King James Version

NRSV   New Revised Standard Version

Vg   Vulgate

A GUIDE TO USING THIS COMMENTARY

Several features have been incorporated into the design of this commentary. The following comments are intended to assist readers in making full use of this volume.

Pericopes of Scripture

The scriptural text has been divided into pericopes, or passages, usually several verses in length. Each of these pericopes is given a heading, which appears at the beginning of the pericope. For example, the first pericope in this commentary is Romans 9:1-5 "Paul Anguishes over His Own People." This heading is followed by the Scripture passage quoted in the English Standard Version (ESV). The Scripture passage is provided for the convenience of readers, but it is also in keeping with Reformation-era commentaries, which often followed the patristic and medieval commentary tradition, in which the citations of the reformers were arranged according to the text of Scripture.

Overviews

Following each pericope of text is an overview of the Reformation authors' comments on that pericope. The format of this overview varies among the volumes of this series, depending on the requirements of the specific book(s) of Scripture. The function of the overview is to identify succinctly the key exegetical, theological and pastoral concerns of the Reformation writers arising from the pericope, providing the reader with an orientation to Reformation-era approaches and emphases. It tracks a reasonably cohesive thread of argument among reformers' comments, even though they are derived from diverse sources and generations. Thus, the summaries do not proceed chronologically or by verse sequence. Rather, they seek to rehearse the overall course of the reformers' comments on that pericope.

We do not assume that the commentators themselves anticipated or expressed a formally received cohesive argument but rather that the various arguments tend to flow in a plausible, recognizable pattern. Modern readers can thus glimpse aspects of continuity in the flow of diverse exegetical traditions representing various generations and geographical locations.

Topical Headings

An abundance of varied Reformation-era comment is available for each pericope. For this reason we have broken the pericopes into two levels. First is the verse with its topical heading. The reformers' comments are then focused on aspects of each verse, with topical headings summarizing the essence of the individual comment by evoking a key phrase, metaphor or idea. This feature provides a bridge by which modern readers can enter into the heart of the Reformation-era comment.

Identifying the Reformation Authors, Texts and Events

Following the topical heading of each section of comment, the name of the Reformation commentator is given. An English translation (where needed) of the reformer's comment is then provided. This is immediately followed by the title of the original work rendered in English.

Readers who wish to pursue a deeper investigation of the reformers' works cited in this commentary will find full bibliographic detail for each Reformation title provided in the bibliography at the back of the volume. Information on English translations (where available) and standard original-language editions and critical editions of the works cited is found in the bibliography. The Biographical Sketches section provides brief overviews of the life and work of each commentator, and each confession or collaborative work, appearing in the present volume (as well as in any previous volumes). Finally, a Timeline of the Reformation offers broader context for people, places and events relevant to the commentators and their works.

Footnotes and Back Matter

To aid the reader in exploring the background and texts in further detail, this commentary utilizes footnotes. The use and content of footnotes may vary among the volumes in this series. Where footnotes appear, a footnote number directs the reader to a note at the bottom of the page, where one will find annotations (clarifications or biblical cross references), information on English translations (where available) or standard original-language editions of the work cited.

Where original-language texts have remained untranslated into English, we provide new translations. Where there is any serious ambiguity or textual problem in the selection, we have tried to reflect the best available textual tradition. Wherever current English translations are already well rendered, they are utilized, but where necessary they are stylistically updated. A single asterisk (*) indicates that a previous English translation has been updated to modern English or amended for easier reading. We have standardized spellings and made grammatical variables uniform so that our English references will not reflect the linguistic oddities of the older English translations. For ease of reading we have in some cases removed superfluous conjunctions.

GENERAL INTRODUCTION

The Reformation Commentary on Scripture (RCS) is a twenty-eight-volume series of exegetical comment covering the entire Bible and gathered from the writings of sixteenth-century preachers, scholars and reformers. The RCS is intended as a sequel to the highly acclaimed Ancient Christian Commentary on Scripture (ACCS), and as such its overall concept, method, format and audience are similar to the earlier series. Both series are committed to the renewal of the church through careful study and meditative reflection on the Old and New Testaments, the charter documents of Christianity, read in the context of the worshiping, believing community of faith across the centuries. However, the patristic and Reformation eras are separated by nearly a millennium, and the challenges of reading Scripture with the reformers require special attention to their context, resources and assumptions. The purpose of this general introduction is to present an overview of the context and process of biblical interpretation in the age of the Reformation.

Goals

The Reformation Commentary on Scripture seeks to introduce its readers to the depth and richness of exegetical ferment that defined the Reformation era. The RCS has four goals: the enrichment of contemporary biblical interpretation through exposure to Reformation-era biblical exegesis; the renewal of contemporary preaching through exposure to the biblical insights of the Reformation writers; a deeper understanding of the Reformation itself and the breadth of perspectives represented within it; and a recovery of the profound integration of the life of faith and the life of the mind that should characterize Christian scholarship. Each of these goals requires a brief comment.

Renewing contemporary biblical interpretation. During the past half-century, biblical hermeneutics has become a major growth industry in the academic world. One of the consequences of the historical-critical hegemony of biblical studies has been the privileging of contemporary philosophies and ideologies at the expense of a commitment to the Christian church as the primary reading community within which and for which biblical exegesis is done. Reading Scripture with the church fathers and the reformers is a corrective to all such imperialism of the present. One of the greatest skills required for a fruitful interpretation of the Bible is the ability to listen. We rightly emphasize the importance of listening to the voices of contextual theologies today, but in doing so we often marginalize or ignore another crucial context—the community of believing Christians through the centuries. The serious study of Scripture requires more than the latest

Bible translation in one hand and the latest commentary (or niche study Bible) in the other. John L. Thompson has called on Christians today to practice the art of "reading the Bible with the dead."[1] The RCS presents carefully selected comments from the extant commentaries of the Reformation as an encouragement to more in-depth study of this important epoch in the history of biblical interpretation.

Strengthening contemporary preaching. The Protestant reformers identified the public preaching of the Word of God as an indispensible means of grace and a sure sign of the true church. Through the words of the preacher, the living voice of the gospel (*viva vox evangelii*) is heard. Luther famously said that the church is not a "pen house" but a "mouth house."[2] The Reformation in Switzerland began when Huldrych Zwingli entered the pulpit of the Grossmünster in Zurich on January 1, 1519, and began to preach a series of expositional sermons chapter by chapter from the Gospel of Matthew. In the following years he extended this homiletical approach to other books of the Old and New Testaments. Calvin followed a similar pattern in Geneva. Many of the commentaries represented in this series were either originally presented as sermons or were written to support the regular preaching ministry of local church pastors. Luther said that the preacher should be a *bonus textualis*—a good one with a text—well-versed in the Scriptures. Preachers in the Reformation traditions preached not only about the Bible but also from it, and this required more than a passing acquaintance with its contents. Those who have been charged with the office of preaching in the church today can find wisdom and insight—and fresh perspectives—in the sermons of the Reformation and the biblical commentaries read and studied by preachers of the sixteenth century.

Deepening understanding of the Reformation. Some scholars of the sixteenth century prefer to speak of the period they study in the plural, the European Reformations, to indicate that many diverse impulses for reform were at work in this turbulent age of transition from medieval to modern times.[3] While this point is well taken, the RCS follows the time-honored tradition of using *Reformation* in the singular form to indicate not only a major moment in the history of Christianity in the West but also, as Hans J. Hillerbrand has put it, "an essential cohesiveness in the heterogeneous pursuits of religious reform in the sixteenth century."[4] At the same time, in developing guidelines to assist the volume editors in making judicious selections from the vast amount of commentary material available in this period, we have stressed the multifaceted character of the Reformation across many confessions, theological orientations and political settings.

Advancing Christian scholarship. By assembling and disseminating numerous voices from such a signal period as the Reformation, the RCS aims to make a significant contribution to the ever-growing stream of Christian scholarship. The post-Enlightenment split between the study of the Bible as an academic discipline and the reading of the Bible as spiritual nurture was foreign

---

[1]John L. Thompson, *Reading the Bible with the Dead* (Grand Rapids: Eerdmans, 2007).
[2]WA 10,2:48.
[3]See Carter Lindberg, *The European Reformations*, 2nd ed. (Malden, MA: Wiley-Blackwell, 2010).
[4]Hans J. Hillerbrand, *The Division of Christendom* (Louisville, KY: Westminster John Knox, 2007), x. Hillerbrand has also edited the standard reference work in Reformation studies, OER. See also Diarmaid MacCulloch, *The Reformation* (New York: Viking, 2003), and Patrick Collinson, *The Reformation: A History* (New York: Random House, 2004).

to the reformers. For them the study of the Bible was transformative at the most basic level of the human person: *coram deo.*

The reformers all repudiated the idea that the Bible could be studied and understood with dispassionate objectivity, as a cold artifact from antiquity. Luther's famous Reformation break-through triggered by his laborious study of the Psalms and Paul's letter to the Romans is well known, but the experience of Cambridge scholar Thomas Bilney was perhaps more typical. When Erasmus's critical edition of the Greek New Testament was published in 1516, it was accompanied by a new translation in elegant Latin. Attracted by the classical beauty of Erasmus's Latin, Bilney came across this statement in 1 Timothy 1:15: "Christ Jesus came into the world to save sinners." In the Greek this sentence is described as *pistos ho logos*, which the Vulgate had rendered *fidelis sermo*, "a faithful saying." Erasmus chose a different word for the Greek *pistos*—*certus*, "sure, certain." When Bilney grasped the meaning of this word applied to the announcement of salvation in Christ, he tells us that "immediately, I felt a marvellous comfort and quietness, insomuch as 'my bruised bones leaped for joy.'"[5]

Luther described the way the Bible was meant to function in the minds and hearts of believers when he reproached himself and others for studying the nativity narrative with such cool unconcern:

> I hate myself because when I see Christ laid in the manger or in the lap of his mother and hear the angels sing, my heart does not leap into flame. With what good reason should we all despise our-selves that we remain so cold when this word is spoken to us, over which everyone should dance and leap and burn for joy! We act as though it were a frigid historical fact that does not smite our hearts, as if someone were merely relating that the sultan has a crown of gold.[6]

It was a core conviction of the Reformation that the careful study and meditative listening to the Scriptures, what the monks called *lectio divina*, could yield transformative results for *all* of life. The value of such a rich commentary, therefore, lies not only in the impressive volume of Reformation-era voices that are presented throughout the course of the series but in the many particular fields for which their respective lives and ministries are relevant. The Reformation is consequential for historical studies, both church as well as secular history. Biblical and theological studies, to say nothing of pastoral and spiritual studies, also stand to benefit and progress immensely from re-newed engagement today, as mediated through the RCS, with the reformers of yesteryear.

Perspectives

In setting forth the perspectives and parameters of the RCS, the following considerations have proved helpful.

Chronology. When did the Reformation begin, and how long did it last? In some traditional accounts, the answer was clear: the Reformation began with the posting of Luther's Ninety-five

---

[5]John Foxe, *The Acts and Monuments of John Foxe: A New and Complete Edition*, 8 vols., ed. Stephen Reed Cattley (London: R. B. Seeley & W. Burnside, 1837), 4:635; quoting Ps 51:8; cited in A. G. Dickens, *The English Reformation*, 2nd ed. (University Park, PA: The Pennsylvannia State University Press, 1991), 102.
[6]WA 49:176-77, quoted in Roland Bainton, "The Bible in the Reformation," in *CHB*, 3:23.

Theses at Wittenberg in 1517 and ended with the death of Calvin in Geneva in 1564. Apart from reducing the Reformation to a largely German event with a side trip to Switzerland, this perspective fails to do justice to the important events that led up to Luther's break with Rome and its many reverberations throughout Europe and beyond. In choosing commentary selections for the RCS, we have adopted the concept of the long sixteenth century, say, from the late 1400s to the mid-seventeenth century. Thus we have included commentary selections from early or pre-Reformation writers such as John Colet and Jacques Lefèvre d'Étaples to seventeenth-century figures such as Henry Ainsworth and Johann Gerhard.

Confession. The RCS concentrates primarily, though not exclusively, on the exegetical writings of the Protestant reformers. While the ACCS provided a compendium of key consensual exegetes of the early Christian centuries, the Catholic/Protestant confessional divide in the sixteenth century tested the very idea of consensus, especially with reference to ecclesiology and soteriology. While many able and worthy exegetes faithful to the Roman Catholic Church were active during this period, this project has chosen to include primarily those figures that represent perspectives within the Protestant Reformation. For this reason we have not included comments on the apocryphal or deuterocanonical writings.

We recognize that "Protestant" and "Catholic" as contradistinctive labels are anachronistic terms for the early decades of the sixteenth century before the hardening of confessional identities surrounding the Council of Trent (1545–1563). Protestant figures such as Philipp Melanchthon, Johannes Oecolampadius and John Calvin were all products of the revival of sacred letters known as biblical humanism. They shared an approach to biblical interpretation that owed much to Desiderius Erasmus and other scholars who remained loyal to the Church of Rome. Careful comparative studies of Protestant and Catholic exegesis in the sixteenth century have shown surprising areas of agreement when the focus was the study of a particular biblical text rather than the standard confessional debates.

At the same time, exegetical differences among the various Protestant groups could become strident and church-dividing. The most famous example of this is the interpretive impasse between Luther and Zwingli over the meaning of "This is my body" (Mt 26:26) in the words of institution. Their disagreement at the Colloquy of Marburg in 1529 had important christological and pastoral implications, as well as social and political consequences. Luther refused fellowship with Zwingli and his party at the end of the colloquy; in no small measure this bitter division led to the separate trajectories pursued by Lutheran and Reformed Protestantism to this day. In Elizabethan England, Puritans and Anglicans agreed that "Holy Scripture containeth all things necessary to salvation: so that whatsoever is not read therein, nor may be proved thereby, is not to be required of any man" (article 6 of the Thirty-Nine Articles of Religion), yet on the basis of their differing interpretations of the Bible they fought bitterly over the structures of the church, the clothing of the clergy and the ways of worship. On the matter of infant baptism, Catholics and Protestants alike agreed on its propriety, though there were various theories as to how a practice not mentioned in the Bible could be justified biblically. The Anabaptists were outliers on this subject. They rejected infant baptism altogether. They appealed to the example of the baptism of Jesus and to his final words as recorded in the Gospel of Matthew (Mt 28:19-20): "Go therefore, and make disciples of all nations, baptizing them in the name of the Father, and of the Son, and of the Holy Spirit, teaching them to observe all that I have commanded you." New Testament Christians, they argued, are to follow not only the commands of Jesus in the Great Commission, but also the exact order in which they were given: evangelize, baptize, catechize.

These and many other differences of interpretation among the various Protestant groups are reflected in their many sermons, commentaries and public disputations. In the RCS, the volume editors' introduction to each volume is intended to help the reader understand the nature and significance of doctrinal conversations and disputes that resulted in particular, and frequently clashing, interpretations. Footnotes throughout the text will be provided to explain obscure references, unusual expressions and other matters that require special comment. Volume editors have chosen comments on the Bible across a wide range of sixteenth-century confessions and schools of interpretation: biblical humanists, Lutheran, Reformed, Anglican, Puritan and Anabaptist. We have not pursued passages from post-Tridentine Catholic authors or from radical spiritualists and antitrinitarian writers, though sufficient material is available from these sources to justify another series.

Format. The design of the RCS is intended to offer reader-friendly access to these classic texts. The availability of digital resources has given access to a huge residual database of sixteenth-century exegetical comment hitherto available only in major research universities and rare book collections. The RCS has benefited greatly from online databases such as Alexander Street Press's Digital Library of Classical Protestant Texts (DLCPT) as well as freely accessible databases like the Post-Reformation Digital Library (prdl.org). Through the help of RCS editorial advisor Herman Selderhuis, we have also had access to the special Reformation collections of the Johannes a Lasco Bibliothek in Emden, Germany. In addition, modern critical editions and translations of Reformation sources have been published over the past generation. Original translations of Reformation sources are given unless an acceptable translation already exists.

Each volume in the RCS will include an introduction by the volume editor placing that portion of the canon within the historical context of the Protestant Reformation and presenting a summary of the theological themes, interpretive issues and reception of the particular book(s). The commentary itself consists of particular pericopes identified by a pericope heading; the biblical text in the English Standard Version (ESV), with significant textual variants registered in the footnotes; an overview of the pericope in which principal exegetical and theological concerns of the Reformation writers are succinctly noted; and excerpts from the Reformation writers identified by name according to the conventions of the *Oxford Encyclopedia of the Reformation*. Each volume will also include a bibliography of sources cited, as well as an appendix of authors and source works.

The Reformation era was a time of verbal as well as physical violence, and this fact has presented a challenge for this project. Without unduly sanitizing the texts, where they contain anti-Semitic, sexist or inordinately polemical rhetoric, we have not felt obliged to parade such comments either. We have noted the abridgement of texts with ellipses and an explanatory footnote.

While this procedure would not be valid in the critical edition of such a text, we have deemed it appropriate in a series whose primary purpose is pastoral and devotional. When translating *homo* or similar terms that refer to the human race as a whole or to individual persons without reference to gender, we have used alternative English expressions to the word *man* (or derivative constructions that formerly were used generically to signify humanity at large), whenever such substitutions can be made without producing an awkward or artificial construction.

As is true in the ACCS, we have made a special effort where possible to include the voices of women, though we acknowledge the difficulty of doing so for the early modern period when for a variety of social and cultural reasons few theological and biblical works were published by women. However, recent scholarship has focused on a number of female leaders whose literary remains show us how they understood and interpreted the Bible. Women who made significant contributions to the Reformation include Marguerite d'Angoulême, sister of King Francis I, who supported French reformist evangelicals including Calvin and who published a religious poem influenced by Luther's theology, *The Mirror of the Sinful Soul*; Argula von Grumbach, a Bavarian noblewoman who defended the teachings of Luther and Melanchthon before the theologians of the University of Ingolstadt; Katharina Schütz Zell, the wife of a former priest, Matthias Zell, and a remarkable reformer in her own right—she conducted funerals, compiled hymnbooks, defended the downtrodden and published a defense of clerical marriage as well as composing works of consolation on divine comfort and pleas for the toleration of Anabaptists and Catholics alike; and Anne Askew, a Protestant martyr put to death in 1546 after demonstrating remarkable biblical prowess in her examinations by church officials. Other echoes of faithful women in the age of the Reformation are found in their letters, translations, poems, hymns, court depositions and martyr records.

Lay culture, learned culture. In recent decades, much attention has been given to what is called "reforming from below," that is, the expressions of religious beliefs and churchly life that characterized the popular culture of the majority of the population in the era of the Reformation. Social historians have taught us to examine the diverse pieties of townspeople and city folk, of rural religion and village life, the emergence of lay theologies and the experiences of women in the religious tumults of Reformation Europe.[7] Formal commentaries by their nature are artifacts of learned culture. Almost all of them were written in Latin, the lingua franca of learned discourse well past the age of the Reformation. Biblical commentaries were certainly not the primary means by which the Protestant Reformation spread so rapidly across wide sectors of sixteenth-century society. Small pamphlets and broadsheets, later called *Flugschriften* ("flying writings"), with their graphic woodcuts and cartoon-like depictions of Reformation personalities and events, became the means of choice for mass communication in the early age of printing. Sermons and works of devotion were also printed with appealing visual aids. Luther's early writings were often accompanied by drawings and sketches from Lucas Cranach and other artists. This was done "above all for the sake of children and simple folk," as Luther

---

[7]See Peter Matheson, ed., *Reformation Christianity* (Minneapolis: Fortress, 2007).

---

put it, "who are more easily moved by pictures and images to recall divine history than through mere words or doctrines."[8]

We should be cautious, however, in drawing too sharp a distinction between learned and lay culture in this period. The phenomenon of preaching was a kind of verbal bridge between scholars at their desks and the thousands of illiterate or semiliterate listeners whose views were shaped by the results of Reformation exegesis. According to contemporary witness, more than one thousand people were crowding into Geneva to hear Calvin expound the Scriptures every day.[9] An example of how learned theological works by Reformation scholars were received across divisions of class and social status comes from Lazare Drilhon, an apothecary of Toulon. He was accused of heresy in May 1545 when a cache of prohibited books was found hidden in his garden shed. In addition to devotional works, the French New Testament and a copy of Calvin's Genevan liturgy, there was found a series of biblical commentaries, translated from the Latin into French: Martin Bucer's on Matthew, François Lambert's on the Apocalypse and one by Oecolampadius on 1 John.[10] Biblical exegesis in the sixteenth century was not limited to the kind of full-length commentaries found in Drilhon's shed. Citations from the Bible and expositions of its meaning permeate the extant literature of sermons, letters, court depositions, doctrinal treatises, records of public disputations and even last wills and testaments. While most of the selections in the RCS will be drawn from formal commentary literature, other sources of biblical reflection will also be considered.

Historical Context

The medieval legacy. On October 18, 1512, the degree *Doctor in Biblia* was conferred on Martin Luther, and he began his career as a professor in the University of Wittenberg. As is well known, Luther was also a monk who had taken solemn vows in the Augustinian Order of Hermits at Erfurt. These two settings—the university and the monastery—both deeply rooted in the Middle Ages, form the background not only for Luther's personal vocation as a reformer but also for the history of the biblical commentary in the age of the Reformation. Since the time of the Venerable Bede (d. 735), sometimes called "the last of the Fathers," serious study of the Bible had taken place primarily in the context of cloistered monasteries. The Rule of St. Benedict brought together *lectio* and *meditatio*, the knowledge of letters and the life of prayer. The liturgy was the medium through which the daily reading of the Bible, especially the Psalms, and the sayings of the church fathers came together in the spiritual formation of the monks.[11] Essential to this understanding was a belief in the unity of the people of God throughout time as well as space, and an awareness that life in this world was a preparation for the beatific vision in the next.

---

[8]Martin Luther, "Personal Prayer Book," LW 43:42-43* (WA 10,2:458); quoted in R. W. Scribner, *For the Sake of Simple Folk: Popular Propaganda for the German Reformation* (Cambridge: Cambridge University Press, 1981), xi.

[9]Letter of De Beaulieu to Guillaume Farel (1561) in *Theodor Beza nach handschriftlichen und anderen gleichzeitigen Quellen*, ed. J. W. Baum (Leipzig: Weidmann, 1851), 2:92.

[10]Francis Higman, "A Heretic's Library: The Drilhon Inventory" (1545), in Francis Higman, *Lire et Découvrir: la circulation des idées au temps de la Réforme* (Geneva: Droz, 1998), 65-85.

[11]See the classic study by Jean Leclercq, *The Love of Learning and the Desire for God* (New York: Fordham University Press, 1961).

The source of theology was the study of the sacred page (*sacra pagina*); its object was the accumulation of knowledge not for its own sake but for the obtaining of eternal life. For these monks, the Bible had God for its author, salvation for its end and unadulterated truth for its matter, though they would not have expressed it in such an Aristotelian way. The medieval method of interpreting the Bible owed much to Augustine's *On Christian Doctrine*. In addition to setting forth a series of rules (drawn from an earlier work by Tyconius), Augustine stressed the importance of distinguishing the literal and spiritual or allegorical senses of Scripture. While the literal sense was not disparaged, the allegorical was valued because it enabled the believer to obtain spiritual benefit from the obscure places in the Bible, especially in the Old Testament. For Augustine, as for the monks who followed him, the goal of scriptural exegesis was freighted with eschatological meaning; its purpose was to induce faith, hope and love and so to advance in one's pilgrimage toward that city with foundations (see Heb 11:10).

Building on the work of Augustine and other church fathers going back to Origen, medieval exegetes came to understand Scripture as possessed of four possible meanings, the famous *quadriga*. The literal meaning was retained, of course, but the spiritual meaning was now subdivided into three senses: the allegorical, the moral and the anagogical. Medieval exegetes often referred to the four meanings of Scripture in a popular rhyme:

> The letter shows us what God and our fathers did;
> The allegory shows us where our faith is hid;
> The moral meaning gives us rules of daily life;
> The anagogy shows us where we end our strife.[12]

In this schema, the three spiritual meanings of the text correspond to the three theological virtues: faith (allegory), hope (anagogy) and love (the moral meaning). It should be noted that this way of approaching the Bible assumed a high doctrine of scriptural inspiration: the multiple meanings inherent in the text had been placed there by the Holy Spirit for the benefit of the people of God. The biblical justification for this method went back to the apostle Paul, who had used the words *allegory* and *type* when applying Old Testament events to believers in Christ (Gal 4:21-31; 1 Cor 10:1-11). The problem with this approach was knowing how to relate each of the four senses to one another and how to prevent Scripture from becoming a nose of wax turned this way and that by various interpreters. As G. R. Evans explains, "Any interpretation which could be put upon the text and was in keeping with the faith and edifying, had the warrant of God himself, for no human reader had the ingenuity to find more than God had put there."[13]

With the rise of the universities in the eleventh century, theology and the study of Scripture moved from the cloister into the classroom. Scripture and the Fathers were still important, but they came to function more as footnotes to the theological questions debated in the schools and brought together in an impressive systematic way in works such as Peter Lombard's *Books of Sentences* (the standard theology textbook of the Middle Ages) and the great scholastic *summae* of the

---

[12]Robert M. Grant, *A Short History of the Interpretation of the Bible* (New York: Macmillan, 1963), 119. A translation of the well-known Latin quatrain: *Littera gesta docet/Quid credas allegoria/Moralis quid agas/Quo tendas anagogia.*
[13]G. R. Evans, *The Language and Logic of the Bible: The Road to Reformation* (Cambridge: Cambridge University Press, 1985), 42.

thirteenth century. Indispensible to the study of the Bible in the later Middle Ages was the *Glossa ordinaria,* a collection of exegetical opinions by the church fathers and other commentators. Heiko Oberman summarized the transition from devotion to dialectic this way: "When, due to the scientific revolution of the twelfth century, Scripture became the *object* of study rather than the *subject* through which God speaks to the student, the difference between the two modes of speaking was investigated in terms of the texts themselves rather than in their relation to the recipients."[14] It was possible, of course, to be both a scholastic theologian and a master of the spiritual life. Meister Eckhart, for example, wrote commentaries on the Old Testament in Latin and works of mystical theology in German, reflecting what had come to be seen as a division of labor between the two.

An increasing focus on the text of Scripture led to a revival of interest in its literal sense. The two key figures in this development were Thomas Aquinas (d. 1274) and Nicholas of Lyra (d. 1340). Thomas is best remembered for his *Summa Theologiae,* but he was also a prolific commentator on the Bible. Thomas did not abandon the multiple senses of Scripture but declared that all the senses were founded on one—the literal—and this sense eclipsed allegory as the basis of sacred doctrine. Nicholas of Lyra was a Franciscan scholar who made use of the Hebrew text of the Old Testament and quoted liberally from works of Jewish scholars, especially the learned French rabbi Salomon Rashi (d. 1105). After Aquinas, Lyra was the strongest defender of the literal, historical meaning of Scripture as the primary basis of theological disputation. His *Postilla,* as his notes were called—the abbreviated form of *post illa verba textus,* meaning "after these words from Scripture"—were widely circulated in the late Middle Ages and became the first biblical commentary to be printed in the fifteenth century. More than any other commentator from the period of high scholasticism, Lyra and his work were greatly valued by the early reformers. According to an old Latin pun, *Nisi Lyra lyrasset, Lutherus non saltasset,* "If Lyra had not played his lyre, Luther would not have danced."[15] While Luther was never an uncritical disciple of any teacher, he did praise Lyra as a good Hebraist and quoted him more than one hundred times in his lectures on Genesis, where he declared, "I prefer him to almost all other interpreters of Scripture."[16]

Sacred philology. The sixteenth century has been called a golden age of biblical interpretation, and it is a fact that the age of the Reformation witnessed an explosion of commentary writing unparalleled in the history of the Christian church. Kenneth Hagen has cataloged forty-five commentaries on Hebrews between 1516 (Erasmus) and 1598 (Beza).[17] During the sixteenth century, more than seventy new commentaries on Romans were published, five of them by Melanchthon alone, and nearly one hundred commentaries on the Bible's prayer book, the Psalms.[18] There were two developments in the fifteenth century that presaged this development and without which it

---

[14]Heiko Oberman, *Forerunners of the Reformation* (Philadelphia: Fortress, 1966), 284.

[15]Nicholas of Lyra, *The Postilla of Nicolas of Lyra on the Song of Songs,* trans. and ed. James George Kiecker (Milwaukee: Marquette University Press, 1998), 19.

[16]LW 2:164 (WA 42:377).

[17]Kenneth Hagen, *Hebrews Commenting from Erasmus to Bèze, 1516–1598* (Tübingen: Mohr, 1981).

[18]R. Gerald Hobbs, "Biblical Commentaries," *OER* 1:167-71. See in general David C. Steinmetz, ed., *The Bible in the Sixteenth Century* (Durham: Duke University Press, 1990).

could not have taken place: the invention of printing and the rediscovery of a vast store of ancient learning hitherto unknown or unavailable to scholars in the West.

It is now commonplace to say that what the computer has become in our generation, the printing press was to the world of Erasmus, Luther and other leaders of the Reformation. Johannes Gutenberg, a goldsmith by trade, developed a metal alloy suitable for type and a machine that would allow printed characters to be cast with relative ease, placed in even lines of composition and then manipulated again and again, making possible the mass production of an unbelievable number of texts. In 1455, the Gutenberg Bible, the masterpiece of the typographical revolution, was published at Mainz in double columns in gothic type. Forty-seven copies of the beautiful Gutenberg Bible are still extant, each consisting of more than one thousand colorfully illuminated and impeccably printed pages. What began at Gutenberg's print shop in Mainz on the Rhine River soon spread, like McDonald's or Starbucks in our day, into every nook and cranny of the known world. Printing presses sprang up in Rome (1464), Venice (1469), Paris (1470), the Netherlands (1471), Switzerland (1472), Spain (1474), England (1476), Sweden (1483) and Constantinople (1490). By 1500, these and other presses across Europe had published some twenty-seven thousand titles, most of them in Latin. Erasmus once compared himself with an obscure preacher whose sermons were heard by only a few people in one or two churches while his books were read in every country in the world. Erasmus was not known for his humility, but in this case he was simply telling the truth.[19]

The Italian humanist Lorenzo Valla (d. 1457) died in the early dawn of the age of printing, but his critical and philological studies would be taken up by others who believed that genuine reform in church and society could come about only by returning to the wellsprings of ancient learning and wisdom—*ad fontes*, "back to the sources!" Valla is best remembered for undermining a major claim made by defenders of the papacy when he proved by philological research that the so-called Donation of Constantine, which had bolstered papal assertions of temporal sovereignty, was a forgery. But it was Valla's *Collatio Novi Testamenti* of 1444 that would have such a great effect on the renewal of biblical studies in the next century. Erasmus discovered the manuscript of this work while rummaging through an old library in Belgium and published it at Paris in 1505. In the preface to his edition of Valla, Erasmus gave the rationale that would guide his own labors in textual criticism. Just as Jerome had translated the Latin Vulgate from older versions and copies of the Scriptures in his day, so now Jerome's own text must be subjected to careful scrutiny and correction. Erasmus would be *Hieronymus redivivus*, a new Jerome come back to life to advance the cause of sacred philology. The restoration of the Scriptures and the writings of the church fathers would usher in what Erasmus believed would be a golden age of peace and learning. In 1516, the Basel publisher Froben brought out Erasmus's *Novum Instrumentum*, the first published edition of the Greek New Testament. Erasmus's Greek New Testament would go through five editions in his lifetime, each one with new emendations to the text and a growing section of annotations that expanded to include not only technical notes about the text but also theological comment. The influence of Erasmus's Greek New

---

[19]E. Harris Harbison, *The Christian Scholar in the Age of the Reformation* (New York: Charles Scribner's Sons, 1956), 80.

Testament was enormous. It formed the basis for Robert Estienne's *Novum Testamentum Graece* of 1550, which in turn was used to establish the Greek *Textus Receptus* for a number of late Reformation translations including the King James Version of 1611.

For all his expertise in Greek, Erasmus was a poor student of Hebrew and only published commentaries on several of the psalms. However, the renaissance of Hebrew letters was part of the wider program of biblical humanism as reflected in the establishment of trilingual colleges devoted to the study of Hebrew, Greek and Latin (the three languages written on the *titulus* of Jesus' cross [Jn 19:20]) at Alcalá in Spain, Wittenberg in Germany, Louvain in Belgium and Paris in France. While it is true that some medieval commentators, especially Nicholas of Lyra, had been informed by the study of Hebrew and rabbinics in their biblical work, it was the publication of Johannes Reuchlin's *De rudimentis hebraicis* (1506), a combined grammar and dictionary, that led to the recovery of *veritas Hebraica*, as Jerome had referred to the true voice of the Hebrew Scriptures. The pursuit of Hebrew studies was carried forward in the Reformation by two great scholars, Konrad Pellikan and Sebastian Münster. Pellikan was a former Franciscan friar who embraced the Protestant cause and played a major role in the Zurich reformation. He had published a Hebrew grammar even prior to Reuchlin and produced a commentary on nearly the entire Bible that appeared in seven volumes between 1532 and 1539. Münster was Pellikan's student and taught Hebrew at the University of Heidelberg before taking up a similar position in Basel. Like his mentor, Münster was a great collector of Hebraica and published a series of excellent grammars, dictionaries and rabbinic texts. Münster did for the Hebrew Old Testament what Erasmus had done for the Greek New Testament. His *Hebraica Biblia* offered a fresh Latin translation of the Old Testament with annotations from medieval rabbinic exegesis.

Luther first learned Hebrew with Reuchlin's grammar in hand but took advantage of other published resources, such as the four-volume Hebrew Bible published at Venice by Daniel Bomberg in 1516 to 1517. He also gathered his own circle of Hebrew experts, his *sanhedrin* he called it, who helped him with his German translation of the Old Testament. We do not know where William Tyndale learned Hebrew, though perhaps it was in Worms, where there was a thriving rabbinical school during his stay there. In any event, he had sufficiently mastered the language to bring out a freshly translated Pentateuch that was published at Antwerp in 1530. By the time the English separatist scholar Henry Ainsworth published his prolix commentaries on the Pentateuch in 1616, the knowledge of Hebrew, as well as Greek, was taken for granted by every serious scholar of the Bible. In the preface to his commentary on Genesis, Ainsworth explained that "the literal sense of Moses's Hebrew (which is the tongue wherein he wrote the law), is the ground of all interpretation, and that language hath figures and properties of speech, different from ours: These therefore in the first place are to be opened that the natural meaning of the Scripture, being known, the mysteries of godliness therein implied, may be better discerned."[20]

The restoration of the biblical text in the original languages made possible the revival of scriptural exposition reflected in the floodtide of sermon literature and commentary work. Of even

---

[20]Henry Ainsworth, *Annotations upon the First Book of Moses Called Genesis* (Amsterdam, 1616), preface (unpaginated).

more far-reaching import was the steady stream of vernacular Bibles in the sixteenth century. In the introduction to his 1516 edition of the New Testament, Erasmus had expressed his desire that the Scriptures be translated into all languages so that "the lowliest women" could read the Gospels and the Pauline epistles and "the farmer sing some portion of them at the plow, the weaver hum some parts of them to the movement of his shuttle, the traveler lighten the weariness of the journey with stories of this kind."[21] Like Erasmus, Tyndale wanted the Bible to be available in the language of the common people. He once said to a learned divine that if God spared his life he would cause the boy who drives the plow to know more of the Scriptures than he did![22] The project of allowing the Bible to speak in the language of the mother in the house, the children in the street and the cheesemonger in the marketplace was met with stiff opposition by certain Catholic polemists such as Johann Eck, Luther's antagonist at the Leipzig Debate of 1519. In his *Enchiridion* (1525), Eck derided the "inky theologians" whose translations paraded the Bible before "the untutored crowd" and subjected it to the judgment of "laymen and crazy old women."[23] In fact, some fourteen German Bibles had already been published prior to Luther's September Testament of 1522, which he translated from Erasmus's Greek New Testament in less than three months' time while sequestered in the Wartburg. Luther's German New Testament became the first bestseller in the world, appearing in forty-three distinct editions between 1522 and 1525 with upward of one hundred thousand copies issued in these three years. It is estimated that 5 percent of the German population may have been literate at this time, but this rate increased as the century wore on due in no small part to the unmitigated success of vernacular Bibles.[24]

Luther's German Bible (inclusive of the Old Testament from 1534) was the most successful venture of its kind, but it was not alone in the field. Hans Denck and Ludwig Hätzer, leaders in the early Anabaptist movement, translated the prophetic books of the Old Testament from Hebrew into German in 1527. This work influenced the Swiss-German Bible of 1531 published by Leo Jud and other pastors in Zurich. Tyndale's influence on the English language rivaled that of Luther on German. At a time when English was regarded as "that obscure and remote dialect of German spoken in an off-shore island," Tyndale, with his remarkable linguistic ability (he was fluent in eight languages), "made a language for England," as his modern editor David Daniell has put it.[25] Tyndale was imprisoned and executed near Brussels in 1536, but the influence of his biblical work among the common people of England was already being felt. There is no reason to doubt the authenticity of John Foxe's recollection of how Tyndale's New Testament was received in England during the 1520s and 1530s:

---

[21]John C. Olin, *Christian Humanism and the Reformation* (New York: Fordham University Press, 1987), 101.

[22]This famous statement of Tyndale was quoted by John Foxe in his *Acts and Monuments of Matters Happening in the Church* (London, 1563). See Henry Wansbrough, "Tyndale," in *The Bible in the Renaissance*, ed. Richard Griffith (Aldershot, UK: Ashgate, 2001), 124.

[23]John Eck, *Enchiridion of Commonplaces*, trans. Ford Lewis Battles (Grand Rapids: Baker, 1979), 47-49.

[24]The effect of printing on the spread of the Reformation has been much debated. See the classic study by Elizabeth L. Eisenstein, *The Printing Press as an Agent of Change* (Cambridge: Cambridge University Press, 1979). More recent studies include Mark U. Edwards Jr., *Printing, Propaganda and Martin Luther* (Minneapolis: Fortress, 1994), and Andrew Pettegree and Matthew Hall, "The Reformation and the Book: A Reconsideration," *Historical Journal* 47 (2004): 1-24.

[25]David Daniell, *William Tyndale: A Biography* (New Haven: Yale University Press, 1994), 3.

The fervent zeal of those Christian days seemed much superior to these our days and times; as manifestly may appear by their sitting up all night in reading and hearing; also by their expenses and charges in buying of books in English, of whom some gave five marks, some more, some less, for a book: some gave a load of hay for a few chapters of St. James, or of St. Paul in English.[26]

Calvin helped to revise and contributed three prefaces to the French Bible translated by his cousin Pierre Robert Olivétan and originally published at Neuchâtel in 1535. Clément Marot and Beza provided a fresh translation of the Psalms with each psalm rendered in poetic form and accompanied by monophonic musical settings for congregational singing. The Bay Psalter, the first book printed in America, was an English adaptation of this work. Geneva also provided the provenance of the most influential Italian Bible published by Giovanni Diodati in 1607. The flowering of biblical humanism in vernacular Bibles resulted in new translations in all of the major language groups of Europe: Spanish (1569), Portuguese (1681), Dutch (New Testament, 1523; Old Testament, 1527), Danish (1550), Czech (1579–1593/94), Hungarian (New Testament, 1541; complete Bible, 1590), Polish (1563), Swedish (1541) and even Arabic (1591).[27]

Patterns of Reformation

Once the text of the Bible had been placed in the hands of the people, in cheap and easily available editions, what further need was there of published expositions such as commentaries? Given the Protestant doctrine of the priesthood of all believers, was there any longer a need for learned clergy and their bookish religion? Some radical reformers thought not. Sebastian Franck searched for the true church of the Spirit "scattered among the heathen and the weeds" but could not find it in any of the institutional structures of his time. *Veritas non potest scribi, aut exprimi*, he said, "truth can neither be spoken nor written."[28] Kaspar von Schwenckfeld so emphasized religious inwardness that he suspended external observance of the Lord's Supper and downplayed the readable, audible Scriptures in favor of the Word within. This trajectory would lead to the rise of the Quakers in the next century, but it was pursued neither by the mainline reformers nor by most of the Anabaptists. Article 7 of the Augsburg Confession (1530) declared the one holy Christian church to be "the assembly of all believers among whom the Gospel is purely preached and the holy sacraments are administered according to the Gospel."[29]

Historians of the nineteenth century referred to the material and formal principles of the Reformation. In this construal, the matter at stake was the meaning of the Christian gospel: the liberating insight that helpless sinners are graciously justified by the gift of faith alone, apart from any works or merits of their own, entirely on the basis of Christ's atoning work on the cross. For Luther especially, justification by faith alone became the criterion by which all other doctrines and

---

[26]Foxe, *Acts and Monuments*, 4:218.
[27]On vernacular translations of the Bible, see *CHB* 3:94-140 and Jaroslav Pelikan, *The Reformation of the Bible/The Bible of the Reformation* (New Haven: Yale University Press, 1996), 41-62.
[28]Sebastian Franck, *280 Paradoxes or Wondrous Sayings*, trans. E. J. Furcha (Lewiston, NY: Edwin Mellen Press, 1986), 10, 212.
[29]BoC 42 (BSLK 61).

practices of the church were to be judged. The cross proves everything, he said at the Heidelberg disputation in 1518. The distinction between law and gospel thus became the primary hermeneutical key that unlocked the true meaning of Scripture.

The formal principle of the Reformation, *sola Scriptura*, was closely bound up with proper distinctions between Scripture and tradition. "Scripture alone," said Luther, "is the true lord and master of all writings and doctrine on earth. If that is not granted, what is Scripture good for? The more we reject it, the more we become satisfied with human books and human teachers."[30] On the basis of this principle, the reformers challenged the structures and institutions of the medieval Catholic Church. Even a simple layperson, they asserted, armed with Scripture should be believed above a pope or a council without it. But, however boldly asserted, the doctrine of the primacy of Scripture did not absolve the reformers from dealing with a host of hermeneutical issues that became matters of contention both between Rome and the Reformation and within each of these two communities: the extent of the biblical canon, the validity of critical study of the Bible, the perspicuity of Scripture and its relation to preaching, and the retention of devotional and liturgical practices such as holy days, incense, the burning of candles, the sprinkling of holy water, church art and musical instruments. Zwingli, the Puritans and the radicals dismissed such things as a rubbish heap of ceremonials that amounted to nothing but tomfoolery, while Lutherans and Anglicans retained most of them as consonant with Scripture and valuable aids to worship.

It is important to note that while the mainline reformers differed among themselves on many matters, overwhelmingly they saw themselves as part of the ongoing Catholic tradition, indeed as the legitimate bearers of it. This was seen in numerous ways including their sense of continuity with the church of the preceding centuries; their embrace of the ecumenical orthodoxy of the early church; and their desire to read the Bible in dialogue with the exegetical tradition of the church.

In their biblical commentaries, the reformers of the sixteenth century revealed a close familiarity with the preceding exegetical tradition, and they used it respectfully as well as critically in their own expositions of the sacred text. For them, *sola Scriptura* was not *nuda Scriptura*. Rather, the Scriptures were seen as the book given to the church, gathered and guided by the Holy Spirit. In his restatement of the Vincentian canon, Calvin defined the church as "a society of all the saints, a society which, spread over the whole world, and existing in all ages, and bound together by the one doctrine and the one spirit of Christ, cultivates and observes unity of faith and brotherly concord. With this church we deny that we have any disagreement. Nay, rather, as we revere her as our mother, so we desire to remain in her bosom." Defined thus, the church has a real, albeit relative and circumscribed, authority since, as Calvin admits, "We cannot fly without wings."[31] While the reformers could not agree with the Council of Trent (though some recent Catholic theologians have challenged this interpretation) that Scripture and tradition were two separate and equal sources of divine revelation,

---

[30]LW 32:11-12* (WA 7:317).
[31]John C. Olin, ed., *John Calvin and Jacopo Sadoleto: A Reformation Debate* (New York: Harper Torchbooks, 1966), 61-62, 77.

they did believe in the coinherence of Scripture and tradition. This conviction shaped the way they read and interpreted the Bible.[32]

Schools of Exegesis

The reformers were passionate about biblical exegesis, but they showed little concern for hermeneutics as a separate field of inquiry. Niels Hemmingsen, a Lutheran theologian in Denmark, did write a treatise, *De methodis* (1555), in which he offered a philosophical and theological framework for the interpretation of Scripture. This was followed by the *Clavis Scripturae Sacrae* (1567) of Matthias Flacius Illyricus, which contains some fifty rules for studying the Bible drawn from Scripture itself.[33] However, hermeneutics as we know it came of age only in the Enlightenment and should not be backloaded into the Reformation. It is also true that the word *commentary* did not mean in the sixteenth century what it means for us today. Erasmus provided both annotations and paraphrases on the New Testament, the former a series of critical notes on the text but also containing points of doctrinal substance, the latter a theological overview and brief exposition. Most of Calvin's commentaries began as sermons or lectures presented in the course of his pastoral ministry. In the dedication to his 1519 study of Galatians, Luther declared that his work was "not so much a commentary as a testimony of my faith in Christ."[34] The exegetical work of the reformers was embodied in a wide variety of forms and genres, and the RCS has worked with this broader concept in setting the guidelines for this compendium.

The Protestant reformers shared in common a number of key interpretive principles such as the priority of the grammatical-historical sense of Scripture and the christological centeredness of the entire Bible, but they also developed a number of distinct approaches and schools of exegesis.[35] For the purposes of the RCS, we note the following key figures and families of interpretation in this period.

Biblical humanism. The key figure is Erasmus, whose importance is hard to exaggerate for Catholic and Protestant exegetes alike. His annotated Greek New Testament and fresh Latin translation challenged the hegemony of the Vulgate tradition and was doubtless a factor in the decision of the Council of Trent to establish the Vulgate edition as authentic and normative. Erasmus believed that the wide distribution of the Scriptures would contribute to personal spiritual renewal and the reform of society. In 1547, the English translation of Erasmus's *Paraphrases* was ordered to be placed in every parish church in England. John Colet first encouraged Erasmus

---

[32]See Timothy George, "An Evangelical Reflection on Scripture and Tradition," *Pro Ecclesia* 9 (2000): 184-207.

[33]See Kenneth G. Hagen, "'De Exegetica Methodo': Niels Hemmingsen's *De Methodis* (1555)," in *The Bible in the Sixteenth Century*, ed. David C. Steinmetz (Durham: Duke University Press, 1990), 181-96.

[34]LW 27:159 (WA 2:449). See Kenneth Hagen, "What Did the Term *Commentarius* Mean to Sixteenth-Century Theologians?" in *Théorie et pratique de l'exégèse*, eds. Irena Backus and Francis M. Higman (Geneva: Droz, 1990), 13-38.

[35]I follow here the sketch of Irena Backus, "Biblical Hermeneutics and Exegesis," *OER* 1:152-58. In this work, Backus confines herself to Continental developments, whereas we have noted the exegetical contribution of the English Reformation as well. For more comprehensive listings of sixteenth-century commentators, see Gerald Bray, *Biblical Interpretation* (Downers Grove, IL: InterVarsity Press, 1996), 165-212; and Richard A. Muller, "Biblical Interpretation in the Sixteenth and Seventeenth Centuries," *DMBI* 22-44.

to learn Greek, though he never took up the language himself. Colet's lectures on Paul's epistles at Oxford are reflected in his commentaries on Romans and 1 Corinthians.

Jacques Lefèvre d'Étaples has been called the "French Erasmus" because of his great learning and support for early reform movements in his native land. He published a major edition of the Psalter, as well as commentaries on the Pauline Epistles (1512), the Gospels (1522) and the General Epistles (1527). Guillaume Farel, the early reformer of Geneva, was a disciple of Lefèvre, and the young Calvin also came within his sphere of influence.

Among pre-Tridentine Catholic reformers, special attention should be given to Thomas de Vio, better known as Cajetan. He is best remembered for confronting Martin Luther on behalf of the pope in 1518, but his biblical commentaries (on nearly every book of the Bible) are virtually free of polemic. Like Erasmus, he dared to criticize the Vulgate on linguistic grounds. His commentary on Romans supported the doctrine of justification by grace applied by faith based on the "alien righteousness" of God in Christ. Jared Wicks sums up Cajetan's significance in this way: "Cajetan's combination of passion for pristine biblical meaning with his fully developed theological horizon of understanding indicates, in an intriguing manner, something of the breadth of possibilities open to Roman Catholics before a more restrictive settlement came to exercise its hold on many Catholic interpreters in the wake of the Council of Trent."[36] Girolamo Seripando, like Cajetan, was a cardinal in the Catholic Church, though he belonged to the Augustinian rather than the Dominican order. He was an outstanding classical scholar and published commentaries on Romans and Galatians. Also important is Jacopo Sadoleto, another cardinal, best known for his 1539 letter to the people of Geneva beseeching them to return to the Church of Rome, to which Calvin replied with a manifesto of his own. Sadoleto published a commentary on Romans in 1535. Bucer once commended Sadoleto's teaching on justification as approximating that of the reformers, while others saw him tilting away from the Augustinian tradition toward Pelagianism.[37]

Luther and the Wittenberg School. It was in the name of the Word of God, and specifically as a doctor of Scripture, that Luther challenged the church of his day and inaugurated the Reformation. Though Luther renounced his monastic vows, he never lost that sense of intimacy with *sacra pagina* he first acquired as a young monk. Luther provided three rules for reading the Bible: prayer, meditation and struggle (*tentatio*). His exegetical output was enormous. In the American edition of Luther's works, thirty out of the fifty-five volumes are devoted to his biblical studies, and additional translations are planned. Many of his commentaries originated as sermons or lecture notes presented to his students at the university and to his parishioners at Wittenberg's parish church of St. Mary. Luther referred to Galatians as his bride: "The Epistle to the Galatians is my dear epistle. I have betrothed myself to it. It is my Käthe von Bora."[38] He considered his 1535 commentary on Galatians his greatest exegetical work, although his massive commentary on Genesis

---

[36]Jared Wicks, "Tommaso de Vio Cajetan (1469-1534)," *DMBI* 283-87, here 286.

[37]See the discussion by Bernard Roussel, "Martin Bucer et Jacques Sadolet: la concorde possible," *Bulletin de la Société de l'histoire de protestantisme français* (1976): 525-50, and T. H. L. Parker, *Commentaries on the Epistle to the Romans, 1532–1542* (Edinburgh: T&T Clark, 1986), 25-34.

[38]WATR 1:69 no. 146; cf. LW 54:20 no. 146. I have followed Rörer's variant on Dietrich's notes.

(eight volumes in LW), which he worked on for ten years (1535–1545), must be considered his crowning work. Luther's principles of biblical interpretation are found in his *Open Letter on Translating* and in the prefaces he wrote to all the books of the Bible.

Philipp Melanchthon was brought to Wittenberg to teach Greek in 1518 and proved to be an able associate to Luther in the reform of the church. A set of his lecture notes on Romans was published without his knowledge in 1522. This was revised and expanded many times until his large commentary of 1556. Melanchthon also commented on other New Testament books including Matthew, John, Galatians and the Petrine epistles, as well as Proverbs, Daniel and Ecclesiastes. Though he was well trained in the humanist disciplines, Melanchthon devoted little attention to critical and textual matters in his commentaries. Rather, he followed the primary argument of the biblical writer and gathered from this exposition a series of doctrinal topics for special consideration. This method lay behind Melanchthon's *Loci communes* (1521), the first Protestant theology textbook to be published. Another Wittenberger was Johannes Bugenhagen of Pomerania, a prolific commentator on both the Old and New Testaments. His commentary on the Psalms (1524), translated into German by Bucer, applied Luther's teaching on justification to the Psalter. He also wrote a commentary on Job and annotations on many of the books in the Bible. The Lutheran exegetical tradition was shaped by many other scholar-reformers including Andreas Osiander, Johannes Brenz, Caspar Cruciger, Erasmus Sarcerius, Georg Maior, Jacob Andreae, Nikolaus Selnecker and Johann Gerhard.

The Strasbourg-Basel tradition. Bucer, the son of a shoemaker in Alsace, became the leader of the Reformation in Strasbourg. A former Dominican, he was early on influenced by Erasmus and continued to share his passion for Christian unity. Bucer was the most ecumenical of the Protestant reformers seeking rapprochement with Catholics on justification and an armistice between Luther and Zwingli in their strife over the Lord's Supper. Bucer also had a decisive influence on Calvin, though the latter characterized his biblical commentaries as longwinded and repetitious.[39] In his exegetical work, Bucer made ample use of patristic and medieval sources, though he criticized the abuse and overuse of allegory as "the most blatant insult to the Holy Spirit."[40] He declared that the purpose of his commentaries was "to help inexperienced brethren [perhaps like the apothecary Drilhon, who owned a French translation of Bucer's *Commentary on Matthew*] to understand each of the words and actions of Christ, and in their proper order as far as possible, and to retain an explanation of them in their natural meaning, so that they will not distort God's Word through age-old aberrations or by inept interpretation, but rather with a faithful comprehension of everything as written by the Spirit of God, they may expound to all the churches in their firm upbuilding in faith and love."[41] In addition to writing commentaries on all four Gospels, Bucer published commentaries on Judges, the Psalms, Zephaniah, Romans and Ephesians. In the early years of the Reformation, there was a great deal of back and forth between Strasbourg and Basel, and both

---

[39]CNTC 8:3 (CO 10:404).

[40]*DMBI* 249; P. Scherding and F. Wendel, eds., "Un Traité d'exégèse pratique de Bucer," *Revue d'histoire et de philosophie religieuses* 26 (1946): 32-75, here 56.

[41]Martin Bucer, *Enarrationes perpetuae in sacra quatuor evangelia*, 2nd ed. (Strasbourg: Georg Ulrich Andlanus, 1530), 10r; quoted in D. F. Wright, "Martin Bucer," *DMBI* 290.

---

were centers of a lively publishing trade. Wolfgang Capito, Bucer's associate at Strasbourg, was a notable Hebraist and composed commentaries on Hosea (1529) and Habakkuk (1527).

At Basel, the great Sebastian Münster defended the use of Jewish sources in the Christian study of the Old Testament and published, in addition to his famous Hebrew grammar, an annotated version of the Gospel of Matthew translated from Greek into Hebrew. Oecolampadius, Basel's chief reformer, had been a proofreader in Froben's publishing house and worked with Erasmus on his Greek New Testament and his critical edition of Jerome. From 1523 he was both a preacher and professor of Holy Scripture at Basel. He defended Zwingli's eucharistic theology at the Colloquy of Marburg and published commentaries on 1 John (1524), Romans (1525) and Haggai–Malachi (1525). Oecolampadius was succeeded by Simon Grynaeus, a classical scholar who taught Greek and supported Bucer's efforts to bring Lutherans and Zwinglians together. More in line with Erasmus was Sebastian Castellio, who came to Basel after his expulsion from Geneva in 1545. He is best remembered for questioning the canonicity of the Song of Songs and for his annotations and French translation of the Bible.

The Zurich group. Biblical exegesis in Zurich was centered on the distinctive institution of the *Prophezei*, which began on June 19, 1525. On five days a week, at seven o'clock in the morning, all of the ministers and theological students in Zurich gathered into the choir of the Grossmünster to engage in a period of intense exegesis and interpretation of Scripture. After Zwingli had opened the meeting with prayer, the text of the day was read in Latin, Greek and Hebrew, followed by appropriate textual or exegetical comments. One of the ministers then delivered a sermon on the passage in German that was heard by many of Zurich's citizens who stopped by the cathedral on their way to work. This institute for advanced biblical studies had an enormous influence as a model for Reformed academies and seminaries throughout Europe. It was also the seedbed for sermon series in Zurich's churches and the extensive exegetical publications of Zwingli, Leo Jud, Konrad Pellikan, Heinrich Bullinger, Oswald Myconius and Rudolf Gwalther. Zwingli had memorized in Greek all of the Pauline epistles, and this bore fruit in his powerful expository preaching and biblical exegesis. He took seriously the role of grammar, rhetoric and historical research in explaining the biblical text. For example, he disagreed with Bucer on the value of the Septuagint, regarding it as a trustworthy witness to a proto-Hebrew version earlier than the Masoretic text.

Zwingli's work was carried forward by his successor Bullinger, one of the most formidable scholars and networkers among the reformers. He composed commentaries on Daniel (1565), the Gospels (1542–1546), the Epistles (1537), Acts (1533) and Revelation (1557). He collaborated with Calvin to produce the *Consensus Tigurinus* (1549), a Reformed accord on the nature of the Lord's Supper, and produced a series of fifty sermons on Christian doctrine, known as *Decades*, which became required reading in Elizabethan England. As the *Antistes* ("overseer") of the Zurich church for forty-four years, Bullinger faced opposition from nascent Anabaptism on the one hand and resurgent Catholicism on the other. The need for a well-trained clergy and scholarly resources, including Scripture commentaries, arose from the fact that the Bible was "difficult or obscure to the unlearned, unskillful, unexercised, and malicious or corrupted wills." While forswearing papal claims to infallibility, Bullinger and other leaders of the magisterial Reformation saw the need for a kind of Protestant magisterium as a check against the tendency to read the Bible in "such sense as everyone shall be persuaded in himself to be most convenient."[42]

Two other commentators can be treated in connection with the Zurich group, though each of them had a wide-ranging ministry across the Reformation fronts. A former Benedictine monk, Wolfgang Musculus, embraced the Reformation in the 1520s and served briefly as the secretary to Bucer in Strasbourg. He shared Bucer's desire for Protestant unity and served for seventeen years (1531–1548) as a pastor and reformer in Augsburg. After a brief time in Zurich, where he came under the influence of Bullinger, Musculus was called to Bern, where he taught the Scriptures and published commentaries on the Psalms, the Decalogue, Genesis, Romans, Isaiah, 1 and 2 Corinthians, Galatians and Ephesians, Philippians, Colossians, 1 and 2 Thessalonians, and 1 Timothy. Drawing on his exegetical writings, Musculus also produced a compendium of Protestant theology that was translated into English in 1563 as *Commonplaces of Christian Religion*.

Peter Martyr Vermigli was a Florentine-born scholar and Augustinian friar who embraced the Reformation and fled to Switzerland in 1542. Over the next twenty years, he would gain an international reputation as a prolific scholar and leading theologian within the Reformed community. He lectured on the Old Testament at Strasbourg, was made regius professor at Oxford, corresponded with the Italian refugee church in Geneva and spent the last years of his life as professor of Hebrew at Zurich. Vermigli published commentaries on 1 Corinthians, Romans and Judges during his lifetime. His biblical lectures on Genesis, Lamentations, 1 and 2 Samuel, and 1 and 2 Kings were published posthumously. The most influential of his writings was the *Loci communes* (*Commonplaces*), a theological compendium drawn from his exegetical writings.

The Genevan reformers. What Zwingli and Bullinger were to Zurich, Calvin and Beza were to Geneva. Calvin has been called "the father of modern biblical scholarship," and his exegetical work is without parallel in the Reformation. Because of the success of his *Institutes of the Christian Religion* Calvin has sometimes been thought of as a man of one book, but he always intended the *Institutes*, which went through eight editions in Latin and five in French during his lifetime, to serve as a guide to the study of the Bible, to show the reader "what he ought especially to seek in Scripture and to what end he ought to relate its contents." Jacob Arminius, who modified several principles of Calvin's theology, recommended his commentaries next to the Bible, for, as he said, Calvin "is incomparable in the interpretation of Scripture."[43] Drawing on his superb knowledge of Greek and Hebrew and his thorough training in humanist rhetoric, Calvin produced commentaries on all of the New Testament books except 2 and 3 John and Revelation. Calvin's Old Testament commentaries originated as sermon and lecture series and include Genesis, Psalms, Hosea, Isaiah, minor prophets, Daniel, Jeremiah and Lamentations, a harmony of the last four books of Moses,

---

[42]Euan Cameron, *The European Reformation* (Oxford: Oxford University Press, 1991), 120.

[43]Letter to Sebastian Egbert (May 3, 1607), in *Praestantium ac eruditorum virorum epistolae ecclesiasticae et theologicae varii argumenti*, ed. Christiaan Hartsoeker (Amsterdam: Henricus Dendrinus, 1660), 236-37. Quoted in A. M. Hunter, *The Teaching of Calvin* (London: James Clarke, 1950), 20.

Ezekiel 1–20, and Joshua. Calvin sought for brevity and clarity in all of his exegetical work. He emphasized the illumination of the Holy Spirit as essential to a proper understanding of the text. Calvin underscored the continuity between the two Testaments (one covenant in two dispensations) and sought to apply the plain or natural sense of the text to the church of his day. In the preface to his own influential commentary on Romans, Karl Barth described how Calvin worked to recover the mind of Paul and make the apostle's message relevant to his day:

> How energetically Calvin goes to work, first scientifically establishing the text ("what stands there?"), then following along the footsteps of its thought; that is to say, he conducts a discussion with it until the wall between the first and the sixteenth centuries becomes transparent, and until there in the first century Paul speaks and here the man of the sixteenth century hears, until indeed the conversation between document and reader becomes concentrated upon the substance (which must be the same now as then).[44]

Beza was elected moderator of Geneva's Company of Pastors after Calvin's death in 1564 and guided the Genevan Reformation over the next four decades. His annotated Latin translation of the Greek New Testament (1556) and his further revisions of the Greek text established his reputation as the leading textual critic of the sixteenth century after Erasmus. Beza completed the translation of Marot's metrical Psalter, which became a centerpiece of Huguenot piety and Reformed church life. Though known for his polemical writings on grace, free will and predestination, Beza's work is marked by a strong pastoral orientation and concern for a Scripture-based spirituality.

Robert Estienne (Stephanus) was a printer-scholar who had served the royal household in Paris. After his conversion to Protestantism, in 1550 he moved to Geneva, where he published a series of notable editions and translations of the Bible. He also produced sermons and commentaries on Job, Ecclesiastes, the Song of Songs, Romans and Hebrews, as well as dictionaries, concordances and a thesaurus of biblical terms. He also published the first editions of the Bible with chapters divided into verses, an innovation that quickly became universally accepted.

The British Reformation. Commentary writing in England and Scotland lagged behind the continental Reformation for several reasons. In 1500, there were only three publishing houses in England compared with more than two hundred on the Continent. A 1408 statute against publishing or reading the Bible in English, stemming from the days of Lollardy, stifled the free flow of ideas, as was seen in the fate of Tyndale. Moreover, the nature of the English Reformation from Henry through Elizabeth provided little stability for the flourishing of biblical scholarship. In the sixteenth century, many "hot-gospel" Protestants in England were edified by the English translations of commentaries and theological writings by the Continental reformers. The influence of Calvin and Beza was felt especially in the Geneva Bible with its "Protestant glosses" of theological notes and references.

During the later Elizabethan and Stuart church, however, the indigenous English commentary came into its own. Both Anglicans and Puritans contributed to this outpouring of biblical studies.

---

[44]Karl Barth, *Die Römerbrief* (Zurich: TVZ, 1940), ii, translated by T. H. L. Parker as the epigraph to *Calvin's New Testament Commentaries*, 2nd ed. (Louisville, KY: Westminster John Knox, 1993).

The sermons of Lancelot Andrewes and John Donne are replete with exegetical insights based on a close study of the Greek and Hebrew texts. Among the Reformed authors in England, none was more influential than William Perkins, the greatest of the early Puritan theologians, who published commentaries on Galatians, Jude, Revelation and the Sermon on the Mount (Mt 5–7). John Cotton, one of his students, wrote commentaries on the Song of Songs, Ecclesiastes and Revelation before departing for New England in 1633. The separatist pastor Henry Ainsworth was an outstanding scholar of Hebrew and wrote major commentaries on the Pentateuch, the Psalms and the Song of Songs. In Scotland, Robert Rollock, the first principal of Edinburgh University (1585), wrote numerous commentaries including those on the Psalms, Ephesians, Daniel, Romans, 1 and 2 Thessalonians, John, Colossians and Hebrews. Joseph Mede and Thomas Brightman were leading authorities on Revelation and contributed to the apocalyptic thought of the seventeenth century. Mention should also be made of Archbishop James Ussher, whose *Annals of the Old Testament* was published in 1650. Ussher developed a keen interest in biblical chronology and calculated that the creation of the world had taken place on October 26, 4004 B.C. As late as 1945, the Scofield Reference Bible still retained this date next to Genesis 1:1, but later editions omitted it because of the lack of evidence on which to fix such dates.[45]

Anabaptism. Irena Backus has noted that there was no school of "dissident" exegesis during the Reformation, and the reasons are not hard to find. The radical Reformation was an ill-defined movement that existed on the margins of official church life in the sixteenth century. The denial of infant baptism and the refusal to swear an oath marked radicals as a seditious element in society, and they were persecuted by Protestants and Catholics alike. However, in the RCS we have made an attempt to include some voices of the radical Reformation, especially among the Anabaptists. While the Anabaptists published few commentaries in the sixteenth century, they were avid readers and quoters of the Bible. Numerous exegetical gems can be found in their letters, treatises, martyr acts (especially *The Martyrs' Mirror*), hymns and histories. They placed a strong emphasis on the memorizing of Scripture and quoted liberally from vernacular translations of the Bible. George H. Williams has noted that "many an Anabaptist theological tract was really a beautiful mosaic of Scripture texts."[46] In general, most Anabaptists accepted the apocryphal books as canonical, contrasted outer word and inner spirit with relative degrees of strictness and saw the New Testament as normative for church life and social ethics (witness their pacifism, nonswearing, emphasis on believers' baptism and congregational discipline).

We have noted the Old Testament translation of Ludwig Hätzer, who became an antitrinitarian, and Hans Denck that they published at Worms in 1527. Denck also wrote a notable commentary on Micah. Conrad Grebel belonged to a Greek reading circle in Zurich and came to his Anabaptist convictions while poring over the text of Erasmus's New Testament. The only Anabaptist leader with university credentials was Balthasar Hubmaier, who was made a doctor of theology (Ingolstadt, 1512) in the same year as Luther. His reflections on the Bible are found in his numerous

---

[45] *The New Scofield Reference Bible* (New York: Oxford University Press, 1967), vi.
[46] George H. Williams, *The Radical Reformation*, 3rd ed. (Kirksville, MO: Sixteenth Century Journal Publishers, 1992), 1247.

writings, which include the first catechism of the Reformation (1526), a two-part treatise on the freedom of the will and a major work (*On the Sword*) setting forth positive attitudes toward the role of government and the Christian's place in society. Melchior Hoffman was an apocalyptic seer who wrote commentaries on Romans, Revelation and Daniel 12. He predicted that Christ would return in 1533. More temperate was Pilgram Marpeck, a mining engineer who embraced Anabaptism and traveled widely throughout Switzerland and south Germany, from Strasbourg to Augsburg. His "Admonition of 1542" is the longest published defense of Anabaptist views on baptism and the Lord's Supper. He also wrote many letters that functioned as theological tracts for the congregations he had founded dealing with topics such as the fruits of repentance, the lowliness of Christ and the unity of the church. Menno Simons, a former Catholic priest, became the most outstanding leader of the Dutch Anabaptist movement. His masterpiece was the *Foundation of Christian Doctrine* published in 1540. His other writings include *Meditation on the Twenty-fifth Psalm* (1537); *A Personal Exegesis of Psalm Twenty-five* modeled on the style of Augustine's *Confessions*; *Confession of the Triune God* (1550), directed against Adam Pastor, a former disciple of Menno who came to doubt the divinity of Christ; *Meditations and Prayers for Mealtime* (1557); and the *Cross of the Saints* (1554), an exhortation to faithfulness in the face of persecution. Like many other Anabaptists, Menno emphasized the centrality of discipleship (*Nachfolge*) as a deliberate repudiation of the old life and a radical commitment to follow Jesus as Lord.

Reading Scripture with the Reformers

In 1947, Gerhard Ebeling set forth his thesis that the history of the Christian church is the history of the interpretation of Scripture. Since that time, the place of the Bible in the story of the church has been investigated from many angles. A better understanding of the history of exegesis has been aided by new critical editions and scholarly discussions of the primary sources. The *Cambridge History of the Bible*, published in three volumes (1963–1970), remains a standard reference work in the field. The ACCS built on, and itself contributed to, the recovery of patristic biblical wisdom of both East and West. Beryl Smalley's *The Study of the Bible in the Middle Ages* (1940) and Henri de Lubac's *Medieval Exegesis: The Four Senses of Scripture* (1959) are essential reading for understanding the monastic and scholastic settings of commentary work between Augustine and Luther. The Reformation took place during what has been called "le grand siècle de la Bible."[47] Aided by the tools of Renaissance humanism and the dynamic impetus of Reformation theology (including permutations and reactions against it), the sixteenth century produced an unprecedented number of commentaries on every book in the Bible. Drawing from this vast storehouse of exegetical treasures, the RCS allows us to read Scripture along with the reformers. In doing so, it serves as a practical homiletic and devotional guide to some of the greatest masters of biblical interpretation in the history of the church.

The RCS gladly acknowledges its affinity with and dependence on recent scholarly investigations of Reformation-era exegesis. Between 1976 and 1990, three international colloquia on the

---

[47]J-R. Aarmogathe, ed., *Bible de tous les temps*, 8 vols.; vol. 6, *Le grand siècle de la Bible* (Paris: Beauchesne, 1989).

history of biblical exegesis in the sixteenth century took place in Geneva and in Durham, North Carolina.[48] Among those participating in these three gatherings were a number of scholars who have produced groundbreaking works in the study of biblical interpretation in the Reformation. These include Elsie McKee, Irena Backus, Kenneth Hagen, Scott H. Hendrix, Richard A. Muller, Guy Bedouelle, Gerald Hobbs, John B. Payne, Bernard Roussel, Pierre Fraenkel and David C. Steinmetz. Among other scholars whose works are indispensible for the study of this field are Heinrich Bornkamm, Jaroslav Pelikan, Heiko A. Oberman, James S. Preus, T. H. L. Parker, David F. Wright, Tony Lane, John L. Thompson, Frank A. James and Timothy J. Wengert.[49] Among these scholars no one has had a greater influence on the study of Reformation exegesis than David C. Steinmetz. A student of Oberman, he has emphasized the importance of understanding the Reformation in medieval perspective. In addition to important studies on Luther and Staupitz, he has pioneered the method of comparative exegesis showing both continuity and discontinuity between major Reformation figures and the preceding exegetical traditions (see his *Luther in Context* and *Calvin in Context*). From his base at Duke University, he has spawned what might be called a Steinmetz school, a cadre of students and scholars whose work on the Bible in the Reformation era continues to shape the field. Steinmetz serves on the RCS Board of Editorial Advisors, and a number of our volume editors have pursued doctoral studies under his supervision.

In 1980, Steinmetz published "The Superiority of Pre-critical Exegesis," a seminal essay that not only placed Reformation exegesis in the context of the preceding fifteen centuries of the church's study of the Bible but also challenged certain assumptions underlying the hegemony of historical-critical exegesis of the post-Enlightenment academy.[50] Steinmetz helps us to approach the reformers and other precritical interpreters of the Bible on their own terms as faithful witnesses to the church's apostolic tradition. For them, a specific book or pericope had to be understood within the scope of the consensus of the canon. Thus the reformers, no less than the Fathers and the schoolmen, interpreted the hymn of the Johannine prologue about the preexistent Christ in consonance with the creation narrative of Genesis 1. In the same way, Psalm 22, Isaiah 53 and Daniel 7 are seen as part of an overarching storyline that finds ultimate fulfillment in Jesus Christ. Reading the Bible with the resources of the new learning, the reformers challenged the exegetical conclusions of their medieval predecessors at many points. However, unlike Alexander Campbell in the nineteenth century, their aim was not to "open the New Testament as if mortal man had never seen

---

[48]Olivier Fatio and Pierre Fraenkel, eds., *Histoire de l'exégèse au XVIe siècle: texts du colloque international tenu à Genève en 1976* (Geneva: Droz, 1978); David C. Steinmetz, ed., *The Bible in the Sixteenth Century* [Second International Colloquy on the History of Biblical Exegesis in the Sixteenth Century] (Durham: Duke University Press, 1990); Irena Backus and Francis M. Higman, eds., *Théorie et pratique de l'exégèse. Actes du troisième colloque international sur l'histoire de l'exégèse biblique au XVIe siècle, Genève, 31 août–2 septembre 1988* (Geneva: Droz, 1990); see also Guy Bedouelle and Bernard Roussel, eds., *Bible de tous les temps*, 8 vols.; vol. 5, *Le temps des Réformes et la Bible* (Paris: Beauchesne, 1989).

[49]For bibliographical references and evaluation of these and other contributors to the scholarly study of Reformation-era exegesis, see Richard A. Muller, "Biblical Interpretation in the Era of the Reformation: The View From the Middle Ages," in *Biblical Interpretation in the Era of the Reformation: Essays Presented to David C. Steinmetz in Honor of His Sixtieth Birthday*, ed. Richard A. Muller and John L. Thompson (Grand Rapids: Eerdmans, 1996), 3-22.

[50]David C. Steinmetz, "The Superiority of Pre-Critical Exegesis," *Theology Today* 37 (1980): 27-38.

it before."[51] Rather, they wanted to do their biblical work as part of an interpretive conversation within the family of the people of God. In the reformers' emphatic turn to the literal sense, which prompted their many blasts against the unrestrained use of allegory, their work was an extension of a similar impulse made by Thomas Aquinas and Nicholas of Lyra.

This is not to discount the radically new insights gained by the reformers in their dynamic engagement with the text of Scripture; nor should we dismiss in a reactionary way the light shed on the meaning of the Bible by the scholarly accomplishments of the past two centuries. However, it is to acknowledge that the church's exegetical tradition is an indispensible aid for the proper interpretation of Scripture. And this means, as Richard Muller has said, that "while it is often appropriate to recognize that traditionary readings of the text are erroneous on the grounds offered by the historical-critical method, we ought also to recognize that the conclusions offered by historical-critical exegesis may themselves be quite erroneous on the grounds provided by the exegesis of the patristic, medieval, and reformation periods."[52] The RCS wishes to commend the exegetical work of the Reformation era as a program of retrieval for the sake of renewal—spiritual réssourcement for believers committed to the life of faith today.

George Herbert was an English pastor and poet who reaped the benefits of the renewal of biblical studies in the age of the Reformation. He referred to the Scriptures as a book of infinite sweetness, "a mass of strange delights," a book with secrets to make the life of anyone good. In describing the various means pastors require to be fully furnished in the work of their calling, Herbert provided a rationale for the history of exegesis and for the Reformation Commentary on Scripture:

> The fourth means are commenters and Fathers, who have handled the places controverted, which the parson by no means refuseth. As he doth not so study others as to neglect the grace of God in himself and what the Holy Spirit teacheth him, so doth he assure himself that God in all ages hath had his servants to whom he hath revealed his Truth, as well as to him; and that as one country doth not bear all things that there may be a commerce, so neither hath God opened or will open all to one, that there may be a traffic in knowledge between the servants of God for the planting both of love and humility. Wherefore he hath one comment[ary] at least upon every book of Scripture, and ploughing with this, and his own meditations, he enters into the secrets of God treasured in the holy Scripture.[53]

Timothy George
General Editor

[51]Alexander Campbell, *Memoirs of Alexander Campbell*, ed. Robert Richardson (Cincinnati: Standard Publishing Company, 1872), 97.
[52]Richard A. Muller and John L. Thompson, "The Significance of Precritical Exegesis: Retrospect and Prospect," in *Biblical Interpretation in the Era of the Reformation: Essays Presented to David C. Steinmetz in Honor of His Sixtieth Birthday*, ed. Richard A. Muller and John L. Thompson (Grand Rapids: Eerdmans, 1996), 342.
[53]George Herbert, *The Complete English Poems* (London: Penguin, 1991), 205.

INTRODUCTION TO ROMANS 9–16

Christians have long clashed over and celebrated the first half of Romans, in which Paul addresses sin, justification, faith, grace, law and gospel.[1] Although the latter half of Romans has not attracted the same attention, Paul provides material for significant Reformation discussion and disputes: election and predestination, the relationship between the Jews and the Gentiles in God's salvific plan, political theology, and Christian ethics. "Saint Paul in this epistle simply wants to sum up the entire Christian, evangelical teaching," the Lutheran pastor Cyriacus Spangenberg wrote, "and to prepare an entryway into the entire Old Testament."[2] Accordingly the reformers will touch on an ocean of topics in this volume; however, we will only focus on four in this introduction to help light the reader's path: predestination, the relationship between the Jews and Gentiles, the ministry of the Word, and Christian ethics.

On Predestination: "Before the Foundation of the World"

Ever since Augustine's (354–430) dispute with Pelagius (d. c. 418), the Western church has puzzled over the relationship between divine sovereignty and human freedom.[3] No theological debate is more charged and complex in this regard than election. Pelagius denied original sin, teaching that unaided by God's grace human beings are able not only to will to be perfect but also to be perfect in this life. He believed that Augustine's anthropology excused human beings for their sin and did not take seriously Jesus' command, "Be perfect as your Father in heaven is perfect" (Mt 5:48). Augustine, in contrast, insisted on the total priority and necessity of God's grace for human ability, willing and acting—he even conceded that a person could be sinless in this life but only by

---

[1]Recently the first half of Romans has become especially disputed on account of the new perspective on Paul (NPP). In general, the NPP claims that Second Temple Judaism understood "works of the law" to refer not to works performed to earn salvation, but rather to preserve covenant boundaries and mark those who were included in the covenant. Thus the NPP reads Paul as more focused on a correct understanding of inclusion in the covenant than on grace. Scholars who advocate the NPP tend to use Luther and the reformers as scapegoats for how the church has incorrectly interpreted Scripture. However, that Luther reads more of himself into Paul's epistles than what Paul actually meant has become an unproved truism in these circles. Ironically readers of NPP literature are more likely to find caricatures of Luther than an even-handed historical treatment of this student of Scripture. For a recent attempt to bring the biblical studies guild into conversation with the reformers, see Michael Allen and Jonathan A. Linebaugh, eds., *Reformation Readings of Paul: Explorations in History and Exegesis* (Downers Grove, IL: IVP Academic, 2015). For more on the NPP, see Stephen Westerholm, *Perspectives Old and New on Paul: The "Lutheran" Paul and His Critics* (Grand Rapids: Eerdmans, 2004).
[2]Cyriacus Spangenberg, *Außlegung der Ersten Acht Capitel der Episteln S. Pauli an die Römer* (Strasbourg: Samuel Emmel, 1566), 5r.
[3]That Augustine's position on divine sovereignty and human responsibility developed over his career in the context of disputes complicates how to summarize Augustine's view and has led to disagreement in the tradition and the contemporary historical guild. See Matthew Levering, *The Theology of Augustine: An Introductory Guide to His Most Important Works* (Grand Rapids: Baker Academic, 2013), 71-87; Matthew Levering, *Predestination: Biblical and Theological Paths* (Oxford: Oxford University Press, 2011), 44-54.

God's grace. He saw Pelagius as nullifying Jesus' death and resurrection as well as the Holy Spirit's work.[4] Despite several condemnations of Pelagianism these disputes concerning the priority and necessity of God's grace continued after the deaths of Augustine and Pelagius. At the Second Council of Orange (529), the controversy came to an end: so-called semi-Pelagianism—that human beings can reach out to God unaided and unprovoked, to which he responds with grace—was anathematized. The council fathers also anathematized "with all detestation" that God predestines some to evil—a view that could be derived from Augustine's writings but not one that he explicitly defended.[5]

While the reformers held a spectrum of views concerning election and predestination, all of them saw themselves as Augustine's heirs; none of the reformers would have accepted the Pelagian label.[6] For the reformers, the priority and necessity of grace was nonnegotiable. Nevertheless, there is a spectrum of views among them—some monergistic (God acts alone), some synergistic (a combination of divine and human action).[7]

Double predestination. Some reformers interpreted Augustine as maintaining that predestination is unconditioned by human works and choice, but that God, in his mercy and wisdom, predestines some to salvation and others to condemnation.[8] While this "dreadful decree" causes mortals to tremble, according to these theologians, God's word clearly teaches this.[9] Human beings cannot plumb the inscrutable reasons God chooses to act in this way, and these reformers censored their critics accordingly. John Calvin quipped that if some take issue with this decree, "let

---

[4]Augustine confronted Pelagius with an array of biblical passages: "Deliver us from evil" (Mt 6:13); "I do not nullify the grace of God, for if righteousness were through the law, then Christ died for no purpose" (Gal 2:21); "God's love has been poured into our hearts through the Holy Spirit" (Rom 5:5); that Christ came for the sick (Mt 9:12-13); and that God destroys the wisdom of the wise (1 Cor 1:18-31). Peter Brown reminds us that we should be careful about conflating Pelagianism with Pelagius: "Pelagianism as we know it, that consistent body of ideas of momentous consequences, had come into existence; but in the mind of Augustine, not of Pelagius" (*Augustine of Hippo: A Biography* [Berkeley: University of California Press, 1967], 345).

[5]Henry Bettenson and Chris Maunder, eds., *Documents of the Christian Church*, 3rd ed. (Oxford: Oxford University Press, 1999), 67. Scholars regularly remind their readers how unhelpful a label semi-Pelagianism is, quipping that this view could just as accurately be labeled "semi-Augustinianism." For example, see Jaroslav Pelikan, *The Christian Tradition*, 5 vols. (Chicago: University of Chicago Press, 1971–1989), 1:318. On the dispute between Augustine and Pelagius, see further Pelikan, *Christian Tradition*, 1:278-331; Brown, *Augustine of Hippo*, 340-82.

[6]Of course, this does not mean that none of them might have been guilty of (semi-)Pelagian views. The medieval debates concerning predestination shaped how the reformers talked about this doctrine, especially the semi-Pelagian assertion "to do what is in oneself" (*facere quod in se est*). See Heiko A. Oberman, *The Harvest of Medieval Theology: Gabriel Biel and Late Medieval Nominalism* (Grand Rapids: Baker, 2000), 185-217; Levering, *Predestination*, 68-97.

[7]In his treatment of predestination Levering categorizes the perspectives into five different groups: (1) God's foreknowledge preserves the free human response to grace; (2) God's transcendent priority, willing to save some but permitting others to rebel; (3) God wills to save some and wills to destroy others; (4) God's loving desire for all human beings and his transcendence; and (5) universalism. See Levering, *Predestination*, 10. Levering argues that the position that balances the biblical, theological and pastoral issues is as follows: "God's eternal love for each and every rational creature has no deficiency of stinginess, and God from eternity predestines some to union with him and permits others to rebel permanently" (ibid., 11).

[8]See Pelikan, *Christian Tradition*, 1:297-98. Some scholars challenge this consensus, arguing that Augustine did not explicitly affirm reprobation as a decree, but instead associated it with divine permission. For example, see Levering, *Theology of Augustine*, 80n21; A. Trapè, "Augustine of Hippo," in *Encyclopedia of Ancient Christianity*, 3 vols., ed. Angelo Di Berardino (Downers Grove, IL: IVP Academic, 2014), 1:292-99. See also Alister E. McGrath, *Reformation Thought: An Introduction*, 4th ed. (Oxford: Wiley-Blackwell, 2012), 191-205.

[9]See LCC 21:955; CO 2:704. For Calvin's treatment of predestination, see further *Institutes* 3.21–25 (LCC 21:920-1008; CO 2:678-744).

them answer why they are men rather than oxen or asses."[10] Human beings can only marvel at the way and will of God, singing his praises and seeking refuge in his promises. John Calvin, Theodore Beza and their heirs are most well known for holding this stance. However, Martin Luther in his debate with Desiderius Erasmus also argued for this position—much to the chagrin of his students.[11] After this debate, Luther demurred from stating his position so explicitly; instead he pointed questioners back to the wounds and words of Christ. At table in 1532, Luther mocked the idea that God should explain himself to us: our scales are insufficient.

> Why, if he had to answer everybody's questions he would be a most wretched God. Let us look to the word of God and in it find refuge from the "Wherefore?" We ought to know his word, but should not inquire into his will, which is often hidden. That would be to measure wind and fire in our scales.[12]

Single predestination. Other reformers found it unfitting of God's goodness to attribute the condemnation of sinners to God's will. They maintained that Augustine taught that God in his wisdom predestines some to salvation, while permitting others to rebel, thus condemning themselves. The *Formula of Concord* clearly teaches this position, saying that predestination is only a comfort for believers and that if it is taught in a way that makes people arrogant or despairing, it has been taught incorrectly.[13] Some Reformed confessions, like the Gallic and Belgic, agree that reprobation is a function of divine permission not divine decree.[14] Philipp Melanchthon, Jerome Bolsec (d. 1585) and Peter Martyr Vermigli also teach this position.[15]

Excursus: Erasmus and the freedom of the will. Erasmus found Luther's statements about the human will abhorrent. Particularly the theses from the Heidelberg Disputation (1518), that "free will, after the fall, exists in name only, and as long as it does what it is able to do, it commits a mortal sin. Free will, after the fall, has power to do good only in a passive capacity, but it can always do evil in an active capacity."[16] To Erasmus this seemed to eradicate human action and freedom, thus making God the author of sin. While asserting that ethical issues are more important than doctrinal disputes, Erasmus entered into controversy with Luther concerning the freedom of the human will. First, Erasmus defines freedom of choice (*liberum arbitrium*) as "a power of the human will by which a man can apply himself to the things which lead to eternal salvation, or turn away from them."[17] Then he expounds the diverse biblical passages with the principle that human effort and divine grace are joined. "I prefer the view of those who do attribute much to free

---

[10]John Calvin, *Institutes* 3.22.1; LCC 21:933.

[11]At the Colloquy of Montbéliard (1586), Beza met with Jakob Andreae to try to clarify several differences between the Reformed and Lutheran camps, not least concerning predestination. Beza read portions of Luther's *Bondage of the Will* to support his argument.

[12]WATR 2:585, no. 2656a; quoted from H. G. Haile, *Luther: An Experiment in Biography* (New York: Doubleday, 1980), 203.

[13]See BoC 517-20.

[14]See *Creeds* 3:366-67, 401.

[15]Previously, scholars included Heinrich Bullinger in the single predestination camp; however, Cornelius Venema has shown that Bullinger taught double predestination. See Cornelius P. Venema, *Heinrich Bullinger and the Doctrine of Predestination: Author of "The Other Reformed Tradition"?* (Grand Rapids: Eerdmans, 2002).

[16]LW 31:40 (WA 1:254).

[17]Erasmus, *On the Freedom of the Will*, LCC 17:47.

choice, but most to grace."[18] In turn, Luther found Erasmus's view abominable. He viciously attacked what he understood to be Pelagianism.

> Your book struck me as so cheap and paltry that I feel profoundly sorry for you, defiling as you were your very elegant and ingenious style with such trash, and quite disgusted at the utterly unworthy matter that was being conveyed in such rich ornaments of eloquence, like refuse or ordure being carried in gold and silver vases.[19]

Conditional predestination. In contrast to how Reformed theologians like Calvin and Beza understand God's election—namely, an eternal immutable decree by which God freely chooses some for salvation and others for damnation—Arminians teach that predestination is conditioned by God's foreknowledge of a person's faith or unbelief, and that God's grace enables and completes faith, but human beings can resist God's grace.[20] "Predestination . . . is the decree of the good pleasure of God in Christ," Jacobus Arminius states, "by which he resolved within himself from all eternity, to justify, adopt and endow with everlasting life, to the praise of his own glorious grace, believers on whom he had decreed to bestow faith."[21] Thus Arminians affirm a form of synergism—not to be confused with works righteousness or Pelagianism—human beings cooperate with God by not resisting his grace in Christ.[22] Those who believe in Christ will be saved; those who do not believe will be condemned.[23] In some respects, this understanding of predestination bears similarities to Erasmus's views in *Freedom of the Will.*

Radicals. As in most things, the radicals held diverse views concerning predestination.[24] Still generally they tended to affirm more of a role for human free will—from something akin to Arminius's *not resisting grace* (e.g., Hubmaier), to what seems more semi-Pelagian (e.g., Denck). None of them seem to have held outright Pelagian views; all sought to emphasize the importance of God's grace. Some Italian Anabaptists, however, accepted the bondage of the will and predestination.[25]

Despite the diversity of positions on this doctrine, all the reformers sought to add predestination to the pastoral toolkit. "He [God] chose us in him [Christ] before the foundation of the

---

[18]Desiderius Erasmus, *On the Freedom of the Will,* LCC 17:96; cf. p. 90. See Brian A. Gerrish, "Piety, Theology and the Lutheran Dogma: Erasmus's Book on Free Will," in *The Old Protestantism and the New: Essays on the Reformation Heritage* (Chicago: University of Chicago Press, 1982), 11-26.

[19]Martin Luther, *On the Bondage of the Will,* LCC 17:102.

[20]Calvin called it "absurd" to make predestination dependent on foreknowledge or vice versa (*Institutes* 3.21.5; LCC 21:926). On Arminius's understanding of predestination, see Roger E. Olson, *Arminian Theology: Myths and Realities* (Downers Grove, IL: IVP Academic, 2006), 179-99; Keith D. Stanglin and Thomas H. McCall, *Jacob Arminius: Theologian of Grace* (Oxford: Oxford University Press, 2012), 94-140, esp. 134-39. Stanglin and McCall call Arminius's perspective "conditional predestination" (134). These scholars argue that Arminianism should not be called semi-Pelagian or Pelagian; see Olson, *Arminian Theology,* 18, 141-46; Stanglin and McCall, *Arminius,* 157-64.

[21]Disputation 15: On Divine Predestination; Arminius, *Works,* 1:565.

[22]Olson, *Arminian Theology,* 17-18, 165-66; Stanglin and McCall, *Arminius,* 152-53.

[23]Stanglin and McCall summarize the order of God's decrees according to Arminius as "create; permit the fall; appoint Christ as foundation of election to redeem; save, in Christ, (the class of) penitent believers and condemn unbelievers; provide means [i.e., grace] for repentance and faith; save or condemn single, specific individuals foreknown to believe or not believe" (*Arminius,* 140).

[24]On Anabaptist views of human nature, see Thomas N. Finger, *A Contemporary Anabaptist Theology: Biblical, Historical, Constructive* (Downers Grove, IL: InterVarsity Press, 2004), 468-90.

[25]Finger, *Contemporary Anabaptist Theology,* 41.

world, that we should be holy and blameless before him" (Eph 1:4). Of this each believer must be certain. Rather than trying to grasp at God's hidden will, in times of trial the believer must look to Christ and say, "For me Christ was born, Christ has died, Christ has risen again." Appealing to the inscrutable mystery of God's providence, the reformers admonished their followers to gaze on God's mercy in Christ. Human reason cannot grasp the hidden counsels of God. Thankfully God has condescended to us, revealing himself in Christ, the Word and the sacraments.

The Call of the Nations: "Branches Were Broken Off So That You Might Be Grafted In"

For the reformers, Jesus Christ is the substance of Scripture. Accordingly they understood the church to be the true Israel, and in this sense Christians are true Jews. "We have been grafted into the church of Israel—she is our mother," Wolfgang Musculus teaches. "We receive her abundance; not she ours."[26] They considered the patriarchs and matriarchs of Israel as their own fathers and mothers in the faith. For example, one Lutheran pastor, Justus Menius, in his commentary on 1 Samuel states that "Scripture records the saints' weakness and sin . . . for our consolation, certainly, so that it might rouse our faith, lest we despair at the sight of our sin or some other weakness."[27] For Menius the communion of saints includes Old Testament believers. However, in those Jews who rejected Christ and the prophets, the reformers also saw a theology of works righteousness; thus these Jews served as a paradigm for the reformers' opponents, who rejected justification by faith alone.

God has granted favor and special benefits on the Israelites (Rom 9:4-5); nevertheless, "God has consigned all to disobedience, that he may have mercy on all" (Rom 11:32). According to the flesh all human beings are children of wrath; therefore, to be of the carnal seed of Abraham benefits no one. Life and blessing come with being of the spiritual seed of Abraham; this comes only by faith, itself a gift of God. And so the Lord makes a people for himself from Jews and Gentiles—a message writ large over all Scripture. Time and again the reformers repeat the biblical admonition that to be a child of God is not the result of one's effort and merit; God's will and wisdom accomplish this alone. So Paul places law and gospel side by side in his horticultural metaphor (Rom 11:17-24): grafted into the tree, you participate in the lifeblood of Christ—you are God's beloved child; but God is no respecter of persons, so do not arrogate this privilege to your own merit or worth—you too could be lopped off. "Let the one who boasts, boast in the Lord" (1 Cor 1:31).

On anti-Judaic sentiment. While not all the reformers were equally vitriolic toward the Jews, almost all of them said things that are shocking today.[28] "The first half of the sixteenth century was above all a time of exclusion," R. Gerald Hobbs observes.[29] Throughout Europe Jews were ostracized if not exiled; the reformers were socialized to see Jews as "the other," and few of the

---

[26]Wolfgang Musculus, *In epistolam Apostoli Pauli ad Romanos commentarii* (Basel: Johannes Herwagen, 1562), 196-97.
[27]RCS OT 5:98.
[28]For some examples, see RCS OT 7:lii-lv. Modern Lutherans have distanced themselves from Luther's unfortunate anti-Judaic legacy. For example, in the introduction to *On the Jews and Their Lies*: "Such publication is in no way intended as an endorsement of the distorted views of Jewish faith and practice or the defamation of the Jewish people which this treatise contains" (see further LW 47:123-36, here p. 123). See also Eric Gritsch, *Martin Luther's Anti-Semitism: Against His Better Judgment* (Grand Rapids: Eerdmans, 2012).
[29]R. Gerald Hobbs, "Conrad Pellican and the Psalms: The Ambivalent Legacy of a Pioneer Hebraist," *Reformation & Renaissance Review* 1, no. 1 (1999): 96.

reformers broke this mold.[30] In no way do we thus mean to condone their bias and bigotry toward the Jews. However, this reminds us that their time and culture must be understood in their own right, before we move to assess whether and in what way to appropriate their ideas today.

Ministry of the Word: "Behold, I Have Put My Words in Your Mouth"

God chooses to work through ordinary means. The reformers regularly remind us, therefore, that God delights to work through human beings.[31] When the preacher speaks, God speaks—of course, only so far as he speaks in accordance with Scripture (Rom 12:6).[32] Luther regularly remarked that God's Word must be spoken and heard, not merely read: "The church is a mouth house, not a pen house, for since Christ's advent the gospel is preached orally, while before it was hidden in written books. It is the nature of the new covenant and the gospel that it is to be preached and urged orally with a living voice."[33] The Scriptures are alive. Believers experience this truth in prayer and preaching, for the Holy Spirit—who is not to be separated from God's Word—stirs up readers and hearers in faith. And it is no coincidence that God works in this way. "The gospel does not fall by chance like rain from the clouds," Calvin comments; "rather it is delivered by human hands to wherever it is sent by God."[34]

"Whatever was written in former days was written for our instruction, that through endurance and through the encouragement of the Scriptures we might have hope" (Rom 15:4). The reformers oriented their approach to and use of Scripture around verses like this (also 2 Tim 3:16-17; Ps 119:105). In their preaching and teaching, they regularly reminded their congregants and students that Scripture is for them, for their correction and for their instruction.

This normative Word of God, which rules and orders the people of God, comes as law and gospel (an insight especially prevalent among Lutheran exegetes).[35] Every Christian must learn to distinguish law from gospel. Admittedly no easy task! When a student admitted that he was struggling to distinguish law from gospel, Luther teased him: "Yes, dear master Hans, as soon as you can do that, then you will be a doctor! (And he stood up and removed his beret.) As soon as you can do that, I will say to you: 'Dear Herr Doctor Johann, you are a learned man. Paul and I still haven't progressed so far.'"[36] Nevertheless, the general principle is simple enough, as Tilemann Hesshus succinctly puts it: "Law consigns all to sin and unbelief; however, the gospel announces

---

[30]See Heiko Oberman, *The Roots of Anti-Semitism: In the Age of Renaissance and Reformation*, trans. James I. Porter (Philadelphia: Fortress, 1984).

[31]Kaspar von Schwenckfeld, who taught that the Holy Spirit works without mediation, is anomalous. He insisted that nothing external can produce internal certainty, and so he claimed that external symbols, rites and ceremonies were unnecessary. Theologians across the confessional landscape vehemently condemned Schwenckfeld's doctrine of the internal word.

[32]The reformers insisted that faithful interpretation must be ruled by the faith, which they often summarized with the Apostles' Creed. Any interpretation that departed from this trinitarian faith revealed in Jesus Christ, the Word of God, must be rejected. See further below pp. 127-28, 132-35; RCS OT 7:xlvi-lii.

[33]"Gospel for the First Sunday in Advent," LW 75:51 n. 72* (WA 10,1.2:48). In the final edition of the Church Postil (1540), this section was removed.

[34]*Commentary on Romans* 10:15, CO 49:205 (cf. CTS 38:398-99).

[35]The reformers did not equate law with the Old Testament and gospel with the New Testament.

[36]WATR 2:131, no. 1557 (cf. Haile, *Luther*, 191). The student is Johannes Schlaginhaufen (d. 1560), who also recorded this table talk.

God's lovingkindness to all."[37] He unpacks this by saying that law and gospel are to be distinguished according to the time of their revelation, the condition of their promises and their effects. The law was revealed to Adam and Eve and written into every human heart; the gospel remained a mystery until its revelation in our Lord Jesus Christ. The law promises God's love and favor as well as eternal life only to those who keep the whole law perfectly; the gospel promises the same things but unconditionally ("it destroys our works"). The law reveals God's judgment, our iniquity and eternal death; the gospel frees us from sin, wrath, death, Satan's tyranny and hell, placing us in the kingdom of light and life.[38] Once one reads Scripture in this manner, then, according to Luther's jest, one becomes more learned than every saint.

Christian Ethics: "Put On the Lord Jesus Christ"

"Whatever does not proceed from faith is sin" (Rom 14:23). The reformers are adamant that this includes love. Unless it is conditioned and formed by faith, love goes astray, no matter how well intentioned. In Romans 12–15, according to the reformers, Paul explains his teaching concerning good works, that is, Christian love. United to Christ, believers are grafted into the Good Tree, so that they can only bear his good fruit. Just as Christ did not insist on what is his—as true God from true God—but instead "emptied himself, by taking the form of a servant," and "humbled himself by becoming obedient to the point of death, even death on a cross" (Phil 2:7-8), so also should we empty ourselves in service to God and neighbor. Of course, this is only possible by God's grace and Spirit, for "the love of God does not find but creates what is lovable to it," Luther declared, but "the love of human beings comes into existence by what is lovable to it."[39]

Most of the reformers frame Paul's doctrine in Romans 12–15 within the context of the second table of the Ten Commandments. That is, those commandments summarized by our Lord as "You shall love your neighbor as yourself" (Mt 22:39). Thus the majority of these commentators affirm the third use of the law: baptized Christians should use the law by God's Spirit as an aid to live godly, sober and righteous lives.[40] The first two uses of the law are the civil use (to promote external morality even among unbelievers) and the theological use (to reveal and convict one of one's sin). Some claimed that the third use of the law negated the grace of the gospel, which frees people of the law's demands. Most Reformed and some Lutheran theologians, however, countered that those whom God has justified he will sanctify. And he has ordained the law for this purpose too.

> His delight is in the law of the LORD,
>   and on his law he meditates day and night. (Ps 1:2)

---

[37]Tilemann Hesshus, *Explicatio Epistolae Pauli ad Romanos* (Jena: Gunther Huttich, 1571), 366v-367r.

[38]Hesshus, *Explicatio Epistolae Pauli ad Romanos*, 88v-90r.

[39]Heidelberg Disputation (1518), LW 31:45* (WA 1:354).

[40]This became controversial among Lutherans, even before Luther's death; however, the *Formula of Concord* affirms the third use of the law (see BoC 502-3, 587-91). Modern Lutheran theologians disagree whether the *Formula* faithfully represents Luther and whether this is a wise doctrine. For a helpful summary of the debate, particularly its role in the American Lutheran denominational divide, see Scott R. Murray, *Law, Life, and the Living God: The Third Use of the Law in Modern American Lutheranism* (St. Louis: Concordia, 2001). In contrast, Lowell C. Green reaches contradictory conclusions about the meaning of Article 6 and its relationship to Luther; see Green, "The 'Third Use of the Law' and Elert's Position," *Logia* 22, no. 2 (2013): 27-33.

Excursus: On government. That Jesus is Lord over all aspects of life the reformers assumed. How to apply this truth to politics, however, is tricky, for nearly all the reformers taught that Christians must distinguish between the spiritual and worldly kingdoms.[41] Each realm has a form of government particular to it. In the spiritual realm before God the preaching of the Word and the administration of the sacraments promote freedom and equality; in the worldly realm before human beings law and reason preserve physical life. One must distinguish in which realm one is acting and who is the appropriate authority of that realm; thus one realm does not rule over the other. "The king could be rebuked by the priest," David Whitford summarizes, "but the priest could also be chastised for his malfeasance by the king."[42] Still one must act in accordance with one's office; thus private citizens are not authorized to resist authority actively. According to the reformers, this was a key problem with the Peasants' War; they were acting outside of their office, and thus promoting disorder. In political matters, too, the reformers stressed that God acts through the ordinary means that he has ordained for his creatures.

Within this general agreement, the reformers advocated three different postures toward secular authority: (1) a positive understanding of the magistrates with an emphasis on civil submission (e.g., Erasmus and Luther); (2) a positive understanding of the magistrates that made more room for resistance by reading Romans 13 through Acts 5 (e.g., Calvin and Beza); and (3) a negative understanding of the magistrates coupled with the claim that government is for the righteous and that Christians should withdraw from the worldly realm (e.g., Menno Simons and Michael Sattler). One other political theology rejected the consensus concerning the two kingdoms; instead a government's legitimacy was predicated on correct Christian living, which it was sanctioned to coerce (e.g., Thomas Müntzer).[43] Most of the reformers considered this outrageous and wrongheaded theology, and would have affirmed Luther's sentiment in this sermon on Matthew 24:

> He says this so that the disciples wouldn't think that Christ's kingdom would be a worldly or physical kingdom. And it is a very necessary preface and warning which he gives his disciples here. For not only the disciples were mired in this delusion, but also the Chiliasts, Valentinians and Tertullians all fooled around with these thoughts, that before the Last Day it would happen that Christians alone would possess the earth, and that there will be no ungodly. They were moved to these thoughts because the ungodly are so fortunate in the world—they have kingdoms, worldly authority, wisdom and power—but compared to them, Christians are regarded as nothing. So they thought: "Hey, the godless will all be stamped out, so that the pious can live in peace!" . . . They have twisted these passages to mean that Christ's kingdom would be one of worldly peace and tranquility, and some of them have tied this peace to a thousand-year period.[44]

---

[41]See Paul Althaus, *The Ethics of Martin Luther*, trans. Robert C. Schultz (Philadelphia: Fortress, 1972), 39-82; Dolf Britz, "Politics and Social Life," in *The Calvin Handbook*, ed. Herman J. Selderhuis (Grand Rapids: Eerdmans, 2009), 440-41.

[42]David M. Whitford, "Robbing Paul to Pay Peter: The Reception of Paul in Sixteenth Century Political Theology," in *A Companion to Paul in the Reformation*, ed. by R. Ward Holder (Leiden: Brill, 2009), 581.

[43]This categorization is dependent on ibid., 573-606, esp. p. 575.

[44]WA 47:561 (cf. LW 68:271-72); citing Mt 24:7; Is 2:4; Ps 85:10-11; Is 9:7.

We would like to add a final note about gendered language. In keeping with the guidelines of this series we have translated terms which refer to humanity as a whole in ways that avoid masculine constructions.[45] At times, however, we have kept some gendered constructions, which reflect sixteenth-century culture but not necessarily contemporary views on gender issues.

❖   ❖   ❖

As an entrée to the commentary that follows, we would like to end with Cyriacus Spangenberg's panegyric for Romans:

> In sum, this epistle is a light. It shines before the dull and the ignorant to teach them, to enlighten them and to give them correct understanding. It is a truly well-stocked apothecary and herbal bath. If someone has trials and troubles in his heart and conscience, here he will find the right *garden angelica*, not pagan, but holy goldenrod, the true *Angelica* and the Holy Spirit's root, precious living water and bread from heaven, and a compress against every kind of harm. . . .
>
> And who is able fully to laud this holy and divine writing? Yes indeed, everything is in it: spirit, life and power. And although a number of the worldly wise and scribes (like Erasmus and others) do not relish the sweetness of this epistle—and thus judge strangely concerning St. Paul's style and skill in speech—all the same, on account of the aforementioned reasons and manifold benefit, we should seize and teach what is really presented to us in this epistle. We should follow it, let it be faithfully commended to us, diligently apply ourselves to it, ponder it with seriousness and humility. Additionally we should call on GOD for his Spirit and live in obedience with his Spirit. God will certainly act in this way for those who are his, and will let us experience all manner of blessing through Christ Jesus our Lord. Amen.[46]

We pray that you will take up this book and read so that "together you may with one voice glorify the God and Father of our Lord Jesus Christ" (Rom 15:6).

Philip D. W. Krey
Peter D. S. Krey

---

[45]See above, general introduction, p. xxvi.

[46]Spangenberg, *Außlegung der Ersten Acht Capitel der Episteln S. Pauli an die Römer*, 5r-v. See also Robert Kolb, "God's Select Vessel and Chosen Instrument: The Interpretation of Paul in Late Reformation Lutheran Theologians," in *A Companion to Paul in the Reformation*, ed. R. Ward Holder (Leiden: Brill, 2009), 187-211.

COMMENTARY ON ROMANS 9–16

OVERVIEW: In the latter half of his letter to the church in Rome, Paul addresses some complex questions regarding the implications of the gospel of Jesus Christ for both corporate and Christian life. With pastoral concern he elucidates Christ's fulfillment of the Law and the Prophets, the thorny issue of the acceptance of the Gentiles and the rejection of the Jews who did not believe in Christ, Scripture's definition of the church, and the relationship between Christians of varying understandings and giftings. Seeking to renew and preserve the church, the reformers read the apostle's words carefully, prayerfully applying them to their own context: for example, the continued unbelief of some Jews, Catholic resistance to the free gospel of salvation in Christ apart from any human merit and the need to proclaim the gospel faithfully without encouraging arrogance or despair. Unsurprisingly, in these ancient sacred pages Reformation theologians and pastors are not disappointed; they find words "for our learning, that we through patience and comfort of the Scriptures might have hope" (Rom 15:4 KJV). Even if this lofty subject matter—especially of God's election and grace—overwhelms and transcends human reason, nevertheless every creature should be silent and marvel at God's goodness and mercy in his acts of creation and redemption. "O Lord, I am not proud; I have no haughty looks. I do not occupy myself with great matters, or with things that are too hard for me. But I still my soul and make it quiet, like a child on its mother's breast; my soul is quieted within me. O Israel, wait on the Lord, from this time forth for evermore" (Ps 131 BCP).

Prolegomena: Text, Theology and Traditions

ROMANS IS THE DOOR AND KEY TO SCRIPTURE. MARTIN LUTHER: If you want to engage successfully in theology and the study of Sacred Literature and you do not want to dash against a closed or sealed passage of Scripture, then above all things you should learn to understand sin correctly. And the epistle to the Romans should be your door and key to holy Scripture, otherwise you will never reach a proper understanding and knowledge of Scripture. Once you have done this, however, you will understand what a great evil sin is and that on account of sin God sent his Son to blot out sin by the blood of the Son of God—that indescribable sacrifice. LECTURES ON GENESIS.[1]

IN THIS EPISTLE PAUL ADDRESSES THE WEAK AND THE STRONG. MARTIN LUTHER: So that we may understand this epistle properly and clearly, we should know that the Romans to whom St. Paul writes were converted to Christ partially from the Jews and partially from the Gentiles. At that time there were many Jews living in every land, as Acts 17 shows, and especially in Rome. Now after the apostle has taught them faith and good works correctly in the whole epistle, he makes some exhortations at the end of the epistle. So that he may preserve them harmoniously in faith and good works, he takes up the reasons that might produce discord and separate them from the unity of the Spirit. There are two reasons that still today, as in

---

[1]WA 44:507 (cf. LW 7:280).

all times, strive against the unity of the Spirit, against faith and against good works. Therefore we must see them and note them well.

The first reason is that some Jewish converts, though they heard that in the New Testament all kinds of food, days, clothing, vessels, persons, places and manners are free; and that only faith makes us godly in God's sight; and that the laws about eating meat and fish, about special days and clothes, about places and vessels, were entirely abolished—nevertheless their weak conscience and imperfect faith were still so severely ensnared because of long-standing customs that they could not use this freedom. They worried that they would sin if they acted differently than their previous customs.

Similarly, both Jews and Gentiles, because of the same weakness, dared not eat the bread and meat that had been offered to idols by unbelievers, even though it was for sale in the market and was sold there. They thought that if they ate they would be honoring the idols and denying Christ, though it was in truth nothing. All food is clean and a good creature of God, whether in the hands of Gentiles or Christians, whether offered to God or to the devil.

On the other hand, the second reason is that those who knew these things and had a stronger faith did not pay attention to the weak, but used their freedom all too boldly and with contempt for the weak by eating and drinking without distinction whatever came before them, which was also correct. But it was incorrect that they did not avoid the weak, but confused them. When the weak saw that they were so bold, they could neither follow nor remain behind. If they followed, their weak conscience would stand in the way and say, "It is sin; do not do it." If they did not follow, then their conscience again would stand in the way and say: "You are not a Christian, for you do not do what the other Christians do. Your faith must not be correct." See, thus they could neither stay behind nor run ahead; whatever they did, their conscience was against them. Now, to act against conscience is the same as acting against faith and is a grievous

sin. The Church Postil (1540): Second Sunday in Advent.[2]

On Civil and Gospel Righteousness.

Philipp Melanchthon: It is very helpful to note when reading all of Scripture that there is a twofold righteousness. The first is a civil righteousness, for we will call it that for clarity's sake, whenever human reason does good works or civil works. But human reason does not see any other righteousness than that. And so it deems that works of that kind suffice for our justification before God. But it does not value any other worship of God other than offering those civil works, such as not stealing, not killing, not lying, not committing adultery, obeying the authorities and restraining pleasures. And it has decided that God's wrath is placated by such works. Meanwhile, it does not see the uncleanness of the human heart, that it has no fear of or trust in God, and that it has a sinful longing and evil desires of every kind. Therefore the godly have always been at odds with the world. The godly teach some other righteousness beyond that hypocrisy of works. The world, in contrast, teaches the hypocrisy of works to such a degree that it teaches that those works placate the wrath of God and justify a person before God.

But the gospel shows a far different righteousness, which is called the righteousness of faith. For the gospel teaches that Christ, the Son of God, was given on our behalf and that righteousness in God's eyes is believing that our sins are forgiven us for Christ's sake, that is to say, that for Christ's sake we are received into the Father's grace. Meanwhile, the gospel makes clear our sins and condemns not only outward faults but also the uncleanness of the heart. It shows that the human heart is devoid of the fear of God and is devoid of trust in God. It shows the baseness of human desire inflamed with passion in our members. And so it says that we cannot placate God's wrath by the hypocrisy of our works, and it shows us another righteousness

---

[2]LW 75:64-65* (WA 10,1.2:63-64; E2 7:42-43); citing Acts 17:5, 13, 17.

utterly hidden and unknown to the world, namely, what Paul calls the righteousness of faith. THE ARGUMENT IN ROMANS.[3]

THREE CHIEF DIFFICULTIES OF THIS EPISTLE. DESIDERIUS ERASMUS: But the difficulty of this letter equals and almost surpasses its utility. And this seems to me to be the case for three reasons in particular. First, nowhere else is the order of speech more confused; nowhere is the speech more split by the transposition of words; nowhere is the speech more incomplete through absence of an apodosis, about which Origen complains time and again, as he struggles and labors everywhere in difficulties of this kind.[4] Whether this should be attributed to Tertius, in his role as interpreter or as recorder, or to Paul himself, I leave to others to judge. Paul plainly acknowledges his inexperience in discourse, though he begs his ignorance to be excused. Furthermore, so far from aiming at a discourse composed by human skill, he actually thought that he ought to avoid it, lest it detract in any way from the glory of the cross. And for this reason Origen thought that it was superfluous to search for polished composition in Paul.[5] . . . Another factor that contributed to these difficulties of the language was Hebrew, the idioms of which Paul is constantly bringing in, speaking Greek in such a way that nonetheless you sometimes recognize it is Hebrew.

The second cause of difficulty, in my opinion, is the obscurity of things that are hard to put into words; because of them, no other letter is handicapped by more frequent rough spots or is broken by deeper chasms. So much is this the case that he himself, having abandoned something that he had started to say, is compelled to exclaim at one point: "Oh, the depth of riches!" And furthermore as a prudent man he so touches on certain mysteries as to display them as though through a window only, accommodating his speech to the situation of the times and to the capacity of those to whom he writes. Paul knew and saw certain things that it was unlawful for one to say, and he knew to what extent milk and to what extent solid food were needed. He knew the stages of growth in Christ, and what had to be applied to each one. . . .

I believe that a third reason is his frequent and sudden change of masks, while he considers now the Jews, now the Gentiles, now both; sometimes he addresses believers, sometimes doubters; at one point he assumes the role of a weak man, at another of a strong man; sometimes that of a godly man, sometimes of an ungodly man. The result of all this is that the reader, wandering about as though in some kind of confusing labyrinth or winding maze, does not see very well whence he has entered or how he may leave. Origen, in my opinion not less truly than elegantly, compares Paul to a man who leads a stranger into some very powerful ruler's palace: a confusing place, owing to various kinds of winding passageways and to the recesses from the rooms.[6] However, from afar he displays certain things from a most abundant treasury of wealth; he brings some things closer, but is unwilling that others be seen. Often, moreover, after having entered in through one door, he exits through another, so that the stranger himself wonders where he has come from, where he is or what way he should go out.

Even the apostle Peter acknowledges this in his second letter, testifying that there are certain things hard to comprehend in the Pauline letters, which those who are not very learned and not very strong might distort to their own ruin. We for our part have attempted to remove the difficulties to the best of our ability, except for certain words that are so peculiar to the language of Paul that they cannot be expressed in more than one way; these for example: faith, grace, body, flesh, member, spirit, mind, feeling, to build and other of this kind that, although it was not possible to change outright, we have striven to soften as much as possible. But now let us hear the man himself, speaking like a Roman

---

[3]MO 15:443-46.
[4]See PG 14:833.
[5]PG 14:1059.

[6]PG 14:1008.

to the Romans, no, rather, to all, in terms quite blunt and clear. THE ARGUMENT OF ROMANS.[7]

Paul Turns His Attention to Questions of Election (of the Gentiles)

AN ABRUPT SHIFT IN PAUL'S LETTER. JOHN CALVIN: Paul begins to remove the offenses that might have diverted human minds from Christ. For the Jews, for whom he was appointed according to the covenant of the law, not only rejected him but also regarded him with contempt, and for the most part hated him. So one of two things seemed to follow: either there was no truth in the divine promise, or Jesus, whom Paul preached, was not the Lord's Christ who had been promised to the Jews specifically. This twofold knot Paul fully unties in what follows. He, however, so handles this subject as to refrain from all bitterness against the Jews, lest he excoriate their minds. Still he concedes absolutely nothing to them that might harm the gospel. He allows them their privileges in such a way as not to detract anything from Christ. But he passes abruptly to this subject, so that there appears to be no connection to the discourse. He, however, so begins this new subject as if he had already mentioned it.

It happened in this way: having finished handling doctrine, he turned his attention to the Jews, and being astonished at their unbelief as at something monstrous he burst out into this sudden proclamation, as if it were a subject he had already handled. Because there was no one who would not immediately have thought: "If this be the doctrine of the Law and the Prophets, how is it that the Jews so stubbornly reject it?" In addition, it was known everywhere that everything Paul had said so far about the law of Moses and the grace of Christ was more odious to Jews than that through their consent the Gentile's faith should be nourished. It was therefore necessary to remove this obstacle, lest it should impede the advance of the gospel. COMMENTARY ON ROMANS 9.[8]

A NEW DISCUSSION ABOUT THE CHURCH AND THE CALL OF THE GENTILES. PHILIPP MELANCHTHON: An entirely new discussion is begun. Although he at times repeats and interweaves the doctrine of justification, he chiefly treats two other matters: Who truly are the people of God (or which is the true church), and the calling of the Gentiles.... There are at all times two bodies of the church, the one of the true church, the other of the one that has the title but that persecutes the true church. The church, which bears the title, has great authority, great power. Therefore, lest the weak be deceived, it is necessary that the godly be fortified against this external appearance in order that they may understand which is the true church, who are the true people of God.

It is also now being argued:

Major Premise: The church cannot err.

Minor Premise: The assembly of the bishops and priests and of their adherents is the church.

Conclusion: Therefore this assembly cannot err.

They prove the minor premise by the fact that for many centuries these alone were in the ministry of the Word; they have the examples of the fathers, etc., so they are the church. Here it is necessary to show that although they hold the position of the ministry, they do not have the ministry of the gospel if they teach wicked things, and neither are they the church. It is not a small offense that this highest honor—the title of church—is taken from popes, princes and all the most beautifully ordered clerical estate and this august title is conferred on a few who are poor and calamity-ridden, and who indeed seem to be rebelliously shouting against the ordinary form of the church. By this offense many

---

[7]CWE 42:12-14* (LB 7:777-78); alluding to 1 Cor 2:1-5; 2 Cor 12:4; 1 Cor 3:2; 2 Pet 3:15-16; quoting Rom 11:33.

[8]CTS 38:332-33* (CO 49:169).

are being scared away from the gospel and from the true church. Therefore people must be taught about election, that the true church is not any and every crowd, but those who are elected and called to the gospel, who retain the true Word of God and fight for it against the wisdom and power of the world.

That is the occasion for Paul's discussion here. For the Jews were pressing these two arguments, that they were the people of God, and unless things were better for the entire Jewish state, the promises had not yet been fulfilled. Similarly, because they are the seed of Abraham, the promise does not pertain to the Gentiles. Here Paul opposes a contrary statement, that the people of God is a certain multitude chosen through mercy, called through the gospel and sanctified through the Holy Spirit. The people of God are not made by fleshly propagation and the worship of the law. This is the sum and substance of the statement and the principal proposition. Therefore he is speaking of the effect of election, that the true church has been elected through mercy, and he takes away two causes, fleshly propagation and the law.

Here he argues about predestination, about the freedom of the human will and about certain other matters—the general and the special activity of God and contingency. It is useful to consider the things that are said about such great matters, but those things are to be chosen piously and in the fear of God, since they are taught in the Scriptures, have the testimony of received and approved writers, and are profitable for consciences. . . . The writers do not disagree about the reprobation of the wicked, but all confess that the cause of reprobation in those who are damned is their wicked will and their sins. However, in the matter of the cause of predestination or election of those who are to be saved, they do not speak in the same way. . . .

The mercy of God is the cause of election, as Paul clearly teaches here and elsewhere: If it is of works, it is no longer of grace. For the church is not dependent on human counsel or on human powers, but God in Christ loved and chose those who are to be saved. Here two questions about election torment the mind. The first is about worthiness or

merit. The mind argues: If I were worthy, sufficiently pure or had merited well, I would declare that I also would receive mercy and the other benefits that have been promised. This trial arises from the judgment of the law, which requires worthiness and merits. Here it is very useful to hold fast to the teaching of the gospel about gratuitous mercy. The gospel of gratuitous mercy is proclaimed not to drive minds to despair, but in order that it might be a remedy for our mistrust and despair. And mercy is shown not in order that we might do nothing, or so that we might not accept the Word, but in order that our worthiness might be taken away and that the benefit of God might be certain.

The other cause of unrest comes from particularity. Because we hear that mercy is the cause of election, and that few are elected, we experience even greater anguish and wonder whether God shows partiality. Why does he not have mercy on all? To this attack also there should be opposed the universal promises of the gospel, which teach that God offers salvation to all on account of Christ and freely, according to the passage: "The righteousness of God through faith in Jesus Christ on all and over all." And elsewhere: "The same Lord of all is rich toward all." Likewise: "Everyone who will call on the name of the Lord," etc. These universal statements must be opposed to the temptation stemming from particularity. Thereafter we must declare that one must not judge about the will of God from reason without the Word of God. Likewise, just as about justification, so also about election, one must not judge from reason or from the law, but from the gospel.

When we wonder: if merits make no difference, then why is not mercy shown to all? I answer: As far as the Word and the promise are concerned, we must hold fast to universality. But not all attain the benefits because very many people resist the Word. And it is evident that resistance is an act of the human will, because God is not a cause of sin.

If we speak for the benefit of the conscience according to our judgment, let us say as we say about justification: That those who believe are righteous, so the elect do not resist the calling, but believe the gospel, and do not in the end reject it. Nevertheless, it must be held in the meantime that to believe and not to resist are results that come about when the Holy Spirit impels. I am speaking about our judgment, which does not search out the hidden majesty without the Word, but looks at the God who calls through the promise and apprehends his will in the Word, which is universal. Thus Paul says: "It is not of him who wills and runs, but of God who has mercy"; that is, mercy is indeed the cause of election, not our willing and running. Nevertheless, these things are done in the will and in running, not in resisting. COMMENTARY ON ROMANS (1540).[9]

DEFINING TERMS: FOREKNOWLEDGE, PROVIDENCE AND PREDESTINATION. TILEMANN HESSHUS: The foreknowledge of God is the name for God's infinite wisdom and knowledge, by which he foresees and observes from eternity all the things that will be—evil as well as good—no less than he sees present things, nor is any outcome of events able to be hidden from him. "I am God," he says in Isaiah 46, "who from the beginning announces the latter things, and from the very origin those things that have not yet occurred. I speak and it is deemed my counsel, and I do whatever I will."

But providence is the name for the divine reason and care with which he upholds and governs this entire world, holds individual creatures in his hand and will, governs all things in accordance with his good will and divine counsel, gathers the church in the world, rules the saints by his Spirit, permits the wicked to behave wantonly for a while (until he appoints a boundary and a limit for them), helps good things and honors them with rewards, permits evils and punishes them. David describes this providence with these words: "The Lord looked down from heaven; he saw all the children of men. From his well-furnished dwelling he looked down on all who dwell

on earth. He makes their hearts one by one; he understands all their works" (Psalm 33). Again, Matthew 10: "All the hairs of your head are numbered."

But election (*eklogē*) or predestination, or the determination beforehand (*prohorisis*), or the purpose (*prothesis*) or a foreordaining (*taxis*) is the eternal counsel of God by which before the foundation of the world, without any respect to people's merits or works, but purely out of his immense mercy in his Son Jesus Christ he chose for himself a certain number of people, whom he intended to call according to the good pleasure of his will through the preaching of the gospel and to lead by faith to eternal life and glory and decided to leave the remaining multitude of fallen people to their destruction. Thus Luke says in Acts 13: "And as many as had been appointed to eternal life believed." And Paul says in Ephesians 1: "Through whom we also were adopted as it was appointed, predestined according to his purpose, who works all things according to the counsel of his will." It is concerning this election that we are now concerning ourselves. ON THE PREDESTINATION OF THE SAINTS: DEFINING TERMS.[10]

WHEN SHOULD THE DOCTRINE OF ELECTION BE TAUGHT? TILEMANN HESSHUS: All the articles of faith, but especially this doctrine about the election of the saints, are a mystery hidden to the entirety of human reason and far exceeds every capacity of human genius. Consequently, it must be sought, learned and drawn not from the books of the philosophers or the pleasing arguments of the wise of this world, but only from the Word of God, in which God has revealed out of his immense kindness his hidden mysteries, that is, as much as he wanted us to know. The Baptist[11] says,

---

[9]Melanchthon, *Commentary on Romans*, 185-88* (MO 15:677-80); citing Rom 3:22; 10:12, 13; 9:16.

[10]Hesshus, *Explicatio Epistolae Pauli ad Romanos*, 274v-275r; citing Is 46:9-10; Ps 33:13-15; Mt 10:30; Acts 13:48; Eph 1:4-5.

[11]Hesshus seems to have understood Jn 1:15-18 as a paragraph, thus attributing Jn 1:18 to John the Baptist. Modern English translations place Jn 1:15 in parentheses, on account of subtle grammatical reasoning (the *hoti* clauses of Jn 1:16-17 correspond to Jn 1:14). Luther grouped Jn 1:15-18 together as a paragraph (see WADB 6:326-27); Bullinger and Calvin seem to have agreed

"Nobody has ever seen God; the only-begotten Son who is in the bosom of the Father, he himself has made him known to us" (Jn 1). Again, "Nobody knows the Father except the Son" (Mt 11). . . . Therefore let us remember that our minds ought to be called away from those arguments that human reason admires, when we think about election. For what would be more foolish than from ignorant and blind reason to cobble together and invent the hidden and eternal counsel of God concerning how the church of the saints is gathered? As if there would be more wisdom and righteousness in filthy humanity than in the most holy God!

Therefore let us hear God with all reverence as he testifies about his own act of election and reveals the mysteries of his will. And let us recognize that whatever is not revealed in express words by the Son of God, the apostles and the prophets is not only uncertain but also clearly false, and abusive against the divine majesty. David says, "[Your word] is a light to my feet." This principle ought to hold sway in every aspect of religion, but especially in this article. Nor will we be ashamed to admit a humble and godly ignorance in those matters in which investigation is audacious and the presumption of knowledge is harmful.

God does not begrudge us the unapproachable light of his hidden wisdom, but he considers our weakness, which cannot endure the infinite splendor of his divine majesty. He said to Moses, "You cannot see my face, for no human being will see me and live." Therefore let us rather thank God because he has not concealed anything of those matters that pertain to our obtaining eternal salvation, but has revealed all things most clearly through his Son. But he has removed far from our sight for our own advantage those things that can be left unknown without any loss to our salvation and that we cannot perceive or endure in the fragility of this life.

After we have warned that this doctrine about the predestination of the saints ought to be drawn only from the fonts of Israel, one must now add in what order that doctrine ought to be set forth before people. By all means we must take care that consciences that have not yet been instructed in necessary doctrine and confirmed in the very beginnings of religion not be snatched away in the stormy treatment of this doctrine into labyrinths of arguments from which they cannot escape.[12]

"I spoke to you as to infants in Christ; I gave you milk to drink," said Paul. Therefore the mental capacity of the hearers must be taken into consideration. And he teaches us by his own example in this epistle when is the time to set forth this doctrine. ON THE PREDESTINATION OF THE SAINTS: THE SOURCE AND ORDER OF THIS DOCTRINE.[13]

(CTS 34:50 [CO 47:16-17]; Heinrich Bullinger, *In divinum Iesu Christi Domini nostri Euangelium secundum Ioannem, Commentariorum libri X* [Zurich: Froschauer, 1543], 13v). Lefèvre d'Étaples disagrees, stating that "these [Jn 1:16-18] are not the words of John the Baptist, but of John the Evangelist" (*Commentarii initiatorii in quatuor Evangelia* [Basel: Andreas Cratander, 1523], 287r). And Beza avoids making a judgment: "But I leave it to the reader to judge whether these [Jn 1:16-18] are rather the words of the Evangelist" (*Annotationes maiores*, 1:349).

[12]Hesshus primarily means correct instruction according to the Scriptures and the faith; see *Formula of Concord*, "Solid Declaration, Rule and Norm" (BoC 527).
[13]Hesshus, *Explicatio Epistolae Pauli ad Romanos*, 275v, 276r-v; citing Jn 1:18; Mt 11:27; Ps 119:105; 1 Cor 3:2.

9:1-5 PAUL ANGUISHES OVER HIS OWN PEOPLE

I am speaking the truth in Christ—I am not lying; my conscience bears me witness in the Holy Spirit—²that I have great sorrow and unceasing anguish in my heart. ³For I could wish that I myself were accursed and cut off from Christ for the sake of my brothers,ᵃ my kinsmen according to the flesh. ⁴They are Israelites, and to them belong the adoption, the glory, the covenants, the giving of the law, the worship, and the promises. ⁵To them belong the patriarchs, and from their race, according to the flesh, is the Christ, who is God over all, blessed forever. Amen.

a Or *brothers and sisters*

OVERVIEW: How Paul begins the difficult and painful discussion of the rejection of his people shows the reformers his rhetorical dexterity. As if he were smearing honey on the brim of a cup of bitter medicine, Paul speaks to his readers with kindness and gentleness in anticipation of the looming condemnation.[1] Through this strategy—which he often wields—he disarms a potentially hostile audience, so that they might receive his message more readily. He is no enemy of the Jewish nation, no despiser of Mosaic law. On the contrary, he loves the law, and he longs for his Jewish brothers and sisters to understand it fully, that all the advantages and benefits of Israel point to Christ. To prove how serious he is, he even wishes that he would be damned that they might live (*resignatio ad infernum*).

Paul's praise for the Jewish people reaches its pinnacle in the confession that Jesus of Nazareth, who is God and man, is their brother. These commentators cannot help but see the careful theological grammar Paul uses in Romans 9:5—later affirmed and canonized by the Council of Chalcedon (451). According to his human nature, Christ belongs to the fleshly heritage of the patriarchs; according to his divine nature, he is eternally blessed. The apostle skillfully holds together Christ's natures—distinguishable but inseparable—in the unity of his person. Israel's greatest blessing is that the eternal God chose to condescend into human flesh in their midst. "Shout, O Israel! . . . The King of Israel, the LORD is in your midst!" (Zeph 3:14-15 ESV).

9:1-2 *The Truth in Christ About Predestination*

PAUL SWEARS TO TELL THE TRUTH. DAVID PAREUS: "I tell you the truth in Christ." Since the apostle is about to speak concerning the rejection of the Jews and the substitution of the Gentiles, he uses a holy and serious protestation, such as is not found elsewhere in the Scripture. He was led to do so not by fear but by necessity. He knew that he was hated by the Jews on the score that he had defected from Moses to Christ owing to his inconstancy and was teaching a gospel out of hatred for the law. From this understanding it could appear that he wanted to insult the Jews out of some ill-will and flatter the Romans. In order to deflect such suspicions, he most solemnly prefaces his remarks concerning his more-than-human affection toward the Jews, showing that that was far from the case, that he was laboring here with some *epichairekakia* ["joy over a neighbor's

---

[1]For this analogy, see the *English Annotations* on Rom 10:1 and Bullinger on Rom 11:1.

misfortune"] so that he was very grieved by the blindness of his people and their destruction, which he was prepared to redeem by giving up his own salvation. But in order that it may not be thought a trivial matter, and in order to win over their embittered souls instead, he confirms his statement with an oath, and at the same time piles up and proclaims the excellent praises of the Hebrews. Nonetheless, he comes to the point where he shows that they lack only one thing— without which the other things are of no benefit— namely, that they are hostile to Christ. . . .

With an oath he begins his complaint about the grief and torture of his heart because of his people's rejection, which we said was the main point of his introduction. And he explains the reasons for his great grief. "I tell you the truth." By taking an oath he averts the suspicion that his grief is feigned. He is saying, "I am not pretending at all, but I truly attest to my grief." "I am not lying." Someone can tell the truth and neverthe-less lie by saying a true thing that he thinks is false. For lying is going against one's own mind. For this reason the apostle attests the truthfulness in his words and the sincerity in his mind. He invokes three witnesses of the truth: "Christ," whom he will soon call "God blessed forever." He therefore appeals to the judgment seat of God. "His conscience," which is like a thousand wit-nesses—and the worst torture if it is wronged. And "the Holy Spirit," who cannot deceive or be deceived, since he is the Spirit of truth. Com-mentary on Romans 9:1.[2]

Christ Grants a Good Conscience.

Domingo de Soto: If you should happen to look at the composition of the Greek word, you might perhaps say it means, "as my conscience calls Christ as a witness" or "as Christ gives witness at the same time." But the meaning is not that the conscience and Christ give witness at the same time, but rather that Christ is the author of truth for the conscience. In order to remove this ambigu-

ity, the interpreter translated it by this phrase, "as my conscience calls Christ as a witness," which has the same meaning. Therefore he adds the testimony of the conscience as an explanation of the next word, "I am not lying," for speaking contrary to one's conscience is lying. But because the conscience can sometimes be mistaken, he adds, "In the Holy Spirit." Just a little earlier he had said, "The Holy Spirit bears witness to our spirit," because he is undoubtedly infallible. Therefore, just as when he says, "My conscience bears witness," its meaning is that he said, "I am not lying," so also when he says, "In the Holy Spirit," it is an explana-tion of the previous word, "in Christ Jesus," because the Spirit is poured into us by the virtue of Christ. Commentary on Romans 9:1.[3]

Joy in Suffering.

Martin Luther: From this text it is very clear that love is found not only in sweetness and delight but also in the greatest sorrow and bitterness. Indeed it rejoices and delights in bitterness and sorrow, because it regards the misery and suffering of others as if it were its own. Thus Christ even in the final and worst hour of his suffering was aglow with his deepest love, indeed according to blessed Hilary, it filled him with the greatest joy to suffer the greatest pain. For thus it is that "God is wonderful in his saints," so that he causes them, at the very time they are suffering the greatest pains, also to experience the greatest joys. Scholia on Romans 9:2.[4]

Saddened, Paul Struggles to Speak.

John Calvin: Paul dexterously manages to cut short his sentence so that he does not yet fully express what he was going to say. It was not yet suitable to mention the destruction of the Jewish nation openly. . . . He thus intimates a great measure of sorrow as imperfect sentences are for the most part full of pathos. But he will presently express the cause of the sorrow, after having more fully testified

---

[2]Pareus, *In Epistolam ad Romanos*, 819-21.

[3]Soto, *In Epistolam ad Romanos*, 254.
[4]LW 25:379 (WA 56:388); citing Hilary, *De Trinitate* 10.45 (PL 10:379); Ps 68:35.

his sincerity. The perdition of the Jews caused very great anguish to Paul, though he knew that it happened through the will and providence of God.

We hence learn that the obedience we render to God's providence does not prevent us from grieving at the destruction of the lost, though we know that they are thus doomed by the just judgment of God. For the same mind is capable of being influenced by these two feelings. When it looks to God it can willingly bear the ruin of those whom he has decreed to destroy; and when it reflects on these human beings it grieves their punishment. Therefore they are greatly deceived who say that godly people should be apathetic and heartless [*apatheian kai analgēsian*], lest they should resist the decree of God. COMMENTARY ON ROMANS 9:2.[5]

DIFFERENT FORM, SAME SUBSTANCE. TILE-MANN HESSHUS: Since Paul is about to enter into a dispute about the gracious election of God and he is about to show that the children of God are not born out of a fleshly procreation and that the keeping of Mosaic rituals does not bring salvation, he first attests concerning his love toward the Jewish nation. For the Pharisees had been convinced that Paul was the chief enemy of the Jewish people, and they suspected that Paul was spreading abroad a new kind of teaching with the purpose of oppressing the Jews and wiping out the whole Mosaic order.

In order to free himself of this suspicion, he testifies with an oath that a boundless sorrow has overtaken him because of the blindness, stubbornness and destruction of his people. This grief is so great that he wishes to save his own people at the cost of his own eternal destruction. But nobody can declare a more ardent love than placing the other person's safety above their own. With this most ardent feeling, the apostle tries to invite the Jews to consider his teaching. And he shows that it is not out of some private grudge with the intention of harming the Jews that he is spreading abroad the teaching of the justification of a person before God by faith and apart from the works of

the law and that he abolishes circumcision and makes the Gentiles equal to the Jews and welcomes them into the fellowship of the church. Rather, it is because he was divinely commanded to do so, and the salvation of the whole church demands it.

To be sure, the minds of the wise are horribly offended when they hear that the old order (whether of the church or the government) is being overthrown by a new kind of teaching. And since the church and polity of Moses was established by God himself, not only were the Pharisees and political rulers offended but also the apostles themselves were greatly grieved, because they saw that that polity and temple along with all its ceremonies were coming to ruin. What is more, Paul sees not only the overturn of the polity but especially the people's dreadful blindness and destruction. But here the Holy Spirit warns us not to be offended by the overthrow of the earlier regime, whether of the church or of the state, but always to pay attention to hearing the teaching and keeping it pure and sincere, not being scared off by the wicked people's being offended, but putting the glory of God and the salvation of the church ahead of all other things. COMMENTARY ON ROMANS 9:1-3.[6]

9:3-4 The Vast and Glorious Riches of Earthly Israel

CHRIST'S LOVE REFLECTED IN PAUL. JACQUES LEFÈVRE D'ÉTAPLES: Paul considered the so marvelous, so inseparable and insurmountable love of God and Christ toward us, and furthermore considered that out of zeal for his brothers according to the flesh he had been a persecutor of Christ (who had been so kind and extremely loving toward him), to such a degree that he was willing to be separated from Christ for their sake and for the sake of the ancestral traditions. Therefore he was not able not to be overcome with the greatest sadness and constant grief of heart, as someone who reflects that he has been so greatly ungrateful in the face of such great kindness. Therefore the love of Paul is not what is inseparable or insur-

---

[5]CTS 38:334-35* (CO 49:170).

[6]Hesshus, *Explicatio Epistolae Pauli ad Romanos*, 310v-311v.

mountable from every creature, but the love of Christ toward us, who lovingly causes the persecuting to rest and embraces the adversary. ANNOTATIONS ON ROMANS 9:1-3.[7]

WHAT DOES *ANATHEMA* MEAN? JOHN COLET: Here the apostle earnestly desires, yes longs intensely, that the Jews also, even though they refused to be called, may at length through divine grace be reckoned among the number of the called and of those who trust in God. This is what, out of his great love towards them, he now longs for; yes, even on condition that if only they be saved, he himself may be made accursed and an offering and victim for them, to be sacrificed for the propitiation of God. For this is the meaning of the Greek word *anathema*, since the verb *anathematize* ... denotes both "to execrate" and also "to devote," that is, to assign and to dedicate. An anathema ... is a victim over which one makes an oath. EXPOSITION OF ROMANS.[8]

PAUL'S FERVENT LOVE FOR HIS PEOPLE. JOHN CALVIN: Paul could not have expressed a greater ardor of love than what he testifies here. That is surely perfect love that does not refuse to die for the salvation of a friend. But there is another word added, *anathema*, which proves that he speaks not only of temporal but also of eternal death; but he explains its meaning when he says "from Christ," for it signifies a separation, and what is it to be separated from Christ, but to be excluded from the hope of salvation? It was then proof of the most ardent love that Paul hesitated not to wish for himself that condemnation which he saw impending over the Jews, in order to deliver them. ... Many indeed doubt whether this was a lawful desire; but this doubt may be thus removed: the settled boundary of love is that it proceeds as far as the conscience permits; if then we love in God and not without God's authority our love can never be too much.

And such was the love of Paul; for seeing his own nation endued with so many of God's benefits, he loved God's gifts in them, and them on account of God's gifts, and he deemed it a great evil that those gifts should perish, hence that his mind being overwhelmed he burst forth into this extreme wish. COMMENTARY ON ROMANS 9:3.[9]

SACRIFICIAL LOVE. DAVID PAREUS: This is an example of the most vigorous love toward the brothers, by which we all ought to be bound in aiding our brothers' salvation. It is very appropriate for shepherds to be devoted to their sheep, and such is the case in the example of Christ the Great Shepherd. But in his case alone did he mourn thoroughly as an example of such great love. He alone, out of pure love for us and indeed for his enemies, poured out his life for our salvation. But this is not a trivial argument for the divinity of Christ. For by God alone can there be an *anathema* or curse; only God can cast body and soul into hell. Therefore, because the apostle wishes that he were anathema to Christ, he indicates that Christ is true God, whose friendship means eternal blessing and whose rejection means an eternal curse. COMMENTARY ON ROMANS 9:3.[10]

GOD'S YES HIDDEN UNDER HIS NO. MARTIN LUTHER: Those who are truly righteous in that they abound in love achieve this resignation without great sadness. For because of their abounding love for God they make all things possible, even enduring hell. And by reason of this facility they immediately escape the penalty of this kind. Indeed they have no need to fear being damned, for they willingly and happily submit to damnation for the sake of God. Rather it is they who are damned who try to escape damnation.

For even Christ suffered damnation and desertion more than all the saints. And it was not

---

[7]Lefèvre d'Étaples, *Epistola ad Rhomanos*, 85r.
[8]Colet, *An Exposition of St Paul's Epistle to the Romans*, 33-34*.
[9]CTS 38:335-36* (CO 49:170-71).
[10]Pareus, *In Epistolam ad Romanos*, 824.

easy for him to suffer, as some imagine. For he really and truly offered himself for our eternal condemnation to God the Father for us. And according to his human nature he acted in no way different than a human being to be eternally damned to hell. And on account of this love of his toward God, God immediately raised him from death and hell and thus devoured hell. This all his saints should imitate, some to a lesser and some to a greater degree, for the more perfect they have been in their love, the more readily and easily they can do this. But Christ underwent this with the greatest difficulty of all. Hence in many passages he complains about the agonies of hell.[11]

Those who shrink from this interpretation are still being ruled by the fancies of their flesh, thinking that to love oneself is to want or hope first of all for something good for oneself; but they do not understand what this kind of good is, and thus they do not know what it is to love. For to love is to hate oneself, to condemn oneself and to wish the worst, in accord with the statement of Christ: "Whoever hates his life in this world will keep it in eternal life." But if someone says: "I do not love my life in this world because I am seeking what is good for it in the life to come," I reply: You are doing this out of love for yourself, which is a worldly love, and therefore you still love your life in this world. Whoever loves himself in this way truly loves himself: he loves himself not in himself but in God, that is, in accord with the will of God, who hates, damns and wills evil to all sinners, that is, to all of us. For what is good in us is hidden, and that so deeply that it is hidden under its opposite. Thus our life is hidden under death, love for ourselves under hate for ourselves, glory under ignominy, salvation under damnation, our kingship under exile, heaven under hell, wisdom under foolishness, righteousness under sin, power under weakness. And universally our every assertion of anything good is hidden under the denial of it, so that faith

may have its place in God, who is a negative essence and goodness and wisdom and righteousness, who cannot be possessed or touched except by the negation of all our affirmatives. SCHOLIA ON ROMANS 9:3.[12]

PAUL CHALLENGES THE ISRAELITE DEFINITION OF THE TRUE CHURCH. PHILIPP MELANCHTHON: We establish this as the aim [of the text]: it teaches that one must distinguish the true and elected church from the one that has the title and the fleshly prerogatives. This is a necessary teaching against the magnificent show that the false church puts forth, namely, its antiquity, the examples of the fathers and the consensus of the crowd. When these things meet our eyes, let us distinguish the churches as Paul here distinguishes the people of God. The true people has been elected through mercy; it is the people that has the gospel.

But the Jews contended that they were the people of God because they were descendants of Abraham, had the law, the fathers, examples and miracles. From this they reasoned as follows:

Major Premise: Christ has not yet come, because when Christ comes he will save the people.

Minor Premise: The people has not been saved, but a certain few seditious persons boast they have been saved.

Conclusion: Therefore Christ has not yet come.

Here Paul responds to the minor premise and teaches that the people had been elected through mercy, not on account of fleshly prerogatives or because of the law. If the discussion of Paul is to be referred to this understanding, it will be easier, and it can be transferred to our use in order that we may learn which is the true church.

Paul begins with a very serious complaint, in which he testifies that he is grieved by the destruction of his nation. All holy men [*sancti viri*] suffer

---

[11]Luther is likely referring to the Psalms. On Luther's immediate christological interpretation of the Psalms, see RCS OT 7:xlviii-xlix.

[12]LW 25:382-83 (WA 56:392); citing Jn 12:25.

intense grief when they consider that so great a
multitude of human beings is being damned, and
wonder at this secret counsel that the church is
such a tiny crowd, weak and downcast. Chiefly it
was a matter of grief to those born in this people
that this nation should be rejected, since the
fathers and the prophets came from it. Here let us
ponder Paul's argument in order that we may learn
to fear God. If God did not spare those who were
descendants of the fathers and of the prophets,
about whom the promises openly spoke, how
much less will he spare the Gentiles. COMMEN-
TARY ON ROMANS (1540).[13]

THE HONOR OF ISRAEL, GOD'S FAITHFULNESS.
JOHN CALVIN: The whole drift of Paul's discourse
is to this purpose, that though the Jews by their
defection had produced an ungodly divorce
between God and themselves, yet the light of
God's favor was not wholly extinguished, according
to what he had also said in Romans 3. They had
indeed become unbelievers and had broken his covenant, but still their unfaithfulness had not
rendered void the faithfulness of God. For he had
not only reserved for himself some remnant seed
from the whole multitude, but had as yet continued, according to their hereditary right, the name
of a church among them.

But though they had already stripped themselves of these ornaments, so that it availed them
nothing to be called the children of Abraham, yet
as there was a danger, lest through their fault the
majesty of the gospel should be depreciated among
the Gentiles, Paul does not regard what they
deserved, but covers their baseness and disgraceful
conduct by throwing veils over them, until the
Gentiles were fully persuaded, that the gospel had
flowed to them from the celestial fountain, from
the sanctuary of God, from an elect nation. For the
Lord passing by other nations had selected them as
a people for himself, and had adopted them as
children, as is often testified by Moses and the
prophets. And not content simply to give them the

name of children, the Lord calls them sometimes
the first-begotten, and sometimes his beloved....
By these words he means, not only to set forth his
kindness toward the people of Israel, but rather to
exhibit the efficacy of adoption, through which the
promise of the celestial inheritance is conveyed.
COMMENTARY ON ROMAN 9:4.[14]

WHAT DOES PAUL MEAN BY THE COVENANTS?
DOMINGO DE SOTO: Indeed, he weaves together
the qualities of sons in a picturesque and orderly
manner. But in Greek it reads in the plural:
diathēkai, "testaments." Now the same noun in the
plural means "distributions of inheritances that are
discharged after the death of the testator," but in
the singular it also means "an agreement among
living people" and "the inheritance itself." Thus,
perhaps in order that it would mean "the agree-
ments and covenants of God that he had made
with them," the translator rendered it as "testament."
For this reason Origen says, "Each time they sinned,
they seem to have been disinherited." And again,
"Each time God was propitiated, called them back
and led them back to the inheritance of his
possession, God must be believed to have repaired
the testament." And God made a covenant with
Abraham and the other fathers, as was related in
Genesis. Other interpreters, when they read the
plural noun, apply the word to the two testaments,
namely the old and the new testaments, which Paul
comments on. The first of those testaments was
granted to them, but the second was promised.
Nonetheless, if you read the singular, "testament,"
understand it to mean the Old Testament. COM-
MENTARY ON ROMANS 9:4.[15]

COVENANTS AND PROMISES, LAW AND GOS-
PEL. TILEMANN HESSHUS: "Testaments or
Covenants": There can be no doubt that he
understands the law and the gospel. For these are
the two covenants that God fashioned with the
people of Israel: one on Mount Sinai according to

---

[13]Melanchthon, *Commentary on Romans*, 188-89* (MO 15:681).

[14]CTS 38:339-40* (CO 49:172); citing Rom 3:3; Ex 4:22; Jer 31:9.
[15]Soto, *In Epistolam ad Romanos*, 257; citing Gal 4:21-31.

the Ten Commandments, in which he promised life and all good things on the condition that the law be fulfilled; the other, by which he promised the Messiah and offered freely for his sake the forgiveness of sins and the inheritance of eternal life to all who believe. The giving of the law is one kind of agreement or testament. It was an immense act of kindness that God renewed his law from heaven and informed us of his will.

The worship regulations, such as the ceremonies and rites prescribed by Moses, pertain to the old testament. Only in this people were true acts of worship—pleasing to God—being offered to God. For God had commanded them, and they were taking place in such a way that the promise of the Messiah shone forth. The Lord detested the other rituals done by the other nations. "The promises": they are the other kind of testament, namely, the new testament, by which God promises the forgiveness of sins and eternal life through the Messiah. COMMENTARY ON ROMANS 9:4.[16]

GOD'S GREAT LOVE FOR THE CHILDREN OF THE PROMISE. JACQUES LEFÈVRE D'ÉTAPLES: The great love of God and kindness toward the Jews: He wanted to embrace and glorify them. And in no other nation did the Lord appear in the flesh, with the result that he himself could say, "I was not sent except to the sheep of the house of Israel who have perished." Testaments were written with them. The Scripture indeed speaks about the old one: "Our Lord wrote a covenant with us at Horeb." But it also speaks about the new one: "A festival for the house of Israel and a new covenant for the house of Judah, not like the one I wrote with your fathers." And the first giving of the law was transmitted by Moses. The second law will go out from Christ out of Zion, as it had been written: "And the word of the Lord from Jerusalem." Worship, that is, a manner of worship, was given to them so that they might worship the true God, while others worshiped not God but demons, for (he says) all the gods of the heathen are demons. And he made

promises to them; nearly all the prophets are witnesses thereof. Their fathers were Abraham, Isaac and Jacob, from whom Christ the Lord wanted to trace his genealogy according to the flesh. For according to his divinity he had an eternal origin from the Father. And if the rest of the blessings seem trivial, nonetheless this is a great proof of his love toward them: Christ, who is God blessed above all things, deigned to take on flesh from them. But you will say, "If the promises concerning Christ were made to them and yet they did not receive him, as it is written, 'He came to his own and his own did not receive him,' then the proclamation of God was made void." By no means. For the children of the promise are understood to be those who emulate the faith of Abraham, not merely those who descend from Abraham according to the flesh, and they are true Israelites and sons and seed of Abraham—not by the flesh, but by the Spirit. ANNOTATIONS ON ROMANS 9:4-5.[17]

9:5 The God-Man Belongs to Israel

A CLEAR WITNESS OF CHRIST'S DIVINITY. THE ENGLISH ANNOTATIONS: A most evident testimony and pregnant proof of Christ's divinity! Blush for shame, says Oecumenius, and be confounded, O you wretched miscreant Arius, when you hear Christ glorified by the apostle with the title of God, in the singular number, with the article *ho*, "the God," or "only God" and "God over all" and blessed forever. ANNOTATIONS ON ROMANS 9:5.[18]

THE PREMIER GLORY OF THE JEWS IS THAT CHRIST IS THEIR BROTHER. JOHN CALVIN:

---

[16]Hesshus, *Explicatio Epistolae Pauli ad Romanos*, 312v-313r.

[17]Lefèvre d'Étaples, *Epistola ad Rhomanos*, 85v; citing Mt 10:6; Deut 5:2; Jer 31:31-32; Is 2:3; Jn 1:1-11.

[18]Downame, ed., *Annotations*, BBB3r*. Oecumenius (sixth century), probably a well-educated layman from Isauria in Asia Minor, authored the earliest extant Greek commentary on Revelation. See further William C. Weinrich, ed., *Revelation*, ACCS NT 12 (Downers Grove, IL: InterVarsity Press, 2005), xvii-xxix; Oecumenius, *Commentary on the Apocalypse*, trans. John N. Suggit, FC 112 (Washington, DC: Catholic University of America Press, 2006).

They who apply this to the fathers, as though Paul meant only to say that Christ had descended from the fathers, have no reason to allege. For his object was to close his account of the preeminence of the Jews by this encomium—that Christ proceeded from them. It was not a thing to be lightly esteemed, to have been united by a natural relationship with the Redeemer of the world. If he had honored the whole human race, in joining himself to us by a communion of nature, much more did he honor them, with whom he had a closer bond of union. It must at the same time be always maintained that when this favor of being allied by kindred is unconnected with godliness, it is so far from being an advantage that on the contrary it leads to a greater condemnation. COMMENTARY ON ROMANS 9:5.[19]

THREE INTERPRETATIONS OF "WHO IS GOD OVER ALL." DESIDERIUS ERASMUS: This passage can be construed in three ways. First the clause "who is above all" *ho ōn epi pantōn* may be joined to the preceding words and separated from the subsequent in this manner: "From whom is Christ according to the flesh—Christ who is above all" or "who was above all." To forestall any suspicion that Christ's honor was diminished through the human nature which he assumed, Paul added with a view to his divinity, "who is above all." This construction attributes divinity to Christ, because nothing is above all except God alone. For *epi* is used in place of *epanō*. Then after a period, there would follow "God be blessed forever," so that this would be an expression of thanks as a result of the contemplation of love toward the human race so great that God wished God the Son to assume a human body for our sake. But on this reading the article in *ho ōn* ["the one being"] is virtually superfluous; [while] in *theos eulogētos* ["God be blessed"], it is lacking.

In the second reading the entire passage sticks tightly together: "From whom is Christ according to the flesh, which Christ, since he is God above all, is . . . blessed forever." This reading very clearly

pronounces Christ God; but it would be easier if *hos ōn* ["who being"] had been written in place of *ho ōn* ["the one being"].

The third reading has no difficulties, at least on linguistic grounds—"from whom is Christ according to the flesh"; here a period ends the sentence. Then from a consideration of such great goodness of God, an expression of thanks is added, *ho epi pantōn theos, eulogētos eis tous aiōnas*, that is "God who is above all be blessed forever." Thus we would understand that the law that was given and the covenant and the prophets and finally Christ sent in human body—all of these things God, through an ineffable plan, provided to redeem the human race. Here if you take God to be the whole sacred Trinity (a meaning that frequently occurs in Sacred Literature, as when we are commanded to worship and serve God alone) Christ is not excluded. But if ["God" here] means the person of the Father (as is frequently true in Paul, especially when Christ or the Spirit is mentioned in the same passage) although from other passages in Scripture it is clearer than day that Christ, no less truly than the Father or the Holy Spirit, is called God, nevertheless this particular passage does not effectively refute the Arians, since nothing prevents it from being referred to the person of the Father. And so that those who claim from this passage that it is clearly demonstrated that Christ is openly called God, seem either to place little confidence in the witness of other scriptural texts; or to attribute no intelligence to the Arians, or they have not considered carefully enough the apostle's language. There is a similar passage in [2 Corinthians] 11, where he says that the Father is blessed forever: "God and the Father of our Lord Jesus Christ, who is blessed forever." For in the Greek there, "blessed" can be referred only to the Father. ANNOTATIONS ON ROMANS 9:5.[20]

---

[19]CTS 38:341* (CO 49:173-74).

[20]CWE 56: 242-43*; citing 2 Cor 11:31. Arius (c. 250–336) taught that the Father created the Son and thus the Son is wholly distinct, separate and subordinate to the Father. The Council of Nicaea (325) condemned this teaching; however, it did not settle the question of Christ's substance. Some advocated that the Son is of similar substance (*homoiousios*); others recognized that the

PROOF OF THE UNION OF CHRIST'S TWO NATURES IN HIS PERSON. TILEMANN HESSHUS: Since the Mosaic polity was founded for the sake of the Messiah, the Son of God, so it was the chief glory of this people that Christ, the Almighty God, was born of the Jews. Also, it was the greatest sin of this people that they did not welcome the only-begotten Son of God, but defiled him with their blasphemies and crucified him. But in this passage Paul teaches the doctrine of the two natures in Christ, the human and the divine, united in one person. Christ is from the Jews according to the flesh; therefore Christ is true man, having flesh and blood, body and soul. He is also the eternal and almighty God above all things, begotten from the essence of the eternal Father. And these two natures are one person.[21] Therefore from this passage one must derive the teaching of the communication of attributes. COMMENTARY ON ROMANS 9:5.[22]

THE UNITY OF NATURES IN CHRIST'S PERSON. JOHANNES BRENZ: Here Paul describes and demonstrates the person of Christ with few but indeed clear, distinct words, that he is true God and true man. For he says it in this way, "From their race Christ descended according to the flesh." If that's true, then he must be a true man. Right after that he adds, "Who is God over all, praised in eternity." So then, Christ, according to his person, is true man and true God; yes, the man Christ is true God. And this is not just in name alone but also by the very reality itself. How else could he say "praised in eternity"? Indeed we cannot say such about any human being. Thus "the fullness of deity dwells bodily in him," as Paul says of Christ in Colossians 2.

However, when we say, "the man Christ is God," we want to demonstrate two things. First, the eternal, only-begotten Son of God, the second person in the divine essence, took on himself man or, as the epistle to the Hebrews says, the seed of Abraham, so that God and man became one inseparable person. Second, the Son of God poured the fullness of his deity on this man, whom he took on himself in the unity of his person, and made him omnipotent, omniscient, omnipresent, yes, a present Lord and Ruler. That is what we understand . . . when we say that the Son of Man is one person with the Son of God.

Yes, that's exactly what we otherwise call the *communicatio idiomatum*, that is, a sharing and bond of the attributes of both natures in the one person of Christ. In this way and in such a form the Son of God took on himself man, so that he shared all his attributes, or as Paul says it, the whole fullness of his divinity bodily—however, without any harm and comingling of both substance and natures of the divinity and humanity. EXPOSITION OF ST. PAUL'S EPISTLE TO THE ROMANS.[23]

THIS PASSAGE CLEARLY TEACHES THE HYPOSTATIC UNION. DAVID PAREUS: The limitation "according to the flesh" teaches that in addition to his flesh there is in Christ another nature, a divine one, according to which he does not have his origin from among the Jews. The Greek article *to* ["the"]

Father and Son share the same substance (*homoousios*). The Council of Constantinople (381) canonized the latter.

[21]Almost certainly a printing error—adding *divinae* after *duae naturae*—rendered this sentence heterodox: "And these two divine natures are one person." No one during the Reformation taught there were two divine natures in Christ. Hesshus clearly would have rejected such a statement, as shown earlier in this comment and throughout his other *works* (for example, see RCS OT 7:23-24). We have therefore emended the text to reflect accurately Hesshus's own theology.

[22]Hesshus, *Explicatio Epistolae Pauli ad Romanos*, 315r.

[23]Brenz, *Erklerung der Epistel S. Pauls an die Römer*, 563; citing Col 2:9; Heb 2:16. *The communicatio idiomatum* (i.e., communication of properties in Christ's person) concerns the relationship between Christ's human and divine natures. Reformed theologians hold that Christ's natures are united in his person, but there is no exchange of attributes between the natures. While affirming that the traits of one nature cannot be predicated of the other, Lutheran theologians argue that the inseparability of the hypostatic union entails that the human nature of Christ partakes in the divine nature. See Richard A. Muller, *Dictionary of Latin and Greek Theological Terms Drawn Principally from Protestant Scholastic Theology* (Grand Rapids: Baker, 1985), 72-74; David J. Luy, *Dominus Mortis: Martin Luther on the Incorruptibility of God in Christ* (Minneapolis: Fortress, 2014), esp. 178-94.

emphatically indicates that here there is some different meaning than earlier in verse 3. "Who is God blessed above all." Because he had restricted Christ's origin from the Jews to his flesh or humanity, he also adds a reference to that according to which Christ does not originate from the Jews, namely, his divine nature, for he is not a mere human being, but also true God, existing in two natures in the unity of the person. It was opportune for him to mention here Christ's divinity so that it might become apparent what sort of superiority the Jews had, in that Christ wanted to take on his flesh from the Jews: namely, because Christ was both man and God. But lest it be thought that he is calling him God in an unusual sense, in the way that magistrates and kings are called "gods" inasmuch as they are agents of God, he designates him with the epithet of "true God": "The God who is *epi pantōn*, 'above all people' or 'above all things'"—which amounts to the same thing. He teaches that Christ is superior to all creatures and things. *Eulogētos*, "Blessed for ever." And from Romans 1:25 it is obvious that this ascription belongs to the true God alone, where God the Creator is honored with the same ascription. Heretics have labored from long ago to escape this divine praise of Christ. Erasmus also detracts not a little from it in his comments. . . .

This passage, if any, is very clear about the person of Christ, the *theanthrōpos* ["God-Man"].

First, he teaches that Christ is the true and eternal God, blessed above all things forever, who alone is God the creator (1:25). Second, but he is also true man, endowed with flesh and a human soul, the offspring of Jewish ancestors. Third, he exists in two true, distinct natures that are joined hypostatically, the divine and human natures, because the same person originated from the fathers who is also God blessed forever. Fourth, finally, all divine and human things correspond in Christ according to their distinct natures. COMMENTARY ON ROMANS 9:5.[24]

ETERNAL PRAISE. DESIDERIUS ERASMUS: Christ is a man in such a way that at the same time he is also God, not the god peculiar to this or that nation, but the God of the whole world, and a God who is one with the Father. He is in command of all, and all these things are carried out by his inscrutable wisdom. Because of such an unusual love for the human race, praise and thanksgiving are owed to him for all eternity. Amen. PARAPHRASE ON ROMANS 9:5.[25]

---

[24]Pareus, *In Epistolam ad Romanos*, 827-28.
[25]CWE 42:53*.

9:6-29 THE MYSTERY OF ELECTION

[6]But it is not as though the word of God has failed. For not all who are descended from Israel belong to Israel, [7]and not all are children of Abraham because they are his offspring, but "Through Isaac shall your offspring be named." [8]This means that it is not the children of the flesh who are the children of God, but the children of the promise are counted as offspring. [9]For this is what the promise said: "About this time next year I will return, and Sarah shall have a son." [10]And not only so, but also when Rebekah had conceived children by one man, our forefather Isaac, [11]though they were not yet born and had done nothing either good or bad—in order that God's purpose of election might continue, not because of works but because of him who calls— [12]she was told, "The older will serve the younger." [13]As it is written, "Jacob I loved, but Esau I hated."

[14]What shall we say then? Is there injustice on God's part? By no means! [15]For he says to Moses, "I will have mercy on whom I have mercy, and I will have compassion on whom I have compassion." [16]So then it depends not on human will or exertion,[a] but on God, who has mercy. [17]For the Scripture says to Pharaoh, "For this very purpose I have raised you up, that I might show my power in you, and that my name might be proclaimed in all the earth." [18]So then he has mercy on whomever he wills, and he hardens whomever he wills.

[19]You will say to me then, "Why does he still find fault? For who can resist his will?" [20]But who are you, O man, to answer back to God? Will what is molded say to its molder, "Why have you made me like this?"[21]Has the potter no right over the clay, to make out of the same lump one vessel for honorable use and another for dishonorable use? [22]What if God, desiring to show his wrath and to make known his power, has endured with much patience vessels of wrath prepared for destruction,[23]in order to make known the riches of his glory for vessels of mercy, which he has prepared beforehand for glory— [24]even us whom he has called, not from the Jews only but also from the Gentiles? [25]As indeed he says in Hosea,

"Those who were not my people I will call 'my people,'
and her who was not beloved I will call 'beloved.'"
[26]"And in the very place where it was said to them, 'You are not my people,'
there they will be called 'sons of the living God.'"

[27]And Isaiah cries out concerning Israel: "Though the number of the sons of Israel[b] be as the sand of the sea, only a remnant of them will be saved, [28]for the Lord will carry out his sentence upon the earth fully and without delay." [29]And as Isaiah predicted,

"If the Lord of hosts had not left us offspring,
we would have been like Sodom
and become like Gomorrah."

a Greek not of him who wills or runs   b Or children of Israel

---

OVERVIEW: All the reformers saw themselves as Augustine's heirs: the creation, causation and completion of every good work requires God's grace.[1] Each decried Pelagian and semi-Pelagian views of election and the human will. Nevertheless the reformers held a spectrum of views on predestination and election. Some reformers—like Calvin, Beza, Bucer and Luther in his debate with Erasmus—retrieve Augustine's understanding of predestination: unconditioned by human works and human choice, God in his mercy and wisdom predestines some to

---

[1]For a more sustained treatment on the range of teaching concerning predestination, see above, pp. xlv-xlix.

salvation and others to condemnation.[2] They admit that this is a "dreadful decree."[3] Nevertheless, ministers of the Word are called to teach the fullness of God's Word, and they believe Scripture clearly teaches this doctrine. Human beings cannot penetrate the reasons for this counsel of God. Other reformers—like the authors of the *Formula of Concord*—found such a harsh formulation of God's predestination to rob believers of assurance, to push them to arrogance or despair. These theologians affirm that God in his mercy and wisdom predestines some—unconditioned by human works and human choice—to salvation, while he permits others to rebel, thus condemning themselves.

Erasmus worries that such strong emphasis on God's action alone (monergism) in election negates human freedom, perhaps even making God the author of evil. In his debate with Luther, couched in denials and condemnations of the twin errors of Pelagianism and semi-Pelagianism, he wrote, "I prefer the view of those who do attribute much to free choice, but most to grace."[4] The Remonstrants—often called Arminians—agree in some sense with Erasmus; however, they limit the human role to merely not resisting God's grace in Christ. While generally affirming a role for human free will, the Anabaptists hold diverse views on predestination from something like the Remonstrant view to what might seem semi-Pelagian.

Despite the diversity of positions on this doctrine, all the reformers seek to add predestination to the pastoral toolkit. "God chose us in Christ before the foundation of the world, that we should be holy and blameless before him" (Eph 1:4). Of this each

believer must be certain. Rather than trying to grasp at God's hidden will, in times of trial the believer must look to Christ and say, "For me Christ was born, Christ has died, Christ has risen again." Appealing to the inscrutable mystery of God's providence, the reformers admonished their followers to gaze on God's mercy in Christ. Human reason cannot grasp the hidden counsels of God. Thankfully God has condescended to us, revealing himself in Christ, the Word and the sacraments.

PREFATORY REMARKS ABOUT PREDESTINATION. JOHANN WILD: Up to this point Paul has taught how sin ought to be recognized and where a cure ought to be sought. Now he reveals to whom this salvation pertains, a fact that we can learn from no other place than from predestination. Therefore, before we enter into the matter of predestination, we must first take note of some things.

First, just as not all who passed through the sea from Egypt entered the Promised Land, so not all who are baptized are saved. This is what the parables about the tares, the dragnet, the marriage feast, the ten virgins, etc. indicate. And there is the word of Christ: "Many are called," etc. Therefore it is not enough to be received into the number of the faithful by people, unless you should also happen to be received by God into the book of life. See Revelation 3:20-21 about this. And this being written in the book of life is nothing other than predestination. Second, predestination cannot be investigated by human reason. Nor is that astonishing, if indeed we find it difficult to investigate the things that are on earth, etc. All things are difficult. Read 4 Esdras 4 and Job 38–39 about this. Third, since predestination is inscrutable to human nature, it follows that it is dangerous to speak about it, as experience itself shows. For there is nothing that offends the carnal more. For this reason, the wise man says, "Do not seek out those things that are higher than you." For he who investigates majesty will be quashed by its glory, and whoever throws a stone up in the air will have it fall on his head.

Fourth, one must not speak stubbornly, but with fear about such mysteries of so great a

---

[2]See Pelikan, *Christian Tradition*, 1:297-98. Some scholars challenge this consensus, arguing that Augustine did not explicitly affirm reprobation as a decree, but instead associated it with divine permission. For example, see Levering, *Theology of Augustine*, 80n21; A. Trapè, "Augustine of Hippo," in *Encyclopedia of Ancient Christianity*, 3 vols., ed. Angelo Di Berardino (Downers Grove, IL: IVP Academic, 2014), 1:292-99.
[3]See LCC 21:955; CO 2:704. For Calvin's treatment of predestination, see further *Institutes* 3.21–25 (LCC 21:920-1008; CO 2:678-744).
[4]Desiderius Erasmus, *On the Freedom of the Will*, LCC 17:96; cf. p. 90.

magnitude. By all means, Paul seems to restrain the carnal person from speaking about these matters. "O human being, who are you to answer God?" It is as if he were to say, "As much as you are a human being and mere clay, you cannot understand with all the saints what the length and breadth [of God's love is]." Therefore first take care that you are a child of God and his friend, for we do not reveal secrets to slaves, but to children and friends. And "blessed are the pure in heart, for they themselves will see God." "But the unspiritual person does not understand any of those things that are spiritually judged." A Christian has rather many other things about which he can usefully speak and ask about.

Fifth, a godly person is truly not troubled at all by worry over predestination, but entrusts himself entirely to God, saying with David, "If I will have found favor in the eyes of the Lord," etc. "If not," etc. This is denying oneself perfectly.

Sixth, whoever wishes to speak about predestination usefully and without any danger, let him observe the Pauline order, so that first he considers himself to be a sinner, then recognizes the grace of God through Jesus Christ, etc., and then at last considers predestination. For whoever recognizes that all people are sinners by nature and so deserving nothing but punishment will not dispute over why God showed grace to this individual and not to another, but will thank God, since he did not condemn all, but revealed Christ to him, etc.

Seventh, predestination is learned nowhere more certainly than from Christ, for he revealed this hidden and divine counsel and decree, namely whom God wishes to be saved and whom he does not. He says, "Whoever does not believe in the Son has already been judged." "But whoever believes is not condemned." Again, "The Father has given all judgment to the Son." Again, "this is the will of the Father, so that all who see the Son," etc. Again, "Every branch in me that does not bear fruit he removes," etc. Why then are you vexed about predestination? Run to Christ, believe in him, be incorporated into Christ, bear fruit in Christ, remain in life, and you are certain that you have

been predestined. If you do not do these things, you are a reprobate. Exegesis of Romans 9.[5]

Reprobation, Too, Should Be Understood as Predestination. Martin Bucer: God chose us in Christ before the foundations of the world were laid, having predetermined us to adoption as sons. Predetermination, then, which we commonly call "predestination," is that act of designation on the part of God whereby in secret counsel God designates and actually selects and separates from the rest of humankind those who are drawn to his Son, Jesus our Lord, and ingrafts them into him (having brought them into this life at his own good time), and whom, when thus drawn and ingrafted, God will regenerate through Christ and will sanctify to fulfill God's purposes. This, then, as I have said is the predestination of the saints.

There is in addition a general predestination. *Proorismos* means simply "predetermination," and God accomplishes all things by his predeterminate counsel. . . . If you require a definition of this general predetermination it is the assigning of each thing to its own purpose, whereby before creating them God destines all things separately from eternity to some fixed use. In this sense there is even a predestination of the wicked, for just as God forms also out of nothing, so God forms them for a definite end. God does everything in wisdom, not excepting the predetermined and good use of the wicked, for even the godless are the tools and instruments of God, and "God has made everything for its own purpose, even the wicked for the day of evil." The theologians, however, refuse to call this "predestination," preferring "reprobation" instead. Nonetheless, God does all things well and wisely, and so does nothing except by chosen design. God gave Pharaoh up to a depraved mind and raised him up for the purpose of showing divine power in

---

[5]Wild, *Exegesis in Epistolam ad Romanos*, 203r-205r; citing Sir 3:23; Prov 25:27; Sir 27:25; Rom 9:20; Eph 3:18-19; Jn 15:14-15; Mt 5:8; 2 Cor 2:14; 2 Sam 15:25; Jn 3:18; 6:47; 5:22; 6:40; 15:2.

punishing him; Esau too God hated before he had done any evil. Scripture speaks in terms as plain as these. Indeed, who will deny that when God formed these and all the wicked God foreknew before making them the purposes for which God wished to use them, and that God ordained and destined them for those ends? So what prevents us from calling it "predestination" in their case too? At any rate, none of the wicked does God fail to put to good use, and in every act of sin on our part there is some good work of God.

… Many assert predestination only of the saints and not reprobation of the wicked … because it seems to them unworthy of God to say that he has predetermined anyone to perdition. Nevertheless, Scripture does not shrink from stating that God abandons certain human beings to a depraved mind and works in them to their ruin; why then is it unworthy of God to say that he had also decided in advance to abandon them to a depraved mind and work in them to their ruin? But it is intolerable to human reason that some by God should be hardened, blinded and given up to a reprobate mind, and this is why it is thought impious to ascribe to God the predetermining and destining of anyone to these fates. …

We must accordingly reject the judgment of reason in this area, and confess that the judgments of God are "a great abyss" and inscrutable, yet righteous. For God is just in all ways, even when to our reason it seems otherwise. Therefore we must confess that God justly demands of us a holy life adorned with every virtue, and justly also hardens, blinds and abandons to a spirit of depravity whom God will, and finally justly condemns and punishes them, while to us is to be assigned all the blame for our perdition. AN INQUIRY CONCERNING PREDESTINATION.[6]

DREADFUL DECREE. JOHN CALVIN: I ask: whence does it happen that Adam's fall irremediably involved so many peoples, together with their infant offspring, in eternal death unless because it so pleased God? Here their tongues, otherwise so loquacious, must become mute. The decree is dreadful indeed, I confess. Yet no one can deny that God foreknew what end man was to have before he created him, and consequently foreknew because he so ordained by his decree. If anyone inveighs against God's foreknowledge at this point, he stumbles rashly and heedlessly. What is there to accuse the heavenly Judge because he was not ignorant of what was to happen? If there is any just or manifest complaint, it applies to predestination. And it ought not to seem absurd for me to say that God not only foresaw the fall of the first man, and in him the ruin of his descendants, but also meted it out in accordance with his own decision. For as it pertains to his wisdom to foreknow everything that is to happen, so it pertains to his might to rule and control everything by his hand. INSTITUTES 3.23.7.[7]

GOD IS NO RESPECTER OF PERSONS, AND GOD IS FOR US. JOHANN WILD: Paul begins to discuss the matter of predestination. As soon he has set forth the matter itself, he thereupon removes the arguments of the flesh. His chief thesis is that "it is not a matter of the one who wills or of the one who runs, but of God who has mercy." That is to say, the fact that one person is predestined to glory instead of another person is not owing to his nature or his parents or lineage or his merits, but to the mercy and voluntary election of God. That it is not nature is obvious because we are all the same as far as nature is concerned, namely, children of wrath. For how was Peter better by nature than Judas was? That it is not based on parents or lineage is obvious because not all are elected who are born of upright parents, nor are all damned who are born of evil parents. The example of Isaac is relevant to this matter. Again, concerning Jacob and Esau, if predestination were based on the parents, then also Ishmael and Esau would have been predestined. But that it is not based on merits is obvious because Peter was

---

[6]Bucer, *Common Places*, 96-98*; citing Rom 9:22, 13, 17; 11:33.

[7]LCC 21:955-56* (CO 2:704).

predestined from eternity when he had not yet merited anything but was not even born. The example drawn from Jacob and Esau is also relevant to this point. What did Jacob merit? Therefore it is agreed that election does not consist of works but of the grace of the one calling. Therefore it is truly said, "It is not a matter of the one who wills," etc. For this reason Paul says, "By grace are you saved, not by works." Also pertinent to this matter is what is said: "I will have mercy on whom I want to," etc. That is, "I will offer grace out of mercy on the one whom out of mercy I have predestined, and the one to whom I here offer grace out of my mercy I will glorify in the future out of the same mercy." Behold, you are hearing nothing other than mercy and grace. The godly recognize this. He says, "Your mercy will go before me." Again, "Your mercy is before my eyes." Again, "Your mercy follows me. Therefore I will not hope in the bow nor in my sword," etc. Again, "Their arm will not save them, but yours will, and the illumination of your face, because you have delighted in them." But you say, "If it is not of the one who wills, etc., then I do not want to will or to run anymore." To the contrary, one ought to run all the more, the more certainly we know that our salvation depends on the will of God. Listen to Paul: "We are God's handiwork, created for good works," etc. But you say, "You are driving me to despair when you attribute all things to God. Who knows whether he wants to help me?" To the contrary, he is for us. If the matter rested on our merits, who would not despair? But now since it depends on grace and the good will of God, who does not dare to hope? Scripture after all teaches that God is rich in mercy. Again, "there is mercy and abundant redemption with him." Again, "He does not forget to show mercy." Again, "because the earth is full of the mercy of the Lord," and "his mercy is from generation to generation, indeed, from eternity and to eternity." EXEGESIS OF ROMANS 9:6-13.[8]

GOD'S ETERNAL AND IMMUTABLE COUNSEL. GALLIC CONFESSION: We believe that from this corruption and general condemnation in which all human beings are plunged, God, according to his eternal and immutable counsel, calls those whom he has chosen by his goodness and mercy alone in our Lord Jesus Christ, without consideration of their works, to display in them the riches of his mercy; leaving the rest in this same corruption and condemnation to show in them his justice. For the one group is no better than the other group, until God discerns them according to his immutable purpose which he has determined in Jesus Christ before the creation of the world. Neither can any human being gain such a reward by his own virtue, as by nature we can not have a single good feeling, affection or thought, unless God has first put it into our hearts. ARTICLE 12.[9]

GOD'S ETERNAL PREDESTINATION AND ELECTION. FORMULA OF CONCORD: This predestination is not to be probed in the secret counsel of God but rather to be sought in the Word, where it has also been revealed. However, the Word of God leads us to Christ, who is the "Book of Life" in whom are inscribed and chosen all who shall be eternally saved, as it is written, "He chose us in Christ before the foundation of the world."

This Christ calls all sinners to himself and promises them refreshment. He is utterly serious in his desire that all people should come to him and seek help for themselves. He offers himself to them in his Word. He desires them to hear the Word and not to plug their ears or despise his Word. To this end he promises the power and the activity of the Holy Spirit, divine assistance in remaining faithful and attaining eternal salvation. . . .

A Christian should only think about the article of God's eternal election to the extent that it is revealed in God's Word. The Word holds Christ before our eyes as the "Book of Life," which he opens and reveals for us through the preaching of

---

[8]Wild, *Exegesis in Epistolam ad Romanos*, 207r-209r; citing Ps 59:10; 26:3; 44:6, 3; 130:7; 33:5; 100:5.

[9]*Creeds* 3:366-67; alluding to Rom 3:2; 9:23; 2 Tim 2:20; Tit 3:5-7; Eph 1:4; 2 Tim 1:9; Ex 9:16; Rom 9:22; Jer 10:23; Eph 1:4-5.

the holy gospel, as it is written, "Those whom he has chosen, he has also called." In Christ we are to seek the Father's eternal election. He has decreed in his eternal, divine counsel that he will save no one apart from those who acknowledge his Son Christ and truly believe in him. We should set aside other thoughts, for they do not come from God but rather from the imagination of the evil foe. Through such thoughts he approaches us to weaken this glorious comfort for us or to take it away completely. We have a glorious comfort in this salutary teaching, that we know how we have been chosen for eternal life in Christ out of sheer grace without any merit of our own, and that no one can tear us out of his hand. For he has assured us that he has graciously chosen us not only with mere words. He has corroborated this with an oath and sealed it with the holy sacraments. In the midst of our greatest trials we can remind ourselves of them, comfort ourselves with them and thereby quench the fiery darts of the devil. . . .

Accordingly we believe and maintain that those who present the teaching of God's gracious election to eternal life either in such a way that troubled Christians cannot find comfort in it but are driven to faintheartedness or despair, or in such a way that the impenitent are strengthened in their arrogance, are not preaching this teaching according to the Word and will of God, but rather to their own reason and at the instigation of the accursed devil, because (as the apostle testifies) "whatever was written was written for our instruction, so that by steadfastness and by the comfort of the Scriptures we might have hope."

Therefore we reject the following errors. First, when it is taught that God does not want all people to repent and believe the gospel. Second, that when God calls us, God does not seriously intend that all people should come to him. Third, that God does not desire that everyone should be saved, but rather that without regard to their sins—only because of God's naked decision, intention and will, some are designated for damnation so that there is no way that they could be saved. Fourth, that the cause of God's election does not lie exclusively in God's mercy

and the most holy merit of Christ but rather that there is also a cause in us, because of which God has chosen us for eternal life. These are blasphemous, horrible and erroneous teachings, which take way from Christians all the comfort that they have in the holy gospel and in the use of the holy sacraments. Therefore these errors are not to be tolerated in the church of God. ARTICLE II: ELECTION.[10]

9:6a *The Word Cannot Return Void*

CLARIFYING THE QUESTION. JACOBUS ARMIN-IUS: It is necessary to properly settle the question that is in dispute between the apostle and the Jews, for this will be of great importance to the whole matter. The question is not "Are most of the Jews rejected?" or "Is the word of God of no effect?" For the apostle confesses that it would be impious even to admit the latter thought, and the former he will later prove by the clear testimony of Scripture. The real question, however, embraces both of these: "Will the word of God fail, even if most of the Jews are rejected?" Yet even this is not sufficient, as the answer to this question does not settle the whole dispute or exhaust all the difficulties. For, if the apostle, by force of his arguments, should prove that some and indeed most of the Jews are rejected, and yet the word of God remains sure, another question remains: "Does not the word of God fail if the Jews who are rejected are those who with the greatest zeal seek the righteousness of the law?" That question must still remain, as it would be easy for the Jews to make an exception to the solution of that question: "Though the word of God may remain sure, if many of the Jews are rejected, yet we cannot be included in the number, otherwise the word of God will fail." Adding this element completes the real question thus: "Does the word of God become of no effect if the Jews who are rejected by God are those who seek righteousness, not of faith, but of the law?" ANALYSIS OF ROMANS 9.[11]

---

[10]BoC 517-19*; citing Phil 4:3; Rev 3:5; Eph 1:4; Mt 11:28; Rom 8:30; Jn 10:28-29; Rom 15:4. See further, BoC 640-56.
[11]Arminius, *Works*, 3:529-30*.

GRACE IS FROM GOD ALONE. DOMINGO DE
SOTO: In [this section of this chapter] Paul
establishes this point concerning the origin of grace,
namely, that it does not have its origin by the
merits of people, but from the predestination of
God. Thus, when he recounted the numerous
privileges of the Jews, he went on to explain how all
those things occurred to them by the grace of God.
And furthermore, when he lamented their
wretched downfall, he anticipates their argument
so that they would not conclude that the promises
of God (which he mentions now among the other
gifts) had been uncertain and in vain. For he had
promised to the fathers salvation through the seed
of Abraham and Israel; therefore, if such a large
number of their posterity was deprived of that
faith and salvation, those promises seem to have
been void. Therefore he cuts off this conclusion in
advance, saying, "But the Word has not failed
God"; that is to say, "I am not so deeply saddened
by your departure that my confidence in the
promises of God has collapsed through you or that
my confidence in those promises has been broken
or weakened by your guilt." COMMENTARY ON
ROMANS 9:6-13.[12]

LOOK TO GOD'S WORD AND BELIEVE!
PHILIPP MELANCHTHON: [It's as if he were
saying]: Although I deplore the destruction of
the nation, I do not command anyone to despair.
Rather, I exhort all to believe. For I do not think
that none of the Jews can be saved. Rather the
promise still pertains to us; it is not void. If only
you would believe the promise! For as many as
do will be saved. COMMENTARY ON ROMANS
(1540).[13]

THE WORD OF GOD IS UNFAILING. WOLF-
GANG MUSCULUS: We should note this passage,
so that in all disputations we depend on the
certainty of God's Word, knowing that it cannot
fail. Now something is said to fail when it is

invalid. For example, concerning the kingdom of
Christ, Scripture says that it stretches to the end
of the earth. It doesn't look that way; nevertheless, it is true, for the Word of God cannot fail.
Therefore everywhere there are some godly
people. When people argue about the certainty
of God's Word, either one side or the other is
wrong. So then, if the Word of God seems
obscure and doesn't seem to fit together, we
would rather blame our weakness and ignorance
than the Word of God. COMMENTARY ON
ROMANS 9:6.[14]

9:6b-9 Children of God Through the Promise, Not Through the Flesh

LOOK ONLY TO CHRIST. TILEMANN HESSHUS:
Christ is the sole foundation of the church.
Therefore, when we look for the church, we should
not consider matters according to fleshly birth but
according to the promise and Son of God Jesus
Christ. COMMENTARY ON ROMANS 9:8.[15]

THE TRUE CHURCH IS ELECTED BY GOD.
PHILIPP MELANCHTHON: This is the chief
proposition in which he answers the objection
concerning which is the true people of God. The
Jews contended that they were the people of God,
that they were the church and that the promises
pertained to them alone. Paul responds that the
elect are the people of God, and he distinguishes
the true people from those who have the title. The
true church must be distinguished from that
kingdom which has the title but which makes way
against the true church.

Paul states the proposition clearly: The sons of
God are not made by fleshly propagation, not by
natural gifts or merits, but by the election of God.
In order to clarify this statement, he leads us to
Scripture so that we may see how God at all times
separated some by his election. God did this to

[12]Soto, *In Epistolam ad Romanos*, 258.
[13]Melanchthon, *Commentary on Romans*, 189* (MO 15:681).
[14]Musculus, *In epistolam Apostoli Pauli ad Romanos commentarii*, 158.
[15]Hesshus, *Explicatio Epistolae Pauli ad Romanos*, 317v.

prepare a church and to show that the church does not come into being by human counsel. If sons were made by nature or merits, there would have been no need for God to separate the son of his promise from the rest.

The Chaldeans and the Egyptians were not inferior to Isaac in natural gifts or merits. Alexander the Macedonian, Fabius and Scipio were better endowed with natural gifts than we, and yet they did not have the gospel. Therefore the church is by election, not by natural gifts or merits. COMMENTARY ON ROMANS (1540).[16]

REJECTED BUT NOT FORSAKEN. TILEMANN HESSHUS: This is an anticipation of his later argument by which he warns us that his testimony should not be taken to mean that he was forgetful of the prophetic discourses, which expressly predicted the rejection of this his people; instead he says these things only because he most ardently awaits the preservation and salvation of his people. Therefore he now calls himself back from that immense grief, which he embraces owing to the destruction of his own people, and he turns his mind to the Word of God and teaches these two things based on it. First, the church or the assembly of the elect does not depend on the carnal propagation of the seed of Abraham or on a form of polity or on Mosaic ceremonies, but on the eternal, gracious election of God and on the promise of the Messiah. Second, his people have not been so rejected that none of them could be saved any more through Christ, but the external form of the polity was removed so that the Gentiles might be taken into the fellowship of the church and only the unbelievers were rejected. If someone is converted to Christ, they are not excluded from the king-

dom and benefits of the Redeemer, so that by the example of the Gentiles they may rather be provoked toward faith in Christ. COMMENTARY ON ROMANS 9:6.[17]

TRUE ISRAELITES. DAVID PAREUS: "Israel" in its first occurrence in this verse means "Jacob," understood as an individual, but in its second occurrence means "the descendants of Jacob," understood in a collective sense. There are those who want to make this line of argumentation to be understood in a typical sense, that is to say, that a distinction between the children of God has been foreshadowed in them. But it is a matter of exegesis. He is proving that the promise did not perish because of the rejected Jews because there was a division of the Israelites, for God had once foretold this and it had been part of his eternal counsel. To be sure, an unlimited promise was made to the Israelites. But not all born in the flesh from Israel are true Israelites, but only those who are children of the promise, that is, who receive the promise by faith. Therefore the promise suffers no hardship and the veracity of God cannot be questioned, even if carnal Israelites are condemned. Meanwhile the promise confirmed to the children of the promise, the true Israelites, remains.

"Nor because they are the seed of Abraham." Earlier he had distinguished between true Israelites and carnal ones. Now he also divides the seed of Abraham, because they were always saying, "We are the seed of Abraham." All were the seed of Abraham, but not all were the children of Abraham. How so? Because God restricted the right to sonship to Isaac and excluded Ishmael, who was the seed of Abraham, but not his son. COMMENTARY ON ROMANS 9:6-7.[18]

ACCORDING TO THE FLESH OR THE SPIRIT? TILEMANN HESSHUS: Here now he enters the dispute about election and the true church of

---

[16]Melanchthon, *Commentary on Romans*, 189* (MO 15:682). Alexander the Great (366–324 BC), tutored by Aristotle to be a philosopher king, hellenized the known world. Quintus Fabius Maximus (c. 280–203 BC), dictator of Rome—an emergency office appointed by the Senate—engaged Hannibal only indirectly by attacking supply lines, wisely saving Rome from a much greater army. Cornelius Scipio Africanus (236–183 BC), a great military strategist, defeated Hannibal at the Battle of Zama (c. 202 BC).

[17]Hesshus, *Explicatio Epistolae Pauli ad Romanos*, 315r-v.
[18]Pareus, *In Epistolam ad Romanos*, 832.

God: what it is, whence it arises, what establishes it, on what it depends. "Not all who are of Israel are Israel." That is to say, not all who have been born of Jacob by fleshly procreation are true Israelites, elect for eternal life, nor are those who are the seed of Abraham necessarily sons, that is, heirs of the promise. Here he sets forth two kinds of Israelites and two kinds of sons of Abraham. The first are those who are such according to the flesh; the second are those who are such according to the Spirit and the promise. And here the apostle Paul teaches that not all who have been born of the seed of Abraham, Isaac and Jacob are living members of the church and destined for eternal life. For the church of God is not created, established and propagated by carnal procreation, but only by God's eternal election, his promise and the Spirit. For from eternity, owing to his boundless mercy, God chose for himself those whom he predestined to life to be his sons. And through his promise and the Holy Spirit he gave them a new birth and adopted them as sons, who will be the heirs of eternal bliss. Therefore he recognizes nobody as his son and heir of life except one born again by the Word and Spirit. This is a noteworthy and clearly necessary chapter of doctrine, showing us the origin of the church and what is the true and elect church—about which there has always been a major controversy among humankind—and refuting multiple kinds of errors of the human mind. Reason disputes various things concerning the gathering of the church. And because it sees that governmental authority is established, defended and transferred to others either by fleshly generation or adoption or notable virtue, labors, victories or the advice and election of the governed, and similar means, it imagines in its mind that the method of establishing and extending the church is the same. COMMENTARY ON ROMANS 9:7.[19]

WHO ARE THE CHILDREN OF THE PROMISE?

JOHN CALVIN: The promise was so given to Abraham and to his seed that the inheritance did not belong to every seed without distinction; it hence follows that the defection of some does not prove that the covenant does not remain firm and valid.

But that it may be more evident on what condition the Lord adopted the posterity of Abraham as a peculiar people to himself, two things are to be here considered. First, the promise of salvation given to Abraham belongs to all who can trace their natural descent to him, for it is offered to all without exception. For this reason they are rightly called the heirs of the covenant made with Abraham; and in this respect they are his successors or, as Scripture calls them, the children of the promise. For since it was the Lord's will that his covenant should be sealed, no less in Ishmael and Esau than in Isaac and Jacob, it appears that they were not wholly alienated from him; except, it may be, you make no account of the circumcision, which was conferred on them by God's command; but it cannot be so regarded without dishonor to God. But this belonged to them, according to what the apostle had said before, "whose are the covenants," though they were unbelieving; and in Acts 3 they are called by Peter, the children of the covenants, because they were the descendants of the prophets.

Second, the children of the promise are strictly those in whom its power and effect are found. Thus Paul denies here that all the children of Abraham were the children of God, though a covenant had been made with them by the Lord, for few continued in the faith of the covenant; and yet God himself testifies, in Ezekiel 6, that they were all regarded by him as children. In short, when a whole people are called the heritage and the peculiar people of God, what is meant is that they have been chosen by the Lord, the promise of salvation having been offered them and confirmed by the symbol of circumcision; but as many by their ingratitude reject this adoption, and thus enjoy in no degree its benefits, there arises among them another difference with regard to the fulfillment of the promise. That it might not then

[19]Hesshus, *Explicatio Epistolae Pauli ad Romanos*, 315v-316r.

appear strange to anyone that this fulfillment of the promise was not evident in many of the Jews, Paul denies that they were included in the true election of God. COMMENTARY ON ROMAN 9:6.[20]

THE PROMISE TO ABRAHAM PERTAINS TO ALL THE PREDESTINED. JUAN DE VALDÉS: By saying "the children of promise" St. Paul means those who believe in God's promises, imitating Abraham in that he believed in the promise. And those, he says, are they whom God holds to be Abraham's seed, and in thus fulfilling for them what he promised Abraham, he fulfills his promise to Abraham.

The righteous are called "the children of the promise" because the promise made to Abraham belongs especially to them, as though God had had them all present at the time he made the promise to Abraham. So that being "children of the promise" pertains to predestination, the predestined are the children of the promise and the children of the promise are predestined. COMMENTARY ON ROMANS 9:6-8.[21]

EXTRAORDINARY BIRTH. TILEMANN HESSHUS: By the testimony of Scripture he proves his argument and demonstrates the difference between the birth of Isaac and that of Ishmael. Ishmael was conceived and born in the usual method of nature. But Isaac was born in an extraordinary way from the sterile Sarah, past her childbearing prime. But the divine promise rendered Sarah fertile, and so Isaac was the son of the promise. Thus only those who are born of the promise through the Holy Spirit and follow in the footsteps of Abraham's faith are likewise the spiritual sons of Abraham. Paul advises us that we must accurately consider the divine promise that was the reason for Isaac's birth. And he had in mind not only the birth of Isaac but rather mainly the birth of the Messiah (the blessed seed) and of the whole church, and considered that God named

those who would be born of Isaac "the seed of Abraham" for a peculiar reason. And the promise given to Abraham concerning Isaac was speaking not only concerning the multiplication of the seed, the conquest of the land of Canaan and the establishment of a kingdom, but was chiefly showing that the Messiah, Jesus Christ, would come, in whom the eternal Father gathers the eternal church and establishes a spiritual kingdom. COMMENTARY ON ROMANS 9:9.[22]

9:10-12 God Works in Ways Abhorrent to Human Wisdom

SCRIPTURES CONFIRM PREDESTINATION. JUAN DE VALDÉS: St. Paul confirms what he has stated, that the promise made to Abraham does not affect or interest those who are Abraham's seed by fleshly generation, but those who are so by God's election, giving a very striking example. It is as if he should say, What is to be understood concerning Abraham's two sons is also to be understood concerning Isaac's two sons, Jacob and Esau. It is true that while they were the two sons of Isaac, Abraham's son, concerning whom the promise was made, and while they both were children of one mother, and even both conceived in one act of coitus, God chose Jacob and rejected Esau. And he did this before they came from their mother's womb, in order that it might be clear that the election of the one and the reprobation of the other did not depend on the good works of the one or on the bad works of the other, but solely on the will of God....

This is what St. Paul means by these words, and I think that everyone interested in the election of God understands by them (and even without them) the very same. Others, whom it does not interest, do not desire to understand them, nor do they desire to hear them. So then, I understand it to be a mark of a godly mind, and of predestination, to sense that there is predestination, and to rejoice in it; it is a mark of an ungodly mind, and of

---

[20]CTS 38:344-45* (CO 49:x); citing Acts 3:25; Ezek 6:9.
[21]Valdés, *Commentary upon Romans*, 154* (*Commentario de Romanos*, 184).

[22]Hesshus, *Explicatio Epistolae Pauli ad Romanos*, 316r.

reprobation, not to be willing to admit predestination and to regret it.

I understand, moreover, that pious people recognize the justice of God in predestination, recognizing that God is just, while impious people recognize injustice in God, in predestination itself. While pretending to be pious, they will not admit it, and when constrained to admit it by holy Scripture, they admit it with certain conditions, and with certain additions, so that it virtually comes to the same as though they had not admitted it. COMMENTARY ON ROMANS 9:10-13.[23]

PROMISES POINT TO JESUS. PETER MARTYR VERMIGLI: "The older will serve the younger." This seems to be a temporary promise. However, we have not seldom taught that the foundation and basis of these earthly promises is the promise concerning Christ and the acquisition of eternal salvation through him. And from this the following can be gathered. For if you consider the rule of primogeniture, you will not find that Jacob fulfills it. Never in his entire life did he rule over his brother Esau. Rather when he returned from Mesopotamia he was a suppliant to his brother Esau, and he begged that he might obtain mercy from him. Esau seems to have been far more powerful than he. Nevertheless, concerning their descendants it should not be doubted that the promise happened, for in the time of David and Solomon the Jews gained dominion over the Edomites. However, if these things should be applied to the apostle's argument, they must be understood concerning the promise of Christ and eternal joy. For Paul does this, lest it seem to contradict the divine promise, that a few of the Jews would be accepted into the gospel, since the far greater portion of them were excluded. COMMENTARY ON ROMANS 9:12.[24]

THREE ERRORS REFUTED. DOMINGO DE SOTO: But here the thought could strike someone: since

the love of God toward us is eternal, why in the world did he retreat to setting forth an example from children who were not yet born, since indeed it is equally true about adults that, before we do any good, we have been loved by God, by whose love we are made good? Now the answer is that God wanted to reveal to us those secrets of his as Paul explains them here, in a manner suitable for our intelligence. For if he had given as an example Cain and Abel, to pick one example, or David and Saul, or Nebuchadnezzar and Pharaoh, someone would perhaps be able to think that their foreseen divergence in merits had been the reason that he had predestined the one but rejected the other. But in these people, who did not prevail by any use of their freedom, he revealed the matter most visibly, namely, that when one of them was chosen and the other was hated before either had merited anything, and there was no mention made of a foreseeing of their merits, we can see clearly the mystery of predestination in this fact, as if it had been written on a tablet, namely, that neither the influence of merits nor a foreseeing of them was a reason for this difference, nor was the decision made in the case of adult human beings who could use reason, but rather the cause was the will alone of the one loving and calling them. The passage in Ephesians agrees well with this: "He chose us in Christ before the foundation of the world, so that we might be holy," that is, he chose us not because of our foreseen holiness, but his election was the cause of our holiness, as we will explain as fully as we can.

Therefore three errors are refuted by this one clause. First is the error of the Manicheans, who ascribe the diversity of people's talents and the things that befall them to the stars of their birth. Against that idea is the word of Jeremiah: "Do not fear the signs of the heaven, which the heathen fear." The second error is what, for example, is reported to have been Origen's, namely, that the diversity in human beings came to be because of the merits of the souls that had been created at the same time as the angels and had done various things outside the body. And the third error is that of the Pelagians, namely, that some people were loved and others

---

[23]Valdés, *Commentary upon Romans*, 155-56* (*Commentario de Romanos*, 185-86).

[24]Vermigli, *In Epistolam ad Romanos*, 351-52 (cf. *A Commentarie upon the Epistle to the Romanes*, 250v).

hated owing to their preceding merits. For against the Manicheans he does what Paul says: "When they had not yet been born." And against the second error this is added: "They had done nothing good or bad." But against Pelagius he appends, "Not based on works but on the one who calls." COMMENTARY ON ROMANS 9:10-13.[25]

PAUL'S THREE PROPOSITIONS IN THIS PASSAGE. JOHN CALVIN: Paul's first proposition is "As the blessing of the covenant separates the nation of Israel from all other people, so God's election makes a distinction between human beings in that nation, while he predestines some to salvation and others to eternal condemnation." The second proposition is "There is no other basis for this election than the goodness of God alone and also, after Adam's fall, his mercy, which embraces whom he pleases without any regard for their works." Third, "The Lord in his unmerited election is free and exempt from the necessity of imparting the same grace to all equally. Rather, he passes by whom he wills, and whom he wills he chooses." COMMENTARY ON ROMANS 9:11.[26]

9:13 *Jacob I Loved, But Esau I Hated*

THE COVENANT DOES NOT NECESSARILY EXCLUDE ISHMAEL AND ESAU. TILEMANN HESSHUS: A second line of argument is taken from the example of Jacob and Esau, by which he proves that the church depends on the gracious election of God, not on carnal birth or on the strength of the will or the merits of one's works. The proof drawn from Ishmael and Isaac was a clear one; it proved that the question of who are the sons of God is determined by the promise of God. But this proof is even clearer: for Rebekah conceived and carried offspring from the one Isaac, our father, and when she inquired of the Lord, before the children were born and had not done anything good or evil, the divine voice answered,

"The older shall serve the younger," that is, Jacob was chosen to be the people of God and the promise of the Messiah was transferred to him. But Esau was made a servant and not taken into the people of God. Therefore it is most abundantly clear that birth from the holiest parents does not make someone a living member of the church. For as far as his birth was concerned, Esau was the firstborn of Isaac. Nor do the works or merits of people do anything in establishing the elect church and the heirs of eternal life. For when the boys were not yet born and had not done anything good or evil, Rebekah was told, "The older will serve the younger." That is to say, he chose the one and neglected the other. He took Jacob into the covenant and the people of God, but he did not take Esau into the people of the covenant. Paul adds the reason so that he might support his thesis that it was according to God's election, not due to their works: "but it was spoken to her by the one who called." Here the apostle teaches most expressly that the election of those who will be saved depends by no means on the honor of the flesh or on the merits of their works but on the pure, gracious election of God; God does not consider any of our works or merits, but considers only his most generous purpose, mercy and will.

If someone should object here that this passage in Moses is speaking about a physical benefit, by which Jacob was graced by God more than Esau in a particular manner, namely, that from Jacob the people of God and the blessed seed would be born, that his offspring would conquer the land of Canaan and possess the kingdom, they ought to know that the Holy Spirit always considers mainly the spiritual in the divine promises and that Christ, the blessed seed, is the fulfillment of every polity and of all the divine promises. Therefore, just as it is owing to the pure election and mercy of God that Jacob was taken into the covenant, that he along with his offspring were made into the people of God, and that he received the promise of the Messiah who would be born, so also it was a spiritual grace and it was owing to God's gracious

---

[25]Soto, *In Epistolam ad Romanos*, 261-62; citing Eph 1:4; Jer 10:2. [26]CTS 38:349* (CO 49:177).

election that Jacob was predestined to eternal life, that he was called to the ministry of the gospel, that faith was kindled in him and that he acquired eternal salvation through his son, the Messiah, owing to God's good pleasure alone.

But as to the fact that Esau was not taken into the external covenant and did not receive the promise of the Messiah, but was subjected to the authority of Jacob, one cannot accuse God of injustice on this score, for he owed him nothing. Instead he could have learned that eternal salvation was to be sought in the mercy of God alone, if Esau wanted to hope for it (Genesis 36). And by all means we ought to hope that Ishmael and Esau were at last led to repentance and to place their faith in the promised Redeemer—which teaching they had learned from their fathers Abraham and Isaac—and so obtained salvation through the mercy of God, even if they lacked the privilege of the promise given to Jacob. COMMENTARY ON ROMANS 9:10-12.[27]

COOPERATE WITH GOD'S WILL. JACQUES LEFÈVRE D'ÉTAPLES: If God by his purpose and foreknowledge loved Jacob and hated Esau, that would not mean that he was sinful and unjust, would it? By no means, but he was just toward each of them. In Jacob, who was good, he was just in showing his mercy. In Esau, who was hard-hearted and boorish and pursued his own desires, he was just in showing justice. In the former he showed his love so that he might turn all to goodness and piety. In the latter he showed his hatred so that he might frighten all away from evil. And a human being always has God as his helper toward the good, no matter what he does, whether good or evil. But when he does the good, he cooperates with God, but when he does evil, he works without God and contrary to divine help. It is no different than if some good father helped his two sons in their abilities by education, sound pieces of advice and exhortations to live well, and

one son obeyed his father and did good work, but the other son was disobedient and did evil. The son who did good cooperated with his good father. And the son who did evil worked without his father and contrary to the help of his father. This is what God did and much more. To Esau as much as to Jacob he gave all the good things that led to good, and he gives the same to every mortal. But whoever gives also gives for this purpose, namely, so that he may be helpful to himself, right? But whoever does good and is accepted by God is accepted not by his own work or his own will, but by the pity of God and his will. For the will of God is infinitely good, but ours is finite and (if I may put it this way) of no goodness. Therefore it is fair that every acceptance and every justification come from the will of God. ANNOTATIONS ON ROMANS 9:11-13.[28]

GOD FOREKNOWS OUR ACTIONS AND PREDESTINES ACCORDINGLY. HANS DENCK: Why then did God hate Esau before he was even born, yes, before he could have done any evil? He himself answers, "I knew that you would transgress, therefore I have called you evil from your mother's womb." Why did he love Jacob? The answer of the Lord, "Before I had formed you in your mother's womb, I knew you; therefore I have consecrated you before you were born." He knew well beforehand that Jacob would not sin, even though he might well have sinned; on this account he loved him. And just as Esau's sin and that of all perverse human beings was known by God from the very beginning, so also was their punishment and death. For God punishes no one undeservedly. And just as the righteousness of Jacob and all the elect was known by God from the beginning, so also was their reward, the kingdom and eternal life prepared. But no one is crowned unless he first fights. DIVINE ORDER (1527).[29]

---

[27]Hesshus, *Explicatio Epistolae Pauli ad Romanos*, 318v-319v; citing Gen 25:23.

[28]Lefèvre d'Étaples, *Epistola ad Rhomanos*, 85v-86r.
[29]Denck, *Selected Writings*, 249-50; citing Rom 9:11-13; Is 48:8; Jer 1:5; Gen 18:23; Mt 25:34; Jn 14:2; 2 Tim 2:15.

THOSE WHO SAY GOD FOREKNOWS OUR ACTIONS AND PREDESTINES ACCORDINGLY ARE LIARS.

TILEMANN HESSHUS: Since election itself is the clearest proof of all of God's gracious mercy and immense kindness, we must detest the audacity and wickedness of people who try out of their own mind to fashion the idea that the reason for election is people's merits. According to this idea, God saw from eternity who would obey his divine will and who would be wicked, and so he chose for life those whom he saw would be godly, but destined for destruction those whom he foresaw would be wicked.

Augustine relates this opinion with these words of Pelagius. "Pelagius says, 'Therefore, God knew in advance who would be holy and blameless by the choice of their free will, and so he chose them before the foundation of the world in his own foreknowledge, by which he foreknew that they would be people of that sort. Therefore,' he says, 'before they had been predestined, he chose them as sons, because he knew beforehand that they would be holy and blameless. At any rate, God himself did not make them holy, nor did he foresee that he would make them holy, but rather he foresaw that they would be holy.'" Also Origen has spread abroad this opinion, and rather many people have followed him, inasmuch as it agrees with human reason. And the papist writers cling to this opinion tooth and nail.

The patrons of free will and the synergists[30] seem to speak more circumspectly (at least in their opinion) when they say that God indeed did not regard our merits in election, but took into account the assent of the will, for God elected to eternal life those whom he foresaw would believe the gospel and assent to the working of the Holy Spirit, but he destined to eternal damnation those whom he foresaw would fight against the gospel and the Holy Spirit. And thus they make the assent of the will the cause for election.

But this opinion of the synergists does not differ one whit from the opinion of Origen, Pelagius and the papists. For whether they call it godliness or the assent of the will or faith, they make the reason for election to lie within us—a false opinion against which the whole sacred Scripture loudly protests. For it shows that the reason for election lies within God, not ourselves. "You did not choose me," says Christ, "but I chose you." And to the one paying attention to the words of Paul ("Just as he chose us in Christ before the foundation of the world so that we might be holy and blameless"), the matter is not obscure: we were not chosen because we were going to be holy, but rather in order that we might be holy. . . .

For Paul urges that our election ought to be ascribed only to the mercy and purpose of God. And, in order to exclude every ground in ourselves, he says, "When we were not yet born, nor had done anything good or bad." And lest anyone divide the benefits of election between God and a human being, as if the principal reason were the mercy in God's will, but the lesser principal reason were found in the human's will, he further excludes every zeal and attempt of the human will: "It is not of he who wills nor of he who runs, but of God who has mercy." ON THE PREDESTINATION OF THE SAINTS: THE REASON FOR ELECTION.[31]

GOD'S ETERNAL AND UNCONDITIONED CALL.

DAVID PAREUS: Here the concept of "election" and "calling" are used in the same sense. The idea that he calls "according to their election" ought to be

---

[30]During the 1550s and 1560s, students of Luther and Melanchthon sparred over the role of the will in salvation; these debates are known as the synergistic controversy. In later editions of his *Loci Communes* Melanchthon gave more attention to the will's Spirit-enabled obedient cooperation in God's grace. He did not see this as contradicting Luther's monergism (i.e., salvation by grace through faith); however, in light of the Interim some Lutheran theologians saw this as a disguised return to medieval Catholicism. The controversy reached its peak in 1560 when Viktorin Strigel, under house arrest for his Philippist view of the will, debated Matthias Flacius (1520–1575). Article 2 of the *Formula of Concord* settled the debate, stating that only by God's work—through his ordained means, namely, the preaching and hearing of his Word—are human beings saved (BoC 491-94, 543-62). See further OER 4:133-35.

[31]Hesshus, *Explicatio Epistolae Pauli ad Romanos*, 283r-v, 284v-285r; citing Jn 15:16; Eph 1:4.

understood to be the opposite of "according to their rejection." For the election of one is the abandonment or rejection of another. For election is not the taking of all, but a separation of some (who are approved) from others. Therefore the meaning is this: The cause of the two divine pronouncements was so that the intention of God, whereby he had chosen Jacob and rejected Esau, would remain established. This is obvious, for he had denied that either evil or good deeds had been the reason for this distinction. Therefore he did not choose Jacob because of his good deeds, nor did he fail to choose Esau because of his evil deeds, because again he sets forth each divine pronouncement in the effects of God's intention: "Jacob I loved, but Esau I hated." And at last he will soon compare the just hardening with the mercy. Therefore he posits that we must consider and adore the entire mystery of God's purpose or of divine predestination from the statements of fact (*hypothesis*) of the sons of Abraham and Isaac, but he will soon draw a definitive conclusion (*thesis*) when he will say, "It does not depend on the one willing," etc.[32] "He has mercy on whom he wills, and he hardens whom he wills." Indeed, it is something imperceptible to human reason and even contrary to it, because people cannot grasp how God arranges everything most wisely and justly not only outside of humanity but also in the human race, so that nothing good or evil happens to anyone apart from his purpose. Nor are they able to endure that the free will of a human being is subjected to the divine counsel, because they want to be *autexousioi* ["absolutely free"] and they want themselves to be the cause of their own salvation or damnation. But the apostle reconciles these things very well. For there is not any difficulty in this dispute, provided that human reason submits itself to God and recognizes that God is the most just governor of all things, whose will is

the height of fairness and the rule of justice. Therefore let us observe the suppositions of this passage (*hypotheses*) in a few words:

1. The promises of the gospel have indeed been given to the whole church, so that grace and salvation in Christ may be offered to all, but the promises are not fulfilled in all because they have the added condition of faith and conversion to God, which is not fulfilled in all.

2. Therefore, even if the greater portion of Christians should lose the promises of the gospel and thus become condemned by Christ, nonetheless the promises have not on that account failed or been rendered void.

3. Not all Christians or children of Christians are also children of God, but only the children of the promise, and so the Christian church always consists of children of the flesh and children of God.

4. The children of the promise are those who receive the promise of the gospel with faith and who are born anew of God by the power of the promise through the Word and the Holy Spirit, just as Isaac was born of Sarah by the power of the promise.

5. This division of sons in the church started from the beginning in the sons of Adam (Cain and Abel), of Noah, of Abraham, of Isaac and of Jacob, and this division will remain until the end of the world, because in the field of our Lord the weeds grow always with the wheat and on the last day one of two women working at the mill will be taken and the other left behind and one man of two lying in a bed will be taken and the other will be left behind.

6. However, it is not owing to human nature, since all are equally guilty and wicked, all are children and vessels of wrath after the fall. But it is owing to the grace of God that some are called to Christ through the Word and others are not, and that some who are called are drawn efficaciously through the Spirit, that is, they are granted faith and repentance, while others are not.

---

[32]In Greek philosophy, a *hypothesis* was something presumed either because it was axiomatic or because it was a set of facts agreed on by all participants in the debate; a *thesis* was a conclusion that could be drawn from the facts, but it had to be proven, since more than one *thesis* could be drawn from a particular *hypothesis*.

7. The grace of calling does not come from the free will or effort of human beings, but from the will of God who calls: "Who set you apart," etc.

8. The will or free will[33] of God who calls is his plan according to the election in Christ, that is, it is the counsel of God by which he separated some from others out of the mass of human beings doomed to destruction. He separated them by choosing some and leaving others behind. This plan is called predestination, and it contains within it both election and rejection or reprobation. Isaiah 41:9: "You are my servant. I have chosen you and have not rejected you."

9. This plan of making a distinction is eternally in God, before the foundations of the world were laid, before human beings were created or born.

10. And this plan is so firm that it cannot be changed or hindered by anything created.

11. The cause that moves God to make this plan of distinguishing between people was not the foreseen worthiness or unworthiness of people, for he saw that all in the mass destined for perdition to be equally unworthy of love or grace.

12. Nor was there some other foreseen prerogative, for when Jacob and Esau were equal in this regard, God made a distinction between them, loving the one and turning away from the other.

13. Nor were there some foreseen good or evil merits, because it is not based on works. And the merits of all were bad, and the merits of none were good.

14. Nor was it that their faith in Christ was foreseen, since this is given by God to the elect according to his plan. Therefore faith is an effect of election. But an effect cannot be its own cause. Nor was it based on the foreseen lack of faith, because that is naturally the state of all.

15. But election is only the will of God calling and having mercy on those whom he wills and hardening those whom he wills.

This last statement human reason can in no way endure, but accuses God of injustice and cruelty. Therefore the apostle will henceforth defend the matter.

But *let us observe* that the apostle does not set forth this whole mystery based on his own talent, but based on the Scripture, whose oracles and histories he connects.

Let us learn then the following: (1) This mystery must be learned not from philosophy, but from the Scripture. (2) Therefore only in the church should it be taught and made known. Outside the church and outside of Scripture it will be deemed folly or even blasphemy. Therefore it is not the case that we should countenance the cavil and sophistry of human reason in opposition to this doctrine. (3) Scripture ought to be the only norm for dogmas and controversies. For if the apostle did nothing *ektos graphōn* ["outside the Scriptures"], how much less may we? (4) The Old Testament is the foundation of the New. The New Testament is the fulfillment and illustration of the Old. And this is true in general. COMMENTARY ON ROMANS 9:13.[34]

EXTERNAL BENEFITS. TILEMANN HESSHUS: Here again I advise that these testimonies speak about a temporal and external benefit, namely, the promise of the Messiah connected to a certain family, the public form of the church and a certain kingdom. For insofar as it pertains to a spiritual blessing and participation in salvation, neither Ishmael nor Esau was excluded from it. This is clear from the fact that both of them were

---

[33]The *arbitrium* ("free will," as it is translated in this passage) is a stronger term than *voluntas* (translated "will"). The two terms may be used interchangeably, but when they are distinguished, the latter embraces all the inclinations that we may have (but may or may not follow), while the former emphasizes the decision-making power of the will. Thus, a person might find the *voluntas* telling him to eat, but the *arbitrium* determines whether the person will. Nearly all Christians at the time of the Reformation would acknowledge that our *voluntas* is somehow or other enslaved or hindered by sin, but the magisterial reformers emphasized that not only our *voluntas*, but our *arbitrium* was enslaved. Humanists like Erasmus could not accept such a notion. See further Muller, *Dictionary of Latin and Greek Theological Terms*, 330-31.

[34]Pareus, *In Epistolam ad Romanos*, 836-39.

circumcised and retained the teaching of Abraham. Nonetheless, Paul correctly adapts these testimonies to this matter of the election of the saints to life, for they clearly show that all the kind benefits of God depend only on God's gracious election, mercy and good pleasure. COMMENTARY ON ROMANS 9:13.[35]

9:14 Is God Unjust Then?

THE LABYRINTH OF PREDESTINATION. JOHN CALVIN: The flesh cannot hear of this wisdom of God without being instantly disturbed by numberless questions, and without attempting in a manner to call God to account. We hence find that the apostle, whenever he treats of some high mystery, obviates the many absurdities by which he knew human minds would be otherwise possessed. For when people hear anything of what Scripture teaches concerning predestination, they are especially entangled with very many impediments. Indeed the predestination of God is in reality a labyrinth, from which the minds of human beings can by no means extricate themselves. But so unreasonable is the curiosity of people, that the more perilous the examination of a subject is, the more boldly they proceed, so that when predestination is discussed, as they cannot restrain themselves within due limits, they immediately, through rashness, plunge themselves, as it were, into the depth of the sea. What remedy then is there for the godly? Must they avoid every thought of predestination? By no means! For as the Holy Spirit has taught us nothing but what it behooves us to know, the knowledge of this would no doubt be useful, provided it is confined to the Word of God. Let this then be our sacred rule, to seek to know nothing concerning it, except what Scripture teaches us. When the Lord closes his holy mouth, let us also stop that way, and go no further. COMMENTARY ON ROMANS 9:14.[36]

REASON ACCUSES GOD OF INJUSTICE. TILEMANN HESSHUS: When human reason hears furthermore that Jacob and Esau were born in the same condition and that neither was better than the other, but that nonetheless one was preferred to the other—one was chosen and the other left behind—it is gravely offended and accuses God of injustice, as being one who behaves whimsically in the most serious matters, as tyrants do and as is contrary to the norm of justice. For reason thinks in proportion to its own wisdom—or rather its stupidity. It thinks that equals should get equal gifts. Either both individuals who were born from the corrupt mass of humanity ought to be left behind or both ought to be chosen. This objection often creeps into not only profane minds but even into the mind of all the saints owing to the fact that "the unspiritual person does not perceive the things that belong to the Spirit of God, for they are folly and it is not possible for them to perceive it." Paul refutes this objection in this passage and shows that there is no injustice with God, even if the election of the saints disagrees with the judgment of reason, for he does no injury to anyone and the entire kindness of election is a gracious gift and is owing solely to the grace of God. But mercy by no means wars with justice. And God does not owe anyone anything; if he were to elect nobody or bestow his kindness on no one, he nonetheless could not be accused of injustice. Furthermore, Christ in Matthew 20 refutes in the same way the malice of the human way of thinking, which finds fault with the kindness of God: "Friend," he says, "didn't you agree with me on a denarius? Take what is yours and go. But I want to give to this last one as I gave to you. Or may I not do what I want with my own money? Or is your eye so evil because I am so good?" COMMENTARY ON ROMANS 9:14.[37]

THE LORD'S GOODNESS AND OMNISCIENCE. MARTIN BUCER: We know by experience even that

---

[35]Hesshus, *Explicatio Epistolae Pauli ad Romanos*, 318r-v. [36]CTS 38:353-54* (CO 49:180).

[37]Hesshus, *Explicatio Epistolae Pauli ad Romanos*, 320v-321r; citing 1 Cor 2:14; Mt 20:13-15.

God alone is good, and that therefore everything that is true and right and good is his work alone. It is he who brings it about, by the breath of his powerful inspiration, that some things are distinguished only in certain respects and function only with certain properties, that others possess life as well, others again are endowed with the senses, while human beings enjoy also the faculties of reason and intellect. He likewise infuses into human beings diverse abilities of mind and body, for in some he inspires excellence in the liberal arts, in others a signal refinement of character, in others again the prowess of bravery; some he renders preeminent in erudition and learning, and others still outstanding for yet other talents. But those whom he chooses for himself for eternal life he first inspires to depend on him in all things and look to him at every moment, as they devote themselves solely to the task of fitting their lives for the role in which he has cast them. He also especially equips and empowers them for those particular gifts whose exercise he has ordained for unfolding his goodness to humankind. COMMENTARY ON ROMANS.[38]

9:15-18 *God Has Mercy on Whom He Will*

DO NOT BE ANXIOUS; THE LORD WILL CHOOSE. MARTIN LUTHER: Paul seems by these words to be rebuffing those who are anxious and curious about the predestination of themselves or others, as if to drive them away from thoughts and questions about predestination. As the common saying goes: to whom it comes it comes, and whom it hits it hits. It is as if he were saying: "No one will know to whom I will be merciful and to whom I will be gracious, nor can anyone be certain about it because of his merits or works or anything else." Thus this word is one of fear and humiliation. Therefore we must note that in the Hebrew the first mentioned expression "I will show mercy" means to be merciful in the sense that he who shows mercy gives a benefit or a free gift even to him who has not offended or committed a sin, but is only in need and poor. SCHOLIA ON ROMANS 9:15.[39]

RULE OF EQUITY APPLIES TO DEBTS NOT GIFTS. PHILIPP MELANCHTHON: Paul sees that these things are far too high for human reason to perceive. Therefore he interrupts himself, and puts forth and refutes a common argument that must come into the mind of all sane people. If Esau and Jacob are equals, then God should have chosen or rejected both, because a just judge renders equal things to equals. Paul refutes this in this way: Equal things are rendered to equals when a debt is paid. In the case of a gift or when something is done through mercy, there is no need to render equal things to equals.

Thus also Christ in the parable about those brought into the vineyard shows that through mercy equal things are given to persons who are not equals. In accord with this understanding this saying is cited: "I will have mercy on whom I will have mercy," that is, on whom it seems good to me to take pity, as if he said, "Salvation comes by mercy, not through a debt." And he adds the conclusion: "It does not depend on anyone's willing or running, but on God who takes pity." This statement testifies that human beings are chosen and called through mercy in order that they may will and run. COMMENTARY ON ROMANS (1540).[40]

DIVINE MONERGISM. TILEMANN HESSHUS: From the previous testimonies of Scripture he draws a conclusion, namely, that the benefit of election and the entire salvation of a person in no way depends on people's will, running or efforts, but on God's mercy alone. "It is not a matter of him who wills," that is, the will or zeal or effort or human assent are not the reason for eternal salvation, but it depends only on the most merciful will of God. Those who explain this passage to

---

[38]Bucer, *Common Places of Martin Bucer*, 151.

[39]LW 25:387* (WA 56:397). See further David C. Steinmetz, "Luther and Augustine on Romans 9," in *Luther in Context*, 2nd ed. (Grand Rapids: Baker, 1995), 18-19.
[40]Melanchthon, *Commentary on Romans*, 190* (MO 15:682-83); citing Ex 33:19.

mean "It is not a matter of only the one who runs but also of him who shows mercy" flagrantly corrupt this passage. Contrary to Paul's intention they divide the benefit of salvation between God and humans, even though Paul excludes every cooperation of the human will in acquiring salvation and ascribes this favor to the mercy of God alone.

Also those who seek a defense for their synergism[41] from this passage do violence to the Scripture. They posit that a person can wish and run of their own accord in order to obtain salvation. For Paul did not forget what he had said to the Philippians: "It is God who works in us both to will and to do." Therefore Paul urges that eternal salvation does not originate in the will, running or attempt of a human being, but only in God's election, purpose and mercy. To be sure, there is a will and a running in a person, but it is perverse, preposterous and carnal. The Pharisees ran and pursued righteousness, but with a perverse zeal. They resisted the grace of God and their own salvation more than they sought it according to God's Word. Therefore it does not follow from Paul's statement that a human being can truly attain their salvation of their own powers or attempt what they should do to obtain salvation. Willing and running in the flesh is much different from that which is willing and running in the Spirit. Paul's thought is that whatever the will or running or attempt of a carnal human there is in pursuing salvation, it nonetheless does not help our salvation at all, unless salvation is found only in the gracious mercy of God. Commentary on Romans 9:16.[42]

Rubbish to Deny Free Will. Balthasar Hubmaier: We see here thoroughly and clearly what great rubbish all those have produced and introduced into Christendom to this point who deny the freedom of the will in people and say how this freedom is an empty and idle name and is nothing in itself. For thereby our God is shamed and blasphemed as if he like a tyrant penalized and condemned humanity for something that it was impossible for them to will or to do. Thereby is also lifted and overthrown the justifiable charge that Christ will use against all the godless on the Last Day, when he says, "I was hungry and you did not feed me." For then they could all too easily excuse themselves and answer: "It was, however, impossible for us, for you have robbed us of willing and working the good because of Adam. For we were also foreseen from eternity in your unchanging wisdom and thereto ordained that we should not feed you." Likewise: Judas Iscariot, when he betrayed you, and Pilate when he had to sentence you although you were innocent. "What do you now accuse us of, since we are not guilty, but you yourself who have made and used us as an unworthy vessel, and now so that your eternal wisdom and providence remain true and just, we must go as damned ones into the eternal fire with the devil and confirm your foreknowledge."

Through the denial of the free will manifold cause is given to the malevolent to lay all their sins and evil deeds on God, saying, "That I practice harlotry and adultery is the will of God. What God wills must take place. Yes, who can counter his will? Were it not his will, then I would not sin. If it is his will, then I will stop sinning." Not to mention that by this erroneous opinion many people are misled into laziness and great despair, so as to think that since I cannot will or do anything good, and since all things happen out of necessity, I will thus remain therein. If God wants to have me, then he will freely draw me. If he does not, then my will is in vain and unfruitful. Yes, such people are waiting also for a special, unusual and miraculous drawing of God, which he would use with them, as if the sending of his holy Word were not enough to draw and summon them. All of which is the work of such an evil, crafty and blasphemous devil that I do not know whether a more harmful Satan for the hindrance of all righteousness and godliness could rise up on earth

---

[41]On the synergistic controversy, see above p. 31n30.
[42]Hesshus, *Explicatio Epistolae Pauli ad Romanos*, 320r-v [sic 322r-v]; citing Phil 2:13.

among Christians. Through this false opinion a great part of the holy Scriptures is overthrown and made powerless. May the all-powerful, good and merciful God graciously aid us against such serious error and crush it with the breath of his mouth, through Jesus Christ our Lord. Amen. FREEDOM OF THE WILL (1527).[43]

A PASTORAL CONCERN ABOUT HUMAN WILL. MARTIN LUTHER: It does not follow from this text that a person's willing and running achieves nothing, but rather that it is not a matter of their own power. The work of God is not nothing. But a person's willing and running is the work of God. For Paul is speaking here about willing and running according to God, that is, about the life of love and the righteousness of God. But any other kind of willing and running is nothing—no matter how intensely those who do not will and run in the way of God will and how vigorously they run. For these things are not of God and are not pleasing to him. . . .

Nevertheless I am warning you that anyone whose mind has not yet been purged should not rush into these speculations, lest they fall into the abyss of horror and hopelessness. Instead, they should first purge the eyes of their heart in their meditation on the wounds of Christ. I myself would not even read these things if the lectionary and necessity did not compel me to do so. For this is very strong wine and the most complete meal, solid food for those who are perfect, that is, the most excellent theology, of which the apostle says: "Among the mature we impart wisdom." But I am a baby who needs milk, not solid food. Whoever is a child like me should do the same. The wounds of Christ, "the clefts of the rock," are sufficiently safe for us. SCHOLIA ON ROMANS 9:16.[44]

MAN BETWEEN GOD AND THE DEVIL. MARTIN LUTHER: In short, if we are under the god of this world, away from the work and Spirit of the true God, we are held captive to his will, as Paul says to Timothy, so that we cannot will anything but what he wills. For he is that strong man armed, who guards his own palace in such a way that those whom he possesses are in peace, so as to prevent them from stirring up any thought or feeling against him; otherwise, the kingdom of Satan being divided against itself would not stand, whereas Christ affirms that it does stand. And this we do readily and willingly, according to the nature of the will, which would not be a will if it were compelled; for compulsion is rather (so to say) "unwill" [noluntas]. But if a Stronger One comes who overcomes him and takes us as his spoil, then through his Spirit we are again slaves and captives—though this is royal freedom—so that we readily will and do what he wills. Thus the human will is placed between the two like a beast of burden. If God rides it, it wills and goes where God wills, as the psalm says: "I am become as a beast (before you) and I am always with you." If Satan rides it, it wills and goes where Satan wills; nor can it choose to run to either of the two riders or to seek him out, but the riders themselves contend for the possession and control of it. . . .

But if we are unwilling to let this term [that is, "free will"] go altogether—though that would be the safest and most God-fearing thing to do—let us at least teach people to use it honestly, so that free choice is allowed to a human being only with respect to what is beneath them and not what is above them. That is to say, a human being should know that with regard to their faculties and possessions they have the right to use, to do or to leave undone, according to their own free choice, though even this is controlled by the free choice of God alone, who acts in whatever way he pleases. On the other hand in relation to God, or in matters pertaining to salvation or damnation, a human being has no free choice, but is a captive, subject and slave either of the will of God or the will of Satan. ON THE BONDAGE OF THE WILL.[45]

---

[43]CRR 5:447-48* (QGT 9:296-97); citing Mt 25:42.
[44]LW 25:389-90* (WA 56:399-400); quoting 1 Cor 2:6; alluding to 1 Cor 3:1-2; Song 2:14; Ex 33:22. See Steinmetz, "Luther and Augustine on Romans 9," 19.

[45]LCC 17:140, 143*; citing 2 Tim 2:26; Lk 11:21, 18; Ps 73:22-23.

Free Election Is Not Ineffectual in Us.
John Calvin: They are, however, to be condemned who remain secure and idle on the pretence of giving place to the grace of God; for though nothing is done by their own striving, yet that effort which is influenced by God is not ineffectual. These things, then, are not said that we may quench the Spirit of God, while kindling sparks within us, by our waywardness and sloth; but that we may understand that everything we have is from him, and that we may hence learn to ask all things of him, to hope for all things from him and to ascribe all things to him, while we are prosecuting the work of our salvation with fear and trembling. Commentary on Romans 9:16.[46]

Receive Scripture as God's Voice.
David Pareus: "Scripture says" stands for *God says in Scripture*. Because Scripture is the Word of God. This refutes the blasphemous sophistry of the Jesuits: "A judge of controversies must speak. Scripture does not speak but is mute letters. Therefore Scripture cannot be a judge of controversies." Their assumption is false. For Scripture *says* to Pharaoh. Thus Scripture is not mute, but speaks. For God speaks in it and through it. Therefore Scripture must be heard as the voice of God, which is certainly judge. Commentary on Romans 9:17.[47]

The Example of Pharaoh.
Tilemann Hesshus: A fourth argument is taken from the example of Pharaoh and is confirmed by the testimony of Scripture by which he proves that it depends only on the purpose and will of God that someone is chosen and ordained to life. If indeed God should leave in damnation those whom he wills, just as he did not choose Pharaoh for life, but left him in damnation, nonetheless he used this reprobate person for his glory and the edification of the church. For he exalted him with wealth, power, a kingdom and honor, but did not give him his Spirit, but rather by offering him outwardly the light of his Word, he blinded him more and more and drove him into a rage so that he attempted to oppress the people of God shrewdly and keep them forcefully in slavery. But God did this with the intention that his immense power would be better known in the world and that the freeing of the church from the hand of so mighty a tyrant would be more famous and thus the knowledge of God would be spread abroad in the world. Therefore it lies in the choice and will of God to make some vessels of mercy and to permit others to be vessels of wrath, such as Pharaoh was. Nonetheless, he knows how to use most wisely those vessels of wrath for the increase of his glory and the benefit of the church. Commentary on Romans 9:17.[48]

God's Revealed and Hidden Wills.
Balthasar Hubmaier: The Scripture that says no one may resist his will does not refer to the revealed will of God, but it refers to the hidden will. Where one now confuses and mixes the two wills with one another there soon follows out of that a notable misunderstanding, error and confusion of Scriptures. Therefore one should wisely divide the judgments in the Scriptures and ruminate truly on them in order to know which Scriptures point to the secret will of God or to the preached.

The schools call the revealed power and will of God an ordered power and will. Not that the first will is unordered, for everything that God wills and does is orderly and good. He is not subject to any rule. His will is itself a rule of all things. Therefore they call the will "ordered" since it occurs according to the preached Word of the holy Scriptures in which he revealed his will to us. From that now comes the division wherein one speaks of the hidden and revealed will of God. Not that there are two wills in God, but thus the Scripture serves us and accommodates itself to speak according to our human ignorance so that we know that although God is almighty and can do all things omnipotently, nevertheless, he wills not to act toward us poor people according to his

---

[46]CTS 38:357-58* (CO 49:182).
[47]Pareus, *In Epistolam ad Romanos*, 852.
[48]Hesshus, *Explicatio Epistolae Pauli ad Romanos*, 330v-331r.

omnipotence, but according to his mercy, as he has sufficiently testified the same to us through his most beloved Son and through all those who point to him in the Old and New Testaments. . . .

Well then let us treat the division of the two wills with an example. According to his secret will the almighty and hidden God could set Peter in hell and, on the other hand, Judas or Caiaphas into heaven and do injustice to no one. We are in his hand. But according to his revealed will he cannot send the embattled Jacob away from him without the blessing. He must be merciful also to the weeping David and has to forgive him his sins, so that he be found to be just in his speaking when he is judged. He also could not dispatch the heathen woman from him unheard. So great and mighty is the power and dignity of the prophecies of God who has become human and been revealed through his Word, who cannot deny himself, or heaven and earth must first fall into pieces. Not that our will, word or work are so high and valuable in themselves, but so powerful and forceful are the divine prophecies in all the believers. Therefore God is captured, bound and overcome with his own Word by believers. In the Scriptures that is called "God being in our midst." FREEDOM OF THE WILL (1527).[49]

To Will and Foreknow Are Different, but Not for God.

DESIDERIUS ERASMUS: Violence is not . . . done to our own will if the course of events is in the hand of God, or if he turns the endeavors of human beings in another direction than they had intended, in accordance with his secret purpose. So just as he turns the efforts of the wicked to the benefit of the godly, so the efforts of the good do not attain the end they seek, unless they are aided by the free favor of God. Without a doubt this is what Paul meant by "So it depends not on human will or exertion, but on God's mercy." The mercy of God preveniently moves the will to will, and accompanies it in its effort, gives it a happy issue. And yet meanwhile we

will, run, follow after—yet what is our own let us ascribe to God to whom we wholly belong.

They sufficiently explain the difficulty about foreknowledge by saying that it does not impose necessity on our will. . . . For prescience is not the cause of things that happen, for it befalls us to foreknow many things that do not happen because we foreknow them, but rather we foreknow them because they are going to happen. Thus the eclipse of the sun does not happen because astrologers predict its occurrence, but they predict its occurrence because it was bound to happen. On the other hand, the question of the will and the determination of God is more difficult.

For God to will and foreknow are the same thing; in some way it must be that he wills what he foreknows as future, and what he does not hinder, though it is in his power to do so. And this is what Paul means by "Who can resist his will" if he has mercy on whom he wills and hardens whom he wills? Truly, if there were a kind who carried into effect whatever he willed, and nobody could resist him, he could be said to do whatever he willed. Thus the will of God, since it is the principal cause of all things that take place, seems to impose necessity on our will. Nor does Paul solve the question, but simply rebukes the questioner: "But who are you, O man, to answer back to God?" Indeed, he rebukes the impious complainer as if the master of a house should say to a froward slave: "What business is it of yours why I give this order? Just do what I command!" He would reply very differently to a prudent and faithful servant, modestly seeking to learn from his master why he wished a thing to be done that at first sight seemed useless. God willed Pharaoh to perish miserably, and he willed rightly, and it was right for him to perish. Yet he was not forced by the will of God to be obstinately wicked.

It is as though a master, knowing the depraved mind of a servant, should commit to him a task, in which an opportunity to sin would be given, in which he might be taken and punished as an example to others. He foreknows that he will follow his inclinations and sin, and will him to

---

[49]CRR 5:472-73, 474* (QGT 9:416-18); citing Gen 32:29; Ps 51; Mt 15:28; Lk 21:33; Rom 8; Mk 9:23; Mt 18:18.

perish, and even wills him in some way to sin. Yet the servant is not excused by this, since he sins from his own wickedness. For he has already previously deserved punishment and is to be publicly punished now that his wickedness is exposed. For what will you take to be the origin of merits where there is perpetual necessity and where there never was free will? What we have said, however, of events, which God often makes to turn out differently from what human beings intended, though true in many cases, is not always true, and in fact happens more frequently with evil things than with good. The Jews crucifying the Lord intended to destroy him entirely; this wicked design God turns to the glory of his Son and the salvation of the whole world. But the centurion Cornelius, who sought with good works the favor of the Divine Being, obtained his wish. And Paul, at the end of his course, gained the crown that he sought.

Here I am not discussing whether God, who is without any argument the primary and highest cause of all things that are made, so acts in some cases by secondary causes that he himself meanwhile does not intervene at all, or whether he so works all things that secondary causes only cooperate with the principal cause, without being otherwise necessary. Certainly it cannot be doubted that God can, if he will, turn the natural issue of secondary causes in another direction. So he can make fire grow cold and moist, water to harden and dry up, the sun to be darkened, rivers to freeze, rocks to melt, poison to heal and food to kill, just as the same fire from the Babylonian furnace revived the three children and burned the Chaldeans. Whenever God acts like this, we call it a miracle. So he can take away taste from the palate and judgment from the eyes, stun the powers of the mind, memory and will, and make them do what seems good to him. . . . What rarely happens does not make a general law. And yet in these cases, whatever God wills, he wills for good reasons, even though they are sometimes hidden from us. This will none can resist, but his ordained will . . . human beings often do resist. Did not Jerusalem resist when it refused to be gathered together when God willed? ON THE FREEDOM OF THE WILL.[50]

GOD ACTS ACCORDING TO HIS GOOD PLEASURE. MARTIN LUTHER: How miserably Diatribe[51] is tormented here; to avoid losing free choice she twists herself into all sorts of shapes. At one moment she says that there is a necessity of consequence but not of the consequent; at another that there is an ordained will, or will signified, that can be resisted and a will purposed that cannot be resisted. At another the passages quoted from Paul are not opposed to free choice, for they are not speaking of human salvation. At another the foreknowledge of God presupposes the necessity, while at yet another it does not. At another grace preveniently moves the will to will, accompanies it on its way and gives it a happy issue. At another the first cause does everything, and at yet another it acts through secondary causes while remaining itself at rest. In these and similar bits of juggling with words, her only aim is to gain time by distracting our attention for a while from the main issue to something else. She credits us with being as stupid and senseless or as little concerned about the subject as she is herself. Or else, just as little children in fear or at play will put their hands over their eyes and then imagine that nobody sees them because they see nobody, so in all sorts of ways Diatribe, who cannot bear the rays or rather lightning flashes of the clearest possible words, pretends that she does not see the real truth of the matter, hoping to persuade us also to cover our eyes so that even we ourselves may not see.

But these are all signs of a mind under conviction and rashly struggling against invincible truth. . . . Diatribe may pretend and pretend again, quibble and quibble again, as much as she likes, but if God foreknew that Judas would be a traitor, Judas necessarily became a traitor, and it was not in the power of Judas or any creature to do differently or to

---

[50]LCC 17:66-68*.
[51]Luther personifies Erasmus's defense of free will—*De libero arbitrio diatribē* (Basel: Froben, 1524)—by this name.

change his will, though he did what he did willingly and not under compulsion, but that act of will was a work of God, which he set in motion by his omnipotence, like everything else. For it is an irrefutable and self-evident proposition that God does not lie and is not deceived. There are no obscure or ambiguous words here, even if all the most learned men of all the centuries are so blind as to think and speak otherwise. And however much you boggle at it, your own and everyone else's conscience is convinced and compelled to say that if God is not deceived in what he foreknows, then the thing foreknown must of necessity take place; otherwise, who could believe his promises, who would fear his threats, if what he promises or threatens does not follow necessarily? Or how can he promise or threaten if his foreknowledge is fallible or can be hindered by our mutability? Clearly this very great light of certain truth stops everyone's mouth, puts an end to all questions, ensues the victory over all evasive subtleties.

We know, of course, that the foreknowledge of human beings is fallible. We know that an eclipse does not occur because it is foreknown, but is foreknown because it is going to occur. But what concern have we with that sort of foreknowledge? We are arguing about the foreknowledge of God; and unless you allow this to carry with it the necessary occurrence of the thing foreknown, you take away faith and the fear of God, make havoc of all the divine promises and threatenings, and thus deny his very divinity. But even Diatribe herself, after a long struggle in which she has tried every possible way out, is at length compelled by the force of truth to admit our view when she says: "The question of the will and the determination of God is more difficult. For God to will and to foreknow are the same thing. And this is what Paul means by 'Who can resist his will if he has mercy on whom he wills and hardens whom he wills?' Truly if there were a king who carried into effect whatever he willed, and nobody could resist him, he could be said to do whatever he willed. Thus the will of God, since it is the principal cause of all things that take place, seems to impose necessity

on our will." So says she; and we can at last thank God for some sense in Diatribe.

What, then, has now become of free choice? But again this eel wriggles suddenly away by saying: "Paul, however, does not solve this question, but rebukes the questioner, 'O man, who are you to answer back to God?'" What a beautiful evasion! Is this the way to treat Holy Writ, pontificating like this on one's own authority, out of one's own head, with no Scripture proofs and no miracles, and in fact corrupting the very clearest words of God? Does not Paul solve this question? What then does he do? "He rebukes the questioner," she says. Is not that rebuke the most unqualified explanation? For what was the point of that question about the will of God? Was it not whether it imposes a necessity on our will? But Paul replies that that is precisely the case: "He has mercy," he says, "on whom he wills, and whom he wills he hardens. It depends not on man's willing or running, but on God's mercy." And not content with this explanation, he proceeds to introduce people who bring objections against it in favor of free choice (prating that there are then no merits and we are damned through no fault of our own, and so forth), in order to put a stop to the murmurings and indignation by saying: "You will say to me, then, Why does he still find fault? Who can resist his will?'" Do you see the character he puts on? When they hear that the will of God implies necessity for us, they murmur blasphemously and say: "Why does he still find fault?" That is to say, why does God insist, urge, demand, complain as he does? Why does he accuse, why does he blame, as if we people could do what he demands if we would? He has no just cause for this faultfinding; let him rather accuse his own will, let him find the fault there, let him put the pressure on there. For who can resist his will? Who can obtain mercy when he does not will it? Who can melt if he wills to harden? It is not in our power to change, much less to resist, his will, which wants us hardened and by which we are forced to be hardened, whether we like it or not. . . .

I admit that the question is difficult, and indeed impossible, if you wish to maintain at the same time both God's foreknowledge and humankind's freedom. For what could be more difficult, nay more impossible, than to insist that contradictories or contraries are not opposed, or to find a number that was at the same time both ten and nine? The difficulty is not inherent in our question, but is sought out and imported, precisely as the ambiguity and obscurity of the Scriptures is sought for and forcibly imported into them. Paul is thus putting a check on the ungodly, who are offended by this very plain speaking when they gather from it that the divine will is fulfilled by necessity on our part, and that very definitely nothing of freedom or free choice remains for them, but everything depends on the will of God alone. The way he checks them, however, is by bidding them be silent and revere the majesty of the divine power and will, in relation to which we have no rights, but which in relation to us has full right to do whatever it pleases. Not that any injustice is done to us, since God owes us nothing, has received nothing from us and has promised us nothing but to do his will and pleasure. On the Bondage of the Will.[52]

A Fixed Number of Elect. Tilemann Hesshus: Therefore Holy Scripture clearly and without any circumlocutions attests that a certain number—and that a small number compared to the multitude of the ungodly—was elected by God before the foundation of the world for the fellowship of eternal life. For Paul says, "The solid foundation of God stands, having this inscription: The Lord knows who are his...." "Just as he chose us in Christ before the foundations of the world were laid, so that we might be holy and blameless before him in love, as he predestined us for the adoption of sons according to the good pleasure of his will." From these clear passages it is necessary to posit that God from eternity determined beforehand and predestined a certain number of elect people. Christ too has this number in mind in John 17: "I have kept those whom you gave me, and none of them has perished except for the son of perdi-

tion so that the Scripture might be fulfilled." ... That he has numbered them most precisely—who can doubt that God counts the saints in his census, to whom he will impart his wisdom, life, heavenly joy, kingdom, glory and eternal bliss? And unless you would take away from God his foreknowledge of all things and his infinite wisdom, which would be an act of extreme wickedness, you cannot deny that God knew for certain from eternity how many and who the elect are who will enjoy eternal glory with God. Paul certainly affirms that the purpose of God according to election stands firm; therefore God can by no means be deceived. As Christ attests, God prepared an eternal kingdom for his elect before the foundations of the world were laid. Therefore he knows them all and has foreseen those for whom he has prepared those things.

This is true, notwithstanding the fact that we are not talking in a literal sense when we say that God foresees the future, for there are neither past things nor future things with God, but all things are present. But if he sees as present whatever will happen in all eternity, it is necessary that the number of those to be saved cannot lie hidden from his wisdom. Christ says, "No one will snatch my sheep from my hand." Therefore also the Lord knows the number of those who are his own (Jn 6). On the Predestination of the Saints: A Fixed Number of the Elect.[53]

God's Name Is Glorified in Both Paul and Pharaoh. Juan de Valdés: St. Paul cites what holy Scripture states concerning Pharaoh to prove, that just as God has some people whom he employs as vessels of mercy, so he likewise has other people whom he employs as vessels of wrath, glorifying God's name by means of both. In saying "vessels" I understand instruments. Pharaoh was an impious vessel of wrath. God through the penalties and punishments with which he chastised Pharaoh manifested his omnipotence. So, by means of Pharaoh, God glorified his name. ... St. Paul was

---

[52]LCC 17:239-42*; citing Rom 9:20, 16.

[53]Hesshus, *Explicatio Epistolae Pauli ad Romanos*, 281r-v; citing 2 Tim 2:19; Eph 1:4-5; Jn 17:12; 10:28.

likewise a vessel of mercy and in his conversion and in the nations whom he converted, God manifested his omnipotence. So by means of St. Paul, he glorified the divine name. The same may be said . . . of all the other persons in whom God has outwardly manifested his omnipotence, in whatever way it may have been.

So, I understand that in the same way that there are some among the ungodly who—not being incited—are not external vessels of wrath, because God does not manifest his omnipotence in them externally, so also there are some among the saints, who—neither being inspired nor moved by the Holy Spirit to external manifestations—are truly pious and just, but they are not external vessels of mercy, because God does not demonstrate his omnipotence in them. The ungodly are generally internal vessels of wrath in this present life, but in the life to come they will be so externally too, while the saints are likewise internal vessels of mercy in the present life, but in the life eternal they too will be so, outwardly, for they both shall glorify the glory of God, but differently. . . . So among the ungodly those who are external vessels of wrath in this present life is accidental; it is peculiar to some and not others. And among the saints those who are external vessels of mercy in this present life is accidental; it is peculiar to some and not others. Commentary on Romans 9:17-18.[54]

9:19-21 How Can God Justly Condemn?

Begin at the Beginning: Jesus Christ.

Martin Luther: What an unquenchable fire it is, whenever a person begins to debate [about predestination]! And the more one debates about it, the more one despairs. Our Lord God is so

opposed to this debate that against it he has placed baptism, his Word, his sacraments and seals; on these things we must stand. I am baptized; I believe in Jesus Christ—what does it matter to me if I'm predestined or not? He has given us a foundation on which we should steady our feet: Jesus Christ; through him we climb to heaven. He is the only way and entrance to the Father. So when, in the devil's name, we begin first to build above, on the roof, despising the foundation, that's why we fall. If we could only believe the promises, that God has spoken them and consider him alone as the speaker, then we would glorify his Word. But when we see his Word in the mouth of a human being, for us, it's the same as if a cow were lowing. Table Talk: Konrad Cordatus (1532).[55]

Why Do You Quarrel with God? Philipp

Melanchthon: Paul adds the conclusion: "Therefore he has mercy on whom he wills; whom he wills, he hardens." This conclusion is not understood equally so far as the causes are concerned but of the effect of the election, that some are elected, while others, who are adversaries of the gospel, are hardened.

First you should learn about the phraseology. For the Hebrews, transitive verbs most commonly have the meaning of permitting. For instance: "Lead us not into temptation," that is, do not permit us to be led into it. Likewise, "You have made us to go astray," that is, you allowed us to fall into error. Thus "to harden" means "not to liberate" others; instead they are permitted to fight against God in order that they may perish. Therefore "whom he wills he hardens" means that he does not set them free, does not convert them because they continue to fight against God who is calling them.

Second, Paul is not saying here that the cause of hardening or reprobation is not in the ungodly. Prudence must be exercised here, and one must think that the cause of hardening or reprobation is in the ungodly themselves because they do not

---

[54]Valdés, *Commentary upon Romans*, 160-61* (*Commentario de Romanos*, 190-92). Valdés is distinguishing between what is "accidental" to a thing and what is "essential" to a thing—that is, what can be removed without altering the thing's nature and what cannot be removed without altering the thing's nature. So, Valdés means that if someone is a vessel of wrath or mercy in this life, that does not mean that according to their person they must be such; it does not necessarily correspond to their nature.

[55]WATR 2:562, no. 2631b.

cease to resist God, who is calling them. These things that Paul says are certain, that there is a great number that is hardened or rejected, which fights against the Word of God. If someone obeys the Word of God, he is not in that number.

Let us learn here what the judgment is about those who fight against the Word of God. Because they fight against it, they are hardened and show that they are of the number of the reprobate.

When he says, "Whom he wills, he hardens," he immediately adds the objection: If hardening occurs by the will of God, that multitude cannot be converted; if it cannot be converted, then is it accused? He answers, conceding that it cannot be converted, namely, from necessity of the consequence, as if he said: "It is true that the multitude is rejected and that it cannot be converted, because it has been rejected; but it has been rejected on account of its own ungodliness. If someone obeys God, who is calling, he is not of that number." Thus he answers by way of a concession, and adds the ultimate cause why God ordained things in this way: in order that both the wrath and the mercy might be more clearly seen.

I apply Paul's answers this way: "Why do you quarrel with God?" That is, when you see this extraordinary counsel of God according to which he chooses few and rejects many, you should obey God and fear his judgment, lest you be offended by the example of the multitude. Know that God is showing mercy in saving us, and is showing his wrath in punishing those who do not obey.

This is the least intricate explanation. It should not be thought that there is no hardening or reprobation in the ungodly themselves, nor does Paul say this. Also the picture of the clay and the potter does not imply that the wicked do nothing, but it fits insofar as from the one mass of the human race God saves some according to his decision and damns others. The causes cannot be entirely accommodated to an analogy. For the idea must be retained that God is not the cause of sin. This also must be held fast: the promise is universal. Thus Paul himself later adds the reason: Israel is perishing because it is unwilling to accept the

gospel. While pursuing righteousness it does not achieve it, because it is not of faith, etc. Here he expressly sets down the cause of reprobation, namely, because they fight against the gospel. COMMENTARY ON ROMANS (1540).[56]

A RESPONSE TO PROTESTANT READINGS.
DOMINGO DE SOTO: But nonetheless here a most grave doubt stubbornly remains, namely, that Paul not only is deliberately not answering the present question at all, but seems to be deflecting and avoiding an answer to the previous question (if one may speak about Paul in this way). For to stick with his example, although a vessel may be made for dishonor, it would not be able to ask its maker and accuse him of injustice because he made it to be such when he owed nothing to it. Nonetheless, if a potter were to find fault with the shape and shoddiness of the vessel, it would have been able to excuse itself justly and even scatter aspersions against the maker who wanted to make it that way. In a similar manner, the sensual and reprobate person would be able to say to God, "Granted, that there is no injustice in you when you condemn me in this way, nonetheless that is no reason why you invent a charge against me and blame me for being such a being as you made me to be." Therefore Paul ought to have answered this second objection and not evaded the question and fled back to the first one.

Good God, how many absurd and downright inconceivable things those Lutherans are contriving here. Listen to Bucer, among others, on this passage, where he contends that hardened and reprobate people perform evil deeds under God's design and even his compulsion and yet sin no less. He says, "Granted that what we may not be able to understand is no less the very truth," and it is for this reason that he says that Paul does not know how to reply. Therefore, listen to that Lutheran: in what sense he reads this phrase, "Who will resist his will?" He takes it to mean "Who will resist the will of God when he wants

---

[56]Melanchthon, *Commentary on Romans*, 191-92* (MO 15:683-85).

Pharaoh or any other wicked person to sin?" It is as if he were to say, "It is necessary that he sins so that he is driven to it." "Thus, for that reason," he says, "God hardened Pharaoh so that he would want to disobey God's own command. Indeed, God himself made that good-for-nothing person fight against him. And so while he was not obeying God, Pharaoh was doing what God wanted him to do. Indeed, Pharaoh was not even able to permit the people to leave, since God disposed him to act that way." Nor did Bucer dare to ascribe this only about the reprobate Pharaoh, but he goes on to confirm the same thing concerning David. Namely, he says that God sent it into his heart to count the people, whom he numbered under compulsion, or else God would have been frustrated in his own work. And Pharaoh sinned no less seriously than David did. But if we are not able to understand this inherent quality of fault in a work done under compulsion, Bucer says that we should not be astonished when Paul says, "O man, who are you?" We are obligated to believe it no less unhesitatingly. Look at their monsters and consider that they lack no open ears into which they vomit such ideas. So that we may pass over the rather many things that I put together against these monstrosities in the recently cited chapters of book one of *Concerning Nature and Grace*, let me ask: Is anyone at all bold enough to think that when God ordered Pharaoh so earnestly through Moses to let his people go, he did not mean what he was expressing in his command?[57] For then that command would be a fiction, which is not something befitting God. Now if God wanted Pharaoh not to obey him, then, when Pharaoh did not obey God's command, he would have obeyed God's will no less; and so by sinning he would not have sinned—which is a contradiction. COMMENTARY ON ROMANS 9:21-22.[58]

FAULTY HUMAN REASON ATTACKS GOD.

DAVID PAREUS: The refutation of the third calumny, by which human reason attacks God for judgments that seem harsh and unfair, is much more virulent than earlier. *First*, human reason accused him of inconstancy if he rejected the Jews. *Next* it accused him of injustice if he did not choose all. Now it accuses him of cruelty if he hardens those whom he will and nonetheless is angry at the hardened people. He first moves his audience and then refutes their objections with simple questions for the sake of emphasis. "Therefore, will you say to me" perceives that human reason can make out of God's mercy and hardening an opportunity to reproach God's judgments as tyrannical. If God stirred up, hardened and ruined Pharaoh apart from his own guilt and if he hardens whomever he will, Pharaoh and the hardened will be free from fault, at any rate. For they are not able to resist his will; he himself will be cruel if he punishes the innocent or destroys those whom he has made to be guilty. This is that subtlety of reason by which even today (albeit blasphemously) there is a protest by some against the judgments of God. . . .

Before we hear the apostle's reply, let us reduce this twofold objection to standard [syllogistic] form:

[First Syllogism]

Major Premise: God is wrong to be angry at those who are hardened by his will.

Minor Premise: Pharaoh and the reprobate are hardened by the will of God.

Conclusion: Therefore God is wrong to be angry at them.

[Second Syllogism]

Major Premise: Human beings do not deserve to be punished by God for whatever cannot be avoided by human beings.

---

[57]Domingo de Soto, *De natura et gratia* (Paris: Foucher, 1549), 1r-94v. Soto prepared this account for the Council of Trent, restating (unfairly) and responding to thirty-five alleged Protestant theses.
[58] Soto, *In Epistolam ad Romanos*, 266-67.

Minor Premise: The hardening of Pharaoh and of the reprobate occurs by the immutable will of God, which no one can resist.

Conclusion: Therefore the hardened do not deserve to be punished.

To respond briefly to the first syllogism: It commits the fallacy of four terms. The major premise is concerned about the will in the sense of "a commandment" or "watchword." The minor premise, which is concerning the will in the sense of "God's good pleasure" or his decree, is true. But concerning this matter the major premise is false, because the will of God's good pleasure is primal righteousness, and it is impossible that it would ever be unjust, however much human reason may growl.[59]

As for the second syllogism, the major premise must be clarified: "Human beings do not deserve to be punished by God for whatever cannot be avoided by human beings," namely, if they themselves should wish to avoid it and are not carried along wholeheartedly to that very goal. But just as the reprobate are not able to avoid their hardening, so neither do they want to avoid it. They are not hardened unwillingly or under compulsion, but of their own entire will, and they harden themselves.[60]

But a fuller explanation about these things is found below in the explanation of difficult matters. COMMENTARY ON ROMANS 9:19.[61]

IN PUNISHMENT AND PITY GOD IS MERCIFUL.
JACQUES LEFÈVRE D'ÉTAPLES: This is Paul's first refutation of the question, especially to the inexperienced: namely, one must not irreverently dispute against God, whether he creates one individual for mercy or another for his justice. It both pleases God to have pity and to punish. But life is in his will and wrath in his indignation. To be sure, even when he punishes, he is merciful, and when he shows mercy he is just. But when you sin, you do not wish to be accused and you do not wish to be punished. But you are accused for the reason that you sin of your own free will, and divine help had been prepared to help your weakness so that you would not sin. And you are punished for the reason that God is just and you did not sin by his will but by your own. He wants you to be good, and he always aids you for this purpose; your will is by itself the cause of your sin and your hardening. It is not the will of God that is the cause, unless by chance you might wish to say that it is an accidental and permissive cause, but that is not what it means to be a cause.[62] God wants all people to be saved, and much more than a father wants his own sons to be saved, inasmuch as he has made and created us. And how could he want us to sin,

---

[59]A valid syllogism must have three and only three terms: a major, a minor and a middle term. The major term and the middle appear in the major premise, and the minor term and the middle appear in the minor premise, while the conclusion has the major and minor terms. In addition, each term must be used in the same sense throughout. If a word is used in two different senses, the syllogism is said to commit the fallacy of four terms. The specific fault here is in the ambiguous middle. "Will" is used in two different senses. If the hardening took place because of some arbitrary rule that God made, as the critics assume in the major premise, they would have a point. But in truth the hardening of which the minor premise speaks takes place because of God's good pleasure (*beneplacitum*), which is reflected in his eternal decree (*decretum*) and is no mere temporary commandment (*mandatum*) or watchword (*signum*), the latter being something that would change every day in a military camp. God's good pleasure is the font and source of all righteousness and cannot be called into question as a derivative law might.
[60]Here Pareus does not question per se the validity of the syllogism, but argues that the major premise is incorrect as stated or is at least overly broad. If the major premise were revised to meet Pareus's explanation, the minor premise would

also have to be adjusted (in order to remain a valid syllogism) to say that Pharaoh and other hardened individuals were hardened against their will—something that would be false.
[61]Pareus, *In Epistolam ad Romanos*, 857, 858-59.
[62]Lefèvre is making two distinctions here: between the substantial and the accidental, and between the permissive and the express will of God. The former distinction is used to make the point that God is not substantially the cause of sin. As the one by whom all humans "live, move and have their being," he is the cause of all actions, including evil actions, but with the latter he can be considered a cause only insofar as he is the cause of actions, not the cause of the content of those actions. The second distinction is used to make the point that God permits some actions that he does not desire, but allows humans to undertake, nonetheless. But when philosophers and theologians speak of causation, they usually exclude such remote factors, or else one would soon have to speak of the flapping of a butterfly's wings as being as much of a cause for a hurricane as ocean currents and evaporation.

when the divine word says, "You are not a God that desires iniquity?" Therefore, if you sin, you sin against his will. But if you behave well, you behave according to his will. He wants you to behave well, but freely. For that reason he does not implant in you the necessity to behave well. Much less does he implant in you the necessity to behave badly. How, therefore, does a wicked person speak against God, if he has mercy on him whom he wishes to do so and he hardens him whom he wishes, "Who will resist his will?" Such thinking implies that if someone is bad, God wanted him out of necessity to sin, when in reality God does not want him to sin either out of necessity or of his own free will. Such thinking also implies that if someone is good, God wanted him to be good out of necessity. Truly, God did not want such a thing; instead, he wants him to be good of his own free will and he helps him for this very purpose. Why then does God harden some, abandon others, or wish to harden or abandon them? Clearly, like a father at long last abandons incorrigible sons after a long delay and displays in them his power and proper punishment, so also God displays the same in the case of the obstinate and arrogant, whom also for this reason he at last abandons. He does this because any delay would not benefit them in any way, but rather would increase their penalty. And he pities others and wants to pity them, as a father takes pity on obedient children or those children who have come to their senses and turned from disobedience. So also God wishes to pity the obedient and those who have returned to their senses, so that he may show in them the riches of his glory, as in vessels that he prepared for his glory. From the obedient the mercy of God is discerned; from the disobedient, God's justice and power. ANNOTATIONS ON ROMANS 9:19-21.[63]

WHO DO YOU THINK YOU ARE? DAVID PAREUS: In Augustine, [*De diversis quaestionibus octoginta tribus*] question 68,[64] the Marcionite and Man-ichaean heretics once brought forth the censure that Paul failed here and did not have anything to answer the cunning arguments that were raised against him. But away with such blasphemous talk! But Augustine (in his *Enchiridion*, chapter 99[65]) sufficiently refutes this idea. The apostle speaks from the Holy Spirit—and the Holy Spirit never fails. To the contrary, he judges these objections to be so crass that he artfully beats them back. By his apostolic authority he has enough wherewith to refute human audacity; nonetheless he so defends God from every accusation of iniquity that he at the same time explains the most serious reasons why they ought to just give up and go home. COMMENTARY ON ROMANS 9:20.[66]

GOD'S PERFECT JUSTICE TRANSCENDS HUMAN REASON. TILEMANN HESSHUS: Because the sublime judgment of God that he uses in gathering and sanctifying the church is clearly hidden from and alien to human intelligence, reason cannot grasp it, but rather straightaway barks at God, summoning his works to court and finding fault with his fairness and justice. For it does not understand the hideousness of sin or the harshness of divine judgment or the boundlessness of mercy or the bottomless depths of divine wisdom. Therefore, when it accuses God of injustice, it thus frees itself of every blame and clearly absolves itself. It says, "If God pities whomever he wishes to and hardens whomever he wishes, and so it depends not on the choice and will of a person but of God, that someone is either chosen to life or left in damnation, therefore God has no reason to be angry at the reprobate. And why does he rebuke godless people with such vehemence? How will he exercise judgment? For nobody can resist his will." The apostle reminds reason of its origin and restrains and refutes this blasphemous wantonness of reason, which threatens to bring suit against God the Creator. What is more unjust than for a work to sue its maker? Therefore, since God is the

---

[63]Lefèvre d'Étaples, *Epistola ad Rhomanos*, 86v; citing Ps 5:4.
[64]See PL 40:70-74.
[65]NPNF 3:268-69.
[66]Pareus, *In Epistolam ad Romanos*, 859.

creator of humankind, a human being may not in any way pursue a lawsuit against his Maker. Wicked and haughty people are not worthy even to be refuted, because they set their lawsuit in motion out of pure arrogance and petulance toward God. They are justly restrained by this harsh punishment because a piece of clay is unworthy to demand explanations for its formation from its maker.

With this serious rebuttal Paul teaches the godly that we understand the lofty and hidden mystery of election most correctly only when we consider the immense majesty of God and in turn confess the worthlessness of our nature and we entrust ourselves entirely to the divine will and power and allow ourselves to be shaped as clay is handled and shaped by the potter.

Nonetheless, reason cannot obtain from this fact a means by which it might be free of blame. For the entire mass from which God makes some to be vessels for honor and destines others for ignominy is infected and polluted with sin. God considers that in the beginning human nature was pure, just and upright, without any disgrace of sin. But of its own initiative and free will it rejected this innocence and stained itself with sin and sank itself into death. But it is out of this mass of humanity, contaminated by sin, that God forms vessels of mercy destined for glory. By this work of his he shows his boundless mercy and wisdom. From the same corrupt mass of humanity he leaves behind other vessels for ignominy and his just judgment, doing no one any injustice. Therefore a human being does not have any grounds for complaining. In vain the wicked strive to excuse themselves and release themselves from blame. On the Last Day God will exercise his judgment with perfect justice. COMMENTARY ON ROMANS 9:19-21.[67]

THE ANALOGY OF THE POTTER AND CLAY. DA-VID PAREUS: Who will direct a case against God here? The reason for the consequence is twofold: First, from the analogy between God and the potter—how does a potter relate to God?—and,

second, from the analogy between God's right over his creations and the potter's right over the clay. A potter has an absolute right over the clay, which he did not make and is not even able to make. Why then will God not have an absolute right over the creatures he made and makes by his absolute power? A potter's prerogative is to fashion clay, but not to create it. But God creates, fashions and appoints the mass of humanity in his absolute power, as he wills. Now Paul alludes to the passage of Jeremiah 18, where it is asserted that the potter has the right over the clay to produce a pot and again to pull it apart and form it differently.

Therefore by this simile two things are solidly taught. First, as the potter by his sheer will forms from the same clay a dish for noble uses and an earthen pot for ignoble uses, so God by his sheer will—and indeed by a greater right—forms out of the same mass of humanity some people to be vessels of glory and others to be vessels of ignominy, that is, he elects some people, converts them and endows them with salvation in Christ, but he does not elect others, but leaves them in death, rejects them and damns them for their sins. Second, as the potter does this without any injustice nor is he held to give an account for his action, nor do the vessels have the right to demand an explanation, so God is not unjust or cruel because he elects, rejects, has pity and hardens whom he wills, but in those whom he elected he is very good and in those whom he left behind and hardened he is in no wise culpable.

"But," you say, "the apostle has not yet solved the problem, but made it worse. Even if a pot could not demand from its maker, 'Why did you make me this way?' the potter nonetheless does not have the authority to get angry at the pot because it is just as he made it." The answer: A simile does not mean the two things are the same. If a pot remains as its maker made it, it does not offer him the occasion for getting angry at it. Even so, the potter has the right of tearing it apart of his own free will. But if the pot also began to stink either from itself or from some other source or if it acquired some

---

[67]Hesshus, *Explicatio Epistolae Pauli ad Romanos*, 324r-325r.

blemish, would not the potter rightly be angry at it? So even if a human being had remained as God had formed him, God nonetheless would have the right of destroying him, but would not God rightly be angry at a human being ruining himself by his sin? Commentary on Romans 9:21.[68]

9:22-24 Vessels of Wrath and Mercy

Election Not Submitted for Human Judgment. John Calvin: Paul briefly shows, that though the counsel of God is in fact incomprehensible, yet his unblamable justice shines forth no less in the perdition of the reprobate than in the salvation of the elect. He does not indeed give a reason for divine election, so as to assign a cause why this person is chosen and that one rejected; for it was not fitting that the things contained in the secret counsel of God should be subjected to human judgment; and, besides, this mystery is inexplicable. He therefore keeps us from curiously examining those things that exceed human comprehension. He yet shows that as far as God's predestination manifests itself, it appears perfectly just. Commentary on Romans 9:22.[69]

God Patiently Suffers the Wicked. Juan de Valdés: In that expression, "he has endured with much patience," I think St. Paul's meaning is that God—with the intent of using the wicked to reveal his glory—does not chastise the wicked as soon as they fall into wickedness, or, more properly speaking, when they resolve to be wicked. As if he should say, "God did not punish Pharaoh by taking away his life, when he resolved to resist the will of God, instead he sent Pharaoh diverse punishments, until the end when he drowned Pharaoh in the sea." And it is in this waiting for the wicked to fill up the measure of their iniquity that St. Paul understands God to exercise long-suffering and patience. Commentary on Romans 9:22-24.[70]

God Prepares the Elect for Glory; The Reprobate Prepare Themselves for Destruction. Domingo de Soto: Dear reader, attentively observe here the distinction between predestination and reprobation. First, there is a distinction with respect to the goal: the goal of reprobation is to show anger, but the goal of predestination is to show mercy. Therefore there is also a difference in what God employs, for God employs anger against the one group, but mercy toward the other. But there is a third difference in regard to God's preparation. For the same people whom God predestines he also prepares for the goal, namely, by calling, helping and moving them forward through good works. But he does not prepare in like manner for damnation those whom he rejects. For the bad works for which they are condemned are their own deeds. And so he does not say here that because he wanted to show wrath, he wanted to make the reprobate vessels of wrath and fit them for destruction. To the contrary, in order to show that their works were products of their own free will with the result that they are contrary to God's own will, he says, "He bore with them." And he alludes to Pharaoh, by whom he encompasses all haughty people who heap up sins upon sins. God does not remove them from his midst straightway, but he puts up with them by delaying their punishment. And insofar as it pertains to him, it is that he draws them to repentance by his kindness (according to Paul's phrase in chapter 2) and long-suffering, but their hardening is the cause for God wanting (though incidentally) to show his wrath abundantly in them. For this reason he calls them "vessels of wrath," just as the elect were called "a vessel of election" for the opposite reason. For he sticks to the example of the potter, so that those whom he had called "vessels of reproach" he now names "vessels of wrath," that is, those who have made themselves fit to be filled with the wrath of God. Commentary on Romans 9:22.[71]

[68]Pareus, *In Epistolam ad Romanos*, 861-62.
[69]CTS 38:357-58* (CO 49:182).
[70]Valdés, *Commentary upon Romans*, 165* (*Commentario de Romanos*, 196).
[71]Soto, *In Epistolam ad Romanos*, 269.

DIVINE PREPARATION AND PERMISSION.
DOMINGO DE SOTO: Predestination is a kind of
providence—a certain part of providence that
applies to an individual. For while providence is
some general, eternal arranging of matters into
their proper goals (whether the goal is natural or
supernatural), predestination (as it is used in the
conversations of the saints) is the particular
destining of a rational creature toward its final goal,
to which it is led by the leading and favor of God
beyond its own nature. But reprobation is also the
eternal will of God's permitting some people to
wander away from that final goal by their own free
will. Thus the goal of predestination (as Paul
teaches us here) is to show the glory and mercy of
God, but the goal of reprobation is to manifest his
righteousness and patience. COMMENTARY ON
ROMANS 9:23.[72]

**THE SWEET CONFIDENCE OF RECEIVING GOD'S
CALL.** DAVID PAREUS: But who indeed are those
vessels of mercy? "We are," he says, "Whom he has
called." From our calling we recognize that we are
among those vessels because the vessels whom he
predestined he also called, as Romans 8:30 had
said. Therefore now he passes on a presupposition
of this doctrine, a presupposition that is altogether
comforting, namely, that one ought not to judge
concerning God's eternal election a priori, that is,
from the hidden counsel of God, which cannot be
ascertained in itself, but a posteriori, that is, from
its effects in us and others, that is, the calling, faith,
justification, new birth and other benefits of Christ
that are revealed to us by the gospel. That is where
the sweetest *plērophoria* ["full confidence"] of faith
is born. For if God's plan is firm and his election is
immutable, our faith and salvation will remain at
any rate firm and immutable. Thus are refuted the
ill-considered outcries of some that the doctrine of
divine predestination is an abyss, that it cannot be
understood, that it ought not to be taught in the
church, that people are being sent off to investigate
a matter hidden by God, that it drowns people in

despair, etc. The apostle now shows these things to
be false and wicked. Therefore this is the summary:
As many as perceive that they have been called to
faith in Christ and obey the call (whether they
come from the Jews or the Gentiles) have an
infallible testimony in their hearts that they are
vessels of mercy that God has prepared for glory.
COMMENTARY ON ROMANS 9:24.[73]

IN ELECTION ALL ARE EQUAL. JUAN DE
VALDÉS: The expression "whom he has called" is
very significant. I understand it to mean that we
are brought to accept the grace of the gospel and to
be vessels of mercy prepared for glory, not by any
effort of our own, but by God's calling. It should
also be noted that, in calling both Jews and
Gentiles, God removes all distinction, for he will
not allow hierarchical distinction of persons among
them. COMMENTARY ON ROMANS 9:22-24.[74]

9:25-26 *Becoming God's People*

THE ELECT CHURCH OF JEWS AND GENTILES.
PHILIPP MELANCHTHON: After he has set down
the thesis that the people of God is the church of
the elect, he now comes to the hypothesis that the
elect are from among Jews and Gentiles. He proves
this with the testimonies of Scripture in order to
show that the gospel pertains to the Gentiles. First
he quotes this passage from Hosea. The testimony
is sufficiently clear. The reader must be reminded
of this in passing. As often as the call of the
Gentiles is spoken of, one must know that grace is
being commended, that we are pleasing not on
account of the law, but freely on account of Christ.
COMMENTARY ON ROMANS (1540).[75]

GOD'S CALL NOT OUR MERIT. JOHANNES
BUGENHAGEN: Here we see that the people of God
are elected by God's calling, not their merits.... For

---

[72]Soto, *In Epistolam ad Romanos*, 269-70.

[73]Pareus, *In Epistolam ad Romanos*, 870-71.
[74]Valdés, *Commentary upon Romans*, 165-66* (*Commentario de
    Romanos*, 197).
[75]Melanchthon, *Commentary on Romans*, 192* (MO 15:685); citing
    Hos 2:23; 1:10.

the Gentiles were not called the people of God according to the reckoning of time. At that time they were not counted among the people of God, but before God, from eternity they were God's people, because he has loved them since before the foundations of the earth. . . . Therefore you see here that by grace alone these titles are commended to us, because first we are made the people of God, then beloved, afterward sons and heirs. COMMENTARY ON PAUL'S LETTER TO THE ROMANS.[76]

A GREAT HONOR. PETER MARTYR VERMIGLI: Now it is no small dignity to be admitted into the people of God, for it depends on this: that we believe in God, that we have our faith sealed with the sacraments, that we publicly believe and confess, that we publicly and privately pray to and worship our God. And in this way we live as his Word commands us and his Spirit prompts us. COMMENTARY ON ROMANS 9:26.[77]

9:27-29 Only a Remnant

A HARD WORD. JOHN CALVIN: Paul proceeds now to . . . what he was unwilling to begin with, lest he should too much exasperate their minds. And it is not without a wise contrivance that he adduces Isaiah as exclaiming, not speaking, in order that he might excite more attention. But the words of the prophet were evidently intended to keep the Jews from glorying too much in the flesh. For it was a thing dreadful to be heard, that of so large a multitude a small number only would obtain salvation. For though the prophet, after having described the devastation of the people, lest the faithful should think that the covenant of God was wholly abolished, gave some remaining hope of favor; yet he confined it to a few. But as the prophet predicted of his own time, let us see how Paul could rightly apply this to his purpose.

It must be in this sense: when the Lord resolved to deliver his people from the Babylonian captivity, his purpose was that this benefit of deliverance should come only to a very few of that vast multitude; which might have been said to be the remnant of that destruction, when compared with the great number that he suffered to perish in exile. Now that temporal restoration was typical of the real renovation of the church of God; yea, it was only its commencement. What therefore happened then is to be now much more completely fulfilled as the very progress and completion of that deliverance. COMMENTARY ON ROMANS 9:27.[78]

PROMISE KEEPER. DESIDERIUS ERASMUS: No matter how great the crowds of those who fall away, it will not upset the promise of God. To break one's word in promises is characteristic of human beings, but God is one who fulfills completely whatever he has said, and in full measure—not cheating, but truly and justly. . . . Shadows seem to have an element of deception and the law speaks at length; it promises, it foreshadows, instructs, warns and consoles. But Christ has been sent and has fulfilled once and for all what was promised, has embodied what was foreshadowed and has reduced the lengthy list of instructions to the single precept of evangelical love. PARAPHRASE ON ROMANS 9:27-28.[79]

GOD HIDES LIFE UNDER DEATH. TILEMANN HESSHUS: Paul retained the customary translation of the Septuagint. But in Hebrew it is rendered, "Destruction will be decreed, overflowing with righteousness. For the Lord will bring about destruction—and that a complete destruction—in the whole land." The prophet is foretelling the destruction and annihilation of the Jewish nation, for the Israelites were imagining that the Mosaic polity and their kingdom would last forever, even if they engaged in wickedness of every kind. Therefore Isaiah warns that they are greatly in error, since indeed God had certainly decreed and determined that he would overturn

---

[76]Bugenhagen, *In Epistolam Pauli ad Romanos interpretatio*, 114r; citing Eph 1:4.
[77]Vermigli, *In Epistolam ad Romanos*, 396 (cf. *A Commentarie upon the Epistle to the Romanes*, 281v).
[78]CTS 38:373-74* (CO 49:190-91).
[79]CWE 42:57-58; citing Is 28:22.

and abolish the polity of Moses along with all its ceremonies and laws and destroy the people themselves, even to the point of slaughter. Nonetheless, God governed the destruction and overthrow of his people by virtue of his marvelous and immense wisdom so that the righteousness of God would then overflow; that is, it would flow forth most abundantly and take over the whole earth. These things have been fulfilled, as Isaiah had prophesied. For the Lord brought about destruction; that is, he made an end to the Mosaic polity: he abolished the priesthood of Aaron, overturned the temple, and extirpated and wiped out the whole Jewish nation. But this very devastation was a flood of righteousness. That is to say, in the very destruction of the Jewish nation, by which it seemed that the entire church would perish, the font of righteousness and all of Christ's benefits flowed forth generously and richly. For the Messiah himself is raised from the dead and seated at the right hand of the Father; he pours out the Holy Spirit visibly over the apostles and the church. The apostles and the Jews who had been converted to God spread abroad the light of the gospel through the whole earth. Gentiles are chosen for fellowship with the church. Not only did many of the Jews but also rather many Gentiles from all kingdoms and nations embraced the teaching of the gospel. They were freed from sin and death and pursued righteousness and eternal life. Never, at any other time since the founding of the church, has the church flourished to such a degree and grown so marvelously as at the time when the Jewish nation was destroyed and the apostles were teaching the gospel.

Therefore it is not the case that we fear that the church will die as empires fall or a dispute arises between churches or scholars. For God knows how to govern events in such a way that those things that we think will bring the most certain demise to the church will give it the greatest growth. COMMENTARY ON ROMANS 9:27-28.[80]

THE OLD TESTAMENT TYPOLOGICALLY INTIMATES THE GOSPEL. JUAN DE VALDÉS: In these authoritative passages quoted by St. Paul from Old Testament Scripture, consider principally what he intends to prove by them. He has proved by the Hosea passage that the calling of the Gentiles to the grace of the gospel had already been prophesied. By the Isaiah passage, he intends to prove that it had been already prophesied that all the Jews were not to be saved, but a certain number of them, and that this number was to be small. Now it is not to be said that Isaiah means that very few of the very many who were children of Israel or Israelites would escape God's punishment after the Babylonian captivity—because that's what the prophets said in the Scriptures. It seems that they trick human curiosity by apparently intimating one thing, while they effectively teach Christian simplicity by intimating another.

I say this because just as the exodus of the people of Israel from Egypt symbolizes to me the ungodly person's departure from ungodliness, and the entrance and residence of this same people in the land of promise symbolizes to me the entrance and residence of the godly person in the grace of the gospel, so likewise the captivity of the Israelites in Babylon symbolizes to me the captivity of the bodies of Christians in the grave and the return of the Jews to Jerusalem symbolizes to me the return of Christians to eternal life. So then, I recognize that the prophets (in what they have said of that captivity and of that return to Jerusalem) were more intent on prophesying what should come to pass upon the return of Christians to their bodies in order to enter eternal life, than upon what should occur at the return of the Jews to Jerusalem. COMMENTARY ON ROMANS 9:27-28.[81]

TINY FLOCK CONFIRMED BY ISAIAH. TILEMANN HESSHUS: With another testimony of Isaiah he proves the same thing, namely, that the church does not depend on the multitude of the

---

[80]Hesshus, *Explicatio Epistolae Pauli ad Romanos*, 337r-v; citing Is 10:22-23.

[81]Valdés, *Commentary upon Romans*, 167* (*Commentario de Romanos*, 198-99); alluding to Hos 1:10; 2:23; Is 1:9.

Jewish people, but rather that God has rejected and destroyed the greater portion of that nation, and that nonetheless he has chosen and preserved a remnant for himself from that nation. Furthermore, it is a singular act of God's kindness and an achievement of his that God did not reject and destroy the entire nation. Just as nobody was saved from Sodom and Gomorrah, so nobody of the whole Jewish nation would have been saved and all would have perished by their own free will unless the Lord had preserved a seed for himself out of his singular mercy and kindness, that is, unless he had adopted some of them to be sons of God through the Holy Spirit. Therefore these ones are the sons of God, the elect church and the holy seed, who are called and preserved by divine mercy. We must diligently consider this passage concerning the astounding smallness of the church so that we will not be offended by it, but rather know that it pleased God the Father, because he decided to give the kingdom of heaven to a tiny flock. COMMENTARY ON ROMANS 9:29.[82]

THE LORD OF HOSTS. JUAN DE VALDÉS: The holy Old Testament Scripture is accustomed to call God "the Lord of hosts," meaning by hosts all things created in heaven and on earth. Thus God shows his omnipotence, just as a mighty prince makes himself feared by his armies. The holy New Testament Scripture calls God "the Father of our Lord Jesus Christ." And they too call him so who know Christ, the knowledge of whom causes love and not fear.

Here the point to observe is that, when he says "Lord" in the Hebrew, it is God's most holy name, which signifies his essence and his existence, which is self-existent, and gives being and life to everything that exists and lives. COMMENTARY ON ROMANS 9:29.[83]

---

[82]Hesshus, *Explicatio Epistolae Pauli ad Romanos*, 328r.
[83]Valdés, *Commentary upon Romans*, 169* (*Commentario de Romanos*, 201).

9:30–10:4 RIGHTEOUSNESS COMES BY FAITH

[30]*What shall we say, then? That Gentiles who did not pursue righteousness have attained it, that is, a righteousness that is by faith;* [31]*but that Israel who pursued a law that would lead to righteousness[a] did not succeed in reaching that law.* [32]*Why? Because they did not pursue it by faith, but as if it were based on works. They have stumbled over the stumbling stone,* [33]*as it is written,*

"*Behold, I am laying in Zion a stone of stumbling, and a rock of offense;*

and whoever believes in him will not be put to shame.*"

10 *Brothers,[b] my heart's desire and prayer to God for them is that they may be saved.* [2]*For I bear them witness that they have a zeal for God, but not according to knowledge.* [3]*For, being ignorant of the righteousness of God, and seeking to establish their own, they did not submit to God's righteousness.* [4]*For Christ is the end of the law for righteousness to everyone who believes.[c]*

a Greek *a law of righteousness*   b Or *Brothers and sisters*   c Or *end of the law, that everyone who believes may be justified*

OVERVIEW: The foundation stone of God's house—Christ—becomes a stumbling stone to those who strive to please God through human works according to human reason (see Is 28:16; 8:14). Here many of the reformers continue to draw out the implications of the priority of grace in salvation. Until a person has been justified, none of their works can be called good; good works only flow out of faith. Human reason bristles at this teaching. But Jesus calls the sick, not the healthy; the sinners, not the righteous (Mk 2:17). Until human beings correctly understand their condition by God's Word and Spirit, they remain offended by God's wise foolishness: that whoever believes in the crucified and resurrected Christ will be given eternal life.

This requires a correct understanding of the law: its content and its purpose. To help their readers with the law's content and purpose, the reformers deftly wield Paul's statement that "Christ is the end of the law." All Scripture—as a whole and in its parts—is about Jesus Christ. Apart from Christ Scripture is incomprehensible. "Take Christ out of the Scriptures," Luther asked, "and what will you find left in them?"[1] The law accurately reflects human sin and inadequacy, goading us to look for

help and mediation. Only Christ meets the law's demands, and so only he can help us and mediate for us. In this way the law—all its lessons, commands and promises—leads us to Christ and his righteousness. Not to acknowledge this is to use the law contrary to its purpose. And so the reformers encourage us to repent and believe.

9:30-31 Righteousness by Faith Versus by Law

WATERS OF MERCY. JOHANNES OECOLAMPA-DIUS: The water of grace always flows in valleys of humility and turns away from mountains of pride. Therefore, because the Gentiles did not consider themselves as righteous, they accepted Christ—nevertheless by the mercy of God alone! For they did not have anything by which they should have merited that grace. But the Jews trusted in their many works and were sent away empty. ANNOTATIONS ON ROMANS 9:30.[2]

THE OFFENSE OF RIGHT BELIEF. PHILIPP MELANCHTHON: Here Paul expressly sets down the cause of reprobation, namely, because they are

---

[1]*Bondage of the Will* (1525), LCC 17:110.

[2]Oecolampadius, *In epistolam ad Rhomanos*, 82r.

not willing to believe the gospel. I said above that the picture of the clay is not to be taken in such a way as if the cause of reprobation were not in the human will. For here Paul expressly sets down the cause, and adds the reason that prevents the ungodly from believing: because the gospel accuses human righteousness and worship and sets forth another righteousness. Here the "wise" judge that it is most absurd to take away the praise from righteousness—from outward obedience—and from worship. They see that when worship has been changed, states are changed and destroyed. Therefore they begin to hate and persecute this kind of doctrine as though it were blasphemous, as if it injures the glory of God, abolishes worship, loosens the rein on the license of the people, is seditious and destroys the state. This has always been the chief cause of persecution, and it fired up the Jews very greatly, because they had a law that was divinely given and worship that was divinely ordained.

So now our adversaries persecute us furiously and cruelly because we say that human beings cannot satisfy the law nor be justified in the sight of God on account of good works, but only through faith for the sake of Christ. They also rage all the more when acts of worship are reprehended, such as Masses, monkery and similar things. For when ordinances are changed, the state seems to be made to totter, to be cast down, and to be destroyed, and the glory of God seems to be harmed. From this hatreds are kindled and immense struggles arise. These "offenses" greatly move human reason, which thinks the glory of God is injured and the common society is destroyed. And it is difficult for the saints to strengthen themselves so that these "offenses" do not drive out their faith.

Therefore Paul says afterward: "I confess that the Jews have a zeal." And to the Corinthians he says that the reason why the Jews do not believe the gospel is because they look at the law covered with a veil, that is, because they think the righteousness of the law is righteousness in the sight of God. Because this is disapproved by the gospel they are incited to persecute. Thus Christ becomes a rock of offense because reason thinks it is a

blasphemous and seditious doctrine to disapprove of outward righteousness and worship. COMMENTARY ON ROMANS (1540).[3]

9:32-33 *The Salvific Stumbling Stone*

ERASMUS ERRS HERE. THEODORE BEZA: Listen carefully: Trying to attain their own righteousness, they pursued the law of righteousness. The old translation omitted *nomou*, "the law." Erasmus says, "It was added so that you may understand it to be speaking concerning works that are bereft of faith and truth." But he is arguing as if we would be justified before God due to the works that follow faith, and not rather that once we have been justified, we would on that account do good works. But even much less fitting is the interpretation of the Greeks, who aver that the particle *hōs* ["as"] was added to indicate that the works of the Jews were not truly works of the law. Erasmus also insults the Jews, because he thinks that they received salvation by their own works, apart from the grace of God. But that is not the case, for it appears from the speech of that Pharisee that the Jews thought about merits and grace no differently than the Sophists nowadays do, who set up a combination of free will along with grace and faith with works. ANNOTATIONS ON ROMANS 9:32.[4]

A BARRIER TO SIN AND DEATH. JOHN COLET: St. Paul implies that in their grossness and ignorance of mind, they had rejected the offered truth and in kicking against the stone of stumbling had hurt themselves, not suffering Christ the rock of offense (that is, the rock that was a bar to them when sliding into the abyss) to be an obstacle to their sins; but in thus spurning and, as it were, striking at the stone with their feet, that it might be removed out of the way, lest it should hinder their headlong fall to death, they stumbled so heavily on it and inflicted such a wound on themselves that it

---

[3]Melanchthon, *Commentary on Romans*, 193-94 (MO 15:686-87); citing Rom 10:12; 2 Cor 3:15.
[4]Beza, *Annotationes majores*, 2:114.

was necessary for that mischief long afterward to remain in them, as a mighty argument of their folly and guilt. Exposition of Romans.[5]

Rock of Offense. Tilemann Hesshus: The prophet Isaiah calls Christ "a stone of stumbling and a rock of offense" ... not because Christ could be the cause of anyone's downfall, rather because the kingdom of Christ clearly stands in opposition to the judgment of reason. And so the wise of this world are seriously offended by him. People search for riches and pleasures, but Christ, wherever Christ lays his head, has none of those things. "Anyone who wants to follow me," he says, "must take up his cross." Powerful rulers long for Christ's kingdom and teaching to be the kind of thing that will not create any strife or turmoil, and will not be offensive to the minds of those in power. But the kingdom and teaching of Christ cannot exist in this world without struggles, for the world opposes Christ with all its strength, and because Satan holds human nature captive, it is annoyed to be reproached for its impiety. As a result, the powerful reject Christ, along with his teaching and his whole kingdom, as he is an instigator of riots and a hindrance to salutary peace. Intellectuals and philosophers long for a gospel that agrees with the judgment of reason. But all the teaching of Christ concerning his person, kingdom, benefits, judgment and eternal life has been set far beyond all the ability of the human intellect. And all these things seem utterly absurd to our reason. Those who are holy and righteous in the eyes of the world do not want to be stripped of praise for their righteousness. They search for the kind of Christ who will admire their righteousness and holiness and deem them worthy of eternal rewards. However, because Christ proclaims the kind of teaching that condemns the righteousness and holiness of the whole world, and because he alone, in the office of Mediator, offers true righteousness and holiness before God, they curse him. Commentary on Romans 9:32-33.[6]

Our Rock. Johann Wild: Christ is the stone—the most precious stone of election, the foundation stone, the cornerstone, the stone of offense and the stone of pulverizing. Exegesis of Romans 9:33.[7]

The Word *Freely* Is Always Implied. Philipp Melanchthon: In these statements about faith, the little word *freely* [*gratis*] should always be understood. Let us not think, "If I shall be sufficiently worthy, then I will believe," for this is not putting confidence in Christ, but trusting in one's own worthiness. Therefore he says: "Whoever believes in him," that is, whoever trusts in him— that God is favorable toward us on account of Christ, not on account of our own worthiness—he will be saved. Commentary on Romans (1540).[8]

Never Put to Shame? Johannes Brenz: Has no one ever been put to shame who believed in Christ? Answer: indeed, many have been put to shame—even Christ when he was hanged on the cross. But Isaiah and Paul here do not mean that kind of shame, but are speaking about the vocation of Christ and what belongs to it. And this is the meaning: that no one will be put to shame who submits to Christ and his calling, for which he came down to earth. Now Christ came into the world, first, to atone for our sin, then, to hold and receive us in death and, finally, to receive us into eternal life. Therefore, whoever seeks the forgiveness of sins from Christ and believes that they are forgiven by God for Christ's sake, and believes that through him one will receive eternal life, will certainly not be put to shame. If someone, however, outside of the purposes of Christ looks for something else with a different hope, that one will be put to shame. If one were to believe that stones could be changed into bread or gold nuggets, that would of course put someone to shame. The reason is that Christ did not come into this world to change stones into gold or bread; that was not his

---

[5]Colet, *An Exposition of St. Paul's Epistle to the Romans*, 53*.
[6]Hesshus, *Explicatio Epistolae Pauli ad Romanos*, 329v-330r.

[7]Wild, *Exegesis in Epistolam ad Romanos*, 214v.
[8]Melanchthon, *Commentary on Romans*, 194* (MO 15:687).

purpose. But if we believe that our sins are atoned for by Christ, that death has been conquered, and that for Christ's sake we will receive eternal life, we believe rightly—and precisely this belongs to the office of Christ. Accordingly we will not be put to shame, but receive eternal life. St. Paul's Epistle to the Romans.[9]

10:1 *Paul Deeply Desires the Salvation of the Jews*

Honey on the Brim. The English Annotations: Intending to set forth the Jews as an example of marvelous obstinacy, the apostle begins with a sweet insinuation, as it were anointing the brim of the cup with honey, out of which they were to drink a bitter poison. Annotations on Romans 10:1.[10]

Honey Catches More Flies Than Vinegar. David Pareus: By this example of the apostle preachers are taught that the souls of their hearers must be diligently prepared so that they might be well disposed to the person of those teaching and persuaded by their benevolence, especially when a troublesome and disagreeable matter must be handled, so that when they have to refute errors or rebuke vices their hearers will understand that nothing was said against them out of ill-will, but everything was said out of a zeal for aiding them to salvation. Otherwise what is said scarcely enters their minds, even if it is very salutary. Concerning this matter the precepts of the rhetoricians ought to be consulted. Commentary on Romans 10:1.[11]

Imitate Paul's Example. Peter Martyr Vermigli: Rhetoricians use this method: so that they say nothing rough or unpleasant, first with some color they soften their audience. Now the scorpion—that deadly beast—clasps [its prey] with its forearms or its front claws, so that it can

strike better with its tail and thrust in its venomous sting. So why do we not more tightly embrace our neighbors with kindness and love as closely as possible, so that we might heal them? Commentary on Romans 10:1.[12]

We Long for the Salvation of the Clergy. Johannes Bugenhagen: That is, "I want nothing other than that the Jews would be saved, and I pray for this in my heart—that is, before God." And today we say many things against the clergy (as they call them) condemning their works of righteousness; nevertheless, at the same time we seek their salvation and grieve in our hearts for them like Paul toward the Jews. Commentary on Paul's Letter to the Romans.[13]

10:2-3 *Zeal Without Knowledge*

What Does Paul Mean? Theodore Beza: Therefore, you will say, there is a certain zeal for God, but nonetheless it does not come from knowledge. However, if this is the case, it follows that good (as they call them) intentions, of themselves and without further qualification, are pleasing to God. I reply: As the matter itself indicates, Paul is not excusing the Jews, seeing that he has already said that they had not obtained righteousness and he had begged God to spare them from destruction. Therefore I say that in this passage Paul is speaking in this way not absolutely, but *kata synkrisin* ["in comparison"] and in respect to the feeling of his whole people, not that of individual Jews. Moreover, he attributes a zeal for God to the Jews, that is, the sort of zeal that leads to the glory of the true God but not in the proper way, with the consequence that the fault does not lie in the goal itself as much as in the means—a praise that could not be offered to any other nation. But let us recognize that this praise helps only to the degree that they are deemed worthy in a certain

[9]Brenz, *Erklerung der Epistel S. Pauls an die Römer*, 623-24.
[10]Downame, ed., *Annotations*, BBB3v*.
[11]Pareus, *In Epistolam ad Romanos*, 991-92.
[12]Vermigli, *In Epistolam ad Romanos*, 442 (cf. *A Commentarie upon the Epistle to the Romanes*, 313r).
[13]Bugenhagen, *In Epistolam Pauli ad Romanos interpretatio*, 116v-117r.

respect, even though they nonetheless perish unless saved by grace, despite the fact that they seem to be righteous before those who either do not know the true God or who do not follow him if they do know him. For whence does this error arise except out of some inborn vice—which the Lord justly avenges, even if it were the only fault—or even out of some voluntary stubbornness? Annotations on Romans 10:2.[14]

Zeal and Knowledge Are Necessary.
Martin Luther: We must take note that "to have an enlightened zeal for God" is to be zealous for God in pious ignorance and mental darkness, that is, to regard nothing as so grand and good, even if it appear to be God himself and all his glory, so as not to be always fearful, always prepared to be led and turned and directed to a lesser kind of good. And thus without understanding, without feeling, without thinking, a person must be indifferent to all things, whatever may be required, whether by God or by human beings or by some other creature. Such people do not know how to choose but they expect to be chosen and called. Thus Psalm 17 says, "With the Chosen One you will be chosen." It does not say: "By him who chooses you will be chosen."

These people are gentle and teachable, as gold can be shaped and fashioned to every form. . . . "To have an enlightened zeal" is to know nothing about what one is zealous for. For to know that one does not know, this is the kind of knowledge according to which the Jews do not have zeal. For they know that they know. For whoever knows that he does not know is gentle, teachable, unresisting, ready to give a hand to everyone. Scholia on Romans 10:2.[15]

Word and Spirit.
Tilemann Hesshus: He shows the reason for his love toward his people and, at the same time, the reason for their rejection. "I bear them witness," he says, "that they burn with a zeal for God, and they try to uphold and observe the law. They fight for ceremonies and sacrifices but

without full knowledge, that is, not according to a true understanding of the divine word, not from the true Spirit and faith." Here young people need to learn what true zeal is. It is without a doubt an earnest and burning love for God and his name, arising from true faith in God and kindled by the Holy Spirit. Incited and stirred up by the Holy Spirit, disparaging all dangers to his life, this person strives to uphold and defend God's name and glory.

This zeal must be ruled by the light of the divine Word, by true faith and by impulses arising from the Holy Spirit. The impulses of the human heart, though they might be more vigorous, serve the glory of God much less. Scripture condemns the inappropriate zeal of Saul when he slaughtered the Gibeonites, for he was not ruled by the Word and the leading of the Holy Spirit.

It must be seen, therefore, that zeal is to be ruled by the Word of God, and by true faith, and it should not proceed from the impatience of our flesh but from the inspiration of the Holy Spirit. The Jews had a certain sort of zeal for keeping and upholding the law, but they did not understand the intention of the law. They were without repentance, without faith in Christ. Instead they set themselves against justification by faith, which the law urges above everything else. Commentary on Romans 10:2.[16]

Zeal Mixed with Error.
Philipp Melanchthon: He adds a complaint about the destruction of the nation, as above, and ascribes to it a zeal, that is, eagerness for piety, but connected with an error. The error is the chief one in the articles of faith, namely with respect to the nature of Christ's office and kingdom, whence forgiveness of sins comes, what is true righteousness and what sin is. A great threat is added against those who defend wicked opinions about the righteousness of the law, when he says: "They have not submitted themselves to the righteousness of God." He clearly condemns all who oppose the true doctrine about the righteousness of faith. Commentary on Romans (1540).[17]

---

[14]Beza, Annotationes majores, 2:114-15; citing Jn 2:17.
[15]LW 25:404-5* (LW 56:413-14); citing Ps 17:26 (Vg).

[16]Hesshus, Explicatio Epistolae Pauli ad Romanos, 331v-332r.
[17]Melanchthon, Commentary on Romans, 195* (MO 15:687-88).

Seek God Wisely. John Calvin: See how they went astray through inconsiderate zeal! They sought to set up a righteousness of their own; and this foolish confidence proceeded from their ignorance of God's righteousness. Notice the contrast between the righteousness of God and that of people. We first see that they are opposed to one another, as things wholly contrary, and cannot stand together. It hence follows that God's righteousness is subverted as soon as people set up their own. And again, as there is a correspondence between the things contrasted, the righteousness of God is no doubt his gift; in the same way, the human righteousness is what they derive from themselves, or believe that they bring before God. Then whoever seeks to be justified through himself does not submit to God's righteousness. For the first step toward obtaining the righteousness of God is to renounce our own righteousness. Why do we seek righteousness from somewhere else, unless necessity compels us? Commentary on Romans 10:3.[18]

10:4 The Law's Telos Is Christ

The Meaning of Telos. Desiderius Erasmus: *Telos* in this passage means "consummation" and "perfection," not "destruction." . . . For what has been completed and perfected with all the things usually required, this the Greeks call *teleion*. Christ is the culmination, therefore, of the law. And in the case of the Psalms that bear the title *In finem* ["to the end"], they suppose that something quite hidden, quite secret must be tracked down. What Paul here calls *telos* he elsewhere calls *plērōma* ["fulfillment"]. Annotations on Romans 10:4.[19]

The Law's Demands Met in Christ. Philipp Melanchthon: Christ gives what the law requires. Whoever believes in Christ has what the law demands—righteousness by imputation—and is set free from sin and death. But this liberation is only begun in this life, although the believer is truly righteous by imputation. Commentary on Romans (1540).[20]

In What Sense Is Christ the End of the Law? The English Annotations: Christ is said to be the end of the law, partly because all the ceremonies of the law prefigured him and had reference to him as their scope, end and accomplishment. Partly, because by the law ceremonial, moral and judicial the consciences of all who were under the law were convinced of sins, the expiation of which could nowhere be found except in the sacrifice of Christ's death. Or Christ may be said to be the end of the law because the end of the law is perfect righteousness. A person may be justified by it, whose end we cannot attain by ourselves through the frailty of our flesh, but we attain it by Christ who has fulfilled the law for us. Annotations on Romans 10:4.[21]

The Whole and the Parts of the Law Are About Christ. John Calvin: The apostle answers an objection that might have been made against him; for the Jews might have appeared to keep the right way by depending on the righteousness of the law. It was necessary for Paul to disprove this false belief, and that is what he does here. He shows that whoever seeks to be justified by their own works is a false interpreter of the law, because this is why the law had been given: to lead us by the hand to another righteousness. Indeed whatever the law teaches, whatever it commands,

---

[18]CTS 38:383* (CO 49:195-96).
[19]CWE 56:277* (LB 6:617); citing Rom 13:10. Erasmus translates this verse as "the perfection of the law is Christ." His comment about psalm titles refers to the LXX's rendering of *lamnaṣēaḥ* as *eis to telos*. Modern English translations use "choir director" and similar phrases; however, contemporary commentators continue to puzzle over the precise meaning of *lamnaṣēaḥ*, since the root *nṣḥ* has a wide semantic range (e.g., "to lead," "glory," "eternity," "blood"). The LXX rendering *eis to telos*, according to Hans-

Joachim Kraus, "is completely enigmatic." The Christian exegetical tradition has long interpreted this phrase christologically. For early modern treatments of this psalm superscription, see RCS OT 7:37-38; for a modern analysis, see Hans-Joachim Kraus, *Psalms 1–59: A Commentary*, trans. Hilton C. Oswald (Minneapolis: Augsburg, 1988), 29-30.
[20]Melanchthon, *Commentary on Romans*, 195* (MO 15:688).
[21]Downame, ed., *Annotations*, BBB3v*.

whatever it promises, it always has Christ as its main object. Therefore all its parts must be applied to him. But this cannot be done, unless being stripped of all righteousness and troubled by the knowledge of our sin we seek free righteousness from him alone.

From this it follows that the wicked abuse of the law was justly condemned in the Jews who absurdly fashioned into an obstacle what was supposed to be an aid. Yes, it appears that they had shamefully mutilated the law of God. They rejected its soul and seized the dead body of the letter. Even though the law promises reward to those who observe its righteousness, still after having proved all guilty it substitutes another righteousness in Christ—which is not acquired by works but is received by faith as a free gift. Here we have then a remarkable passage, which proves that the law in all its parts refers to Christ. Consequently no one can rightly understand it who does not continually aim at this target. COMMENTARY ON ROMANS 10:4.[22]

THE LAW MUST REFER TO CHRIST. TILEMANN HESSHUS: Most diligently must we attend to this remarkable statement of the apostle: "The end of the law is Christ." For not only does he teach what is the principal use of the divine law, but he also brilliantly expounds the whole Law, Moses and all the Prophets. He reminds us that the whole law of God refers to Christ—that is, the whole law should serve us in this way: to force us to run to Christ the Mediator. And when we seize Christ, we satisfy the law. And the law demands nothing more from us than this.

Therefore when we read in Moses, "You shall love the Lord your God with all your heart, and your neighbor as yourself," it should be understood in this sense: "As a human being, you are certainly required to love God with your whole heart, and your neighbor as yourself, but because you have not fulfilled this word—nor can you because of your corrupt nature—you deserve

damnation. Fear, therefore, the wrath of God, acknowledge your uncleanness and repent in earnest. Then flee to the Mediator promised in the gospel. Remember that he has fulfilled the law in your place, and satisfied the judgment of God for your sins. Believe in him, so that his obedience will be imputed to you. Thus in Christ you will have the end and fulfillment of the law."

Thus, when we hear in Moses, "Cursed is everyone who does not remain in all these things which are written in this book of the law," these words should be understood in this way: "Yes, you must acknowledge and confess, O human being, that you have not kept—nor are you able to keep—all that is written in the law. Therefore you lie under a divine curse, which will thrust you into hell. But run to the Mediator, Jesus Christ! He is the end of the law. He has become a curse for us, so that we might receive the blessing promised to Abraham." And in sum the whole law must refer to Christ. COMMENTARY ON ROMANS 10:4.[23]

HOW, WHY AND FOR WHOM IS CHRIST THE END OF THE LAW? DAVID PAREUS: Now we must consider, first, in what sense Christ is said to be the end of the law, second, to what purpose and, third, for whom and how? For the apostle covers these three points in this brief sentence, which he will confirm with the Scriptures in the following explanation.

First, [in what sense is Christ the end of the law?] Those who say that Christ is the end, that is, the abolition, of the law are telling the truth, but not simply so, since there is one law that is moral and another that is ceremonial and civil. Concerning the ceremonial law, the statement is true, but the same is not the case with the moral law. Therefore an end is the opposite of a beginning and has a meaning that is divided into four parts: (1) An end is the extremity of an object or its terminus, as a point is said to be the end of a line, death is the

---

[22]CTS 38:384-85* (CO 49:196).

[23]Hesshus, *Explicatio Epistolae Pauli ad Romanos*, 333v-334r; citing Deut 6:5; Lev 19:18; Deut 27:26.

end of a life, the blessed isles[24] are the end of land, and the last day is the end of the age.... (2) That on account of which there is motion or what moves an agent is called an end. This is called *hou heneka* ["for the sake of which"].... (3) The aim and goal for which we are cultivated is called an end. Thus the end of faith is said to be the salvation of souls. ... (4) Finally, an end is the perfection and completion of an item, so that *telos* ["end, accomplishment"] is the same as *teleiōsis* ["accomplishment, fulfillment"].... In all these ways Christ is said to be the end of the law; in the first and fourth way he is the end all by himself; in the second and third way he is the end accidentally.[25]

First, Christ is the end of the law, that is, the terminus of the law-mandated ceremonies. For by his sacrifice and offerings he put an end to the types found under the law.... But the apostle is not speaking concerning this end, properly speaking.

Second, Christ is the end of the moral law *hou heneka*, "for the sake of which" the law was given. To be sure, he is the end not in and of himself, but accidentally. Our justification was in and of itself the end of the law, because the law commands perfect obedience and promises life to those who present such obedience. For whoever has done these things will live in them. But the law knows that such righteousness is impossible. And yet nonetheless it demands, urges and threatens a curse unless we offer it: "Cursed is everyone," etc. Why, I ask? Is it to make fun of the weak? No, rather to compel us to flee to Christ by trusting in his mercy and forgiveness. Therefore Christ is the end of the moral law, *hou heneka*, "for the sake of which" it was given—not in and of himself, but accidentally, that is, because of our wickedness, just as medicine is said to be the end of illness accidentally, because illness does not indeed vie for medicine, but directs

the sick person accidentally to medicine, since illness compels the sick person to need it.

Third, Christ is the end of the law as the aim to which the law is directed, also accidentally. For in and of itself the law does not indeed refer sinners to Christ, which it does not know or about whom it is at least certainly silent, but it refers sinners to Satan and the curse. Nonetheless, it accidentally directs us to Christ, insofar as the justification that it promises neither exists nor can be obtained except in Christ. And in this sense the law is said to be a pedagogue leading to Christ.

Finally, in and of himself and in the most appropriate sense, Christ is the end of the law, that is, he is its completion and perfection, because the fulfillment of the law exists and is obtained only in Christ. As he himself says, "I did not come to abolish the law, but to fulfill it." Christ indeed fulfilled the ceremonial law in one way: by being an expiatory sacrifice offered once and for all on the cross. But he fulfilled the moral law in four ways: (1) By the conformity of his nature and life that he himself alone had and has; (2) by his satisfaction for the curse and our sins by his humility and death; (3) by the bestowal of the Spirit, who gives new birth to the elect, which leads to the new obedience of the law; and (4) by purging the teaching of the law of people's corruptions. In this way Christ is the fulfillment of the law....

Second, for what purpose is Christ the fulfillment of the law? For righteousness. There is no true righteousness other than through the fulfillment of the law. There is no fulfillment of the law except in Christ. For there is no human being in whose mouth there is not found deceit or who has exhibited good behavior down to the last point of the law, except for Christ. And he did not earn righteousness for himself, for he himself in himself was eternal righteousness. Therefore it is for others that he is the end of the law for righteousness. That is, he earned righteousness for others. But for whom?

Third, [for whom and how is Christ the fulfillment of the law?] For every individual believing in him. When he says, "for every individual," he wishes that none be excluded. Therefore,

---

[24]In antiquity these islands were believed to be in the extreme west.

[25]Pareus is distinguishing between what is "accidental" to a thing and what is "essential" to a thing—that is, what can be removed without altering the thing's nature and what cannot be removed without altering the thing's nature. So, Pareus means that the law in and of itself (*per se*) does not direct us to Christ, but makes us aware of our need for him (*per accidens*).

he creates a universal righteousness for believers of the Old Testament as well as of the New Testament, for Gentiles as well as Jews. COMMENTARY ON ROMANS 10:4.[26]

THROUGH THE PREACHING OF THE WORD GOD'S PEOPLE ARE UNITED TO HIM. DIRK PHILIPS: Thus the congregation of God has existed from the beginning in Christ, through whom all things are renewed, yes, joined in one body, everything that is in heaven and on earth, and from which God's congregation is built more gloriously and also is expanded. For then the figures have come to an end, but the true being has come forth; the grace and truth have arisen through Jesus Christ. . . . But how this happened and how this erection of the congregation of Jesus Christ has occurred, the Scripture shows us with great clarity, namely, through the right teaching of the divine Word and through the faith that comes by hearing the divine Word, added by the illumination of the Holy Spirit. For no one may enter into the kingdom of God, into the heavenly Jerusalem, that is into the congregation of Jesus Christ, except that he be improved in heart, repents truly and believes the gospel.

Yes, just as God began his congregation on earth in paradise with pure and holy people who were created according to his image and were made in his likeness, so also he still wants to have such people in his congregation who are created after Jesus Christ and are renewed by the Holy Spirit. For although the promised salvation was earned by the Savior Jesus Christ, and although that lost life was bought back through the blood of the unique sacrifice and has been offered to all people in the gospel, nevertheless not every person enjoys the same eternal salvation and eternal life. Only those who are born anew here in this life, through the Word of Jesus Christ, who lets them seek and find with the light of the divine Word, and who follow the voice of their Shepherd, who

are enlightened with the true knowledge of God and his will and accept the righteousness of Christ with a true faith. THE ENCHIRIDION: THE CONGREGATION OF GOD.[27]

UNDERSTAND ELECTION ONLY THROUGH CHRIST AND HIS WORD. TILEMANN HESSHUS: Let us flee to Christ our Redeemer; let us impress the very sweet promises of the gospel onto our hearts. "God so loved the world that he gave his only-begotten Son, so that everyone who believes in him should not perish but have eternal life." . . . Again, "As I live, I do not desire the death of a sinner but rather that he be converted and live." . . . From these promises let us seek consolation against the terrors of the conscience. Then, justified by faith and having acquired peace, let us be eager for the new life in accordance with God's commandments. Let us restrain the desires of the flesh and let us take our minds captive in obedience to Jesus Christ. Let us also make our souls steadfast for moments of tribulation. For all who wish to live piously in Christ will suffer persecution. And let us not be broken by dangers or adverse situations, but let us seek after the true sources of consolation from the gospel. Among those sources of consolation we will also find the teaching concerning the eternal predestination of the saints, which we may use safely and fruitfully in the fear of God and in accordance with his Word.

Let no one say or think, "If I have been elected from eternity, then it is all the same whether I study or despise the gospel, whether I believe in Christ or indulge my doubts, whether I live piously or wickedly—for it is nonetheless necessary for me to be saved. But if I have not been elected, then nothing can help me, even if I learn doctrine with great zeal, die with a firm faith in the merits of Christ and strive to obey the divine law—for nonetheless it is necessary for me to perish." Insolent thoughts of this kind of

---

[26]Pareus, *In Epistolam ad Romanos*, 1000-1003; citing Rom 6:21; Phil 3:19; 2 Cor 11:15; Jn 13:1-38; 1 Pet 1:1-25; Rom 6:22; 1 Tim 1:5; Rom 13:10; Mt 11:1-30; Jn 8:13; Mt 5:17.

[27]CRR 6:356, 357* (BRN 10:386-87); citing Col 1:19-20; Rom 10:4; Col 2:9; Rom 10:18; Mt 3:8; Gal 4:7; Gen 2:8; Heb 2:3-4; 5:12; Tit 2:13; Heb 8:2; 10:19; 1 Pet 1:23; Jas 1:18; Jn 3:3; 8:32; 12:46.

extreme wickedness directed against God, which fight against the Word of God and originate from their author, Satan, and are a chief plague on the soul, ought not to be allowed entrance in any way but must be removed far away and must be denounced at their first appearance.

For God did not reveal the doctrine concerning election so that it might be heedlessly made sport of and his gospel held in contempt, but rather so that we might all the more humbly marvel at his majesty, learn his word all the more diligently and embrace Christ, the book of life. Therefore, let people who give themselves over to carnal security whenever the election of the saints is mentioned know that they are unjust toward the divine majesty, because they wickedly turn upside down and defame the boundless kindness of God, inasmuch as they despise the counsel of God, which leads us to his Word, and follow the deceptions of Satan and bind for themselves snares of despair. Consequently let godly minds watch out for that wickedness and confine themselves within the boundaries of the divine Word, while always applying godly sighs toward God in faith. On the Predestination of the Saints: The Source and Order of This Doctrine.[28]

---

[28]Hesshus, *Explicatio Epistolae Pauli ad Romanos*, 278r-279r; citing Jn 3:16; Ezek 33:11.

10:5-21 THE MESSAGE OF SALVATION TO ALL

[5]For Moses writes about the righteousness that is based on the law, that the person who does the commandments shall live by them. [6]But the righteousness based on faith says, "Do not say in your heart, 'Who will ascend into heaven?'" (that is, to bring Christ down)" [7]or 'Who will descend into the abyss?'" (that is, to bring Christ up from the dead). [8]But what does it say? "The word is near you, in your mouth and in your heart" (that is, the word of faith that we proclaim); [9]because, if you confess with your mouth that Jesus is Lord and believe in your heart that God raised him from the dead, you will be saved. [10]For with the heart one believes and is justified, and with the mouth one confesses and is saved. [11]For the Scripture says, "Everyone who believes in him will not be put to shame." [12]For there is no distinction between Jew and Greek; for the same Lord is Lord of all, bestowing his riches on all who call on him. [13]For "everyone who calls on the name of the Lord will be saved."

[14]How then will they call on him in whom they have not believed? And how are they to believe in him of whom they have never heard?[a] And how are they to hear without someone preaching? [15]And how are they to preach unless they are sent? As it is written, "How beautiful are the feet of those who preach the good news!" [16]But they have not all obeyed the gospel. For Isaiah says, "Lord, who has believed what he has heard from us?" [17]So faith comes from hearing, and hearing through the word of Christ.

[18]But I ask, have they not heard? Indeed they have, for

"Their voice has gone out to all the earth,
    and their words to the ends of the world."

[19]But I ask, did Israel not understand? First Moses says,

"I will make you jealous of those who are not a nation;
    with a foolish nation I will make you angry."

[20]Then Isaiah is so bold as to say,

"I have been found by those who did not seek me;
    I have shown myself to those who did not ask for me."

[21]But of Israel he says, "All day long I have held out my hands to a disobedient and contrary people."

a Or him whom they have never heard

OVERVIEW: The reformers seize hold of Paul's distinction between the righteousness of the law and the righteousness of faith. The law commends works; faith commends the Word. But human beings are unable to perform the works required by the law; only through faith in Christ are human beings made righteous, for only he has fulfilled the demands of the law. Thus our inability to fulfill the righteousness of the law chases us to Christ, the sum and substance of Scripture. His incarnation, crucifixion, death, resurrection and ascension, while not always obvious to reason, are the focus of all Scripture.

Paul models how to interpret Scripture correctly, these interpreters observe, with his treatment of Deuteronomy 30. To ask who will ascend or descend for us is to deny what Christ has already accomplished. Christians are not a people marked by skepticism and unbelief, probing God's Word with reason; rather they are a people who accept Christ's mysterious and miraculous work as a gift from God! And we need not try to find him, for he has come to us. "The Word is near." Through union with Christ all that is his becomes ours.

Now our God has ordained ordinary, even mundane, means for revealing his character and message to us. The reformers highlight the catena of action that God wills, causes and completes through his grace: he commissions preachers to preach, so that hearers can hear and believe, and then they too confess, so that others may also hear. God's grace envelops each step. He harmonizes the external working of the preaching and reading of his Word with the internal working of his Spirit. The work of the Word cannot be opposed to the work of the Spirit. And so believers must be careful, measuring the preaching they hear against the plumb line of the church: holy Scripture. God reveals his will according to his Word, authored by his Spirit. Through the ministry of the Word, God, like a mother to her disobedient children, holds out his arms to us, his dear creatures. "As I live, declares the Lord God, I have no pleasure in the death of the wicked" (Ezek 33:11). Indeed, "he gave his only Son, that whoever believes in him should not perish but have eternal life" (Jn 3:16).

Christ Brings Life in God. Jacques Lefèvre d'Étaples: Thus Moses puts it in Leviticus: "I am the Lord your God. Keep my laws and judgments, for the person who does them shall live in them." But it is one thing to live in them, that is, to live for the law, and another thing to live for God. For before Christ came, the fathers lived in them, that is, they lived for the law. But when Christ came and drew them from the shadows in which they were living by the life of the law, they began to live for God. For the former life was swallowed up, as if it were not a life, by that most excellent life of God and of Christ, like a flickering light is swallowed up by a most excellent light. And one must think thus also about the righteousness of the law and the righteousness of God, which cannot be grasped without faith in Christ. Moses revealed to the Israelites enigmatically the faith and righteousness of Christ, who would descend from the heavens and return from hell. Annotations on Romans 10:5.[1]

The Goal of Scripture: Jesus. Tilemann Hesshus: In this argument we must most diligently attend to the difference between law and gospel—this is the light of all holy Scripture. Now there are three clear differences, as it was shown above in chapter 3. That teaching should be repeated in this passage.[2]

Second, it should be noted in this passage what the chief goal of all holy Scripture is: that our Lord Jesus Christ, crucified, died, raised from the dead, sits at the right hand of the Father; whoever believes in him will be saved. Perhaps it could seem strange to someone that Paul proves his description of the righteousness of faith out of Deuteronomy 30, since in that passage Moses uses legal terminology. "If," he says, "you obey the voice of God, according to all that I command you, so that you love the Lord your God, and so that you walk in his ways," etc. However, by correctly and carefully listening to this sermon of Moses, it will not be difficult to understand that it is all gospel, since he exhorts the Jews to repent, and he promises the mercy of God to those who repent. "If," he says, "you turn to the Lord your God with all your heart, the Lord will also turn back your captivity, and he will be moved deep within by his compassion concerning forgiveness of sin." But he curses sinners. The gospel, however, for those who repent, offers grace and life. And it is not possible at all for true love for God to exist in a human being—which Moses requires in this chapter—unless true faith in God shines forth in him, accepting the forgiveness of sins and understanding that he has been reconciled. From this passage, therefore, Paul most correctly

---

[1]Lefèvre d'Étaples, *Epistola ad Rhomanos*, 88r; citing Lev 18:5.

[2]In his comment on Romans 3:21, Hesshus distinguishes law and gospel according to the time of their revelation, the condition of their promises and their effects. The law was revealed to Adam and Eve and written into every human heart; the gospel remained a mystery until its revelation in our Lord Jesus Christ. The law promises God's love and favor as well as eternal life only to those who keep the whole law perfectly; the gospel promises the same things but unconditionally ("it destroys our works"). The law reveals God's judgment, our iniquity and eternal death; the gospel frees us from sin, wrath, death, Satan's tyranny and hell, placing us in the kingdom of light and life. See Hesshus, *Explicatio Epistolae Pauli ad Romanos*, 88v-90r.

appropriates Moses' description of the righteousness of the gospel or faith. For Moses taught exactly the same thing that Paul presses. Moses testifies, therefore, that the Jews will be blessed, if genuinely moved to repentance they turn back to the Lord and believe his word. Here Paul hands down the same teaching. This is righteousness before God: if anyone, having acknowledged his sin and having truly repented, believes in our Lord Jesus Christ, the promised Mediator, and he is convinced that because of Jesus' death and resurrection he has the forgiveness of sins, righteousness and eternal life.

Nor should it disturb the reader that in Moses the Mediator or the death and resurrection of Christ is not explicitly mentioned, for Moses refers to these things in general according to the Word of God. The scope of the entire Word of God is our Lord Jesus Christ. As Peter eloquently teaches: "To him all the prophets bear witness, that all who believe in him receive the forgiveness of sins in his name." Also, "Search the Scriptures, for they bear witness about me." Therefore, because the head and sum of the entire Word of God is that Jesus Christ is God and man [homo], that he died for our sins and rose again for our righteousness and that all who believe in him have eternal life, Moses wanted nothing other than that the Jews would believe in Christ. And because he commands so often that the Jews love the Lord, he is talking about the Messiah who is Jehovah and is always present with his people. COMMENTARY ON ROMANS 10:5-13.[3]

10:5-7 The Distinction Between Moses' Law and Christ's

ALL OF SCRIPTURE IS ABOUT JESUS. MARTIN LUTHER: Moses does not use these words in this sense, but the apostle out of the abundance of his own feeling and spirit brings out the real kernel, teaching us with a strong argument that the entire Scripture deals only with Christ everywhere, if it is looked at inwardly, even though on the face of it it

may sound differently by the use of shadows and figures. Hence he also says that Christ is the end of the law, as if to say that all Scripture finds its meaning in Christ. That this is absolutely true he proves by the fact that this word which is most alien to Christ yet signifies Christ. SCHOLIA ON ROMANS 10:6.[4]

RIGHTEOUSNESS IS TWOFOLD. DESIDERIUS ERASMUS: For one ought to imagine that righteousness is twofold: the author of the first was Moses and the author of the second is Christ. The former consists in ceremonies; the latter in faith and obedience. The first is a kind of groundwork and beginning of the second, just as the unchiseled slab is the beginning for a future statue or just as a coagulation of blood later grows into a living creature.[5] However, it would be most foolish to cling to the rudimentary when you have at hand what is finished and completed. But Christ is the completion of the whole Mosaic law (which by itself is rudimentary and weak), because he confers true righteousness not through circumcision but through faith. And this path to righteousness is open not only to Jews but to all who believe. PARAPHRASE ON ROMANS 10:5.[6]

RIGHTEOUSNESS OF LAW AND FAITH. MARTIN LUTHER: The apostle is comparing the two kinds of righteousness with each other, so that he attributes works to the righteousness of the law but the Word to the righteousness of faith. For work was required for the law, but faith is required for the Word. (The law was required for the deed, so that we might know what ought to be done, but for faith the Word was required, not so that we might know but so that we might believe.) Thus the first kind of righteousness depends on the work that has been done, but the second on the Word, which we believe. It is this Word he describes, as if to say that the Word which must be believed is nothing else than this: Christ died and is risen again.

---

[3]Hesshus, *Explicatio Epistolae Pauli ad Romanos*, 336v-338r; citing Deut 30:16, 10; Acts 10:43; Jn 5:39.

[4]LW 25:405 (WA 56:414); citing Deut 30:12.
[5]The physician Galen (AD 130–200) argued that flesh and bone were formed from coagulated blood.
[6]CWE 42:60.

This is the reason why these negative and questioning forms of expression include some very strong affirmatives. In this way, "Who will ascend into heaven?" means you should most firmly say that Christ has ascended into heaven, and you will be saved. Do not doubt at all that he has ascended; for this is the Word that will save you. This is the way the righteousness of faith teaches. This is the way of the compendium, the short way to salvation. For the righteousness of the law is long, winding and circuitous, as is signified by the wandering of the children of Israel in the wilderness.

The intent of the apostle is that the total righteousness of human beings, leading to salvation, depends on the Word through faith and not on good works through knowledge. Hence also in all the Prophets God contends against nothing else than that they are unwilling to hear his voice, and through the Prophets he has not commended good works but rather his words and his sermons. Scholia on Romans 10:6.[7]

Distinction Between Faith and Love, Law and Gospel. Philipp Melanchthon: The point at issue in the comparison lies in the two phrases "to do" and "to believe." The righteousness of the law is to do the law, that is, to render perfect obedience according to the law. So, he says, righteousness is described by Moses when he says "doing them," as though he said: "The righteousness of the law is this very obedience by which the things the law prescribes are truly and wholly done: to glorify God, to burn with love of God with all one's heart, to love neighbor, to be without concupiscence, to be without any vicious affect, to be without sin." That is the righteousness the law requires, which human nature is so far from fulfilling that it does not even know what the love of God is. On the other hand, the righteousness of faith is not to be righteous on account of fulfilling the law or on account of our virtues, but it is to believe that we are righteous, that is, accepted by God, on account of Christ.

From this the distinction between faith and love can be seen, and why one must say, "We are just by faith" and how this is to be understood. One must not imagine that "we are just by faith" means that on account of our renewal or our new virtues we are righteous, but instead that we are righteous because of Christ, who can be apprehended in no other way than through faith. To say that we are righteous by love is the same as to say that we are righteous through our virtues, or through our fulfillment of the law. However, it is certain that we do not satisfy the law. Therefore it is necessary that this saying be retained in purity: "We are counted righteous by faith," in order that it may be understood that we are righteous—accepted—not on account of our virtues, but on account of Christ, the Mediator, through mercy, freely. That is what Paul intends in this definition, which he amplified wonderfully by quoting certain words from Deuteronomy. Commentary on Romans (1540).[8]

Words of the Work-Righteous. Martin Luther: Whoever does not believe that Christ has died and rose again to justify us from our sins, says: "Who has ascended to heaven and descended to the deep?" But that's what those who want to be justified by works and not by faith do—although they indeed say otherwise with their mouth but not in their heart. The emphasis is on the phrase "in your heart." Marginal Gloss on Romans 10:6-8 (1546).[9]

No Room for Speculation Apart from the Word. Tilemann Hesshus: Paul and Moses say, "Do not say in your heart, 'Who will ascend into heaven?' (that is, to bring Christ down)." That is, you must not demand private conversations with God; you must not require that Christ be sent again from heaven just to you, to reveal the Father's will to you. Instead you must be satisfied with the Word in which God has abundantly revealed himself and shown his will with infallible testimonies. Nor

---

[7]LW 25:405-7* (WA 56:414-15).

[8]Melanchthon, *Commentary on Romans*, 196* (MO 15:688-89).
[9]WADB 4:61.

should anyone say, "'Who will descend into the abyss?' (that is, to bring Christ up from the dead)." That is, you must not demand that hell expose itself to you and reveal what kind of judgment is in hell. You must not require that Christ die again, and, rising from the dead, submit himself to you for inspection, so that you can see with your own eyes those things that are the secrets of the heavens and the depths. These kinds of cravings are seen in all people, and they bring forth pure unbelief and impiety. And for this reason they should be suppressed. COMMENTARY ON ROMANS 10:6.[10]

Two Doubts to Destroy. DAVID PAREUS: Two types of doubt especially battle our faith and so should be driven off by believers. The first doubt is concerning the ascent into heaven, that is, concerning the grace of God and heavenly salvation, how we might be able to obtain it. "Do not say in your heart." That is, take care not to be full of doubt or to ask out of anxiety. For this is what it means to say in one's heart, "Who will ascend into heaven?" Here he retains the words of Moses, but he explains them in verse 9 through the verb *sōthēsē*, "you will be saved." For this is the meaning: How can I obtain salvation from heaven and in heaven? The second doubt is anxiety and fear concerning the descent into the abyss, that is, concerning the curse and eternal death. For "the abyss" in the New Testament means "hell." . . . Therefore to descend into the abyss means to be abandoned in the curse and death, to be thrust down to those below and damned. In verse 11 the apostle explains this through the verb *kataischynthēsetai*, "he will be put to shame." Christ speaks of it by using the word "be condemned": "Whoever believes will not be condemned," etc. And here the righteousness of faith says, "Take care that you do not say, 'Who will descend into the abyss?'" How may I escape the abyss? Will I perhaps be cast down and damned? He says, "Let these things depart and be far away from those justified by faith. This is the first thing about the nature of faith, because faith directly excludes the papistic *epochēn*

["suspension of judgment"] concerning the grace of God and the fear that is born from that notion, since faith has *plērophorian* ["full confidence"] concerning grace and heavenly salvation. COMMENTARY ON ROMANS 10:6-7.[11]

Do Not Doubt That God Can Be Known. PHILIPP MELANCHTHON: Although the heart knows there is a God, it doubts whether God is concerned about us, denies that the will of God toward us can be known and denies that he hears or saves us. It is apparent enough that these doubts cling to human minds. Therefore the law of God rebukes them and requires faith. "Do not say in your heart: 'Who will ascend into heaven?'" that is, do not be an Epicurean, or think that God is nothing, or doubt whether there is a God, or whether he is concerned about human affairs. Do not think that God is so hidden that his will is not expressed in some word. Do not think that his will is unknown just because he is not discerned with bodily eyes. Do not think that he does not hear, that he does not take pity or does not require this worship, which he taught in his Word, etc.

How then can God be found and apprehended? "The Word," he says, "is near." Hence I lead you to the Word. Hear it, if you believe that God is apprehended and his will is seen when you hear the Word. Believe that this is the will of God, that he wants to be worshiped in this way, that he wants to hear, as he has promised. It is quite clear that this is the meaning in Moses. It is also not doubtful that Moses is here speaking about faith, and that he requires faith. Faith believes not only that there is a God, but also that God wants to be known through his Word, and to be invoked that he wants to hear, that he wants to take pity according to his promise, and that he demands these acts of worship.

These things that are spoken in general, although they contain the doctrine about faith, are nevertheless somewhat obscure, and are voices of the law. Therefore Paul puts forward another Word and mentions the Mediator in order that he may set

---

[10]Hesshus, *Explicatio Epistolae Pauli ad Romanos*, 338v.

[11]Pareus, *In Epistolam ad Romanos*, 1012.

forth gratuitous mercy promised because of Christ. When we acknowledge this, faith becomes certain that we are heard, saved, etc., freely on account of Christ, not on account of the law.

He applies this in this way: "Do not say in your heart, 'Who will ascend into heaven?' for that is to lead Christ down from heaven." This means first: Do not be an Epicurean; then, do not doubt that it is the will of God that Christ should be the Mediator, that God wants to save us because of Christ. If you do not believe that Christ is the Mediator, that he saves us, you pull him down from heaven, you deny that he rules and you accuse God of lying, as if his promises were void. COMMENTARY ON ROMANS (1540).[12]

THE SACRED ANCHOR OF CHRIST'S DEATH, RESURRECTION AND ASCENSION. DAVID PAREUS: Do not say, "Who? Who?" because this would be to deny the foundations of faith. For the apostle sets forth two remedies as foundations for faith against each temptation: Christ's ascension into heaven and his resurrection from the dead, both of which would be called into doubt by such wavering. He shows that the first doubt is incompatible with the ascension of Christ into heaven, because doubting about the way to obtain heavenly salvation is nothing other than ignoring or doubting or denying that Christ has ascended into heaven. How is that so? This line of reasoning seems very subtle, but to the contrary it is a plain and powerful argument for a consequence by going from a denial of the effect to the denial of the cause.[13] The Christian faith holds to this firm foundation, namely, that Christ ascended into heaven and that he ascended for the sake of our salvation, interceding there for us and preparing a place for us. Therefore whoever firmly believes that Christ by his ascension has opened heaven to the faithful is not able to say, "Who will ascend now into heaven?" because they cannot doubt concern-

ing the ascension and intercession of Christ and the Father's grace toward them. But if someone doubts, anxiously asking, "Who will ascend into heaven?" what are they revealing other than that they do not believe that Christ has ascended?

"That is, to bring back Christ from the dead." He shows that anxiety and fear of damnation are diametrically opposed to belief in the resurrection of Christ from the dead, because to have this fear is nothing other than to bring back Christ from the dead, that is, to be ignorant of or to doubt or to deny that Christ has risen from the dead. How is that so? The reason is the same as earlier: an argument from the negation of the effect to the negation of the cause. For by rising from the dead, Christ triumphed over Satan, hell, the abyss and death, not for himself but for his believers (Col 2; Heb 2). Therefore, whoever clings to this by faith does not bristle at the thought of the abyss and death nor anxiously asks, "Who will descend into the abyss?" But whoever wavers denies that Christ died and came back to life. This is the true explanation of this passage.

And this is a second aspect concerning the nature of faith because it does not attach the reason for its *plērophoria* ["certainty"] in itself, that is, in its understanding, but it finds its infallible reason in trusting in the death, resurrection and ascension of Christ. Let us flee to this sacred anchor, as often as the flesh or reason strikes doubt or fear in us.

There is also this other distinction by which the righteousness of faith is separated from the righteousness of the law. For since the latter does not know the ascension and resurrection of Christ and its fruit, it is able to strike nothing but doubt concerning heaven and fear of hell in people. COMMENTARY ON ROMANS 10:6-7.[14]

DO NOT DENY THE RESURRECTION OF THE DEAD! PHILIPP MELANCHTHON: Do not think after the manner of the Epicureans that there is not another life after death; and do not think that human beings cannot be set free from sin and death. If you doubt, you deny that Christ rose from

---

[12]Melanchthon, *Commentary on Romans*, 196-97* (MO 15:689-90).
[13]That is, an argument by *modus tollens*: If "if p, then q" holds, then "not q, not p" holds.

[14]Pareus, *In Epistolam ad Romanos*, 1013-14.

the dead. You imagine that Christ still lies dead, is yet to be resurrected, that he is not the victor over death and sin. The sum and substance of the statement is: Do not doubt that for his sake God truly takes pity on us, remits our sins, hears and saves us. Thus Paul adds to the statement of Moses the gospel about the Mediator, and includes the exclusive word in order that faith may be certain.

Let us oppose this very weighty speech of Paul to our infirmity and doubting, and in it contemplate how great is the wickedness to doubt whether God wants to remit sins, whether he wants to hear, help, save and finally grant us the things he promised through Christ. Every time we pray, let us think about these words: "Do not say, 'Who shall descend into heaven?'" For that would be to bring down Christ. Instead, declare that Christ is truly sitting at the right hand of the Father, that he is our intercessor, that we are heard. When we do this, we learn the power and meaning of this saying. For those who do not pray deny that Christ is sitting at the right hand of the Father, and that he is our intercessor, etc. COMMENTARY ON ROMANS (1540).[15]

DENIAL OF CHRIST'S DESCENT IS DENIAL OF HIS VICTORY. JOHANNES BUGENHAGEN: "Or who will descend into the abyss? (That is, to bring Christ up from the dead)." That is, to say in your heart that there is no one who descended into hell, into death. What else is that than to deny that Christ has died for us? So, therefore, Christ is taken away, to whom will we flee in the end? On whom will we rely to ascend into heaven and flee death? We will suggest to ourselves nothing other than our works and external righteousness, for [without Christ] it cannot happen otherwise than that you will deny Christ as the first victor over death and that through death he was restored in the glory of the Father. You see, therefore, by what counsel Paul cites this: so that we would understand that Moses not only talks about the law or righteousness of the flesh but also concerning other things, that is, what is through faith, so that the mouth of the "righteous"

might be blocked—those who only preach their works in their heart and Christ by their mouth. There cannot be a greater blasphemy against God. And so these words of Paul should be diligently heeded, lest their true meaning escape you. The emphasis and all the force of this passage is in speech, in the heart. It's as if he were saying: I do not want you to doubt God's mercy and kindness toward you; he is the one who makes you righteous and saves you. Do not consider these matters according to your free will or your works. It is necessary that you stand most resolutely on this Rock, lest it happen that you be engulfed by sinking sands and assaulted by tempests. COMMENTARY ON PAUL'S LETTER TO THE ROMANS.[16]

THROUGH FAITH IN CHRIST BY HIS SPIRIT WE ASCEND IN HIS RESURRECTION. JOHN CALVIN: Let us note that Jesus Christ lives in us not only in his power but also in order that all that is his may be common to us, and especially his resurrection, in which consists the accomplishment of our salvation. St. Paul says that if we do not believe that he is risen, it is as if (to the best of our ability) we dragged him out of heaven. On the contrary, when we believe seriously and without hypocrisy that he is risen and at the same time we know that he is seated at the right hand of God his Father, we know that all power is given to him so we may be maintained and governed by him, that he is our defense against sin and death, and that all the good things that have been given to him, he received in order that he might give us his Spirit, and he distributes to each one of us according to the portion he knows is suitable. See then how in believing without hypocrisy that our Lord Jesus Christ is risen—because we know that he has power to guard us against every thing that could hurt is—when we are in his protection we are so confident that we are able to despise the devil and all our enemies, even death will be happy and a passage to celestial life for us. Then we know that all he possesses has been given to him in complete

---

[15]Melanchthon, *Commentary on Romans*, 197-98* (MO 15:690-91).

[16]Bugenhagen, *In Epistolam Pauli ad Romanos interpretatio*, 119r-v.

fullness so that he may give it to us as alms according to the poverty he knows to be in us. It is true that we will not have such perfection of them as he, but it is enough that he knows what is good and proper for us, and that we may be nourished by him daily until we are united with him in his glory in another fashion than we are now. SERMON ON MATTHEW 28:1-10 (APRIL 14, 1560).[17]

10:8-11 The Word Is Near; Believe!

BY GOD'S WORD AND SPIRIT. PHILIPP MEL-ANCHTHON: One must not imagine that God sends the Holy Spirit without his Word. Paul leads us to the ministry and to the spoken word. God is found nowhere outside of his Word or without his Word; he wants to be known through it. By means of this instrument he wants to work. Therefore let us seek God through the Word in every temptation, and let us resist with the Word. And let us declare that this certainty is the will of God that is set forth in his Word. He is saying this about a very great thing, namely, about salvation: "The Word is near, in your mouth," and "The word of faith that we preach." COMMENTARY ON ROMANS (1540).[18]

FAITH AND CONFESSION ARE CONNECTED. PETER MARTYR VERMIGLI: This is not said in order that we should believe that the gospel is not joined with the law, for how could repentance be preached? Rather it is written for this reason: because the principal part of the apostles' ministry revolves around faith's righteousness. And when it is said, "This is the word of faith that we preach," through a certain emphasis it is explained that the doctrine of the gospel in no way opposes the law of Moses—indeed, on the contrary, they fit together very well! Not only is it said that the word is near in your heart, but also in your mouth. Paul most fittingly accommodates this to his proposition, for he says this has to do with confession, which

immediately follows true and efficacious faith. COMMENTARY ON ROMANS 10:8.[19]

UNITY OF THE PROPHETIC AND APOSTOLIC WORD. TILEMANN HESSHUS: "But the word is near you, in your mouth and in your heart." That is, "But you should be satisfied with such illustrious revelations, so many repetitions of the promise, such a clear word, such plain testimonies, in which God has revealed his will most clearly, namely, that he wants to receive us into his grace and to save us through his only-begotten Son, the Mediator." And so Paul describes the nature and quality of true faith to us, which must not depend on the external senses or experience; instead everything concerning this has been revealed in the word. In it we must rest, remain and anchor our feet. "This," he says, "is the word of faith that we preach." Now here he explains what this word is, which faith should constantly contemplate: without a doubt our Lord Jesus Christ. That the eternal Father gave his only-begotten Son to the world, subjected him to death for the sins of the whole human race and raised him from the dead, so that all who believe in him should not perish but have eternal life. Immediately this word was revealed in the Garden of Eden: "The seed of the woman will crush the head of the serpent." This word was given to Abraham: "In your seed all the nations will be blessed." Moses urged this same word of salvation: "The Lord God is a merciful, gracious, generous God, of great compassion and truthfulness, who pardons iniquity and sins." Also, "The Lord will raise up a prophet for you like me; he will speak in my name, you will listen to him." The same word Paul also preached, for he taught that the Son of God Jesus Christ, according to the prophecies of the prophets, was betrayed, died and on third day raised again; all who believe in him have the forgiveness of sins and eternal life.

And so Paul first proves that his teaching about Jesus Christ depends on the testimonies of the

---

[17]Elsie Anne McKee, ed. and trans., *John Calvin: Writings on Pastoral Piety*, Classics of Western Spirituality (New York: Paulist Press, 2001), 122-23 (SCal 7:97); citing Rom 10:6-7.
[18]Melanchthon, *Commentary on Romans*, 198* (MO 15:691).

[19]Vermigli, *In Epistolam ad Romanos*, 452 (cf. *A Commentarie upon the Epistle to the Romanes*, 320r-v).

prophets. Then he exposits Moses himself, that, pressed and formed by the word of God, he pressed the teaching about our Lord Jesus Christ. In addition, he teaches that Jesus Christ is the eternal and omnipotent God, since he is indeed the one whom Moses so often calls "Jehovah." He bears witness to this concerning the agreement of all the prophets and apostles, that they all confessed absolutely the same doctrine, without a doubt concerning our Lord Jesus Christ, according to the saying of Peter. All the prophets bear testimony to this: all who believe in his name receive the forgiveness of sins. COMMENTARY ON ROMANS 10:8.[20]

ONE LORD JESUS CHRIST AND ONE GOD OUR FATHER. THEODORE BEZA: "Lord Jesus," *Kyrion Iēsoun.* That is, you regard him alone as your Lord and Savior. For besides not only the irreverent but even devils themselves are able to believe and profess him to be the Lord and Jesus.

"God," *ho theos,* that is, the Father, who is said to have raised Christ from the dead, not so that the divinity of the Son might be discounted, but so that the counsel of the Father on how to redeem us might be seen in the resurrection of the Son. ANNOTATIONS ON ROMANS 10:9.[21]

THE EXTERNAL WORKS OF THE TRINITY ARE INDIVISIBLE. DAVID PAREUS: Here and in many other passages Paul ascribes raising up to God, for divine power raises up, which is common to the Trinity. And Paul does not restrict the name of God to the person of the Father. For the Father raised the Son through the Son. The Son raised himself through the Spirit of holiness. *For whatever the Father does, the Son also does.* COMMENTARY ON ROMANS 10:9.[22]

PAUL CENTERS THE GOSPEL IN JESUS' RESURRECTION. JUAN DE VALDÉS: This Paul states to be

the word of faith that dwells in the Christian's mouth and heart: what is preached in the gospel. . . . I understand this profession to consist in confessing that Christ is the Word of God, by whom God created all things, agreeing with the passage, "All things were made by him." He is the Son of God, according to the Father's declaration: "This is my beloved Son, in whom I am well pleased." He is the head of the Christian church. He is King of God's people, agreeing with those words, "All power is given to me in heaven and on earth." And a person is saved by believing, not by merely confessing with the mouth but with the heart, thus consenting with the mind "that God has raised him from the dead."

Now I understand St. Paul not to state that one should believe that Christ died, because this was generally known and obvious; instead one should believe that Christ rose from the dead, for this is what was called into question, and this is what confirms Christ's authority. It is thus by his resurrection that he has demonstrated the wretchedness, the humility and the poverty in which he lived. And he has illustrated, too, the ignominy with which he died, since he is the first that has risen from the dead not to die again.

Here it is worthy of deep consideration that St. Paul establishes all Christian faith in one's belief in Christ's resurrection. And rightly so, for once this is believed one easily submits oneself to everything else, the resurrection being, as it were, a voucher for everything that Christ said and did throughout his life. COMMENTARY ON ROMANS 10:9.[23]

THE CENTRALITY OF THE RESURRECTION. PETER MARTYR VERMIGLI: The resurrection of the Lord is a sort of bond and tether by which the preceding and following articles concerning the faith of our salvation are beautifully tied together. For if Christ has risen again, it follows that he died for our sins, and that his sacrifice was pleasing to God. And these things could not have happened unless he had

[20]Hesshus, *Explicatio Epistolae Pauli ad Romanos,* 338v-339v; citing Jn 3:16; Gen 3:15; 22:18; Ex 34:6-7; Deut 18:15; 1 Cor 15:3-4; 1 Pet 1:10-12.
[21]Beza, *Annotationes majores,* 2:115.
[22]Pareus, *In Epistolam ad Romanos,* 1017-18.

[23]Valdés, *Commentary upon Romans,* 182-83* (*Commentario de Romanos,* 214-15); quoting Jn 1:3; Mt 17:5; 28:18.

first assumed human flesh to redeem the human race and had truly become human. And if he has risen again, he has eternal life, he ascended to the Father. And it is not for no reason that he is with the Father in heaven! Indeed there, as he had promised, he is present for us as our help, and he prepares a place for us. COMMENTARY ON ROMANS 10:9.[24]

FAITH AS INSTRUMENT. TILEMANN HESSHUS: Paul's statement clearly destroys the idea that through faith a preparation happens, so that then we are made righteous through something else—for example, infused love (as the papists claim) or essential righteousness (as Osiander claims). For he does not say that preparation happens through faith, but that through faith righteousness itself is seized, and that by faith we are justified. Nor does Paul want either our own virtue or the indwelling of God to be our right-eousness.[25] On the contrary, this fantasy he attacks most fiercely with all his strength in the entire letter! Instead he teaches that our righteousness is what has been offered to us in the Word: the forgiveness of sins given through Christ, which we embrace and apply to ourselves by faith, only as an instrument. COMMENTARY ON ROMANS 10:10.[26]

LOVE STIRS UP FAITH. DESIDERIUS ERASMUS: When these people so immensely exaggerate faith and love in God, our ears are not offended, for we judge that the fact that the life of Christians is everywhere so corrupted by sins proceeds from no other cause than that our faith is so cold and torpid, since it makes our belief in God a matter of words, and floats on our lips, according to Paul: "For one believes with the heart and so is justified." I will not specifically argue with those who refer all things to faith as the fountain and head of all, even though to me faith seems to be born from charity and charity in turn from faith: certainly charity nourishes faith just as oil feeds the light in a lantern; the more

strongly we love him, the more freely do we trust him. Nor are there lacking some who think of faith as the beginning of salvation rather than the sum. ON THE FREEDOM OF THE WILL.[27]

FAITH AND CONFESSION ARE DISTINGUISH-ABLE BUT INSEPARABLE. JUAN DE VALDÉS: Faith in your heart is principally necessary, and just as necessary is confession with your mouth. But these words of St. Paul should not be understood so restrictedly that it suffices to confess the Lord Jesus with your mouth without having him in your heart; nor does it suffice to believe with your heart in Christ's resurrection without confessing him with your mouth. Nor should it be understood that confession with your mouth without heartfelt faith is sufficient for salvation. Rather, it is to be understood that God requires both these things: your heart and your mouth. Your heart so that you may believe and your mouth so that you may confess what you believe. And by this faith and by this confession God gives you two things: justification (because you believe with the heart) and salvation (because by confessing with the mouth what you believe, you thereby fortify your own faith and increase it). COMMENTARY ON ROMANS 10:10.[28]

FAITH SHINES LIKE THE SUN. TILEMANN HESSHUS: For when the sun has risen it is impossible that it not pour forth its light and scatter its rays, in the same way, when faith has been kindled in one's heart through the Holy Spirit, it is impossible that the radiance of good works and new life not radiate and shine from it. For through faith, not only is the forgiveness of sins received, but also the Holy Spirit. And the Holy Spirit does not leave a person in death, but revives and renews them, and stirs up their mind, their will and their heart to the love of God, to prayer, to thanksgiving, to eager confession of the name of

[24]Vermigli, *In Epistolam ad Romanos*, 452 (cf. *A Commentarie upon the Epistle to the Romanes*, 320v).
[25]See *Formula of Concord*, Article 3 (BoC 494-98, 562-74, esp. 572).
[26]Hesshus, *Explicatio Epistolae Pauli ad Romanos*, 340r-v.

[27]LCC 17:89.
[28]Valdés, *Commentary upon Romans*, 184-85* (*Commentario de Romanos*, 216-17).

Christ and to all good works. COMMENTARY ON ROMANS 10:10.[29]

THE NECESSITY OF FAITH AND CONFESSION.
DAVID PAREUS: He explains and confirms each part and shows how confession coheres with faith, while he puts what had been the latter in front of what had been the former, putting the cause before effect and thus correcting the previous order, as it were.[30] First, one believes, then confession follows. Both are necessary. Faith is necessary for righteousness, and confession is necessary for salvation. Just now he was attributing salvation to each in common, but now he divides the effect, not according to their parts but according to their stages. For righteousness is the beginning of salvation. He most properly attributes it to faith, because by faith we are justified, that is, we obtain the forgiveness of sins by Christ's merit, which is the first step of salvation. For no access to God is appointed except to the one to whom iniquities are forgiven, if indeed God is a consuming fire. He ascribes salvation to confession, not because salvation is not also owing to faith, but because we, having been justified by faith, obtain salvation, that is, new birth and heavenly glory by our confession, that is, by calling on God and by the obedience of faith. For by "confession" one properly understands the calling on the name of Jesus, as will become obvious in verse 13: "Whoever calls on the name of the Lord *sōthēsetai* ['will be saved']". But by "salvation" is understood all the steps of salvation except for the first one, that is, righteousness, which is acquired by faith. However, he emphatically says, "With the heart one believes, and with the mouth one makes confession," distinguishing each as regards their proper location or subject, and thus explaining further the words of Moses concerning the mouth and heart. One does not believe merely by the tongue or brain, but by the heart. However, the heart in the Hebrew way of speaking means "the part that wills and desires." Nor is the confession made only inwardly in the heart, but also outwardly with the mouth in the ears of the church and of the world. Faith lies hidden inside, but confession speaks on the outside. The *kardiognōstēs* ["knower of hearts"] knows our faith, but people judge our confession. "It is believed" is said impersonally or passively, with the subject understood to be "the resurrection of Christ" or "that Christ was raised from the dead." What is "it is believed for righteousness"? The same as above, in 4:5. Faith is imputed as righteousness, or righteousness (which is the forgiveness of sins) is received by faith. "One confesses unto salvation," namely, the salvation obtained in Christ. COMMENTARY ON ROMANS 10:10.[31]

SCRIPTURE: THE SOLE INFALLIBLE NORM.
DAVID PAREUS: He continues to confirm by the opinions of Scripture what he had said concerning faith and the salutary effect of confession. Scripture, he says, promises salvation to those who believe and call on God. But the Scripture is not able to be broken (Jn 10:35). Therefore, it is truly believed for righteousness, etc. . . . Again, let us observe here that the Scripture above in 9:17 is not a mute or inert letter, as the Jesuits blasphemously aver, but it is the living Word of God. The apostle says, "For the Scripture says"; therefore the Scripture speaks, with God certainly speaking through it. Therefore why should it not adjudge controversies between us and say to the parties, "You are in error" and "you are holding to the truth"? For by using the singular "you" in verse 9—"if you believe," etc.—it addresses each and every one. But that it is the norm of dogmas— and indeed the only norm—is confirmed from this passage. For up to this point the apostle has confirmed from Scripture alone all the dogmas of the faith, going nearly point by point. But by this process alone all the dogmas of the faith are being thoroughly proved in an infallible manner; that alone is the infallible norm of the dogmas of the faith. Such is the force of Scripture alone. Traditions are not like that, because they are uncertain, fallible, changeable, not to mention wicked for the most part.

---

[29]Hesshus, *Explicatio Epistolae Pauli ad Romanos*, 341r.
[30]Paul speaks first of "confessing with one's mouth" and then of "believing in one's heart"; however, technically the latter is the cause of the former.

[31]Pareus, *In Epistolam ad Romanos*, 1019-20.

Therefore Scripture alone, not traditions, ought to be the norm. COMMENTARY ON ROMANS 10:11.[32]

HASTE AND SHAME AMOUNT TO THE SAME SENSE. TILEMANN HESSHUS: What the apostle translates "will not be put to shame," in Hebrew is "he will not hasten." Clearly the sense is the same, for the prophets and the apostle want to say this: Whoever believes in Christ will not be overcome by death and the devil; instead he will conquer and obtain eternal life and salvation. When the voice hastens, it indicates fear, hurry and flight of a violated and fettered conscience, which, beholding its own sins and feeling the wrath of God, hastens to flee from the world, and nevertheless is trapped and entangled. Faith however removes this hurry and flight, and it begets confidence and boldness to call on God. COMMENTARY ON ROMANS 10:11.[33]

10:12-13 *The One True Lord Is Lord of All*

THE LORD IS NOT BOUND TO GEOPOLITICAL BOUNDARIES. DESIDERIUS ERASMUS: You see that the substance of this matter does not depend on ceremonies but on faith. Even Isaiah testifies to this when he says about Christ: "Whoever believes in him will not be put to shame." When he says, "whoever," does he not destroy every difference between Jew and Greek? When he says, "believes," but does not say, "has been circumcised," or something similar, does he not then render ceremonies of the law obsolete? Faith alone is required, and faith can be common on an equal basis to all. For God is not only the Lord of the Jews but equally of all. His kindness must not be limited by such narrow boundaries that it should be extended to the Hebrews alone and then exhausted. On the contrary, his abounding and overflowing goodness is immense, not toward one or another nation, but to all peoples of whatever nation, provided that by sincere trust in the divine power

they implore his help.... The word of the prophet excludes no human race. Whoever calls on the Lord with a believing mind will attain salvation, whether Jew or Greek or barbarian. And on the other hand, whoever does not call on the Lord will perish. PARAPHRASE ON ROMANS 10:11-13.[34]

CHRIST'S RICHES ARE FOR BOTH JEW AND GENTILE. JUAN DE VALDÉS: There is no difference between Jew and Greek, since salvation is promised not to those who work but to those who believe. Paul says that this equality exists because Christ is Lord of both Jews and Greeks, through his obedience he reconciled both with God, from the enmity that they had toward God through Adam's disobedience, and through their own particular disobediences. So that by "Lord" Christ is to be understood....

Again, I understand them to invoke Christ, who, knowing the righteousness of God and their own unrighteousnesses, submit themselves to the righteousness of God. They seek to be justified through Christ, and in Christ, so they commit themselves to the justice of God executed in Christ, and they invoke Christ as their Mediator.

The riches of Christ, Paul says, are that he will save all who invoke his name, justifying them, raising them up again, giving them immortality and eternal life. These are the riches of Christ that I understand God to communicate to those who are members of Christ, as he communicates light through the sun to those who have eyes clear enough to see it. COMMENTARY ON ROMANS 10:12-13.[35]

INVOKE THE LORD'S NAME! DAVID PAREUS: He had proved the salutary effect concerning faith. Now he goes on to prove from Scripture, concerning the calling on God, which earlier he had called confession. At the same time by the prophecy of Joel 2:32 he confirms what he had said just now about all who call on God: "Whoever calls on the name of the Lord will be freed, for on Mount Zion and in Jerusalem

---

[32]Pareus, *In Epistolam ad Romanos*, 1021-22.
[33]Hesshus, *Explicatio Epistolae Pauli ad Romanos*, 343r-v; citing Is 28:16 (cf. Is 49:23; Joel 2:26-27).
[34]CWE 42:61*; citing Is 28:16.
[35]Valdés, *Commentary upon Romans*, 186-87* (*Commentario de Romanos*, 218-19).

there will be escape or freedom." The Hebrew *ymlt*, "will escape, will be freed," the LXX *sōthēsetai* ["will be saved"] is an instance of the consequence appearing before the antecedent. For whoever escapes danger is saved. This is a promise of eternal, not temporal, freedom. For the whole prophecy is about the kingdom and benefits of the Messiah, as Peter interprets it in Acts 2. Therefore freedom from sin, death and Satan is promised—but to whom? To the Jews only? To all who call on him. Call on whom? The name of Jehovah, that is, for those who implore the mercy of Jehovah for Christ's sake. This prophecy not only confirms the present argument of the apostle, but also others: that a religious invocation ought not to be directed to anyone except to Jehovah so that it may be salutary; and that in the church alone is the invocation of God and salvation. For the church is Mount Zion and Jerusalem, in which alone is given escape amid the ruins of the whole earth. COMMENTARY ON ROMANS 10:13.[36]

WHY THOSE WHO CALL ON HIM? PHILIPP MELANCHTHON: First we must observe that he stresses the universal particle, and remind ourselves that the promises are universal. Second, we must consider what the purpose of this new statement is, and whether the statement "Everyone who will call" agrees with the gospel.

I answer: this is a new prophecy, distinguishing the gospel from the law, because the law also teaches us to call on God, with the condition of perfect obedience. But this prophecy promises salvation to those who call on God, to those whom the law formerly could not help, and who are still such that they cannot render the obedience that the law demands. To those he now promises salvation if they call on the name of God, that is, if they call on him as the Lord who reveals himself in his Word he gave to the fathers, which he handed down in the coming of his Son.

Here it is necessary that calling on God be understood together with that little word *freely*. For it demands that we believe that we are heard and

saved *freely*, because of the promised Lord. This promise must be opposed to the law, as if he said: "Because the law could not help you, because you are under sin and death, salvation by another way is promised. God will give a teacher, he will pour out his Spirit, and by calling on the Lord, you will be saved from these very evils, from sin and death, from which the law did not set you free."

That is the simple and true meaning of the promise. Therefore it squares with the gospel, and adds a measure of light to the definition of the righteousness of faith that he handed down above: The righteousness of the law is to do the law. But the righteousness of faith is to call on the Lord and to declare that on account of the Son of God we are set free from sin and death and from wrath, from which the law could not set us free.

The promise will become sweet when the little word *freely* is understood in it. Calling on God is to be practiced in this way, lest our own unworthiness scare us off, so we may know that it is a command of God that we should call on him. Likewise, that it is commanded that we believe that we are heard because of Christ, not because of our own worthiness. Therefore let us obey God and render him acts of worship. When we call on him, let us remember that we are bringing unworthiness and sins, and let us pray that we may be set free and heard because of Christ. When we do this we are at the same time repenting. Now it is easy to reconcile the dissimilar statements: God does not hear sinners, namely, those who call on him without repentance and without faith. COMMENTARY ON ROMANS (1540).[37]

10:14-15 *The Beautiful Feet of the Gospel Envoy*

ARGUMENT BUILT ON JOEL. TILEMANN HESSHUS: The foundation of this *gradatio*[38] is the testimony of Joel: "Everyone who calls on the name

---

[36]Pareus, *In Epistolam ad Romanos*, 1024.

[37]Melanchthon, *Commentary on Romans*, 200-201* (MO 15:693-94).
[38]*Gradatio* ("climax") is a rhetorical strategy that builds an argument from the least important to the most important in a chain or ladder. For example, A . . . B; B . . . C; C . . . D.

of the Lord will be saved." By this word the prophet attributes invocation of God even to the Gentiles, and he promises salvation to them too. From this Paul concludes, however, that true invocation cannot happen without the light of faith in the Mediator. For "in Spirit and truth the Father must be called on," and "no one comes to the Father except through the Son." And faith cannot exist without the external ministry of the Word, for this is the instrument through which God kindles faith in the hearts of believers. And the preaching of the Word cannot exist unless God sends heralds, for those who run of their own will without God's command do not advance God's Word but instead their own fabrications. By this series—since they are closely interconnected—it is obvious that God has revealed his merciful will exhibited in the Mediator also to the Gentiles, and that God wants not only the Jews but all nations to repent, believe the gospel and be saved through Christ. COMMENTARY ON ROMANS 10:13-15.[39]

CHAIN OF PREACHING. DAVID PAREUS: All these questions imply a negative answer. As if he were saying, "They are not able to call on God." The whole section is a *gradatio*, from a denial of causes to a denial of effects.

Those who do not call on God are not saved, according to Joel's oracle.

Those who do not believe do not call on God.

Those who do not hear the Word of God do not believe.

Those to whom the Word is not preached do not hear.

There is no preaching to those to whom preachers of the Word are not sent.

Therefore those to whom preachers of the Word are not sent will not be saved.

This is entirely stated in the negative, but it is not on that account ineffective, for in the negative statements the corresponding affirmative statements ought to be understood.

Therefore those who want to be justified ought to call on God.

Those who want to call on him ought to believe.

Those who want to believe ought to hear the Word.

One must preach to those who ought to hear the Word.

Preachers must be sent to those to whom there must be preaching.

Therefore the first instrument of salvation is the sending of preachers; next, the preaching of the Word; third, the hearing of the Word; fourth, faith; finally, calling on God. By these steps one ascends to righteousness and salvation. Those who spurn these means are robbed of salvation. Nonetheless, in all these means we are uniquely called back to heeding the grace of God. For he gives those things to those to whom he wishes to give it by his extraordinary providence. And the beginning is found in the sending of preachers. But this sending is from God. For it belongs to him to rouse up and send messengers to people. Therefore, if God does not send preachers, who will preach? Who will hear the Word? Who will believe? Who will call on him? Who will be saved? Nobody, to be sure. Therefore the entire series of our salvation flows from God and depends on him. Also the honor, need and efficacy of the ministry is commended. For through the ministry, to whom belongs the task of the preaching of God's Word, God works in the elect hearing, faith, calling on him and salvation. COMMENTARY ON ROMANS 10:14.[40]

GOD CALLS HIS PREACHERS. JOHN CALVIN: Paul indicates that this is proof and pledge of divine love when God condescends to any nation with the preaching of his gospel. And no one is his preacher, but those whom he has stirred up by his special providence. For that reason there is no doubt that God visits that nation in which the gospel is announced. But because Paul by no means treats the lawful call of anyone, it would be pointless to discuss this topic more specifically here. It is

[39]Hesshus, *Explicatio Epistolae Pauli ad Romanos*, 344v; citing Joel 2:32; Jn 4:24; 14:6.

[40]Pareus, *In Epistolam ad Romanos*, 1025-26.

sufficient to remember this alone: the gospel does not fall by chance like rain from the clouds; rather it is delivered by human hands to wherever it is sent by God. COMMENTARY ON ROMANS 10:15.[41]

THE MINISTRY OF THE WORD IS GOD'S ORDINARY MEANS. PHILIPP MELANCHTHON: Paul adds the manner in which the benefits of Christ come to us, namely, through the ministry of the Word of God. This foremost passage about the necessity and the dignity of the ministry must be most diligently noted in order that we may know in what way God works in us, and may not seek other illuminations outside of the Word, nor grant entrance to imaginations and opinions about God without a sure word of God. This precept about the Word of God is wide open, for it is difficult for a person to stand fast by the Word of God and to say for certain that what he sets forth in the Word is the will of God, and so he easily slips into other imaginations. Thus Eve, thinking lightly of the Word, adds the imagination: "Perhaps God does not think so harshly." So it happens in many articles. . . .

We must know that God does not want his will about sin and about grace to be known and apprehended in any other way except in the Word, and that the Holy Spirit works through the Word. Let us hold this rule fast, and for this great reason show all honor to and defend the public ministry of the Word. And let us always keep these statements before our eyes: "Faith comes from hearing, hearing the Word of God." Likewise: "How shall they hear without a preacher?" Likewise: "How beautiful are the feet of those who preach the gospel of peace." COMMENTARY ON ROMANS (1540).[42]

TWO VIEWS OF THE MINISTRY OF THE WORD. TILEMANN HESSHUS: Here we must consider the difference between human judgment and the judgment of the Spirit concerning the ministry of the gospel. The world not only holds the ministry in contempt, but also furiously hates, blasphemes, persecutes and tries with all its power to destroy it as a hindrance to peace and the instigator of all discord and tumult. But the Holy Spirit proclaims that nothing is more beautiful or lovely than these heralds, for they announce peace and blessing. That is, they are ambassadors who announce the forgiveness of sins given because of Christ. They preach reconciliation with God, and they teach how peace of conscience and eternal blessing can be obtained. The prophet even nods to the effect of the promise of the gospel to show the difference between the Mosaic law—which only breeds terror in the conscience—and the promise of the gospel—which brings peace. COMMENTARY ON ROMANS 10:13-15.[43]

THE FEET OF THE WORD ARE THE VOICES OF PREACHERS. MARTIN LUTHER: What is meant by the term "feet"? According to the first interpretation, the term refers to the attitude and the devotion of those who preach, which must be free of all love of money and glory. But according to the Hebrew, which is more accurate, although the term *feet* can be taken in a literal sense, namely, that the coming of preachers of good things is something desirable for those who are tortured by sins and an evil conscience, yet more correctly the term can signify their very words themselves or the sounds and the syllables, the pronunciation of the words of those who preach, for their voices are like feet or vehicles or wheels by which the word is carried or rolled or it walks to the ears of the hearers. Hence he says, "Their voice goes out through all the earth." If it went forth it must have feet. And again, "His word runs swiftly." Whatever runs has feet. The word runs, therefore the word has feet, which are its pronunciations and its sounds. This must be the case, for otherwise Isaiah 32 would be absurd: "Happy are you who sow beside all waters, who let the feet of the ox and the ass range free." And Psalm 91 reads: "You will tread on the lion and the adder, the young lion and the serpent you will

---

[41]CO 49:205 (cf. CTS 38:398-99).
[42]Melanchthon, *Commentary on Romans*, 201-2* (MO 15:694-95); citing Rom 10:17, 14, 15.

[43]Hesshus, *Explicatio Epistolae Pauli ad Romanos*, 345v.

trample underfoot." This is not done except through the Word. For while the hearer sits quietly and receives the Word, the "feet" of the preacher run over them, and they crush them to see whether they can make them better. Thus Micah 4 reads: "Arise and thresh, O daughter of Zion, for I will make your horn iron and your hoofs bronze; and you shall beat in pieces many peoples." The term *threshing* here is understood in the sense of the ox treading out the grain with his feet. Thus the feet of the church as it preaches are voices and words by which it cuts and shakes up the people and "beats them to pieces." And the church does this with nothing else than with words and voices. But they are "beautiful" and desirable to those whose consciences are pressed down by sins. SCHOLIA ON ROMANS 10:15.[44]

10:16-17 *Faith Comes by Hearing*

THE POWER OF GOD AND ORDINARY MEANS. DAVID PAREUS: "It is by hearing," that is, by the external hearing of the Word faith is generated in the hearts of the elect as the Spirit of God works inwardly. Preachers speak the doctrine of the Word to the ears; the ears bring the matter to the mind, but it is blind when it comes to understanding divine matters. The Spirit of God is present through the doctrine drawn from the ears and he illumines the mind so that it can perceive so that it can give assent, as the Spirit also opens the heart and inclines the obstreperous will to acquiesce to and delight in the things it is perceiving. Thus the gospel is called the power of God, that is, an instrument of the power of God, by which it kindles faith in the minds and hearts of the elect unto salvation. COMMENTARY ON ROMANS 10:17.[45]

HEARING IS THE SOURCE OF FAITH. PETER RIEDEMANN: According to the words of Paul, faith comes from diligently listening to the preaching of God's Word, which comes from the mouth of God and is spoken by those whom God sends. Here, however, we do not speak of the literal but of the living Word that pierces soul and spirit, the Word put by God in the mouth of his messengers. The same Word prepares for salvation, that is, it teaches us to know God. From this knowledge, faith springs up, grows and increases, and with faith comes knowledge, so that the one who has faith lives and walks in God, and God in that person. These intertwine and grow together, leading people to God and planting them in God. CONFESSION OF FAITH.[46]

HEARING NECESSARY BUT NOT SUFFICIENT. TILEMANN HESSHUS: This is an *occupatio*, by which he counters a silent objection.[47] Although Paul had linked the sending of preachers, the preaching of the Word, hearing of the Word and faith in the Word as sequential causes and effects, the Jews could object: "If, therefore, faith comes from hearing and preaching, then you should not reprimand our unbelief, since prophets have always been sent to this people, and the Word of God has perpetually resounded among our people." But Paul replies: "Faith indeed comes from hearing, but it does not follow from this that all who hear embrace the Word with true faith; for there is not a physical connection of causes. Many despise the Word. Many resist the Holy Spirit. Many furiously persecute the Word. Isaiah also deeply lamented this concerning the people of Israel, 'Who has believed by hearing us?' With amazement he wonders at the scarcity of believers in the people of Israel. And so it is not enough to hear and know the promise, instead it must be seized with true faith, as the Gentiles do." . . .

Here then we should learn that by no means does faith come from the power of free will or

---

[44]LW 25:417* (WA 56:425-26); citing Ps 19:4; 147:15; Is 32:20; Ps 91:13; Mic 4:13. Luther is referring to a "foot" of poetry, a unit of meter. Thus, the poetry of preachers has a beautiful cadence.
[45]Pareus, *In Epistolam ad Romanos*, 1033.

[46]CRR 9:85; citing Heb 4:12; Jer 1:4-10; 2 Tim 3:14-17; Jn 17:6-8, 1 Jn 4:16-21; Eph 3:17-19.
[47]*Occupatio* or apophasis is a rhetorical device where someone brings up an argument by denying it.

philosophy and other histories of the world; instead it is kindled by the Word of God, for the Holy Spirit alone is the efficient cause of faith. "By grace you have been saved" through faith and without a doubt that you believe is the gift of God. The instrumental causes are the Word of God and human hearing; the mind and will are not the efficient cause, but a submissive subject, in whom God works according to his wonderful mercy and goodness. Therefore the synergists[48] err, who assert three concurrent causes of faith: the Holy Spirit, the Word of God, and the mind and will. And thus they ascribe to the power of free will what belongs only to the Holy Spirit alone. COMMENTARY ON ROMANS 10:16-17.[49]

GOD, NOT HUMAN BEINGS, AUTHORIZES THE WORD AND THE RESPONSE. JUAN DE VALDÉS: The feet of those who preach the gospel do not cease to be beautiful, because not everyone believes what is preached to them. Paul means to say that the unbelief of some does not diminish the dignity of those who are sent by God to preach, since God's purpose is for those to whom the good news is sent should believe. This he proves from the authority of Isaiah, who also says that not everyone believed who heard what he— on God's behalf—told them; but his authority was not lessened because of that account. . . . Using Isaiah's expression, St. Paul infers that a person cannot believe, unless he be told what it is he must believe; mere telling is inadequate unless the individual telling him be inspired, moved and sent by God to tell him it. The entire interaction depends only on the will of God, who inspires the speaker to speak and the hearer to listen. . . .

Even for it to be a human being's word it must be spoken by a human being; so also for it to be the Word of God, it must be spoken by the Spirit of God, through the mouth of whoever announces it. Thus in the holy Scriptures the apostles and ministers of Christ are called the mouth of God. God speaks by them and in them. By this one should understand well what God says through Isaiah: "The Word that shall go forth from his mouth shall not return to him void, but it shall accomplish what he pleases." And from this we should understand how necessary it always is that, following the advice Christ gave to his disciples and that he gives to all of us, we should ask God to send people among us who will speak the words of God. May they speak under the inspiration of God, not as the human spirit teaches, speaking instead according to God's experience, not human knowledge. COMMENTARY ON ROMANS 10:16-17.[50]

INTERNAL FAITH AND EXTERNAL WORD ARE PARTNERS NOT OPPONENTS. MARTIN LUTHER: Out of his great mercy God has given us the pure gospel, the noble and precious treasure of our salvation. This gift evokes faith and a good conscience in the inner self, as is promised in Isaiah 55, that his word will not go forth in vain, and Romans 10, that "faith comes through preaching." The devil hates this gospel and will not tolerate it. Since he has not succeeded hitherto in opposing it with the power of the sword, he now, as indeed always, seeks victory by deceit and false prophets. I ask you, Christian reader, to observe carefully. If God wills I will help you to discern the devil in these prophets so that you can yourself deal with him. It is for your good, not mine, that I write. Follow me thus.

Now when God sends forth his holy gospel he deals with us in a twofold manner, first outwardly, then inwardly. Outwardly he deals with us through the spoken word of the gospel and through material signs, that is, baptism and the sacrament of the altar. Inwardly he deals with us through the Holy Spirit, faith and other gifts. But whatever their measure or order, the outward factors should and must precede. The inward experience follows and is effected by the outward. God has determined to give the inward to

---

[48]On the synergistic controversy, see above p. 31n30.
[49]Hesshus, *Explicatio Epistolae Pauli ad Romanos*, 346r, 347r; citing Is 53:1; Eph 2:5.

[50]Valdés, *Commentary upon Romans*, 189-90* (*Commentario de Romanos*, 222-23); quoting Is 55:11.

no one except through the outward. For he wants to give no one the Spirit or faith apart from the outward word and sign instituted by him, as he says in Luke 16, "Let them hear Moses and the Prophets." Accordingly Paul can call baptism a "washing of regeneration" in which God "richly pours out the Holy Spirit." And the spoken gospel "is the power of God for salvation to everyone who has faith."

Observe carefully, my brother, this order, for everything depends on it. However cleverly this factious spirit imagines that he highly regards the Word and Spirit of God and passionately declaims about love and zeal for the truth and righteousness of God, he nevertheless has as his purpose to reverse this order. His insolence leads him to set up a contrary order and . . . seeks to subordinate God's outward order to an inner spiritual one. Casting this order to the wind with ridicule and scorn, he wants to get to the Spirit first. "Will a handful of water, he says, make me clean from sin? The Spirit, the Spirit, the Spirit must do this inwardly. Can bread and wine profit me? Will breathing over the bread bring Christ in the sacrament? No, no, one must eat the flesh of Christ spiritually. The Wittenbergers are ignorant of this. They make faith depend on the letter." Whoever does not know the devil might be misled by these many splendid words to think that five holy spirits were in the possession of Karlstadt and his followers. AGAINST THE HEAVENLY PROPHETS (1525).[51]

BETTER TO GO TO THE SERMON THAN MASS. JOHANN ECK: Know that it is far better to guide a child to the sermon than to the Mass—although you should do both. Now there is one child who hears Mass again and again until he turns fourteen years old, but he hears no sermon, and then there is another child who hears fourteen years of sermons, but no Mass; which will be a better Christian? Without a doubt the one who listens to preaching! For he knows much more about faith.

Faith comes from hearing, Saint Paul tells us and the Lord through Isaiah: "My Word that goes out from my mouth will not return empty." THE SIXTEENTH SERMON: ON VIOLATING THE FOURTH COMMANDMENT.[52]

THE CHURCH IS ESTABLISHED BY THE WORD. HEINRICH BULLINGER: Therefore since faith comes by hearing, and hearing by the Word of God, and that distinctly, the church cannot possibly spring up or be built up by the decrees and doctrines of humans. Hence we affirm that only the Word of God is apt for the building up of the church of God. Human doctrines set up human churches, but Christ's Word builds up the Christian church. For the human doctrines proceed from flesh and blood. But Peter confessing with a true faith, and therefore grounded on Christ, who is the foundation of the church, heard these words from Christ himself: "Flesh and blood have not revealed these things unto you, but my Father who is in heaven." . . . Therefore let us hold that the church is not built by human decrees, but founded, planted, assembled and built only by the Word of Christ. OF THE HOLY CATHOLIC CHURCH.[53]

SCRIPTURE'S AUTHORITY DERIVES FROM GOD NOT PEOPLE. RUDOLF GWALTHER: From all this it is sufficiently proved that the holy Scriptures have their source and origin from God, so from this it must follow that they have their authority and dignity from themselves and not from human beings—as some falsely imagine. Such people might say that if the Christian church had not accepted the gospel, then it would not be dignified and authoritative enough of itself, that we should believe it. They support their opinion with holy Augustine, who allegedly said: "I would not have believed the gospel if the church did not believe

---

[51]LW 40:146-47* (WA 18:135-37); citing Is 55:1; Rom 10:17; Lk 16:29; Tit 3:5; Rom 1:16.
[52]Eck, *Christenliche Predigen*, 5:32r-v; alluding to Rom 10:17; quoting Is 55:11. By fourth commandment, Eck means "Honor your father and mother."
[53]LCC 24:307-8; Mt 16:17; Gal 1:16; 1 Cor 2:5; Jn 8:47; 18:37; 10:5; Mt 15:9.

it."[54] And accordingly they urge this hard, so that they make the church a judge over the Scriptures, and then they want to conclude from this that they have power and might to establish new ordinances and statutes beyond and next to Scripture, since they are not subject to the Scriptures, but the Scriptures are subject to them.

But this is not only a coarse error and falsehood, but also a profound blasphemy through which human beings place themselves not merely next to God but even over him. For . . . Scripture is inspired by God and comprehends God's will and word. Now should a person have power as a judge to invalidate the Scriptures, they would then receive their authority from human beings. Then it must clearly follow that human authority is greater than God's authority, and that the church's ordinances should be more valid than those God has ordained. Now is this not to place what is created above the Creator, and to subject God along with his Word and statutes to sinful human beings? Is it still true then that the Scriptures say, "All people are liars, but God alone is true"? And how can those who by nature are liars make the truth powerful with their authority? Is the saying of Peter still true that says, "Believers—that is, the Christian church—have been born from the imperishable seed of the Word of God"? If, however, the church and the assembly of believers have arisen from the Word of God, which is encompassed in the Scriptures, then in no way can it be that the Scriptures receive their authority from those who through it have been born children of God and true believers. CONCERNING THE HOLY SCRIPTURES AND ITS SOURCE.[55]

WHAT ABOUT THE MUTE, DEAF AND INFANTS? DAVID PAREUS: Another contested matter arises from verses 13-17: Since people are not saved except by calling on God and believing in him, but faith

comes from hearing, are therefore the mute, deaf and infants devoid of salvation, since they cannot call on God, hear or believe?

Reply: Here the apostle is discoursing concerning the instruments of faith and salvation in adults, and indeed the ordinary instruments it is necessary for those who vie for salvation to use. But charity will not soon despair of the salvation of those in the church who are deprived of those means by a defect of age or of their senses through no fault of their own. For God does not even restrict his grace to those means to such a degree that he would not be able to confer it apart from them to whomever he wishes. And as far as infants of the church are concerned, the grace of the covenant stands in place of hearing, faith and calling on God. Nothing prevents faith from being conferred on the deaf and mute elect either by immediate grace or by objects and other means by which the church is properly attentive. For the Spirit blows where he wills, and the groans and sighs of the heart take the place of calling on God in the case of the mute. For if the nestlings of the raven call on God, why cannot mute people? Also, the Scripture attributes to infants the act of calling on God: "Out of the mouth of infants and nursing babes you have perfected your praise." But how will they call on him in whom they do not believe? Therefore there ought to be no doubt that they have faith in their own way. COMMENTARY ON ROMANS 10.[56]

10:18 Have They Heard?

THEY CANNOT CLAIM IGNORANCE. THE ENGLISH ANNOTATIONS: As for the Jews who have not believed, what can be said of them? Is it because they have heard nothing of the gospel? Surely not, for the gospel, like the sun, has cast its beams over the whole world. May we not therefore say that the fault lies in they themselves, who rejected that light of saving knowledge, which the Gentiles have embraced? The apostle answers that this is not to

---

[54]"I should not believe the gospel except as moved by the authority of the Catholic Church" (Augustine, *Against the Epistle of Manichaeus, Called Fundamental* 5.6 [NPNF 4:131]).

[55]Gwalther, *Von der heiligen Gschrifft*, c2v-c3v; citing Rom 3:4; 1 Pet 1:23; Rom 10:14; Gal 1:8.

[56]Pareus, *In Epistolam ad Romanos*, 1059; citing Ps 8:2.

be denied, seeing Moses protested the very same of old. ANNOTATIONS ON ROMANS 10:18.[57]

THE HISTORICAL SENSE DOES NOT PRECLUDE THE PROPHETIC SENSE. DAVID PAREUS:

It seems that the wording of the psalm does not correspond to the apostle's purpose, since the psalm does not speak about the preaching of the apostles, but about the preaching of the heavens, by which they proclaim the glory of God.

Reply: . . . In order to preserve the evidence of this passage, Augustine and rather many of the fathers say that the psalm allegorically understands the word "heavens" to mean "the apostles," and the words "their voice" to mean "the preaching of the gospel," and the word "sun" to mean "Christ." But there is no need to flee to an allegorical explanation, because the apostle is perhaps not citing the words of the psalm, but rather only alluding to them, as he often does. For this reason he does not say, "As it is written," as he is accustomed to do when citing a passage as proof. Not a few interpreters follow this opinion. Origen in chapter 6 of his Romans commentary . . . says: "One must take note of the habit of the apostle: when he takes some entire string of words from the Scripture, he does not always take it as it was set up in its original passage." Or he is making an argument from similarity: If the voice of the heavens once went out into all the world, why shouldn't the voice of the gospel do so today? Or he is arguing from the lesser to the greater: by the degree that the voice of the gospel is greater, seeing that by it the apostles tell the glory of God much more clearly. In my judgment Paul by his apostolic spirit recognizes prophecy in that statement of the Psalms. *Historically*, to be sure, David is describing there the glory of God shining back in the handicraft by which the world was made. But nothing prevents it from being a prophecy about the preaching of the apostles that would go out into all the world during the reign of the Messiah, as the preterite "has gone out" is used instead of the future "will go out," in the customary interchange of tenses that the Hebrews use. COMMENTARY ON ROMANS 10.[58]

THE CHURCH OF SCRIPTURE. TILEMANN HESSHUS:

Therefore as a result of this proclamation of the gospel, the Gentiles have accepted the faith. And by having his Word sent to the nations, God has testified that he has chosen a church for himself not only from the Jews but also from the Gentiles. For the Father did not give the Son some meager portion of the human race, but the whole world! . . . "The Father loves the Son," John says, "and has given all things into his hand." Therefore no one should believe that he has been excluded from the kingdom of Christ, for whoever imagines that the kingdom of sin extends wider or is more powerful than the kingdom of Christ wrongs Christ.

In the Psalms there is a *qawām*—that is, their rule, measuring line, canon.[59] In this way the Holy Spirit directs the doctrine of the prophets and apostles, for this should be the only rule and measuring line according to which the structure of the whole church should be established and directed. This rule is most right and certain. Nor does it allow itself to be bent according to human desires, according to the will of the powerful, according to the conventions of various peoples, but rather it remains the same among all peoples, in all realms. Nor does it ever deceive, because it was not contrived by human cleverness; rather it was revealed and prescribed by God through the Holy Spirit. Nor are apostles or other bishops permitted to invent new doctrines or to establish

[57]Downame, ed., *Annotations*, BBB4r*; citing Mt 5:45; Ps 19:4-6.

[58]Pareus, *In Epistolam ad Romanos*, 1061-62.

[59]Hesshus translates *bĕcol-hāʾāreṣ yāṣāʾ qawām* as "Throughout all the earth goes their rule [*regula*]." Most modern as well as early modern Hebraists amend *qawām* ("their measuring line") to *qalām* ("their voice"). In his comment on Psalm 19, Hesshus identifies this "most straight and sure measuring line" of the prophets, apostles and ministers of the Word as "the Word of God revealed by God through the Son of God" (*Commentarius in libros Psalmorum* [Helmstadt: Lucius, 1586], 88v). See further John Goldingay, *Psalms*, Baker Commentary on the Old Testament Wisdom and Psalms (Grand Rapids: Baker Academic, 2006), 1:282; Hans-Joachim Kraus, *Psalms 1–59: A Commentary*, trans. Hilton C. Oswald (Minneapolis: Augsburg, 1988), 267-68, 271-72.

articles of faith out of their own heads, but rather only according to this rule should the church, which is the house of God, be built everywhere. COMMENTARY ON ROMANS 10:16-18.[60]

CLARIFICATIONS ABOUT THE INTERPRETATION OF PSALM 19. JOHN CALVIN: This passage of Paul gave occasion to the ancients to explain the whole psalm allegorically, and posterity has followed them, so that, without doubt, the sun going forth as a bridegroom from his chamber is Christ and the heavens are the apostles. They who had most piety, and showed a greater modesty in interpreting Scripture, thought that what was properly said of the celestial architecture has been transferred by Paul to the apostles by way of allusion. But as I find that the Lord's servants have everywhere with great reverence explained Scripture, and have not turned them at pleasure in all directions, I cannot be persuaded that Paul has in this manner misconstrued this passage. I then take his quotation according to the proper and genuine meaning of the prophet, so that the argument will be something of this kind. God has already from the beginning manifested his divinity to the Gentiles, though not by the preaching of human beings, yet by the testimony of his creatures; for though the gospel was then silent among them, yet the whole workmanship of heaven and earth did speak and make known its author by its preaching. It hence appears that the Lord, even during the time in which he confined the favor of his covenant to Israel, did not yet so withdraw from the Gentiles the knowledge of himself, but that he ever kept alive some sparks of it among them. He indeed manifested himself then more particularly to his chosen people, so that the Jews might be justly compared to domestic hearers, whom he familiarly taught as it were by his own mouth; yet as he spoke to the Gentiles at a distance by the voice of the heavens, he showed by this prelude that he designed to make himself known at length to them also.

But I do not know why the Greek translator rendered the word *qawām* ["their line"] as *phthongon autōn*, "their sound," for it means a line, sometimes in building and sometimes in writing. As it is certain that the same thing is mentioned twice in this passage, it seems to me probable that the heavens are introduced as declaring by what is written as it were on them, as well as by voice, the power of God. For by the word going forth the prophet reminds us that the doctrine, of which the heavens are the preachers, is not included within the narrow limits of one land, but is proclaimed to the utmost regions of the world. COMMENTARY ON ROMANS 10:18.[61]

ALL THE WORLD? DAVID PAREUS: Another contested matter arises from verse 18: how can the voice of the apostles be said to have gone out throughout the world when not even now has the gospel been preached in India, America, Brazil, Japan, etc.?

Reply: The apostle is not stating that the gospel was spread abroad once and for all in his own lifetime into all the parts of the world. He himself preached from Jerusalem through all the regions up to Illyria[62] (Rom 15:19). Mark preached the gospel in Egypt, Thomas in India, Matthew in Ethiopia and others elsewhere. Twice the apostle writes the same thing in Colossians 1:6, 23. But if today the barbarians do not have the gospel, it does not follow that their ancestors never had it, because very many other nations lost it by their ingratitude. But what if we should say that the new world was sunk before the times of Ptolemy and remained hidden, but were recently uncovered and occupied by neighboring barbarians? For it is not altogether likely to be true that those lands could not have been discovered by the sailings of the ancients. But it is certain that many parts of the world now lie hidden, submerged by water, that once were inhabited and were accessible. But how is it

---

[60]Hesshus, *Explicatio Epistolae Pauli ad Romanos*, 347v-348r; citing Jn 3:35; Ps 19:4.

[61]CO 49:207-8 (cf. CTS 38:402-4). See further CTS 8:312-15 (CO 31:196-98).
[62]Illyria was a Roman province, roughly the location of the former Yugoslavia.

astonishing if we were to say the reverse, namely, that there were some lands that had previously lain buried emerged from the water? But I also leave this matter undecided. COMMENTARY ON ROMANS 10.[63]

10:19 *Have They Understood?*

THE FOLLY OF JEWS AND GENTILES. HULDRYCH ZWINGLI: Paul directs the sermon to the Jews. But the Jews said, perhaps, that they had not heard. Indeed I would show them from the Scriptures that their excuse is vain. God speaks through Moses that he would provoke the Jewish people through a people who were not his and would anger them through a foolish people, namely, by preaching his gospel to the Gentiles. The people are called a foolish people, because they worship vain and foolish idols, which is the height of foolishness, namely to worship the god that you yourself have made. In the same way the Gentiles are foolish in this, that they were ignorant of the will and law of God. To know the will of God is the highest wisdom. ANNOTATIONS ON ROMANS 10:19.[64]

EVEN THE PROPHETS KNEW THE GENTILES WOULD PARTICIPATE IN THE PROMISE. JUAN DE VALDÉS: Now that in the time of the gospel these words of Moses are specifically fulfilled, the truth of this appears from personal experience, which shows us how greatly those who professed Judaism were indignant and angry at the call of the Gentiles to the grace of the gospel. So much so that even to those who had accepted the gospel—even the apostles themselves—it seemed to be most extraordinary that the Gentiles should be admitted to the grace of the gospel. St. Paul thoroughly proves by this authority that the call of the Gentiles to the grace of the gospel had been prophesied in the law itself.

When St. Paul says, "Did Israel not understand?" I take it to mean that we are to understand the publication of the gospel throughout the world, with the admission of the nations to participation in it. . . . He might also mean Christianity, the preaching of the gospel. Then St. Paul would mean that the Hebrews could not excuse themselves by saying that they had no knowledge of the gospel since it is evident that both Moses and Isaiah had knowledge of it. COMMENTARY ON ROMANS 10:19.[65]

PAUL KNOWS THAT THEY KNOW. WOLFGANG MUSCULUS: He had already asked above "Have they not heard?" and he had shown that all the Jews had most certainly heard, since the sound of gospel preaching had already spread throughout the whole globe by that time. Now by this he wanted to prove that the Jews were utterly blinded. Now he shows superfluously, not only that the Jews had heard the preaching of the gospel, but also that they now argued about these things and by these things the Jews had been especially offended. . . . Namely that the Gentiles should be called to faith and that they should be rejected on account of their unbelief. And he proves this by two witnesses whom the Jews did not dare to oppose—now that they were dead, although while they were alive, they treated them most wickedly. He clearly shows that Moses and Isaiah preached the same things. Now since reading Moses and the Prophets was most familiar to the Jews, he rightly finds them guilty for being ignorant of them; consciously and knowingly they are willing to perish and to resist the grace of God. . . . Therefore that he says, "Did Israel not understand?" is the same as if he would say, "Did Israel only hear the preaching of the gospel and not also understand that these things are happening now in the calling of the Gentiles and their rejection?" Israel clearly understood. For they were not able to use their ignorance of Moses and the Prophets as a pretext. But all these things Moses and the Prophets preached most brilliantly. Therefore they know, and

---

[63]Pareus, *In Epistolam ad Romanos*, 1062-63.
[64]Zwingli, *In plerosque Novi Testamenti Libros*, 454.

[65]Valdés, *Commentary upon Romans*, 192-93* (*Commentario de Romanos*, 225-26).

they knowingly oppose the truth. COMMENTARY ON ROMANS 10:19.[66]

GOD'S DEFINITION OF FOOLISHNESS: HUMAN MERIT. MARTIN LUTHER: These are words of grace, that is, they have been spoken to commend grace, because God saves no one but sinners, he instructs no one but the foolish and stupid, he enriches none but paupers, and he makes alive only the dead; not those who merely imagine themselves to be such but those who really are this kind of people and admit it. For it really was a fact that the Gentiles were not the people of God and were a foolish nation, so that, being saved without any merits or zeal of their own, they might acknowledge the grace of God.

But the proud who trust in their own merits and wisdom become very angry and grumble because to others is given freely when they are undeserving what they themselves sought with such great zeal. As Christ expresses it in the Gospel in the parable of the older son who turned away from his prodigal brother and did not want him to come in, and also in the parable of those men who when they had received the denarius for the whole day's work complained because the master treated the last comers equally with the first. But the really foolish ones are those who are presumptuous only about themselves and do not rejoice over the salvation of others. And by the same token they prove that they are seeking God not for the sake of God but for their own sake, that is, because of the love of concupiscence and their comfort (that is, impurely) and they are even proud of this impurity and loathsomeness of theirs; that is, they are twice as loathsome as the people whom they despise. For were they really seeking God, they would not look down on the salvation of others but would rejoice in it and find pleasure in it, because they would see that they pleased God, and his pleasure must be desired more than anything else. SCHOLIA ON ROMANS 10:19.[67]

10:20-21 God Still Waits

LISTEN, YOU BLIND AND HAUGHTY PEOPLE! JUAN DE VALDÉS: God is always doing this very thing: calling to himself some of the many who neither seek him nor remember him, while rejecting many, who pretend to seek him and to remember him. . . . These things should be considered by those who, puffed up by their own reason and fleshly wisdom, pretend to know everything—not only what is written with human wisdom, where they have authority, but even what is written by the Holy Spirit, where they have no authority at all. They are like blind people, trying to judge between shades of colors. COMMENTARY ON ROMANS 10:20.[68]

THE MEANING OF GOD'S OUTSTRETCHED HANDS. JUAN DE VALDÉS: God stretches forth his hands universally to all the nations on earth. With temporal blessings he gives them the fruits of the earth in great abundance. Now I understand God to have stretched forth his hands to the Hebrew people in a special manner. He gave them things outside nature's usual course, like water out of the rock, manna and the quail, etc. He miraculously favored them with wondrous signs in heaven and on earth. I likewise understand that God stretches forth his hands in a special manner to the Christian people. He, either through himself or through the agency of an individual or many individuals (members of the same people), gives them an abundance of spiritual gifts, increasing their faith by knowledge of God and by the knowledge of Christ; and increasing their love through the union between them and God, whereby people come to be pure love and charity, just as God is pure love and charity.

Since this stretching forth of the hands is wholly internal, and is experienced within the soul, the gifts are internal too. Those who experience this learn that the Christian people are never

---

[66]Musculus, *In epistolam Apostoli Pauli ad Romanos commentarii*, 186.
[67]LW 25:418-19* (WA 56:427).

[68]Valdés, *Commentary upon Romans*, 194* (*Commentario de Romanos*, 226-27); alluding to Mt 8:19-21.

incredulous, doubting God's promises. "Neither are they rebellious," opposing themselves to the will of God. Indeed, they are always faithful and obedient, believing in God's promises and relying on them. They are obedient in everything that they know to be the will of God. Those who are not faithful and obedient to God in this way, or those who do not desire and strive to be so, they, not being Christ's, are not the Christian people, however much they may pride themselves as such, and persuade themselves that they are so. . . .

I will add this, that just as when some of us stretch forth our hands to others, by being generous to them, and intend by this to attract them to follow us, and to love us, so also when God stretches forth God's hands to us, we should consider that God intends by this to attract us, so that we may follow, serve, adore and love God. Those who do not consider this when God stretches forth his hands to them are unbelieving, unfaithful, ungodly and totally blind. COMMENTARY ON ROMANS 10:21.[69]

GOD AS MERCIFUL AND MOTHERLY. DAVID PAREUS: "All day I have stretched out my hands" is anthropopathy[70] and a metaphor from mothers who call back their unruly children to them with their outstretched arms. He means then the infinite benefits by which God has lured them to himself: The preaching, promises, exhortations and threats of the prophets, by which they labored in vain to call them back from their sins and to lead them to repent. By this action he commends God's immeasurable goodness to us, so that God can absolutely not be blamed for their destruction, because even to the rebellious he stretches out his hands—and yes all day long! That is, he invites them to faith and repentance by his word and benefits—and frequently and for a long time—so that in the end their stubbornness is inexcusable. It is, however, anthropopathy. COMMENTARY ON ROMANS 10:21.[71]

THE REPROBATE HAVE ONLY THEMSELVES TO BLAME. TILEMANN HESSHUS: One ought not to charge God with being the reason for the damnation of the reprobate. For God is not the reason for anyone's destruction, but rather God is greatly grieved that a person has sunk themselves into death and willingly invited their own destruction. God created Adam in his own image and likeness and bestowed on him those greatest goods: righteousness, freedom, joy and life. And he appointed him for the fellowship of eternal companionship with God. Nor did God bestow these greatest gifts on Adam alone, but his entire posterity. He also added dire threats so that he would guard those good gifts all the more carefully. But he made humankind subject to his own free will and placed before him good and evil, life and death, so that his obedience toward God might be all the more noteworthy. Nor does God appoint any person to doom, unless they have been polluted and contaminated by sin. Nor did the foreknowledge of God, which foresaw that humankind would fall and the ungodly would resist the Word and remain under God's wrath, impose on them a need to sin or give them any reason to distrust him. ON THE PREDESTINATION OF THE SAINTS: THE REASON FOR THE CONDEMNATION OF THE REPROBATE.[72]

---

[69]Valdés, *Commentary upon Romans*, 195-96* (*Commentario de Romanos*, 228-29).
[70]That is, attributing human feelings to God.
[71]Pareus, *In Epistolam ad Romanos*, 1039-40.
[72]Hesshus, *Explicatio Epistolae Pauli ad Romanos*, 302r-v [sic 293r-v].

11:1-10 THE REMNANT OF ISRAEL

I ask, then, has God rejected his people? By no means! For I myself am an Israelite, a descendant of Abraham,[a] a member of the tribe of Benjamin. [2]God has not rejected his people whom he foreknew. Do you not know what the Scripture says of Elijah, how he appeals to God against Israel? [3]"Lord, they have killed your prophets, they have demolished your altars, and I alone am left, and they seek my life." [4]But what is God's reply to him? "I have kept for myself seven thousand men who have not bowed the knee to Baal." [5]So too at the present time there is a remnant, chosen by grace. [6]But if it is by grace, it is no longer on the basis of works; otherwise grace would no longer be grace.

[7]What then? Israel failed to obtain what it was seeking. The elect obtained it, but the rest were hardened, [8]as it is written,

> *"God gave them a spirit of stupor,*
> *eyes that would not see*
> *and ears that would not hear,*
> *down to this very day."*

[9]And David says,

> *"Let their table become a snare and a trap,*
> *a stumbling block and a retribution for them;*
> *[10]let their eyes be darkened so that they cannot see,*
> *and bend their backs forever."*

a Or *one of the offspring of Abraham*

OVERVIEW: God is gracious, and he keeps his promises. The reformers here clarify Paul's use of logic and Scripture to prove God's gracious steadfast love—no matter how things might seem. These commentators expound the apostle's argument that matters before God are not the same as they seem before human beings. Paul argues by *modus tollens*[1]: if God has abandoned his people, then Paul would be abandoned; however, Paul has not been abandoned, thus God has not abandoned his people. Nestled within this observation, the reformers remind pastors not to trust their eyes, but to trust their faith. "Are you able to drink the cup that I am to drink?" (Mt 20:22). They might be so plagued by strife and stress that like Elijah they would rather die than continue in their office; nevertheless, they must not consider the results of their faithful ministry, for God alone grants the growth (1 Cor 3:7). Instead they must diligently attend to the ministry of the word, only observing whether the people are still willing to hear the Word preached.

Paradoxically, when the church looks healthy, it is often disease ridden; when it seems to be dying, it is clothed in strength and power. Only by God's goodness and mercy is the church preserved.

In their comments on this passage the reformers again see the need to prove and reaffirm the Augustinian claims about the priority and sufficiency of grace. Paul leaves no room for human merit. He explicitly opposes grace to works. Satan strives to obscure the gospel by sneaking in human merit through many different strategies (for example, Aristotelian causes). But these commentators exorcise this demonic teaching with Paul's word and Augustine's support: "The grace of God absolutely does not exist unless it be absolutely free."[2] Once a person is justified through faith in Christ, then good works flow from this faith.

And again our exegetes praise Paul's skill in the Scriptures. God's Word alone proves doctrine, and it alone interprets itself and doctrine. On account of human sinfulness, sometimes the clear and

---

[1]That is, if "if p, then q" holds, then "not q, not p" holds.

[2]Augustine, *On Original Sin* 28 (NPNF 5:246*).

bright Scriptures seem dark, but they reveal what is necessary for salvation. Believers must allow the Holy Spirit to prepare this table before them, lest it become a snare.

Paul Proclaims Promise to the Jews.
Tilemann Hesshus: Now Paul has clearly proved by the testimonies of holy Scripture that the Gentiles belong to the kingdom of Christ, that now through faith they have been adopted into the fellowship of the church, but that the Jews have been cast aside because of their unbelief, so that they are not the people of God. And he has preached about the severity of God toward the unbelief of the Jews with sufficient gravity. So lest he entirely deprive the Jews of hope of returning to God and obtaining his mercy, Paul teaches that in the very severity of God his kindness toward the Jewish people shines forth. For he has not utterly rejected his people, so that not one of them could be saved, but only so that they would repent, give up their stubborn lives of unbelief, return to the Lord Messiah with their whole heart and believe in Jesus Christ, the Son of God, who was crucified and raised again. Then he testifies to them that the gates of divine grace stand wide open . . . and that they are going to have precedence before the Gentiles as the sons of the promise and natural branches. So far this entire epistle of Paul has focused on this, so that it would call the Jews and Gentiles to repentance and invite them to faith in Christ.

First he proves this mitigation of the previously imposed severe judgment by his own example. Accordingly, although he is an Israelite of the tribe of Benjamin, he turned to God, not only obtaining the forgiveness of sins, but also being set apart as a distinguished apostle of Jesus Christ. And so it is evident that God has not completely rejected the Jews, but demands that they repent and believe the gospel. Then they will not only not be excluded from the grace of the Messiah but even in a certain way will enjoy a privilege. This is why Paul frequently says, "first the Jew, then the Greek."

And Christ says: "Let the children be fed first." Commentary on Romans 11:1.[3]

Elected According to God's Mercy.
Philipp Melanchthon: He tones down the above complaint about the falling away of the people and testifies that the promise still belongs to the people, and that many will follow it, namely, those who believe. First he argues from his own example: I am an Israelite, and I have received the promise, so Israelites are able to obtain it. The other reason is taken from the example of the time of Elijah. Thus he reminds us that the church is always small, and that the number and power of the wicked is much greater.

He adds the teaching that the church has not been elected on account of the law, on account of the form of government, but that the people of God that accepts the gospel by faith has been elected. He adds that the cause of election is mercy, not the law, not the form of government, as was said above about the distinction between the two peoples. The synagogue has the title "people of God," and wages war against the true people and the true church. We need to be prepared against this offense, and forearmed in order that we may know that the church is not that crowd which persecutes the gospel, even if they have the worship and form of government. Commentary on Romans (1540).[4]

11:1-4 *Has God Rejected His Own People?*

Paul's Gospel Tonic. Heinrich Bullinger: Here he introduces a consolation, lest the Jews, having been frightened too greatly, utterly despair; perhaps by this method he might even be able to win some of them. For those things he has written so far concerning the rejection of the Jews he did not write to enrage them, but rather to win them and to cast out false hope. Just as medicinal tonic

---

[3]Hesshus, *Explicatio Epistolae Pauli ad Romanos*, 349r-v; citing Mk 7:27.
[4]Melanchthon, *Commentary on Romans*, 204 (MO 15:697); citing 1 Kings 19:10-18.

has a bitter taste, so also the gospel has its bitterness—but not too much. Thus the apostle, the most celebrated herald of the gospel of God, introduces such a very elegant consolation in this passage. The main point is that God has not rejected his people whom he has foreknown. COMMENTARY ON ROMANS 11.[5]

PASTORS, BEAR WITH YOUR STUBBORN PEOPLE; PEOPLE, DON'T BE STUBBORN. DAVID PAREUS: Let pastors learn to pray for their people and patiently bear their weakness—indeed, their obstinacy—and not easily descend to prayers against their people so that the pastors may not sin by an immature zeal. But let the hearers take care not to provoke pastors by their stubbornness and compel God to intervene against them, for God does not despise at all the groans of his servants. Concerning this, the apostle admonishes us not to force pastors who keep watch over our souls to carry their duty with groaning (Heb 13:17). "For," he says, "that would be *alysitelēs,* 'useless,' for you, indeed even harmful." COMMENTARY ON ROMANS 11:2.[6]

PAUL'S SYLLOGISM. WOLFGANG MUSCULUS: He proves by this example that God has not abandoned his people. It's as if he says: "If he had abandoned his people—that is, whoever is an Israelite—he would have abandoned me too. So while no hope for salvation seemed to be left for me ('for I too am an Israelite'), he has not abandoned me, but received me into his grace. Therefore he has not abandoned his people."

Now from his example he gathers the conclusion that he wanted to prove, that God has not rejected his people. And "for I too am an Israelite" would be the major premise, which is: If God has rejected his people, he has rejected me too.... And the minor premise, which he does not state, would be: But he has not rejected me. From this it is concluded: Therefore he has not rejected his people. This syllogism is by consequent—where through

refutation of the consequent the antecedent is refuted. COMMENTARY ON ROMANS 11:1.[7]

GOD CAUSES, ENABLES AND COMPLETES OUR SALVATION. PETER MARTYR VERMIGLI: This should not be understood as simple knowledge, for even those who are damned are not hidden from God. Instead this knowledge has a connection with approval. And they are said to have been foreknown who have been received by God and whom he has separated from the rest as his people whom he will save. For this reason Augustine in his book *On the Gift of Perseverance* alters this verb "he has foreknown" to "he has predestined."[8] Those who want election to be dependent on foreseen works say that those whom God foreknew would believe and live godly and holy lives are picked out. But these ideas have been refuted at length above, so instead let us hold the opposite understanding. We believe therefore that we accept God's truth and live godly lives because we have been chosen, and not that we have been chosen because we will believe. On God our salvation must depend; it does not even have its beginning from us. Christ said (as it is written in John): "Those you have given to me I have not lost." That is, if they do not hear me, if they perish, they are not those whom you have given me. COMMENTARY ON ROMANS 11:2.[9]

THREE LESSONS FROM ELIJAH. TILEMANN HESSHUS: Because God confirms that he preserves worshipers for himself, Paul concludes that salvation does not proceed from our free will but from the grace and election of God. This history of Elijah and Paul's line of argument teaches that we will always be astounded by the smallness of the church, just as the prophets and apostles themselves were bewildered by this. Thus the verses of

---

[5]Bullinger, *In Romanos Epistolam,* 135r-v.
[6]Pareus, *In Epistolam ad Romanos,* 1076.

[7]Musculus, *In epistolam Apostoli Pauli ad Romanos commentarii,* 189.
[8]Augustine, *A Treatise on the Gift of Perseverance* 47 (NPNF 5:544).
[9]Vermigli, *In Epistolam ad Romanos,* 469 (cf. *A Commentarie upon the Epistle to the Romanes,* 333r); citing Jn 18:9.

Isaiah: "The Lord will cause gleanings to be left in the Valley of Rephaim, it will be like when an olive tree is shaken, he causes two or three berries to remain in the highest bough, four or five on its fruit-bearing branches, says the Lord God of Israel."

Second, this history reminds us that the church is not preserved by diligence, zeal or human counsel, but only by divine goodness and mercy. For unless the immeasurable goodness of God illuminates some by his Word and Spirit and preserves them in the faith, the entire human race would voluntarily rush headlong into destruction, so that no one would believe the teaching of Christ.

Third, we learn from this passage that we should not judge the size of the church or the fruits of our labor in ministry by appearances or the church's external state. Instead this judgment should be relinquished to God. Often when we suppose that the church is flourishing, God, who examines every heart, judges far differently. On the other hand, when we fear that the church is being thoroughly destroyed, before God it is clothed in strength and shines brilliantly. COMMENTARY ON ROMANS 11:2-5.[10]

TOIL, TROUBLE AND DISCOURAGEMENT HOUND THE MINISTERS OF THE WORD. PETER MARTYR VERMIGLI: It repeatedly happens to the pious that, swept away by excessive zeal, they complain to God on account of the good fortune of the impious—as if God seems to despise his own cause. Today this happens to us too. We suppose that we alone are left, for all Italy, France and Spain seem to be enslaved to superstitions and antichrist; but it is not so. The church has not been razed, although she is oppressed by great tyranny. And in those places there are many thousands of honest men [*virorum*], who in difficulties and oppression most chastely keep their faith in God. . . .

The things that happened in the time [of Elijah] were very similar to the things Paul experienced. Obviously the entire kingdom of the ten tribes had gone astray, and in the kingdom of Judah very few who were passionate and zealous for true piety remained, like in the early days of the apostles nearly everyone could have seemed to be strangers to Christ. Certainly Elijah had wanted to die, nor are many ministers found to be any different. On account of the troubles of their calling and the impudence and incredulity of the people, many ponder forsaking their ministry, toiling also in weakness—on account of which this prophet of ours seems to have been so disheartened that he begged to die. However, let ministers know that they must remain in their calling as long as the strength of their body allows, and as long as they are not forced out. For as long as they are able to bear to hear the Word of God, the human beings and congregation entrusted to them should not be forsaken in any circumstance. But if they are all to a man despisers and they will not suffer the Word of the Lord to be preached, then, as Christ commanded the apostles, shake the dust off your feet against them and leave. Still as long as there are some who want to endure the pastor preach and handle the Word of God, the pastor must not yield his ministry. . . . By the example of this prophet we are able to know how many troubles ministers must endure in governing the church—and truly not slight or common troubles, but those before which death seems preferable! With what great trouble and zeal we should imagine that Christ said: "O unbelieving generation, how long will I endure you?" COMMENTARY ON ROMANS 11:4.[11]

"TO THE IMAGE OF BAAL." THEODORE BEZA: *tē Baal*. Erasmus translates it correctly this way, for the feminine article indicates that the Greek word *eikoni* ["image"] must be read. But among the Hebrews the word "Baal" *bʾl* (*bahal*) designates him under whose power we are, as a slave is under his master's power or a wife under her husband's. From that usage it came about that it is now understood to mean an idol to which idolaters sell themselves entirely. But even nowadays those who

---

[10]Hesshus, *Explicatio Epistolae Pauli ad Romanos*, 350r-v; citing Is 17:5-6.

[11]Vermigli, *In Epistolam ad Romanos*, 470-71 (cf. *A Commentarie upon the Epistle to the Romanes*, 333v-334r); citing Lk 9:41.

call on the Virgin Mary by no other name than "our Lady" profess the same thing, and they customarily do not invoke other saints unless they append the title "lords" or "patrons" to them, to whom they transfer the worship that is due to God. ANNOTATIONS ON ROMANS 11:4.[12]

SEARCH SCRIPTURE DILIGENTLY. PETER MARTYR VERMIGLI: Now finally to finish our treatment of this passage I thought we should be admonished to search the Scriptures with the same diligence with which we see Paul treat them. For unless he had read these things with the greatest attention, he would not have been able to discuss them so skillfully. COMMENTARY ON ROMANS 11:4.[13]

11:5-6 All Election Is by Grace

GRACE AND WORKS ARE MUTUALLY EXCLUSIVE. TILEMANN HESSHUS: In this passage we should diligently attend to the argument that Paul composes from the term *grace*. For he places these two things diametrically opposed to one another: to be chosen and saved by grace and to be saved by works. He says, "If we are saved by grace, then it is not by works; but if by works, then not by grace." For these things contradict one another: to grant something freely out of mercy and to pay wages for work out of obligation. And so both cannot be true.

In this argument, first the apostle clearly teaches in what sense he wants to take the term *grace*: not how the papacy takes it, as infused qualities or

newness of life; but as the gratuitous mercy, favor and clemency of the eternal God, by which—without any of our work, worthiness and merit—God freely pardons our sins, receives us in his grace, pronounces us righteous and confers on us the inheritance of eternal life. And so in this passage the Council of Trent is convicted of open blasphemy. The council pronounces anathema on all who assert that the grace by which we are justified means only the favor of God—indeed the antichrist's kingdom does not fear contradicting the most plain teaching of the Holy Spirit.[14]

Next in this passage Paul exposes the delusion of those who mix human merits with the grace of God, and invent out of their own mind without any testimony of holy Scripture that justification happens to us partly by the grace of God, partly by our own merit. From this comes the following false statements. First, we are justified freely by God's mercy, but then by love. Also, indeed we are primarily justified freely by God's mercy, but less so on account of our works. Also, we are not justified by faith alone, but by faith formed by love and improved works. Also, good works are so necessary for justification and salvation that without them no one can be saved. Also, the mercy of God is indeed the efficient cause of our justification; the merit of Jesus Christ the [material][15] cause; the formal cause of our justification, however, by which we are pleasing before God, is the good works themselves and newness of life. These and similar fanatical opinions, which Satan uses to obscure the gospel, Paul clearly refutes in this passage, because he shows that these contradict one another: to accept favor [*beneficium*] freely and to be justified by merit on account of works. He says, "If by grace, then not by works." And so what madness is this! To imagine that we are justified partly by grace, partly by works, or that good works are necessary for salvation? Paul adds this reason: "Otherwise grace will not be grace." For grace is what is freely given without merit. From

---

[12]Beza, *Annotationes majores*, 2:120. Modern biblical scholars believe that by using a feminine article before Baal, Paul implies *aischynē* ("shame"). This parallels the Hebrew custom of using *bōšet* ("shame") as a euphemism for pagan gods (for example, see 2 Sam 2:8; 3:8). See further C. E. B. Cranfield, *A Critical and Exegetical Commentary on the Epistle to the Romans*, International Critical Commentary (Edinburg: T&T Clark, 1985), 2:547; Joseph A. Fitzmyer, *Romans: A New Translation with Introduction and Commentary*, Anchor Bible 33 (New York: Doubleday, 1993), 605; Douglas J. Moo, *The Epistle to the Romans*, New International Commentary on the New Testament 38 (Grand Rapids: Eerdmans, 1996), 676n25.

[13]Vermigli, *In Epistolam ad Romanos*, 472 (cf. *A Commentarie upon the Epistle to the Romanes*, 335r).

[14]Council of Trent, sixth session, chapter 9, "Against the Vain Confidence of the Heretics," and canon 9.

[15]The printer likely incorrectly used *meritoriam* here, rather than *materiam*.

this comes Augustine's expression (most worthy of praise and full of piety), which taken from this argument he repeats several times: "Grace will not be grace in any way unless it is free in every way."[16]

Therefore the very term *grace* excludes all merit of works and even all necessity for the presence of works. For if all grace is free and does not in any way permit merit, our works are necessarily not required for salvation. On the other hand Paul presses, "But if by works, then it is not by grace, otherwise works are not works." To exclude any merit of works, he presses also the term *works*, for what we obtain by our works we do not owe to grace. As Bernard piously and rightly has said: "How can she be full of grace if what she has is not from grace?"[17] O God of grace, whatever you assign to merits, I do not want merit that would exclude grace! And so this is a most powerful proof that without any merit, but by God's grace and mercy we are justified.

If anyone wonders why Paul places grace and works in contradiction to each other, since works are the effect of free justification, he should know that Paul does not want this: that the grace of God and the works of human beings should contend with each other, but that free justification and justification by merit of works should be diametrically opposed to one another. That's why God has shown mercy on us, because we could not be saved by our works. That's also why Christ has died for our sins, because we could not achieve salvation by our own strength. Therefore whatever you ascribe to works, you detract from both the mercy of God and the merit of Jesus Christ. For this reason Paul says: "If justification is by works of the law, Christ died for no reason." COMMENTARY ON ROMANS 11:6-7.[18]

FORESEEN WORKS CONSTRAIN FREE GRACE. JOHN CALVIN: This amplification is derived from a comparison between things of an opposite character. For such is the case between God's grace and the merit of works, that whoever establishes the one overturns the other. But if no regard to works can be admitted in election without obscuring the gratuitous goodness of God, which he designed to be commended so much to us, what can those frenzied minds who make the cause of election the worthiness in us that God foresees say to Paul? Whether you offer future or past works, this declaration of Paul, which says that grace leaves nothing to works, will oppose you. Here Paul does not so much argue about our reconciliation with God, nor about the means or relative causes of our salvation, but rather he ascends to why God before the foundation of the world chose only some and passed by others. Elsewhere he denies that God has been led to this distinction by anything other than his own good pleasure. For he contends that as much room is made for works, so much is taken away from grace.

From this it follows that foreknowledge of works are wrongly mixed with election. For if God chooses some and rejects others because he has foreseen them to be worthy or unworthy of salvation, then having established the reward for works, the grace of God will not reign alone, but mutilated it will only be a part of the cause of our election. For as Paul has reasoned before concerning the justification of Abraham, where reward is paid, grace is not freely bestowed. Now he draws his argument from the same fountain, that if works are taken into account when God adopts a certain number of human beings into salvation, reward is owed, and therefore not a free gift. COMMENTARY ON ROMANS 11:6.[19]

CHRIST ALONE. TILEMANN HESSHUS: To be sure, the sole cause and only source for the election of the saints is the immense mercy of God, but that mercy was made manifest in such a way that it is to be seen only in Jesus Christ, the Son of God. For he chose us and predestined us for the adoption as sons in his beloved Son and through his Son and because of his Son. Not only has no person been elected apart from the Son of God,

---

[16]For example, *On Original Sin* 28 (NPNF 5:246).
[17]Bernard of Clairvaux, *Song of Songs Sermon* 67.10 (PL 183:1107). Bernard is preaching on Song 2:16 here.
[18]Hesshus, *Explicatio Epistolae Pauli ad Romanos*, 351r-352v; citing Gal 2:21.

[19]CTS 38:414-15* (CO 49:214-15); citing Rom 4:1-12.

Jesus Christ, but also the mercy of God toward the mass of humanity polluted by sin cannot even be understood apart from Christ. Therefore one ought not to inquire about election apart from Christ, but one must determine that we were chosen before the foundation of the world in Christ alone, that is, because of the intercession of the Son of God in the following manner: Christ would be appointed our mediator and sacrificial victim for the sins of the world, and the church would be gathered by the Spirit and power of Christ, be united with him, be consecrated to him for all eternity and serve his glory in true righteousness and holiness. Paul clearly teaches this (Eph 1). ON THE PREDESTINATION OF THE SAINTS: ALL ARE SAVED WHO ARE CHOSEN IN CHRIST.[20]

11:7-10 *The Mystery of Divine Sovereignty and Human Responsibility*

INCOMPREHENSIBLE COUNSELS. JOHN CALVIN: Paul labors to prove here that those who were blinded were not blinded because it was warranted by their wickedness, but because they were rejected by God before the foundation of the world. This knot you may untie quickly in this way: that the origin of impiety, which so provokes God's fury, is the perversity of nature after it has been forsaken by God. Paul, therefore, while speaking of eternal reprobation, has not without reason referred to those things that proceed from it, as fruit from the tree or a river from its source. Indeed the ungodly on account of their sins are punished with God's just judgment, blindness. But if we seek the source of their ruin, we must come to this: that cursed by God, through all their deeds, words and purposes, they cannot accumulate and add anything but a curse. Indeed the cause of eternal reprobation has been so hidden from us that nothing remains for us but to marvel at the incomprehensible counsels of God. . . . They act foolishly who, as soon as a word is said about relative causes, try on account of this pretext to bury the matter of reprobation, which

lies hidden from our senses. COMMENTARY ON ROMANS 11:7.[21]

SEEK CORRECTLY. PETER MARTYR VERMIGLI: He concludes his argument this way: not all the Jews are saved, but those whom he has foreknown—I mean, the elect. But if they sought him, how did they not find him? Because they sought him incorrectly. They sought a Messiah who would rule the world with glory and pomp, who would make them rich, who would subject all nations to their rule. They sought their own gain, namely, to have bread from Christ. They sought to worship the Messiah and God differently than it was ordered in Sacred Literature. . . . So because they sought him incorrectly, it is not surprising that they did not find him. And for that reason when Christ said, "Seek and you will find, ask and you will receive, knock and it will be opened to you," the adverb *correctly* should be added. We must ask correctly, we must seek correctly and we must knock correctly, otherwise we will be frustrated. COMMENTARY ON ROMANS 11:7.[22]

SCRIPTURE IS ITS OWN INTERPRETER. DAVID PAREUS: Let us learn first from the method of the apostle the purpose and use of the Scriptures. I said earlier that the Scriptures ought to be uniquely the norm and guideline for us in those things that pertain to faith. Besides this one must diligently note their twofold use. The first is the power to prove dogmas. The apostle makes a claim to this use in the Scriptures when he cites them to confirm his thesis. Therefore no proof for dogmas in the church ought to be received from any other source than from the Scriptures. But those things are to be taken from the Scriptures that either are expressly contained in them or are deduced from them by an evident and necessary consequence. The second use is the power to interpret and explicate dogmas, indeed the Scriptures themselves.

---

[20]Hesshus, *Explicatio Epistolae Pauli ad Romanos*, 285r-v.

[21]CTS 38:417* (CO 49:216).
[22]Vermigli, *A Commentarie upon the Epistle to the Romanes*, 336v-337r* (*In Epistolam ad Romanos*, 474); citing Jn 6:26; Mt 7:7.

The Jesuits seem (in their opinion) to argue very ingeniously concerning the interpreter of the Scriptures, whom they want to be the pope alone. They accuse the Scriptures of ambiguity and talk a lot about how the right of interpretation does not reside in the Scriptures because it is concerning the Scriptures' interpretation that the question is raised. And yet this is childish sophistry. The question is being raised concerning the interpretation of Scripture, but not of the whole book all at once, but rather of this particular passage now and of that passage next. Nevertheless, the interpretation of one Scripture passage is given through another. For it explains itself in turn: what seems more obscure in one passage is rendered more clearly in another. Therefore let there be a comparison of Scripture passages and all will be clear, at least it will be sufficiently clear for the knowledge of salvation. Paul does this. "The rest grew callous," he says. This is an obscure Scripture passage. He illuminates it by another Scripture passage from Isaiah 29: "He gave them a spirit of deep sleep." And this seems obscure, and so he illuminates it by another, from Isaiah 6: "So that they may not see with their eyes," etc. This is a necessary observation at this time. COMMENTARY ON ROMANS 11:8.[23]

DRUNKEN STUPOR. PETER MARTYR VERMIGLI: The metaphor is drawn from those who strive to make others drunk by goading them to drink more, and perhaps their drink is laced to make them act like idiots. But this alone is the difference: human beings act unjustly when they do this, but God does this most justly. COMMENTARY ON ROMANS 11:8.[24]

STUPOR, SATAN AND SEDITION. PHILIPP MELANCHTHON: A spirit of remorse is an angry spirit, embittered with hatred of God and the gospel. For there is a certain dreadful bitterness of hate in enemies of the gospel, such as is described in Cain, Pharaoh and similar persons. First, it is

because the devil inflames those attacks. Second, because human reason itself is vehemently offended by the dissolution of acts of worship and of the state. It imagines the doctrine to be blasphemous and seditious, for they think the glory of God is injured by a change in acts of worship. . . . Changes of acts of worship change also the form of government, and now it certainly tears the church apart. Each brings forth immense hatred because it is thought to harm the glory of God, and others are grieved that the authority of the church is shaken, that the order of the church is being destroyed. COMMENTARY ON ROMANS (1540).[25]

A RAGING AND BLINDED SPIRIT. TILEMANN HESSHUS: When he says "a spirit of disquiet," I think that Paul is looking at a passage in Isaiah 29: "The Lord has mixed a spirit of deep sleep or dullness for them, and he has closed their eyes so that they cannot see." With these words, the prophet prophesied the blinding of the Jews at the time of the Messiah's advent. Isaiah calls the horrible stupor of the heart "a spirit of deep sleep or lethargy," on account of which the hectic heart is not able to ponder or understand God's Word. Paul says "a spirit of disquiet" to explain the mind of the prophet more fully. Moreover, a spirit of disquiet and horrible anguish are joined with the most bitter hatred of God and the truth; and there is a seething rage within the person. As the Pharisees and high priests, whom Stephen accused of killing Christ, were cut to the heart and stirred into a rage, so also Judas, Ahithophel, Pharaoh and Saul were overwhelmed by a spirit of disquiet—nothing more tragic than this can be said! For anguish, fury and madness are mixed with grief so that although the heart feels immeasurable anguish, nevertheless it does not come to its senses, but rather rages at God and at itself and at all creatures. It wishes that there were no God and that no created thing existed.

O Lord Jesus Christ, crucified for us and raised again, do not let this sort of spirit be poured out on us! But instead grant us repentance, kindle faith in

[23]Pareus, *In Epistolam ad Romanos*, 1096-97.
[24]Vermigli, *In Epistolam ad Romanos*, 475 (cf. *A Commentarie upon the Epistle to the Romanes*, 337v-338r).

[25]Melanchthon, *Commentary on Romans*, 204 (MO 15:697-98).

us and grant us a spirit of grace and prayer, a spirit of wisdom and the fear of God, so that we would believe in you and live with you in all eternity. Amen. COMMENTARY ON ROMANS 11:8.[26]

PAUL OBJECTS TO AN OBJECTION. JOHN CALVIN: Paul adds "down to this very day," lest anyone should object that this prophecy has already been fulfilled, and so it is incorrectly applied to the time of the proclamation of the gospel. He anticipates this objection, adding that it is not only the blindness of one day, which is described there, but also that it has endured with the incurable obstinacy of the people even to Christ's advent. COMMENTARY ON ROMANS 11:8.[27]

TABLES OF EGYPTIANS, JEWS AND CATHOLICS. PHILIPP MELANCHTHON: "Table" signifies that in which human beings chiefly find repose, which seems to bring comfort, help, restoration and quiet. Thus the table of Pompey was the king of Egypt, the one with whom he sought refuge, by whose aid he hoped he would be safe, but it turned out to be his destruction. As for the Jews, their table was the law and their form of government at the time and the most glorious title "people of God." They knew that these things had been divinely handed down and had been so long defended, and they thought that they could not be changed. Therefore they condemned the doctrine, which seemed to be against them, and hoped they would be victors, as their fathers held fast the minds that were caught in a net of evil persuasion, and afterward destroyed them, etc. And now the title "church" is the table of the adversaries of the church. It ensnares minds with a false persuasion, and it will be their destruction. COMMENTARY ON ROMANS (1540).[28]

SCRIPTURE BECOMES A SNARE. CARDINAL CAJETAN: This is the sense [of Paul's use of Psalm 69 here]. "Let their tables," the faith of the Jews—

that is, sacred Scripture, which is the table of their credulity—"become a snare." . . . "And a stumbling block," that is, an obstacle to dash against. "And a retribution for them," that is, justly as their merits demand. For sacred Scripture—which was given to the Jews to kindle faith, to enlighten them concerning what should be believed—on account of the sin of the Jews has been transformed into a snare, restraining them, so that they do not believe in the Messiah. COMMENTARY ON ROMANS 11:9.[29]

TRAPPED AND BLINDED BY THEIR HARD HEARTS. TILEMANN HESSHUS: The table is the prophetic and apostolic teaching and the whole ministry of the gospel, which is set with the most delicious dishes to feed and nourish our soul, so that we will not die of hunger but live forever. "You have prepared before me a table against those who trouble me." But this table—which restores and revives the godly—for the ungodly and the despisers of Christ becomes a snare, a deception, a stumbling block and retribution, for by the very teaching of the prophets and apostles the ungodly are increasingly blinded, hardened and whipped into a fury, so that they are unable to believe. Indeed this happens not because of the preaching of doctrine, but because of the wickedness of the human heart. This wickedness robs the heart of the Holy Spirit, by whom it hears the very excellent sermons of the prophets; thus it fans the flames of hatred against the gospel. And it becomes the law of God, which punishes contempt for God's Word. "Let their eyes become darkened," he says, "so that they cannot see, and bend their backs forever." That is: "May you punish them with blindness of mind, so that they are unable to see the truth. Burden and bend their backs, so that they are not able to lift their eyes to heaven, to grasp knowledge of God and to repent." These kinds of dreadful imprecations are nothing other than a most sure prophecy that this is going to happen to all despisers of the gospel and enemies of the church.

---

[26]Hesshus, *Explicatio Epistolae Pauli ad Romanos*, 353v-354r; citing Is 29:10.
[27]CTS 38:418-19* (CO 49:217).
[28]Melanchthon, *Commentary on Romans*, 205 (MO 15:698).

[29]Cajetan, *In Sacrae Scripturae Expositionem*, 5:65.

Now here it is disputed whether the foundation and fault for sin can be placed on God in any way, for God is said to blind eyes, stop up ears, to transform a table into a snare, to bend the back. But this most true statement must always be held firmly with both hands: in no way is God the cause of sin, nor does he will sin, nor does he impel our minds to sin, nor does he approve of sin; rather, he is truly and terribly angry with all sins. For it is an unchanging rule: "You are not a God who wills iniquity." COMMENTARY ON ROMANS 11:9-10.[30]

SPIRIT-LED IMPRECATIONS. WOLFGANG MUSCULUS: In this passage we see that the saints were impelled by the Spirit of God, to loath the wicked enemies of the truth and glory of God, thus also to utter imprecations on these wicked and dreadful people. This is well known: "I hate them with a perfect hatred." Consequently there is no reason why some dread to read these things in the manner of imprecations, and think that they should be read in the manner of prophecy. And if we compare what happened to the Jews by God's just judgment to those imprecations, we see that those things the saints, by the Holy Spirit, pray against the impious enemies of God to be in the form of prophecy. For the Spirit of God—by whom the saints are led into these affections—knows what is going to happen to the impious.

And therefore he stirs up the saints by his inspiration to imprecate. Such imprecations of the saints are contained in a number of other passages in Scripture, like Moses against the conspiracy of Dathan and Abiram, Elisha against the attendants of the impious king, and Peter against Ananias and Sapphira. COMMENTARY ON ROMANS 11:8-10.[31]

DO NOT DESPISE THE GOSPEL. PHILIPP MELANCHTHON: This means burden them more and more with errors, offenses, sins and calamities. Finally, oppress them with eternal servitude, lest they begin again to bloom, lest they recover their authority and rule. The Anabaptists furnish a clear example. They brought forth new errors. Then they added the foulest offenses, sedition, lusts and blasphemies so that now their madness might become manifest until they were finally utterly destroyed. Similar things happened to the Jews after they persecuted the gospel. Let the threat of such dreadful punishment warn us not to despise the gospel, lest we bring down such punishments on ourselves. COMMENTARY ON ROMANS (1540).[32]

---

[30]Hesshus, *Explicatio Epistolae Pauli ad Romanos*, 354r-355r; citing Ps 23:5; 5:4.

[31]Musculus, *In epistolam Apostoli Pauli ad Romanos commentarii*, 192; citing Ps 139:22. On the question of imprecation, see also RCS OT 7:280-84, 422-23.

[32]Melanchthon, *Commentary on Romans*, 205 (MO 15:698). Melanchthon is referring here to shocking—though anomalous—events like the kingdom of Münster (1534–1535). For a brief treatment see RCS NT 6:liii-liv; for an in-depth reconstruction, see George H. Williams, *The Radical Reformation*, 3rd ed. (Kirksville, MO: Sixteenth Century Journal Publishers, 1992) 561-82.

11:11-24 GENTILES GRAFTED IN

[11]So I ask, did they stumble in order that they might fall? By no means! Rather through their trespass salvation has come to the Gentiles, so as to make Israel jealous. [12]Now if their trespass means riches for the world, and if their failure means riches for the Gentiles, how much more will their full inclusion[a] mean!

[13]Now I am speaking to you Gentiles. Inasmuch then as I am an apostle to the Gentiles, I magnify my ministry [14]in order somehow to make my fellow Jews jealous, and thus save some of them. [15]For if their rejection means the reconciliation of the world, what will their acceptance mean but life from the dead? [16]If the dough offered as firstfruits is holy, so is the whole lump, and if the root is holy, so are the branches.

[17]But if some of the branches were broken off, and you, although a wild olive shoot, were grafted in among the others and now share in the nourishing root[b] of the olive tree, [18]do not be arrogant toward the branches. If you are, remember it is not you who support the root, but the root that supports you. [19]Then you will say, "Branches were broken off so that I might be grafted in." [20]That is true. They were broken off because of their unbelief, but you stand fast through faith. So do not become proud, but fear. [21]For if God did not spare the natural branches, neither will he spare you. [22]Note then the kindness and the severity of God: severity toward those who have fallen, but God's kindness to you, provided you continue in his kindness. Otherwise you too will be cut off. [23]And even they, if they do not continue in their unbelief, will be grafted in, for God has the power to graft them in again. [24]For if you were cut from what is by nature a wild olive tree, and grafted, contrary to nature, into a cultivated olive tree, how much more will these, the natural branches, be grafted back into their own olive tree.

a Greek *their fullness*   b Greek *root of richness*; some manuscripts *richness*

OVERVIEW: With Paul's vivid horticultural metaphor, the reformers admonish their audience to guard against arrogance. This passage, according to the reformers, removes any possible reason for boasting by again underscoring God's monergism. As a gardener cultivates a tree, deciding which branches are too lifeless and which branches might fit in well, so our Lord tends to his church. Several commentators implicitly distinguish law from gospel in this metaphor. First, those in-grafted should fear. In and of themselves they are no different from the branches cut away to make space for them; they too are but dead branches when severed from the life-giving tree of Christ's cross. Second, those in-grafted should praise and love God! They are nourished by the revitalizing blood of that tree and filled with its faith-granting Spirit. And so these foreign branches should cling to God's promises in Christ, acknowledging that apart from God's Son and Spirit they are unable to live and believe. Day by day, sustained by the trunk, they grow from grace to grace and glory to glory.

11:11-12 Paul Longs for the Full Inclusion of the Jews

GOD'S CHALLENGE. PHILIPP MELANCHTHON: The proposition set forth above is repeated. The Jews were not caused to stumble in order that the race might perish. The reason is sharply delineated and has an obvious meaning. For the argument is taken from the ultimate cause of the reception of the Gentiles, in this way: the Gentiles have been received in order that the Jews might be challenged to believe when they see that the gospel is efficacious in the Gentiles. Therefore it is necessary that there be some remnants among the Jews who will believe. For what need would there have been to challenge the Jews if none were going to believe?

Paul appends the consequence in this way: if their downfall served to challenge them, then there is some remnant that is unharmed, that is, there must be some part that can be healed. This idea can also be enlarged from the minor premise: If their downfall served the acceptance of the Gentiles, how much greater will the safety be of those who obeyed when they were challenged, because God challenged them for this purpose, that he might heal them and render them whole and unharmed. COMMENTARY ON ROMANS (1540).[1]

DIMINUTION AND FULLNESS. THEODORE BEZA: He explains what he understands by the phrase "the apostasy of the Jews," namely, the substitution of this people, because so few embraced the gospel, since the majority dashed against this rock, as it were. For the people who do not worship God in Christ are deemed to be not a people, with the result that the Jews are deservedly said to have been reduced to a small number by their haughtiness. But to their small number is juxtaposed the coming fullness, namely, when the whole nation will draw near to Christ for their common advantage. The same thing was determined concerning the fullness of the Gentiles, which he will mention below, in verse 25. But one must diligently note in this line of argumentation that the apostle undoubtedly is distinguishing between the nation of the Jews and that of the Gentiles in general, but is not speaking about individual human beings, and is evaluating the condition of those nations based on that diminution and fullness. Consequently, as long as the diminishment lasts, the Gentiles or Jews who had been removed are said to be grafted in, albeit under the fullness, although, if you should happen to look at individual people who came once to Christ and learned from him, such a person will never be cast out. ANNOTATIONS ON ROMANS 11:12.[2]

11:13-16 By Ministering to the Gentiles Paul Ministers to the Jews

AN EXHORTATION TO HUMILITY. TILEMANN HESSHUS: This wordy sermon is a most grave exhortation to the Gentiles. They should not squander this new benefit—that they have been given by the light of the gospel and that they have been accepted into the fellowship of the church—with pride and carelessness. They should not revile the Jews. Instead in the fear of God they should ponder how unworthy of this benefit of God they are and what great lovingkindness and mercy the eternal Father has shown them! Next they should contemplate the most grave severity of God, who did not spare his own people, but cut them off and cast them aside on account of their unbelief. And from this example they should learn for themselves what it's good for, how easily they could lose this remarkable blessedness and glory through carelessness and unbelief, and thus that they should strive to persevere in faith in God, fear of God and calling on God.

This Pauline exhortation we—who born not of the Jews but of Gentiles have entered the fellowship of the church—must always remember. The eternal Father has declared his immense lovingkindness and goodness to us. For although our ancestors not only worshiped idols, like the Gentiles, but were also polluted by the great craze for idolatry under the Roman antichrist, nevertheless he granted us the light of his gospel, called us to the fellowship of the church and placed us in the kingdom of his Son Jesus Christ, who shares righteousness, life and joy with us.

O omnipotent, merciful and most holy God, Father of our Lord Jesus Christ, I confess that I am wholly unworthy of such immense kindness of yours. Yes, to you through our Lord Jesus Christ I give thanks with my whole heart, that you have called me to the fellowship of the church, that you have given me your Son and that you have illuminated me with your Holy Spirit. O Lord Jesus, keep my soul, rule my heart with your Holy Spirit, increase and strengthen

---

[1]Melanchthon, *Commentary on Romans*, 205-6 (MO 15:698-99).
[2]Beza, *Annotationes majores*, 2:122.

my faith, so that to the end of my life I would persevere in faith, give thanks to you eternally and glorify your name! COMMENTARY ON ROMANS 11:13-24.[3]

THE MINISTRY TO GENTILES IS FOR THE BENEFIT OF THE JEWS. MARTIN LUTHER: How does he magnify his ministry? By glorying in the fact that even though the Jews have fallen, he is announcing to the Gentiles the riches of Christ. For he seems to be reproving the Jews for receiving nothing and diminishing themselves and making themselves sinners, whereas through his ministry the Gentiles have been made rich. Therefore, if such great good had come out of the Gentiles through his ministry, whereas it was taken away from the Jews, by this action he is surely proving the greatness of his ministry. But he does not glorify in such a way that he thereby brings pleasure to himself, but he does it for the salvation of others, so that the Jews, when they hear that they have fallen and that the Gentiles have been made rich and have accepted their riches, might be stimulated to seek the riches of the same ministry. But they would not be so stimulated if he said he had ministered something worthless to the Gentiles or that the Jews had lost nothing. SCHOLIA ON ROMANS 11:13.[4]

UNDERSTAND THIS SIMPLY. PHILIPP MEL-ANCHTHON: What Paul is saying is this: "I glorify my ministry, that is, I teach with great confidence and diligence the gospel by which the glory of God is adorned and shown, in order that I may challenge the flesh, that is, the Jews." And he adds an amplification from the minor premise: If their rejection was profitable, how much more glorious will their restitution be since it will be, as it were, a resurrection from the dead. This is the simple and least involved interpretation. COMMENTARY ON ROMANS (1540).[5]

HEREDITARY HOLINESS IS A FUNCTION OF THE COVENANT. JOHN CALVIN: Now as a result of this comparison between the honor of the Jews and the Gentiles, he annuls the arrogance of the Gentiles and pacifies the Jews, as much as he is able. For he shows that in no respect do the Gentiles surpass the Jews—however much they might allege any privilege of honor of their own. On the contrary, if it were a competition, the Gentiles would be left very far behind. In this comparison we should remember that one person is not compared with another person, but one nation with another nation. Therefore, if they are compared with one another, they will be found equal in this: that they both are equally sons of Adam. The only difference is that the Jews have been separated from the nations to become a special people for the Lord. And so they were made holy by the sacred covenant and adorned with special honor, with which God did not deem fit for the Gentiles at that time. But because the vitality of the covenant seemed meager then, he commands us to consider Abraham and the patriarchs, among whom surely God's blessing was not empty or void. Therefore Paul concludes that from Abraham and the patriarchs a hereditary holiness had passed to all their descendants. This conclusion would not be valid if it were only made concerning the person, and the reason for the promise had not been considered. For it is not the case that because the father is righteous he immediately transmits his uprightness to his son. Instead because the Lord by this agreement made Abraham holy for himself, so that his seed also would be holy, and so he has conferred holiness not only on his person but also on his entire offspring, the apostle does not wrongly infer that in their father Abraham all Jews have been made holy.

To confirm this, he offers two analogies: the first taken from the ceremonies of the law, the second borrowed from nature. For the firstfruits, which were offered, made the entire heap holy; similarly from the roots the goodness of the sap is diffused to the branches. And descendants have the same relationship with their parents, from whom they

---

[3]Hesshus, *Explicatio Epistolae Pauli ad Romanos*, 359v-360r.
[4]LW 25:426-27* (WA 56:434).
[5]Melanchthon, *Commentary on Romans*, 206 (MO 15:699).

originate, as the heap has with the firstfruits and the branch with the trees. Therefore it is not surprising if in their father the Jews were made holy.

Here there will be no difficulties, if you understand *holiness* not to be what properly belongs to nature, but what flowed from the covenant. It truly may be said, I admit, that the Jews are naturally holy, because among them their adoption is hereditary. But now concerning our first nature, we know that according to it all are cursed in Adam. For that reason the honor of an elect people, properly speaking, is a supernatural privilege. COMMENTARY ON ROMANS II:I6.[6]

CALVIN CONFUSES SPIRITUAL AND FLESHLY HOLINESS. TILEMANN HESSHUS: What Calvin argues in this passage—that a hereditary holiness was transferred to all the descendants of Abraham and that the entire people of Israel was sanctified in Abraham—is different from the mind of Paul. Paul is not speaking about the spiritual nobility of Israelite ancestry, since naturally the sons of Israel as much as the Gentiles were sons of wrath and subject to the curse. And so incorrectly and against the mind of Paul, Calvinists conclude from this passage that the children of faithful Christians are holy from their mother's womb—even before baptism. For Paul explicitly says concerning the Gentiles and Jews (and himself!): "By nature we all were sons of wrath." And Christ says: "Everything born of the flesh is flesh." Spiritual holiness is not transferred by fleshly generation, but by spiritual rebirth. For this reason Christ says: "Unless a person is born again by water and the Spirit, he will not enter the kingdom of God."

Persuaded by the clear testimony of Scripture, Calvin acknowledges that a righteous person does not transmit uprightness to his sons. But that he says that this is caused by the power of the promise—that the sons of holy people are holy— is clearly useless, for the promise without application is void. The promise had been given to the whole world. "The seed of the woman will crush the head of the serpent." Nevertheless, this promise has benefited no one, nor did it make anyone holy, except those who have applied it to themselves in faith. Thus the promise, "I will be your God and the God of your seed," does not make the sons of Abraham according to the flesh holy from their mother's womb; instead, it is talking specifically about Abraham's spiritual seed, born again through faith, in which Abraham excelled. To this seed God binds himself in this way: that he willingly cares for them as God, if they keep his covenant. That is, if, having followed in the footsteps of Abraham's faith in the Messiah who will bless the nations, they believe. For the entire promise must be seized by faith; without faith the promise is void.

Therefore the promise does not make the sons of Abraham according to the flesh holy from the womb—just as the first promise concerning the seed crushing the head of the serpent did not make Cain holy from the womb. And that promise, "Whoever believes in the Son has eternal life," does not now make the sons of the righteous holy from their mother's womb before baptism.

Therefore in this passage Paul is not talking about spiritual holiness, but about legal, external or Mosaic holiness, which has a certain congruence with the ceremonial law. For the law calls holy what has been devoted to holy things, and whatever was permitted for the saints to use. It called common, profane and illicit those things not permitted for the saints to use. Therefore Paul wants to say that those things offered as firstfruits to God are holy; it is permitted to use them with thanksgiving. In the same way, when God chose the patriarchs and prophets and made them righteous as a kind of firstfruits of the people of Israel, he testified that by no means would he reject the entire people of Israel, but that from them he would select those whom he will save for his own gracious purpose.

"If the root is holy, so are the branches." He is not talking about spiritual holiness, but about legal holiness. It's as if he were saying: "If God can use

---

[6]CTS 38:425-27* (CO 49:220-21).

the root, he can use the branches in his own sanctuary. For according to the law, if the roots are holy, the branches and fruit are holy." If someone were to understand these things about spiritual holiness, then the most absurd ideas would follow. COMMENTARY ON ROMANS 11:13-24.[7]

TITHES AND HOLY GOODS; BAPTISM AND HOLY CHILDREN. DAVID PAREUS: The mass itself is holy, the branches are holy too, according to the formula of the covenant: "I will be your God and your seed's God." Therefore it should not be doubted, if they are now cast aside, they will be accepted again. If now they have died, they will be brought back to life again from the dead.

First, by the law of firstfruits the Jews were admonished and we are admonished that the fruits of the earth and all that is born do not owe their success to us; rather they are bestowed by God, to whom then some portion must be owed by the law of acknowledgment and gratitude, so that the use of the rest would be holy and healthy for us. Formerly God claimed the firstfruits and tithe for himself through the Mosaic law. This law has been removed. Yes indeed. But for that reason God's right to our crops has not been removed. And so as those things that we offer to God and the poor in God's name are holy—voluntary obedience or firstfruits or the tithe or some civic obligation—so through the holy firstfruits or tithe, the rest of the mass has been made holy for us.

Second, the covenant honor of the church passing from parents to their children is taught and confirmed. For as the promises made to the parents and to their children, by the law of the covenant, formerly pertained to the Jewish church, so today they pertain to the Christian church. And so from the holy roots the branches are made holy; from Christian parents Christian children are made holy. Otherwise the apostle would not argue this to be so. He confirms this again in 1 Corinthians 7: "Otherwise your children would

be unclean, but now they are holy." From this the great difference between children of the church and children of pagans is clear; it is as different as between holy and profane. According to this law, to the children of the Jews pertained the right of the covenant and the city of God, circumcision, the promises and other privileges given to the patriarchs by God according to the promise: "I will be your God and your seed's God." St. Peter used this argument to console the Jews who were cut to the heart on Pentecost: they should not despair, but should be baptized and accept the forgiveness of their sins in faith from Christ. According to the same law, to the children of Christians pertains the right of the covenant, God's promise, baptism and other privileges of the city of God, by the same promise: "I will be your God," etc. If not, a worse condition would be established in this new church than in the old church. And so, according to this law, our children are to be baptized and made holy. The children of the Turks are profane and outsiders; they are not given in baptism until they become children of the church. COMMENTARY ON ROMANS 11:16.[8]

THE APOSTLES ARE THE FIRSTFRUITS OF THE JEWS. MARTIN LUTHER: The Latin word *delibatio* is here used for the Greek *aparchē*, that is, "first-fruits," or what is offered from the first and best of the crop. And this is a more apt and fitting way to describe the meaning of the apostle than the term *delibatio*. It is as if he were saying: If the apostles are holy people who have been taken from among the Jews as the firstfruits and as the most precious part, as it were, then the whole nation, since they are of the same stock and nature, must not be despised because of their unbelief. SCHOLIA ON ROMANS 11:16.[9]

---

[7]Hesshus, *Explicatio Epistolae Pauli ad Romanos*, 360v-361v; citing Gen 3:15; 17:1-8; Jn 3:36.

[8]Pareus, *In Epistolam ad Romanos*, 1110-12; citing Gen 17:1-8; 1 Cor 7:14; Acts 2:37-41. Pareus's reasoning echoes Calvin's argument that baptism (the sign of the new covenant) and its benefits must be at least as good as circumcision (the sign of the old covenant) and its benefits. See *Institutes* 4.16.4; LCC 21:1327 (CO 2:978-79).

[9]LW 25:427* (WA 56:435).

11:17-18 Branches Grafted In

The Sacred Tree of Jews and Gentiles.
Jacques Lefèvre d'Étaples: Jeremiah insinuates that the community of the Hebrews is rightly called an olive tree, speaking thus about it: "The Lord called your name 'a luxuriant, beautiful, fruit-bearing, and splendid olive tree.'" And this spiritual grafting is remarkable and contrary to physical in-grafting. For in a physical in-grafting a fertile branch is grafted into a wild tree, and the branch does not draw its condition from the trunk, but rather what was inserted preserves its nature. Indeed, from an infertile trunk a tree that has received grafted branches is made more fertile. However, in the spiritual grafting that Paul is talking about here, it happens in the opposite way. For what is inserted does not retain its nature, but imitates the fecundity of the trunk and its condition, deriving nothing from itself but from the trunk. Therefore, if the grafting in of the Gentiles were similar to a physical grafting, they would perhaps have something in themselves from which they might be able to boast. But since the opposite is true, they do not have anything in themselves from which they might be able to boast, but only in the trunk. But the trunk in which the church and all the children of the church are planted is Christ.

If you make the church the bride, Christ is the groom. If you make the church the body, Christ is the head. If you make the church a temple or a city, Christ is the cornerstone, the mountain, the foundation. If you make the church an olive tree, Christ is the trunk that carries it in himself, makes it fertile and waters it. And if we look carefully at this spiritual olive tree, the Jews have the first parts, inasmuch as they are natural parts of the tree. The Gentiles have the second parts, since they are branches that have been grafted into the tree. And that is a great reason for us both to love and to fear. To love, when we consider the kindness of God toward us, who were not natural branches, to be sure, but God grafted us into the sacred olive tree. But also to fear, when we consider the harsh severity of God's justice concerning the Jews, the natural branches of the olive tree, which he cut off from the sacred olive tree. And he did it for us because of our faith, but for the Jews because of their unfaithfulness. How then will we not fear that we will be cut off and lopped off, if we fall from the faith, since we are not the natural branches? And how would we not see that, if faithful Jews are found, they would be grafted better than us into their own, natural olive tree? This is an argument from the lesser to the greater; it follows of necessity. Annotations on Romans 11:16-21.[10]

Our Mother Church. Wolfgang Musculus: And this passage reveals not only that the one church is made from Jews and Gentiles, but also that we have been grafted into the church of Israel—she is our mother. We receive her abundance; not she ours. We both share this abundance, that is, the heavenly grace, by which we are nourished. And as many of us who have been chosen for life and true piety obtain it. There is no other God, there is no other grace, there is no other Spirit, there is no other piety, nor other Mediator and Redeemer of the old covenant than of the new covenant. Commentary on Romans 11:17.[11]

The Holy Trunk Remains. John Calvin: Paul wisely mitigates the severity of the case, by not saying that the whole top of the tree was cut off, but that some of the branches were broken, and also that God took some here and there from among the Gentiles, whom he set in the holy and blessed trunk. Commentary on Romans 11:17.[12]

Fruitless Without Faith. Wolfgang Musculus: "Although you were a wild olive tree"—that's what we would be outside of faith in Christ: some barren wild olive tree. Commentary on Romans 11:17.[13]

---

[10]Lefèvre d'Étaples, *Epistola ad Rhomanos*, 90v*; citing Jer 11:16.
[11]Musculus, *In epistolam Apostoli Pauli ad Romanos commentarii*, 196-97.
[12]CTS 38.428* (CO 49:221).
[13]Musculus, *In epistolam Apostoli Pauli ad Romanos commentarii*, 197.

11:19-21 If Natural Branches Have Been Lopped Off, How Much More the Grafted Branches!

REPRESS ARROGANCE AND UNBELIEF. DESIDERIUS ERASMUS: Why are the Jews plucked from the olive tree? Because they refused to believe. Why are the Gentiles grafted in? Because they obeyed the gospel. This is what Paul himself argues: "They were broken off because of their unbelief." That is undoubtedly in either case because they refused to believe. To those plucked off he gives the hope that they may be grafted in if, abandoning their unbelief, they choose to believe, and to those grafted in he instills fear lest they may fall if they turn themselves from the grace of God. "You," he says, "stand fast only through faith. So do not become proud, but stand in awe." . . . All this shows clearly that Paul's sole object here is to repress the arrogance at once both of the Gentiles and the Jews. ON THE FREEDOM OF THE WILL.[14]

TRUST GOD'S GOODNESS NOT YOURS. JOHN CALVIN: This is a most powerful reason to beat down all self-confidence. For the rejection of the Jews should never come across our minds without striking and shaking us with dread. For what ruined them, but that through supine dependence on the dignity that they had obtained they despised what God had appointed? They were not spared, though they were natural branches; what then shall be done to us, who are the wild olives and aliens, if we become arrogant beyond measure? But this thought, as it leads us to distrust ourselves, so it tends to make us cleave more firmly and steadfastly to the goodness of God. COMMENTARY ON ROMANS 11:21.[15]

HUMILITY, DOWNFALL AND COMFORT. PHILIPP MELANCHTHON: Now he turns to the Gentiles. He exhorts them not to despise the Jews out of carnal security, nor run securely up against God, trusting in this title, that they are the people of God or the church. Thus now the popes promise themselves in carnal security that they are the church, and as a result of this opinion they establish and do many things against the Word of God. God will without doubt punish this wickedness according to the second commandment. As Ezekiel says: "On account of us the name of God is in bad repute among the heathen."

What Paul here prophesies about the downfall of the church of the Gentiles shows the outcome. The church in Asia and Africa, having scarcely been founded, was destroyed by the rage of Muhammad. In Europe it is being dreadfully oppressed by idolatry and ungodliness, by the profanation of the Masses, the invocation of the saints, by the superstitious opinions of human acts of worship, by ignorance of the doctrine of faith.

But we should comfort ourselves in the midst of these offenses with the fact that the promises of the gospel are always valid for believers, and that there is always some true church, namely, those who repent and truly believe. Christ promises that the church will always remain and that the promises are immutable. COMMENTARY ON ROMANS (1540).[16]

11:22-24 The Kind and Just Gardener

HAVE COMPASSION FOR THE LOPPED OFF BRANCHES. MARTIN LUTHER: In opposition to this many people are proud with marvelous stupidity when they call the Jews dogs, evildoers or whatever they like, while they too, and equally, do not realize who or what they are in the sight of God. Boldly they heap blasphemous insults on them when they ought to have compassion on them and fear the same punishments for themselves. Moreover, as if they are certain concerning themselves and others, they rashly pronounce themselves blessed and the others cursed. Such

---

[14]LCC 17:70*; citing Rom 11:20, 25.
[15]CTS 38:430* (CO 49:222).

[16]Melanchthon, *Commentary on Romans*, 206-7 (MO 15:699-700); citing Ezek 36:23.

today are the theologians of Cologne,[17] who are so stupid in their zeal that in their articles, or rather in their inarticulate and inept writings, they say that the Jews are accursed. Why? Because they have forgotten what is said in the following chapter: "Bless, and do not curse," and in another place: "When reviled, we bless; when slandered, we try to conciliate." They wish to convert the Jews by force and curses, but God will resist them. SCHOLIA ON ROMANS 11:22.[18]

NO ROOM FOR PRIDE—OR DESPAIR. DAVID PAREUS: This is the final conclusion of the speech (spoken in reply to the earlier conclusion), which he treats at length all the way to the end from his hope for the restoration of the Jews. You will be cut off if you do not remain in the faith. They, in contrast, will be inserted again if they do not remain in unbelief. Therefore you do not have any reason to extol yourself or to despise them. Therefore, just as hypocrites and apostates have something to fear, so those who have fallen away by their lack of faithfulness have something to hope in, provided they return to God in repentance and faith. Therefore he forbids us to despair about the salvation of any human being, no matter how cut off or alienated from the faith. And so he forbids us to despair about the conversion of even the Jews. Much less, however, should we despair of our own salvation, even if the flesh and the world attempt to cut off our faith. For nobody who desires salvation is rejected, as John 6 says: "The one coming to me I will not cast out." Nobody who has been cast out will be forsaken by God but

will be inserted again, provided that he does not remain in unbelief. Therefore the apostle gives hope to the rejected Jews for their restitution, namely, that God will raise them up and draw them to faith in Christ.

But what are we to say? The condition seems uncertain if they do not remain. For perhaps they will remain—and that too seems impossible. For a branch that has been cut off is not able to insert itself again into the tree. A dead branch cannot make itself alive, an unbeliever cannot reject his unbelief and pour faith into himself. Therefore this seems to be no consolation. To be sure, Chrysostom, who defends free will excessively here out of his debt to Greek philosophy, in general leaves it in a person's capability to remain in faith and to reject unbelief; here they do not have anything by which they can escape or that they can say in reply so that this consolation may remain firm, unless they confess with the apostle that our conversion, our faith and our endurance lies in the power and will of God alone. For this is what the apostle further teaches, confirming that that condition is neither impossible nor doubtful. It is *not impossible* because God can graft them back in. Thus in the matter of conversion and faith he draws us away from human preparations, capacities, strengths, attempts, zeal and will, and draws us to God alone. For God is he who works to will and to do. Therefore he does not say, "They will be grafted in again, if they do not remain in unbelief, and they will not remain in unbelief because it is in their hands; they can convert themselves, come to their senses and believe." Nevertheless, a bad tree cannot bear good fruit; a leopard cannot change its spots; a branch that has been lopped off cannot graft itself back in. And yet all unbelievers are bad trees, spotted leopards and lopped-off branches. COMMENTARY ON ROMANS 11:23.[19]

---

[17]Led by Jewish convert Johannes Pfefferkorn (1469–1523), the Dominican theologians of Cologne sought to impel the conversion of the Jews through the destruction of their books. While gaining the support of the emperor in 1509, an extended controversy was sparked with Hebraist Johannes Reuchlin, who recognized the importance of Jewish texts for Christian exegetes and ridiculed the supporters of this measure for their reactionary and ignorant opinions.
[18]LW 25:428-29* (WA 56:436); citing Rom 12:14; 1 Cor 4:12-13.

[19]Pareus, *In Epistolam ad Romanos*, 1124-25; citing Jn 6:37; Jer 13:23; Mt 7:18.

11:25-36 THE MYSTERY OF ISRAEL'S SALVATION

[25]Lest you be wise in your own sight, I do not want you to be unaware of this mystery, brothers:[a] a partial hardening has come upon Israel, until the fullness of the Gentiles has come in. [26]And in this way all Israel will be saved, as it is written,

"The Deliverer will come from Zion,
    he will banish ungodliness from Jacob";
[27] "and this will be my covenant with them
    when I take away their sins."

[28]As regards the gospel, they are enemies for your sake. But as regards election, they are beloved for the sake of their forefathers. [29]For the gifts and the calling of God are irrevocable. [30]For just as you were at one time disobedient to God but now have received mercy because of their disobedience, [31]so they too have now been disobedient in order that by the mercy shown to you they also may now[b] receive mercy. [32]For God has consigned all to disobedience, that he may have mercy on all.

[33]Oh, the depth of the riches and wisdom and knowledge of God! How unsearchable are his judgments and how inscrutable his ways!

[34] "For who has known the mind of the Lord,
    or who has been his counselor?"
[35] "Or who has given a gift to him
    that he might be repaid?"

[36]For from him and through him and to him are all things. To him be glory forever. Amen.

a Or brothers and sisters   b Some manuscripts omit now

OVERVIEW: The reformers marvel at and puzzle over God's Israel, the church. That God has consigned all to disobedience so that he could have mercy on all is a mystery that should cause every mortal to tremble. How strange that by this decree God is no respecter of persons! In this way he removes any opportunity for human merit in salvation. We all fall short. The reformers warn us that we should not try to measure God's justice with our puny human standards. "Who is this that darkens counsels by words without knowledge?" (Job 38:2). Instead we should memorize this succinct statement of divine doctrine—the law and the gospel—and ponder in our hearts these lofty words and teachings. God's plan for our salvation is incomprehensible, and it cannot be improved.

The apostle ends his treatment of election in praise, the reformers observe. Our Lord has mercifully crafted fences for us to remain within, namely, his Word. And even within these boundaries there is more than enough for human beings to ponder. "Deep calls to deep" (Ps 42:7). The reformers pray that by his Word and Spirit God would correct our ignorance and calm our outrage. We cannot know the hidden will of God, yet we must remember that his hidden will does not contradict his revealed will, which he has given us for his glory in his mercy.

In Paul's closing benediction the reformers see the highest doctrine of Christian faith: the Trinity. While other passages are more helpful for constructing, affirming and proving the doctrine of the Trinity, they remark, it is fitting and right to read it here too. The apostle's words point to the fact that the external works of the Trinity are indivisible (*opera Trinitatis ad extra sunt indivisa*); together God the Father and God the Son and God the Holy Spirit effect their one will and purpose. "Holy, holy, holy is the LORD of hosts; the whole earth is full of his glory!" (Is 6:3).

11:25-28 The Paradox of Israel and the Nations

PROPHECY OF FUTURE CONVERSION. PHILIPP MELANCHTHON: Paul adds a prophecy about the conversion of the Jews, which should perhaps be understood in this way: It will come to pass that later, before the end of the world, some from among the Jews will be converted. But I do not know whether he wants to say that there will be a conversion of a great multitude around the time of the end of the world. Since this is a mystery, let us commit it to God. The prophecy of Isaiah preaches about the liberation of the people, namely, about that liberation which the gospel actually describes, that is, about the remission of sins. It is a sweet statement because it teaches clearly that in the new testament forgiveness of sins is to be preached. This liberation of the people is to be understood as extending from the beginning of the preaching of the gospel until the end. COMMENTARY ON ROMANS (1540).[1]

GOD'S PROMISE TO ABRAHAM. THEODORE BEZA: That is to say, "until" defines the amount of time, which indeed seems now for the most part to have been completed. For (I ask you) how few nations are there today in the world who do not profess Christ, at least nominally? But meanwhile the people of the Jews, although they have been scattered across the whole globe and tossed to and fro most wretchedly, cannot say nonetheless (as all who come to us from Asia and Africa universally confirm) how populous and numerous that people is, so that even now that blessing made to Abraham in Genesis 22:7 exerts itself. But who would not see that this is not being done rashly by God, and that today that nation employs against those who profess the gospel a cruelty and rage that clearly deserves that somehow, just as we once succeeded the Jews who had been cast out by their profession, they in turn will now succeed us? But what the apostle calls the "fullness of the Gentiles"

I have already explained above, in verse 12. However, he uses the word "enter" in accordance with the custom of Scripture, which speaks about the assembly of the church as if it were in some certain place. ANNOTATIONS ON ROMANS 11:25.[2]

PAUL PROPHESIES THE FALL OF THE GENTILE CHURCH. TILEMANN HESSHUS: To stir up more vigorously the Gentile's diligence and zeal in keeping the faith, Paul prophesies concerning the fall of the church of the Gentiles, and predicts that horrible darkness will follow again. He also reminds us concerning the future that some of the Jews will always turn to the Mediator Jesus Christ. For God wants to be visible in his church continually, and most just is his severity in punishing the contempt of his gospel—whether this most grievous sin is committed by Jews or by Gentiles. Next he wants his immense mercy to shine on the world, by which he calls human beings to repentance, illumines and saves those who were most worthy of eternal rejection. And the whole church's history and those things that we see daily clearly testify that Paul has prophesied in the Spirit of God concerning most serious matters. As also in other epistles he predicted with eloquent words the terrible darkness that will follow. While the apostles themselves were still instructing the church and handing down the gospel, many imposters arose.

These imposters corrupted the chief articles [of the faith], and scattered dangerous errors among the common people. Many from the circumcision faction argued that the observance of the law was necessary to obtain righteousness. Ebion and Cerinthus denied Christ's divine nature. Hymeneus and others denied the resurrection of the flesh. Immediately after the apostles a great multitude of heretics arose in the church of the Gentiles; they obscured and corrupted the chief parts of heavenly doctrine, and they dragged with them a huge number of erring people into eternal destruction. Finally, in the East, the Muhammadan barbarity and blasphemy and, in the West, the craze for

---

[1] Melanchthon, *Commentary on Romans*, 207* (MO 15:700); citing Is 59:20-21.

[2] Beza, *Annotationes majores*, 2:125-26.

idolatry and superstition of the monks ravaged and ruined the chief churches in the world. Because Paul in the Spirit foresaw so great a fall of the church of the Gentiles, the Gentiles were stirred up to call on and fear the true God in all seriousness, that they not grow arrogant and self-assured, but in all zeal try to preserve the gospel's purity. COMMENTARY ON ROMANS 11:25.[3]

"ISRAEL" MEANS THE PEOPLE OF GOD. JOHN CALVIN: Many understand this of the Jewish people, as though Paul had said that religion would again be restored among them as before. I, however, extend the word *Israel* to all the people of God, according to this meaning: "When the Gentiles shall come in, the Jews also shall return from their defection to the obedience of faith; and thus shall be completed the salvation of the whole Israel of God, which must be gathered from both; and yet in such a way that the Jews shall obtain the first place, being as it were the firstborn in God's family." This interpretation seems to me the most suitable, because Paul intended here to set forth the completion of the kingdom of Christ, which is by no means to be confined to the Jews, but is to include the whole world. He does not confirm the whole passage by this testimony of Isaiah, but only one clause: that the children of Abraham shall be partakers of redemption. But if one takes this view, that Christ had been promised and offered to them, but because they rejected him, they were deprived of his grace; yet the prophet's words express more, even this: that there will be some remnant, who, having repented, shall enjoy the favor of deliverance. COMMENTARY ON ROMANS 11:26.[4]

THE UNITY AND USE OF SCRIPTURE. DAVID PAREUS: He also introduces Scripture passages to confirm the mystery. Wasn't it enough for faith in the mystery that the apostle affirmed it by the Spirit of God? It was enough, to be sure. Nonetheless, as he has done everywhere up until now, he

summons the prophetic Scriptures, repeating that phrase, "As it is written," so that he might make clear what he said in his defense to King Agrippa, "I am saying nothing other than those things that the Prophets and Moses foretold would happen."

First, let this strengthen us concerning the harmony and concordance of the prophetic and apostolic Scriptures. Nothing is told in the New Testament pertaining to salvific faith that had not been foretold in the Old. Nothing was promised in the Old that is not taught as fulfilled in the New. Thus the apostolic Scripture is nothing other than a commentary on the prophetic Scripture. The New Testament is nothing other than an illustration and fulfillment of the Old. Therefore there is one testament, one Scripture, one faith, one church—which must be held onto against the fanatics, the enemies of Moses and the Prophets.

Second, he entrusts to us again the honor and use of the sacred Scriptures, that from them alone *asphaleian* ["assurance"] and certainty ought to be sought and obtained. For whatever is said in matters of faith outside of the Scriptures is rejected and approved with equal ease. Therefore the Scriptures define our faith as an immovable boundary and the first truth that norms all others, and every theological doctrine and demonstration in the end necessarily is resolved by going to the Scriptures alone. This is the sentiment and consensus of all antiquity. COMMENTARY ON ROMANS 11:26.[5]

THE PROPHETS' PROPHECY OF THE MESSIAH. TILEMANN HESSHUS: The testimony of the prophet Isaiah proves that the Son of God was established by the Father as the deliverer of the entire church, and that for this he would be sent: to take away sins as well as to save the unworthy. From this it follows that the Jews who had been elected to life Christ would free from sin and save—and not just Gentiles. The prophecy of the prophet not only speaks of deliverance but also about the whole office of the Messiah and about the time of the Messiah's advent. He was sent for this: to take away from Jacob his sins, that is,

---

[3]Hesshus, *Explicatio Epistolae Pauli ad Romanos*, 362r-363r.
[4]CTS 38:437-38* (CO 49:226-27); citing Is 59:20-21.

[5]Pareus, *In Epistolam ad Romanos*, 1132-33; citing Acts 26:22.

to deliver the church from sin, death, the wrath of God and the curse of the law. And in this way through faith he would freely justify and save the unworthy. Jesus Christ exercised his office for all ages, gathering a church from all nations. . . . This distinguished prophecy of Isaiah pertains to the entire church altogether, and so also to the Gentiles. In this passage Paul certainly urges the conversion of the Jews in accordance with Isaiah's prophecy, and most correctly. For the name Jacob not only means the entire church, gathered from all nations, which is the spiritual Jacob, but also especially those who from the people of Israel turn to God. Therefore it is correctly gathered from this testimony, that some Jews will always be converted to Christ.

Indeed Paul is chiefly concerned with quoting the testimony of a passage in Isaiah 59. But at the same time he touches other prophecies of the Prophets concerning the kingdom and office of the Messiah. He elucidates and explains these, especially the prophecy in Isaiah 43: "I am the one who blots out your sins." Also, Jeremiah 31: "This is my covenant: I will pardon their sin, and I will not record their iniquities." And Isaiah 53: "Because he has born their sins himself." And Micah: "Who is a God like you? Who pardons and removes sins from the remnants of his inheritance?" These and similar passages of the Prophets Paul considered with a single glance. For that reason this remarkable explanation of the prophetic prophecies and the distinguished description of the kingdom of Christ should be noted here.

First, the apostle teaches that Jesus Christ is the eternal and omnipotent God, who says in the Prophets: "I am the Lord your God, who blots out your sin." And: "Who is a God like you, who takes away iniquity?" Second, he teaches from where the Messiah is going to come and where he'll teach and begin his kingdom, namely, from Judea and in Zion. Third, he teaches, that the Messiah's kingdom is spiritual, not worldly. For the Messiah was not promised to seize the world's empires and to establish Jewish governors over these provinces. Instead he is promised to be the Deliverer who rescues us from sin, from death, from Satan's tyranny, and to restore righteousness, joyfulness and eternal

life for us. Fourth, he shows that the Jews have no privilege over the Gentiles in justification; rather they too are sinners, and they need the Deliverer and Mediator, who freely pardons sins and justifies. Fifth, he shows the distinction between the old testament or covenant and the new, for he proves from the Prophets what the new covenant consists of, that God freely remits and removes iniquities. Also the old covenant does not speak of the free remission of sins but requires perfect obedience, and threatens the horrible wrath and curse of God on sinners. Therefore the new differs from the old testament in every way. Sixth, he teaches that God always preserves in the human race the church, and both from Jews and from Gentiles he will turn some to faith in Jesus Christ. COMMENTARY ON ROMANS 11:26-27.[6]

GOD KEEPS HIS PROMISES. JOHN CALVIN: He shows that the worst feature in the Jews ought not to subject them to the contempt of the Gentiles. Their chief crime was unbelief. But Paul teaches us that they were thus blinded for a time by God's providence, so that a way to the gospel might be made for the Gentiles—and still they were not forever excluded from the favor of God. He then admits that they were for the present alienated from God on account of the gospel, so that thus the salvation, which at first was deposited with them, might come to the Gentiles. Yet God was not unmindful of the covenant that he had made with their fathers, and by which he testified that according to his eternal purpose he loved that nation. This he confirms by this remarkable declaration, that the grace of the divine calling cannot be made void. COMMENTARY ON ROMANS 11:28.[7]

OUR GOD IS INERRANT AND IMMUTABLE. DESIDERIUS ERASMUS: God formerly made a covenant with this nation, and having once sanctified that covenant he will not allow it to become null and void through the fault of some

---

[6]Hesshus, *Explicatio Epistolae Pauli ad Romanos*, 364r-365r; citing Is 59:20-21; 43:25; Jer 31:33-34; Is 53:4; Mic 7:18.
[7]CTS 38:440* (CO 49:228).

who behave themselves in a way unworthy of the promises. . . . For they did not fall from the grace of God to such an extent that they cannot be reconciled. Very many of them do not accept the gospel of Christ but adhere to the letter of the law, and are thus enemies of God; and (lest you scoff at them) this has worked to your advantage, because when they rejected the gospel it was offered all the sooner to you. However, they are descended from holy men and belong to the one nation that God chose for himself from among all nations as his own; commended by these things, they are beloved by God. Consequently they will be received more easily into grace if they recover their senses, because God has promised to their fathers what we are preaching. For God does not, in our human way, promise a gift or receive into adoption only to repent later and change his mind. He is absolutely immutable, for just as he never errs, neither does he ever need to repent. He will remember his promise as soon as they cease to reject it. . . . It is wrong to gloat over the fallen, especially if their fall has worked to your advantage. Rather we should rejoice when they come to their senses. PARAPHRASE ON ROMANS 11:28-29.[8]

11:29-32 God's Immutable and Unfathomable Election

GOD'S UNCHANGING PROMISES. TILEMANN HESSHUS: This is a remarkable sentence concerning the certainty and immutability of the divine promises. God has promised that he would gather a church from the descendants of Abraham. So, even though the Jews defiled themselves with horrible iniquities—they discarded the gospel, persecuted the prophets and crucified the Messiah—nevertheless, on account of his immense steadfastness, lovingkindness and truthfulness God does not change his verdict, but gathers to himself a church from the Israelites, the persecutors and executors of his own Son. Therefore no one, on

account of his indignity, should consider themselves excluded from the kingdom of the Messiah; no one should doubt the unchanging truth and eternal certainty of the divine promises.

From this we should also learn that the promises of spiritual goods are always valid for us, and that the way of salvation stands open for us through Christ. And this is so even if the goods of this life should be denied us or snatched from us, as Job piously says: "Even if he slays me, nevertheless, I will hope in him." For although the Jews lost their kingdom, their state, their ancestral home and all earthly blessing; nevertheless, salvation is not denied to them, if only they turn to Christ the Mediator in true faith. COMMENTARY ON ROMANS 11:29.[9]

ASSURANCE AND CONSOLATION CONCERNING GOD'S CALL. DAVID PAREUS: He proves the love of God for this nation from the immutability of the divine counsel. At the same time, what he had earlier called "the election and the fathers," here he calls "the gifts and calling," and thus he interprets himself. He does not understand "gifts" to mean any old gifts, but the gifts that flow from the grace of election. He does not understand the "calling" to be an external calling (for this often fails) but the internal calling that is always efficacious, which takes place through the Spirit. Concerning this calling he had said, "Those whom he had predestined, these he called, justified and glorified." These are *ametameleta* ["irrevocable"], that is, they are immutable insofar as they pertain to God. This is a metonymy of effect for cause. For repentance is the cause of a change, but we do not change those things for which we do not repent. But it is not possible that God would repent of his calling. Why? Because it flows from his very good, extremely wise and immutable counsel. Therefore it is immutable. Haymo puts it this way: "Repentance is understood to be a change. Therefore the gifts and calling of God are without change in

---

[9]Hesshus, *Explicatio Epistolae Pauli ad Romanos*, 365v-366r; citing Job 13:15.

those concerning whom it was earlier said, 'Those whom he predestined he also called,' not in those concerning whom it is said, 'Many are called, but few are chosen.'"

Here is a noteworthy consolation for the godly concerning the *asphaleia* ["assurance, certainty"] of our faith and our salvation. For if the gifts of election have been given to us one time by God, he will never repent of them; therefore he will never remove them. But what if we ourselves should reject them? What God gives he not only does not take away, but also preserves. But if God is preserving us, we will not reject the gifts, and we are not even able to reject them because we do not want to do so, for God does not bring about in us a will to reject them but rather a zeal to persevere. This is what Peter says: "You are being guarded by God's power for salvation through faith." Calvin makes this a hendiadys: "Gift and calling" is to be understand as meaning "the gift of calling." COM-MENTARY ON ROMANS 11:29.[10]

THE LORD USES BOTH JEWS AND GENTILES FOR THE BENEFIT OF THE OTHER. THOMAS WILSON: The pith and sinews of this argument consists in the following: there is as much or rather more force in what is the good to produce a good effect than there is in what is evil to bring about a good end. Therefore the blindness of the Jews, although it is a sin, yet because it was God's work, had an end that was so good that it brought the conversion of the Gentiles. COM-MENTARY ON ROMANS.[11]

HUMAN JUSTICE CANNOT JUDGE DIVINE JUSTICE. JOHN CALVIN: They play with the frivolous argument that, since God is Father of all, it is unjust for him to forsake any but those who by

their own guilt previously have deserved this punishment. As if God's generosity did not extend even to pigs and dogs! But if it is a question of humankind, let them answer why God bound himself to one people, to be their Father; also why he picked a small number out of these, like a flower. But their own passion to speak evil prevents these revilers from considering that "God makes the sun rise on the good and the evil," so that the inheritance is entrusted to those few to whom he will sometime say, "Come, blessed of my Father, inherit the kingdom," etc. They also object that God hates nothing he has made. This I concede to them; yet what I teach stands firm: that the reprobate are hateful to God, and with very good reason. For, deprived of his Spirit, they can bring forth nothing but reason for cursing. They add that "there is no distinction between Jew and Gentile," and that consequently God's grace is extended to all indiscriminately. Provided, to be sure, that they admit, as Paul states, that "God calls people both from the Jews and from the Gentiles according to his good pleasure," so that he is bound to no one. In this way we also dispose of their objection made in another place, that "God has shut up all things under sin, that he may have mercy on all"; that is to say, because he wills that the salvation of all who are saved be ascribed to his own mercy, although this benefit is not common to all. Now when many notions are adduced on both sides, let this be our conclusion: to tremble with Paul at so deep a mystery; but, if froward tongues clamor, not to be ashamed of this exclamation of his: "Who are you, o human being, to argue with God?" For as Augustine truly contends, they who measure divine justice by the standard of human justice are acting perversely. INSTITUTES 3.24.17.[12]

YOU ARE RESPONSIBLE FOR YOUR RESPONSE TO THE WORD. HANS DENCK: Such work is accomplished by the Word of God, which preaches

[10]Pareus, *In Epistolam ad Romanos*, 1135-36; citing 1 Pet 1:5. Compare Haymo, *Commentary on Romans* 11:29; PL 117:466. It is unclear whether Haymo the bishop of Halberstadt (d. 853) or Haymo of Auxerre (d. ca. 878) wrote this work; Pareus would have thought Haymo of Halberstadt, the more well-known figure and student of Alcuin (d. 804), the author. See Calvin, *Commentary on Romans* 11:29, CTS 38:440; CO 49:228.
[11]Wilson, *Commentary upon Romanes*, 989*.
[12]LCC 21:986-87*(CO 2:728); citing Mt 5:45; 25:34; Rom 10:12; 9:24; 11:32; Gal 3:22; Rom 9:20; Pseudo-Augustine, *Of Predestination and Grace* 2 (MPL 45:1667).

damnation to humankind, saying, "You have inflicted this on yourselves. Do not therefore blame someone else. You deserve to suffer what you yourselves have willed." DIVINE ORDER (1527).[13]

ALL THE ELECT FROM THE JEWS AND GENTILES.
THEODORE BEZA: "Them all," *tous pantas*, that is, first the Jews, then those Greeks, namely, the elect concerning whom he has been discoursing, as also the appended article demonstrates. Therefore the meaning is not that God wishes to have pity on all human beings one by one and that there is no particular election in the eternal counsel of God (which is a ridiculous thing to think, since there can be no election of all human beings without exception), but rather that we may know that all who are saved, whether from among the Jews or from among the Greeks, are saved in no other way than by mercy, since all people in themselves are guilty of eternal death. The old translation [i.e., the Vulgate] rendered it as "everything." The same meaning remains, however, inasmuch as the apostle speaks in this way in Galatians 3:28. It is a universal particle limited to those people concerning whom there is discussion, namely, with the intention of removing a distinction between people groups.[14] Therefore those who abuse this testimony in order to overturn the eternal predestination of God, by which he destined some for mercy and others for the severity of his judgment, miss the point altogether. The Vulgate reads *ta panta*, that is, "everything," as also does the Codex Claromontanus, but the meaning stays the same as the phrase *tous pantas* ["all (people)"], as in John 12:32. ANNOTATIONS ON ROMANS 11:32.[15]

THE LAW AND GOSPEL IN A SENTENCE.
TILEMANN HESSHUS: This very grave sentence not only explains the reason why God permitted

first the Gentiles then the Jews to fall into such great disbelief and error—without a doubt so that he made it clear that human beings are not justified by works or merit but only by God's lovingkindness and mercy. But also the entire argument, which he has handled so far, he finishes with this remarkable conclusion, and gathers together the whole argument in this very brief summary: "God has consigned," he says, "all to unbelief." That is, the whole world is guilty before God, and all lack the righteousness and glory of God. Neither are Jews righteous, nor do heathens have anything to boast about before God. However, God offers his lovingkindness to the entire human race. "So that he may have mercy on all," he says. God hinders no one from the fountain of his goodness.

This is the briefest summary of the entire heavenly doctrine, encompassing both law and gospel at once. For the law consigns all to sin and unbelief; however, the gospel announces God's lovingkindness to all. Therefore such a noble sentence, which contains in itself all the principal parts of heavenly doctrine, should be imprinted on our heart. And the weight of these words and this doctrine, which the apostle here clearly hands down, should be pondered and observed. COMMENTARY ON ROMANS 11:32.[16]

FREE AND UNIVERSAL. PHILIPP MELANCHTHON: This is the closing word, in which there is an equalizing of Gentiles and Jews. Confidence in merits is taken away from both. He exhorts all to repent. Thereafter he sets forth comfort equally to all. There is most profound teaching in each part, for to be confined under sin is not to be understood without fear, but embraces guilt, fears, and judgment on and punishments of sin, as if he said: "All are guilty, all will be subjected to the judgment of God, to death and afflictions."

So David was confined under sin when he was driven into exile, when he was troubled by dreadful pains. In these afflictions, this comfort that is

---

[13]Denck, *Selected Writings*, 252*; citing Ps 2:5-6; Hos 9:1-17; Rom 11:32.
[14]Beza is arguing that "all" does not mean "all" in an absolute sense (that is, "all the people in the world") but rather "all those saved," and that in this latter subset of humanity all receive their salvation by grace.
[15]Beza, *Annotationes majores*, 2:128

[16]Hesshus, *Explicatio Epistolae Pauli ad Romanos*, 366v-367r.

taught here must be held fast above all things. For it teaches about the cause of afflictions and judgment, and about its outcome. He says that we are subjected to these evils because of sin, but not in order that we may perish.

He adds the manner of the liberation. It is promised by gratuitous mercy, in order that the comfort may be sure. He commands us to believe that we are justified and saved through mercy, not because of our worthiness or merits. Yes, he commands us who are confined under sin, who are truly guilty, to flee to mercy, not to spurn the offered mercy, but to declare that we receive remission of sins freely, because of Christ.

This statement will become clear and sweet when we put it to use, when in true fears and afflictions we feel that it pertains to us, and we will support ourselves by this promise of mercy. It is a useful statement, and it should be used in all afflictions because it reminds us of the ultimate cause of afflictions, and also of gratuitous mercy.

The little word *universal* should also be observed in order that we may know that the promise is universal, and in order that we, each and every one, may truly include ourselves in this universality. COMMENTARY ON ROMANS (1540).[17]

11:33-35 The Depths and Heights of God's Wisdom

GOD'S WISDOM. PHILIPP MELANCHTHON: An exclamation is added in order that he may rein in human arrogance and human thoughts about the counsel of God, by which he wonderfully established and governs his church. For many things offend human reason, for example, that only a few—and those being downtrodden people—make up the people of God, and that so great a multitude—which is outstanding in terms of number, virtue and glorious deeds—is damned. The Jews were strangely offended when they heard that the synagogue had been rejected, since it had the most honorable title "people of God." Also

now the minds of very many people are offended, and they murmur when they hear that those who hold the title "church" are not the church.

To these offenses Paul opposes this exclamation, in which he teaches that we should subject ourselves to the wisdom and the Word of God, and that we should not fall away from the Word, even if we do not understand why God governs the church according to such a wonderful plan.

We should do both, acknowledge the greatness of God's wrath in the rejection of so many peoples, for so many centuries and so many persons. Let this wrath admonish us to fear, lest we despise the Word of God. Again, let us also acknowledge the mercy, that God has afterward renewed his Word and finally disseminated it in the whole world. Let us be strengthened by this testimony of the mercy, and declare that God truly wants to receive us, truly wants to make us his people and truly wants to save those who call on him.

This is the sum and substance of the Pauline exclamation by which he meets the offenses and forbids human judgments about this secret counsel of God. Likewise he forbids arrogance, lest we trust that we become the people of God on account of fleshly prerogatives or merits, as the bishops contend that they are the church on account of the succession. COMMENTARY ON ROMANS (1540).[18]

GOD IS THE AUTHOR OF EVERY GOOD THING. DESIDERIUS ERASMUS: God takes thought for the salvation of humankind by a plan we cannot understand but that could not possibly be better. For he wishes his own kindness to be felt by us in such a way that we are not able to claim anything for ourselves. For whatever is evil may be imputed to our own vice. On the other hand, whatever is good proceeds from God as from its source and is conferred through him as through its author. All good things are in him as the guardian and protector of gifts, so that human beings can claim

---

[17]Melanchthon, *Commentary on Romans*, 207-8* (MO 15:700-701).

[18]Melanchthon, *Commentary on Romans*, 208 (MO 15:701-2).

for themselves no portion or praise from this, since beginning, middle and end belong to God. Therefore to him alone are owed honor, praise and glory for all eternity. Thus it is impious for human beings to claim anything for themselves. PARAPHRASE ON ROMANS 11:34-36.[19]

THE THOUGHTS OF GOD ARE BEYOND OUR GRASP. JACOBUS ARMINIUS: The thoughts of God and his will (both what he wishes to be done by us and what he has resolved to do concerning us) are of free disposition, which is determined by the divine power and liberty inherent in himself. Since he has, in all this, called in the aid of no counselor, those thoughts and that will are of necessity "unsearchable and past finding out." ORATION 3: THE AUTHOR AND THE END OF THEOLOGY.[20]

REMAIN WITHIN THE LIMITS OF GOD'S REVEALED WORD. TILEMANN HESSHUS: With this exclamation he finally tears apart the debate over the free election of God and the justification of human beings through faith. God has established fixed boundaries for human beings: how far they should proceed in their knowledge and investigation of the divine will and counsel. For what is sufficient for us to obtain salvation the eternal Father has revealed to us through the Son. Truly the full wisdom of the Father, which is infinite, the Son has not revealed; nor are we able to grasp it in this mortal life. Therefore God wants us to remain within the limits laid down for us; nor should we rush into the secret counsels of God. And as in all the other articles of faith there are a vast number of things that absolutely cannot be comprehended by shrewdness of mind, but must simply be believed, so also in this article concerning the predestination of the saints, reason struggles vainly with it and dashes against it indiscriminately, unless the Word of God shines forth.

Therefore, in short, Paul warns that we must avoid investigating the divine will without the Word. We should not ask why God has chosen this person, but has passed over that person. Why should the thief be called at the end of his life after so many iniquities, but Saul, Joash and Judas should be cast aside after illustrious deeds? Why did he love Jacob, but he hated Esau? We must not explore why God for so many thousands of years has permitted so many nations to go their own way. We must not investigate why God has chosen so few, while so great a multitude perish. Nor why the ungodly multitude excels in positions of power, wealth and glory. Nor why he permits devils to prowl with such fury in this wretched nature. It is sufficient for us to know that there is no unrighteousness in God. And so the immeasurable and impenetrable wisdom of God should be adored rather than the secrets of his divine counsel be explored.

"Whoever probes majestic matters," says Solomon, "will be overwhelmed by their glory." Therefore we should acknowledge our frailty and remember that we are human beings who cannot capture and comprehend the whole divine Majesty. We should thank God that he reveals his will in his Word, so far as is necessary for us to obtain salvation. Now we should remain within the limits of his revealed Word, and we should not go beyond it, nor should we jump these fences out of curiosity. "I keep myself," says David, "in the Word of your lips, away from the works of human beings, away from the path of thieves." Again: "Your Word is a lamp to my feet." Again, Christ says: "They have Moses and the Prophets; let them hear them."

From this passage a distinction is correctly deduced: there is the revealed will of God and the secret, unknown will of God. Not that there are contradictory wills in God concerning the same matter! However, because God has not revealed the entirety of his wisdom, because he has revealed his mind in the law and gospel, his wisdom should not be examined and it is most certain and most infallible. But still his wisdom and mind are

---

[19]CWE 42:68-69.
[20]Arminius, *Works*, 1:87*.

infinite; knowledge of them is not necessary to obtain salvation. Concerning these things, Paul and Isaiah say: "Who has known the mind of the Lord?" And they forbid us from probing it. Commentary on Romans 11:33-36.[21]

Search the Revealed, Not the Hidden Will of God. David Pareus: This is as if he were to say, "Nobody." However, we recognize him from his word and works. We recognize them after the fact, but only in part, as much as suffices for our salvation. Infinite mysteries remain hidden in the mind of God, which nobody should presume to investigate. Thus 1 Corinthians 2:16 says, "Who knows the mind of the Lord or will teach him? But we have the mind of Christ." "For nobody has ever seen God; the Son who is in the bosom of the Father has revealed him to us." Therefore concerning the mind of the Lord we only know as much as Christ has revealed to us. But whatever is dreamed up or imported into the church beyond Christ's teaching is not from the mind of the Lord but from human invention, whether it is brought forth by the authority and name of the pope or of councils. And so this is the *first reason* restraining our rashness, lest we arrogate for ourselves the power of judgment concerning the most wise and most inscrutable judgments of God, as if we were blind people pronouncing judgments about colors. For human perspicacity, compared to the immense wisdom of God, is pure folly, pure blindness and pure darkness. Commentary on Romans 11:34.[22]

Mystery of Mysteries: The Gift of Faith. Marguerite de Navarre:

Therefore, come, O blessed Saint Paul,
who has tasted so plentifully of this sweet honey,
blind for three days and in celestial ecstasy,
come and correct my ignorance and weakness.

What did you see during your heavenly vision?
Listen to his response: "O most heavenly expanse,
divine wealth from the great treasury,
source of all wisdom,
fountain of sacred science,
your mind and your ways are,
according to our methods and means,
well beyond our understanding."
O most wonderful Saint Paul, you who are so wise,
you astonish us that your words go no further
in interpreting the divine mysteries.
Tell us: What can we hope for one day from this love?
Listen to what he had to say:
"However worthy,
no human eye has ever seen,
nor human ear ever heard
what God has prepared for
and promised to us for the end of time."
Have you nothing further to add? "Nothing."
What he has told us of the ineffable
serves to inspire our love and admiration,
that which he can neither declare nor name,
drawing our hearts, affections and aspirations
toward what we cannot ourselves see,
indeed, imagine or feel:
the will to die as martyrs.
O mighty gift of faith, from which such good comes,
that we possess what we do not have.
Faith gives hope of certain truth,
which in turn engenders perfect love.
And, as we know, God is love.
And if that loves abides in us, then so too does God.
He lives in us, and we in him;
we are all in him and he is in us.
And if we possess him through faith,
such possession is not within our power to define.
The Mirror of the Sinful Soul.[23]

[21]Hesshus, *Explicatio Epistolae Pauli ad Romanos*, 369r-370r; citing Prov 25:27; Ps 17:4; 119:105; Lk 16:29.
[22]Pareus, *In Epistolam ad Romanos*, 1141-42.
[23]Marguerite de Navarre, *Selected Writings*, 145-47; citing Acts 9; 1 Jn 4:7-12.

11:36 The Ministry and Majesty of the Triune God

THE ONE TRIUNE GOD. JACQUES LEFÈVRE D'ÉTAPLES: This is a confession of the most divine Trinity. He implies, "from him through the Son himself and into the Holy Spirit himself." "From him" shows the Power from which all things are directed; "through him" shows the Wisdom through which all things are directed; and "to him" shows the Goodness to which all things are directed. And when he appends, "To him be glory forever," there is a confession of the divine Unity. Therefore to the very most divine Trinity and Unity: all honor and glory forever and ever. Amen. ANNOTATIONS ON ROMANS 11:36.[24]

DEEP MEANING IN THESE PREPOSITIONS. DESIDERIUS ERASMUS: The old theologians philosophize about these three prepositions. Thomas interprets "from him" as "from the first cause of all things"; "through him" as "the one working and administering"; "in him" as "in the end." . . . He is not, however, far from the opinion of Origen, who explicates in this way: "In the phrase 'from him,' he points to the very fact that we exist; 'through him,' however, to the fact that our lives are ordered through his providence; and 'in him' to the fact that the perfection and end of all will be in him, at the time when God will be all in all."[25] Thomas points out that the preposition *de* ["from"] has nearly the same meaning as *ex*, except that it adds [the notion of] participation in the substance. ANNOTATIONS ON ROMANS 11:36.[26]

GRAMMATICAL DETAILS. THEODORE BEZA: *In ipsum, eis auton* ["into him"]; Vulgate, *In ipso, en autō* ["in him"]. I do not approve of the latter reading. For I think that here he means the purpose of all God's deeds, namely, God himself, to whose glory are ascribed all things whatsoever that

are in heaven or in earth, just as all things were also made by him and are governed by him. But these things are understood not only strictly in relation to the creation and governance of objects, but especially concerning his new works that he has brought forth in his elect. ANNOTATIONS ON ROMANS 11:36.[27]

TRADITIONAL TRINITARIAN LOCUS. TILEMANN HESSHUS: The doctrine concerning the three persons of the Divinity is usually repeated in this passage—as if Paul had said that all things exist from the Father, through the Son and in the Spirit. However, the doctrine concerning the three persons of the Divinity is handed down with greater clarity in other passages. Nor should those phrases—from the Father, through the Son and in the Spirit—be pressed with too much curiosity. For without too much concern, the apostles accept other passages concerning the persons. *Hō men gar dia tou pneumatos didotai logos sophias* ["for to one person through the Spirit is given the Word of wisdom"].[28] Again, Psalm 33: "By the Word of the Lord the heavens were made, and by the Spirit of his mouth all their host." Colossians 1: *ta panta en autō synestēken* ["in him all things hold together"]—speaking about the Son.

And also the doctrine concerning the creation and conservation of all things should be observed here. For Paul testifies that all things have been formed by God and are preserved through him. Commentary on Romans 11:36.[29]

ALL CREATION FOR GOD'S GLORY. DAVID PAREUS: He renders an account of the preceding sentence from a comparison of all creations (and

---

[24]Lefèvre d'Étaples, *Epistola ad Rhomanos*, 91r.
[25]PG 14:1202.
[26]CWE 56:318 (LB 6:628); citing Thomas Aquinas, *Super Epistolam ad Romanos lectura*, 11.5.
[27]Beza, *Annotationes majores*, 2:129.
[28]Here *logos sophias* is rendered literally, for Hesshus is highlighting verses that mention the persons of the Trinity without much fanfare. Luther translated this phrase idiomatically as "to speak of wisdom" (WADB 7:119). Modern English translations variously render this phrase: "the word of knowledge" (CEB, KJV, NASB); "the utterance of knowledge" (ESV, NRSV); and "a message of knowledge" (NIV).
[29]Hesshus, *Explicatio Epistolae Pauli ad Romanos*, 370r-v; citing 1 Cor 12:8; Ps 33:6; Col 1:17.

therefore of people) to God. He says, "There is a Creator of all things, for he made all things out of nothing so that the things that had not existed might come into being. Therefore all things are from him, as from a first principle. Therefore he receives nothing from anyone to whom he gives life, movement and breath. All things also exist through him, because he sustains and preserves all things by his power, for in him we live, move and exist." *Di hou* and *di autou*: "through whom, through him": This is ascribed not only to the Son in 1 Corinthians 8:6 and Colossians 1:20 but also to the Father in this passage and in 1 Corinthians 1:9. Therefore it designates not the instrument of creation (as the Arians want it to mean), but the efficient cause. Finally, all things aim for him as for their goal. For he made all things for his own sake, even the

wicked for the evil day. Therefore he will not be harmed if he should reduce even the world itself to nothing for the sake of his glory. COMMENTARY ON ROMANS 11:36.[30]

A SUCCINCT SUMMARY OF THE TRINITY.
MARTIN LUTHER: This statement concerning the Trinity is profound—incomprehensible to common people. Yet this passage depicts the Trinity excellently! Every creature's essence is formed and directed by God. From God, because he is Creator; through Christ, because he is Mediator; in the Holy Spirit, because all things are given to us in him. TABLE TALK (1537).[31]

---

[30]Pareus, *In Epistolam ad Romanos*, 1143-44.
[31]WATR 3:437-38, no. 3591.

12:1-2 A LIVING SACRIFICE

I appeal to you therefore, brothers,^a by the mercies of God, to present your bodies as a living sacrifice, holy and acceptable to God, which is your spiritual worship.^b ²Do not be conformed to this world,^c but be transformed by the renewal of your mind, that by testing you may discern what is the will of God, what is good and acceptable and perfect.^d

a Or *brothers and sisters*   b Or *your rational service*   c Greek *age*   d Or *what is the good and acceptable and perfect will of God*

OVERVIEW: Here Paul begins a discourse on Christian ethics (Rom 12–15). Even in the structure of Paul's letter, the reformers see that justification precedes sanctification. Until the Holy Spirit rules the mind and conquers human reason, all works— no matter how good they might appear—apart from faith are sin. And so the reformers commend Paul's redefinition of "reasonable" to us: reasonable worship is worship performed in faith according to the Word. Christian reason is subject to faith. Reasonable worship means that the external acts reflect the internal realities. With this reframing of worship comes a new meaning of sacrifice. In Christ human beings are redeemed for obedience to God, not continued enslavement to sin. "How can we who died to sin still live in sin?" (Rom 9:6). Now the reformers who so strongly emphasized divine monergism press human responsibility. Yes, the Lord is sovereign and establishes our paths (Prov 16:9); still he chooses to use ordinary means: us. We are responsible. Our commentators show no naiveté about continued sin in this life, even after justification, and they remind us that even our fits and starts of obedience are pleasing to God—because of our Mediator, Jesus of Nazareth. In Christ we are no longer our own, so we should stop living like it. "And those who belong to Christ Jesus have crucified the flesh with its passions and desires" (Gal 5:24). Only then will we truly live.

THE HOLY SPIRIT'S ORDERED CATECHESIS.
TILEMANN HESSHUS: The Holy Spirit constantly follows this order in explaining heavenly doctrine: in the first place he censures people for their sin, reveals the wrath of God and calls all to repentance. In the second place he shows us the Redeemer and his benefits, and he promises to all who flee with a true faith to the Redeemer forgiveness of sins, righteousness and eternal life. In the third place, after consciences have been cheered and strengthened by the comfort of the gospel, then he passes on the teaching about good works. He teaches what sort of obedience God requires of the faithful and diligently urges them so that each believer may be eager for good works.

The Holy Spirit followed this order also in this epistle. In the first three chapters he convicted the world about sin and called all to repentance. At the end of the third chapter and then all the way up until chapter 12 he splendidly explained the teaching about the justification of a human being before God. He showed that the promise of the gospel was without cost; he explained the benefits of the Redeemer; he taught that appropriation of these benefits takes place only by faith; and he showed the solid consolations against sin. But now he hands down the doctrine concerning good works. For the Son of God redeemed us from the wrath of God and the curse of the law but not with this goal in mind, namely, that we might serve sin, but rather so that, once we had been snatched from the power of Satan and given the Holy Spirit, we might render obedience to God in true righteousness and holiness. COMMENTARY ON ROMANS 12.[1]

---

[1]Hesshus, *Explicatio Epistolae Pauli ad Romanos*, 370v-371r.

IN CHRIST YOU ARE RIGHTEOUS; LIVE LIKE IT! PETER MARTYR VERMIGLI: Physicians first cleanse an ulcer of pus and secretions, then they daub it with soothing ointments. In the same way, Paul first refuted their arrogance—those who trust that they can be made righteous either by law or by philosophy through human strength—with a piercing argument. Now therefore he turns to urge us to a holy life and good works—by which we are renewed and made perfect by righteousness that dwells in us. And so he first establishes the doctrine of justification; then, after that's finished, he exhorts us to the fruits of good works and zeal for good works.

Our opponents should at least learn from this method of the apostle that good works do not precede justification. For first we must be regenerated, then we must bear the fruit of renewal. And this part should not be neglected, for it is added to the superior part as its fruit. Why does God make us righteous and regenerate us through faith in Christ? So that we continue to dwell in sin? When Aulus Fulvius had withdrawn his son from Catiline's rebels to kill him, he said: "For Catiline I did not beget you, but for your fatherland."[2] In the same way God did not regenerate us for sin, but for innocence and holiness. Therefore Paul asks us in this chapter—and on account of God—that we live worthily of God's benefits. . . . When we were dead in sin and were absolutely unable to raise or heal ourselves, he of his pure lovingkindness made us righteous through Christ. And to accomplish this, his one, only and dearly beloved Son suffered, was delivered into death—a most shameful death on the cross—for us. And his goodness toward us is so great that before the foundations of the world were laid he chose and predestined us to eternal joy. By these most excellent benefits of God we are stirred up to conduct ourselves in a manner worthy and suitable of them. COMMENTARY ON ROMANS 12:1.[3]

THE NEW OBEDIENCE FLOWS FROM REGENERATION. PHILIPP MELANCHTHON: First the remission of sins, justification and the gift of the Holy Spirit must be accepted by faith on account of Christ, freely. Afterward it is necessary that the new obedience follow, which is a certain beginning of fulfilling the law. Therefore the commandments are taught after the doctrine concerning faith.

But why must the commandments be taught, since it is the Spirit who obeys God? I answer: First, there is need for the Word, in order that the carnal part be coerced. Thereafter it is necessary that the doctrine of repentance be constantly taught, and the remnants of sin in us mortified, so that repentance may increase. In the third place, there is need of the Word for the righteous, through which they are taught what works please God, and through which spiritual impulses are aroused. Therefore, after the doctrine of the gospel and faith has been set forth, also the commandments or the law are taught. COMMENTARY ON ROMANS (1540).[4]

EXCURSUS ON GOOD WORKS. PHILIPP MELANCHTHON: Here now the doctrine of good works must be known—what kind of works are demanded, and how they can please. First, what kind. For demanded are the good works that have been divinely taught, within and without, namely, fear of God, faith, love, repentance, patience and calling on God. These inner impulses are not found in the ungodly, even if external civil discipline is present. Therefore one must diligently consider what kind of works should be found in believers.

But in what way do they please? This teaching is necessary for the church. . . . Both must be held fast: first that we are not righteous because of our virtues or works, and that sin still clings to us, which also defiles good works. Therefore knowledge of our infirmity and repentance ought to increase in us. Next, although we are not righteous because of our virtues, after we have been reconciled by faith and are righteous, even beginning

---

[2] In accordance with Roman law, Aulus Fulvius's father ordered his son's execution for joining Catiline's rebellion (63 BC); see Sallust, *The War with Catiline*; LCL 116:85-86.

[3] Vermigli, *In Epistolam ad Romanos*, 581 (*A Commentarie upon the Epistle to the Romanes*, 410v); citing Eph 2:5.

[4] Melanchthon, *Commentary on Romans*, 209* (MO 15:702).

obedience is pleasing. This is not because it satisfies the law or is without defect, but because of our High Priest, Christ, who intercedes for us, etc.

This teaching is a great comfort for the godly, and the greatness of the mercy exhorts us to perform good works. For when a godly mind hears that even a small and contaminated measure of obedience is an act of worship of God and a sacrifice, it will without doubt be incited to furnish it with greater zeal. COMMENTARY ON ROMANS (1540).[5]

12:1a-b *True Worship Is Sacrificial Living*

OUR LIFE IS A PRAYER BEFORE GOD. JUAN DE VALDÉS: That the whole life of a Christian should be a continual prayer, for his mind is necessarily kept in constant communion with God and with Christ, desirous of the glory of God and of Christ; a continual fast, for one ought always to be attentive to abstaining from things that inflate the flesh with pride against the spirit, such as the excesses of the table, vanity in dress and the joys and pleasures of the world; a continual feast, for one must always be inwardly glad and rejoice in virtue of the peace that one finds in one's conscience through reconciliation with God, which one enjoys through Christ. CHRISTIAN INSTRUCTION FOR CHILDREN.[6]

TRUE OBEDIENCE ACCORDING TO FAITH NOT REASON. TILEMANN HESSHUS: The Holy Spirit begins the exhortation to eagerness for doing good works with a description of the true, spiritual obedience toward God, which is not some dead semblance of virtue, but rather a living and holy righteousness, pleasing to God and in line with the norm of divine wisdom. For even if human reason sometimes understands the distinction between honorable and base things, attempts to stir people toward virtue and even adorns praiseworthy deeds with great commendations of the heathen (such as the justice of Aristides, the moderation of Camillus, the chastity of Scipio, the temperance of Atticus,

the faithfulness of Regulus and the clemency of Caesar), nonetheless human reason does not understand what true virtue is and how it can and ought to flourish. Without the light of the divine Word, reason does not know what sort of works and what forms of worship God demands. It does not know God himself, to whom all obedience must be directed. It does not know the promise of reconciliation and faith, without which nobody can please God. It does not know the Holy Spirit, who alone produces true virtue. It does not know the standard of the divine law, with which each work and each impulse must agree.

Therefore the virtues—be they ever so notable—of all the heathen and unregenerate people are nothing other than dead images, letters and pictures that lack life, and sins before God. For they arise solely out of the impure flesh; but whatever is not of faith is sin, and without faith it is impossible to please God. Furthermore, true worshipers will worship the Father in Spirit and truth. Therefore the virtues of the heathen must be distinguished by far from the works of the saints. Let these illustrative differences be in view. COMMENTARY ON ROMANS 12:1.[7]

TRANSLATION DELIBERATION. DESIDERIUS ERASMUS: The Latin Vulgate translation reads *exhibere*: "that you present your bodies." Chrysostom and Theophylact point out that *parastēnai* is properly used of those who furnish war horses to a

---

[5]Melanchthon, *Commentary on Romans*, 209-10* (MO 15:702-3).
[6]*Valdés' Two Catechisms*, 185.

[7]Hesshus, *Explicatio Epistolae Pauli ad Romanos*, 371v-372r. Hesshus continues with several pages explaining the difference between works of heathens and of Christians according to their respective efficient, formal and final causes. Aristides (early fifth century BC) was an Athenian statesman nicknamed "the Just" and was praised for his honesty. Marcus Furius Camillus was an exiled Roman who helped his native city defeat the Gauls in 390 BC. Scipio Africanus was presented with a voluptuous prisoner of war, but rather than have his way with her returned her to her fiancé. Marcus Attilius Regulus (d. 250 BC) was captured by the Carthaginians but paroled to deliver a message to the Roman senate; he delivered it, but urged the Romans not to surrender; nonetheless, he himself kept his word and returned to Carthage, even though it meant his death by torture. Julius Caesar (100–44 BC) was known for sparing many people who had fought against him in the civil war.

general. Thus I have translated *praebere* ["to furnish"]. If you reflect that in baptism we have renounced the desires of the flesh and dedicated ourselves to Christ, the word *exhibere* ["to present"] is appropriate, and it admonishes us to make good our profession. Or again, if we have in mind that there is an allusion to the ancient custom of burnt offerings, in which the priest placed the victim on the altar while God consumed it with fire from heaven, the word *present* fits well. What has once been devoted to God should not be used for any other purpose; just as the one who has furnished horses for a commander in war has nothing to do with them in the future, one cannot recall for personal use what one has once turned over. Chrysostom has also observed that Paul did not say *poiēsate*, that is, "make your bodies a sacrifice," but *parastēsate*, that is *tradite* ["hand over"], so they no longer belong to you but come under the control of God. And it would be sacrilege to appropriate anew to the service of the devil what you once furnished to your commander, God, for fighting the devil. At the same time we are admonished to take care to treat our bodies in such a way that they are instruments suitable for the divine will and worthy to be presented before God's eyes. ANNOTATIONS ON ROMANS 12:1.[8]

What Does Paul Mean by "Your Bodies"?

DAVID PAREUS: This is a Hebrew synecdoche for "you entirely," or by "bodies" he understands (as earlier) the carnal desires that reside in the body and exert themselves chiefly through the body. Therefore, placing our bodies as a sacrificial victim for God, that is, as a sacrifice, means mortifying fleshly longings and desires. COMMENTARY ON ROMANS 12:1.[9]

Paul Commends Priestly Discipline to All Believers.

JOHANN SPANGENBERG: Here Paul speaks of [displacing the body and dulling and killing its evil lusts and desires] in a very different manner than in his other letters. In Galatians he calls it crucifying the flesh with its lusts; in Ephesians and Colossians he calls it putting off the old self and killing your earthly members. Here however he calls it making a sacrifice, and he praises this sacrifice with the very highest and holiest words. . . . He does this so that with such mighty words he would stir us up more strongly to the fruits of the faith, for the whole world considers the priestly office the noblest and highest office, as in truth it is. Why does he hold up sacrifice so high? Because sacrificing is the main work. For in baptism God consecrated us all as priests and anointed us all with the Holy Spirit. Thus he also wants us to carry out this priestly office and priestly works, namely, to pray for one another, to instruct one another and to offer our bodies as a living sacrifice to God.

What would papists say to this, that all Christians are priests? They can say what they like. Saint Paul knows absolutely nothing about papist Mass-priests and slaughter-priests. There is no apostle, neither Peter nor Paul, who were priests of the Mass.[10] These are human inventions. They have aped the Jews. And through these external ceremonies—consecrating, anointing, sprinkling, burning incense, differentiating time, place, person, clothes, food, etc.—they have made a pure Judaism out of Christianity. That, of course, was not Christ's intention. With his death and resurrection he freed us from such things. Then the pope comes with his entourage and turns Christians into Jews again. That is wrong. All Christians are priests, both men and women, consecrated not by human beings, but by God in baptism, anointed not with oil or chrism, but with the Holy Spirit. As Saint Jerome writes, "Baptism is the lay priesthood." Not chrism but the new birth makes a true priest. EPISTLE FOR THE FIRST SUNDAY AFTER EPIPHANY.[11]

---

[8] CWE 56:320*.
[9] Pareus, *In Epistolam ad Romanos*, 1226-27.

[10] Spangenberg is not dismissing ordained offices; instead he is distinguishing between the pastoral office and a merely ceremonial role.
[11] J. Spangenberg, *Postilla Teütsch*, 4:64r-65v; citing Gal 5:24; Eph 4:22; Col 3:5; Jerome's *Dialogue Against the Luciferians* (PL 23:158; NPNF2 6:321).

SPIRITUAL SACRIFICES OF THE SPIRITUAL PRIESTHOOD. JOHANN WILD: Now he teaches the foremost of all works to be the mortification of the body, and he calls this by a new and extraordinary name: an offering. In other passages he calls it either crucifixion or putting off of the old self. He did this not without reason. For, in the first place, through this he reminds us of our dignity: through Christ we have become kings and priests, a royal priesthood and a spiritual priesthood, so that we may offer spiritual sacrifices, etc. They err who imagine that the external church does not need bishops, pastors, teachers and ministers. They err who say that these sorts of offices are common.[12] And so Peter says "spiritual priesthood." If the name priest delights you, pray passionately for all things, teach yourself and your peers, baptize yourself through the remembrance of the first baptism, commune yourself with the sacrament through meditation on Christ's suffering. Offer a sacrifice of praise and mortification. These are the things that belong to your priesthood.

"Present your bodies," he says. Not just your hand, tongue, etc. And he does not mean only your body, but also your soul and everything. And do not present your body in just any manner, but as a sacrificial victim—by this word death is indicated. Therefore slay your body as a sacrificial victim. First, the members of the body (the external body and senses) that cause offense should be removed—indeed, not through a physical sword but through careful guarding and restraining of the senses. Second, the internal vices of the soul should be slain: wrath, vengeance, desire, concupiscence,

hatred, avarice, pride, etc. Third, also reason itself and our own will and its affections should be slain. See how many sacrificial victims you find in yourself! Our body is a living sacrifice. EXEGESIS OF ROMANS 12:1.[13]

OUR SPIRITUAL SACRIFICE. DESIDERIUS ERASMUS: As long as the law remained carnal God allowed the bodies of beasts to be sacrificed to him. But since the law has begun to be spiritual, sacrifices must be made to God with spiritual victims. Sacrifice your disposition to pride rather than a young calf, slay your boiling anger instead of a ram, immolate your lust instead of a goat, sacrifice to God the lascivious and seductive thoughts of your mind instead of pigeons and doves. These are sacrifices truly worthy of a Christian; these are victims pleasing to Christ. God is spirit and is won over by gifts of the Spirit. PARAPHRASE ON ROMANS 12:1.[14]

12:1c What Is "Reasonable" Worship?[15]

REASON IS SUBJECT TO FAITH. MARTIN LUTHER: Saint Paul here calls all sacrifices, works and worship "irrational," if they happen without faith and knowledge of God. MARGINAL GLOSS ON ROMANS 12:1 (1546).[16]

DEEDS OF REASONABLE WORSHIP. TILEMANN HESSHUS: He calls it furthermore "reasonable worship," so that he may distinguish the obedience of the saints from the external sacrifices and slaughtering of cattle, whether those things were done by the Levites, or the Pharisees without faith, or the heathen. And so he demands true, solid, internal and spiritual obedience from the justified. For he calls it their "reasonable worship," in which God is recognized by the mind and worshiped by

---

[12]Wild is criticizing a common misconception of the priesthood of all believers. Luther agrees with Wild: "It is true that all Christians are priests, but not all Christians are pastors" (*Commentary on Psalm 82*, 1530; WA 31,1:211). For Luther, the priesthood of all believers means that all Christians have unmediated access to Jesus Christ, and united to him by faith all Christians participate in his ministry; nevertheless God in his wisdom has ordained an ordered external ministry, and Christians should not despise it. See further Luther's *Freedom of a Christian* (1520), LW 31:333-77 (WA 7:42-73 [Latin]; cf. the German text, pp. 20-38); Paul Althaus, *The Theology of Martin Luther*, trans. Robert C. Schultz (Philadelphia: Fortress, 1963), 313-18.

[13]Wild, *Exegesis in Epistolam ad Romanos*, 230r-231r; citing 1 Pet 2:5.
[14]CWE 42:69.
[15]Most of the reformers render *logikēn* as "reasonable." Today this is translated variously: "spiritual" (NRSV, ESV, NASB), "true and proper" (NIV), "appropriate" (CEB) or "reasonable" (KJV, NKJV).
[16]WADB 4:67.

faith—not merely honored with the lips or external gestures.

But when he calls all the deeds of the godly a "sacrificial offering," he is speaking about a sacrifice *eucharistikō* ["of thanksgiving"]. For there are two types of sacrifices. One is the prefiguring sacrifices, such as all the offerings in the law; the other is the true, living, holy sacrifice, which Paul here calls *logikēn latreian* ["reasonable worship"]. However, there is also a twofold living sacrifice. One is the *hilastikon* ["propitiatory"], namely, the obedience and suffering of the only Son of God, by which the wrath of God was appeased, as it was said, "When he will have given his life as an offering for sin, he will see his offspring." The other is the *eucharistikon* ["thanksgiving"], namely, all the good works of the saints, which are done according to the Word of God in trust in the Redeemer, with the purpose of honoring God. David says, "Offer sacrifices of righteousness and hope in the Lord," and "the sacrifice for God is a troubled heart; a troubled and humbled heart, O God, you will not despise." But when he orders us to offer our bodies to God as a living sacrifice, he embraces every good deed in general and indeed advises us that we ought to feel that we are not burdening our abilities, bodies and life, as if we were sacrificing a whole burnt offering to God at all times, for we owe God our life and all things, and we have been dedicated and consecrated to him. When Paul endures immense labors and troubles in his journeys and explains that he is in various dangers so that he may spread abroad the light of the gospel, he sacrifices his body to God, if indeed he endures all things in faith for the glory of God. And all the good works of the saints offered in true faith in Jesus Christ and directed to the glory of God are sacrifices pleasing to God, for it is necessary to mortify the desires of the flesh in order for us to be able to serve God.

That this forbids us to imitate the attitudes of this world is a general rule that follows of necessity. For the world feigns some zeal for virtue and puts on a mask, as it were, of noteworthy duty and righteousness, although it is most alien to true righteousness. But if it pays to the poor, it carries

great mercy and generosity in front of itself, but it is either seeking after worldly glory or hunting after some other advantage. COMMENTARY ON ROMANS 12:1.[17]

THE COST OF PURE WORSHIP. JOHANN SPANGENBERG: As it happens in the external priesthood, few truly practice and perform the priestly office; so it also happens here. All Christians—men and women, young and old—have the priestly name. But the priestly office? That sacrifice they don't rush to. Everyone is horrified of it. What is the reason? It costs life and limb, honor and friends, and everything that the world has. How Christ rendered this office on the cross—no one wants to do that. No one wants to choose and accept pain and trouble for joy, death for life, shame for honor, enemies for friends, like Christ did for our sake. Thus it is a difficult office and a costly sacrifice....

Here he distinguishes the sacrifices of the old and new testaments. The sacrifices of the old testament were cows, calves, bulls, goats, sheep, lambs, etc.—completely irrational animals. But in the new testament there should be no other sacrifice than the old Adam alone who here on earth should be dulled and killed with all his evil lusts, desires and inclinations; he must die to sin and become a new creature of God, and he must patiently bear every cross, suffering and misery sent by God.... The sacrifice of the new testament should be a living, holy, well-pleasing offering, a reasonable act of worship, not an act of worship that uses irrational, dead animals, like the Jewish sacrifices. Also not an act of worship that uses external ecclesial pomp and the dead ceremonies of the papists and monks; nor a self-invented act of worship, of a self-chosen cross, like that of Baal and Moloch worshipers, and of the Turkish priests. Instead it should be an act of worship that is established in God's Word, which proceeds from a pure, believing heart, and strives to glorify God and to help and comfort neighbors, like the act of

---

[17]Hesshus, *Explicatio Epistolae Pauli ad Romanos*, 373r-v; citing Is 53:10; Ps 4:6; 51:17.

worship described by Saint James: "Pure and undefiled worship before God the Father is this: to visit orphans and widows in their affliction and to keep oneself unstained by the world." EPISTLE FOR THE FIRST SUNDAY AFTER EPIPHANY.[18]

THE HEART OF CHRISTIAN PHILOSOPHY: WE ARE GOD'S. JOHN CALVIN: Even though the law of the Lord provides the finest and best-disposed method of ordering a person's life, it seemed good to the Heavenly Teacher to shape his people by an even more explicit plan to that rule which he had set forth in the law. Here, then, is the beginning of this plan: the duty of believers is "to present their bodies to God as a living sacrifice, holy and acceptable to him," and in this consists the lawful worship of him. From this is derived the basis of the exhortation that "they be not conformed to the fashion of this world, but be transformed by the renewal of their minds, so that they may prove what is the will of God." Now the great thing is this: we are consecrated and dedicated to God in order that we may thereafter think, speak, meditate and do nothing except to his glory. For a sacred thing may not be applied to profane uses without marked injury to him.

If we, then, are not our own but the Lord's, it is clear what error we must flee, and whither we must direct all the acts of our life.

We are not our own: let not our reason nor our will therefore sway our plans and deeds. We are not our own: let us therefore not set it as our goal to seek what is expedient for us according to the flesh. We are not our own: insofar as we can, let us therefore forget ourselves and all that is ours.

Conversely, we are God's: let us therefore live for him and die for him. We are God's: let his wisdom and will therefore rule all our actions. We are God's: let all the parts of our life accordingly strive toward him as our only lawful goal. O, how much has that person profited who, having been taught that he is not his own, has taken away dominion and rule from his own reason that he

may yield it to God! For, as consulting our self-interest is the pestilence that most effectively leads to our destruction, so the sole haven of salvation is to be wise in nothing and to will nothing through ourselves but to follow the lead of the Lord alone.

Let this therefore be the first step, that a person depart from himself in order that he may apply the whole force of his ability in the service of the Lord. I call "service" not only what lies in obedience to God's Word but also what turns the human mind, empty of its own carnal sense, wholly to the bidding of God's Spirit. While it is the first entrance to life, all philosophers were ignorant of this transformation, which Paul calls "renewal of the mind." For they set up reason alone as the ruling principle in human beings, and think that it alone should be listened to; to it alone, in short, they entrust the conduct of life. But the Christian philosophy bids reason give way to, submit and subject itself to the Holy Spirit so that the person himself may no longer live but hear Christ living and reigning within him. INSTITUTES 3.7.1.[19]

12:2 True Worship Transfigures Your Mind

PAUL'S TWOFOLD PURPOSE IN THIS VERSE. CYRIACUS SPANGENBERG: With his command he does two things. First, he warns us about what we should avoid. Second, he admonishes us about what we should diligently attend to. The warning sounds like this: do not be like those of this world. That can well be taken to heart by a preacher, who should not only admonish for the good, but also warn about the bad. . . . Since therefore, beside the devil and our corrupted flesh, most of all the world by its example turns people away from God, so very faithfully Paul warns us, saying: "Do not be conformed to this world." He speaks explicitly about this world, in which we now live, and indeed, equally lets us understand that there is still another and better world, where things will clearly

---

[18]J. Spangenberg, *Postilla Teütsch*, 4:66r-v, 68r-69r; citing Jas 1:27.

[19]LCC 20:689-90* (CO 2:505-6); citing 1 Cor 6:19; Rom 14:8; Eph 4:23; Gal 2:20.

be different and toward it we should also orient our thoughts. So watch out that we do not conform to this world. And for the Christians in Rome this warning was very necessary for the time, because they lived in such a place where the most powerful and mighty people on earth lived, who daily lived their lives in arrogance and sensual pleasure, where one also never saw and heard anything else but pleasure, lust and corruption with all kinds of luxury and ostentatious display. And it is certainly a good warning for our time, and necessary as well, where everything is coming undone and everyone does what they want. LAST EIGHT CHAPTERS OF ROMANS.[20]

THE NATURAL LIMITS OF NONCONFORMITY. SEBASTIAN FRANCK: Some get to the place where they will have nothing to do with the heathen, not only in fasting, celebrating, living, eating, drinking, etc. They also establish rules about how simple clothes have to be, how each is to be made and how many folds the skirt should have. Like the monks, they have rules governing eating, drinking, silence, speaking and clothes. And when one of their wives gives birth to a child, she is not to be modest, or to draw a curtain as the heathens do. They quote the Scripture "and be not conformed to this world," as though faith changed the nature, customs and laws of the outward person. Or as though Paul meant that we should walk on our head, eat with our feet, speak with our hands and do all the work of nature differently from the world when he says you are not to be like them, etc. Paul means the vain and wicked ways and practices of the world that we are not to be like, for what is considered great in the world is an abomination before God. Not all practice these fantasies but only a few, the others allowing nature its right at these points. ON THE ANABAPTISTS.[21]

DAILY WE GROW IN THE THEOLOGY OF THE CROSS. JOHANN SPANGENBERG: The world can

neither see nor hear this sacrifice; it looks askance at it from both sides; it does not have our mind and spirit in itself at all. But we still have a strong mind and intention of the world in ourselves. Therefore it is necessary for us to pay attention that we follow neither the ways of the world nor our reason and good intentions. Instead we must always subdue our mind and will, acting differently from what our reason and will prescribes, so that we are found to be unconformed to the world. And thus we are daily transformed and renewed in our minds.

What does "transformed and renewed in mind" mean? That daily we cherish more and more what the world and reason hate, because daily we prefer more and more to become poor, sick, rejected, fools and sinners. And finally we consider death better than life, foolishness more precious than wisdom, shame more noble than honor and poverty more blessed than wealth. This mind the world does not have. Instead it thinks about everything much differently, and it remains in this old mind, unchanged and unrenewed, old and hardened like a stone. . . .

There is a big difference between God's will and our will. The world cannot be satisfied with this life, but a Christian says with Saint Paul, "Here we do not have an enduring city." The world fears the cross; a Christian desires it and sighs with that hermit that God had forgotten him, because he had not been sick for a whole year. For the world all suffering lasts too long, but a Christian says with Saint Paul, "I consider the suffering of this time not worth comparing to the glory, which will be revealed to us." The world cries: "O Lord, let me live a long life. Give me luck, well-being and health. Let everything go well," etc. But a Christian says with Saint Paul, "I desire to depart and be with Christ." EPISTLE FOR THE FIRST SUNDAY AFTER EPIPHANY.[22]

HEAVENLY DOCTRINE MATURES THE NEWLY BORN IN CHRIST. DAVID PAREUS: To be sure, this will of God is contained and described in the

---

[20]C. Spangenberg, *Außlegung der Letsten Acht Capitel der Episteln an die Römer*, 176v.
[21]CRR 10:235*.

[22]J. Spangenberg, *Postilla Teütsch*, 4:69r-70v; citing Heb 13:14; Rom 8:18; Phil 1:23.

law. For he understands and sets forth the revealed will as a rule. But a mind that has not been reborn does not understand it all, but the wisdom of the flesh does not in any way want to be subjected to it, for it is enmity to it (Rom 8). But the will of God is not entirely in the law, but to the contrary the better part is contained in the gospel and furthermore is unknown to people's minds. Therefore the new birth is especially necessary. But this does not take place except by the assiduous and diligent examination of the divine will, that is, meditation on, investigation of and obedience to heavenly doctrine. But assiduous calling on God is also required for this. This will of God from the law and the gospel is recognized as a rule for us. If we follow this North Star[23] of our faith and actions, we will not go astray. Therefore the study of heavenly doctrine is demanded of us here. COMMENTARY ON ROMANS 12:2.[24]

FOLLOW TRUTH, THAT IS, CHRIST, CAREFULLY. DESIDERIUS ERASMUS: If you examine all the cares, joys, hopes, fears, ambitions and opinions of humankind, you will find them all full of error. They call good evil and evil good; they make the sweet bitter and the bitter sweet; they make light darkness and darkness light. And it is by far the greatest part of humankind that is involved. But you must both despise them if you do not wish to be like them, and pity them if you desire them to be like you, and to echo the words of Augustine, at times one must weep for those who should be mocked, and at times one must mock those who deserve our tears.[25]

. . . You are very close to danger and on the verge of slipping if you begin to look around you at what most people are doing or if you try to discover what they are thinking. Since you are one of the sons and daughters of life and light, let the dead bury the dead, let the blind, the leaders of the blind, fall with them into the ditch. Be careful not to turn the eyes of your heart from your model Christ in any other direction. You will not go astray if you follow the lead of Truth. ENCHIRIDION.[26]

---

[23]*Cynosura*, "dog's tail," another name for Ursa Minor or the Little Dipper.
[24]Pareus, *In Epistolam ad Romanos*, 1232.

[25]PL 38 945.
[26]CWE 66:93*; citing Is 5:20; Rom 12:2; Jn 12:36; Eph 5:8; Mt 8:22; Lk 9:60; Mt 15:14.

12:3-8 GIFTS OF GRACE

3For by the grace given to me I say to everyone among you not to think of himself more highly than he ought to think, but to think with sober judgment, each according to the measure of faith that God has assigned. 4For as in one body we have many members,a and the members do not all have the same function, 5so we, though many, are one body in Christ, and individually

members one of another. 6Having gifts that differ according to the grace given to us, let us use them: if prophecy, in proportion to our faith; 7if service, in our serving; the one who teaches, in his teaching; 8the one who exhorts, in his exhortation; the one who contributes, in generosity; the one who leads,b with zeal; the one who does acts of mercy, with cheerfulness.

a Greek *parts*; also verse 5   b Or *gives aid*

OVERVIEW: In his discussion of the gifts of the Spirit, Paul builds on the truth that in Christ we are not our own: we belong to the body of Christ. The reformers seize this metaphor with gusto. We need each other, for God has dispersed abilities throughout his church. And our gifts are not given for our own use—does the eye look at itself?—but for the edification of the entire body. Thus we help others by fulfilling our own tasks in their proper sphere, not by usurping another member's task or calling. While some are ordained for higher offices and others for lower offices, according to our commentators, this does not create an asymmetrical power relationship. Parishioners listen to their pastors; pastors preach to their parishioners. This is fitting and right. Both pastors and parishioners are equal before God, and they are called to fulfill their God-given vocation. To continue with the body metaphor, how ridiculous would it be for an ear to try to speak? Believers, therefore, must remain modest. While some gifts are seen as more honorable than others, they are all still gifts, given to each in mercy. "What do you have that you did not receive? If then you received it, why do you boast as if you did not receive it?" (1 Cor 4:7). Therefore be humble and teachable. The arrogance of an unteachable spirit plagues the church; all heresies arise from it.

The reformers focus especially on Paul's phrase "according to the analogy of faith"—today usually

rendered as "in proportion to (your) faith" (Rom 12:6). In the tradition this has long been used as the standard of correct biblical exegesis, for prophecy is chiefly understood as biblical interpretation.[1] "Faithful interpretation is guided by the rule of faith," Craig Farmer writes, "the trinitarian, christological and evangelical scope of Scripture's content and meaning that arises from it and in turn makes sense of the whole and the parts."[2] Any preaching or teaching that does not square with this rule is false teaching, not God's Word. Many of our commentators here simply equate the analogy of faith with the Apostles' Creed.[3] To some today this might seem like eisegesis. However, the reformers paid careful attention to the grammatical, historical

---

[1]For more on the threefold meaning of "prophecy," see RCS OT 5:96-97.

[2]RCS NT 4:li; see also RCS OT 7:xlvi-lii.

[3]For them faith includes both the active and passive aspects of faith, that is, the faith by which we believe and the faith that we believe—*fides qua creditur* and *fides quae creditur*, respectively. Although some leave room for the passive sense, modern commentators tend to emphasize the active understanding as self-evident in this passage—thus they supply the possessive pronoun *your*. Fitzmyer, however, calls the passive understanding of faith "the best interpretation." See C. E. B. Cranfield, *A Critical and Exegetical Commentary on the Epistle to the Romans*, International Critical Commentary (Edinburg: T&T Clark, 1985), 2:619-21; Joseph A. Fitzmyer, *Romans: A New Translation with Introduction and Commentary*, Anchor Bible 33 (New York: Doubleday, 1993), 647-48; Douglas J. Moo, *The Epistle to the Romans*, New International Commentary on the New Testament 38 (Grand Rapids: Eerdmans, 1996), 765-66.

and literary features of the biblical text. Still, to take the dual authorship of the Bible seriously meant for the reformers that Scripture must be approached with the Holy Spirit's presuppositions, namely, the faith. According to most of our forebears in faith, to try to exegete and translate Scripture apart from the faith ensures false and even damaging results. "Do not interpretations belong to God?" (Gen 40:8).

The Gifts of the Spirit Are for the Benefit of the Church.
David Pareus: So far there has been a general entreaty. A special ordinance will follow concerning the right use of spiritual gifts and functions in the church. At that time various *charismata* ["spiritual gifts"] were flourishing, which were being given to the faithful through the apostles by the imposition of hands for the edification of the church. But not all people were employing them for this purpose, owing to their ambition or negligence. To the contrary, they got carried away with some gifts, while despising others, as is evident both from this very exhortation and also other similar ones, especially 1 Corinthians 12–14 and Ephesians 4. Therefore he urges that no one disturb the church with their gifts, for whose edification he has received them. He strengthens this exhortation with apostolic authority, which he says was given to him by God, lest someone dare to interrupt. "Through the grace that was given to me." It is as if he were to say, "in the name of God, whose ambassador I have been appointed." "To each of you or among you." He commands those who have gifts or public offices as a group and individually, for it is obvious that the commandment from the following verses is directed to them. He binds together the great and the lowly, lest anyone should remove himself on the pretext of his degree or honor. For the more someone excels in gifts or office, the more they are in need of the reins of modesty, with which the apostle speaks to us here. Commentary on Romans 12:3.[4]

12:3 Focus on God's Call, Not Your Worth

Humility and Order in the Body of Christ.
Jacques Lefèvre d'Étaples: Whoever is above what is proper and his own rank and who seeks after an office of his own seems and thinks himself to be wise in his own eyes assumes office for himself and is haughty and does not retain a sense of humility commensurate with the faith. But one ought to know that all the faithful are like one body, whose head is Christ. Therefore the perception of the whole body ought to flow from Christ in all members. And whoever does not belong to Christ is not a member of the head, but is a foreign part. And just as one member of the body does not usurp the action of another member, so one rank in the church ought never to usurp what belongs to another. Otherwise it is behaving haughtily and thinking more than is fair and confusing good order. But those of the lower ranks ought to be content with the duties of the lower ranks; those of the higher ranks ought to be content with the duties of the higher ranks; the sacred ranks, with sacred matters; the secular ranks, with secular matters; and everyone ought mutually to assist in their own functions, so that the members of the body might mutually help one another, love each other and agree with one another. Annotations on Romans 12:3.[5]

Humility of Teachers and Rulers.
Tilemann Hesshus: Earlier he had preached in general about zeal for godliness and all virtues. So now he handles in particular certain matters and hands down maxims for living. But in the first place he instructs those who are in charge of others in the ministry of teaching and in the church with what modesty, faith and diligence they ought to execute their office and lead others. For when those placed in authority over the church fail in their duties, not only do they scandalize others but they also disturb the church and hinder its edification.

---

[4]Pareus, *In Epistolam ad Romanos*, 1233-35.

[5]Lefèvre d'Étaples, *Epistola ad Rhomanos*, 92v.

Therefore in the first place he exhorts the rulers of the church to true modesty or humility, which is the virtue of the first commandment, so that they certainly recognize their own weakness, ponder from whom they have received their gifts, do not think arrogantly about themselves, do not act haughtily beyond their place, do not insert themselves into other people's callings, do not attribute to themselves a singular wisdom, learning and diligence, do not (because of an overconfidence in their talents) undertake matters not entrusted to them, and do not despise others as lower than themselves. Arrogance is most harmful in every line of work, but it is an especially harmful plague in the church. From arrogance heresies, schism and contentions customarily arise and at last devastate the church. Paul of Samosata[6] knew more than he ought to have. For he despised the other pastors of the church, thought himself alone to be learned, and overconfident in his talents he invented a new error. In this way Nestorius[7] knew more than was just and by his arrogance disturbed the whole church to such a degree that calm was not able to be restored for many centuries. So the Roman pontiffs have horribly devastated the church with their arrogance and haughtiness and turned the ministry of teaching into political governance. Therefore let us obey Paul's precept and each think modestly about ourselves and not despise others. Let us recognize that others are also salutary instruments of God. And let us not employ the gifts conferred on us for our own advantage, but for the common use of the church. Let us not pedantically show the keenness of our talent. Let us not chase after a reputation for eloquence or singular wisdom, but let us modestly perform our duties in the fear of God in accordance with that measure which God has imparted to us. COMMENTARY ON ROMANS 12:3.[8]

WHAT DO YOU HAVE THAT YOU HAVE NOT RECEIVED? DAVID PAREUS: There follow arguments of exhortation, which are remedies of arrogance and curiosity. At the same time he explains what it means to be sober-minded, namely, to be wise according to the measure of faith received from God. *Hekastō hōs*, "to each one as," is a transposition of the particle *hōs* ["as"] for *hōs hekastō* ("as to each one"), a transposition commonly found in the apostle elsewhere, as in 1 Corinthians 3:5, etc. There are almost as many thoughts as there are words. He says, "God distributed to each one." *Emerisen*, that is, he apportioned. So he says in 1 Corinthians 7:17. Therefore let everyone think that whatever they have they have from God. He has established God as a household manager who distributes in his house to individuals a ration of victuals, labors and rewards. Let each one pursue it and be content with it. Therefore, just as it is not appropriate to bury the talent received from God, as that worthless servant did, so it is also not appropriate to be carried away by the talent one has received. But those who are growing haughty are like Aesop's crow that showed off itself in feathers that belonged to other birds.[9] Against those haughty ones it is said, "Who set you apart? What do you have that you have not received? He made allotments to each." He did not make allotments to one or to you alone, but to each. There is nobody in the family of God who has not received a talent, public or private. God has distinguished offices in the church so that some teach and others listen, some are in charge and others are under authority, just as in verses 6-7 the apostle will mention distinct offices. Therefore let each person think that the talent was entrusted not to them alone but also to their fellow servants. Thus each one who labors diligently in their station will have something; whoever despises or hinders another will not have anything.

"The measure of faith." Faith here has a broad meaning: both knowledge of Christ's teaching and the condition brought about of this faith that

---

[6]Paul of Samosata (d. 275) taught a form of modalism known as monarchianism. He believed that there was only one God and that Jesus had been adopted in his baptism.

[7]Nestorius (d. 450) denied the full personal union of the two natures in Christ.

[8]Hesshus, *Explicatio Epistolae Pauli ad Romanos*, 374v-375v.

---

[9]Carl P. E. Spring, *Luther's Aesop* (Kirksville, MO: Truman State University Press, 2011), 37, 48-49, 57, 66.

justifies and finally the gifts that were once given by faith to the faithful along with faith and baptism. *Metron pisteōs*, "the measure or portion of faith," is contrasted to the fullness or perfection of the gifts. Nobody has this fullness because God has not given it to anyone, but a certain measure to all individually, more to some and less to others. First Corinthians 7:7: "Each one has his own gift from God; one of one kind and another of another kind," according to which the grace and mercy of God is greater in one than in another. The parable of the varying amounts of talents pertains to this passage: one received ten, another five, yet another one. Therefore let nobody be arrogant as if they alone possessed all things. COMMENTARY ON ROMANS 12:3.[10]

No Man Is an Island. JOHANN SPANGEN-BERG: It is as if he wanted to say: "Although the gifts and works are dissimilar and varied, no one should therefore think himself superior, so that he would not create sects among Christians. But each person should abide in the measure of their faith and serve others with their gifts, and in that way the unity of love and the simplicity of faith remain constant. No one should neglect his own works or abilities." EPISTLE FOR THE FIRST SUNDAY AFTER EPIPHANY.[11]

12:4-5 Christ's Body Has Many (and Diverse) Members

Christ's Spirit Animates Believers. JUAN DE VALDÉS: That all those who belong to the church, inasmuch as they are members of Christ and have the spirit of Christ, are children of God, are just, pious and holy, partaking of what is in Christ, in him as head and in them as members. For this reason they are called Christian, the most exalted and divine name that can be given to humans on earth. CHRISTIAN INSTRUCTION FOR CHILDREN.[12]

Members of One Head. HEINRICH BULL-INGER: Paul, in order most properly to express for us and as it were to set before our eyes this unity and agreement of the members, uses a parable of a human body. . . . In 1 Corinthians 12 he expounds more fully and plainly the conjunction of the Head and members and that mainly by the same parable of the members a human body, expressing it very eloquently, and witnessing that between the highest members of the church and the lowest there is a great and fitting agreement and also a diligent care and assistance that is both continual and most faithful. From all this it appears that the marks of the true and lively church of Christ are the communion of the Spirit of Christ, sincere faith and Christian charity, without which no one is a partaker of this spiritual body. And by these things you may easily judge whether you are in fellowship of the church or not. OF THE HOLY CATHOLIC CHURCH.[13]

The Grace of the Body. TILEMANN HES-SHUS: With an elegant metaphor taken from the human body, he teaches that it is fitting for each person to consider modestly what sort of gift they have received from God, in what part of the body they have been placed and over which task they have been set, and then pursue it modestly and faithfully. No one ought to rush into or force their way into greater callings out of arrogance or restlessness. Feet do not take for themselves the duties of the eyes. The hand does not take the duties of the heart or liver for itself. But the individual members serve their own place in a most beautiful harmony and without arrogance, meddlesomeness, envy or contempt. So each one ought to serve their own place and apply to the common edification of the church this gift that they have received from God. Paul calls "grace" those offices in the church and the gifts conferred on individuals through the Holy Spirit, so that everyone can apply themselves fruitfully to the task entrusted to them, for God

---

[10]Pareus, *In Epistolam ad Romanos*, 1236-37.
[11]J. Spangenberg, *Postilla Teütsch*, 4:71r.
[12]*Valdés' Two Catechisms*, 184*.

[13]LCC 24:306-7; citing 1 Cor 12:12-13.

confers all gifts freely. COMMENTARY ON
ROMANS 12:4-6.[14]

INDIVIDUALS ARE EMPOWERED AND LIM-ITED FOR THE COMMON GOOD. JOHN CALVIN:

The very thing that he had previously said of
limiting the wisdom of each according to the
measure of faith he now confirms by a reference
to the vocation of the faithful. For we are called
for this end: that we may unite together in one
body, since Christ has ordained a fellowship and
connection between the faithful similar to what
exists between the members of the human body;
and as human beings cannot of themselves come
together into such a union, he himself becomes
the bond of this connection. As then is the case
with the human body, so it ought to be with the
society of the faithful. By applying this similitude,
he proves how necessary it is for each to consider
what is suitable to their own nature, capacity and
vocation. While this similitude has various
functions, it should be especially applied to the
present matter: as the members of one body—
and they are all distinct—have distinct abilities,
but no single member either possesses all abilities
at once, or assume other members' offices for
itself, so also God has distributed various talents
to us. By this act of distinction he has established
the order that he wants to be observed among us,
so that each person would conduct themselves
according to the measure of their ability and not
force themselves into another person's office. Nor
should one person desire to have all things at
once, content with their lot; they should willingly
abstain from usurping the offices of others.
Nevertheless, when he notes with eloquent
words the communion that is among us, at the
same time he also indicates what great zeal there
ought to be, so that the abilities that each
member possesses would contribute to the
common good of the body. COMMENTARY ON
ROMANS 12:4.[15]

THE METAPHOR OF THE BODY. DAVID PAREUS:

We, all the faithful, are one body in Christ, that is,
under Christ our head, and we are individually
members of one another. Therefore let each be wise
in proportion to their own portion; let no one
despise or hinder anyone; let all not individually
serve themselves but other members, and let them
employ their talent for the edification of the whole
church. The eye does not see itself or see for itself,
but for the members and the body. The hand does
not touch itself or touch for itself, but for the body.
The foot does not carry itself but the body. So let us
not serve ourselves but the members and the body. It
is not a rare thing in every manner of speaking for a
communion to be called a body, because it is like a
body. Thus the communion of saints is the mystical
body of the church because it has something that is
like the head and something that is like parts of the
body. *Christ is the head*; the faithful are members of
Christ and each other, first because just as members
stick to the head through the ligaments of nerves
and arteries, so all are held together by the bond of
the Holy Spirit with Christ the head and with one
another in a mystical way, and second because all are
united outwardly in the unity of faith, the sacraments and charity with Christ and one another. One
must relate these things to the apostle's aim, namely,
that no one would get carried away by their own
gifts if they should happen to have more, for it
would be foolish for the head to get all carried away
because it is the head. His aim is also that no one
would despise another person who has fewer gifts,
for it would be unfair for the head to insult the
stomach or the foot because they are in a lower place.
Finally, his aim is that all would relate all their own
gifts to the public edification, just as all parts of a
body work harmoniously for the health of the body.
This is the foundation of Christian love; arrogance is
what plagues it. If we who are many are one body,
we with an equal right have a share in the head of
Christ. If we are members of one another, let us
foster a mutual Christian love. COMMENTARY ON
ROMANS 12:4.[16]

---

[14]Hesshus, *Explicatio Epistolae Pauli ad Romanos*, 375v-376r.
[15]CTS 38:458* (CO 49:237-38).

[16]Pareus, *In Epistolam ad Romanos*, 1238-39.

THE METAPHOR APPLIED TO THE MINISTRY OF THE WORD. JOHANN SPANGENBERG: Through this parable Saint Paul wants to say how many members constitute the body and yet remain only one body. So also there are many servants and yet only one Christian church, whose head is Christ. In the body there are eyes, ears, mouth, nose, hands and feet. So also in Christianity there are bishops, pastors and preachers. Each member has its own office. The eye sees. The ear hears. The mouth speaks. The hands work. The feet walk. So also in Christianity each prelate has their own office and calling. The eyes are bishops and preachers; the ears, parishioners; the hands, rulers; the feet, subjects. Now if the foot hurts, the eyes look at it, the hands grasp it, the mouth calls for help, etc. And so it should also happen in Christianity. One should help carry another person's load and burden. One accepts another person's distress and concerns as one's own. One should help, serve and advise others with words and deeds. In this way God wants to be our dear Father and Patron, and he wants us to be his children—yes, accepting us as true living sacrifices in his kingdom, in eternal life. EPISTLE FOR THE FIRST SUNDAY AFTER EPIPHANY.[17]

12:6 *The Analogy of Faith*

ALL OTHER PROPHECIES ARE FALSE. CARDINAL CAJETAN: The Greek term translated *rationem* ["reasoning"] in the Vulgate means "analogy," that is, proportional reasoning. The best use of the gift of prophecy is always to examine whether it is proportional to the faith. For prophets who deviate from a method that squares with the faith you should consider false prophets rather than prophets. And because they are in discord with the proportion of Christian faith, all such prophecies must be cast aside. COMMENTARY ON ROMANS 12:6.[18]

THE STANDARD OF THE CHRISTIAN FAITH. JOHN CALVIN: In fact all gifts have their own defined limits, to depart from these is to corrupt these gifts. But because Paul's speech here is a bit confused, we can arrange it, so that the conclusion begins like this: "Therefore whoever has the gift of prophecy should examine it according to the analogy of faith; whoever has the gift of ministry should use it for ministering; whoever has the gift of teaching should use it for teaching," etc. Whoever will consider this goal will appropriately keep himself within the bounds of his gifts. However, this passage is variously understood.

For there are those who understand prophecy as the ability to divine the future, which flourished during the first beginnings of the gospel in the church, saying that at that time the Lord wanted to commend the dignity and excellence of his kingdom in every way. And that "according to the analogy of faith" is added, they believe should be applied to all members. I, however, prefer to follow those who extend this word [that is, "prophecy"] even more broadly to the particular gift of revelation, so that anyone is able to engage deftly and skillfully the office of interpreter in explaining the will of God. And so prophecy today in the Christian church is generally nothing other than the right understanding of Scripture and the particular ability to explain it, since all the ancient prophecies and all the oracles of God have been finished in Christ and his gospel. For in this sense Paul used it when he said: "I wish you spoke in tongues, even more that you prophesy." "In part we know, and in part we prophesy." Nor does it seem that Paul here wanted to enumerate only those astonishing graces by which Christ ennobled his gospel in the beginning; rather we see that he refers only to those ordinary gifts, which remain in the church perpetually. . . .

He is able to admonish here those who prophesy in church, that they should shape their prophecies according to the rule of faith, lest in anything they deviate from this standard. By the word "faith" he means the first principles of religion; whatever teaching is not found to correspond with

---

[17]J. Spangenberg, *Postilla Teütsch*, 4:71v-72r.
[18]Cajetan, *In Sacrae Scripturae Expositionem*, 5:70.

these is condemned as falsehood. COMMENTARY ON ROMANS 12:6.[19]

PASSIVE OR ACTIVE FAITH? THEODORE BEZA: The word *tēs analogias* ["of the analogy"] can be explained in two ways, namely, first, in the sense of a certain "appropriateness" or "congruence," or, second, in the sense of what he had earlier called *metron*, "a measure." If you follow the first of these interpretations, the apostle meant the true standard of prophecy, that is, of discerning the true interpretation of the Scriptures from a false interpretation, namely, whether they are forced in line with the *autopista* axioms[20] of the Christian faith that have been included in the creed that they call the Apostles' and that was written at the beginning of the proclamation of the gospel as a summary of the gospel and so is deservedly called the norm and rule of faith by Tertullian.[21]

But if we were to embrace the second meaning of this word, we would say that after Paul admonished in general that each person consecrate themselves to God and keep themselves within the lanes of their lot, he now explains it part by part. Therefore, first he recalls the ecclesiastical functions, which he divides into two kinds or two groups, namely, the prophetic and the diaconal. By the term "prophecy" he encompasses those things that pertain to the task of teaching, but by the term "diaconate" he encompasses the other ecclesiastical tasks that the apostles gave up in Acts 6:2-4. Now since there is not just one function in the task of teaching, but there are various degrees, and in the one and same function the measure of the Spirit is not equal, so the apostle admonished the prophets to prophesy in proportion to their faith, that is, each one should cling to the measure of their own revelation, so that no one individual should seem in their opinion to know all things. But if this admonition had been kept in the church, it would never have fallen into those dangers from which

now it has scarcely begun to emerge and into which same place one must certainly still fear that it will fall back, unless what the apostle commanded in 1 Corinthians 14:30-33 takes place.

In other respects, the word "prophecy" is often understood in a narrower sense, as in Ephesians 4:11 and 1 Corinthians 12:23, and "service" (*diaconia*) is to the contrary understood in a much broader sense, so that it encompasses all ecclesiastical tasks, and even the very calling of apostles. For certainly we ought to serve God in public and in private, as above in chapter 11, verse 13; Acts 6:4; 12:25. Our apostle applies a similar division of the ecclesiastical functions into these two categories in Philippians 1:1 and 1 Timothy 3, calling "bishops" those whom here he calls "prophets," to whom clearly the ministry of preaching was entrusted, while he understands the others under the title "deacons." Peter too speaks in this way: 1 Peter 4:11. ANNOTATIONS ON ROMANS 12:6.[22]

THE NORM OF ALL PROPHECY. DAVID PAREUS: This is explained in two ways. First, that the *analogia pisteōs* ["analogy of faith"] is the same as what had been stated earlier as *metron pisteōs* ["measure of faith"], that is, the revelation of the truth and the gifts granted to each one. Each one would be affirming as much as they know, and concerning that of which they are certain they would discourse in proportion to the measure of faith granted to them by God and would prophesy concerning the dogmas. Ephesians 4 speaks this way: "according to the measure of the gift of Christ." The Syriac translation renders this meaning: "according to the measure of his faith," which Martyr[23] follows, so that "faith" here means that knowledge of which God has made those whom he has placed in the office of teaching partakers, so that as he teaches or exhorts or consoles, he would not offer anything to the people except for those things that God had suggested, namely, by his inspiration and revelation, so that they would not

---

[19]CO 49:238-39 (CTS 38:459-61); citing 1 Cor 14:5; 13:9; 14:32. See further LCC 20:12-13 (CO 2:12-13).
[20]That is, axioms trustworthy in and of themselves.
[21]Tertullian, *Prescription Against Heretics* 12–13 (ANF 3:249).

[22]Beza, *Annotationes majores*, 2:131-32.
[23]See Vermigli, *In Epistolam ad Romanos*, 589-90.

dare to teach, either what they themselves do not understand or what they themselves have invented. That saying of Peter is applicable here: "Whoever speaks, let him speak as the oracles of God." Again, "if someone should happen to think differently, God will reveal this to them too." This interpretation is sufficiently fitting and the opinion is entirely necessary. If our forebears had observed it and if all teachers were observing it today, we would not have so many human fancies, so many abuses or so many controversies in the church.

But the apostle seems to have said this earlier in this very same verse, that we have spiritual gifts according to the grace given to us. And an analogy is not the same as a *metron* ["measure"], for a measure pertains to one item being measured. But an *analogy* is the resemblances between two items. But the apostle by all means seems to be saying something more, that is, he is prescribing a norm to which all prophecy ought to be directed. By *faith*, therefore, some understand the rule of Scripture and the axioms of faith, such as are summarized in the creed of the apostolic faith and have the manifest truth drawn from the Scriptures. However, an *analogy* of faith is an evident harmony and consensus on the main headings of the faith, with which anything true is in harmony and whatever is discordant is false and adulterated. One must prophesy in the church according to this analogy. This rule applies to every prophecy. Therefore all interpretations, disputes, questions and opinions in the church are examined according to the norm of holy Scripture and the Apostolic Creed, so that they may conform to this norm.

Thus Luther translates it, "Let the explanation be in accordance with the faith." Calvin explains it in this way: "By the word 'faith' he means the first axioms of religion, by which whatever doctrines will have been apprehended unable to make an answer will be convicted of falsehood." Denis the Carthusian does not differ much: "According to the rule of faith," that is, "according to the aim and exigency of the catholic faith. For prophecy is ordained for the strengthening of the faith and properly looks to those things that pertain to salvation, which is its

aim, which faith teaches." Haymo distorts the apostle's thinking: "according to the rule of faith," that is, "just as faith merited," an idea he seems to have picked up from Ambrose, who makes the passage here to mean the merit of faith. Theophylact wanders off from the purpose of this passage: "according to the proportion of faith," that is, "as each one has faith, so he receives grace." He says, "For grace is not simply poured out but, taking a measure from those who receive it, flows out only as much as the room it will find in the vessel of faith offered to it." This is an idea he has drawn from Chrysostom. Notwithstanding that it was just said that God will distribute to each a measure of the faith, it has to be added from elsewhere: "as he wills." Therefore faith itself and the vessel of faith, whether narrow or full, that each one has and that each one thinks little of, is given by God and created by him, because all is grace, not of ourselves. Bellarmine . . . says: "According to the rule of faith," so that no one may prophesy anything contrary to the faith, as false prophets do. But if we leave out these statements, the teaching of this passage is very clear. COMMENTARY ON ROMANS 12:6.[24]

THE CHURCH'S OFFICES ARE NORMED BY THE ONE FAITH. PHILIPP MELANCHTHON: In the enumeration he prescribes rules for certain persons, for instance, prophets. Prophecy signifies revelation, predictions about future events or interpretation of Scripture, for which there is also need of some revelation. No one knows what true faith is, what true comfort for the conscience is or true knowledge of sin, without a divine impulse. And some have clearer impulses than others.

Now he teaches that the interpretation of the Word of God should be analogous, that is, in agreement with the faith. It should not depart from the articles of faith, nor extinguish the true knowledge of Christ or faith in Christ. In earlier times, Ebion, Paul of Samosata and others who contended that there was only a human nature in Christ departed from the faith. Thereafter the

---

[24]Pareus, *In Epistolam ad Romanos*, 1242-44.

Arians, who denied that the Son of God was God by nature; the Manichaeans, who imagined two gods and condemned marriage, courts and eating meat. Thus they imagined that people are righteous not by faith but by such observances.

The Pelagians departed from the analogy of faith because they denied that there is such a thing as original sin and imagined that the law of God is satisfied through such rational works as people can perform as well as possible. They felt that a person merited the remission of sins by these works, and that he is righteous on account of rational works; they taught nothing at all of justifying faith. They added that people are righteous and saved without the Holy Spirit.

These Pharisaical opinions destroy the gospel of Christ completely. For Christ was given us because we do not satisfy the law and because we are not righteous because of the law. A different righteousness is set forth, namely, that we are accounted just by faith on account of Christ. Because Pelagian opinions take away the benefits of Christ they certainly are not according to the analogy of faith. COMMENTARY ON ROMANS (1540).[25]

THE ANALOGY OF FAITH DOES NOT BIND THE SPIRIT'S MOUTH. MARTIN LUTHER: People consider it an honor to teach others. And so each one seeks and wants to teach. That is the greatest misfortune in the church so far as the understanding of Scripture is concerned. For these people, Paul prescribes this limit: "If anyone is a preacher and has the office of teaching others what the Word is, let him above all see to it that he preach nothing which is not in accord with the faith." Whatever is taught, whatever is heard, should fit with the faith. Otherwise, if it is not "in harmony with the faith"—if it does not agree with the faith—the hearers should know that as well, so that they may say, "That agrees with my faith in every respect." And yet Paul says, "Preaching should be analogous with the faith." He does not bind the mouth of the Holy Spirit. But know this: if the

Holy Spirit makes you a prophet, then he will not lead you off into the woods but will teach you what agrees with faith in Christ. When the Holy Spirit was promised to the apostles, Jesus said, "When the Paraclete has come, he will direct you into all truth"—but not beyond the Word. Therefore, even if you boast of the Spirit, if you do not have the Word of God, you are a heretic. The principle for discerning the Spirit is easy: namely, to what extent he teaches the Word of God. "He will glorify me," Jesus says. The Holy Spirit has various revelations, but all must agree with the faith, which is that the Holy Spirit glorifies the Son of God. . . .

This is what must be taught: that all prophecies yield themselves to the faith, so that it may be said, "This or that may be taught, but the faith is the teacher so that our doctrine may be confirmed through the faith." You shall not be the one who is master of the holy Christian church; but where God's Word and faith is, there God will confirm it. If you will not hear the Word, what harm is that to me? If I preach the Word and faith of Christ, then I am confirmed as a doctor. I will teach you nothing; you will not say on the Last Day: "Dr. Martin taught me this," but, "Jesus Christ said this through the mouth of the pastor. I do not believe in Dr. Martin, but in the Father, the Son and the Holy Spirit, who speak through the apostles and through preachers." SERMON ON THE SECOND SUNDAY AFTER EPIPHANY 1545.[26]

ALL PROPHECY MUST CONFORM TO CHRIST'S WORD AND SPIRIT. MENNO SIMONS: The word of Christ, alone, is sufficient for me. If I do not follow his testimony, then, truly, all that I do is useless. And even if I had such visions and inspirations, which is not the case, even then it would have to be conformable to the Word and Spirit of Christ, or else it would be mere fantasy, deceit and satanic temptation. THE REASON MENNO SIMONS DOES NOT CEASE TEACHING AND WRITING.[27]

[25]Melanchthon, *Commentary on Romans*, 214-15* (MO 15:708-9).

[26]LW 58:216-17, 220* (WA 49:682, 684); citing Jn 16:13, 14.
[27]Simons, *Complete Works*, 248*.

12:7-8 *Use Your Gifts for the Benefit of the Body*

On Teaching and Exhorting. Martin Luther: We teach those who still do not know, and we exhort those who already know, so that they can progress. Marginal Gloss on Romans 12:7-8 (1522).[28]

On Serving. Tilemann Hesshus: If the ministry in the church has been entrusted to us, let us give attention to serving. In the early church the name "deacons" was given to the stewards of the resources of the church who served at tables and offered food to widows and other poor people from the resources of the church. Nowadays those who distribute the sacraments are called "deacons." Therefore Paul's belief is this: just as each person has been called to some task in the church, so they ought to look especially to this so that they may serve with a ready and faithful mind and not seek their own advantage, but always look to the church's needs, edification and fruit. Lawrence was a faithful deacon of the church, who preferred to pour out his life rather than to hand over the treasury of the church to a tyrant. Faithfulness in explaining the Scriptures and diligence in ministry pertains to the third commandment. Commentary on Romans 12:7.[29]

Prophecy as Teaching and Exhortation. David Pareus: He now presents two kinds of prophecy: the office of teaching, which is properly that of teachers, and the office of exhorting, which is properly that of the pastors of the church. For he also distinguishes teachers and pastors in Ephesians 4. They were distinct gifts of the Holy Spirit: To some was given a very clear revelation and under-standing of doctrine. They alone were devoting themselves to the duties of teaching, as they explained the chief points of religion and formed the faith of the church. They were also called "catechists." To others was imparted the *dynamis* ["power"] of exhorting, comforting, arguing, correcting and finally forming the life and character of the faithful. However, the apostles excelled in each capacity, and they are truly the common parts of the office of bishop. For that reason they are combined in 1 Corinthians 14: "Whoever prophesies speaks for edification," that is, for instruction, comfort and exhortation. Nonetheless, it does not hinder anything if today the parts that pertain to teaching are entrusted to certain individuals who are stronger than others in the *dynamei hermeneutikē* ["interpre-tive ability"], while the administration of the sacraments is entrusted to others, and pastoral care to still others. For not all people possess the same capability. For there is a manifest distinction between the teachers of scholars and pastors of the churches. Therefore not without merit does the apostle distinguish between the two. The precept was this: let whoever exercises the office of teaching or pastor be sober-minded, carrying out his work modestly and diligently, without arrogance, pride, tyranny or *polypragmosynē* ["meddlesomeness"]. Commentary on Romans 12:7.[30]

A Serious and Weighty Task. Tilemann Hesshus: He further instructs the ministers of the church: the interpreters of sacred Scripture, whom he calls "prophets," have the first place. Then he admonishes teachers and exhorters about their office. These people I understand to be those who educate the youth and catechumens in the catechism and who thereupon urge the people to prayers, godliness, patience and constancy. Paul urges them to be mindful of their task to which they have been called. Let whoever teaches not pursue subtleties or engage in idle questions or engage in unnecessary contentions, but look solely

---

[28]WADB 4:66.
[29]Hesshus, *Explicatio Epistolae Pauli ad Romanos*, 377v-378r. The prefect of Rome ordered Lawrence of Rome (d. AD 258) to forfeit the treasures of the church. He asked for time to gather them; at the end of the allotted time he showed the prefect the poor members of the church. Unamused, the prefect ordered Lawrence's execution. See further RCS OT 7:388 n. 34.

[30]Pareus, *In Epistolam ad Romanos*, 1246-47; citing Eph 4:11-16; 1 Cor 14:3.

to building up the church in the faith. Let him not play with deceits or hide his opinion, but let him speak clearly and unambiguously, and then let him revisit and inculcate the articles of faith. Let him who exhorts not always say pleasing things to his hearers or impart jokes and witticisms. Let him not be trifling in character, but let him exhort the church to every kind of virtue with as much seriousness and severity as he can, both in his speech and morals (for antiquity well said, *Ou logos, alla ho tropos esti ho peithōn tou legontos,* that is, "not the speech but the character of the speaker has the power to persuade"), and let him reproach sins according to God's word and only seek the correction of the church. COMMENTARY ON ROMANS 12:7.[31]

PASTORAL AND TEACHING OFFICES DIFFER IN APPLICATION. THE ENGLISH ANNOTATIONS: Here Paul divides prophets into doctors and pastors. The doctors simply searched into the meaning of Scripture, but the pastors, besides the exposition of the text or the commenting on it, also applied the sense of the Scriptures to the special use of their hearers. The former resemble lecturers in the university; the latter, our preachers. ANNOTATIONS ON ROMANS 12:8.[32]

CHURCH LEADERS MUST WATCH VIGILANTLY. JOHANN SPANGENBERG: Ruling is nothing other than looking after all the offices of the Christian congregation, ensuring that things are going right, namely, that God's Word is preached purely and clearly, the sacraments are offered rightly and alms are distributed orderly. This office belongs to bishops. . . . Truly they must not be lazy or sluggish, but rather diligent, vigilant and assiduous. It depends on the wagoner, if the horses and wagon should move well, so also with the prelates of the Christian faith. If the wagoner falls asleep, allowing the wagon and horses to go their own way, especially on a dangerous street, there's not

much good to hope for. So also if the bishops, shepherds and prelates sleep, the devil will take advantage. EPISTLE FOR THE SECOND SUNDAY AFTER EPIPHANY.[33]

ON GIVING, RULING AND MERCY. TILEMANN HESSHUS: Let each person discharge his duty. For he is still speaking about those who are preeminent in the church. "He who gives generously," that is, he who distributes the alms of the church to the poor—let him discharge this office. Let him not seek his own profit or put people in obligation to him. Let his gifts not imitate talons. Let him not indulge his desires or respect persons, but let him be equal toward all poor.

"He who is in charge, let him act with zeal," that is, let him discharge his task with great diligence. Here Paul speaks about the rulers of the church, who were the censors of morals and elders in the church, who along with the pastors or bishops exercised judgment over the church. From these he requires zeal and diligence. For as it says in the proverb: "The eye of the master feeds the horse." And Solomon says in Ecclesiastes 10: "By laziness the roof will deteriorate, and by a slackening of the hands the house will leak." Diligent vigilance is especially necessary for a person in charge, for people's petulance is boundless and must be restrained at once; if by negligence some sin is committed in governing, it is restored to integrity with difficulty.

"He who shows mercy," that is, he who takes care of the sick and does them good, let him discharge that duty with joy. Let him not do it with an unwilling, morose, difficult spirit, but with a lively and ready spirit. And let him know that he serves Christ himself; it has truly been said: *chariton de te thymos aristos,* that is, "when it comes to acts of kindness a friendly willingness is the most pleasing thing of all." It is a great consolation to the sick when they see someone discharging their duties with a lively spirit. On the other hand,

[31]Hesshus, *Explicatio Epistolae Pauli ad Romanos,* 378r-v.
[32]Downame, ed., *Annotations,* CCCIr*.

[33]J. Spangenberg, *Postilla Teütsch,* 4:75v-76r; citing 1 Tim 3:4-6; Mt 13:25.

it saddens them greatly if they notice that they perform their duties with a sad face. All these duties I put under the heading of the third commandment, for they pertain to the public ministry in the church. Commentary on Romans 12:8.[34]

Social Welfare. John Calvin: By *metadidountas* ["those who contribute"] . . . Paul does not mean those who give lavishly from their own property, but deacons who were in charge of distributing the common resources of the church. By *eleountas* ["those who show mercy"], he means widows and other ministers who were put in charge of caring for the sick according to the ancient church's custom. For there were two different tasks: to acquire the poor's necessities, and to attend to the management of their care. To the former he attributes simplicity, by which, without deceit or respect of persons, they would faithfully administer what was entrusted to them. He

wanted them to render their duties with cheerfulness, lest by their irritable attitude—which frequently happens—they detract from the grace of their office. For as nothing comforts the sick or otherwise afflicted more than whenever they see cheerful and eager souls care for them, in the same way if they discern despondence in the face of those who care for them, they will feel despised. Commentary on Romans 12:8.[35]

Why Does Paul List Ruling Last? Johann Spangenberg: Through the Holy Spirit he sees well that the spiritual prelates would abandon preaching, teaching and admonishing and seize onto ruling—against the command of Christ. Thus, to remind them of these words of Christ, he places ruling last and the other offices—preaching, teaching and admonishing—first. But Paul's reminder had just as much effect as Christ's command. Epistle for the Second Sunday After Epiphany.[36]

---

[34]Hesshus, *Explicatio Epistolae Pauli ad Romanos*, 378v-379r; citing Eccl 10:18.

[35]CO 49:240 (cf. CTS 38:462-63). See further RCS NT 6:lii-liii.
[36]J. Spangenberg, *Postilla Teütsch*, 4:76v; citing Lk 22:25-26.

12:9-21 MARKS OF THE TRUE CHRISTIAN

⁹Let love be genuine. Abhor what is evil; hold fast to what is good. ¹⁰Love one another with brotherly affection. Outdo one another in showing honor. ¹¹Do not be slothful in zeal, be fervent in spirit,ᵃ serve the Lord. ¹²Rejoice in hope, be patient in tribulation, be constant in prayer. ¹³Contribute to the needs of the saints and seek to show hospitality.

¹⁴Bless those who persecute you; bless and do not curse them.¹⁵Rejoice with those who rejoice, weep with those who weep. ¹⁶Live in harmony with one another. Do not be haughty, but associate with the lowly.ᵇ Never be wise in your own sight. ¹⁷Repay no one evil for evil, but give thought to do what is honorable in the sight of all. ¹⁸If possible, so far as it depends on you, live peaceably with all. ¹⁹Beloved, never avenge yourselves, but leave itᶜ to the wrath of God, for it is written, "Vengeance is mine, I will repay, says the Lord." ²⁰To the contrary, "if your enemy is hungry, feed him; if he is thirsty, give him something to drink; for by so doing you will heap burning coals on his head." ²¹Do not be overcome by evil, but overcome evil with good.

a Or *fervent in the Spirit* b Or *give yourselves to humble tasks* c Greek *give place*

OVERVIEW: The reformers focus on three things here: love, prayer and peace. Justified and loved by God, Christians must love their neighbor—even foreigners, the unlovable and their enemies. Christian love does not act with the expectation of compensation, for believing in a God who is no respecter of persons, believers should also be no respecter of persons (by God's grace!). But this goes against our nature; therefore, our commentators commend constant prayer—in public and private, with our mouth and mind. Through prayer Christians commune with the Lord, casting all their burdens on him and receiving peace. "God is our refuge and strength, a very present help in trouble" (Ps 46:1).

Paul admonishes us to strive for peace. The reformers stress the qualifiers "if possible" and "as far as it depends on you" (Rom 12:18). Peace must not come at the cost of the church's faith, our neighbor's well-being or the state's order. Peace at such a high price is sin. However, barring these exceptions, we are commanded not to insist on our rights, to remember that judgment is the Lord's jurisdiction and that the Lord alone knows the heart.

12:9-13 Be Diligent and Fervent in Love

LOVE WITHOUT APPEARANCES. THE ENGLISH ANNOTATIONS: Now he comes to the duties of the second table, which he derives from charity, which is the fountain of them all. He describes it as sincerity, hatred of evil, earnest study of good things and good affection to help our neighbor. It can be asked why the apostle here added the epithet "sincere," or without dissimulation, to love rather than to other virtues. The answer is twofold. It is either because they are all comprised in love, or because there is almost no person who does not make some show of love or friendship to their neighbor without some kind of secret rancor or malice in their heart. ANNOTATIONS OF ROMANS 12:9.[1]

GENUINE LOVE PROCEEDS FROM THE HOLY SPIRIT. TILEMANN HESSHUS: Up to this point he has been teaching bishops, teachers and governors of the church. Now he also teaches how individual hearers and believers ought to be eager for virtue. And he begins first with sincere love. This is the bond of perfection and truly is the foundation for the other virtues. Love for one's neighbor is

[1]Downame, ed., *Annotations*, CCCIr*.

commanded in the second table, which is summarized in the words "Love your neighbor as yourself." The world too often holds in front of itself the love for one's neighbor, but all things in the world are feigned by artificial means, kept under wraps and painted in false colors. Nothing is sincere, nothing is pure. Thus the proverb has been coined: "Flee those whom you believe to be trustworthy and you will be safe." Similarly, *memnēson apistein* ["Remember not to trust anyone"]. And the godly ought to be strangers to every form of pretense and to hate the embellishment of a painted candor. They must reflect that God searches the heart. And the love of the godly ought to proceed from the Holy Spirit, for in the Spirit nothing is faked or feigned.

It is a general commandment that he says: "Oppose evil; cling to the good." For when we see all dishonest and base deeds—not only external high crimes, but also internal hidden deceits and evil activities, as they call them—he wants us to the contrary to join ourselves to whatever is praiseworthy, good, honorable and godly. And let us never allow ourselves to be moved from zeal for true virtue. COMMENTARY ON ROMANS 12:9.[2]

LOVE ONE ANOTHER! TILEMANN HESSHUS: He repeats the commandment about true love, for love is the root of all duties. He says, let there be such love among you Christians as there usually is among brothers who share the same mother. For if nature itself kindles such sparks of mutual love among brothers and kinsfolk, how much greater sparks of love ought the Holy Spirit to kindle, since we have been given a second birth by him and adopted as sons of God. COMMENTARY ON ROMANS 12:10.[3]

DO NOT BE LAZY IN SHOWING LOVE. MARTIN LUTHER: Note how love keeps nothing for itself and seeks only those things that are in the interest of others. He has taught us above how we ought to bestow our goods and talents for the benefit of others, namely, by contributing, by showing mercy, by showing love and so forth, and then how we should bestow honor and good report among ourselves. Now he teaches that one should offer himself, saying that to help, to serve and to succor with our own body, so to speak, is to support and stand by those who are in need. On the other side are the Absalomites, that is, the fathers of peace and those who are not willing to be disturbed and helpful over the needs of others. If they do something, they do it unwillingly and grudgingly, as we see in legal actions, lawsuits and the like. Those who snore and yawn and are lukewarm in all their efforts are the people who break this command, and they achieve nothing by their works but only dissipate them. People of this kind are also hateful to human beings, to say nothing of God. SCHOLIA ON ROMANS 12:11.[4]

SERVING TIME OR THE LORD? THE ENGLISH ANNOTATIONS: In some editions, it is not *kyriō* but *kairō*, that is, serving the time. We might not understand this reading if the apostle called us to be temporizers, and to apply ourselves to the corrupt customs and manners of the times. Instead, the apostle's exhortation is for us to be timely in all our actions and to undertake them at the most appropriate occasion, as he exhorts elsewhere, to walk wisely toward outsiders, redeeming the time, because the days are evil. But in the most ancient copy of Thecla, and generally in most correct editions, the word is not *kairō*, but *kyriō*, not the time but the Lord.[5] And the meaning is that we should have no other aim or scope in all our actions than his service, and whatsoever our employment be, we are to consider with all diligence, as servants of the Lord, what his service and honor requires. ANNOTATIONS ON ROMANS 12:11.[6]

---

[2]Hesshus, *Explicatio Epistolae Pauli ad Romanos*, 379v.
[3]Hesshus, *Explicatio Epistolae Pauli ad Romanos*, 380r.

[4]LW 25:455-56* (WA 56:463); citing 2 Sam 13:22; Prov 18:9.
[5]Thecla, a fourth-century Egyptian martyr, is often cited as the scribe for the *Codex Alexandrinus*, which contains the LXX and much of the New Testament.
[6]Downame, ed., *Annotations*,CCC1r*; citing Col 4:5; Eph 5:16; Ps 2:11; Eph 6:7.

HOPE. TILEMANN HESSHUS: Hope is a virtue of the first commandment, by which we strengthen ourselves in adversities by confidence in divine mercy, seek and await a lessening of our troubles as God wills, and consider based on God's promises that we certainly will be freed from all troubles. It is said about Stephen: "He went triumphant in spirit and lessened his losses by his hope."[7] COMMENTARY ON ROMANS 12:12.[8]

BE CONSTANT IN PRAYER. MARTIN LUTHER: This is spoken in opposition to those who read the Psalms without any heart. We must be on our guard that the prayers of the church do not become more of a hindrance than a help. First, because we offend God more by reading them when our heart is not in it, and second, because we are deceived and made secure by the appearance of these things as if we had truly prayed properly. Thus we will never become attached to the desire for true prayer, but when we pray these things, we think we have prayed and are in need of nothing more. This is a terrible danger. And in return for these things we then at our leisure and in security consume the income and the pensions and the subsidies of the people!

This is the reason he inserted the word "constant," a great watchword that must be noted and respected by all, and especially by clerics. This word signifies that we must put real work into our praying, and it is not in vain, as the ancient fathers have said, "There is no work like praying to God."[9] Therefore when a man wants to enter the priesthood, he must first consider that he is entering a work that is harder than any other, namely, the work of prayer. For this requires a subdued and broken mind and an elevated and victorious spirit. But at this point the lawyers introduce a nice explanation, that to pray the hours is not commanded, but rather to "read" them or to "say" them is. For in this manner they encumber the canon

law with words and snore on in peace. But even if we omit the canonical hours, we need to say something about prayer.

Prayer is of two kinds. There is the vocal prayer, of which it is presently the custom to say that a virtual intention is sufficient—a nice cover for laziness and negligence![10] For on the basis of this, in the first place, they must by force tear from themselves the good intention, and then being satisfied with this, they give up every other attempt.

And in this type of prayer there is a threefold attentiveness: the material (or sensual) attentiveness, whereby one pays attention only to the words, as monks and others such as simple laypeople do, who do not understand even the Lord's Prayer. And this is real prayer no more than the material is the real thing, that is, according to its own nature, it is not prayer in the proper sense of the word, but only in an extrinsic sense, by which every other good work can be called prayer. To pray in this way is merely to perform an act of obedience, which makes it pleasing to God. Such prayer is not to be despised, and it is good in many other ways. First, because it drives away the devil, even if only recited in the simplicity of the heart, that is, if "it is sung in the Spirit" and thus brings the Holy Spirit to us. This is symbolized in David's playing the harp before Saul, for the devil cannot endure even having the Word of God read, as we know from many examples. "For one who speaks in a tongue speaks to God." Second, because the divine word by nature affects the soul, even if it is not understood, for it is a word of grace, as we read in Psalm 45: "Grace is poured on your lips." . . . Third, it gives to the intellect and the emotions an occasion that they would not have otherwise, as we see it symbolized in the minstrel of Elisha. Fourth, although many people who pray this way do not have the full emotional effect of these words, yet they often have a common and elevated spirit toward God.

[7]This is a famous line from Pietro Bembo (1470–1547), an influential Italian cardinal and poet.
[8]Hesshus, *Explicatio Epistolae Pauli ad Romanos*, 382r.
[9]*Vitae Patrum V, Verba Seniorum* XII, 2 (PL 73:941).

[10]Luther uses the twofold Scholastic classification of prayer: *oratio vocalis* and *oratio mentalis*; that is, prayers spoken out loud (for example, in worship) and prayers spoken in the heart (for example, in private devotion).

There is also the intellectual attentiveness, whereby one gives attention to the sense and meaning of the words. The better educated and intelligent must pay attention to this, for each must pay his talent to God.

Then there is the spiritual or emotional attentiveness, whereby one is attentive to the emotional or spiritual effect of the words, as when one laments with those who lament, rejoices with those who rejoice, shouts for joy with those who are shouting for joy and accommodates oneself to every moment of the words. This is true prayer. Of these two points the apostle says, "I will sing with the spirit, and I will sing with the mind also." By using the expression to "sing with the spirit" he is calling attention to the sensual attentiveness, apart from intellectual attentiveness, which is intimately connected with emotional attentiveness, as in the case of devout nuns and uneducated people. By using the expression "to sing with the mind" he is describing the intellectual attentiveness, which can be aroused both with and without the spirit. The mental prayer is the ascent of the mind, as well as the spirit, to God. This is the prayer of which the apostle is speaking here when he says: "Be constant in prayer." In this passage he is emphasizing that Christians should engage in frequent as well as diligent prayer, for "to be constant" means not only to take a great deal of time, but also to urge, to incite, to demand. Just as there is no work for which Christians ought to be more frequent, so no other work requires more labor and effort and therefore is more efficacious and fruitful. For here "the kingdom of heaven has suffered violence, and men of violence take it by force." For prayer in my opinion is a constant violent action of the spirit as it is lifted up to God, as a ship driven upward against the power of a storm. . . .

This violence decreases and disappears, to be sure, whenever the Spirit draws and carries our heart upward by grace, or surely, when a present and major anxiety compels us to take refuge in prayer. And without these two factors, prayer becomes a most difficult and tedious thing, but its effect is tremendous. For true prayer is omnipotent, as our Lord says: "For everyone who asks receives," etc. Thus we must all practice violence and remember that he who prays is fighting against the devil and the flesh. SCHOLIA ON ROMANS 12:12.[11]

THE NECESSITY OF PRAYER. JOHN CALVIN: It is therefore by the benefit of prayer that we reach those riches which are laid up for us with the heavenly Father. For there is a communion of people with God by which, having entered the heavenly sanctuary, they appeal to God in person concerning God's promises in order to experience where necessity so demands, that what they believed was not in vain, although God had promised it in word alone. Therefore we see that to us nothing is promised to be expected from the Lord that we are not also bidden to ask of God in prayer. So true is it that we dig up by prayer the treasures that were pointed out by the Lord's gospel, and that our faith has gazed on. Words fail to explain how necessary prayer is, and in how many ways the exercise of prayer is profitable. Surely with good reason our heavenly Father affirms that the only stronghold of safety is in calling on God's name. By so doing we invoke the presence both of God's providence, through which God sustains us, weak as we are and well-nigh overcome, and of God's goodness, through which we are received, miserably burdened with sins, unto grace: and in short, it is by prayer that we call on God to be wholly present to us. Hence comes an extraordinary peace and repose to our consciences. For having disclosed to the Lord the necessity that was pressing on us, we even rest fully in the thought that none of our ills is hidden from God, who we are convinced has both the will and the power to take the best care of us. INSTITUTES 3.20.2.[12]

PERSEVERE IN PRAYER. TILEMANN HESSHUS: Calling on God is a virtue of the second commandment, by which we flee in Spirit and truth to the

---

[11]LW 25:458-61* (WA 56:465-68); citing Mt 15:8; Mk 7:6; Is 29:13; 1 Cor 14:15; 1 Sam 16:23; 1 Cor 14:2; Ps 45:2; Song 4:11; 2 Kings 3:14-15; 1 Cor 14:15; Mt 11:12; 7:8. [12]LCC 20:851* (CO 2:625-26); citing Joel 2:32.

eternal Father and by trusting in the Redeemer Jesus Christ we see spiritual and physical goods from God and we consider it certain that God will truly hear us. This is our refuge in every need, as Solomon says, "The name of the Lord is a most mighty tower; the righteous flees to it and is delivered."

Genuine calling on God is not merely one among the greatest virtues, but is also the virtue most needed. And because in the church alone this highest form of worship is offered to God, Paul diligently exhorts the church to practice this calling on God. But he warns us to persevere constantly in prayer, for many people fall away from God because they are not heard at once; they leave off praying with the result that they toil in vain and seek other, forbidden aid or fall into despair. Such a falling away is a manifest sign that their faith was not sincere or was not built on a solid foundation. For it is customary for God to delay help and liberation for some time so that he may test our faith so that then he may have a notable opportunity to show more clearly his kindness and love toward us. And so God trains our patience and obedience.

Therefore Paul commands us to persevere in prayer, as it is said in Psalm 27: "Wait for the Lord; be bold, and let your heart be strong, and wait for the Lord." COMMENTARY ON ROMANS 12:12.[13]

ADVICE FOR AFFLICTION. WOLFGANG MUSCULUS: These commands pertain entirely to times of affliction, and they advise how Christians should handle themselves—not only among themselves, but also toward other Christians subject to afflictions. But if affliction breaks out, first patience is necessary to preserve our spirits. Second, by attentive prayer to God, we beg for God's aid, that he not allow us to be surrounded by the plots of our enemies, but instead that he protect us everywhere. And if anything else be needed in affliction, that we ask for this from God, whether it be firmness of faith or hope or patience or steadfastness of spirit or providence to avoid the trickery

of Satan, etc. Finally it is necessary that even if we are without afflictions, still, we should lift up the needs of the saints, namely, those who are in affliction. He does what he says here. "Sharing the needs of the saints": that is, the needs of the brothers are the same as our own worries. COMMENTARY ON ROMANS 12:12-13.[14]

CARE FOR THE LEAST AMONG YOU. JOHN CALVIN: He returns to the duties of love, the chief of which is to do good to those from whom we expect the least recompense. As it commonly happens that those who more than others are pressed down with want and stand in need of help are especially despised (for the benefits conferred on them are regarded as lost), God recommends them to us in a special manner. It is indeed then only that we prove our love to be genuine, when we relieve needy brothers for no other reason than that of exercising our benevolence. Now hospitality is not one of the least acts of love; that is, that kindness and liberality which are shown toward strangers, for they are for the most part destitute of all things, being far away from their friends. He therefore distinctly recommends this to us. We hence see that the more neglected anyone commonly is by people, the more attentive we ought to be to their wants. COMMENTARY ON ROMANS 12:13.[15]

CONSIDER OTHERS BETTER THAN YOURSELF. JOHN CALVIN: Now in these words we perceive that denial of self has regard partly to people, partly, and chiefly, to God. For when Scripture bids us act toward others so as to esteem them above ourselves, and in good faith to apply ourselves wholly to doing them good, it gives us commandments of which our mind is quite incapable unless our mind be previously emptied of its natural feeling. For such is the blindness with which we all rush into self-love that each one of us seems to himself to have just cause to be

---

[13]Hesshus, *Explicatio Epistolae Pauli ad Romanos*, 382r-v; citing Prov 18:10; Ps 27:14.

[14]Musculus, *In epistolam Apostoli Pauli ad Romanos commentarii*, 218. [15]CTS 38:467* (CO 49:242-43).

proud of himself and to despise all others in comparison. If God has conferred on us anything of which we need not repent, relying on it we immediately lift up our minds, and are not only puffed up but almost burst with pride. The very vices that infest us we take pains to hide from others, while we flatter ourselves with the pretense that they are slight and insignificant, and even sometimes embrace them as virtues. If others manifest the same endowments we admire in ourselves, or even superior ones, we spitefully belittle and revile these gifts in order to avoid yielding place to such persons. If there are any faults in others, not content with noting them with severe and sharp reproach, we hatefully exaggerate them. Hence arises such insolence that each one of us, as if exempt from the common lot, wishes to tower above the rest, and loftily and savagely abuses every mortal human being, or at least looks down on them as inferior. The poor yield to the rich; the common folk, to the nobles; the servants, to their masters; the unlearned, to the educated. But there is no one who does not cherish within themselves some opinion of their own preeminence.

Thus each individual, by flattering themselves, bears a kind of kingdom in their breast. For claiming as their own what pleases them, they censure the character and morals of others. But if this comes to the point of conflict, their venom bursts forth. For many obviously display some gentleness so long as they find everything sweet and pleasant. But just how many are there who will preserve this even tenor of modesty when they are pricked and irritated? There is no other remedy than to tear out from our inward parts this most deadly pestilence of love of strife and love of self, even as it is plucked out by scriptural teaching. For thus we are instructed to remember that those talents which God has bestowed on us are not our own goods but the free gifts of God; and any persons who become proud of them show their ungratefulness. "Who causes you to excel?" Paul asks. "If you have received all things, why do you boast as if they were not given to you?"

Let us, then, unremittingly examining our faults, call ourselves back to humility. Thus nothing will remain in us to puff us up; but there will be much occasion to be cast down. On the other hand, we are bidden so to esteem and regard whatever gifts of God we see in others that we may honor those human beings in whom they reside. For it would be great depravity on our part to deprive them of that honor which the Lord has bestowed on them. But we are taught to overlook their faults, certainly not flatteringly to cherish them; but not on account of such faults to revile those whom we ought to cherish with good will and honor. Thus it will come about that whatever person we deal with, we shall treat them not only moderately and modestly but also cordially and as a friend. You will never attain true gentleness except by one path: a heart imbued with lowliness and with reverence for others. INSTITUTES 3.7.4.[16]

12:14 Bless All People

LOVE THOSE WHO HATE YOU. JOHN CALVIN: He will presently give direction respecting the retaliation of the injuries that we may suffer: but here he requires something even more difficult: that we are not to imprecate evils on our enemies, but to wish and to pray God to render all things prosperous to them, however much they may harass and cruelly treat us. And this kindness, the more difficult it is to be practiced, so with the more intense desire we ought to strive for it. For the Lord commands nothing with respect to which he does not require our obedience; nor is any excuse to be allowed if we are destitute of that disposition, by which the Lord would have his people to differ from the ungodly and the children of this world. This is arduous, I admit, and wholly opposed to human nature; but there is nothing too arduous to be overcome by the power of God, which shall never be wanting to us, provided we neglect not to seek for it. And though you can hardly find one

---

[16]LCC 20:693-94* (CO 2:508-9); citing Phil 2:3; 1 Cor 4:7.

who has made such advances in the law of the Lord that they fulfill this precept, yet no one can claim to be the child of God or glory in the name of a Christian who has not in part attained this mind, and who does not daily resist the opposite disposition. COMMENTARY ON ROMANS 12:14.[17]

12:15-16 Live in Harmony with Everyone

LOVING SYMPATHY. RUDOLF GWALTHER: By these words, to be sure, Paul submits a universal precept in which he commends Christian sympathy to us, so that by this same attitude we would certainly have mutual affection among us, and so we would bear the misfortunes and feelings of others. The unity of the body of the church requires this, which we have often said. In this verse he explains this more diligently with two specifics. The first pertains to joyful and favorable circumstances: "Rejoice," he says, "with those who rejoice." This precept can seem superfluous, but in fact it is necessary. For by nature we are envious and inclined to rivalry, and we usually sneer at the happiness of others; as Christ says about the murmuring laborers, we look with evil eyes at God's generosity and goodness that follows others. Therefore the apostle wants to heal this fault and admonishes that having laid aside every envy and rivalry, we congratulate the happiness of others and look with favor on their joyful successes in the same manner as our own. Those who do this rightly attend to the tranquility of their souls and reconcile themselves to the mind of others. . . .

In the second part of this aphorism he commands us to weep with those who weep, but this is nothing other than to be affected by another's misfortunes as if they were our own. For he explains it this way in this epistle to the Hebrews: "Be mindful of those who are suffering since you are in the same body." The rationale for this precept depends on unity, which for us is in Christ; it extends as much as from faith as it is contained in the bond of love which is moved to pity if we see someone in misery and calamity. SERMONS ON THE EPISTLE TO THE ROMANS.[18]

EXCELLENCE BEFORE GOD COMES THROUGH HUMILITY. JOHN CALVIN: The apostle employs words in Greek more significant, and more suitable to the antithesis, by which he means that it is not the part of a Christian ambitiously to aspire to those things by which he may excel others, nor to assume a lofty appearance. On the contrary, they are to exercise humility and meekness, for by these we excel before the Lord, and not by pride and contempt of the brothers. A precept is fitly added to the preceding; for nothing tends more to break unity than when we elevate ourselves, and aspire to something higher, so that we may rise to a higher situation. I take the term humble in the neuter gender, to complete the antithesis. Here then is condemned all ambition and that elation of mind which insinuates itself under the name of magnanimity. For the chief virtue of the faithful is moderation, or rather lowliness of mind, which always prefers to give honor to others rather than take it away from them. COMMENTARY ON ROMANS 12:16.[19]

DON'T BE A BLOCKHEAD. MARTIN LUTHER: The command against being conceited is directed against opinionated, hard-headed, stiff-necked people, whom in popular language we call blockheads, but whom Scripture describes as "stiff-necked" and "unbelieving." We are all strongly inclined to this fault with a strange propensity, and most rare is the person who does not possess it. In German it is described by the word *steifsinnig*, which means to yield to the advice of no one, even though we are convinced by their reasoning. And even if one uses the opposite method, such people still remain adamant and wait for the chance to rejoice and laugh if the advice of others proves

---

[17]CTS 38:468-69* (CO 49:243).

[18]Gwalther, *In D. Pauli Apostoli Epistolam ad Romanos homiliae*, 177r, 177v; citing Mt 20:1-16; Heb 13:3; Lk 10:25-37.
[19]CTS 38:470-71* (CO 49:244).

wrong. These people are the authors of contention and the most effective disturbers of the peace and destroyers of spiritual unity. SCHOLIA ON ROMANS 12:16.[20]

12:17-19 Vengeance Is the Lord's Alone

OVERCOME EVIL WITH GOOD. JOHN COLET: We must persevere resolutely in goodness and endurance of evil, so that capricious evil may at length be overcome by unswerving good, and what is in truth the weaker thing by its stronger opposite. . . . One who does not see this, but fancies that force must be repelled by force, and war by war, and evil by evil, in this unhappy blindness sees no light. And it may be clearly recognized how great the error in which one is involved from the fact that one will never by any effort attain what one is endeavoring and longing to accomplish, nor in this way, it is most certain, will one ever perceive an end of evils; but rather evils after evils springing up so thickly that the more one toils in extricating oneself by that method, the more will one involve oneself in evils. We are as yet surrounded and almost overwhelmed by so many evils in this world and the cause, which wholly *lies in wickedness*, is none other than this: that in our folly and blindness we do not seek to conquer opposites by opposites but wish rather to increase one evil by another, not perceiving that when we return evil for evil, that we are increasing the evil, not dispelling it. Now the apostle Paul, taught by Christ, saw the marvelous truth of the evangelic precept that evil must not be rendered for evil. EXPOSITION OF ROMANS.[21]

PEACE IN AND OVER ALL THINGS. MARTIN LUTHER: St. Paul speaks and teaches that we Christians ought to live in peace with everyone, as much as it depends on us. This means that we ought to abandon our right for the sake of peace, so that we do not suffer. For peace is more impor-

tant than what is legal; in fact, the laws are established for the sake of peace. LETTER TO ELECTOR JOHN (1532).[22]

THE INTEGRITY OF THE FAITH IS MORE IMPORTANT THAN EXTERNAL PEACE. DAVID PAREUS: "If it is possible." It is as if he were to say, "I know that it is hardly possible always to cultivate peace with contentious people, partly due to the malice of other people, partly due to your own conscience or weakness—indeed it cannot always be done with a good conscience." For he does not want us to keep quiet or pretend for the sake of peace so that we do not give offense, at least if we hear that the truth and the faith are being censured by unbelievers or heretics or if we see that God is offended by wretched morals, our neighbor is being hurt or the church or state is being thrown into confusion. For then such people must be refuted according to our calling, even if controversies follow. COMMENTARY ON ROMANS 12:18.[23]

PAUL QUALIFIES THIS COMMAND. WOLFGANG MUSCULUS: And this pertains to the preceding subject concerning the good and honorable reputation that should be had among all mortals. For contentious people hear everything in a negative light, while those devoted to peace are praised. But he does not strive for peace who avenges himself, or surely, who somehow strikes another first. But because with those who are evil—and thus they also strive for evil and hate peace—it is either impossible or only possible with great difficulty to live in peace, he therefore adds, "if it's possible" (as if he were saying: "I know that sometimes this cannot happen") and "so far as it depends on you." For peace cannot be based on only one person's goodwill; rather it is necessary that both parties strive for it. *One cannot have any more peace than one's neighbor wants.* Therefore this alone is required: that room not be given for discord through our fault.

---

[20]LW 25:464* (WA 56:472); citing Eph 4:3; Phil 2:2.
[21]Colet, *An Exposition of St. Paul's Epistle to the Romans*, 92-93*.
[22]LW 50:45* (WABr 6:260-61).
[23]Pareus, *In Epistolam ad Romanos*, 1261.

That, with all human beings, he declares adequate; the apostle isn't speaking about unanimity of religion. For to live peacefully in matters of religion with all human beings is neither good nor possible, since there are so many forms of worship of different gods and such a variety of opinions about them. However, concerning that external association through which we are connected with mortals, we must strive for peace as long as it is possible, without taking anything from the profession of the Christian religion. Nothing of the Christian religion should be ceded in favor of external peace. COMMENTARY ON ROMANS 12:18.[24]

CHRIST'S PEOPLE ARE FOR PEACE. DORDRECHT CONFESSION (1632): With regard to revenge and resistance to enemies with the sword, we believe and confess that our Lord Christ as well as his disciples and followers have forbidden and taught against all revenge. We have been commanded to recompense no person with evil for evil, nor to return cursing for cursing, but to put the sword into its sheath or, in the words of the prophet, beat swords into plowshares. From this we understand that following the example, life and doctrine of Christ, we may not cause offense or suffering but should instead seek to promote the welfare and happiness of others. If necessary for the Lord's sake, we should flee from one city or country to another; we should suffer the loss of goods rather than bring harm to another. If we are slapped, we should return the other cheek rather than take revenge or strike back. In addition, we should pray for our enemies and, if they are hungry or thirsty, feed and refresh them and thus assure them of our good will and desire to overcome evil with good. In short, we ought to do good, commending ourselves to the conscience of every man and woman, and, according to the law of Christ, do to others as we should wish them to do to us. ARTICLE 14.[25]

12:20-21 Overcome Evil with Good

IF THE WICKED DO NOT DESERVE LOVE, NO ONE DOES! JOHN DONNE: St. Augustine cites and approves that saying of the moral philosopher [Seneca], *Omnes odit, qui malos odit,* "Whoever hates wicked people hates all people."[26] For if a person will love none but honest people, where shall he find any practice, any object of his love? So if a person will hold friendship with none, nor do offices of society to none, but to good-natured and gentle and supple and sociable people he shall leave very necessary business undone. The most difficult and perverse person may be good ad hoc for such or such a particular use. By good company and good usage, that is, by being mingled with other herbs and ingredients, the very flesh of a viper is made an antidote; a viper does not lose his place in medicine because he is poison. A magistrate ceases not to be a magistrate because he is a wicked person. Much less does a person cease to be a person—and thus to have a title to those duties which are rooted in nature—because he is of a wicked disposition!

"God makes his sun to shine on the good and on the bad, and sends rain on the just and the unjust." God has made of one blood all humankind; how unkindly then, how inhumane is it to draw blood! We come too soon to the name of enemy, and we carry it too far. Plaintiff and defendant in a matter of trespass must be enemies. Disputes in a problematic matter of controversy that is not concerned with foundations must be enemies. And then all enmity must imply irreconcilableness; once enemies, friends never again. We come too soon to the name, and we stand too long upon the thing. There are offices and duties even to an enemy. SERMON 63, ON CANDLEMAS.[27]

VARIOUS INTERPRETATIONS OF THIS VERSE. JOHN CALVIN: Paul shows how we may really

[24]Musculus, *In epistolam Apostoli Pauli ad Romanos commentarii,* 220.
[25]CRR 11:304*; citing Mt 5:39, 44; Rom 12:14; 1 Pet 3:9; Is 2:4; Mic 4:3; Zech 9:8-9; Mt 5:39; Rom 12:19-21; 2 Cor 4:2; Mt 7:12.
[26]Ad Macedonium, Epistle 153.14, PL 33:659. See Anna Maria Ferrero, "Lost and Fragmentary *Works,*" in *Brill's Companion to Seneca: Philosopher and Dramatist,* eds. Gregor Damschen and Andreas Heil (Leiden: Brill, 2013), 207-8.
[27]Donne, *Works,* 3:106-7*; quoting Mt 5:45.

fulfill the precepts of not revenging and of not repaying evil, even when we not only abstain from doing injury but when we also do good to those who have done wrong to us. It is a kind of an indirect retaliation when we turn aside our kindness from those by whom we have been injured. Understand as included under the words *food* and *drink* all acts of kindness. Whatsoever then may be your ability, in whatever business your enemy may want either your wealth or your counsel or your efforts, you ought to help them. But he calls him our enemy not whom we regard with hatred but the one who entertains enmity toward us. And if they are to be helped according to the flesh, much less is their salvation to be opposed by imprecating vengeance on them. As we are not willing to lose our toil and labor, Paul shows what fruit will follow, when we treat our enemies with acts of kindness. But some by coals understand the destruction that returns on the head of our enemy when we show kindness to one unworthy, and deal with that one otherwise than that one deserves; for in this manner one's guilt is doubled. Commentary on Romans 12:20.[28]

Sympathy for the Devil. John Donne: Much less does the commandment bind us to the *inimicus homo*, which is the devil, to further him by fueling and advancing his temptations by high diet, wanton company or licentious discourse— and so on the pretense of maintaining our health or cheerfulness invite occasions of sin. St. Jerome tells us of one sense in which we should favor that enemy, the devil, and that in this text we are commanded to do so.[29] *Benevolus est erga diabolum*, he says, "He is the devil's best friend who resists him." For by our yielding to the devil's temptations we submit him to greater torments than if he missed of his purpose upon us, he should suffer. Sermon 63, On Candlemas.[30]

Defeat Evil Through the Spirit. David Joris: This is how to win. Pay close attention. The Lord has given you much wisdom and power from above, in order to come to the victory. This will not come about through the knowledge of the letter, but through that of the Spirit. Of the Wonderful Working of God (1535).[31]

A Neglected Precept. Desiderius Erasmus: Here "good" and "evil" do not refer to a wicked or upright person but indicate kindness itself or injury. Thus one is overcome by evil who does not restrain one's spirit when provoked by injury but is driven to retaliate. One overcomes evil with good who repays evil deeds with good deeds, causing one's enemy to repent and become a friend. This precept, since the human disposition would find it difficult, Paul added with the authority of the Lord—"says the Lord." Christ, too, enjoined the same in the gospel. And yet somehow those who very much think themselves Christians not only neglect this teaching but even laugh at it openly; and those whose ears—pious, no doubt—do not bear to hear censured even the superstitious cult of Christopher, Barbara or Erasmus[32] do not scruple to raise a laugh at these most holy precepts of Christ. And what Socrates taught the heathen before Christ,[33] which was handed down by Christ himself and inculcated so many times by the apostles, Christians laugh at, although Christ distinguished his own from the world chiefly by this mark of identity. But this is not the place for such a lament. Annotations on Romans 12:21.[34]

A General Precautionary Precept. Tilemann Hesshus: This is a general precept: human wickedness should not be stirred up, so that because of some impatience or wrath we act contrary to righteousness; instead by excellence, patience, gentleness, lovingkindness, goodwill,

---

[28]CTS 38:475-76 (CO 49:247-48).
[29]Jerome, *Commentary on Matthew*; PL 26:58.
[30]Donne, *Works*, 3:108-9*.

[31]CRR 7:121.
[32]Three of the fourteen Holy Helpers, saints venerated for their putative healing powers.
[33]Cf. Plato, *Crito* 49C-E; *Republic* 1.335B-E.
[34]CWE 56: 343-44; citing Lk 6:27-35.

generosity and, above all, confidence in God, we should conquer all wickedness. Because many are overcome by the ungratefulness of some people, they are unwilling to do further good works for others. Many are crushed by insults and pretenses, for pretense disturbs wisdom and crushes the strength of their heart, so that they abandon the responsibilities of their vocation. Many on account of offenses inflicted on their homeland wage war. Therefore Paul commands us to take precautions, so that we do not seem to be conquered by human iniquities and impelled to unrighteousness, but so that we always overcome even iniquity with excellence. Consider when

Otto I reigned. He conquered evil with good when his brother Henry laid claim to the kingdom and plotted treachery against Otto: not only did Otto mercifully pardon his brother, but he also gave him Lotharingia and Bavaria. COMMENTARY ON ROMANS 12:21.[35]

---

[35]Hesshus, *Explicatio Epistolae Pauli ad Romanos*, 387r-v. Otto I (912–973) was crowned in 936 as king of Germany and in 962 as the Holy Roman emperor. Despite his father designating him as sole heir, a coalition of dukes questioned the legitimacy of Otto's reign, supporting his young brother Henry as the rightful king of Germany. Otto squelched this opposition and reconciled with his brother; however, Henry plotted an assassination attempt on Otto. The plot was thwarted, and after public penance, Otto pardoned Henry.

13:1-7 SUBMISSION TO AUTHORITIES

Let every person be subject to the governing authorities. For there is no authority except from God, and those that exist have been instituted by God. ²Therefore whoever resists the authorities resists what God has appointed, and those who resist will incur judgment. ³For rulers are not a terror to good conduct, but to bad. Would you have no fear of the one who is in authority? Then do what is good, and you will receive his approval, ⁴for he is God's servant for your good. But if you do wrong, be afraid, for he does not bear the sword in vain. For he is the servant of God, an avenger who carries out God's wrath on the wrongdoer. ⁵Therefore one must be in subjection, not only to avoid God's wrath but also for the sake of conscience. ⁶For because of this you also pay taxes, for the authorities are ministers of God, attending to this very thing. ⁷Pay to all what is owed to them: taxes to whom taxes are owed, revenue to whom revenue is owed, respect to whom respect is owed, honor to whom honor is owed.

OVERVIEW: Paul exhorts the Romans to obey the divinely appointed secular authorities; to oppose secular authority is to oppose God's order. The magisterial reformers, who often worked closely with civil authorities to enact their reforming efforts, likewise argue that civil rulers are ordained by God and do not need the church—whose role is to proclaim the gospel—to legitimize them. In their eyes, to serve public office is a good Christian vocation ordained by God for the common good, and public officials should serve not out of self-interest but for the welfare of others. Only when the governing authorities contradict the commands of God or become tyrannical may Christians resist for "we must obey God rather than human beings" (Acts 5:29).

While acknowledging the original context of Paul's audience the magisterial reformers nevertheless assume that the magistrates are Christian. They respect the wisdom of Cicero and other Romans about governance but share with Augustine a profound ambiguity about whether justice can be attained by governance apart from Christ. Augustine had argued that as excellent as the Roman Republic was it never attained justice because only Christ brings true justice.[1] The magisterial reformers also remind their readers that only those in certain offices, like pastors, should criticize officials; this was not the role of the private citizen. Good order and the maintenance of peace, which are the responsibility of civil authorities, are necessary for worship and the proclamation of the gospel.

The Anabaptist reformers, on the other hand, encouraged at least two attitudes toward government: either to withdraw altogether from the world and form a true Christian community according to biblical models, like the Hutterites, or, like Thomas Müntzer, to build the kingdom of God on earth and if necessary revolt against "ungodly" rulers who resisted them. The magisterial reformers feared that both approaches could lead to disorder, which is partly why they so often persecuted the radicals. With the exception of those who encouraged withdrawal from the world like some Anabaptists, all the reformers agreed that the governing authorities are divinely ordained to protect the people and serve the common good and therefore do not bear the sword in vain. And so the reformers agree with Paul: Christians must pay all such authorities their due—taxes, revenue, respect and honor.

ON CIVIL GOVERNMENT. TILEMANN HESSHUS: The doctrine of civil government is a necessary one in the church. For when the church is gathered

---

[1]For example, see Augustine, *City of God* 19.21 (NPNF 2:415-16).

among people in this life and needs food, drink, hospitality, protection, laws, judges and contracts, one must know from whom authority derives; who established it, preserves it and directs it; what sort of obedience is owed to a magistrate; whether a Christian may discharge civil duties; whether contracts may be drawn up with a good conscience; whether one may summon another to court; and whether civil matters hinder faith and the righteousness of the Spirit. It is necessary to educate consciences about these great matters, especially because many fanatical minds have foully polluted this estate—people like Marcion, Manes, Tatian, Montanus, the Anabaptists, Thomas Müntzer, Heinrich Pfeiffer and even the Roman Antichrist. For they taught that civil rulers in this type of life would be able to obtain salvation only with difficulty. And they have further contended that every civil office ought to be abolished. COMMENTARY ON ROMANS 13: EXCURSUS ON MAGISTRATES.[2]

GOD'S WORD ON CIVIL MATTERS. PHILIPP MELANCHTHON: Life in the state . . . does not belong to the gospel, but to the judgment of reason and the counsel of the magistracy. Passing laws about contracts, successions, court actions, punishments, war and similar civil or forensic things belongs to reason, like matters of architecture or the art of physicians. Nevertheless it is necessary that there be a word of God about the use of these arts for two reasons: that the works of God may be acknowledged and that we may know their use is permitted to the godly, because our works need to have a testimony from the Word of God.

Let readers here note first to what extent the gospel speaks about political matters in general. They should remember that the gospel does not set up any kind of worldly government, but

approves the forms of government of all peoples and the laws about civil matters that are in agreement with reason. Thus it approves of medicine and the art of building. At the same time the gospel teaches the godly properly about spiritual and eternal life in order that eternal life may be begun in their hearts. In public it wants our bodies to be engaged in this civil society and to make sure of the common bonds of this society with decisions about properties, contracts, laws judgments, magistrates and other things. These external matters do not hinder the knowledge of God from being present in hearts or fear, faith, calling on God and other virtues. In fact God put forth these external matters as opportunities in which faith, calling on God, fear of God, patience and love might be exercised.

There is a certain wisdom worthy for a Christian to know. God cast the church into the midst of these occupations because God wants to become known among people in a common society. He wanted all offices of society to be exercises in confession, and at the same time exercises of faith and love.

Minds must become accustomed to think reverently about all the areas of civil society because minds are greatly hurt by fanatical opinions, that governments, laws, courts and contracts are things thought out by human ingenuity and are only instruments of human greed; that governments are instruments for exercising unjust power against those who are weaker; and that courts serve the desire for revenge or avarice. . . . On the contrary we should think honorably of them. They are gifts and ordinances of God, handed down for this purpose first, that this society may be preserved for the purpose of teaching. Second, that these offices of society themselves may be exercises of confession. Third, that in these works we may exercise fear of God, faith, prayer, love, etc. Therefore let us realize that it is wicked to despise or harm these divine things. COMMENTARY ON ROMANS (1540).[3]

---

[2]Hesshus, *Explicatio Epistolae Pauli ad Romanos*, 388r-v. Marcion (c. 85–c. 165) denied the canonicity of the Old Testament as well as much of the New. Manes (fl. third century AD) was the father of the Manichaean religion, which taught that matter was inherently evil. Montanus (fl. second century AD) started an extreme ascetic movement. Thomas Müntzer (d. 1525) embraced a strong apocalypticism that led ultimately to his death; he was aided by Heinrich Pfeiffer (d. 1525).

[3]Melanchthon, *Commentary on Romans*, 216-17* (MO 15:709-10).

COMMON CONFUSION CONCERNING CIVIL GOVERNMENT. WOLFGANG MUSCULUS: The apostle spends almost the entire chapter teaching the obedience owed to magistrates. So diligently and with such focus he taught this because it is likely that certain erring spirits secretly alienated the profession of the Christian name among sedition and conspiracy. Even at that time erring spirits behaved as if it were disgraceful and unlawful for Christians to obey magistrates, so that it was necessary for the apostle to handle this position with such diligence. This plague tempted Jews too, before Christians, concerning which see Josephus. And this tempts many Christians in our own time. However, as it has always been suppressed, so also in our time it has not been able to prevail, because concerning this matter the Lord declares that those who oppose magistrates oppose the power of God. And not only will the efforts of seditious people accomplish nothing against God's ordered rule, but also they bring judgment on themselves. COMMENTARY ON ROMANS 13.[4]

NO EARTHLY KINGDOM. JOHN CALVIN: Because he so carefully handles this subject regarding the formation of Christian life, it seems that he was compelled to do so by some great necessity, which—though the preaching of the gospel always requires this—needed to be addressed especially in that age. There are always tumultuous spirits who believe that the kingdom of Christ cannot be exalted sufficiently, unless all earthly powers are abolished; nor can they enjoy the liberty given through Christ, unless they cast off every human yoke of subjection. Nevertheless this error, before all others, arrested the Jews. It seemed disgraceful to them that the offspring of Abraham—whose kingdom had flourished greatly before the advent of the Redeemer—should now remain in subjection after he appeared. There was something else that alienated the Jews no less than the Gentiles from their rulers: not only that they all abhorred piety but that they also persecuted religion with a most hostile spirit. And so it seemed absurd to acknowledge them as legitimate lords and rulers who strove to snatch the kingdom away from Christ, the only Lord of heaven and earth. For these reasons it is likely that Paul was led to confirm the power of the magistrates with greater care. And first he lays down a general precept by which he summarizes what he is about to say. Then he adds an explanation and proof of his precept. COMMENTARY ON ROMANS 13:1.[5]

13:1-2 All Authority Is from God

INSTRUCTION CONCERNING RULERS. CARDINAL CAJETAN: After Paul has instructed the Romans concerning the use of the body, the matters and gifts of God, he continues with instruction concerning the use of liberty with respect to rulers. Accordingly he warns that if the Romans suppose that they are exempt from the jurisdiction of secular rulers, it does not follow on account of their liberty in Christ. For this reason he instructs them to submit to secular rulers. And while he should have said "every human being," he quite meaningfully says "every soul," so that we would understand that not only our material, not only our body, but also our soul should be subject to secular rulers in those matters that they can lawfully rule. And by saying "all," he excludes no one. COMMENTARY ON ROMANS 13:1.[6]

PAUL RESPONDED TO CHRISTIAN CIVIL DISOBEDIENCE. DESIDERIUS ERASMUS: Paul was aware that some Christians, under the pretext of religion, were refusing the orders of their rulers, and that as a result the established order would be upset and all things thrown into disarray. Therefore he taught that they should obey anyone at all entrusted with public authority, making exception for

---

[5]CTS 38:477-78* (CO 49:248-49). See further Calvin's comment on Acts 1:6, RCS NT 6:8. Luther agrees that Christians must not confuse Christ's kingdom with temporal power and worldly peace, even if it's tempting (see *Sermons on Matthew* 24 [1539]; LW 68:271-72*; WA 47:561).
[6]Cajetan, *In Sacrae Scripturae Expositionem*, 5:72.

[4]Musculus, *In epistolam Apostoli Pauli ad Romanos commentarii*, 223.

the interests of faith and piety. True, these very rulers are pagan and evil; but order is still good, and for the sake of this the godly must sometimes bear even bad rulers. ANNOTATIONS ON ROMANS 13:1.[7]

OUR SOULS OBEY GOD. MARTIN LUTHER: Is there some mysterious reason why he does not say "every person" but rather "every soul"? Perhaps it is because it must be a sincere submission and from the heart. Second, because the soul is the medium between the body and the spirit, so that he thus may show that the believer is exalted once and for all above all things and yet at the same time is subject to them, and thus, being twin born, one has two forms within oneself, just as Christ does. According to the Spirit, he is above all things, and because through faith the believer has subjected all these things to himself in the sense that he is not affected by them nor trusts in them, he compels them to serve him to his glory and salvation. This is to serve God and so to rule and establish the spiritual realm.

The world is conquered and subjected in no better way than through contempt. But this spiritual rule is now so little known that almost everyone with one accord says that the temporal gifts which have been given to the church are spiritual gifts. And now, they regard only these as spiritual and rule by means of them, except that they still carry on their juridical actions, the lightning bolts of their decrees, and their power of the keys, but with much less concern and zeal than they use on their "spiritual," that is, their temporal duties.

Thus the spirit of believers cannot be or become subject to anyone but is exalted with Christ in God, holding all things under its foot, like the woman depicted with the moon under her feet, symbolizing all temporal powers. The "soul," which is the same as the spirit of a human being, insofar as it lives and works and is occupied with temporal matters, ought to be subject for the Lord's sake to every human institution. By this submission it is obedient to God and wills the same thing that he

wills, and thus through this subjection it is victorious over all these things.

Let me digress a little.[8] A person has to be amazed at the impenetrable darkness of our time. Today nothing hurts more, those voracious spendthrifts of our temporal gifts, than when the liberties, laws, edicts or benefices of the church are violated. Then they immediately let fly the lightning bolts of excommunication and with wondrous audacity declare people heretics, enemies of God and of his church and of the apostles Peter and Paul. In the meantime they are utterly unconcerned as to whether they themselves are friends of God or perhaps even greater enemies than those they condemn. To such an extent have they established an obedience and faith under the custody, enlargement and defense of temporal things. You may be guilty of pride, wantonness, avarice, contentions and wrath, and you may possess the whole catalog of vices mentioned by Paul, and even though you may possess them till they cry to heaven, you are a most pious Christian if only you uphold the laws and liberties of the church. But if you neglect them, you are not a faithful son of the church, nor her friend.

Moreover, the secular princes have given great riches to the church and have endowed her leaders with many benefits. But look at this marvel. In the time of the apostles, when priests were eminently worthy of the favor of all people, they still paid taxes and were subject to the governing authorities. But now, when the life they lead resembles nothing so little as the life of priests, they enjoy the rights of special exemptions. Do the successors possess what the predecessors should have had? And the life that the present generation ought to live, did the former generation already demonstrate it sufficiently? By some marvelous exchange the

---

[7]CWE 56:347.

[8]Luther here criticizes the state of the medieval ecclesial court system. This court operated under spiritual law, that is, canon law. Parishioners who did not pay their tithe were summoned to court to settle the matter. If they did not appear in court, they were excommunicated until they came to court and paid their fines and tithe. These court cases had more to do with the church's power and wealth than the spiritual state of believers. Luther is highlighting this incongruity, saying the church should be concerned with the care of souls rather than its bank accounts.

earlier age labored and merited but received no fruit, while the later age enjoys the fruit without working for it or deserving it. I do not say that these privileges are evil, but that in our day they are being given to evil and undeserving men, when once they were bestowed only on those who were good. SCHOLIA ON ROMANS 13:1.[9]

WHAT IS A MAGISTRATE? PETER MARTYR VERMIGLI: A magistrate is a person chosen by God to uphold law and peace, to restrain crime and evil with punishments and the sword, and to promote every kind of virtue. The efficient cause is God. The final cause is the preservation of the law and peace, the defeat of crimes and troubles, and the increase of virtue. The formal cause is the order that divine Providence has appointed in human affairs. The material cause is the human being or person, for whoever is appointed to the magistracy is chosen from among human beings. COMMENTARY ON ROMANS 13.[10]

GOVERN ACCORDING TO GOD'S WORD, NOT HUMAN REASON. JOHANNES BRENZ: Every Christian government should promote and protect the Word of God and devote all its power to it. For since the power of government comes solely from God, as Christ says in John 19 and Paul in Romans 13, so it is always proper, indeed necessary, that one conduct oneself according to the will of him who created the office of government and to rule according to the Word that creates, maintains and rules all creatures. For the reason that the secular sword has been established is to keep its subjects in peace. But how can temporal, secular peace be better maintained than through the word of peace, which pacifies the sinner, the great enemy of God, the highest good? And how can external peace be maintained if one does not have peace of mind and heart toward God, which only happens through the Word of God, which incorporates us into one Christ by the one Holy Spirit? For this reason the Holy Spirit has bestowed on government the majestic title of "gods." . . . This title gives sufficient indication of what the Lord demands of government, namely, that it should rule according to the Word of God, not according to its own reason or opinion. INSTRUCTION CONCERNING THE DISPUTED ARTICLES OF THE CHRISTIAN FAITH.[11]

WHETHER TYRANT OR SAINT, OBEY THE MAGISTRATES. TILEMANN HESSHUS: Political offices are not condemned because of tyrants and their crimes. And do not let people seek pretexts for their own haughtiness, as if all may deny obedience because tyrants hold office, but let us know that we must obey because of God's command both kings and their agents, whenever they command those things which do not conflict with God's Word or with the law of nature. Polycarp did not refuse to render obedience to the emperor, but said, "We Christians have been instructed to show to the powers ordained by God the honor that befits them," but when he was ordered by the governor to sacrifice to idols, he refused because he was forbidden to do so by divine law. COMMENTARY ON ROMANS 13: EXCURSUS ON MAGISTRATES.[12]

ONLY LAWFUL RULERS. CARDINAL CAJETAN: He does not say "to powers" but "to excellent powers" to distinguish from tyrannical powers— that is, the power of those who are not rightly lords, but tyrants. Accordingly their powers are powers,

---

[9]LW 25:468-69* (WA 56:476-77); citing Rom 8:28; 1 Cor 3:22; Rev 5:10; 12:1; 1 Pet 2:13; 2 Tim 3:2.

[10]Vermigli, *In Epistolam ad Romanos*, 603 (*A Commentarie upon the Epistle to the Romanes*, 426v-427r). To answer the question "Why?," Aristotle distinguishes four causes through which the nature of things can be understood: the material cause—the material of which a thing consists; the formal cause—the form of the thing, encompassing its basic attributes; the efficient cause—the thing that brings about motion or change; and the final cause—the reason for which a thing is done. For a statue, the material cause is the stone from which it is made; the formal cause is the shape that it takes once it has been crafted; the efficient cause is the sculptor carving it; and the final cause may be to preserve a memory, to make money or to represent beauty.

[11]Brenz, *Godly Magistrates and Church Order*, 45*; citing Jn 19:11; Rom 13:1; Ex 22:28.

[12]Hesshus, *Explicatio Epistolae Pauli ad Romanos*, 392r-v.

but they are not "excellent powers," rather they are hostile powers, mercenary powers. According to this distinction of hostile powers, he says "excellent powers," so that they would understand . . . that every soul is not subjected to tyrannical powers but to excellent powers, and as it is said by this one word "to legitimate powers." COMMENTARY ON ROMANS 13:1.[13]

OUR GOD IS A GOD OF ORDER. DAVID PAREUS: Therefore in general we are taught that God is the author and lover of good order and the enemy of *ataxia* ["disorder"] and confusion. Consequently, let us love and pursue order as a most beautiful thing in all things, for the things that exist and come into being by order are beautiful and lasting. But let us recognize that every confusion, whether in the powers that be and empires or in other matters, is the work of the devil and is opposed to God and harmful to human affairs. COMMENTARY ON ROMANS 13:1.[14]

TWO REMINDERS. THEODORE BEZA: However, these two are connected, that is, the office of magistrate and the appointment to that office, so that the apostle rightly calls both . . . the ordinance of God in the next verse. But one ought to remember here two things: namely, that this saying of Paul must be understood to apply to legitimate powers by which the human race is ruled where God the Creator advises this arrangement and not to those that are established by tyranny or even by impiety, and that this saying applies to the laws themselves, not to any and all persons who enjoy this power. To be sure, evil magistrates also do not give orders apart from the judgment and ordinance of God, but this has no bearing on Paul's aim here. ANNOTATIONS ON ROMANS 13:1.[15]

GOVERNMENT IS GOD'S GOOD WORK. PHILIPP MELANCHTHON: This proposition of Paul is first that government, that is, the order of rules or the form of the state, is a good thing, which God by his own work both instituted and preserves. Also the order of the movements of the heavenly bodies has both been instituted by God and is preserved by him. When Paul says that governments are from God, we should understand that they are not only permitted by God, as sins are said to be permitted, but that they are rather works of God, instituted and preserved by him, and confirmed through his Word. Paul clearly calls government an ordinance of God, that is, a thing that is instituted by the counsel of God that it may be in harmony with his will, or that it may be approved by him. Sins are not ordained by God; rather they are the violation of his ordinance.

These things are said briefly by Paul, but they are very important. First, it is necessary that this teaching be found in the church, lest a work of God be ascribed to the devil, and so that the works of God and the works of the devil may be distinguished from each other. Second, we know that these offices have been set before us to be exercises of confession, calling on God and other virtues, to become acts of true worship of God. Third, obedience may be strengthened, lest we violate a divine ordinance, and may remember that God is the protector and preserver of his ordinance. Fourth, the government and all of us in civil life may have the comfort that God governs these dangers of civil life, and preserves kingdoms, civil righteousness, and peace in the world, and punishes tyrannies and robberies.

---

[13]Cajetan, *In Sacrae Scripturae Expositionem*, 5:72. Most of the reformers render *exousiais hyperechousais* more literally as "higher powers." Contemporary biblical scholars give a more idiomatic translation, "governing authorities." Some have posited a double referent to the human magistrates and the angelic beings over them, but this hypothesis has generally been rejected (see Douglas J. Moo, *The Epistle to the Romans*, New International Commentary on the New Testament 38 [Grand Rapids: Eerdmans, 1996], 796 n. 22). See further C. E. B. Cranfield, *A Critical and Exegetical Commentary on the Epistle to the Romans*, International Critical Commentary (Edinburg: T&T Clark, 1985), 2:656-60; Joseph A. Fitzmyer, *Romans: A New Translation with Introduction and Commentary*, Anchor Bible 33 (New York: Doubleday, 1993), 666; Moo, *Epistle to the Romans*, 795-96. Luther offers a sort of compromise, "Let everyone be subject to the magistrates who have power over you" (WADB 7:69).
[14]Pareus, *In Epistolam ad Romanos*, 1296.
[15]Beza, *Annotationes majores*, 2:136; citing Gal 3:27; Judg 6:34; Col 3:10-17.

This is a very great comfort to all godly persons in light of the great dangers to governments. The godly should consider the magnitude of these things, namely, that states are overthrown not only by human audacity but much more by the fury of the devil, who is the enemy of discipline and of things honorable. Therefore Christ calls him a murderer. And in Daniel it is written that a good angel defended the Persian kingdom against an evil angel. The devil incites his members to destroy public harmony. Neither should only the authors of danger be considered. Remembering this comfort of the Scripture—that God wants to preserve governments—we should add prayer, as the Scripture teaches in many places. COMMENTARY ON ROMANS (1540).[16]

TWO TYPES OF LAWS. JOHN HOOPER: The laws of magistrates are of two types and sorts: either they concern God or human beings. If they concern or appertain to God, they are either in accordance with the Word of God or contrary to the Word of God. If they are in accordance with the Word of God, it is necessary and requisite, even on pain of damnation, that they must be obeyed. If they are repugnant to the Word of God, they should not be obeyed. Yet human beings should suffer death rather than defend themselves by force and the violent resistance of superior powers, as Christ, his apostles and the prophets did. If the laws concern and pertain to human beings and civil things, they must simply, without exception, be obeyed, except where they are repugnant and contrary to the law of nature, as Pharaoh's laws and commandments were to the midwives, that they should have killed all the male children that the Israelite women brought forth. Because Saint Paul commanded us to give obedience to the higher powers, how worthy of hellfire are those who resist them with hand, heart and tongue. ANNOTATIONS ON ROMANS 13:1.[17]

PERSECUTIONS MUST BE ENDURED. DESIDERIUS ERASMUS: But if persecution by rulers or magistrates should break out against you because of your profession of Christianity, it must be endured even though it did not arise from any fault of yours. But persecutions must not be provoked or invited by refusing to do what these leaders in their own right demand and what can be done without offense to God. The state stands firm through order; it ought not to be disturbed under the pretext of religion. PARAPHRASE ON ROMANS 13:1.[18]

A PRAYER FOR GOD-GIVEN AUTHORITIES. HANS SCHLAFFER AND LEONHARD FRICK: Once more, O most gracious Father, we pray for all governments and rulers of this world to whom you have given and lent authority from above. Grant them, dear Lord, that they may use their power according to your will, not theirs, to protect and care for the poor, the pious and the righteous, to punish evil and evildoers, that they may not wash their hands in the blood of the faithful and innocent, that an orderly and quiet life may exist among us in all blessedness and integrity. KUNSTBUCH: A SIMPLE PRAYER.[19]

13:3-5 If You Do Good, What Worry Do You Have?

ORDER IS GOOD. DESIDERIUS ERASMUS: For just as God wished that there should be order among the members of the body, . . . so in the whole commonwealth in which there are both good and evil, God wished that there be a certain order. And order in itself is good in itself, even if someone abuses a magistracy. Consequently, those who disturb this order fight against God, its author. And those who fight against God will justly pay the penalty. But if you do not wish to be subject to laws or to magistrates, you should not think that you can achieve this by defiance, but rather by innocence. For magistrates have no power by law except over

---

[16]Melanchthon, *Commentary on Romans*, 217-18* (MO 15:711-12); citing Jn 8:44; Dan 10:13, 20-21.
[17]Hooper, *Annotations on Romans 13*, B1r-v*; citing Ex 1.

[18]CWE 42:73.
[19]CRR 12:275.

those who commit an act that is not permitted. Live rightly and the law does not concern you; there is nothing that you should fear from the magistrates. Paraphrase on Romans 13:2-3.[20]

A Ruler's Duties. Tilemann Hesshus: Paul learnedly summarizes the duties of a ruler when he says that a ruler is an adornment for good works, but a terror for evil works. The prophets call this task "doing judgment" and "doing justice." He even calls a ruler the servant and avenger of God for wrath and states that he does not bear the sword in vain. By this noteworthy praise he not only excellently adorns but also teaches him what his task is. They ought to be a reward for good works as ministers of God. That is to say, they ought to defend orphans and widows, deliver the oppressed, maintain the peace, administer justice and defend integrity. And they should be guardians not only of the second table but also of the first table. For that reason he calls them "servants of God." Let a ruler know that it pertains to his office to see to it that the people are taught rightly about God, schools are built, religion is defended, true worship of God is offered, the sacraments are properly administered and the churches are supported. Psalm 24 says, "Lift up your heads, o gates, and the king of glory will come in." Also: "And kings will be your foster fathers and queens your nurses." Inept and obtuse are those who remove the ruler from any care for the church and religion and want him to be occupied with only earthly goods such as herding. To the contrary, the Scripture says, "And now, kings, understand. Learn, you who judge the earth. Serve the Lord with fear." In their power itself and their royal duties the Holy Spirit wants them to serve Christ. Therefore, by all means the care of religion pertains to them. David, Jehoshaphat, Hezekiah, Josiah all behaved in this pious way, because they founded the church, promoted the worship of God, supported armies of teachers and students, protected prophets, repaired the temple, and stirred up the people to

the love of true religion. Constantine the Great, the Theodosiuses and Charles the Great behaved piously, because they undertook the care of the church, called synods to decide controversies, established pay for ministers of the Word, supported scholars and defended godly gatherings with arms. Commentary on Romans 13: Excursus on Magistrates.[21]

What Is Government? Philipp Melanchthon: Up to this point Paul has taught two rules, that authorities or government are good things and approved by God, and also that it must be obeyed, where he includes the teaching about punishment, which he repeats later. Meanwhile he inserts a description of the government—what it is—in this way: The government is a minister of God to us for the good, a protector for defending right actions and for punishing transgressions with the sword, that is, with corporal punishments.

This definition is complete and better than the Aristotelian definition,[22] which is as follows: The government is the guardian of the laws. For Paul adds the efficient cause, that it has been instituted by God. And with respect to the ultimate cause he adds the clear words: "To you for good," where he distinguishes the tyrant from the true ruler. For a magistrate should think that he had been divinely placed in this office so that he should plan what is useful for others, as Aristotle reminds Alexander that he should think that the kingdom had come to him that he might do good to the entire human race, not that he might be unscrupulous and scornful toward others. Daniel also says to the king: "Free yourself from sin though justice and do good to the

[20]CWE 42:74.

[21]Hesshus, *Explicatio Epistolae Pauli ad Romanos*, 392v-393r; citing Ps 24:9; Is 49:23; Ps 2:10-11a. Constantine the Great (272–337) legalized Christianity as well as provided for its support; he also called the First Ecumenical Council in Nicaea in 325 AD. Theodosius I (347–395) made Christianity the state religion of the Roman Empire. Theodosius II (401–450) opposed Nestorianism and Eutychianism. Charlemagne (d. 814) established the Holy Roman Empire and supported a renewal of liturgical and theological studies sometimes called the Carolingian Renaissance.
[22]See above, p. 154n10.

poor." Also the saying of Xenophon is praised, "A good ruler is not different from a good father." Thus a magistrate should think that authority and wealth have come to him not so that he can misuse them to fulfill his desires, but so that he may be able to counsel for the common good, and that right actions may be protected, such as the true worship of God, discipline, the courts and peace.

But in connection with this definition people ask how we know what are right actions. I answer: Paul here avoids a longer discussion and speaks generally in order to approve the laws of all peoples about civil matters, if only they are in agreement with the law of nature. For from it he wants right actions in civil matters to be judged. Therefore he is here teaching the third rule: A Christian is not bound to the Mosaic form of government, but is permitted to use the laws of all nations that are in harmony with reason. A Christian owes obedience to his present government.... He owes obedience to the present laws that are in agreement with reason. Therefore it is permissible to hang thieves; it is permissible to divide inheritances according to our laws, because the gospel does not establish a new, worldly form of government but preaches about eternal and spiritual life. Meanwhile it permits us to use various forms of governments, even at various times of days. Because obedience toward present laws is taught, it is taught also that we may make use of present laws. In Luke 3 service in the Roman army is approved. And in Acts 15 the apostles forbid that the Gentiles should be burdened with the Mosaic form of government. Paul also says: "In Christ there is neither Jew nor Greek." COMMENTARY ON ROMANS (1540).[23]

THIS APPLIES TO SUBJECTS AND LORDS. PHILIPP MELANCHTHON: These things do not pertain only to subjects but also to magistrates. When they become tyrants, they destroy the ordinance of God no less than seditious people do. Their consciences become guilty because they do not obey the ordinance of God, that is, the laws

they ought to obey. The threats set down here pertain also to them. As Scripture says elsewhere: "You are not exercising human judgment but the Lord's. Whatever you judge shall overwhelm you." For this statement must always be kept in mind— that government is an ordinance of God. Therefore whoever violates it sins, whether he be a subject or a superior, and God will impose punishments, for instance, if in church he despises the sacraments.

The severity of this commandment should agitate everyone lest they think that violation of the political estate is a small matter. On the contrary, let us learn that in those who believe in Christ, the works of political and economical life are good works and acts of worship of God, not merely secular works, because society must be preserved in order that God may become known in it. This purpose is not a worldly matter, since all activities of the political life are aimed at this purpose: God wanted them to be exercises of confession and on account of this purpose he imposed them on us. Therefore the prophets demand these works, and even more so than ceremonies. COMMENTARY ON ROMANS (1540).[24]

MAGISTRATES ARE SERVANTS TO ALL. JOHN CALVIN: From this magistrates may learn the nature of their vocation. They are not to rule for their own interest, but for the public good, nor are they granted unbridled power, but it is restricted to the well-being of their subjects. In short, they are responsible to God and to human beings in the exercise of their power. They are entrusted by God as his envoys and do his business, and they must give an account to him. The ministry, then, that God has committed to them also concerns their subjects, and so magistrates are debtors to them as well. And private citizens are reminded that it is through divine goodness that they are defended by the sword of princes against the wrongs of the wicked. COMMENTARY ON ROMANS 13:4.[25]

---

[23]Melanchthon, *Commentary on Romans*, 219-20* (MO 15:713-14); citing Dan 4:7; Lk 3:14; Acts 15:19-21; Gal 3:28.

[24]Melanchthon, *Commentary on Romans*, 221* (MO 15:715-16); citing 1 Pet 2:13-17; Is 1:17.
[25]CTS 38:481* (CO 49:251).

UNJUST MERCY IS MURDER. BALTHASAR HUBMAIER: The judges, governments and executors of justice are called servants of God in Scripture and are not murderers. God judges, sentences and kills through them, and not they themselves. From this it follows that those who do not want to kill the evildoer but let them live are acting and sinning against the commandment: "You should not kill." For whoever does not protect the righteous kills him and is guilty of his death as much as the one who does not feed the hungry. ON THE SWORD.[26]

GOVERNMENT SHOULD PROTECT THE PIOUS AND PUNISH THE WICKED. DIRK PHILIPS: No congregation of the Lord may have domination over the consciences of people with an external sword, nor compel the unbeliever to faith with violence, nor kill the false prophets with sword and fire. But they must judge and exclude with the Lord's Word all who are within the congregation and found to be evil. Anything more than this that happens is neither Christian, evangelical nor apostolic. And if someone wants to say that the authorities have not received the sword in vain, and that God through Moses has commanded to kill the false prophets, to that I answer briefly: the magistrates have not received the sword from God to judge over spiritual matters—for these must be judged by the spiritual only spiritually—but to keep their subjects in good order and to keep peace, protect the pious and punish the wicked. THE ENCHIRIDION: THE CONGREGATION OF GOD.[27]

CHRISTIANS ARE ONLY CITIZENS OF HEAVEN. THE SCHLEITHEIM ARTICLES: We have been united as follows concerning the sword. The sword is an ordering of God outside the perfection of Christ. It punishes and kills the wicked, and guards and protects the good. In the law the sword is established over the wicked for punishment and for death, and the secular rulers are established to wield the same.

But within the perfection of Christ only the ban[28] is used for the admonition and exclusion of the one who has sinned, without the death of the flesh, simply the warning and the command to sin no more.

Not many who do not understand Christ's will for us will ask whether a Christian may or should use the sword against the wicked for the protection and defense of the good or for the sake of love. The answer is unanimously revealed: Christ teaches and commands us to learn from him, for he is meek and lowly of heart and thus we shall find rest for our souls (Mt 11:29). Now Christ says to the woman who was taken in adultery, not that she should be stoned according to the law of his Father (and yet he says, "What the Father commanded me, that I do" [Jn 8:22]) but with mercy and forgiveness and the warning to sin no more, says: "Go, sin no more." We too should proceed in this same way, according to the rule of the ban.

Second, it is asked concerning the sword whether a Christian shall pass sentence in disputes and strife about worldly matters, such as the unbelievers have with one another. The answer: Christ did not wish to decide or pass judgment between brother and brother concerning inheritance, but refused to do so (Lk 12:13). So should we refuse too.

Third, it is asked concerning the sword whether the Christian should be a magistrate if he is chosen for it. This is answered thus: Christ was to be made king, but he fled and did not discern the ordinance of his Father. Thus we should also do as he did and follow after him, and we shall not walk in darkness. For he himself says: "Whoever would come after me, let him deny himself and take up his cross and follow me" (Mt 16:24). He himself further forbids the violence of the sword when he says: "The princes of this world lord it over them, etc., but among you it shall not be so" (Mt 20:25). Further Paul says, "Whom God has foreknown, the same he has also predestined to be conformed to the image of his Son," etc. (Rom 8:30). Peter also says: "Christ has suffered (not ruled) and has left us an example, that you should follow after in his steps" (1 Pet 2:21).

---

[26]CRR 5:515-16.
[27]CRR 6:375*; citing Rom 13:1-7; Deut 15:1-23; 1 Cor 2:13.

[28]That is, excommunication.

Lastly, one can see in the following points that it does not befit a Christian to be a magistrate: the rule of the government is according to the flesh, that of the Christians according to the Spirit. Their houses and dwellings remain in this world; that of the Christians is in heaven. Their citizenship is in this world, that of the Christians is in heaven (Phil 3:20). The weapons of their battle and warfare are carnal and only against the flesh, but the weapons of Christians are spiritual, against the fortification of the devil. The worldly are armed with steel and iron, but Christians are armed with the armor of God, with truth, righteousness, peace, faith, salvation and with the Word of God. In sum: as Christ our Head is minded, so also must be minded the members of the body of Christ through him, so that there be no division in the body, through which it would be destroyed. As it is written of Christ, so must his members be, so that his body may remain whole and unified for its own advancement and building up. For any kingdom which is divided within itself will be destroyed (Mt 12:25). ARTICLE 6: ON THE SWORD.[29]

WRATH ONLY APPROPRIATE FOR MAGISTRATES. PHILIPP MELANCHTHON: The rebaptizers' fundamental opinion is this: that orderly punishment in government is pure sin and tyranny, for wrath is forbidden to the Christian as it stands written in Romans 12. . . . This is the rebaptizers' reason. And such misunderstanding gives them cause to boast their endurance [against governing authority] as great holiness and in addition to condemn all governing authority, for they imagine that the works of all Christians must absolutely be the same. That's pure blindness! It results from incorrect interpretation of Scripture and from their misunderstanding that they don't know how to distinguish between the spiritual reality in the heart and the external estates, which should and must have dissimilar works—as husband and wife, father and child have dissimilar external works—and should nevertheless have God's fear and faith in Christ in the heart.

Thus, since the rebaptizers grasp this saying in which wrath is forbidden, we should know how to respond to this. Namely, all wrath outside this office is forbidden, but wrath in this office is God's command and a holy and good work. Holy Scripture itself teaches us this distinction; it is not fabricated by human beings.

For Paul says about this office which bears the sword: it is God's work and order, and the governing authority is God's servant to punish the wick and protect the pious. From this saying it's clear that such wrath in this office is not sin, but God's command and order and a true, holy service to God. And because this office is not sin, but a good work ordered by God, therefore Christians may hold and wield such an office, as God's other gifts like food and drink, etc. Yes, they must maintain and not destroy this office, for the law must remain in the world to punish the wicked, as Paul says: "The law is laid down for the sake of the unrighteous." Now the office which bears the sword is a part of the law. . . .

From all this it is clear that the saying that forbids wrath means those works outside of this office; the other saying which praises and commands wrath means those works in this office. And it's easy to understand why the works in this office and those outside of this office must be dissimilar, for this distinction is necessary for the maintenance of peace and discipline. What disorder and turmoil would follow if each and every person wanted to be judge and executioner himself! Thus, God has finely and usefully ordered government. THE REFUTATION OF SEVERAL UNCHRISTIAN ARTICLES.[30]

THE WORLD'S WRATH INCOMPATIBLE WITH THE CHURCH'S LOVE. PETER WALPOT: This power [of the keys] Christ gave to his apostles and his congregation, but the power of the sword he never commended to any apostle or disciple or anyone in his congregation. You will search yourself to death if you think you can find it in his

---

[29]CRR 1:39-41*.

[30]Melanchthon, *Verlegung etlicher unchristlicher Artikel*, B4r-C1r; citing Rom 12:19; 1 Tim 1:9. Here Melanchthon refutes that "Christians should not and cannot be part of a governing authority and office which bears the sword" (B3v).

covenant! Now, the ban, as used in the church of Christ, and the sword, as used in the world, are so completely different as evening and morning, they are such incompatible things as death and life. For that reason they may not be mixed together.

The power of the keys, the ban of Christians, through separation purges from the congregation what is evil. The sword of the world purges from the very face of the earth. The Christians' punishment is loving, yes, a brotherly punishment; the sword's punishment is merciless and filled with wrath. After the Christians' ban we can seek and perform repentance again; after the sword or worldly judgment repentance and reformation are eternally abbreviated. The ministers of the keys are vessels of lovingkindness; the ministers of the worldly sword are vessels of wrath. The power of the keys is wielded and held for the benefit of the Christian community, banning greed and personal property. The power of the sword is held for the benefit of greed and personal property, making individual property and individual people. Thus, the power of the sword in past ages under many different names is called "the worldly authority." That is the reason why this office cannot be joined with the unblemished church. For both follow different paths that go opposite ways and never meet. THE GREAT ARTICLE BOOK: ON THE SWORD.[31]

DIFFERENCE BETWEEN SECULAR AND ECCLE-SIAL RULE. TILEMANN HESSHUS: Indeed, there are many differences between the civil order and the ministry of the gospel, which others have rather fully explained. In this passage let this one thing be noted, namely, that the Holy Spirit by his own testimony arms the ruler here with the sword and physical force against all arrogant people and gives him the power of life and death. Paul says, "He does not bear the sword in vain, but is a servant of God, an avenger of wrath against him who practices evil."

Therefore God himself girded the ruler with the sword and gave him the power to kill the guilty.

Thus God told Noah in Genesis 9, "Whoever sheds blood, his blood will be shed by man." God armed King Jehu with a sword and ordered him to wipe out the entire family of Ahab. And David sang, "Blessed be God who teaches my hands for battle and my fingers for war." Again, Psalm 18: "God girded me with strength for war." Again, "You gave me the shield of your salvation."

But the ministers of the gospel by no means are armed with a sword or physical force, but they are only heralds of the word. They ought to reproach sins with the law and comfort terrified minds with the gospel. Christ says, "The kings of the nations exercise dominion, but it shall not be so with you." And Christ says to Peter, "Whoever takes the sword will perish by the sword. COMMENTARY ON ROMANS 13: EXCURSUS ON MAGISTRATES.[32]

GOD ORDAINS BOTH SECULAR AND ECCLE-SIAL OFFICES. PHILIPP MELANCHTHON: It's clear that God has ordered these two offices differently—the preaching office and worldly governing authority. And he has commanded that Christians must be under both offices. Thus, it's a horrid error to mix these offices into one another or to remove and withdraw the one; for they are both God's order and command. For absolutely no person has the power to overturn God's order. THE REFUTATION OF SEVERAL UNCHRISTIAN ARTICLES.[33]

GOD'S COMMAND: THE DIFFERENCE BETWEEN A MURDERER AND A MAGISTRATE. MARTIN LUTHER: This and other errors all spring from this: that we view the estates externally without God's word and according to their works and send God's word packing. Now if a murderer hacks someone's head off, he does not act rightly in this, for he has no command—that is, no word of God—for it.

---

[31]QGT 12:253.

[32]Hesshus, *Explicatio Epistolae Pauli ad Romanos*, 396v; citing Gen 9:6; 2 Kings 9:5-9; Ps 144:1; 18:39, 35; Lk 22:25-26; Mt 26:52.
[33]Melanchthon, *Verlegung etlicher unchristlicher Artikel*, CIV. Here Melanchthon refutes that "Christians should have no other governing authority than the servants of the gospel alone" (CIR).

Indeed he acts against God's word and command, which forbids killing. And so it is murder, pure hell, darkness and death. However, if a prince or judge kills someone, that's by our Lord God's word and command. You yourself do not bear the sword, but God . . . as if it were in God's hand, as if an angel and not a human bore it, because God's word clings to it, which commands to punish the wicked and to protect and defend the pious. A Wedding Sermon (January 8, 1531).[34]

Summary of the Main Point. John Calvin: What Paul first commanded concerning the rendering of obedience to magistrates he now repeats by way of summary but with an addition: they should be obeyed not only for the sake of human obligation but because we should obey God too. He uses "wrath" for the retribution that magistrates can require for contempt of their dignity. It is as if he had said, "And so they must not be obeyed because it is not lawful to oppose the powerful and mighty without punishment, for they are used to enduring injustices that cannot be repelled, but they should be obeyed willingly, because the conscience is obligated by the Word of God to this submission." Therefore even if the magistrate were disarmed, so that it would be possible to assail and condemn him without punishment, it should be attempted no more than if we were to be threatened with punishment immediately. For a private citizen does not have the right to strip authority from the one whom the Lord has placed in power over us. Moreover, this whole discussion concerns civil offices. And so those who exercise dominion over consciences try in vain to establish their sacrilegious tyranny from this passage. Commentary on Romans 13:5.[35]

13:6-7 Pay What You Owe

Do Not Be Wearied by Taxes! Martin Luther: See how good it is to pay taxes and to obey! By this you help to protect the pious and to punish the wicked. And so don't let it irritate you. Marginal Gloss on Romans 13:6 (1546).[36]

God Demands That the Government Be Diligent. Philipp Melanchthon: Here is also an important word about the diligence that is required of magistrates. For Paul says, "They attend diligently to this," that is, to the service of God, that is, to the propagation of true worship and to the defense of discipline and peace, which are divine benefits. And diligent attendance is a great effort of the mind, which does not relax its care, vigilance and labor, even as it is most true that government is a burden to which no human wisdom can be equal. Nevertheless diligence, which he here calls care, is required of magistrates, which God helping is successful. Commentary on Romans (1540).[37]

Second Table of the Law. Philipp Melanchthon: In this saying he embraces all duties that are necessary in society. He commands that we pay the money we owe to anyone in contracts. He commands that we render the duties we owe to the family, citizens, parents, spouse, children and servants. The Decalogue shows what the duties are that are owed to each individual, which he repeats here in order that we may have a sure teaching about which works are necessary. For it is necessary that the conscience have a sure word also about works, according to which they are regulated, lest acts of worship be imagined without a word of God. About such works Christ says: "In vain they worship me with human commandments." Commentary on Romans (1540).[38]

Show Respect! Juan de Valdés: So servants should honor their masters with exterior and interior respect, as I earlier said with regard to children, and this is what St. Peter means. It is also important to counsel masters not to be tyrannical with their servants, but for them to remember that

---

[34]WA 34,1:54.38-40, 56.1-9.
[35]CTS 38:483* (CO 49:251-52).

[36]WADB 4:69.
[37]Melanchthon, *Commentary on Romans*, 223 (MO 15:717).
[38]Melanchthon, *Commentary on Romans*, 223* (MO 15:717-18).

both of them have the same heavenly Father and Lord. They should, therefore, treat them not as slaves but as brothers. Dealing with this commandment, you should also say that everyone is obliged to obey, respect and honor prelates, priests, princes—those persons who administer justice—since they are established by God. Finally, you should say that children and adults should respect and honor their teachers and elders both in age and in dignity, since even nature teaches us this when we naturally call an old man "father" or "uncle" and an old woman "mother" or "aunt." DIALOGUE ON CHRISTIAN DOCTRINE.[39]

THREE ACTS OF HONOR. TILEMANN HESSHUS: Honor is reverence and piety joined with true faith, by which we not only declare our subjection by some kind of external gesture, but rather acknowledge with true affection of the heart that the civil ruler is the ordinance of God and that he was appointed for our good. By our honor we also love and fear him as we would a parent and as one who acts in the place of God on earth; we pray to God for our ruler and for the preservation of the civil order; and we even forgive and cover over their weaknesses and errors. Therefore honor contains three noteworthy actions.

The first is recognizing the wisdom and kindness of God in establishing civil order and to love the ruler as a servant of God and a guardian of your life and property. Joseph not only revered the Egyptian king with an external gesture, but he also loved him with true affection of heart, as a servant of God. Thus Daniel said to the Babylonian king, "O king, live forever."

The second action is to pray daily for the ruler, as God prompts one by his own Spirit, to give thanks that God has given godly and wholesome princes and that he does not permit tyrants to destroy everything as their desires dictate. Thus Jeremiah orders the Jews to pray for the Babylonian king, and Paul says in 1 Timothy 2, "I urge that above all prayers and intercessions be made for all people and for kings."

The third action that pertains to the honor owed to rulers is respect and reverence, so that we do not misinterpret the dubious deeds of a ruler but rather put a good construction on them. Let us even pardon some errors and lapses and ascribe them to the massive burden of the affairs of state and the weakness of human nature. For as Solomon says, "There is no one on earth who does not sin even when doing some act of kindness." COMMENTARY ON ROMANS 13: EXCURSUS ON MAGISTRATES.[40]

---

[39]*Valdés' Two Catechisms*, 85; citing 1 Pet 2:18-21.

[40]Hesshus, *Explicatio Epistolae Pauli ad Romanos*, 394v-395r; citing Dan 3:9; 5:10; Bar 1:11 (cf. Jer 29:7); 1 Tim 2:1-2; Eccl 7:20.

13:8-14 FUFILLING THE LAW THROUGH LOVE

8Owe no one anything, except to love each other, for the one who loves another has fulfilled the law. 9For the commandments, "You shall not commit adultery, You shall not murder, You shall not steal, You shall not covet," and any other commandment, are summed up in this word: "You shall love your neighbor as yourself." 10Love does no wrong to a neighbor; therefore love is the fulfilling of the law.

11Besides this you know the time, that the hour has come for you to wake from sleep. For salvation is nearer to us now than when we first believed. 12The night is far gone; the day is at hand. So then let us cast off the works of darkness and put on the armor of light. 13Let us walk properly as in the daytime, not in orgies and drunkenness, not in sexual immorality and sensuality, not in quarreling and jealousy. 14But put on the Lord Jesus Christ, and make no provision for the flesh, to gratify its desires.

OVERVIEW: Paul refers to the second table of the Ten Commandments as he encourages the individual Christian to love his or her neighbor. The reformers go to great lengths to explain Paul's phrase that "love is the fulfilling of the law," which on its surface might seem to be opposed to the doctrine of justification by grace through faith alone. For most of the reformers, however, our capacity for love comes only from God, who justifies us, at which point we are enabled by his Spirit to turn in love toward our neighbor. Human love of neighbor, therefore, depends on the love of God.

Yet the reformers remind us that we are still sinful and are tempted by the world and its desires. Like Paul they encourage their readers to wake up from sleep and remember that we are baptized and have become new beings with Christ by the power of the Spirit. We grow in this baptismal knowledge as we awaken each day, and this knowledge unites us with the gift of Christ to lighten our darkness. In our baptismal faith we have been grafted into the body of Christ. Some of the reformers even use mystical language to explain what Paul intends: Christ is in us and we are in Christ. In baptism Christ is ours and we are his; participating in this gift by faith, in love we become Christ to each other.

13:8-10 The Twofold Love of God and Neighbor Fulfills the Law

THE TEN COMMANDMENTS ARE TO LOVE GOD AND NEIGHBOR. JUAN DE VALDÉS: The first three commandments referring to God are comprehended in the love of God, because it is clear that the one who loves God will worship only God and will not use God's name except to glorify it and to praise it. He will likewise keep the feast days. These three commandments are the ones called the first table. The other seven are called the second table and are comprehended in the love of one's neighbor. Because we who love our neighbor will certainly not steal, kill or, in short, do any of those things that God there commands us not to do. So that St. Paul appropriately says that one who loves fulfills the law and elsewhere that the fulfillment of the law is love. DIALOGUE ON CHRISTIAN DOCTRINE.[1]

LOVE OF NEIGHBOR DEPENDS ON LOVE OF GOD. JACQUES LEFÈVRE D'ÉTAPLES: He understands concerning that love that is charity. For love (as one of the saints says) reaches toward another person in order that it may be called charity. First it reaches to God, then to neighbor. And on this twofold love, as the salvific eloquence of the Gospel puts it, "the whole law and the prophets depend." The love of

---

[1] *Valdés' Two Catechisms*, 95.

one's neighbor is founded on the love for God, for there is this certain similarity with the love for God, and the other commands are founded on the love of one's neighbor. Nor can there be a perfect love for God without love for one's neighbor, for how can you perfectly love the truth when you do not love its image? And as John, the beloved disciple of God, says, "Whoever does not love their brother whom they see, how can they love God whom they have not seen?" For everyone who along with you was formed in the image of God is your neighbor. And he is all the more your brother if he has undergone the regeneration and reformation of this image. Nor is this love for your brother perfect love if it is without love for God, for a likeness takes its perfection from the real object. Therefore perfect love is directed toward someone else. This does not rule out love for God, and it does not exclude charity toward one's neighbor. And Paul also says concerning this matter: "Whoever loves another," namely, God and neighbor, "has fulfilled the law" and what he appended at the end, "therefore love is the fulfilling of the law." But you will understand these things more readily if we have set forth the precepts that are understood by the term "law" in this way:

1. Love the Lord your God—with all your heart and with all your soul and with all your strength.
2. And love your neighbor as yourself.
3. Hallow the Sabbath.
4. Honor your father and mother.
5. Do not murder.
6. Do not steal.
7. Do not commit adultery.
8. Do not speak false testimony.
9. Do not covet your neighbor's wife.
10. Nor any other thing of his.

You see that the first and second commandment embrace all of love, but the love for neighbor depends on and follows the love for God. ANNOTATIONS ROMANS 13:8-10.[2]

<hr>

[2]Lefèvre d'Étaples, *Epistola ad Rhomanos*, 94v-95r; citing Mt 22:40; 1 Jn 4:20.

LOVE OTHERS AS SUBJECTS, NOT OBJECTS.

MARTIN LUTHER: The commandment "You shall love your neighbor as yourself" is understood in a twofold manner. First, it should be understood as commanding to love neighbor and oneself. But in another sense it should be understood as commanding to love only neighbor according to the example of love for oneself. This is the better interpretation, because man [*homo*] with his natural sinfulness loves himself above all others, seeks his own benefit in everything and loves everything for his own sake, even when he loves his neighbor or his friend, for he seeks his own in him.[3]

Hence this is a most profound commandment, and each person must test himself according to it by careful examination. For through this expression, "as yourself," every pretense of love is excluded. Therefore whoever loves his neighbor on account of his

money		poor	
honor		lowly	clearly has a
knowledge	and does not	unlearned	hypocritical
favor	love the same	hostile	love, not a
power	person if he is	dependent	love for him
comfort		unpleasant	himself.

Rather he loves what his neighbor has for his own benefit, and thus he does not love him "as himself'"—obviously he loves himself, even if he is a pauper, a fool or absolutely nothing. For who is so useless that he hates himself? And yet no one is such a nothing that he does not love himself, and he does not love others in the same way. Therefore this is the hardest commandment, if we really think about it. And so no one wishes to be robbed, harmed or killed, to be the victim of adultery, to be lied to, to be victimized by false testimony or to have his property coveted. But if he does not wish the same way for his neighbor,

<hr>

[3]See further Heidelberg Disputation (1518), LW 31:45; WA 1:354: "The love of God does not find but creates what is lovable to it; the love of human beings comes into existence by what is lovable to it." Tuomo Mannermaa unpacks this further in *Two Kinds of Love: Martin Luther's Religious World*, trans. and ed. Kirsi Stjerna (Minneapolis: Fortress, 2010).

he is already guilty of breaking this command. Therefore this commandment also includes that of Matthew, "All that you wish others would do to you, do also to them, for this is the Law and the Prophets." Thus this commandment when viewed in a superficial and general way seems petty, if however we apply it to particulars it pours forth infinite salutary teachings and directs us most faithfully in everything. But that this commandment is not observed, that it is sinned against countless times, and that it is ignored by those who are thoughtless proves that people do not apply it to their actions, instead they are content with their good intentions. For example, the wealthy lavish priests with treasures for church buildings or memorials. However, if they were to put themselves in the position of the poor and ask themselves whether they would want it donated to themselves rather than to churches, they would easily learn from themselves what they should do. SCHOLIA ON ROMANS 13:10.[4]

What Kind of Love Fulfills the Law?

PHILIPP MELANCHTHON: Many twist this statement against the doctrine of faith because Paul here says that law is fulfilled by love. From this they argue:

Fulfillment of the law justifies.

Love is the fulfilling of the law.

Therefore love justifies.

I answer very briefly to the minor premise: The minor premise is true with respect to love, but not with respect to the kind of love that any human beings demonstrate. Paul says rightly and properly about the ideal, or about the essence, that love fulfills the law, that is, what the law demands. But it does not follow from this that the law is fulfilled by our love, because our love is unclean and far removed from perfection.

Since nobody could furnish perfect love or fulfillment, we need another righteousness, one that by faith apprehends the mercy promised on account of Christ. This faith is fulfillment of the law by way of imputation. The believers are accounted righteous just as if they had fulfilled the law. Thereafter there is added also that faith begins the fulfillment of the law in us, and this beginning is pleasing because we are in Christ. COMMENTARY ON ROMANS (1540).[5]

Forever Indebted to Love.

CYRIACUS SPANGENBERG: The natural or divine debt obliges a person to another, to show all love and all goodness toward them. And this debt a person can never cast off here on earth, nor entirely pay off. Whatever we might do, we remain indebted to our neighbor in love, so long as we live. About this now Paul says: "Owe no one anything, except that you love one another." If you owe anything else, then focus on it with all possible diligence, until it is paid off, so that no one needs to admonish you. However, what love of neighbor requires, do not think that you can empty yourselves of that; rather know that you are always indebted to support your neighbor's good, to bear with them patiently, to construe their errors in the best light, to show them all service, love, help and kindness, and to do all this out of love, without coercion and compulsion. . . .

Chrysostom interprets these words in this way: We do not handle the debt of love the way we do taxes and tariffs—which we give when the time comes that it's due. Rather we must immediately pay [the debt of] love and pay it without delay. And our Lord God does not want it to be paid off, and nevertheless he wants it always to be paid. So then it's never entirely paid; instead we always remain in debt. For it is such a debt on account of the debt of love that we always are paying it, and nevertheless at the same time remain indebted. LAST EIGHT CHAPTERS OF ROMANS.[6]

---

[5]Melanchthon, *Commentary on Romans*, 223-24* (MO 15:718).
[6]C. Spangenberg, *Außlegung der Letsten Acht Capitel der Episteln an die Römer*, 253r-v.

---

[4]LW 25:475-76* (WA 56:482-83); citing Mt 19:19; Lev 19:18; Mt 7:12.

Love Expresses Faith. David Pareus: He concludes the second exhortation with a noteworthy aphorism: "Love is the *plērōma* ["fulfillment"] of the law." Therefore let us love one another in order to fulfill the law, not only in words and with the tongue, but also in truth and in our work. And John develops this nearly unique theme in his three epistles and recommends what Paul says here and elsewhere: "The end of the commandment is love out of a pure heart," because the word *plērōma* ["fulfillment"] used here and the word *telos* ["end, aim"] are used in the same sense. For without love neither knowledge nor faith nor any *charismata* ["spiritual gifts"] of the Holy Spirit come into existence or benefit anyone. He says, "If I should speak in the tongues of angels, but do not have love, I would be a resounding gong," etc. There let the praises and proper effects of love be seen. Therefore not without reason is it inculcated in us so many times. Nonetheless, lest we imagine with the hypocrites that our love merits eternal life, let us think about how far from perfection we all are in this life. Consequently the gospel shows to us that our righteousness and salvation does not lie in our fulfillment of the law, but in the divine remission of our sins. From that premise Augustine puts it very clearly: "All the commandments of God are fulfilled when whatever is not done is forgiven." Commentary on Romans 13:10.[7]

Love and Faith Together Fulfill the Law. Johann Spangenberg: What does St. Paul mean by the words "love is the fulfilling of the law"? This is what he means to say. Love fulfills the law, because it itself is the fulfillment. But faith fulfills the law, because it administers what is needed to fulfill it. "For faith is active through love." Take an example. Water fills a jug, the host also fills the jug; the water in itself, the host by means of the water. In the same way love fulfills the law, and faith fulfills the law; love in itself, faith by means of love and the Holy Spirit. The Pharisees and works-righteous believe that if they only seem to do the works and ceremonies of the law—whatever might happen to the love of neighbor!—then the law has been carried out well enough. But they greatly miss the mark. God takes no pleasure in any work if our heart is not full of love toward our neighbor. Now where such love does not exist—that is, faith is counterfeit and false—there we also do not keep the commandments of God. But where an upright love of neighbor exists, there we perform—without coercion and compulsion—what God wants; there we also keep the commandments of the Second Table of Moses. Epistle for the Fourth Sunday After Epiphany.[8]

Love Perfectly! David Joris: Always make peace, maintain unity and seek love. For this is the fulfillment of the Law and the Prophets. Bear the burden or sickness of each other and fulfill the law of Christ—in which there is hidden strength. Pay close attention to this. Always take care that you are found in love, or you will not be able to stand in the great day of the Lord. If your heart believes in God and if you love him, then you must also love what God has created and what he desires to be done, especially that love be perfected.

People of the world love according to the flesh, on account of their lusts, like whores and villains and thieves. While they love well, it is not a real work; they still prefer to love those who love them, not in the manner here. For if it is to be correct, our lust must be transformed in the Spirit into love for the Lord with all our heart and mind. This will produce fruit in our brothers. Again, not only for those who love us, for we must feel love for our enemies, those who contradict or oppose us. This must be fulfilled by those who believe and boast that they know God. Those who have not done this from

---

[7]Pareus, *In Epistolam ad Romanos*, 1322; citing 1 Jn 3:18; 1 Tim 1:5; 1 Cor 13:1.

[8]J. Spangenberg, *Postilla Teütsch*, 4:90r-91r; citing Gal 5:6. In his *Treatise on Good Works* (1520), Luther illustrates the correlation between love and God's commands: "When a husband and wife really love one another, have pleasure in each other and firmly trust in this love, who teaches them how they are to behave toward each other, what they are to do or not to do, to say or not to say, what they are to think? Confidence alone teaches them all this, and even more than is necessary" (LW 44:26-27*; WA 6:206).

their hearts, who have not prayed thoroughly for our enemies . . . have neither seen nor known him.

For this reason become perfect in everything, including distribution of charity with a voluntary heart and an affectionate spirit. "God loves a cheerful giver." For this reason make your countenance joyful in all your gifts and joyfully bless the Lord with your tithes. . . . Love is not based or hidden in kisses, nor external work, but in the heart. For such cannot be contained but must radiate and shine. What love does is completely pure and acceptable, even when there are no gifts, for it is powerful. Stand in this and let it take you the right way. The Building of the Church (1537).[9]

United in Christ, Love One Another.
Marie Dentière: God wants us to do what seems good and beautiful to us, but only so far as he commands us, and he condemns those who would add to his commandments or take away from them. Not content with that, they come with their ceremonies, called, if you wish, Vespers or Matins, to damn those who make images and all those who have confidence in them. That shows their great damnation, ingratitude and evil, because in giving to their idols, they condemn the poor people. . . . They are like those who sacrificed to Baal in Babylon.

To excuse themselves, they will say, "It is not thus that the law should be understood. David the prophet did not mean us, but the other idolaters of his time. Scripture has several meanings, and it can be understood in several ways. It is not up to women to know it, nor to people who are not learned, who do not have degrees and the rank of doctor; but they should just believe simply without questioning anything." They just want us to give pleasure, as is our custom, to do our work, spin on the distaff, live as women before us did, like our neighbors. For she who lives like her neighbor does neither good nor evil.

Ha! It is certainly true that many of your people will live like that, giving to Scripture many meanings

and giving you a bag to fill up. You would certainly understand Scripture very well [without them], but even we understand and believe it not only simply but even foolishly. I ask, did not Jesus die as much for the poor ignorant people and the idiots as for my dear sirs the shaved, tonsured and mitered? Did he preach and spread my gospel so much only for my dear sirs the wise and important doctors? Isn't it for all of us? Do we have two gospels, one for men and another for women? One for the wise and another for the fools? Are we not one in our Lord? In whose name are we baptized? By Paul or by Apollos, by the pope or by Luther? Is it not in the name of Christ? He is certainly not divided.

There is no distinction between the Jew and the Greek; before God, no person is an exception. We are all one in Jesus Christ. There is no male and female, nor servant nor free man. I am not talking about the body, for there is the Father and the Son, one to be honored and the other to honor; the husband and the wife, she to love and the other to hold her in esteem; the master to command, the servant to serve and obey; the king, prince and lord to rule and judge, the subject to obey, carry, tolerate and pay tribute, taxes, charges and rents, according to God's Word. The person who resists resists God. Epistle to Marguerite de Navarre.[10]

13:11-13 *Arise! Walk in the Sunlight of the Gospel*

The Twofold Task of the Preaching Office: Teaching and Exhortation. Martin Luther: This epistle reading does not teach about faith but about the works and fruits of faith. It shows how a Christian life should be conducted outwardly and bodily on earth among people. Faith teaches how we are to live in the Spirit before God; Paul writes and teaches abundantly and apostolically about that previous to this reading. When we look at this epistle carefully, then, it does not so much teach as incite, exhort, urge and arouse those who already know what they should do. St. Paul divides

---

[9]CRR 7:178-79*; alluding to Mt 22:39-40; Gal 5:13-14; 6:2; Mt 22:37; Mt 5:43-44; 1 Cor 13:8; quoting 2 Cor 9:7.

[10]Dentière, *Epistle to Marguerite de Navarre*, 78-80*.

the preaching office into two parts: teaching and exhortation. Teaching means that one preaches what is unknown so that people know and understand; exhortation means that one incites and urges what everyone already knows. Both parts are necessary for a preacher. The Church Postil (1540): First Sunday in Advent.[11]

Paul's Metaphors. Cardinal Cajetan: He uses the metaphors of night and day, sleep and vigil, comparing the state of guilt with night and sleep, but the state of grace with day and vigil. And negligence corresponds partly with the state of guilt, as sleep fits with night, and the time of grace corresponds partly with God as the beginning of the day (for the plain day will not exist until the future life). And since it is like the beginning of the day, he says, the hour is now at hand for us to be roused from our sleep of negligence. He means that because we know that the opportunity is given to us presently, that we should cast aside those things related to the night; it is right that we pursue the day, through which the entire law is fulfilled. Commentary on Romans 13:11.[12]

Images of Light and Dark. Philipp Melanchthon: By sleep he understands ignorance of the true doctrine. Watchfulness must mean the new knowledge of the gospel and new actions. And that he commands us to wake up signifies that we are being called to great struggles, dangers and watchfulness. But the world, by contrast, becomes all the sleepier when the gospel is heard, and falls asleep again. For carnal security brings forth negligence, through which various evils slip in little by little. He censures this negligence when he commands us to wake up. Therefore he commands afterward to put on the armor of light, for he indicates that a great struggle is necessary, lest we perish. For the armor of light is knowledge of the Word of God, knowledge of God and the other virtues with which those who use the Word of

God fight against the devil. Conversely, the works of darkness are ignorance of God and the evils that this ignorance gives rise to, for there the devil rules. Commentary on Romans (1540).[13]

We and the Patriarchs Believe in the Same Christ. Philipp Melanchthon: Salvation should be understood of Christ himself, and of the ministry of the gospel, not about the effect. Christ has now been revealed, and remission of sins has been openly promulgated and given, and the ministry of the gospel has been instituted. The patriarchs expected and believed that Christ would come. Therefore salvation is closer to us, because Christ has been revealed, and the remission of sins promulgated, and the ministry of the gospel instituted. For the patriarchs knew that Christ would come, and they knew that the forgiveness of sins was wrapped up in the promises, but they did not have the ministry instituted with the express command to remit sins. As for the effect, we must know that the patriarchs were saved by faith in the promised Christ, even as the church is saved after Christ has been revealed. Neither is there any other salvation of the patriarchs, or of the church after Christ has been revealed, but there is only this difference: they believed in a Christ who would come, we in the one who has come. Commentary on Romans (1540).[14]

Nearness Refers to Revelation, Not Faith. Martin Luther: Thus we (that is, the fathers with us) have believed with the same common faith in the one Christ, and still do believe in him, but in different ways. Just as we, because of this common faith in Christ, say, "We have believed," even though we were not alive at that time but "the fathers believed," so in turn they say, "They will hear, see and believe Christ," even though they are not alive in our times but we do that. David says, "I will see your heavens, the work

---

[11]LW 75:13* (WA 10,1.2:1-2; E2 7:25); alluding to Rom 12:7-8.
[12]Cajetan, *In Sacrae Scripturae Expositionem*, 5:74.

[13]Melanchthon, *Commentary on Romans*, 224* (MO 15:718-19).
[14]Melanchthon, *Commentary on Romans*, 224-25* (MO 15:719).

of your hands (that is the apostles[15])," even though he did not experience it. There are many similar passages in which one person applies another person's actions to themselves because of the common faith. In that way they have Christ in their midst and are one flock.

Now when he says, "Salvation is nearer to us now than when we first believed," that cannot be understood of the nearness of having or possessing. The fathers had the same faith and the same Christ. He was just as near to them as to us, as Scripture says, "Christ yesterday, today and forever." That is, Christ has been from the beginning of the world to the end and all are preserved through him and in him. Whoever believes the most, to him he is the nearest, and whoever believes the least, from him salvation is the farthest—according to talk of possession or property. But St. Paul is speaking here of the nearness of revelation: in the time of Christ the promise was fulfilled and the gospel went out into all the world, and through the same, Christ came to all people and was preached publicly. So here he says, "Our salvation is nearer to us now than when it lay hidden in the promise and had not gone out." Thus he says, "The saving grace of God has appeared." That is, it has gone out and been publicly preached, though it had previously been in all the saints. THE CHURCH POSTIL (1540): FIRST SUNDAY IN ADVENT.[16]

Now! JOHN DONNE: There is not a more comprehensive, a more embracing word in all religion than the first word of this text: *now.* . . . It is an extensive word, *now.* For though we dispute whether this *now,* that is, whether an instant be any part of time or no, yet in truth it is all time. Whatsoever is past, was, and whatsoever is future, shall be an instant; and did and shall fall within this *now.*

We consider in the church four advents or comings of Christ, of every one of which we may say now, now it is otherwise than before. First there is

verbum in carne, the Word came in the flesh, in the incarnation. Then there is *caro in verbo,* he who is made flesh comes in the Word, that is, Christ comes in the preaching of it. And he comes again in *carne saluta,* when at our dissolution and transmigration, at our death he comes by his Spirit and testifies to our spirit that we die the children of God. And lastly he comes in *carne reddita,* when he shall come at the resurrection, to redeliver our bodies to our souls and to deliver everlasting glory to both. . . .

Take then this *now,* the first way of the coming of Christ in person—in the flesh into this world—and then the apostle of Christ directs himself principally to the Jews converted to the faith of Christ. He tells them that their salvation is nearer to them now, now that they had seen him come, than when they did only believe that he would come.

Take the words the second way—of his coming in grace into our hearts—and so the apostle directs himself to all Christians. Now, now that you have been bred in the Christian church, now that you are grown from grace to grace, from faith to faith, now that God by his Spirit strengthens and confirms you: *Now is your salvation nearer than when you believed.* That is, when you began to believe, either by the faith of your parents or the faith of the church or the faith of your sureties at your baptism; or when you began to have some notions and impressions and apprehensions of faith in yourself, when you came to some degree of understanding and discretion.

Take the word of Christ's coming to us at the hour of death, or of his coming to us on the Day of Judgment—for those two are the same for our present purpose, because God never reverses any particular judgment—take the word so, and this is the apostle's argument. You have believed, and you have lived accordingly and that faith and that good life has brought salvation nearer to you, that is, given you a fair and modest infallibility of salvation in the nature of reversion. But now, now that you are come to the approaches of death which shall make your reversion a possession, *Now is salvation nearer you than when you believed.* In sum, the text is a reason why you ought to proceed in good and

---

[15]This gloss was removed in the 1540 edits.
[16]LW 75:16-17* (WA 10,1.2:6-7; E2 7:30-31); quoting Ps 8:3; Rom 13:11; Heb 13:8; Tit 2:11; alluding to Col 1:15-17.

holy ways. It works in all three uses of the word. Whether salvation be said to be near us because we are Christians and thus have advantage of the Jews; or near us because we have made some proficiency in holiness and sanctimony; or near us because we are near our end and thereby near a possession of our endless joy and glory, still from all these uses of the word arise religious provocations to perseverance in holiness of life. SERMON 149, TO THE PRINCE AND PRINCESS PALATINE (1619).[17]

THE TRUE DAY IS THE GOSPEL. MARTIN LUTHER: With the word *day* Paul means the gospel, which is a day in which hearts and souls are enlightened.... Who can enumerate the things revealed to us by this "day"? It teaches us everything: what God is, what we are, what has happened, what is in the future. It teaches us about heaven, hell, earth, angels and devils. There we see how to act toward all these things, wherever we go. Yet the devil has deceived us so that we forsake the day and seek truth among philosophers and heathen who, nevertheless, have known not one part of all these things; they blind us with human doctrines and lead us back into the night. There is no light that does not come from this day. Otherwise St. Paul and all of Scripture would not set forth only this "day" and call everything else the "night." THE CHURCH POSTIL (1540): FIRST SUNDAY IN ADVENT.[18]

THREE VICES. JOHN CALVIN: Paul mentions here three kinds of vices, and to each he has given two names: intemperance and excess in living; sexual indulgence and the filth that is yoked to it; envy and contention. If these have in them so much disgrace that even worldly people are ashamed to commit them before the eyes of human beings, it is fitting that we, who dwell in the light of God, always abstain from such things—even when we are withdrawn from the presence of other human beings. COMMENTARY ON ROMANS 13:13.[19]

WHAT ARE "THE WORKS OF DARKNESS"?

JOHANNES BRENZ: Whoever wants to pay attention to the preaching of the gospel sees everything bright and clear. Christ has fully and completely revealed himself in it; he shines as bright as the sun in heaven in it along with all his benefits. Now then, what ought to be done in such bright daylight? And how then should we direct our lives? Saint Paul instructs us, saying: "Let us cast off the works of darkness and put on the armor of light; let us walk honorably as in the daytime." Now here we should consider what the works of darkness are.

First, there is gorging and guzzling.[20] ... And here we must observe what the ancients considered good behavior. In the morning and during the day they remained sober, but whenever they wanted to be merry, they did such at night around dinner time; with them it was a deep disgrace to be drunk. Accordingly they guarded themselves against getting drunk during the day.... But with us Germans, there is a very different opinion! ... For with us, it's now come to the point that we start in the morning and are wasted and wild the entire day. From this comes a proverb: *Drunk by first light, the whole day's a delight.*[21]

Such drunken living, however, suits those of us who want to be Christians very poorly. And Paul here calls it a work of darkness, and not unreasonably but for three reasons. First, drunkenness is a work of darkness because whoever lives this way

---

[17]Donne, *Works*, 6:33-35*.
[18]LW 75:17, 19* (WA 10,1.2:8, 10; E2 7:32, 34).
[19]CTS 38:489-90* (CO 49:256).

[20]Contemporary biblical studies agrees with Calvin that Paul here offers three hendiadyses to describe the works of darkness (i.e., indulgence of the stomach, sex and violence). Many English translations render *kōmois* ("banquet" or "excessive feasting") in a way that does not draw out the sexual implications that the ESV gives with "orgies": for example, "partying" (CEB); "rioting" (KJV); "carousing" (NIV); "reveling" (NRSV). The Luther Bible (1984) still uses *Fressen und Saufen* ("gorging and guzzling") here. See further C. E. B. Cranfield, *A Critical and Exegetical Commentary on the Epistle to the Romans*, International Critical Commentary (Edinburg: T&T Clark, 1985), 2:687-88; Douglas J. Moo, *The Epistle to the Romans*, New International Commentary on the New Testament 38 (Grand Rapids: Eerdmans, 1996), 825. In contrast, Fitzmyer also translates *kōmois* as "orgies"; Joseph A. Fitzmyer, *Romans: A New Translation with Introduction and Commentary*, Anchor Bible 33 (New York: Doubleday, 1993), 681.
[21]That is, *fru voll, thut den gantzen tag woll.*

cannot let themselves be seen before honorable people; they must hole themselves up and shame themselves for their piggish behavior. Second, gorgers and guzzlers cannot endure the light of God's judgment. Third, on account of such vices people—cast into the abyss of hell, into eternal darkness—must be robbed of the light of eternal salvation. My beloved, since it is now day, let us then walk honorably as in the daytime, and cast aside this work of darkness, so that we will not be thrust into eternal darkness.

Second, Saint Paul names harlotry and lechery—that is, whoring and adultery—a work of darkness. This is his reason: those who live this way shirk the light. Now however it is always day, not only because the gospel of Christ has been revealed but also because God the Lord sees all that is hidden, as David testifies about him, saying, "If I ascend to heaven, you are there; if I descend down into hell, you are also there." Accordingly it is fitting that we set aside such works of darkness and live in discipline, honor and chastity.

Third, rancor and envy are also works of darkness, for they cannot suffer or bear either honorable people or the light of God's judgment. Everyone hates rancorous and envious people; no one likes to deal with them. We flee and avoid them. And God's judgment stands: such people are thrust into eternal darkness. And so we should certainly cast aside such works. FIRST SERMON ON THE EPISTLE FOR THE FIRST SUNDAY IN ADVENT.[22]

CHRIST, THE LIGHT OF EVERY SERMON.
JOHANNES BRENZ: Such preaching against vices is not the most distinguished preaching . . . rather everything depends on the preaching of Christ. And wherever this preaching is not in full force, either not much will come of it or the people will just become hypocrites who seek to merit their salvation in good works. In sum this sermon of Christ should and must have the foremost priority; to be sure, other sermons will follow from it. And so, accordingly Paul in his epistle to the Romans

gave a long and beautiful sermon about the Lord Christ and his righteousness, in which we through faith become participants. So he appends this conclusion to it, by which he wants to acknowledge what should follow from true faith in Christ.

And on account of this passage it was thought fit that this appendix be read from blessed Paul today, the first Sunday in Advent. Since during Advent we focus on the coming of Christ, we begin to teach again the Christian faith, how the teaching of the second article—concerning the birth of Christ, concerning his teaching and miracles, concerning his suffering, death and resurrection—is excellently ordered and structured. This appendix, or today's epistle reading, is read so that we should learn to understand from it that this, which Paul reports here, should be understood not only about today but about every day and in every sermon about Christ, whether it's said openly with explicit words. . . . And so whenever we handle the birth of Christ, as well as his suffering and resurrection, we must always contemplate with it, as Paul says, that "now is the time and hour to rise up from your sleep. The night is past, but the day is at hand." Blessed Paul exhorts us that since Christ comes and reveals his gospel and offers us all his benefits, we should no longer deal in gorging and guzzling, harlotry and lechery, nor in rancor and brawling. Instead we should constantly and regularly put on Christ—who is revealed through his birth, suffering, death and resurrection—and be his followers.

Every time Christ is preached to us, a new light is lifted up and lit. Yes, what's more, whenever Christ is preached to us, the bright, beloved Sun emerges again from under the earth and begins to shine by us. Now there's this fact, that whenever the sun rises, it's bright and clear everywhere, and whatever was hidden and unseen at night becomes seen and manifest—even if we don't say anything about it, still we clearly see it. It's like when someone under veil of night breaks into a house and wants to steal; they are indeed hidden, because it's night. But then suppose that in the blink of an eye the sun arose or someone else lit a light, then it would be seen publicly that a thief is present and

---

[22]Brenz, *Kurtze Ausslegung der Epistel*, 2-3; citing Ps 139:8.

wants to steal. We don't need to say anything much; everyone can see it for themselves. It's the same way with sins like drunkenness, gluttony, adultery, lack of self-control, envy, wrath and hatred—these are hidden, no one knows anything about them—what sins and soul thieves they are. But as soon as Christ is preached and this noble, bright Light is lifted up and lit, then it is apparent that they are grisly, great sins and injustices. Now since Christ is constantly preached among us, we should flee these and other sins, always remembering, "Now is the time to rise up from your sleep, and we should walk as in the daytime." And so we see here that preaching Christ and his benefits should always be practiced and performed, for where this takes place, the other sermons will also be found. . . .

In addition, our Lord Christ not only drives out sin by this, that he atones for these and has granted us this atonement, but also through the power and working of the Holy Spirit. Whenever Christ is preached and accepted with faith, we are granted the Holy Spirit, who cedes no ground or space to sins, but instead opposes them. So whenever Christ is preached, we must always remember this appendix, saying, "Let us now set aside the works of darkness and put on our Lord Jesus Christ." SECOND SERMON ON THE EPISTLE FOR THE FIRST SUNDAY IN ADVENT.[23]

FAITH IS THE LIGHT EMANATING FROM THE SUN THAT SEARCHES FOR THE GOSPEL. MARTIN LUTHER: Just as Christ is the sun and the gospel is the day, so faith is the light, or the looking and watching for this day. For it does not help at all when the sun shines and brings day if our eyes fail to perceive its light. Therefore, though the gospel has gone into all the world and preached Christ, nevertheless only those are enlightened who receive it and have risen from sleep through the light of faith. But the sun and the day are useless for those who are sleeping; they receive no light from it and see as little as if there were neither sun nor day. This is now the time and the hour of which Paul says, "Dear brothers, we know that this is the time and hour to wake from sleep," etc. It is a spiritual time and hour, but it has arisen and still arises in this bodily time, in which we rise from sleep and cast off the works of darkness, etc. THE CHURCH POSTIL (1540): FIRST SUNDAY IN ADVENT.[24]

13:14a *Put On Christ and Become Whole*

DOUBLE DRESSING. JOHANN WILD: We put on Christ in two ways: internally through faith, externally through imitation. EXEGESIS OF ROMANS 13:14.[25]

CHRIST'S GARMENTS ARE PEACE AND LOVE. DESIDERIUS ERASMUS: If we cover the body with more decent clothing when the sun rises lest anything should offend the eyes of others, much more now that the light of the gospel is rising should we adorn the mind with a garment of virtues, which is worthy of the light and does not dread the eyes of God. Henceforth let us so arrange our whole life that we cast off the shadows of our former life and that we may be seen walking in a bright light, visible to God, to angels and to people. Let us not yield to extravagance in feasting or to intoxicating drinking parties. Let us not serve filthy sexual desire and lust; let us not quarrel disgracefully among others through contention and mutual envy. For you were subject to all of these as long as you wandered in the shadows of your former life. The soul is improperly clothed in such a style of dress.

Now since you have been incorporated through baptism into Christ, put on Christ himself. Let him whom you have professed shine forth in your whole life. Imitate him whom you have drunk in. He is chastity. He is sobriety. He is peace. He is love. And a garment of such virtues is fitting for this light of the gospel. PARAPHRASE ON ROMANS 13:12-14.[26]

---

[23]Brenz, *Kurtze Ausslegung der Epistel*, 4-6.

[24]LW 75:19* (WA 10,1.2:11; E2 7:34-35).
[25]Wild, *Exegesis in Epistolam ad Romanos*, 253v.
[26]CWE 42:76-77* (LB 7:822).

"Put On" Is a Common Hebrew Metaphor.

Theodore Beza: Paul persists in his use of the metaphor, but otherwise among the Hebrews the noun *lbš* (*labaš*) is customarily used in a certain matter, by whose acquisition we are adorned (as when someone is said to be clothed with glory, salvation, splendor or righteousness) or to the contrary are disgraced (as when we are said to be clothed with confusion, curse or ruin). Nonetheless, there seems to be a particular energy in that formula, inasmuch as we are allowed to possess Christ in such a way that he is in us and we are in him, just as the Spirit of the Lord is said to have clothed Gideon. But in this passage the apostle is indicating the fruits of sanctification that arise from the Spirit of Christ, by which he wants us to be adorned, as he explains more abundantly in Colossians 3. Annotations on Romans 13:14.[27]

Putting On Christ Is a Common and Important Metaphor for Christians.

John Calvin: This metaphor is commonly used in Scripture with respect to what tends to adorn or to deform human beings. Both of which can be understood with regard to clothing. A filthy and torn garment dishonors a person; what is becoming and clean brings him favor. Now to put on Christ means here to be fortified by the power of his Spirit on every side. In this way the image of God—the soul's only adornment—is renewed in us. Paul is considering the purpose of our calling. God by adopting us unites us to the body of his only-begotten Son, indeed for this purpose, so that renouncing our former life we may become new human beings in him. That is why he says in another passage that we put on Christ in baptism. Commentary on Romans 13:14.[28]

Metaphor of Christ as Our Clothing.

Wolfgang Musculus: Truly Paul prefers to admonish those who were baptized into Christ by the very life of Christ. This pertains to the grace of baptism, in which they had put on Christ, so that what they obtained in baptism sacramentally they may in fact express in their own lives. In a beautiful way here he uses the word "put on" as a metaphor. For just as our cloaked body is completely defended and kept in decency and propriety, through the life of Christ, if only we clothe whatever is carnal, shameful and indecent, then either suppress or certainly cover them, lest we are mocked by them with whom we live. This is announced to the unregenerate in baptism. The one who is baptized is straightway freed from them and clothed in new and white clothes after the baptism. Commentary on Romans 13:14.[29]

What Does it Mean to Be Clothed in Christ?

Martin Luther: Paul quickly shows us all the weapons of light piled up when he admonishes us to dress ourselves in Christ. We put on Christ in two ways. First, we dress ourselves in his own virtues—that happens through faith, which relies on the fact that Christ died for us and did all things for us. Not our righteousness but Christ's has reconciled us to God and redeemed us from sin. This way [of putting on Christ] belongs to the teaching of faith; in this way, Christ is given to us as a gift and a pledge. . . . Second, he is our example and pattern, so that we follow him and become like him, clothed in the same virtues he is. . . .

Here is a strong incentive. It'd have to be a rogue who sees his master fasting and enduring hunger, working, watching and being tired while he himself gulps and guzzles, sleeps, is lazy and lives in debauchery. What master could tolerate such conduct in a servant? Or what servant would dare attempt it? That cannot be. We must be ashamed when we see Christ and find ourselves to be so unlike him.

Who can incite and motivate whoever is not warned, admonished and incited by Christ's own example? What will pages and words accomplish with their rustling, if these peals of thunder from Christ's example fail to move us. For that reason

---

[27]Beza, *Annotationes majores*, 2:138.
[28]CTS 38:490* (CO 49:256); alluding to Gal 3:27.
[29]Musculus, *In epistolam Apostoli Pauli ad Romanos commentarii*, 235.

especially Paul added the word *Lord*, saying, "Put on the Lord Jesus Christ," as if he would say: "Do not think so highly and greatly of yourselves—you who are servants—focus instead on your Lord who also does this, but isn't obliged to." THE CHURCH POSTIL (1540): FIRST SUNDAY IN ADVENT.[30]

IN CHRIST WE RECEIVE HIS RIGHTEOUSNESS AND OBEDIENCE. TILEMANN HESSHUS: "Put on the Lord Jesus Christ." Here the apostle embraces in sum every kind of virtue. For to put on Christ means in this passage to have that mind and will in all life's thoughts and actions as our Lord Jesus Christ always had in the Holy Spirit. It means to be directed by the leading of the Holy Spirit and to have Christ before one's eyes in all things, to love all people for Christ's sake, to live in Jesus Christ and to ascribe all things to his glory.

But one ought to know that we put on Jesus Christ in a twofold manner: First, by imputation through faith; second, by new obedience through the renewal of the Holy Spirit. When we believe in our Lord Jesus Christ, that he was crucified for our sins and rose for our righteousness, we put on Jesus Christ, that is to say, the entire suffering and all the obedience of Jesus Christ is imputed to us by God. Clad in it as in a clean garment before God, we are absolved from sin and pronounced righteous before him. Isaiah 61 speaks in this particular sense: "I will certainly rejoice in the Lord, and my soul will be glad in God, my salvation, because he has clothed me with a garment of salvation and surrounded me with a garment of righteousness, as magnificence adorns a groom in priestly clothing and as it adorns a bride decked out with jewels." The prophet embraces each benefit. Christ, as the High Priest (who offered himself as a victim for sin) and as the church's groom (who was adorned with pure righteousness and the fullness of the Holy Spirit), after he placated the wrath of his Father by his death and obedience, clothes us first

with the garment of righteousness and salvation, forgives us our sins and pronounces us righteous by faith before God, just as if we were lacking every sin and had fulfilled the law. "As many of you as were baptized have put on Christ." Again: "We will be more fully clothed, if we will be found not naked" (2 Cor 5). Then he adorns the church, his own bride, with jewels; that is to say, he enlivens her with the Holy Spirit, adorns her with the knowledge of God, prayer, thanksgiving, love, confession, fear, patience, chastity, mildness, generosity, righteousness, truth and virtues of every kind—which the Holy Spirit calls embroidered pieces of clothing and a gilded garment with golden threads. For no gold gleams so brightly; no diamond or ruby glitters so beautifully; indeed, no evening star or morning star shines so brightly as the church's piety, prayer, confession, constancy and patience, all kindled in true faith through the Holy Spirit. In this passage Paul's phrase looks chiefly to the second manner by which the church is clothed, but nonetheless it must also encompass the first manner. For someone cannot put on Christ's holy state of mind unless first they have been reconciled to God through faith and obtained the gift of the Holy Spirit. For first the tree must be made good; then also good fruits follow. COMMENTARY ON ROMANS 13:14.[31]

CHRIST, OUR GARMENT OF LIGHT. DAVID PAREUS: He ought to have recommended opposite works and described the armor of light, but he changes the metaphor and sets before us a garment instead of armor, by which we are able now to be clothed and equipped for walking honorably and armed for fighting. That "garment" is not our works, but our Lord CHRIST with his righteousness, with which we are clad and please God and are righteous. We put on the garment when we place it around ourselves and cover ourselves with it. Therefore we put on Christ like a garment when by faith we apply the merits of Christ to ourselves, for

---

[30]LW 75:23, 25* (WA 10,1.2:15, 17-18; E2 7:39-40, 42); alluding to Gal 3:27; 1 Cor 15:49; Eph 4:22-24. Luther refers his reader to the postil for New Year's Day, see LW 76:3-38, esp. 20-22 (WA 10,1.1:449-503, esp. 474-78; E2 7:294-339, esp. 315-18).

[31]Hesshus, *Explicatio Epistolae Pauli ad Romanos*, 403r-404r; citing Is 61:10-11; Gal 3:27; 2 Cor 5:3.

whom the filth of our sins is covered in the sight of God. We also put on Christ by the sacrament of baptism: "For as many of you as were baptized into Christ have put on Christ," says the apostle in Galatians 3. Lombard says: "Some put on Christ through their baptism only as far as the sacrament is concerned, but others put on Christ also in substance." And he cites the words of Augustine: "Sometimes people put on Christ to the point of receiving the sacrament; other times they do so to the point of sanctifying their life. And both the good and the wicked are able to share in common that first putting on of Christ, but the latter belongs to the good and pious." In the Eucharist the meaning is not so much that Christ surrounds us on the outside like a garment, but rather enters into us (like bread and drink) and joins himself inwardly to us and dwells in us. "For whoever eats my flesh abides in me and I in him," says Christ. And in Ephesians 3: "By faith Christ dwells in our hearts." Augustine says, "It means more to have Christ in the heart than in the home, for the heart is more inward than our home is" (*Sermon de tempore* 144). Origen says: "Whoever has all the virtues has put on Christ," but it is true when stated as pointing to the effects, but not when stated as pointing to the formal cause. For all who have put on Christ are virtuous, but the opposite is not the case, because many are seemingly virtuous. Commentary on Romans 13:14.[32]

The Perfect Union of Christ and the Church. Johann von Staupitz: The bond between Christ and the church is perfect. It's like this: "I take you as mine. I take you for me. I take you into me." Likewise the church or soul says to Christ: "I take you as mine. I take you for me. I take you into me." Thus Christ says: "The Christian is mine. The Christian is for me. The Christian is I." And the bride: "Christ is mine. Christ is for me. Christ is I." . . .

That he is one with us, all Scripture testifies, which says Christ is in us and we in him. Most of all that Christ said that he gave himself to his disciples, so that "they would be one, as I am in them and you, Father, in me, so that they would be made one." . . . Finally, if Christ is I, then I have a right to heaven, I have hope and I boast in the hope of the sons of God. On Eternal Predestination.[33]

13:14b *Guard Against the Flesh's Desires*

The Proper Use of Food and Drink. Desiderius Erasmus: Up to this point you have used certain things for pleasure; hereafter you should use them for the requirements of the body. Before you were guided by your desires to indulge yourselves shamelessly. From now on turn to the same things soberly, only to the extent of your natural needs. The body must be so nourished that it is strong and living, not lascivious. Food and drink should prevent hunger and thirst, they should not invite and nourish lust. Paraphrase on Romans 13:14.[34]

Balance. Johann Wild: He does not forbid provision for the flesh but provision for the desires of the flesh. So, in another passage he does not say, "I kill my body," but "I place it in slavery." Exegesis of Romans 13:14.[35]

Fight the Flesh's Desires. Martin Luther: We are not to gratify the lusts of the flesh, but to make provision for its necessities or in its necessities. The apostle is trying to say that the

---

[32]Pareus, *In divinam Epistolam ad Romanos commentarius*, 1330-31; citing Gal 3:27; Lombard, *Sentences* 4, dist. 4c; Augustine, Sermon 232.7 (PL 38:1111).

[33]Staupitz, *Libellus de Executione eterne predestinationis*, Bir-v; citing Jn 6:56; 15:1-17; 17:21; Rom 5:1-5.
[34]CWE 42:77* (LB 7:822).
[35]Wild, *Exegesis in Epistolam ad Romanos*, 253v; citing 1 Cor 9:27. The ESV softens *doulagōgō* as "keep under control"; Wild renders it more literally, likewise the CEB, NIV, NRSV. Modern commentators note that this verb (as well as *hypōmiazō*), in keeping with v. 26, bears an athletic metaphor; the reformers also were aware of this. See further Joseph A. Fitzmyer, *First Corinthians: A New Translation with Introduction and Commentary*, Anchor Bible 32 (New Haven, CT: Yale University Press, 2008), 374; and Scott M. Manetsch, ed., *1 Corinthians*, RCS NT 9a (Downers Grove, IL: IVP Academic, forthcoming 2017), *in loco*.

flesh should not be encouraged in its lusts. For as Hugo of St. Victor rightly says: "Whoever encourages his flesh nourishes an enemy"; on the other hand, "whoever destroys the flesh kills a friend."[36] It is not the flesh, but the vices of the flesh, that is, the lusts, which must be destroyed. SCHOLIA ON ROMANS 13:14.[37]

CHRISTIAN FREEDOM NEITHER A FIXED FORMULA NOR SELF-INDULGENT. JOHN CALVIN: Away, then, with that inhuman philosophy that, while conceding only a necessary use of creatures, not only malignantly deprives us of the lawful fruit of God's benevolence but also cannot be practiced unless it robs a person of all their senses and degrades one to a block. But no less diligently, on the other hand we must resist the lust of the flesh, which, unless it is kept in order, overflows without measure. It has its own advocates, who, under the pretext of the freedom conceded, permit everything to it. First, one bridle is put on it if it be determined that all things were created for us that we might recognize the author and give thanks for God's kindness toward us. Where is your thanksgiving if you so gorge yourself with banqueting or wine that you either become stupid or are rendered useless for the duties of piety and of your calling? Where is your recognition of God if your flesh boiling over with excessive abundance into vile lust infects the mind with its impurity so that you cannot discern anything that is right and honorable? Where is our gratefulness toward God for our clothing in the sumptuousness of our apparel if we both admire ourselves and despise others, if with its elegance and glitter we

prepare ourselves for shameless conduct? Where is our recognition of God if our minds are fixed on the splendor of our apparel? For many so enslave all their senses to delights that the mind lies overwhelmed. Therefore, clearly, leave to abuse God's gift must be somewhat curbed, and Paul's rule is confirmed, for if we yield too much to these, they boil up without measure or control.

Therefore, even though the freedom of believers in external matters is not to be restricted to a fixed formula, yet it is surely subject to this law: to indulge oneself as little as possible; but on the contrary, with unflagging effort of mind to insist on cutting off all show of superfluous wealth, not to mention licentiousness, and diligently to guard against turning helps into hindrances. INSTITUTES 3.10.3-4.[38]

REMEMBER YOUR HOMELAND. JOHN CALVIN: As long as we bear our flesh, we cannot totally discard care for it. Even though our life is in heaven, still we continue to sojourn on earth. So then, the things that belong to the body must be taken care of, not in a manner other than as aids in our pilgrimage, nor in a way that makes us forget our native country. Even secular people have said that a few things are sufficient for nature, but human appetites are insatiable. Everyone, then, who wishes to satisfy the desires of the flesh must necessarily not only fall into but also be immersed in a vast and deep abyss.

Setting a bridle on our desires, Paul reminds us that the cause of all intemperance is that no one is content with the sober and right use of things. Therefore he has laid down this rule: we are to provide for the needs of our flesh, but not to indulge its lusts. It is in this way that we shall use this world without abusing it. COMMENTARY ON ROMANS 13:14.[39]

---

[36]The Weimar edition reports that these words have not been found in the works of Hugo of St. Victor; this quotation may be from Gregory, *Homilia in Ezechielem*, 2.7; see LW 25:484n14.
[37]LW 25:484* (WA 56:491); citing Prov 29:21.

[38]LCC 20:721-22* (CO 2:530-31).
[39]CTS 38:490-91* (CO 49:256).

14:1-12 DO NOT PASS JUDGMENT
ON ONE ANOTHER

As for the one who is weak in faith, welcome him, but not to quarrel over opinions. ²*One person believes he may eat anything, while the weak person eats only vegetables.* ³*Let not the one who eats despise the one who abstains, and let not the one who abstains pass judgment on the one who eats, for God has welcomed him.* ⁴*Who are you to pass judgment on the servant of another? It is before his own master[a] that he stands or falls. And he will be upheld, for the Lord is able to make him stand.*

⁵*One person esteems one day as better than another, while another esteems all days alike. Each one should be fully convinced in his own mind.* ⁶*The one who observes the day, observes it in honor of the Lord. The one who eats, eats in honor of the Lord, since he gives thanks to God, while the one who abstains, abstains in* honor of the Lord and gives thanks to God. ⁷*For none of us lives to himself, and none of us dies to himself.* ⁸*For if we live, we live to the Lord, and if we die, we die to the Lord. So then, whether we live or whether we die, we are the Lord's.* ⁹*For to this end Christ died and lived again, that he might be Lord both of the dead and of the living.*

¹⁰*Why do you pass judgment on your brother? Or you, why do you despise your brother? For we will all stand before the judgment seat of God;* ¹¹*for it is written,*

*"As I live, says the Lord, every knee shall bow to me,
and every tongue shall confess[b] to God."*

¹²*So then each of us will give an account of himself to God.*

a Or lord   b Or *shall give praise*

OVERVIEW: In this pericope the Reformation commentators address the topic of the weak and the strong: the liberty of faith in the gospel of Jesus Christ should not be used to hinder the weak in faith. The reformers frame this discussion under the rubric of adiaphora, or nonessentials in the faith. These matters are not unimportant, but they are not critical for salvation, like baptism. Like Paul, the reformers do not want the ceremonial and dietary laws to serve as requirements for Christian life, nor do they want those who still need these traditional supports for their faith to be despised by those who were freed from them by the liberating news that Christ set us free from the traditions devised by human authority. In addition, they recognize that people need order in worship, but these regulations should not be confused with the gospel or be required as meritorious.

Paul ends this pericope with an affirmation of Christ's divinity: the one who was born of the Virgin Mary by the power of the Holy Spirit, who suffered death on a cross and who rose again is true God. Jesus is the one to whom every knee will bow and every tongue confess. Our Reformation commentators assume the veracity of Chalcedonian Christology. The Council of Chalcedon (451) settled disputes concerning how Christ could be both God and man by affirming that Jesus' two natures—human and divine—are joined in the unity of his person without confusion, without change, without division, without separation. While elsewhere, like the early church, the reformers vehemently disputed how exactly the relationship of the natures in one person should be understood, nevertheless in this passage they all agree with the ancient teaching of Chalcedon.[1]

---

[1]Their different interpretations of Christ's presence in the Lord's Supper especially reveal these differences. Since according to his human nature Christ ascended to heaven, what does that mean for his presence in the sacrament? Lutheran theologians argued

Ancient Plague of Adiaphora. Wolfgang Musculus: It is an ancient disease in the church that although we very well agree in the primary matters of faith, nevertheless there are controversies on account of indifferent matters, because those who are weak in faith and more superstitious cling to them, and those who have some knowledge of Christian liberty abuse their liberty and by neglecting love become a stumbling block to the weak. And so endless controversy is spawned between the two factions, so that those who seem strong in faith despise the weak, and in turn the weak judge and condemn those who use their liberty. Since it is shameful that Christians skirmish fiercely among themselves over matters not necessary for salvation and meanwhile neglect what is most important in Christianity, namely mutual love, it seemed good to the apostle to settle the controversy and to prescribe his *mišpāt* ["judgment"] to both factions, so that love would be preserved. Now this controversy had arisen either from a wrongheaded ambition for the law, which did not permit some sorts of food to the Jews and commanded the observance of certain days; or certainly from the wicked superstition of false apostles in which they pressed ceremonies of the law and taught that these ceremonies were to be preserved in the church. Then, out of the apostle's teaching he taught freedom from the ceremonies of the law, so that he took into consideration the consciences of Christians, and he led them into sincerity and purity of faith and knowledge of Christ in whom alone there is salvation for all. Commentary on Romans 14.[2]

Hold to the Foundation and Bear the Weak. Tilemann Hesshus: If someone should hold to the foundation and source of our religion,

let them understand the distinction between law and gospel. Let them know what the benefits of the Redeemer are, how a person receives the forgiveness of sins before God and obtains salvation. Let them not defend errors that oppose the articles of faith, but let them allow themselves to be taught from the Word of God. But should they cling to the observation of festivals or the observation of rituals, they ought not to be condemned because of this lack of knowledge and weakness, but rather welcomed and taught as a true member of the church.

Paul himself imparts this rule: "Receive the weak in faith, but not for the purpose of seeking quarrels"; that is to say, do not ward off the weak from the fellowship of the church, and do not disturb them with a maze of debates, but teach them from the Word and bear their weakness with all kindness. Ambrose observed Lent rather superstitiously and thought it was a matter of necessity. That was an error on his part, but he ought not to be condemned for that reason. For in all the godly there is great weakness. Much blindness and ignorance clings to us all.

But we are being transformed from clarity to clarity; that is, little by little a greater light is being kindled in us through the Holy Spirit and our faith is growing stronger. Although Peter was a mighty apostle and had already received the Holy Spirit, he still doubted that he was permitted to eat animals of every kind and to consort with Gentiles. Peter clearly erred in this matter and was chastised by the apostle Paul (Gal 1). But even if the apostle Peter's weakness was pronounced, he nonetheless was not expelled from the church, but rather welcomed and taught—and he accepted instruction from Paul. Thus we ought to be compassionate toward all the weak people in the church so that we may welcome them, bear with them and teach them. The Fifth Rule Concerning Adiaphora.[3]

On Ceremonies. Philipp Melanchthon: Since error about ceremonies brings forth such great and numerous difficulties, it is necessary that

---

that the ascended Christ is ubiquitous and so according to his human nature, he is present in the bread and wine. However, Reformed theologians disagreed; it is inappropriate to say Jesus according to his human nature is present in the eucharistic elements, for after the ascension his body is localized in heaven. Nevertheless, here in this passage reformed and Lutheran theologians alike agree with the ancient teaching of Chalcedon.
[2]Musculus, *In epistolam Apostoli Pauli ad Romanos commentarii*, 235.

[3]Hesshus, *Explicatio Epistolae Pauli ad Romanos*, 416r-417r.

their use be rightly taught. Paul here teaches in sum that neither the Mosaic ceremonies nor similar ones instituted by human beings are to be observed as being necessary, because the righteousness about which the gospel speaks is not observance of Mosaic or similar rites, but knowledge of Christ, new and spiritual life in the heart. In the outer life, while it is lawful to use various intervals of days, it is also permitted to use different rites. He does not want the opinion of righteousness and necessity to be imagined for ceremonies. Neither does he want discord to be sown about rites, either Mosaic or human. This is the sum and substance of this chapter, which does not talk about sacraments, which have a command, because they are signs added to the promises. Likewise they are testimonies of confession, but here also it is profitable that human traditions be distinguished.

There are three kinds of ceremonies. First, there is the kind of traditions which teach something that cannot be done without sin. Such is the tradition about celibacy, since it is imposed on those who are not fit for it. Likewise the profanation of Masses and the worship of the saints. About this kind the rule must be held fast: "We must obey God rather than human beings." Therefore such traditions are condemned by divine authority.

Second, there is the kind of traditions which make rules about things that are adiaphora according to their nature, such as feast days, dress and food. With respect to these, the purposes must be considered. If the purpose is political, they are lawful traditions, as when festival days are observed not as though this were an act of worship, but for the sake of order, that people may know at what time they should come together to hear the gospel and for the Lord's Supper. Since human beings naturally understand order and need to arrange their activities in an orderly manner, church activities also ought to have their order. Neither can life be without such rites and ordinances that make for good order. Therefore also Paul commands: "That in the church all things should be done decently and in good order."

Third, there is the kind of traditions regarding adiaphora that are thought to be acts of worship,

meritorious or necessary. Such traditions obscure the doctrine of the gospel, and the opinion that comes to them makes godless traditions of adiaphora. Therefore they are rightly violated and abolished in order that the false opinion may be corrected, for it is necessary that errors about worship, merits and necessity be rejected. COMMENTARY ON ROMANS (1540).[4]

FOUR DEGREES OF FREEDOM. PHILIPP MELANCHTHON: Here it is necessary also that we speak about Christian liberty. For the purpose of teaching, I distinguish four degrees of Christian liberty. The first is that remission of sins, imputation of righteousness and eternal life are not given on account of the law or our virtues, but freely on account of Christ, only that we should believe that these things come to us on account of Christ. About this degree Christ says: "If the Son makes you free then you are truly free."

The second degree is that in the remission of sins the Holy Spirit is given, who helps us to begin to obey the law of God, rules us and defends us against the snares of the devil. Although this degree is linked to the one above, I distinguish it in the enumeration so that the benefits of Christ may be more clearly seen. Here belongs the saying of Paul: "Where the Spirit of the Lord is, there is liberty." For that lifts up hearts so that they are not oppressed by the terrors of sin, other terrors or death. The Spirit moves them so that they begin to obey God, as is said elsewhere: "The Holy Spirit helps our infirmity." This liberty will be complete after the resurrection. Meanwhile, however, it must be begun in this life in the exercises of faith and prayer. In these exercises it is understood and grows when we sustain ourselves with the Word of God, in order that we may overcome terrors and griefs. These two degrees chiefly constitute Christian liberty and pertain to spiritual and eternal life (which must be begun in this life), and their knowledge affords great comfort to the godly.

---

[4]Melanchthon, *Commentary on Romans*, 226-27* (MO 15:720-21); citing Acts 5:29; 1 Cor 14:40.

The third degree is that the gospel frees us from the ceremonies and the civil or judicial laws of Moses. This degree pertains in some measure to the outer life, but has its cause in the earlier degrees. For the gospel does not require the Levitical ceremonies, because it teaches that we are proclaimed righteous not on account of those rites or other works of ours, but rather by faith through mercy on account of Christ. And since the gospel teaches about spiritual and perpetual righteousness of the heart, it does not require the form of government or the civil laws of Moses, but permits us to use the architecture and medicine of all nations. . . .

The fourth degree of Christian liberty is that while the gospel permits some ordinances about times and practices in the church to be made by human beings in the interest of good order, it wants us to think that these observances are not acts of worship, that they do not merit remission of sins and that they are not righteousness or perfection. Also, except in case of offense, they can be omitted without sin. Concerning this degree Paul teaches in Colossians 2: "Let no one judge you in food, in drink." He is not speaking only about Mosaic rites, but in general about Mosaic and all ceremonies that are instituted in the church by human authority. Therefore he expressly names human traditions later when he says "according to the precepts and doctrines of human beings."

Knowledge of this degree is very necessary for churches to avoid many errors. Human beings are naturally inclined to false acts of worship, and in dangers they take refuge in their own righteousness or merits, so they erroneously think up and heap up acts of worship. Therefore it is necessary that churches be forewarned so that they may truly understand the teaching about faith, true prayer and the worship of faith, and may know that acts of worship instituted without a divine command are displeasing to God. COMMENTARY ON ROMANS (1540).[5]

14:1-3 *Imitate Your Father and Welcome the Weak and the Strong*

WHO ARE THE WEAK? CARDINAL CAJETAN: He calls "weak in faith"—not in body—those who, still insufficiently trained in the liberty of faith, consider some things to be impermissible that nevertheless according to faith's liberty are permissible. Such people are called "weak in faith," because they have been insufficiently strengthened in those things that pertain to the liberty of faith. COMMENTARY ON ROMANS 14:1.[6]

TOLERATE AND GRADUALLY TEACH. PHILIPP MELANCHTHON: As he is about to speak about the use of ceremonies and liberty, he sets down, first of all, an admonition about tolerating the weak. He teaches a precept that is not to be practiced toward wicked persecutors—enemies of the gospel—but toward our members, that is, toward such as permit themselves to be taught and who hear the gospel. He forbids these to be deterred by unusual examples so that they do not embrace the gospel.

He calls him weak in the faith, not yet sufficiently learned in the doctrine of liberty. Furthermore, when he says that such a one is to be raised up lest they fall into a state of doubt, he reminds us of two things that he should not be compelled to do something against his conscience that his conscience disapproves; and that he should be moved forward little by little and be snatched out and set free from the state of doubt. For doubting in any article, if it is not corrected and increases, is a terrible sickness. It casts out faith and causes despair, hatred of the entire gospel and manifest ungodliness. COMMENTARY ON ROMANS (1540).[7]

THE CHURCH IS FULL OF WEAK PEOPLE. TILEMANN HESSHUS: The church of Christ for the greater part consists of the weak. There are few of those sort of people who have been endowed with the singular light of doctrine and great

---

[5]Melanchthon, *Commentary on Romans*, 228, 229-30* (MO 15:722-24); citing Jn 8:36; 2 Cor 3:17; Rom 8:26; Col 2:16, 22.

[6]Cajetan, *In Sacrae Scripturae Expositionem*, 5:75.
[7]Melanchthon, *Commentary on Romans*, 231-32 (MO 15:726).

strength of the Spirit. Often even also among the greatest apostles great weakness is discovered so that the strength of God may become more conspicuous than our weakness. Therefore Paul orders with great diligence that those who are stronger and are better instructed in the doctrine of godliness show their strength in this, namely, that they patiently bear with the weak.

For this is the kindness and mercy of God: he does not reject the feeble but is mightily concerned about them as those who especially need his help and goodness.

Concerning Christ's office the prophet says: "He will not break a bruised reed, and he will not extinguish a smoking wick." Therefore it is most fair that thought be given in the church to the weak. However, those who are openly enemies of the church, persecute the truth, refuse to be taught and raise a horrible clamor against the church's teaching are not to be counted among the weak. Nor are those weak who live in manifest notorious sins.

Nor also to be numbered with the weak are hypocrites and sycophants who turn themselves to the happier side of the ship and accommodate themselves to the times and to the will of the mighty. For they both hate and mock all religion and hope that they can deceive God and people. God does not welcome but hates such people, as David attests (Psalm 5): "The Lord abhors a bloody and deceitful man." Therefore the weak are those who seriously embrace the teaching of the gospel and do not defend idols or errors, but join themselves to the true church and, provided that they hold to the foundation of the faith about the eternal salvation imparted to us by Christ, may nonetheless be ignorant of many things, have doubts in many areas and think incorrectly about many matters. When it is necessary that errors arise, they nonetheless do not defend their errors stubbornly if they are admonished, but allow themselves to be educated and, when they are shown the solid fundamental truths, they acquiesce to the true way of thinking and have an eagerness for living in a godly and holy way....

Therefore Paul orders these weak people in the church to be received as true members of the church of God, and he wants the One who loves them to be taken into consideration so that we do not offend them either by an unjust condemnation or an intemperate use of our freedom. He says, "Welcome the weak." That is to say, do not count them as your enemy; do not exclude them at once from the fellowship of the saints. Do not disturb their conscience with unnecessary debates, but rather bear with them with great patience and pray to the Lord on their behalf so that they may be strengthened. COMMENTARY ON ROMANS 14:1.[8]

COMMUNION FOSTERS FAITH. CARDINAL CAJETAN: "Accept them," that is, join them to you. Not only does he command them not to be expelled but even to be joined to other Christians, for he wants them to be nourished by this union, so that they might grow in faith. COMMENTARY ON ROMANS 14:1.[9]

THE HOUSE OF GOD IS LIKE ANY FAMILY. DAVID PAREUS: By this commandment of the apostle we are admonished first concerning the perpetual condition of the church, because just as in any family there are found full-grown people, small people, healthy and strong people, ill and weak people, so in the house of God, which is the church, such inequality is repeatedly found, so that some appear full-grown and strong and others small and weak. Such has been the constitution of the godly at all times in the church. The reason for this is that God calls some people to faith more quickly and others later in life; some are equipped by God with more gifts and others with fewer gifts; some apply a more burning zeal concerning those matters that must be cultivated, while others apply a more slovenly zeal. Therefore the foolish rigor of the fanatics is disproved who think that the church cannot truly

---

[8]Hesshus, *Explicatio Epistolae Pauli ad Romanos*, 420r-v, 421r; citing Is 42:3; Ps 5:6.
[9]Cajetan, *In Sacrae Scripturae Expositionem*, 5:75.

exist unless where everyone is equally firm in the faith, equally holy in life, or who think the church does not exist where some weeds are seen to sprout with the wheat in the Lord's field.

However, there is this twofold inequality among believers, namely, as regards the faith and as regards behavior. . . . Therefore it is not the case that we should be offended by such inequality in the servants of God. Instead, if we are stronger in faith and godliness, let us boast of the grace of God; if we are weaker, let us recognize our weakness and remember to devote ourselves to a serious zeal for making progress. But whatever advances we have made in the knowledge of faith and in godliness, let us remember that apostolic word: "We know in part; we prophesy in part." And "We all stumble in many things." . . .

Second, we are admonished about the duty of the stronger toward the weaker in faith or life. Nature and fairness itself demands that the latter be kindly received, taught, cared for and corrected. For the same takes place in a family: the parents direct, admonish and teach the children; the healthy bear and care for the sick. Thus it is appropriate that this happen in the Lord's house. The apostle will inculcate this command more openly in 15:1: "We who are strong ought to bear with the weakness of the weak and not indulge ourselves," where he will set the example of Christ before us, who for the sake of our salvation endured burdensome things. Why shouldn't we too patiently endure some weaknesses of our brothers?

Finally, we are admonished about the prudence that must be applied by the stronger when correcting the weaker. "Whoever warns in an unseasonable time causes harm." In a city more harm comes from an imprudent doctor than from an assassin. Calm teaching, prudent admonishing and brotherly correction profit more than an academic dispute, pointed contention and bitter railing. Therefore one must beware of cunning debates, untimely disputes, quarrels, contentions and *logomachiai* ["battles over words"] as plagues on the church. The apostle orders theologians to stay away from these things (1 Tim 6:4; 2 Tim 2:23). For there is no edification

in these things, because there is no love; it is a great stumbling block and disturbance, because it is a very great bitterness and malice. If this plague could be cured or removed in this argumentative age, it would be possible to hope for peace in the church. COMMENTARY ON ROMANS 14:1.[10]

PATIENCE AND FORBEARANCE. DESIDERIUS ERASMUS: It is not proper immediately to place the worst construction on something that may fall short of wickedness. In order that peace and concord exist everywhere among you, some things must be ignored, some endured, some interpreted with more kindness. This forbearance and sincerity has great force to produce a mutual fellowship of life. Peace will never remain firm among us unless in some things one gives way in turn to another, inasmuch as there are various opinions among people. PARAPHRASE ON ROMANS 14:1.[11]

HOW TO DWELL TOGETHER. JOHN CALVIN: Now he moves to a precept especially necessary for the church's instruction: that those who have made greater progress in Christian doctrine accommodate themselves to the more unlearned, and use their strength to support their weakness. For among God's people some are feebler, and unless they are treated with great gentleness and kindness, they lose heart and eventually are estranged from religion. At that time it's quite likely that this especially happened, since churches were mixed together from Jews and Gentiles. Some—long accustomed to the observation of the Mosaic law, having been raised in it from childhood—could not easily abandon these legal customs; others, who had learned absolutely nothing of the sort, refused this unaccustomed yoke.

Moreover, since human beings are inclined to jump from a difference of opinion to brawls and controversies, the apostle shows how those who differ in opinions are able to remain together

---

[10]Pareus, *In divinam Epistolam ad Romanos commentarius*, 1480, 1481-82; citing 1 Cor 13:9; Jas 3:2.
[11]CWE 42:77.

without discord. He prescribes this as the best way: that those who are stronger should take care to assist the weak, and those who have made more progress should bear with the unlearned. For if God strengthens us before others, he does not grant this strength so that we might oppress the weak. Nor is it part of Christian wisdom to be excessively proud and to despise others. Therefore, in this way, he directs this word to those who are more knowledgeable and who have already been strengthened: the greater the grace they receive from the Lord, the greater they are obliged to help their neighbors. COMMENTARY ON ROMANS 14:1.[12]

WHY DO THE WEAK IN FAITH EAT VEGETABLES? CARDINAL CAJETAN: Notice whom he called "weak in faith": whoever distinguishes between one food and another, between one meat and another. And for this reason he says, "he eats vegetables"—among which there is no distinction. And from this it's clear that he's talking about Jews who turned to Christ. Some, with sound faith, ate all foods, even those that had been forbidden in the law of the Jews. But others with weak faith abstained from eating unclean animals among Jews. Because among them no vegetable is unclean, therefore they are described as eating vegetables. COMMENTARY ON ROMANS 14:2.[13]

A MOST HEALTHY COMMANDMENT. TILEMANN HESSHUS: He states with an example what sort of weak people he is talking about. A weak person is not someone who corrupts the articles of faith, as Arius did, or who stubbornly defends errors, as Major did, or who contaminates himself with manifest sins, as Ahab did. Instead, a weak person is someone who holds to the foundation and nonetheless errs in many matters and needs teaching, such as a person who does not yet understand Christian freedom sufficiently and so does not dare to eat everything that is sold in the market, but fears that they will be polluted by meat

sacrificed to idols and so prefers to eat vegetables rather than wound his conscience. Christians were hearing that they ought not to participate in the sacrifices of idols. Therefore, because meat was often being sold, some of which had been sacrificed to idols, they feared that they might also be defiled, even if unwittingly. On the other hand, the Jews who were converted, even if they embraced the gospel, nonetheless were not able to reject at once the ceremonies in which they had been raised. Even if they were sinning by their weakness, he nonetheless does not want them to be excluded from the church, but rather put up with and taught.

This is truly a most healthy commandment. If every person would remember it, there would be more harmony and fewer dissensions. The stronger ought to welcome the weaker, teach them and not throw them into confusion. The weak ought not to judge concerning matters that exceed their grasp. But why? Does it follow that laypeople may not make judgments concerning the teaching, duties and morals of their superiors? Paul does not want to say this, for he is not discussing here about doctrine or life, but about indifferent matters and the use of one's freedom.

By all means, any godly person at all may make a judgment about doctrine. For whoever is a member of the church holds the articles of the faith and has before his eyes the New and Old Testaments. According to this norm, when he makes a judgment about doctrine or morals, he himself does not make the judgment, but rather the Word of God does so, whose witness he himself brings forth. But in this passage he is discussing adiaphora and warns that one ought not to make a pronouncement about someone else's conscience, when the matter is obscure to us.

Whoever does not eat meat shows by that very fact that the doctrine of Christian freedom is unknown to them. Therefore, how does it flow from trusting in God that one is able to judge another person's deed that does not contradict the Decalogue? COMMENTARY ON ROMANS 14:2-3.[14]

---

[12]CO 49:257 (cf. CTS 38:491-92).
[13]Cajetan, *In Sacrae Scripturae Expositionem*, 5:75.
[14]Hesshus, *Explicatio Epistolae Pauli ad Romanos*, 421r-v, 422r. Arius

NEEDLESS AND AVOIDABLE SCHISMS ARISE.
DAVID PAREUS: He explains the pernicious effect
of the disagreement [between the strong and the
weak]. The strong, eating whatever they wanted,
were despising the weak, who were not eating.
They were inviting them to do the same and
laughing at them when they refused as if they
were not true Christians. The weak Christians in
turn opposed them as if they were profane
individuals given over to their gullet. So both were
sinning. This was a great schism that arose out of
a trivial matter, just as an immense blaze easily
arises from a spark. Often on account of indifferent matters (adiaphora) the church was shaken
and pulled asunder. The Roman Pope Victor
stirred up such disturbances over unleavened and
leavened bread that he was seriously scolded by
Irenaeus, as Eusebius attests in book 5, chapter
[24], of his histories. From this cause there arose
in Saxony the sects of the adiaphorists and the
Flacians. A similar struggle concerning indifferent
matters of ritual exercises the English and Scottish
churches still to this day. Nevertheless the apostle
severely makes known to each group that churches
ought not to be disturbed concerning such things,
nor should love be torn apart. . . .

We must take the facts of the case and draw a
conclusion: Although one is free to omit or do
indifferent matters without scandal, the peace of
the church should not be torn apart for that reason,
nor should the faithful condemn or despise each
other; rather, the strong should condescend to the
weakness of others. Nonetheless, lest the strong
clothe themselves in weakness or foster it in others,
let them bear it lightly and prudently correct them
when they can. COMMENTARY ON ROMANS 14:3.[15]

FOLLOW GOD'S EXAMPLE. TILEMANN HESSHUS:
This most serious argument is taken from God's
authority and contains a very sweet and necessary
consolation in itself. He says, "God himself already
welcomed the weak." Therefore what rashness and
inflexibility would cause you to dare to drive him
out? But Paul took this idea from the promise,
"Come to me all you who labor and are heavy
burdened, and I will give you rest" and "He will not
crush a bruised reed or extinguish a smoking wick."

God promised salvation not only to those who
have been endowed with a robust faith, but also
to those who believe in Christ with a somewhat
faint faith. And unless God spared the weaker,
who would be able to be saved? For we are all
weak. Therefore it is appropriate for us to follow
God's judgment and not be stricter than God so
that a strict sentence is not imposed on us.
COMMENTARY ON ROMANS 14:3.[16]

WE TOO ARE WEAK. PHILIPP MELANCHTHON:
Paul testifies that the weak have been welcomed by
God. But he does not mean enemies or persecutors,
but those who hear the gospel, who are teachable
and have the beginnings of the fear of God and
faith in Christ. Thus the apostles were righteous
before Christ's resurrection, although they had their
weaknesses, as is apparent in the Gospel history. Let
us transfer this example to ourselves, and remember
that we also have many weaknesses. Nevertheless,
we do not abandon our faith because of them, since
the Scripture here testifies that the weak are
welcomed, but also admonishes at the same time

(d. 336) denied the essential divinity of Christ. Georg Major
taught that good works were necessary for salvation. While that
statement could be understood to mean that sanctification
follows justification, he was warned not to make the statement
without further qualification, since it could imply that sanctification was the basis for our justification. Major never acknowledged
that it was at best a misleading way of putting things; his views
were condemned in Article 4 of the *Formula of Concord*. On
Ahab, see 1 Kings 17–22.
[15]Pareus, *In divinam Epistolam ad Romanos commentarius*, 1488,

1489. See Eusebius, *Church History* 5.24 (NPNF2 1:242-44).
Pareus cites three schisms as examples of ignoring Paul's
command here: (1) the Quartodeciman controversy, when Pope
Victor I (d. 199) excommunicated the Asian churches that
celebrated Easter on Nisan 14—Irenaeus protested that while it
is more fitting to celebrate the resurrection on Sunday,
nevertheless this variation in practice was not an innovation and
did not harm the faith; (2) the debates over Luther's legacy
between the Philippists ("adiaphorists") and Gnesio-Lutherans
("Flacians"); and (3) the disagreements over the regulative
principle between the Puritans and the Conformists in the
Churches of England and Scotland.
[16]Hesshus, *Explicatio Epistolae Pauli ad Romanos*, 422v; citing Mt
11:28; Is 42:3.

that the weak are to be carried forward little by little. COMMENTARY ON ROMANS (1540).[17]

14:4 God Alone Is Judge

ONLY ACCORDING TO THE WORD. JOHN CALVIN: The power to judge is taken away from us; this extends to both the person and the deed. Nevertheless between the person and the deed there are many differences, for the person—whoever they may be—we should resign to the will of God [arbitrio Dei]. Concerning his deeds it is indeed not permitted to judge them according to our own assessment, but only according to the Word of God. Judgment taken from the Word, however, is neither human nor unfitting. Therefore Paul here wants to prevent us from the temerity of judging, into which some fall, daring to judge a person's deed without God's Word. COMMENTARY ON ROMANS 14:4.[18]

LET GOD'S WORD PRONOUNCE JUDGMENT. TILEMANN HESSHUS: A second argument is taken from the nature of correlatives: It belongs to a lord to pronounce judgment on his own servants, not the servants who belong to another. Weak Christians, who do not yet understand the enjoyment of freedom, and also the stronger Christians, who believe that they may eat all things, are not our own servants, but servants of our Lord Jesus Christ. Therefore it does not belong to us to judge based on our own feelings. Someone may say, "If someone spreads false teaching, does that mean that he is not our servant and therefore we may not pronounce judgment on him?" I reply: We may not judge anyone based on our own feelings. But whenever we judge others based on God's Word, we do not judge, but rather we are witnesses concerning the judgment that our Lord Jesus Christ already brought forth in his Word. Paul says, "If someone teaches another gospel, let him be anathema." Therefore, when we pronounce an anathema on a false teacher convicted of error from God's Word, it is the Word of God itself that condemns. When he says, "But he will stand," he orders us always to hope for the best for our weak brothers and to look to God's immense kindness, who promised help abundantly for all.

However, these things ought not to be twisted, as if the apostle were ordering that a blind eye be turned to all the crimes and scandals in the church and as if he wished that the severity of ecclesiastical discipline be omitted. By no means! For he does not retract the things that he taught elsewhere (2 Thessalonians 3): "Keep away from every brother who lives in an unseemly way." And he himself handed over an incestuous individual to Satan. However, here he is discussing the weakness of the faithful who retain faith and a good conscience. COMMENTARY ON ROMANS 14:4.[19]

JUDGMENT IS CHRIST'S. PHILIPP MELANCHTHON: He forbids us to condemn one another in the use of indifferent things such as rites about foods, days and other things of this kind. . . . Judgment belongs to Christ; therefore we ought not to arrogate judgment to ourselves, namely, about the conscience of another (not about an outward deed that is clearly unlawful). This rule is well known, far and wide, as also that one "judge not." But the offices are not forbidden, namely, teaching, brotherly admonition or the duties of the magistrate. For these have commandments of God and are divinely instituted courts. What is prohibited are private judgments, that is, condemnations outside of these three courts . . . judgments that have originated from a sick mind, ill will or vanity. A judgment that is made by a person must be made about an external unlawful act. However, it is very common in the world that what others say and do lawfully is deceitfully misinterpreted. Paul disapproves of such judgments in the use of indifferent things, and forbids that condemnations be made on

---

[17]Melanchthon, *Commentary on Romans*, 232* (MO 15:726).
[18]CO 49:258-59 (CTS 38:495).

[19]Hesshus, *Explicatio Epistolae Pauli ad Romanos*, 423r-v; citing Gal 1:8; 2 Thess 3:6.

account of dissimilar rites in indifferent matters. COMMENTARY ON ROMANS (1540).[20]

OUR LORD FINISHES WHAT HE STARTS. JOHN CALVIN: Now because he adds "truly he will stand," not only does he command us to refrain from condemning, but he also exhorts us to gentleness and kindness, so that we are always optimistic about those in whom we discern something of God. For the Lord has created hope for us: he will fully strengthen and lead to completion those in whom he has begun the work of his grace. Now that he reasons from God's power, he does not mean this simply, as if he were saying, "God is able to do it, if he wants"; rather he unites God's will with his power—according to the typical custom of Scripture. Nevertheless he does not here assert some everlastingness, as if it were necessary for those whom God has raised up once to stand until the end. Rather he only warns that we should be optimistic and that our judgments should be inclined in this direction—as he also teaches elsewhere: "He who has begun a good work in you will bring it to completion in the end." In sum Paul shows how the judgments of those in whom love is active should be disposed. COMMENTARY ON ROMANS 14:4.[21]

14:5-6 Feasts and Fasts Only Have Meaning in the Lord

OBEY YOUR CONSCIENCE. JOHN CALVIN: He had just spoken about scruples in the choice of food; now he adds another example about the distinction of days. And both were from Judaism. Accordingly because the Lord distinguishes between foods in his law, pronouncing some foods to be unclean and prohibiting their use, and appoints feast days and solemn days, and commands them to be observed, Jews nurtured in the teaching of the law from childhood were

not able to discard reverence for days, to which they had held from birth and had been accustomed their entire lives. They dared not even touch food that they had abhorred for so long. That they had absorbed these beliefs revealed their weakness, for they would have thought differently if they had been established in a certain and clear knowledge of Christian liberty. That they abstained from what they thought unlawful revealed their piety; likewise it would have revealed their audacity and contempt if they had acted contrary to their conscience.

Here therefore the apostle uses the best moderation when he commands each to be certain of their own counsel. By this he means that in Christians there should be such a zeal for obedience that they do nothing but what they believe, or rather are certain is pleasing to God. And it should be well remembered that this is the beginning of right living: if human beings depend on God's command, they should not allow themselves even to move a finger with a doubtful or wavering mind. It is impossible that temerity not immediately break out into disobedience, whenever we dare to go further than we are convinced is lawful for us. If anyone would object, that error is always confused, and so it is impossible for the certainty that Paul requires to exist in the weak, the solution is obvious: such are to be forgiven, but only if they remain within their small measure of faith. For Paul wanted nothing other than to restrain immoderate liberty, by which it happens that many casually, as it were, throw themselves into doubtful and untested matters. Therefore Paul requires this be adopted, that God's will dictate all our actions. COMMENTARY ON ROMANS 14:5.[22]

CERTAINTY BY GOD'S WORD ALONE. TILEMANN HESSHUS: This commandment is a most wholesome and necessary one. For there are many errors in the human mind, and people wander in their thoughts to an astonishing degree and marvelously love their inventions. Many disagree

---

[20]Melanchthon, *Commentary on Romans*, 232-33* (MO 15:277); citing Mt 7:1; Lk 6:37.
[21]CO 49:259 (CTS 38:495); citing Phil 1:6.

[22]CO 49:259-60 (cf. CTS 38:496-97).

with others out of a zeal to argue. Others are delighted by new and bizarre ideas. Therefore Paul draws the godly back from this petulance and orders everyone to be certain of his own opinion, that is to say, to inquire after the solid foundations so that each person may take his thought captive in obedience to Christ. For reason cannot show any certainty in matters of religion, but let everyone seek solid foundations for his opinion from the Word of God. For only God's Word makes our consciences certain about God's will.

Perhaps someone will object that an error is always obscure, and so a weak and erring individual cannot be certain in their own opinion. I reply: It is true that an erring person's conscience is uncertain. And so Paul gives this wholesome commandment, so that those who hesitate may be allowed to be taught and run immediately to the sacred volume, from which they seek certainty of doctrine, and call diligently upon the Lord for illumination and confirmation.

This most serious commandment of Paul clearly refutes the blasphemous error of the Tridentine Council, which established that one ought always to be in doubt about God's will toward us. COMMENTARY ON ROMANS 14:5.[23]

THE LORD JUDGES US. DESIDERIUS ERASMUS: One gives thanks for the freedom to eat whatever is wished, because the evangelical law distinguishes intentions, not foods. Another gives thanks for the benefit of self-control, while because of weakness, avoids intoxication and is restrained within the boundaries of temperance. All are equal in such matters, and no one ought to cross swords with a brother for the sake of protecting one's own opinion. It is enough if the Lord approves; it is up to the Lord to judge things that either are uncertain or must be borne on account of the times. PARAPHRASE ON ROMANS 14:5.[24]

GIVE THANKS! JOHN CALVIN: Notice that he says, "We eat and abstain to the Lord, because we give thanks." So then without giving thanks eating is unclean and abstaining is unclean. It is only the name of God, if invoked, that sanctifies us and all we have. COMMENTARY ON ROMANS 14:6.[25]

SURRENDER EVERYTHING TO GOD. CARDINAL CAJETAN: Observe, prudent reader, that the foremost reason concerning eating has been taken from an analogy to another person's servant; it was against the rashness of judgments. And this applies both against judgments and against disdain in matters of food and similarly in matters of days. And for this reason Paul here grasps everything, showing that all four can be done without sin, only if they are referred to God. And this is true, he declares by analogy, of course also about living and dying. For we are able to use our life as much as our death for God. For the same reason we are able to eat and to abstain, to distinguish days and to treat all days the same—for God. . . . Paul does not speak about possibility [posse] but about actuality [facto]. And he rightly speaks in the first person, so that we should understand that he speaks about those who are like him—that is, those who have been established in God's grace and love. For such people should give all that is theirs to God. COMMENTARY ON ROMANS 14:6-10.[26]

14:7-9 Jesus Is Lord Over Life and Death

SERVANTS OF OUR LORD JESUS CHRIST. TILEMANN HESSHUS: In this passage Paul warns that one must make a distinction between errors that drive out faith and overturn the foundation and errors that do not extinguish the faith but are gradually corrected among the godly. When the false apostles strived earnestly for circumcision and maintained that keeping the law was necessary in order to obtain salvation, it was a fundamental error that overturned all piety. When Hymenaeus

---

[23]Hesshus, Explicatio Epistolae Pauli ad Romanos, 423v-424v*; citing 2 Cor 10:5.
[24]CWE 42:79.

[25]CTS 38:498-99* (CO 49:261).
[26]Cajetan, In Sacrae Scripturae Expositionem, 5:76.

and Philetus maintained that the resurrection had already happened and that one should not await another, it undermined the foundation of the faith. For that reason Paul handed over such people to Satan. But when godly people erred about the keeping of holidays and the eating of food, it did not overturn the foundation. And so this weakness did not extinguish faith or drive a person away from the grace of Christ. This is a very necessary admonition so that we neither tolerate manifest errors in the church nor condemn innocent people because of their weakness. Irenaeus writes that Christ was crucified in his forty-fifth year.[27] He clearly was in error, but he did not violate the articles of the faith. It was Augustine's *sphalma* ["error"] that the baptism of John did not impart forgiveness of sins, but nonetheless he retained the foundation of Christ's teaching. Cyprian rebaptized those who had been baptized among the schismatics and heretics. It was an error, but one with which faith could exist. Tertullian condemned second marriages. But this one error did not extinguish his faith, at least not until he had embraced the madness of Montanus.

In contrast, Origen, who now and then urged a righteousness based on works and denied the resurrection of the flesh and taught other monstrous things against the Scripture, overturned the foundation and fell out of the grace of Christ. Therefore let us prudently distinguish between opinions and examine them in accordance with the analogy of faith. He says, "Nobody lives for himself." The proof for this opinion is an argument from the whole to the part. Our whole life has been consecrated and dedicated to the Lord; whatever we are and however we live, it serves God's glory. Therefore also the individual actions of the saints are rendered to the glory of God. Therefore one must look to the foundation of godliness, whether someone is embracing the sincere teaching of the gospel and whether he is seriously repenting. When we discover this, we ought to promise, as far

as we are concerned, the best things concerning our neighbor and resolve that all his counsels and actions will be directed to the glory of God. Although there are still blemishes in him, such as ignorance and weakness, they ought to be endured.

The idea "Whether we live or die, we are the Lord's" contains a manifold teaching and a noteworthy consolation. For he admonishes us that both in life and in death, in prosperity and adversity, we ought always to look to the Lord and render every individual action to his will and glory. We ought not to seek those thing that are ours. We ought not to strive for our own convenience and pleasures. Instead we should always remember that we are servants of our Lord Jesus Christ. And so we ought to subject our will and our desires to the will of Christ. Paul also shows a notable consolation, indicating that the Lord is always with us, whether we are afflicted or enjoy happy times, whether we die or live. For because "we live for the Lord and die for the Lord," it is certain that the Lord is with his ministers, that he loves them and takes care of them, that he protects them in accordance with his mercy and also preserves them in death.

He further admonishes that God will demand from us sometime a loving account of all our plans, actions and undertakings. Therefore we should not be very concerned about what at last happens to us—whether we are free or oppressed in this world—but we ought to be zealous for this only: that the glory of Christ is always made known. Finally, in this saying he also promises not obscurely that there will be heavenly rewards both in life and in death for those who strive in a godly way. For since we are servants of our Lord Jesus Christ in our whole life and in death, he will never act in such a way that we will seem to have served him without any compensation or to have been defrauded of our just pay.

He further indicates that Christians are by no means plucked away from Christ by death, but rather that once Christ has recognized them as his own, nobody will ever seize them from his hands. In addition to these things, the resurrection of the dead is clearly promised in this statement, for if we

---

[27]This is a reference to the confusing text in *Against Heresies* 2.22.5-6 (ANF 1:391-92).

belong to the Lord when we are dead, it is necessary that we live. For the Lord is not a God of the dead, but of the living. COMMENTARY ON ROMANS 14:6-8.[28]

YOUR ONLY COMFORT IS THAT YOU HAVE BEEN BOUGHT WITH CHRIST'S BLOOD. DAVID

PAREUS: In other words,[29] we have an obligation. His aim is to teach and strengthen the weak, indeed all the faithful. He wants to *teach* for whom and for what purpose we ought to live and die—not for ourselves or privately for our desire or convenience, but for Christ our Lord, so that his glory may be honored by our life and death. He wants to *strengthen and comfort* the godly, so that we may trust that in life and in death we are not a law unto ourselves nor abandoned to ourselves, but we have the Lord who cares for us more greatly than we do for ourselves, who is able and willing to preserve us while alive and to restore us to life when we are dead. I say, "He is able," because he is almighty, he is God, he has driven away death from himself. He is the universal Lord and judge to whom every knee must bow. "He is also willing," because he has taken us for himself and has acquired us as his property, not by a purchase but by his own blood. But nobody neglects a property and especially one bought at great cost. The safeguarding or perishing of a property is a matter of usefulness or loss for a lord. Christ loves our salvation more than we love money. For he did not pay out money but himself for us. A person who pays money for a slave does not care for him excessively for that reason. But would Christ value as worthless the salvation of those whom he redeemed at so great a cost, for whom he prepared a kingdom for himself at such great expense? We have the sweetest *aim*, *summary* and *application* of this passage, from

which the first question of our catechism concerning our one consolation in life and death was drawn. COMMENTARY ON ROMANS 14:7-10.[30]

BE CONFORMED TO CHRIST. DESIDERIUS

ERASMUS: True perfection will be attained if they "desire to be dissolved and to be with Christ," and if in sickness, financial setbacks and all other misfortunes they consider it their glory and happiness to be deemed worthy even in this manner to be conformed to their Head. Therefore it is not so reprehensible to [practice piety] as it is dangerous to stop there and put all your faith in these practices. I tolerate weakness, but with Paul "I point out a more perfect way." If you examine all your actions and ambitions in accordance with this rule and never stop midway until you reach Christ, you will never stray from the true path and you will never do or tolerate anything in life that cannot be turned into an occasion for the practice of piety. ENCHIRIDION.[31]

WE ARE THE LORD'S POSSESSION. DAVID

PAREUS: He confirms by this explanation that none of the faithful live or die for themselves, at the same time that he teaches for whom therefore we do live and die: for Christ our Lord. Now what does "living for the Lord" mean? It means (1) that in life we recognize this Lord as our own, that we are not under our own authority, but are servants subject to this Lord; (2) that we undertake our life and all our actions at the will of this Lord and we serve him; (3) that we ascribe our whole life to the glory and honor of the Lord, as if that is its goal; (4) that finally we consider that in all the labors and hardships of life our Lord cares for us. This is what it means to live for the Lord. But what does "dying for the Lord" mean? The very same thing as living for him: (1) that in death one recognizes that one is the property of this Lord and is confident that one is not dying *adespoton* ["without a

---

[28]Hesshus, *Explicatio Epistolae Pauli ad Romanos*, 425r-426v; citing Gal; 2 Tim 2:17-18.

[29]*Ex analysi*, that is, if we take the words "None of us lives for himself" and translate them into what they really mean. An analysis in Aristotle's logic is the practice of taking an imperfect logical form and transforming it into a perfect one.

[30]Pareus, *In divinam Epistolam ad Romanos commentarius*, 1500. See Heidelberg Catechism q. 1 (Creeds 3:307-8).

[31]CWE 66:64-65; citing Col 1:23; 1 Cor 12:31.

master"]; (2) that we bear patiently disease and death from the hand of the Lord; (3) that we glorify our Lord by whatever kind of death is sent to us, even that of martyrdom; (4) finally that by faith in the Lord we do not reject the hope of life in death, but trust that he will deliver us with death into life. O thrice and four times blessed are we, if we should live thus for the Lord so that we may die for him, because those who die for the Lord live for the Lord! On the other hand, thrice wretched are those who live for themselves, their gullet and stomach, the world and Satan. For they will die for Satan. . . .

There is a logical inference and nonetheless a reason why we live and die for the Lord: namely, because in life and in death we are the property or possession of the Lord. This is the chief point and basis of our consolation, because we are not abandoned, but we have the Lord of life and the overseer and deliverer for our death. The apostle teaches us to exclaim with this statement of trust: "Who will separate us from the love of Christ? Will oppression? Will difficulty? Will the sword?" etc. This consolation escapes the *epochēn* ["suspension of judgment"] and the conjectural confidence of the sophists, who wish us to be uncertain whether in life and in death we are the Lord's. This consolation escapes the fire of purgatory into which they thrust down the dying believers. For those who are the Lord's in life and death are purged by the blood of the Lord from every sin; therefore they do not need a purgation of fire, but are exempt from torments. "For blessed are they who die in the Lord, because they rest from their labors." And "the souls of the just are in the hand of the Lord, nor does grief come into contact with them." COMMENTARY ON ROMANS 14:8.[32]

IN CHRIST'S POWER. JOHN CALVIN: Whether we live or we die, we are in Christ's power. Now he shows how worthily Christ claims this power over us, for he has obtained it by so great a price! By

meeting his death for our salvation he obtained this dominion that cannot be destroyed by death; and by rising again he has taken our whole life as his property. So, by his death and resurrection he has earned this right: that both in death and in life we should serve the glory of his name. COMMENTARY ON ROMANS 14:9.[33]

14:10-12 Everyone Will Confess God as Just Judge

LIKE BROTHERS. TILEMANN HESSHUS: It is a condition similar to that of brothers. Neither excusing nor condemning each other in turn is fitting for them, but rather an ardent and mutual love. Eliab acted unjustly when he made himself judge of his brother David, whom he ought to have defended rather than accused. But Paul says, "Christians are all bound to each other by the bond of brotherhood." For we have one heavenly Father, confess one doctrine, are governed by the leading of the one Holy Spirit, regardless of whether we are strong or weak. Therefore let neither of the two arrogate for himself the right to judge his brother. Let no one condemn the other; let no one judge the conscience of the other. COMMENTARY ON ROMANS 14:10.[34]

TRUE GOD AND TRUE MAN. MARTIN LUTHER: Thus Christ must be true God, for this is what must happen before his judgment seat. MARGINAL GLOSS ON ROMANS 14:11 (1546).[35]

ISAIAH TESTIFIES TO CHRIST'S DIVINITY. PETER MARTYR VERMIGLI: "Every tongue will confess to God," in Hebrew is, "Every tongue will swear to me." But everyone knows that in an oath there is a very clear confession of God, for he is invoked as a witness or rather as a judge. And he is thus invoked to punish perjurers as they deserve. So far, however, we see that not all things have been

---

[32]Pareus, *In divinam Epistolam ad Romanos commentarius*, 1502-3; citing Rom 8:35; Rev 14:13; Wis 3:1.

[33]CTS 38:500* (CO 49:262).
[34]Hesshus, *Explicatio Epistolae Pauli ad Romanos*, 427r; citing 1 Sam 17:28.
[35]WADB 4:73.

subjected to Christ. Yes, it will happen "when he will have had handed over the kingdom to his God and Father."[36] Then everything—even, among other things, the last enemy, death—will be entirely subjected to him. Nevertheless a certain obedience has now begun, and his kingdom is recognized by the assembly of the pious. If therefore many unjust and evil deeds are now committed, nevertheless we should judge nothing before the right time, lest we prejudge the ruling of the Most High Judge. At that time all things, as we hope, that now seem unjust will be made right. From these words of the apostles the divinity of Christ is most clearly intimated. For when he mentions the judgment seat of Christ, he adds "and every tongue will confess to God."[37] The same is much more evident if the actual Hebrew is examined. Before these words are proclaimed—in the person of God—this is written: "Am I not the Lord? And is there not no other God beside me?" So then, because these words pertain to Christ, as Paul testifies, it is most plainly clear that he is God. COMMENTARY ON ROMANS 14:11.[38]

JESUS CHRIST, GOD'S GLORY AND THE COMING KINGDOM. JOHN CALVIN: Now by the prophet's words he demonstrates that all flesh should be humbled on account of the expectation of that judgment—that is shown through bending the knee. Although in the rest of this passage of the prophet the Lord generally foretells that his glory will be made clear among all nations and his majesty will be prominent everywhere, at the time his glory and majesty were concealed among a select few—in some obscure corner of the world, as it were. Nevertheless, if we examine this passage more closely, it is clear that this reality's fulfillment is not now taking place, nor has it ever taken place in this world, nor indeed is this reality to be hoped for in the future. Now God reigns in no other way than through the gospel; and his majesty is rightly honored in no other way than when it is accepted as known from his Word. But God's Word has always had its enemies, who have obstinately opposed it, and its despisers, who have treated it with ridicule as if it were absurd and fantastical. Even today there are many such people, and there always will be. From this it seems that this prophecy has begun to be fulfilled in this present life, but it is far from its completion, until that day of the final resurrection will have shone, when all Christ's enemies will be knocked over to become a footstool for his feet. And this cannot actually happen until the Lord will have sat in judgment. Therefore Paul has rightly accommodated this testimony to the judgment seat of Christ.

And this is an eminent passage for establishing our faith in Christ's eternal divinity. For God is the one speaking there, and this God has proclaimed that he will never give his glory to another. Now if what God here claims for himself alone is fulfilled in Christ, without a doubt he himself manifests himself in Christ. And, of course, the truth of this prophecy was plainly evident when Christ gathered to himself a people from the whole world and restored them to the worship of his deity and the obedience of his gospel. Paul considers this when he says that "God gave to his Christ the name at which every knee should bow." And it will be fully evident, when he will have ascended his judgment seat to judge the living and the dead, for to him all judgment in heaven and earth has been given by the Father. COMMENTARY ON ROMANS 14:11.[39]

---

[36]Lit., *deo et patri; tō theō kai patri*. In his comment on 1 Corinthians 15:24, Vermigli carefully explicates the christological grammar of this phrase "to his God and Father": here Paul is talking about Christ according to his humanity, in the same sense as John 20:17 (Vermigli, *In Selectissimam S. Pauli Apostoli Priorem ad Corinth. Epistolam . . . Commentarii doctissimi* [Zurich: Christoph Froschauer, 1551], 412r). Calvin adds a second interpretive option: that *kai* here should be understood as "namely" (CTS 40:26; CO 49:546). English translations of the Bible have followed the second option (except the NASB), so much so that modern translations simplify the phrase to "God the Father." See also RCS NT 9a, *in loco*.
[37]The majority of Reformation exegetes—Vermigli included—follow the Majority text for v. 10, *tō bēmati tou Christou*, "the judgment seat of Christ." Modern English translations (except the KJV and NKJV) prefer to follow the reading *tō bēmati tou theou* "the judgment seat of God."
[38]Vermigli, *In Epistolam ad Romanos*, 619 (*A Commentarie upon the Epistle to the Romanes*, 438v); citing 1 Cor 15:26, 24; Is 45:5-6.

[39]CO 49:263 (cf. CTS 38:502-3); citing Is 42:8; Phil 2:9-10.

COEQUAL WITH THE FATHER, CHRIST IS THE DIVINE JUDGE. DAVID PAREUS: The question is raised whether there is an argument for the divinity of Christ in this passage [Is 45:23].

Major: To whomever every knee bows is the true God of Israel (Is 45:23).

Minor: To Christ every knee will bow (Rom 14:11; Phil 2:10).

Conclusion: Therefore Christ is the true God of Israel.

György Enyedi, a Samosatene heretic, attempts to overthrow this argument in a twofold manner: first, by denying the minor premise "because," he says, "every knee will bow not to Christ as he sits on the judgment seat but to the God of Israel at that time when Christ will sit on the judgment seat and all will be made to stand before him at the Last Judgment."[40] He proves it, as he says, "because it can happen that someone standing before a judgment seat does not bow his knee for the one sitting on the judgment seat." Again, "because the apostle only wishes to prove with the statement of Isaiah that 'every knee will bow to me' that that judgment that will be carried out before the judgment seat of Christ will be a universal one, which nobody will be able to escape." Again, "because God the Father will truly be the one making the judgment while Christ sits at the judgment seat (Rom 2:16), 'in the day when God will judge people's secrets according to my gospel through Jesus Christ.' So too Acts 17:31."

Reply. Truly this is a very brazen and blasphemous distortion of the Scripture. First, it is false that by the quotation of Isaiah the apostle merely proves a universal judgment that nobody will escape.

For clearly he proves that Christ will be seated at the judgment seat, that he will be the universal and almighty judge, and for that reason ought to be feared by all. Why? Because he is not a mere man, but the God who once said that every knee ought to bow to him. For he confirms what he declared earlier, that Christ rules the living and the dead, and so in verse 12 he calls Christ "God" absolutely, to whom each of us will have to render an account.

Second, it is false that the knees will not have to bow to Christ as he sits on the judgment throne. For it does not logically follow that we will be made to stand at the judgment seat of Christ because every knee will bow to God, unless it is presupposed that Christ is that very God. Nor is it true that the accused bow their knees in front of a court to anyone other than to the judge. But Christ will be the judge of the living and the dead. For that reason the apostle expressly in so many words ascribes the bowing of the knees to Christ as our judge (Phil 2:10): "So that at the name of Jesus every knee may bow."

Third, this blasphemous assertion is from a noncause, namely, that no knee is obligated to bow to Christ inasmuch as God the Father will do the judging. For the Father will judge through the Son in such a way that the Son will judge by his own power: "For the Father has given all judgment to the Son that all may honor the Son, just as they honor the Father." Consequently, every knee will bow to the Father in the Son, for the wicked will cry, "O hills, hide us from the sight of him who sits on the throne and from the wrath of the Lamb" (Rev 6:16). Therefore the Father in the Son will sit on the throne and will judge.

Finally, the heretic, driven back from this blasphemous denial of the minor premise, attempts to weaken the conclusion by saying that the major premise is true concerning him to whom every knee will bow as far as his essence is concerned, but to Christ every knee will bow not as far as his essence is concerned but only as far as his honor is concerned. That is, they will bow to him but not as to a primary and chief judge, but only as to one who has been chosen and appointed as a

---

[40]György Enyedi (1555–1597), supervisor of the Unitarian Churches in Transylvania, was a well-known antitrinitarian. The Samosatene heresy, named after its leading proponent, Paul of Samosata (c. 200–275), denied Christ's full divinity, teaching that Jesus was not preexistent, but a man inhabited by the Word of God. Thus his power and wisdom was of the same substance as God but not a distinct person.

judge. Therefore it does not follow that he is the eternal God, equal to the Father.

But Christ himself refutes this blasphemous sophistry by saying, "The Father does not judge anyone, but has entrusted all judgment to the Son" (John 5:22). And "whatever the Father does, the Son does likewise," proving at length that he is equal to the Father not by a recent gift but by the natural begetting from the Father according to his divinity: "For just as the Father has life in himself, so he has granted also to the Son to have life in himself." But what is the life of God other than the very essence of God? The Father does not have that in himself as a gift but by nature. Therefore also the Son has it from the Father not by a gift of grace, but by an imparting of the nature (John 5:18; 10:33). Consequently the Jews accused him of blasphemy because he was saying that God was *idion*, his own Father, "making himself equal to God, and because, even though he was a human being, he made himself God," not in a secondary sense or in an honorary way (for they would not have threatened him with a charge of blasphemy concerning that) but as that true Jehovah. They understood much more correctly than those heretics that Christ was speaking of his natural equality with the Father. Even if it is not denied that the knees must bow to Christ as to a judge who was chosen and appointed, insofar as he is the mediator and is human, nonetheless it remains true that knees must bow to him as to a primary and chief judge, insofar as he is one God with the Father. COMMENTARY ON ROMANS 14.[41]

CHRIST'S JUDGMENT SEAT. TILEMANN HESSHUS: It is a serious sin to intrude into someone else's calling or office or duties. But this universal judgment belongs to Christ. By it he judges the whole world and each person's conscience, which lies bare to Christ alone, and he distinguishes stubborn error from weakness. Therefore let us entrust the consciences of our brothers to his judgment, especially in adiaphora or in doubtful cases. It is an article of faith that Jesus Christ will come from heaven and judge the whole earth for all their thoughts, actions and plans, and that the living and dead will appear before the judgment seat of Jesus Christ. Therefore one must take note of this clear testimony about this sublime article. But at each and every moment we ought to put in front of our eyes this most serious thought of all, namely, that we may conduct our whole life, all our plans and all our undertakings so that at some time we may be able to render an account to Christ the supreme judge. The testimony that Paul draws from the prophet Isaiah clearly shows that Jesus is that living and almighty God whom the prophets call "Jehovah" and who is the author of our entire salvation. COMMENTARY ON ROMANS 14:10-13.[42]

---

[41]Pareus, *In divinam Epistolam ad Romanos commentarius*, 1573-76.
[42]Hesshus, *Explicatio Epistolae Pauli ad Romanos*, 427v-428r; citing Is 45:23. On the use of "Jehovah" among the reformers, see RCS OT 7:51-52.

14:13-23 DO NOT CAUSE ANOTHER TO STUMBLE

[13]Therefore let us not pass judgment on one another any longer, but rather decide never to put a stumbling block or hindrance in the way of a brother. [14]I know and am persuaded in the Lord Jesus that nothing is unclean in itself, but it is unclean for anyone who thinks it unclean. [15]For if your brother is grieved by what you eat, you are no longer walking in love. By what you eat, do not destroy the one for whom Christ died. [16]So do not let what you regard as good be spoken of as evil. [17]For the kingdom of God is not a matter of eating and drinking but of righteousness and peace and joy in the Holy Spirit. [18]Whoever thus serves Christ is acceptable to God and approved by men. [19]So then let us pursue what makes for peace and for mutual upbuilding.

[20]Do not, for the sake of food, destroy the work of God. Everything is indeed clean, but it is wrong for anyone to make another stumble by what he eats. [21]It is good not to eat meat or drink wine or do anything that causes your brother to stumble.[a] [22]The faith that you have, keep between yourself and God. Blessed is the one who has no reason to pass judgment on himself for what he approves. [23]But whoever has doubts is condemned if he eats, because the eating is not from faith. For whatever does not proceed from faith is sin.[b]

a Some manuscripts add *or be hindered or be weakened*   b Some manuscripts insert here 16:25-27

OVERVIEW: The commentators consider Paul's affirmation that Christians should not use their liberty to scandalize those who believe it necessary to refrain from drinking alcohol or eating certain foods. Despite the fact that in Christ nothing that we eat or drink affects our salvation (even if it was proscribed in the old covenant), we need to be patient with one another and refrain from putting a stumbling block before another believer who may be weaker in faith. To exercise one's Christian liberty over against another Christian is to sin against the second table of the law. For Paul sin is unbelief, or anything that does not proceed from faith. Taking this cue, the reformers discuss the necessity for faith in order to perform good works. In addition, they distinguish between different kinds of sin, including sins of omission and commission. Their overriding concern, however, is that sin is opposed to God's will, which condemns us. We are incapable of overcoming it on our own.

By comparison, all our commentators agree that the kingdom of God comes by God's grace—not human works—as joy, peace, kindness and righteousness. The kingdom of God comes not just for the strong in body or faith but also for the weak. It appears where one least expects to find God—among the weak and the weak in faith, even as salvation appears where one least expects to see God—on the cross.

ON DISTINGUISHING SINS. JACOBUS ARMINIUS: As the law is perceptive of good and prohibitory of evil, it is necessary not only that an action, but that the neglect of an action be accounted a sin. Hence arises the first distinction of sin into that of commission, when a prohibited act is perpetrated, as theft, murder, adultery, etc., and into that of omission, when a person abstains from an act that has been commanded. . . . And since the law is twofold—one "the law of works," properly called "the law"; the other "the law of faith," which is the gospel of the grace of God—therefore sin is either what is committed against the law or against the gospel of Christ. What is committed against the law provokes the wrath of God against sinners; what is committed against the gospel causes the wrath of God to abide on us. The former, by deserving punishment; the latter, by preventing the remission of punishment.

One is a sin *per se*, "of itself"; another, *per accidens*, "accidentally."[1] A sin *per se* is every external or internal action that is prohibited by the law, or every neglect of an action commanded by the law. A sin *per accidens* can be committed either in things necessary or in things indifferent. In things necessary, either when an act prescribed is performed without due circumstances, such as bestowing alms in order to garner praise from human beings, or when an act prohibited by law is omitted, but not for due cause or a just end, such as when one represses one's anger for a moment in order to exact a more cruel vengeance afterward. In things indifferent, a sin is committed when anyone uses them to the offense of the weak.

Sin is likewise divided in reference to the personal object against whom the offense is committed; and it is either against God, against our neighbor or against ourselves. . . . It is further distinguished from its cause into sins of ignorance, infirmity, malignity and negligence. A sin of ignorance is when a person does anything they do not know to be a sin. . . . A sin of infirmity is when through fear, which may befall even a brave person, or through any other more vehement passion and perturbation of mind, they commit any offense. . . . A sin of malignity or malice, when anything is committed with a determined purpose of mind and with deliberate counsel. . . . A sin of negligence is when a person is overtaken by a sin, which encircles and besets them before they can reflect within themselves about the deed. . . .

Closely related to this is the distribution of sin into what is contrary to conscience and what is not contrary to conscience. A sin against conscience is one that is perpetrated through malice and deliberate purpose, laying waste the conscience, and (if committed by holy persons) grieving the Holy Spirit so much as to cause him to desist from

his usual functions of leading them into the right way, and of making them glad in their consciences by his inward testimony. . . . A sin not against conscience is either what is by no means such, and which is not committed through a willful and wished-for ignorance of the law; as the person who neglects to know what they are capable of knowing. Or it is what, at least, is not such in a primary degree, but is perpetrated through rashness, the cause of which is a vehement and unforeseen temptation. DISPUTATION 8: ON ACTUAL SINS.[2]

14:13 Never Cause Fellow Believers to Stumble

LEGALISM AND LOOSE LIBERTY. PHILIPP MELANCHTHON: Now he is speaking only about this one kind [of offense]: when those who are freer abuse their liberty or those who are sterner—who are not enemies of the gospel—criticize the use of liberty. Both are to be admonished. Although the misuse of liberty is to be scolded, there is more wrong on the other side, which also does more harm on account of the appearance of authority. The more rigid wound the consciences of the godly who make use of their liberty. They scare away many simple people from the gospel, and in many cases grieve the Holy Spirit. Since there is much danger on both sides, Christians have need of great diligence lest they sin, either with harsh criticisms or with the misuse of their liberty. Christians should adhere to the fundamental principle, the doctrine, because here the use is an indifferent thing. COMMENTARY ON ROMANS (1540).[3]

SCANDAL. TILEMANN HESSHUS: The definition of "scandal" is well known; it is a work that opposes the Word of God, whether it is false doctrine or a manifest sin against the law of God or an intemperate use of one's freedom. By a scandal the Holy Spirit is grieved in the godly, the consciences of the

---

[1]Arminius is distinguishing between what is "accidental" to a thing and what is "essential" to a thing—that is, what can be removed without altering the thing's nature and what cannot be removed without altering the thing's nature. So, Arminius means that some acts are always in and of themselves sins (*per se*) and some acts are not always sins but can be on account of circumstances (*per accidens*).

[2]Arminius, *Works*, 1:487-89*; citing Rom 3:27; Heb 2:2-3; Mt 6:2; Gal 6:1; Heb 12:1.
[3]Melanchthon, *Commentary on Romans*, 233 (MO 15:727); citing 1 Cor 8:8.

weaker believers are wounded and the fickle are enticed by the example either to an error or to a sin. He is not discussing at all a "Pharisaic scandal," which is a work that agrees with God's Word, whether it is the confession of the truth or a just action, but that evil people interpret wrongly and thereby take the opportunity to blaspheme the name of God and persecute the church. About this kind of "scandal" Tertullian rightly says, "Good things do not scandalize anyone—except an evil mind."[4] Even here Paul is not discussing false doctrine or manifest crimes, but rather the intemperate use of one's freedom, which is a sin against the second table, which commands, "You shall love your neighbor as yourself." COMMENTARY ON ROMANS 14:13.[5]

DISTINGUISH PROPERLY BETWEEN SCANDALS GIVEN AND TAKEN. THE ENGLISH ANNOTATIONS: By this Paul rebukes those malicious judges of others, who occupy their minds with nothing so much as to find fault with their brothers' actions. Instead they should focus their wits on this, that they do not by their disdainfulness or rash censuring either cast their brothers down entirely or give them any offense by their unseasonable use of Christian liberty.

Here the difference between *scandalum datum* and *scandalum acceptum* must be retained. A scandal taken, and not given, is when anyone takes offense at us for discharging our duty as the Pharisees took offense at Christ's teaching and miracles. A scandal given is when by our indiscrete posture toward or unseasonable use of our Christian liberty we minister a just occasion of offense to our brother. ANNOTATIONS ON ROMANS 14:13.[6]

14:14-16 Nothing Unclean in Christ

ALL CREATURES CLEAN FOR THE CHRISTIAN. TILEMANN HESSHUS: Here the apostle first teaches

that when the Messiah had been revealed and taken into heaven, the Mosaic law about the distinction between clean and unclean animals and about all the Levitical ceremonies and furthermore about civil judgments was abolished. For Christ is the end and fulfillment of the law. And Paul says, "You are not under the law, but under grace." "In Christ Jesus neither circumcision nor uncircumcision counts for anything, but faith that is active through love." For Daniel and Eleazar the meat of a hare or pig was unclean, and they would have sinned against their conscience if they had eaten. For at that time the law was still in force. But to Peter it was said, "Do not call unclean what God has made clean."

Next Paul teaches that all creatures are clean for the godly who believe in Christ, and they may make use of them with thanksgiving. Nor do the abuses of the godless contaminate the things themselves. The thief does not contaminate the sun. A priest does not contaminate meat or water or bread or gold by his idolatry, but rather the godly may use all things as needed with thanksgiving. Paul says, "To the pure all things are pure," and "Every created item is good," and "The earth and its fullness belong to the Lord."

In addition to these things, this idea teaches that bishops may not bind consciences by the prohibition of permitted things and by human traditions. For the freedom into which Christ placed us must be defended. Therefore the distinctions of food in the papacy, especially accompanied by the opinion of their necessity and of worship and merit and perfection, opposes this idea of Paul. COMMENTARY ON ROMANS 14:14.[7]

JEWISH UNDERSTANDING OF "COMMON." HULDRYCH ZWINGLI: What Jews call "common" Latins call "profane" those things permitted to everyone equally. On account of this, therefore, what is common to the other nations is, however, forbidden to them. The Jews called forbidden, contaminated

---

[4]Tertullian, *On the Veiling of Virgins* 3 (ANF 4:28).
[5]Hesshus, *Explicatio Epistolae Pauli ad Romanos*, 428v.
[6]Downame, ed., *Annotations*, CCC2r*.

[7]Hesshus, *Explicatio Epistolae Pauli ad Romanos*, 429v-430r; citing Rom 6:14; Gal 5:6; Acts 10:15; Tit 1:15; 1 Tim 4:4; 1 Cor 10:26 (cf. Ps 24:1).

and untraditional food "common." "With common hands, that is, unwashed"; therefore common is unclean. "Nothing," Paul says, "in itself is unclean, for all things are clean to those who are clean, but only to those who think it is unclean is it unclean." Paul says that all things are sanctified, that is, made lawful to eat—even if through prayers and deprecations they've been consecrated to eat, for they are acknowledged as gifts of God, created and given by God for our use. Paul says these things on account of Jews who are still weak, who still waver in the distinction of foods. "To these I am saying," says Paul, "that nothing is unclean and forbidden to those who are in Christ Jesus." ANNOTATIONS ON ROMANS 14:14.[8]

ERRING CONSCIENCES MISJUDGE REALITY.

CARDINAL CAJETAN: "But whoever considers it to be common, to him it is common." According to him, or through Christ, nothing of this kind is unclean. Nevertheless according to the conscience of someone who thinks a certain food is unclean, to him it is rendered unclean.... Food is not rendered unclean on account of conscience, but to him it is rendered unclean—it is rendered forbidden according to his own conscience.... His conscience considers it unlawful. COMMENTARY ON ROMANS 14:14.[9]

UNHEALTHY, UNNECESSARY AND UNHELPFUL

FOOD. JACQUES LEFÈVRE D'ÉTAPLES: In the early church the apostles commanded the Gentiles to keep themselves from meat sacrificed to idols, from blood and from what had been strangled, not on the grounds that they had given a command in such a way that who partook of these things would be sinning and would be sinners by the very act, but so that they would not be exposed to the illusions of demons. So attests Origen in his treatise *Against Celsus*.[10] For these affect the body and its humors, so that demons (if God so allows) are fit instruments

for permitting illusions, so that they experience whatever things have been *energoumenoi*, that is, wrought by an unclean spirit.[11] Therefore it was not a bad thing to refrain from foods of this kind in those times, not because he who did not abstain from them would sin, but so that the body would not be badly affected and fall into dire straits. Indeed, it is not a bad thing to abstain from foods that the sacred Scriptures denounce as impure, not because we hold to a Jewish superstition, such as those who believe that it is a sin to partake of such things, but because they are more impure and unhealthier. What would I want with a muddy eel? What would I want with a reed-like worm? What would I want with a hare that leads to madness? What would I want with pork that would lead to leprosy? What have I to do with a sow's udder and the whole kitchen of Apicius, which drives out health and purity and feeds only intemperance? Let us all embrace healthy and necessary foods, but let us willingly reject unnecessary foods, if we can, even if it is not a sin to enjoy them. For neither enjoying them nor not enjoying them is either a sin or our justification. But if you are a stumbling block for your weak brother because of your food and you make him sorrowful, abstain from that food. For abstaining from food is not a sin, but to violate charity and the love of your neighbor is a sin. And, conversely, if by abstaining from food you harm your brother and you create a weakness—a weakness I call it—so that he believes that what is not a sin is actually sin, then do not abstain. For not abstaining is not a sin, but harming a brother and leading him into error is a sin. ANNOTATIONS ON ROMANS 14:14.[12]

LOVE YOUR NEIGHBOR IN ALL MATTERS.

DAVID PAREUS: Love does not make a brother sad, but avoids all harm. Instead, it is eager to foster, help and strengthen the weak. We see in the body

---

[8]Zwingli, *In Plerosque Novi Testamenti Libros*, 444; citing Mk 7:2; Tit 1:15.
[9]Cajetan, *In Sacrae Scripturae Expositionem*, 5:77.
[10]Origen, *Against Celsus* 8.30 (ANF 4:650).

[11]The ancients held that the body had four fluids (also called humors): blood, phlegm, black bile and yellow bile. They believed that an imbalance of these fluids affected a person's health and temperament.
[12]Lefèvre d'Étaples, *Epistola ad Rhomanos*, 96v. Several cookbooks from late antiquity were ascribed to Apicius, although little is known about him.

how healthy members treat and cherish weaker members. If some member is sick, they touch it lightly, bandage it and heal it. Therefore making your brother sad is not walking according to love, that is, it is not doing for and offering your brother what love demands. Thus here two conditions are commanded for us to observe concerning freedom in indifferent matters. One is that we do not do anything by which the weaker person would saddened, disturbed in conscience, or estranged from the love of one's neighbor or of the faithful. Otherwise an ill-timed freedom becomes a harmful license and creates a stumbling block. The second is that we employ ourselves in indifferent matters with love for our neighbor, which will always persuade us to descend to the weakness of others. COMMENTARY ON ROMANS 14:15.[13]

FOR THE SAKE OF THE GOSPEL. PHILIPP MELANCHTHON: We must beware lest the gospel sound bad to people, for the glory of God is harmed when his Word is reviled, and human progress is hindered. People do not accept a doctrine that they despise. Controversies do not necessarily alienate the minds of the inexperienced and simple from the gospel so that they begin to hate some doctrine as a seedbed of hatreds, but there are also those offenses that do alienate minds. Those who abuse liberty increase the licentiousness of the common people. On the other hand, stern people deter the weak with the virulence of their judgments, etc. He commands us to shun diligently these offenses of minds on account of the glory of the gospel, in order that more may love and embrace the doctrine. COMMENTARY ON ROMANS (1540).[14]

14:17-19 The Kingdom Is Joy and Peace, Not Gobbling and Guzzling

REIGN OF THE HOLY SPIRIT. JUAN DE VALDÉS: By "the kingdom of God" Paul means the rule of the Holy Spirit, for through God's ruling us by his

Holy Spirit, we begin to enter his kingdom. And I say that we begin to enter, meaning that in this present life we take possession of the kingdom of God, and that in the life eternal we shall continue it, rising again glorious, impassible and immortal. COMMENTARY ON ROMANS 14:15-19.[15]

WHAT IS THE KINGDOM'S SUBSTANCE?

CARDINAL CAJETAN: The substance of the kingdom of God does consist in liberty or rather in the use of liberty regarding food and drink. "But righteousness," but the substance of the kingdom of God is righteousness, rendering each his due. "And peace," stillness without occasion for disturbing anyone. "And joy." For these three things are internal, namely, righteousness maintains all virtue, and peace removes all disturbances—within as much as without—and joy is not of this world but "in the Holy Spirit." These form the substance of the kingdom of God, in individuals as much as in groups. For it is called the kingdom of God where God reigns in us. Accordingly, it is true that by internal mighty works he reigns in us and through them we become participants in the kingdom of God. COMMENTARY ON ROMANS 14:17.[16]

PEACE. MARTIN LUTHER: "Righteousness" toward God—it comes through faith or by believing; "peace" toward our neighbor—it comes through love for one another, by accepting and cherishing one another; "joy in the Holy Spirit" toward oneself—it comes through hope, by having confidence in God and not in those things that one does toward neighbor or toward God. Be pleasant toward yourself, peaceful toward your neighbor, righteous toward God. And nothing so disturbs this peace as the temptation and the offense of the brother, especially in those things that injure his conscience. Hence the word peace must be understood in several ways.

[13]Pareus, In divinam Epistolam ad Romanos commentarius, 1516-17.
[14]Melanchthon, Commentary on Romans, 234* (MO 15:729).
[15]Valdés, Commentary upon Romans, 266* (Commentario de Romanos, 305).
[16]Cajetan, In Sacrae Scripturae Expositionem, 5:77.

First, peace with God as above in Romans 5: "Therefore, since we are justified by faith, we have peace with God." This peace is broken by sin. Second, peace with oneself, which a person has through this joy in the Holy Spirit, through hope and patience, as above in Romans 12: "Rejoice in your hope, be patient in tribulation." This peace is disturbed by impatience or through tribulations that are borne impatiently, that is, through love of carnal and useless peace. Third, peace with one's neighbor, which a person has through the mutual fulfillment and upbuilding of mutual love. And it is broken by contempt for the weakness of the other party and through the violation of the conscience of those who have peace with God and themselves through faith and patience, but not with their neighbors. And this in the passive sense, in that they do not leave others in peace. Therefore he would have us not only be at peace but also bring peace, be quiet and modest toward one another. Scholia on Romans 14:17.[17]

Faith over Liberty. John Calvin: Now . . . he teaches that without loss we can abstain from the use of our liberty, because the kingdom of God is not based on such things. What relates either to the building up or to the preserving of God's kingdom should absolutely not be disregarded—no matter what offenses might follow. But if on account of love one may refrain from the use of foods, while God's honor is uninjured, Christ's kingdom is unharmed and piety is unhindered, then those who upset the church on account of foods should not be endured. Commentary on Romans 14:17.[18]

The Kingdom of God Is Peace and Righteousness. David Pareus: The argument is made from the nature of indifferent things. The kingdom of God and our salvation are not situated in them. Therefore we do not have to fight to the death [digladiandum est] for them, as for hearth

and home, but rather we ought to fight to the death for the kingdom of God. In the church we have to discuss one way about indifferent matters and another way about necessary matters. The strong were thinking that they would greatly advance the kingdom of God by protecting their freedom in food and drink, but they would greatly dishonor the glory of God and endanger Christianity by indulging the weak at all. The apostle denies this. The kingdom of God is described in the Scriptures in various ways, but chiefly in two ways: as the *kingdom of glory*, that is, the future state of the elect in heaven, where God will be all in all, and as the *kingdom of grace*, that is, the condition and gathering of a new church militant on earth, which Christ sketches by various pictures in Matthew 13. This is the meaning of Luke 17:20: "The kingdom of God will not come *meta paratēreseōs* ["with observation"]." Here "kingdom of God" can have either meaning. "The kingdom of God is not . . ."; that is, the kingdom of glory is not obtained by food, as Chrysostom explains. Food and drink do not lead you to the kingdom of heaven, or the faith of the church and salvation do not consist of those external things, nor do we please God by our food or abstaining from food, as the apostle seems to explain in 1 Corinthians 8. . . . To summarize: he teaches that it is an indifferent matter whether one eats or doesn't eat something; it is not seemly for the faithful to debate over this matter, as if it were something necessary for the kingdom of God. . . .

In the antithesis he teaches that the kingdom of God consists of far greater matters, doubtlessly spiritual and internal goods necessary for salvation. He understands "righteousness" to be the righteousness of faith, concerning which he has earlier argued to great extent, that is, the free forgiveness of sins and the reconciliation with God by faith in the blood of Christ, as he defined it in 3:25. Nor does he exclude righteousness from being a motive that is begun through the new birth in those justified by faith. For they belong together, like cause and effect, or root and fruit. He understands "peace" to be the internal tranquility of the conscience or *euthymia* ["cheerfulness"] that follows justification, as he had

---

[17]LW 25:504-5* (WA 56:510-11); citing Rom 5:1; 12:12.
[18]CO 49:265 (cf. CTS 38:506).

said earlier in chapter 5: "Justified by faith we have peace with God." At the same time he embraces the external *philēsychian* ["fondness for tranquility"] and zeal for peace, which fosters harmony with the brothers and avoids offenses, because it accompanies faith in this way and is necessary for the faithful so that the peace of the conscience is not disturbed. From these two things a third arises, namely, joy, with which we always exult in the Lord ... and which Christ promised to his disciples as something durable in the midst of their hardships, persecutions and death: "Nobody will take your joy from you." But lest it be thought that he is talking about a civil righteousness, peace or joy, he adds a phrase that I think must be applied to all three: *en pneumati hagiō* ["in the Holy Spirit"], thereby teaching not only that the Holy Spirit is the author of such great goods, as he says to the Galatians ("The fruit of the Spirit is joy, peace, faith," etc.), but also hinting at their form, that they are spiritual goods, far more excellent than any food or drink you may want, which therefore ought not to be disturbed in us or in others by food or drink, nor should they be regarded as inferior in any way to food or drink. COMMENTARY ON ROMANS 14:17.[19]

ONLY ACCEPTABLE IN CHRIST. PHILIPP MELANCHTHON: This passage contains a clear testimony that good works please God. But Paul says expressly "whoever serves Christ" in order to testify that he is speaking about the good works of those who are righteous by faith in Christ, who know that this worship pleases on account of Christ, the Mediator and High Priest. COMMENTARY ON ROMANS (1540).[20]

OBEY THE WORD. TILEMANN HESSHUS: He teaches what are true good works, namely, not merely outward deeds or a choice form of worship or some exercises undertaken by our own free will, but rather works commanded by the express Word

of God, stirred up by the Spirit of God, flowing forth from faith in Christ, and directed to the glory of Jesus Christ and for the edification of the church. Christ says, "True worshipers will worship the Father in spirit and truth." COMMENTARY ON ROMANS 14:18.[21]

THE KINGDOM IS PRESENT IN RIGHTEOUSNESS, PEACE AND JOY. JOHN CALVIN: This argument has been drawn from the effect. Whenever anyone is acceptable to God and approved by human beings, it is impossible that the kingdom of God does not thrive and flourish excellently in him. Whoever serves Christ with a calm and peaceful conscience in righteousness is approved by human beings as much as by God. Therefore, wherever righteousness and peace and spiritual joy are, there the kingdom of God is complete in fullness; therefore it does not consist in corporeal things. Moreover, he says that whoever obeys God's will is pleasing to God. He testifies that he is approved by human beings, because they cannot not testify to this good character, which they see with their eyes. Not that the wicked always show consideration for the children of God. Indeed without any justification they spew forth many insults against them and with forged false accusations they slander the innocent. In short by maliciously construing good deeds they twist them into sins. But here Paul is talking about honest judgment contaminated with no surliness, no hatred, no superstition. COMMENTARY ON ROMANS 14:18.[22]

NO MERE LIST. MARTIN LUTHER: "Let us then pursue what makes for peace," that is, those things that do not disturb others but that edify and calm them. And what are these things? The answer is that love teaches us what they are as the time and place require, for they cannot be specifically detailed. SCHOLIA ON ROMANS 14:19.[23]

---

[19]Pareus, *In divinam Epistolam ad Romanos commentarius*, 1518-20; citing 1 Cor 8:8.
[20]Melanchthon, *Commentary on Romans*, 235* (MO 15:730).
[21]Hesshus, *Explicatio Epistolae Pauli ad Romanos*, 432v-433r; citing Jn 4:23.
[22]CO 49:266 (cf. CTS 38:508).
[23]LW 25:505* (WA 56:511).

HOLY CONSTRUCTION. THEODORE BEZA: The word "building up" is familiar to Paul. By it are meant all the duties that we owe to our neighbor, whether it is so that we may be joined to Christ or so that we, now joined to him, daily grow strong more and more. For the faithful are said to be the temple of God, in which he (namely, through the Holy Spirit) resides, and the whole throng of the faithful is compared to some immense city, that is, new Jerusalem, which is built out of the faithful themselves, as if they were stones, as is divinely written in a very elegant and clear manner in Isaiah 54 and Revelation 21. ANNOTATIONS ON ROMANS 14:19.[24]

14:20-23 Do Not Act Against Faith and Conscience

DO NO HARM. DESIDERIUS ERASMUS: We must not overlook this: it is more praiseworthy to abstain completely from meat and feed on vegetables, and to drink no wine at all, than become the occasion of your brother's ruin by your eating and drinking. PARAPHRASE ON ROMANS 14:20.[25]

BUT ELSEWHERE PAUL SAYS CONFESS! TILEMANN HESSHUS: "Whoever denies me before human beings, I will deny him before my heavenly Father." Again: "I believed on account of what I said." Again: "With the heart it is believed to righteousness, but with the mouth it is confessed to salvation." These words clearly state that God seriously requires that we not only believe in our heart among ourselves, but that we also clearly profess the faith before the world, neglecting all the dangers of our life and fortunes. Why then does Paul say in this passage, "Keep faith to yourself"? Paul is not discussing here doctrine or the articles of faith, nor is he discussing a situation in which our confession is demanded of us, but about indifferent matters and the use of one's freedom among weak Christians. They do not need our confession of Christ,

which they already know, but they ask that we teach them, bear with them and accommodate ourselves to their weakness. It is a far different matter when our enemies demand our confession and try to wipe out the name of Christ. Then one must not dissimulate any longer, but one must produce a very frank confession and by that act show our faith in the Lord Jesus, because we truly and with all our heart put every confidence in him and put the glory of Christ and the eternal salvation of our soul ahead of the goods of this life, just as Christ harshly commands, "Whoever confesses me before people, I will confess him before my heavenly Father." Nor is it truly faith if it hides the confession of Christ's name because of fear of persecution. COMMENTARY ON ROMANS 14:22.[26]

NICODEMITES PERVERT THIS PASSAGE. JOHN CALVIN: It happens through a perverse longing, if we offend our weaker brothers by eating flesh, because no necessity compels us to it. However, it is easily proved how wrongly this passage is distorted by some who conclude that it does not apply to anyone who participates in observing foolish and superstitious ceremonies, so long as they maintain a pure conscience before God. For Paul wanted nothing less, as the context itself proves: ceremonies that have been instituted to worship God are also part of our confession. Now those who wrench faith away from confession strip away from the sun its heat. Paul discusses nothing of the sort here, but instead he only argues about liberty in the use of food and drink. COMMENTARY ON ROMANS 14:22.[27]

---

[24]Beza, *Annotationes majores*, 2:144.
[25]CWE 42:82.

[26]Hesshus, *Explicatio Epistolae Pauli ad Romanos*, 435r-v; citing Mt 10:33; Ps 115:1 Vg; Rom 10:9; Mt 10:32.
[27]CO 49:268 (cf. CTS 38:510-11). Nicodemites were French evangelicals who conformed their external behavior to Catholic standards. For more on Calvin and the Nicodemites, see Mirjam G. K. van Veen, "Calvin and His Opponents," in *The Calvin Handbook*, ed. Herman J. Selderhuis (Grand Rapids: Eerdmans, 2009), 156-58, and Bruce Gordon, *Calvin* (New Haven, CT: Yale University Press, 2009), 181-97, esp. 189-95; John Calvin, "Apology of John Calvin to Messrs. the Nicodemites upon the Complaint That They Make of His Too Great Rigour (1544)," trans. Eric Kayayan, *Calvin Theological Journal* 29, no. 2 (1994): 346-63.

No Shelter for Nicodemites. David Pareus: This place does not support Nicodemites at all, who pretend they have no faith because they are afraid. Nor does it at all support chameleons,[28] who for the sake of profit outwardly pretend to follow any superstitions and religions you can imagine, but inwardly conceal a pure conscience with God. Nor finally does it oppose the commandment of Christ about freely confessing him or the thought of the apostle about the confession of the mouth that leads to salvation. "For here that faith is not understood," says Chrysostom, "that pertains to dogmas, but that has to do with the argument that has been set forth. Concerning the former type of faith he indeed says, 'With the mouth one confesses unto salvation' and 'Whoever denies me before other people, I myself will also deny him.' For the former type of faith is subverted when it has not been confessed, but the latter type of faith is subverted when it is confessed in an ill-timed manner."[29] And so faith here means in particular the knowledge and correct persuasion of freedom in regard to food, days and other indifferent matters, which the apostle called "faith" in verse 2 and "knowledge" and "persuasion" in verse 14. Commentary on Romans 14:22.[30]

This Is Spoken Against Believers, Not Unbelievers. The English Annotations: Although St. Prosper [of Aquitaine] and other divines—both ancient and later—allege this text to prove that all the works of infidels are sins, because they are done by human beings who do not have faith. However, this rule of the apostle helps in some way to discover and refute that error of the papists and Pelagians, who deny all the works of infidels to be sins. Now the proper and genuine meaning of this assertion of the apostle is not, whatever is done by an infidel is sin, but whatever is done by a believer with a wavering conscience without assurance that the work he does is pleasing to God and has warrant from his Word—to him it is a sin. Annotations on Romans 14:23.[31]

Good Works Flow from Faith Alone. Tilemann Hesshus: Paul teaches that no good works precede justification and that good works are not necessary in saving us. For before faith shines in the heart, all things that exist and take place in a human being are sin, but when faith shines, a human being has already been justified before God. Therefore, since everything that is not of faith is sin, it is necessary that all human works of whatsoever sort that precede faith as well as justification are pure sins before God. For faith is the cause and root of good works. Thus Augustine says: "Good works do not precede the one who is to be justified but rather follow the one already justified." Commentary on Romans 14:23.[32]

Conscience, Law and Gospel. Philipp Melanchthon: In this chapter he has often inculcated the rule that we should do nothing contrary to our conscience. Now at the close he adds also that this work should be done from faith. This addition should be considered diligently, for this addition is not sufficiently clear to those who do not know the true teaching of the gospel. For the common people, the statement of Paul is explained as follows: "Whatever is not from faith is sin," that is, whatever is done contrary to conscience is sin. But they do not explain this sufficiently, for they apply it only to the law, that stealing is done contrary to the law, and therefore is a sin, and against the conscience in the person who steals knowingly. This interpretation is true and necessary. For in our actions it is necessary first of all to consult the law in order that we may know what works God forbids or commands, and there is no doubt that works against the law of God are sins.

---

[28]Lit., *Vertumnuses*, an ancient Roman god able to change his appearance to suit his needs.
[29]John Chrysostom, *Homily 26 on Romans* (NPNF 11:531 [PG 60:640]).
[30]Pareus, *In divinam Epistolam ad Romanos commentarius*, 1525-26.

[31]Downame, ed., *Annotations*, CCC2r*.
[32]Hesshus, *Explicatio Epistolae Pauli ad Romanos*, 437r-v; citing Augustine, *De fide et operibus*, 14 (PL 40:211).

But when Paul mentions faith he demands not only the law or knowledge of history but also true faith. He teaches that works commanded or permitted by God must be done in faith, that is, with the confidence that God is propitious to us on account of Christ, the Mediator, and our works are pleasing on account of that High Priest. Therefore it is necessary to apply the statements of Paul not to the law only, but also to the gospel. COMMENTARY ON ROMANS (1540).[33]

No Faith, All Sin. HULDRYCH ZWINGLI: What is permitted to the pious and faithful is not permitted to the impious. On account of their sin, without distinction and with good conscience, they are not able to use food, clothing, days and all external matters. Wherever there is no faith, there neither sin nor the fear of God are considered, everything is a sham and hypocrisy—hounding after glory. The greatest blasphemy against God is not to trust in God, not to believe him. We please God through Christ, and through him we are appointed as sons of God. Now if we are sons of God, how can we doubt that we are beloved and treasured by the Father? Will not everything we do from this confidence be pleasing to God? Whoever does not trust in God does not believe that he is beloved by God—how could his works be approved by God? ANNOTATIONS ON ROMANS 14:23.[34]

Always Sin to Act Against Conscience. DESIDERIUS ERASMUS: Whoever is undecided thinking that one is not permitted to eat is condemned by the judgment of conscience. Why is this one condemned? Because what that person does is done not out of the strength of faith and the constancy of a mind that is well aware of itself, but against the resistance of one's conscience. However, anything that does not come from faith is connected with sin. If a person has doubts about whether or not something is evil, and still does it, even though that particular thing is not in itself evil,

that person nevertheless demonstrates that one would do something genuinely evil if the opportunity arose. PARAPHRASE ON ROMANS 14:23.[35]

Proceed from the Word. JOHN CALVIN: The reason for this condemnation is that work—however splendid and excellent in appearance—is counted as sin unless it is founded on a right conscience. God does not regard the external ostentation, but the internal obedience of the heart. The assessment of our works depends on this alone. Moreover, what kind of obedience is it if anyone undertakes what he is not persuaded is approved by God? Therefore whenever there is such a doubt, the person who proceeds against the testimony of their conscience is justly charged with transgression.

Here the word *faith* stands for a fixed conviction of the mind and, so to speak, a firm assurance—not just any kind, but what has been derived from God's truth. And so anxiety or uncertainty damages all our actions, however beautiful they may otherwise be. Now since a pious mind can never rest with certainty in anything but the Word of God, here all invented acts of worship—and whatever works begotten of the human brain—vanish. As long as whatever is not from faith is condemned, whatever is not supported and approved by the Word of God is rejected. Nevertheless it is indeed not enough that we do what is approved by the Word of God, unless our mind prepares itself eagerly to this work, trusting this conviction. And so, the beginning of living rightly—lest our minds constantly waver—is to rest in God's Word, confidently proceeding wherever it calls. COMMENTARY ON ROMANS 14:23.[36]

Ancient Variants Err. THEODORE BEZA: Here in very many old codices and also in Greek scholias are added three verses that usually close this epistle in the printed editions, namely, 16:25-27. Nonetheless, I do not approve of this reading because the apostle has not yet ended this discourse,

---

[33]Melanchthon, *Commentary on Romans*, 236* (MO 15:730-31).
[34]Zwingli, *In Plerosque Novi Testamenti Libros*, 445-46.
[35]CWE 42:82-83.
[36]CO 49:268-29(cf. CTS 38:512-13).

with the result that it ought to have been attached not to this passage but to 15:13—if the verses do not seem to fit the very end of the epistle. But perhaps this variant reading occurred by a deceitful tactic of Marcion, who wanted the epistle to be brought to an end here, having expunged all the rest that follows to the end of the epistle, as Jerome attests. ANNOTATIONS ON ROMANS 14:23.[37]

---

[37]Beza, *Annotationes majores*, 2:144. Jerome likely followed Origen's treatment of Romans 16:25-27 (see Jerome on Ephesians 3:5 PL 26:481; cf. PL 14:1290); see further *The Commentaries of Origen and Jerome on St. Paul's Epistles to the Ephesians*, trans. and ed. Ronald E. Heine (Oxford: Oxford University Press, 2002), 144n6. On the textual history of this passage, see Bruce M. Metzger, *A Textual Commentary on the Greek New Testament*, 2nd ed. (Stuttgart: Deutsche Bibelgesellschaft, 1994), 470-73; Amy M. Donaldson, "Explicit References to New Testament Variant Readings Among Greek and Latin Church Fathers" (PhD diss., University of Notre Dame, 2009). Marcion (c. 85–c. 165) denied the canonicity of the Old Testament as well as much of the New.

15:1-7 THE EXAMPLE OF CHRIST

We who are strong have an obligation to bear with the failings of the weak, and not to please ourselves. ²Let each of us please his neighbor for his good, to build him up. ³For Christ did not please himself, but as it is written, "The reproaches of those who reproached you fell on me." ⁴For whatever was written in former days was written for our instruction, that through endur-ance and through the encouragement of the Scriptures we might have hope. ⁵May the God of endurance and encouragement grant you to live in such harmony with one another, in accord with Christ Jesus, ⁶that together you may with one voice glorify the God and Father of our Lord Jesus Christ. ⁷Therefore welcome one another as Christ has welcomed you, for the glory of God.

OVERVIEW: Our commentators maintain that Paul's message is clear: having been assured of salvation in Christ Jesus, Christians live for their neighbors and especially their weaker neighbors. The freedom that salvation in Christ provides makes believers servants of all. Thus the reformers agree that unmerited salvation frees us to work for our weaker brothers and sisters. Moreover, they concur that all Christians are called to be imitators of Jesus by God's grace and through the power of the Holy Spirit. The reformers think that Jesus should be viewed first and foremost as our Savior and only then can he provide a clear example for our daily living.

All of the reformers assume Scripture to be true, mighty and authoritative. It is God's Word for God's people: powerful for our instruction, correction and building up (2 Tim 3:16-17). While maintaining this high doctrine of Scripture that witnesses to the Word made flesh, the reformers affirm a limited role for human reason. In their view, reason has a subordinate place in the gospel of salvation revealed to us by God in Christ through Scripture, the preached Word and the sacraments. Nevertheless, they value human reason for human affairs like good government, marriage and commerce.

15:1-3 As Christ Bore Us, So Must We Bear One Another

DENY YOURSELF. CARDINAL CAJETAN: "The infirmities of weakness" refer not to afflictions of feeble bodies, but to afflictions of the soul, in which the weak are less subjected to spiritual matters and endowed with less strength. There are clearly countless such people among Christ's sheep. "Bear with" as *carry*, which can be fulfilled in many ways: sometimes by tolerating, sometimes by having compassion, sometimes by offering help in word and example or even in deed. . . . Paul appoints two obligations appropriate to those who are more perfect. One is positive, namely, to carry the infirmities of the weak. The other is negative, namely, not to please ourselves. And he added this negative obligation, because this antithesis ad-dresses well a barrier to the positive precept. The failings of others naturally displease us, and therefore if we pursue those things that please us, we will not be able to carry the failings of others. And so to remove this barrier to carrying the failings of others, he offers the best remedy: not to seek those things that please us. Both of these are difficult to perform through unfamiliar works, and nevertheless they must be fulfilled. COMMENTARY ON ROMANS 15:1.[1]

FORTIFY AND FEED THE SHEEP AGAINST THE WOLVES. MARTIN LUTHER: Paul here teaches us to have patience and to bear with the weak, and not to act so harshly toward them, but rather to think for a while as they think, become weak with them, and not cause discord in faith over eating and drinking or any

---

[1]Cajetan, *In Sacrae Scripturae Expositionem*, 5:78-79.

other temporal thing, until they grow stronger in faith and recognize their freedom. . . .

Therefore in this matter there is no better rule than love, and you must treat these kinds of people the same way you would treat wolves and sheep. If the wolf had bitten the sheep almost to the point of death, and you were to proceed with rage against the sheep, declaring it wrong for the sheep to have wounds, that it should be healthy; and you were to compel it forcefully to follow the other healthy sheep to the pasture and to the fold, giving no special care—who would not say that you were out of your mind? The sheep might well say: "Certainly it is wrong for me to be wounded, and I should definitely be healthy, but be angry at the one who did this, and help me to get health!"

See, these Romans should do this also and earnestly oppose the teachers and wolves. But they are to accept the weak consciences damaged by such teachings, not compel or ruin them, but gradually heal them, and eventually drive out that teaching. Meanwhile they are to let them be and think with them what they think and not confuse them. THE CHURCH POSTIL (1540): SECOND SUNDAY IN ADVENT.[2]

STRENGTH IS GIVEN TO PROTECT, NOT DESTROY, THE WEAK. DESIDERIUS ERASMUS: If we are so strong that we have no need of a teacher, we must nevertheless beware that while we attack another person's trivial error of superstition we ourselves do not fall into the graver sin of arrogance. Rather, the stronger we are the more we ought to bear the weakness of others. For those who are older or have greater physical strength do not for this reason push around or trample on those who are younger or unequal to them in strength, as if the only reason they had received strength was to enable them to harm anyone they could. Instead the more they excel in strength of body, the more they consider it shameless for themselves to injure a person younger in age or a person weak because of old age.

So in our case, the stronger we are in mental judgment and learning, the more it is proper for us to accommodate ourselves to the weakness of others, instead of becoming insolent in our knowledge and pleasing ourselves, and preferring to worsen the weakness of a brother instead of bearing or healing it. Therefore no one should take satisfaction from their own endowment, as though they had received it for the sake of pride, but rather they should take pains to despise themselves and by accommodating themselves to their neighbor to please them; not giving in to them in every matter, but only insofar as they can help them and make them better. PARAPHRASE ON ROMANS 15:1-2.[3]

THE STRONGER MUST SERVE THE WEAK. TILEMANN HESSHUS: He says, "We who are stronger ought to bear with the frailties of the weak." This is a repetition of the commandment given earlier: "Receive the weak in faith." Again, "Rather resolve that you will not be a stumbling block to anyone." When he says, "we who are stronger," he admonishes us that there are a variety of citizens in the church. In some there is more light and spiritual strength, and in others there is less. Then he warns that the strength of faith and of the Spirit should not be tactlessly shown off or turned into something that would cause one's neighbor to stumble, but rather should be shown in putting up with and bearing the weak. For it is the hallmark of a truly hardy and strong mind not to insult haughtily a weaker person, but to endure with a noble mind the frailty of a weak person and to support them. For it was for this purpose that God granted them hardiness of faith, and this arrangement pleases God's wisdom, namely, that the mightier serve the weaker. The only-begotten Son of God served sinners; angels serve the church; and parents serve their infants.

He says, "We ought not to please ourselves." To be sure, there are rather many haughty and peevish natures that admire only their own gifts, character, plans and actions, but deeply despise whatever

---

[2]LW 75:65-66* (WA 10,1.2:64-65; E2 7:47-49).

[3]CWE 42:83*.

does not originate with them or fit their own habits. This is a serious vice because it opposes the first commandment and because it often becomes an opportunity and occasion for great bouts of discord in the church. When Victor, bishop of Rome, was pleased with himself to an excessive degree and only approved of his own deeds, he tried without any grounds to excommunicate all the churches in Asia because they disagreed with him on the celebration of Easter. But Paul was not pleased with himself, but made himself everything for all. Jerome was more peevish and arrogant, who loved his own opinions too much and defended some false ideas more than was fair. But Augustine was more modest and calmer, and he was more helpful to the church. Therefore Paul demands true humility. Now humility is a virtue of the first commandment that has been kindled by the Holy Spirit by means of a faith that shines, whereby we acknowledge our weaknesses, subordinate ourselves to the divine will, do not carry ourselves above others, but think reverently about them, offer our own honor to other individuals and with a ready mind serve our subordinates. Notable was the example of Joseph's humility in Egypt. Even though he excelled all his contemporaries in wisdom, nonetheless he did not put himself ahead of anyone and did not look down on anyone; and he eagerly helped his brothers who were but cowherds and the people who had sold him into slavery. COMMENTARY ON ROMANS 15:1-2.[4]

---

[4]Hesshus, *Explicatio Epistolae Pauli ad Romanos*, 438v-439v. Hesshus here alludes to two disputes in the early church: the Quartodeciman controversy and the decade-long dispute between Augustine (354–430) and Jerome (d. 420) over Gal 2:11-14. Pope Victor I (d. 199) instigated the Quartodeciman controversy by excommunicating the Asian churches that celebrated Easter on Nisan 14. Irenaeus protested that while it is more fitting to celebrate the resurrection on Sunday, nevertheless this variation in practice was not an innovation and did not harm the faith. See Eusebius, *Church History* 5.24 (NPNF2 1:242-44). Jerome, in agreement with Origen (d. 254) and John Chrysostom (347–407), claimed that Peter playacted as a proxy for Paul to rebuke judaizers in Antioch (the "useful lie" in rhetoric). Augustine worried that this interpretation, which intimates that Paul lies in this passage (against Gal 1:20), might lead simple Christians to the disastrous conclusion that Scripture cannot be trusted, eroding its authority. For an example of Augustine's

LOVE THE SINNER. MARTIN LUTHER: Now, Christian hatred of sin acts in this way. A Christian discriminates between the vices and the person; they think only of eradicating the vices and preserving the person. Therefore they do not flee nor frighten nor reject or despise anyone, but rather welcome him, gladly associate with him, and act toward them in a way that helps them get rid of their vices. They admonish, teach, pray for them. They are patient. They bear with them. And they do nothing other than what they would want people to do for them if they were stuck in the same defects.

A Christian lives only to be useful to other people—not to eradicate them, but their vices. They cannot do this if they will not tolerate anyone nor have anything to do with anyone who is weak. It would be a very strange work of mercy if you wanted to feed the hungry, satisfy the thirsty, clothe the naked, visit the sick and yet did not want to tolerate having the hungry, the thirsty, the naked and the sick come to you or be with you! Thus wanting to tolerate no wicked or weak person around you would be the same as wanting to be useful and helpful to no one for godliness.

Therefore let us learn from this epistle reading that Christian life and Christian love does not consist in finding godly, upright, holy people, but in making godly, upright, holy people. Let it be their work and practice on earth to make such people, whether it calls for admonition, prayer, patience or whatever. Similarly, a Christian does not live to find wealthy, strong, healthy people, but to make the poor, weak and sick into such people. THE CHURCH POSTIL (1540): SECOND SUNDAY IN ADVENT.[5]

IMITATE CHRIST FOR YOUR NEIGHBOR AND TRUE PIETY. DESIDERIUS ERASMUS: This was written in the Psalms, not only so that we might

---

argument, see *Letter 28* to Jerome, NPNF 1:251-52; for Jerome's commentary on Gal 2:11-14, see PL 26:395-407; for a helpful summary and analysis of the debate and sources, see Jason A. Myers, "Laws, Lies and Letter Writing: An Analysis of Jerome and Augustine on the Antioch Incident (Galatians 2:11-14)," *Scottish Journal of Theology* 66, no. 2 (2013): 127-39.
[5]LW 75:69-70* (WA 10,1.2:68-69; E2 7:53-54).

know, but also so that we might imitate and learn from his example by what gentleness our neighbor must be supported and loved until they come of age in Christ, and cease to be a child and feeble. Therefore just as Christ lowered himself to our level so that he might gradually raise us to his own height, so it is proper for us to strive to imitate his example in enticing our neighbor to true piety. PARAPHRASE ON ROMANS 15:3-4.[6]

EMPTY YOURSELF AS CHRIST DID FOR YOU.

HULDRYCH ZWINGLI: Christ laments that he suffered the reproach, which is due us, so that we learn that he did not seek his own, but to serve us even to become ours. In the same way, we should imitate him and do the same. We are not better than our Master. We are therefore not burdened if we should bear evil on account of Christ. For they cannot please the world who serve Christ: "Blessed are you when they utter evil against you." ANNOTATIONS ON ROMANS 15:3.[7]

THE GALL OF DEATH BEFORE CHRIST'S HONEY.

THOMAS MÜNTZER: Whoever is not willing to have the bitter Christ will eat himself to death with honey. . . . For whoever does not die with Christ is not able to rise again with him. ON FICTIONAL FAITH.[8]

CHRIST'S POWERFUL EXAMPLE OF SELF-GIVING.

DAVID PAREUS: It is not rare that the Holy Spirit in the New Testament bends the prophetic oracles from their original sense into another, related sense and so broadens the meaning of a Scripture passage. Therefore the apostle says that the reproach of those finding fault with God fell on Christ with the same meaning by which Christ is said in the Gospel and also in the prophetic Scripture to have borne the sins of us all. "For God put upon him the iniquity of us all, and because of our sins he wanted to afflict him so that we might be healed by his wound. God made him who knew not sin to be sin for us so that we might become the righteousness of

God in him." Christ is "the Lamb of God, *ho airōn*, the one taking away and removing the sins of the world." Therefore the reproaches of those finding fault with God fell on Christ, that is, our sins by which we had hurt the majesty of God were placed on Christ for him to expiate and propitiate. Thus it has greater force as an example: Christ did not bear his own reproaches, but ours, and made atonement and expiation for them. Why then should not we also bear with and correct the weaknesses of the brothers, since no comparison can be made of their weaknesses to our reproaches against God and punishments Christ endured for them. By *oneidismoi* ["reproaches"] we thus understand all the sins and offenses against God. It is a synecdoche where a particular kind of savagery stands for the whole category. For blasphemy is a particular kind of enormous sin. By *oneidizontas theon* ["reviling God"] is meant not only the Jews, but us all, who have hurled reproaches against God. Let us understand that the fact *epepesan ep' eme*, "that our reproaches have fallen on Christ," did not happen rashly or by consequence, as when an insult to a father falls on a son, or by people's impudence only, as when the Jews grimaced at Christ as he called on the cross to God, "Eli, Eli." But it happened first by the eternal counsel of God who placed on his Son, the Redeemer, the reproaches of others, that he might expiate them by the *lytrō* ["redemption"] of his blood, just as he says, "God laid on him," etc. Then it happened by the voluntary obedience of the Son, who took on himself the guilt and penalties for our sins. We have thus the meaning and the application of this oracle. COMMENTARY ON ROMANS 15:3.[9]

15:4 What Is Scripture For?

SCRIPTURE TEACHES RELIANCE ON GOD.

CARDINAL CAJETAN: See, this is the purpose of sacred doctrine: to rely on God both in adversity and in prosperity. COMMENTARY ON ROMANS 15:4.[10]

---

[6]CWE 42:83*.
[7]Zwingli, *In plerosque Novi Testamenti Libros*, 446; quoting Mt 5:11.
[8]Müntzer, *Schriften und Briefe*, 222-23.
[9]Pareus, *In divinam Epistolam ad Romanos commentarius*, 1587-89; citing Is 53:6.
[10]Cajetan, *In Sacrae Scripturae Expositionem*, 5:79.

SCRIPTURE IS FOR US. MARTIN LUTHER: St. Paul says this here because he had introduced the passage from the Psalms about Christ. He did not want anyone to wonder how this passage made sense here, or how it affects us, since it was said about Christ and fulfilled through him. He anticipates that and gives us a general rule for reading Scripture. He says that not only this passage but all of Scripture was written for our instruction. It is true that things are written in it about Christ and about many saints. . . . But these things were not written for their sakes, since they were first written long afterward, and they never saw them. Thus though much was written about Christ, it was not written for his sake, since he does not need it, but for our instruction. The works and the deeds are written about Christ, but for our instruction, so that we would do the same. THE CHURCH POSTIL (1540): SECOND SUNDAY IN ADVENT.[11]

SCRIPTURE IS FOR OUR INSTRUCTION. DAVID PAREUS: Lest it be thought that he has accommodated to our doctrine the oracle of the psalm, which is speaking about David and hardly applies to Christ, he teaches that this is the use of all the prophetic Scripture, so that it may serve our teaching and edification. Nor does he indicate only one application, but several distinct, although interconnected, ones. The first and broadest application looks to forming faith, the rest look to life and constancy in faith. Therefore the first is contemplative and the rest are practical. "The things that were written earlier are intended for our instruction." By "instruction" he does not mean the mathematical sciences, whether esoteric or general knowledge, in which philosophers put the height of their learning and erudition, and the knowledge of which has its own praise and use.[12]

But he means true knowledge of God and of God's will of his works, both of his creation and governance of the world and the redemption of the church through Christ. Eternal life consists of this knowledge (John 17). He teaches that this knowledge ought not to be sought from the cunning disputes of the philosophers, not from the giant volumes of Plato, Aristotle or Theophrastus, but from the Holy Scriptures. COMMENTARY ON ROMANS 15:4.[13]

SCRIPTURE IS FOR OUR BENEFIT AND GROWTH. JOHN CALVIN: This is a wondrous passage. For by it we know that nothing contained in the oracles of God is vain and unfruitful. We also learn at the same time that by reading Scripture we progress in piety and purity of life. Therefore whatever has been handed down in Scripture we should take pains to learn. For it would be to insult the Holy Spirit if we imagine that he has taught anything that is unimportant for us to know. So whatever is taught in Scripture, we should know, tends toward progress in piety. Although he's talking about the Old Testament, nevertheless the same thing should be understood about the apostolic Scriptures too. For if Christ's Spirit is the same everywhere, there is no doubt that now through the apostles, as formerly through the prophets, he has accommodated his teaching for the edification of his people. Moreover, here the fanatical spirits who crow that the Old Testament has been abolished and that it does not apply to Christians whatsoever are quite rightly proved to be liars. For by what audacity will they rob Christians of those things that, Paul testifies, have been appointed by God for their salvation? COMMENTARY ON ROMANS 15:4.[14]

---

[11]LW 75:73* (WA 10,1.2:73; E2 7:59); alluding to Ps 69:9; Heb 11:39-40.

[12]Mathematics in antiquity included more than just arithmetic. It included optics, music, astronomy and geometry—in short, anything where applied mathematics might be used. It was also considered to be the basis of all philosophy. Notice that the sign

at the door of Plato's academy: "Let no one ignorant of geometry enter." Consider also his *Meno* and *Theatetus*, which rely on a keen knowledge of geometry in order to make epistemological and ontological arguments. Ancient philosophers sometimes distinguished between an esoteric knowledge that they imparted only to their most trusted students and a general knowledge that they imparted through their writings.

[13]Pareus, *In divinam Epistolam ad Romanos commentarius*, 1590.

[14]CO 49:271 (cf. CTS 38:516-17).

SCRIPTURE IS NECESSARY AND SUFFICIENT.
TILEMANN HESSHUS: He intersperses a general
admonition about the use of holy Scripture, from
which we ought to draw doctrine and consolation
and apply its individual meanings to us. Therefore
God has revealed his Word, and the church has
handed down the records of the prophets and
apostles so that through this instrument he may
educate us about his will, comfort us in all
difficulties, and awaken faith and the hope of
eternal life. Therefore Paul shows in this passage
what goal God had in mind when he ordered his
word to be written down: clearly it was so that the
church would have firm consolations in all
adversities. Therefore the divinely inspired
Scripture ought not to be read carelessly. Nor
should it be examined just one time, but it should
be read constantly so that we may always have
remedies against diseases at the ready. The apostle
teaches what the energy and efficacy of holy
Scripture are, that it is not a mute teacher or a
dead letter, as the blasphemous papists write, but
rather because God is truly at work through it, it
speaks comfort in people's hearts and awakens the
hope of eternal life, as Paul says in the first
chapter: "The gospel is the power of God for
salvation to everyone who believes." Again, Psalm
119 says: "Be mindful of your word to your servant,
in which you have given me hope; this is my
consolation in my affliction, for your eloquence
has revived me."

Therefore we must detest the *enthousiastōn*
["enthusiastic"] error of the Montanists and
Schwenkfelders who maintain that the Word of
God and holy Scripture are only an exercise for
the external person and that it does not strike
the heart or silence the soul or work salvation,
but that God brings about such enlightening
without any means. For Paul leads us back to the
holy Scriptures and orders us to seek comfort
from it, just as Christ too says, "They have Moses
and the Prophets; let them listen to them." And
Isaiah: "Unless they have spoken this according
to the Word, the morning light will not dawn on
them." That is to say, those who neglect or

despise the ministry of the Word and holy
Scripture will be deprived of true consolation
and fall into despair.

Here Paul refutes that sophistry of the papists,
who contend that not everything has been expounded that is necessary to be known by us for
our salvation. For he attests that the holy Scripture
was entrusted to the church for our doctrine, so
that it would not be some kind of deficient and
uncertain philosophy, but rather that it would be
the perfect doctrine that instructs us sufficiently
about God, the benefits of our Redeemer and the
way eternal life may be obtained. For this is true
doctrine that teaches us who God is, what his will
is and how we may obtain eternal life. For the
apostle embraces all the parts of the Christian
religion when he calls it "doctrine." The entire
Scripture exhorts us to patience. "For our citizenship is in heaven"; that is, we do not have a lasting
place here. To the contrary we have been exposed
to the insults of all because of our religion, and
God wants us to bear the cross in the world. But
patience is a virtue of the first commandment,
kindled by the Holy Spirit, by which we subject
ourselves through an eminent faith to the divine
will, obey God in adverse circumstances (which he
places on us in proportion to his mercy) and
sustain ourselves by trust in the divine promise and
in the hope of eternal life and a mitigation of the
difficulties. When Hezekiah was besieged, he
patiently submitted himself to the divine will and
bore the greatest difficulties courageously—and
did nothing, nonetheless, contrary to God, but
rather sustained himself by the promise of divine
aid and by the hope for future liberation. For hope
is a movement in the heart stirred up the Holy
Spirit by which in an excellent faith or trust in the
Redeemer we acquiesce to the divine promise and
await a sure mitigation of our difficulties, liberation
from them if God wills and at last eternal life.
COMMENTARY ON ROMANS 15:4.[15]

[15]Hesshus, *Explicatio Epistolae Pauli ad Romanos*, 440v-441v;
citing Rom 1:16; Ps 119:49-50; Lk 16:29; Is 8:20; Phil 3:20.

COMFORT. DAVID PAREUS: "By patience and comfort of the Scriptures," that is, what the teaching of the Scriptures actively brings about. . . ."The comfort of the Scriptures" is the teaching that encourages us toward the hope of salvation. I prefer to understand *paraklēsin* to mean "comfort" rather than "exhortation," because shortly thereafter God is called the God of *paraklēseōs* ["comfort"], which does not fit the meaning "exhortation," but does fit the meaning "comfort." Furthermore, he effects patience by the teaching of the Scriptures, when he teaches us about the will of God and about the reasons for and the end of the troubles of this life. For why wouldn't we patiently endure difficulties, when we learn from holy Scripture that they are let loose on us by the hand and providence of the heavenly Father, both as our just deserts and for our own good, leading to salvation? He also brings "comfort" whenever he sets before us the countless promises concerning God's presence, help and liberation from troubles, concerning the salutary outcome of our troubles, and concerning the glory stored up for us at last in heaven. Finally, "hope" is maintained by patience and comfort of the Scriptures, nor is it lost all the way to the end, because "patience" means "not being broken by evils" and "comfort" means "being confident about the salutary outcome of troubles." Now those who are not broken by evils but bravely trust about their deliverance—and do so by faith in the Scriptures—retain hope planted in God as a most firm anchor all the way until the end, until they in joy reach the gate of salvation. The apostle also said as much earlier: "Hope does not put us to shame." COMMENTARY ON ROMANS 15:4.[16]

SCRIPTURE'S CONSOLATION DOES NOT PRECLUDE SUFFERING. MARTIN LUTHER: Paul combines both endurance and the comfort of the Scriptures. Scripture does not remove adversity, suffering and death; indeed, it proclaims nothing but the holy cross—St. Paul calls it "the word of the cross"—therefore endurance is necessary. But this is what it does: in the midst of suffering it comforts and strengthens, so that our endurance does not break down but perseveres and conquers. It makes the soul very comforted, bold and happy to suffer when it hears a comforting word from its God, that he is with it and sides with it.

As long as this life is nothing other than a mortification of the old Adam who must die, endurance will be part of this life. Again, as long as the life to come cannot be perceived, it is necessary that the soul have something in which it can practice endurance, comprehend that life somewhat and cling to it. That something is God's Word, to which the soul clings, in which it remains and in which it crosses from this life into the life to come, as in a reliable ship, and thus remains firm in its hope.

See, that's the right use of Scripture to comfort the suffering, distressed and dying person. From this it follows that whoever has not tasted suffering and dying can know nothing of comfort from Scripture. That comfort is not tasted or perceived by words, but by experience. St. Paul puts "endurance" first, and then "the comfort of the Scriptures," so that we would know that whoever does not want to suffer, but to seek comfort elsewhere, will never taste this comfort. THE CHURCH POSTIL (1540): SECOND SUNDAY IN ADVENT.[17]

15:5-7 United in Christ for God's Glory

GOD OF THE PATIENT. PHILIPP MELANCHTHON: This is a votive offering or prayer, which is a preparation for the close of this topic about the use of ceremonies. We pray that we may be given zeal for both peace and concord. He calls God a God of patience, as if he said: "God of the patient," that is, a God who regards and comforts those who suffer, as Scripture frequently says elsewhere: "The Lord is near to the brokenhearted"; "The poor man commits himself to you; you are the helper of the fatherless"; " 'Because of the misery of the poor and the groan of

---

[16]Pareus, *In divinam Epistolam ad Romanos commentarius*, 1591-92; citing Rom 5:5.

[17]LW 75:75* (WA 10,1.2:75-76; E2 7:61-62); citing 1 Cor 1:18.

the needy, I will now arise,' says the Lord"; "The Lord upholds all who are falling, and raises up all who are bowed down"; "Call on me in the day of trouble; I will deliver you." Let us fix these and similar statements firmly in our minds and declare that they are meant for us. With such promises let us arouse faith within ourselves, and nourish and strengthen it, for faith is nourished and made strong by this kind of exercise. COMMENTARY ON ROMANS (1540).[18]

TILLED BY GOD. PETER MARTYR VERMIGLI: Lest we think that the Scriptures are able by themselves to beget endurance, hope and consolation in us, Paul preaches that God is the true author of these gifts. Indeed he uses the sacred words as lawful instruments, through which he begets these things in our hearts. Nor does he vainly add this sort of prayer, for by it we understand that it is not enough, if we teach correctly and faithfully, unless God grants strength and power to our teaching. For this reason whoever preaches to and teaches the people should also support those whom they instruct with frequent and fervent prayers, so that having been made good soil by God they would receive the seed fruitfully. COMMENTARY ON ROMANS 15:5.[19]

INDIVIDUALISM IS INTOLERABLE TO FAITH IN CHRIST. MARTIN LUTHER: One's own opinion is the cause of all factions, sects, discord and heresy. As people say, "Everyone is well pleased with their own ways, which is why the land is full of fools." Paul here wants to abolish this individual opinion and self-preference. Nothing is more intolerable and pernicious to Christian faith and the church than this opinion. It cannot give in but must undertake its own way, different from the usual way, so that it establishes something of its own in which it cannot be pleased with itself. From that have come the many factions, tassels and fringes, the chapters and monasteries of the world, none of

which are in harmony with the others. Rather, each one is best pleased with their own way and despises the others.

Thus the apostle here wishes that they would be of one mind, and each would please the other . . . and not wrangle against each other with the thought that one regards one thing as proper and good and another a different thing. . . . But I say this only about the things that are free. . . . In the things that are not free, but prohibited or commanded by Christ, there is no room for debate. THE CHURCH POSTIL (1540): SECOND SUNDAY IN ADVENT.[20]

CORRECT AND BENEFICIAL READING OF SCRIPTURE REQUIRES PRAYER FOR GOD'S GRACE. DAVID PAREUS: Paul wishes for a consensus in faith and love from God, for every good gift descends from the Father of lights. He calls him "the God of patience and comfort," which are the effects that he had shortly before attributed to the Scriptures, so that we may not think that the Scriptures themselves of their own power can bring about those effects in us. Properly speaking, God is the author of endurance, comfort and hope in us, so that we are not broken in our minds in unfavorable circumstances, but we may be encouraged by solid comfort and have our hope fixed on God. But he uses the holy Scriptures like a tool, through which he works those things in our hearts. And so he fittingly adds a vow by which he prays that God may grant those things to them, indicating that one needs the particular grace of God in order to read, hear and meditate on the Scriptures in a salutary way—and to obtain this, one needs ardent prayers to God. For God gives his Spirit to those who ask. Thus he admonishes teachers to join diligent prayers with their preaching and interpretation of the Scriptures in the church and schools; he admonishes pupils to approach the hearing and reading of the Word of God with prayers that God by his grace may teach them inwardly through the Scriptures and work faith, comfort, patience and hope in them by his Spirit. For if our zeal and hard work cannot accomplish

---

[18]Melanchthon, *Commentary on Romans*, 288* (MO 15:786-87); citing Ps 34:18; 10:14; 12:5; 145:14; 50:15.
[19]Vermigli, *In Epistolam ad Romanos*, 626-27 (*A Commentarie upon the Epistle to the Romanes*, 444r).

[20]LW 75:77, 79* (WA 10,1.2:77, 79; E2 7:64, 67).

anything in other actions apart from this work of his, as it is said, "Unless the Lord build the house," etc., how much less will one be able to make progress in perceiving the divine mysteries. This is the reason why the heretics, sophists and many others read the Scriptures fruitlessly and for their harm, because God does not grant the effects of the Scriptures. But he does not give them because they read it without prayer and with no desire to learn, but with a zeal to twist the Scriptures and to drag it to what pleases them. COMMENTARY ON ROMANS 15:5.[21]

UNITY IN FAITH BEGETS UNITY IN DEED.
TILEMANN HESSHUS: Such is the corruption of human nature that all admonitions, exhortations and warnings would bear no fruit unless God should happen to smite the heart by the Holy Spirit and bend it toward true obedience and piety. For that reason Paul joins ardent prayer to his warning and hopes that God himself through his Holy Spirit would speak consolation in their hearts at Rome and grant them a pious and holy harmony in Christ Jesus.

When he calls him "the God of patience and comfort," he advises us that true and efficacious comfort and patience originates from God alone, just as he is the giver of life and victor over death and all evils. To be sure, philosophy or human wisdom tries many things to comfort itself, but cannot find any firm and stable comfort, but falls at last into despair, as the examples of great men show. Therefore God alone is the one who shows by his Word and the Holy Spirit a firm and efficacious comfort in all dangers and adversities and instills in souls true patience that subjects itself to God in faith and hope.

He hopes for consensus for them, first in doctrine, then in all plans, actions and zeal, so that there might be one confession and one mind in all things. For while some people approve of their own words and plans too stubbornly, they often cause great commotion in the church. When Meletius

was too dedicated to his own opinion whereby he denied forgiveness to those who apostatized during persecution, he stirred up a savage schism within the church. Jerome stubbornly defended his exegesis about the apostasy of Peter in the epistle to the Galatians, and he would have caused a great disturbance unless Augustine had been more moderate. Theodoret, supporting John of Antioch and finding fault with Cyril's Confession set in motion a serious division. Chrysostom and Epiphanius fought among themselves with hatred and tore the church apart. Therefore one should be zealous for the church's harmony. But the foundation of this harmony ought to be Jesus Christ. For a consensus or harmony outside of Christ is a conspiracy of evil people, which turns into an assault on God and the destruction of the church. But the goal of a true and godly harmony ought to be that God, the Father of our Lord Jesus Christ, be glorified. Therefore one must detest the harmony that takes place when the truth is diminished or suppressed. Hosius of Cordova sinned gravely because he brought a harmony with the Arians in the Synod of Sirmium and approved by subscribing to the ambiguous word *homoios* ["of like nature"]. Correctly it is said in verse:

> *May that love and peace and sacred harmony be cursed*
> *That violates the true teachings of the divine Christ.*

COMMENTARY ON ROMANS 15:5-6.[22]

---

[21]Pareus, *In divinam Epistolam ad Romanos commentarius*, 1592-93; citing Jas 1:17; Ps 127:1.

[22]Hesshus, *Explicatio Epistolae Pauli ad Romanos*, 442r-443r. In 306, Meletius, bishop of Lycopolis, initiated a schism, seeking to usurp Peter, bishop of Alexandria; he was motivated by personal ambition and Peter's lenience in readmitting those who apostasized during the persecutions of Diocletian. On the protracted dispute between Augustine and Jerome over the interpretation of Gal 2:11-14, see above p. 208n4. Theodoret of Cyrus (c. 393–c. 458) and John, patriarch of Antioch (d. 441), supported Nestorius (c. 386–450) in his conflict with Cyril of Alexandria (c. 376–444) over the term *theotokos*, which led to mutual excommunications and the Nestorian schism. John Chrysostom (347–407) pled to return exiled Origenists to communion with the church; Epiphanius (d. 403) in response sought to discredit Chrysostom, ordaining a rival deacon at his church. They exchanged bitter last words as Epiphanius set out for Cyprus: Epiphanius hoped that Chrysostom would be deposed; Chrysostom, that Epiphanius would not return to his

ONLY ACCORDING TO CHRIST. DAVID PAREUS: Now he indicates what he is praying for from God. The Romans judge and despise each other because they disagree about foods and days. Some were thinking one way, others another way. In order to remove this discord he teaches that they ought to remove disagreement; in order to remove this disagreement, he teaches that there ought to be agreement in the faith among them; in order that there may be agreement in the faith, they need the grace of God, who brings it about. Little progress is made in disputes and arguments unless God joins minds together. They had debated much among themselves, but to no avail. Indeed, they had increased the divide. Paul had argued for an agreement for the most serious reasons. He thinks that these things would not lead to peace unless God leads them to agreement. Therefore he hopes that God will grant them *to auto phronein* ["to think the same thing"]. But he adds: *kata ton Iēsoun Christon* ["in accordance with Jesus Christ"], because one ought not to hope for any old agreement, but only that which is in accordance with Christ, that is, in the doctrine of salvation through Christ. Origen says, "It could happen that some people agree together in malice and think of one thing but for the worse. This is not harmony, but a conspiracy."

Would now that God would grant all people to think the same thing according to Christ in the truth! Up until now people have sought out various means for harmony and peace among the discordant Protestant churches, but to no avail. They have argued in various ways about the Lord's Supper, the person of Christ and other controversies, but the wounds have not been healed at all. Why? Because each one is wise in their own eyes; they think about how to protect their own opinions; nor do they seek harmony according to Christ, but according to human emotions contrary to Christ. Nor hereafter must one hope for any fruit from the disputations, parlays and conflicts of the theologians, when we are not praying to God so that we may all learn to think the same thing according to Christ.

But it seems impossible for all to think the same thing. For there are distinctions of gifts. We all prophesy in part. The apostles themselves had diverse thoughts sometimes. And there have always been some disagreements in the Christian church. "For there must be heresies and scandals." True indeed. Nonetheless it is possible and necessary to have an agreement in accordance with Christ, that is, in the doctrine of salvation, in other words, in the chief articles of the faith, of which true knowledge of God and Christ consists. In the remaining indifferent or debatable matters, the faithful can sometimes disagree, as long as the unity of faith and the bond of love is preserved. Therefore if today the things that are necessary for salvation were to be distinguished from those that are not necessary, and if the many theological questions and subtle distinctions about the presence of the body of Christ under the bread, about the oral eating and the eating of the ungodly, about the ubiquitous presence of the flesh of Christ, about the manner of predestination, about the regeneration of hypocrites, etc. were not mixed with the doctrine of salvation, the church would have less of a disturbance and would easily return to harmony. COMMENTARY ON ROMANS 15:5.[23]

UNITY REQUIRES THE SAME SUBSTANCE. DAVID PAREUS: He had hoped for them to have agreement on the teaching of Christ, since that is the mother of true harmony and peace. Now he hopes for that true harmony and describes it and indicates the goal for which it is mainly hoped for and directed. True harmony requires the unity of

---

see. See Socrates Scholasticus, *Ecclesiastical History* 6.12, 14 (NPNF2 2:147, 148); Sozomen, *Ecclesiastical History* 8.15 (NPNF2 2:409). While a champion of anti-Arian orthodoxy throughout his career, Hosius of Cordova (c. 256–c. 358) is mostly blamed for the compromise made at the Fourth Council of Sirmium (358). See for example Hilary, *De Synodis* (NPNF2 9:4-29).

[23]Pareus, *In divinam Epistolam ad Romanos commentarius*, 1593-94; citing 1 Cor 11:19.

heart and the unity of the mouth. It is not enough to say or profess the same thing with the mouth, unless there is the same opinion and one mind. Origen says, "'One mouth' is said to exist where one and the same agreement and speech comes out of the mouths of diverse people." The goal of harmony is the glorification of God. God is not glorified, but blasphemed, by disagreements and strife. For not only those who disagree and strive with one another are thrown into confusion in their prayers so that they cannot glorify God, but also others, who are offended by the disagreements and quarrels, are provoked into blaspheming the truth and God. Therefore let us all eagerly ask with all our heart that God would grant us agreement and harmony in accordance with Christ so that we may be able to glorify God with a tranquil mind and with one heart and mouth, and let us seek that harmony with all zeal. For we have been created and redeemed for the glory of God. Therefore those who do not glorify God revolt from their own purpose. But what shall we say about those who go so far as to blaspheme or cause God to be blasphemed? COMMENTARY ON ROMANS 15:6.[24]

True Worship Is Rooted in the Gospel.
MARTIN LUTHER: Worship is God's praise.[25] It is unconstrained—at table, in the bedroom, at the tavern, in the attic, in the house, in the field, in all places, with all people, at all times. Whoever tells you otherwise lies as much as . . . the devil himself.

But how are we to have honor and praise for God—true worship—if we do not love him and do not receive his benefits? How are we to love him if we do not know him and his benefits? How are we to know him and his benefits if nothing is preached about them and the gospel is hidden away? Where there is no gospel, it is impossible to know God. Then it is also impossible for God's love and praise to be there. Thus it is also impossible for there to be worship.

But this worship cannot be established with interest payments. It cannot be drawn up with laws and statutes. It knows nothing about high and low festivals. Rather, it comes out of the gospel, and just as quickly into the servant of a poor shepherd as into a great bishop. THE CHURCH POSTIL (1540): SECOND SUNDAY IN ADVENT.[26]

Our God Is Father, Son and Holy Spirit.
DAVID PAREUS: "The God and Father of our Lord." In this way he distinguishes the true God of the church from false gods. An explanatory conjunction has been interposed, so that it is understood to mean "God, who is the Father." Or it is a conjunction that delimits "God" and is understood to mean "God—and indeed that God who is the Father of our Lord Jesus Christ." Elsewhere, in sixteen other places, he likewise says *theon kai patera* ["God and Father"]; elsewhere, in nearly the same number of places, he calls him *theon patera* ["God the Father"] without the conjunction. COMMENTARY ON ROMANS 15:6.[27]

United to Christ We Cherish Our Dear Brothers and Sisters in Him.
JOHN CALVIN: Paul returns to exhortation—to strengthen this he still retains the example of Christ. Having received not one or two of us but all of us, he has thus united us, so that we ought to cherish one another, indeed if we want to remain in his bosom. Only then shall we confirm our calling, that is, if we do not separate ourselves from those whom the Lord has bound together. COMMENTARY ON ROMANS 15:7.[28]

---

[24]Pareus, *In divinam Epistolam ad Romanos commentarius*, 1594-95.
[25]*Gottesdienst ist gottis lob.*

[26]LW 75:80* (WA 10,1.2:81; E2 7:68-69).
[27]Pareus, *In divinam Epistolam ad Romanos commentarius*, 1595. In Robert Estienne's *Textus Receptus* (1550), Paul uses *theos kai patēr* ("God and Father") sixteen times including Romans 15:6: Rom 15:6; 1 Cor 15:24; 2 Cor 1:3; 11:31; Gal 1:4; Eph 1:3; 4:6; 5:20; Phil 4:20; Col 1:3; 2:2; 3:17; 1 Thess 1:3; 3:11, 13; 2 Thess 2:16. He uses *theos patēr* (God the Father) eighteen times: Rom 1:7; 1 Cor 1:3; 2 Cor 1:2; Gal 1:1, 3; Eph 1:2; 6:23; Phil 1:2; 2:11; Col 1:2; 1 Thess 1:1 (2x); 2 Thess 1:1, 2; 1 Tim 1:2; 2 Tim 1:2; Tit 1:4; Philem 3. Modern critical editions of the Greek New Testament differ slightly.
[28]CTS 38:519* (CO 49:272).

IMITATE CHRIST AND GLORIFY THE FATHER.
PETER MARTYR VERMIGLI: Here Paul in these prayers . . . treats the purpose of human life, namely, that, sharing the same mind, we all would glorify God and the Lord Jesus Christ. Now he sums up the matter and concludes with a most profitable epilogue. For here not only does he repeat the stated purpose, but he also blends in the example of Christ. Christ, he says, received us while we were frail, fragile and broken. For that reason it is right that we embrace and cherish one another, unless we don't want to be like our illustrious Master. Just like how he sought nothing other than the glory of the Father, when he lifted us up and helped us, so we too in helping our brethren should place nothing else before us, nor consider anything else other than the glory of God and Christ. And Paul's conclusion is so vehement that it's impossible to deny. For if your broken and frail brother has never offended you, but his behavior is generally commendable, certainly you act unkindly, if you do not bear his infirmity. But if he is loathsome to you and by chance has done something on account of which he seems unworthy of your help, still you should consider Christ's example, which he has placed before you, and establish before your eyes the glory of God, which will be illustrated by your kindness. COMMENTARY ON ROMANS 15:7.[29]

REFLECT JESUS' LOVE FOR GOD'S GLORY.
MARTIN LUTHER: St. Paul here asserts that God's honor is established through Christ, because he received us and bore our sins and blotted them out. So we should take on ourselves the sins, burdens and weaknesses of our neighbor, put up with them, emend them and help him. When sinners or the weak hear or experience this, their hearts become cheerful toward God, and they must say: "Why, this is an excellent, gracious God and true Father who has such people and wants them not to judge us poor and weak sinners, not to condemn us, not to despise us, but rather to receive us, help us and go with us, as if our sins and weaknesses were their own. Who would not love, glorify and honor such a God, and from the bottom of the heart entrust all things to him? What is he himself like if he wants his people to act that way?"

See, such praise God wants to obtain through us when we receive one another and when each one considers their neighbor's affairs to be his own. In that way people are incited to believe and those who already believe are strengthened. But where now is that example in the world?! THE CHURCH POSTIL (1540): SECOND SUNDAY IN ADVENT.[30]

---

[29]Vermigli, *In Epistolam ad Romanos*, 627 (*A Commentarie upon the Epistle to the Romanes*, 444r).

[30]LW 75:83-84* (WA 10,1.2:85; E2 7:74).

15:8-13 PRAISE THE LORD, ALL YOU NATIONS!

[8] *For I tell you that Christ became a servant to the circumcised to show God's truthfulness, in order to confirm the promises given to the patriarchs,* [9] *and in order that the Gentiles might glorify God for his mercy. As it is written,*

> *"Therefore I will praise you among the Gentiles,*
> *and sing to your name."*

[10] *And again it is said,*

> *"Rejoice, O Gentiles, with his people."*

[11] *And again,*

> *"Praise the Lord, all you Gentiles,*
> *and let all the peoples extol him."*

[12] *And again Isaiah says,*

> *"The root of Jesse will come,*
> *even he who arises to rule the Gentiles;*
> *in him will the Gentiles hope."*

[13] *May the God of hope fill you with all joy and peace in believing, so that by the power of the Holy Spirit you may abound in hope.*

OVERVIEW: For our commentators, Paul's emphasis on the calling of the Gentiles does not reject the Jews but rather confirms the promises made to Israel while recognizing that Christ alone is the means for salvation, not circumcision, sacrifices or the law. Clearly, then, both Jews and Gentiles need the mercy of God. The calling of the Gentiles also means that the promise is for all who embrace the gospel in faith.

Paul's extension of the gospel to the Gentiles also helps inform the reformers' understanding of the relationship between the Old and New Testaments. God chose the children of Israel, and the Holy Spirit who spoke to them through the prophets now speaks to the church as the people of God in Jesus Christ. The relationship between the testaments is thus one of promise and fulfillment for the children of Israel and the church, which consists of Jews and Gentiles. For this reason the reformers can interpret the phrase "the root of Jesse" as a clear reference to Christ in the Old Testament. By the power of the Holy Spirit, the promise of salvation given to the Jews now extends to all the nations, and the Spirit creates joy and hope in believers.

A PEOPLE OF JEWS AND GENTILES. TILEMANN HESSHUS: The apostle repeats and inculcates his admonition about welcoming the weak and fostering harmony in the church. As he spoke earlier about each in turn—first he warned the stronger not to oppose or disturb the weaker and then he warned the weaker not to loathe peevishly or condemn the stronger—so here he admonishes together all people of whatever rank or from what place they may be that each welcomes the other with godly love in the church so that God may be glorified by all. And again, he sets before their eyes the example of Christ; nothing in the world is a clearer example than it. He welcomed both Jews and Gentiles for God's glory. Even though great stubbornness, haughtiness and weakness resided in the majority of Jews, nonetheless he did not reject them, but showed himself to them, took on human flesh and lived among them, and gathered the church from them. And he did it to show the glory of God. For he was made a servant of the circumcision, and he subordinated himself to every law. He performed miracles among the Jews so as to fulfill the prophecies given to the fathers and to show infallibly the truth of God.

Again, he also welcomed the Gentiles. That is, he joined himself to the church of the Gentiles by accepting baptism, and he sent the apostles to the Gentiles in order to gather among them a church with the same purpose, namely, to show the glory of God, for the Gentiles who were converted to Christ proclaimed the glory of God. But he proves this clause about the gathering of the Gentiles into the church from the testimonies of Scripture, for this article greatly needed to be proved at that time, given that Christ the Shepherd made one flock out of Jews and Gentiles. He says, "So that the Gentiles may glorify God for his mercy, Christ welcomed them."

"For this reason I will confess you among the Gentiles" is a testimony taken from Psalm 18. In that passage the Holy Spirit prophesies about the Messiah, that he would rule not only the Jews but also the Gentiles and would gather a church among them, which would extol God. But where the name of God is extolled, there is the true church of Christ that is ruled by the Holy Spirit and partakes in the benefits of Christ.

"Exult, O Gentiles, with my people" is a testimony from Psalm 67. He says, "Let the nations rejoice and exult in the Holy Spirit, because you judge the people fairly." Therefore he prophesies that the Gentiles would come to know God and be converted to Christ, for nobody can truly rejoice in the Lord unless he has been reconciled to God by faith in Christ.

But when Paul adds "with his people," he is employing his office as interpreter and reminds them that in the very same psalm the Holy Spirit addresses both Jews and Gentiles, and that the Gentiles who are converted to Christ belong no less to Christ's kingdom and are no less a part of God's people than the Jews are.

"Praise God, all you nations." This testimony is taken from Psalm 117, a notable and clear passage whereby he teaches that Gentiles belong to the fellowship of the church and that the Holy Spirit had foretold that Christ would welcome the Gentiles.

"He will be the root of Jesse and he will arise to rule the nations." Because the Jews could not easily believe that the Gentiles would belong to the fellowship of the church and because the Jews shrank from intermingling with the Gentiles because of their base and vice-ridden lifestyle, Paul spends a long time proving this clause so that he may confirm that the Holy Spirit had predicted the calling of the Gentiles here and there in Holy Scripture. He says, "He will be the root of Jesse," that is, the Messiah will be born. "This one will stand prominently" or "he will arise" "to rule the nations." That is, Christ will help not only the Jews but will also bring salvation to the Gentiles, make satisfaction for the sins of the world, bear the entire wrath of God, reconcile the Gentiles too with God, by the proclamation of the promise free them from sin, death, and the power and tyranny of Satan, and grant them the remission of sins, righteousness, the Holy Spirit and eternal life. For he offers all the benefits of Christ the king to the Gentiles when he says, "The root of Jesse will stand prominently," or as Paul interprets it, "to rule the nations." He says, "The Gentiles will hope in him." Clearly here Isaiah foretells that not only will the gospel be preached to the Gentiles and they will be taken into fellowship with the church, but also that they will partake of all of Christ's benefits. COMMENTARY ON ROMANS 15:7-12.[1]

15:8-9a Christ's Servanthood Confirms God's Glory

PROMISED TO THE JEWS, BUT GIVEN ALSO TO THE GENTILES. MARTIN LUTHER: Why do you say that? Without a doubt so that no one would despise the Jews, but rather welcome them, because Christ welcomed them and did not despise them, and was even promised, shown and given as their own preacher, servant and apostle. What do you say, then, about Gentiles? I do not say that anything was promised to them, but I do say that they praise and have God's mercy, which was given to them without a promise, as Scripture reports.

---

[1]Hesshus, *Explicatio Epistolae Pauli ad Romanos*, 443r-444v; citing Ps 18:49; 67:3-4; 117:1; Is 11:10.

Therefore no one should despise them, but rather welcome them, because God welcomed them and does not despise them.

Now, since Christ has become common to all, Jews and Gentiles, though for different reasons, so we also should be common among one another. Each should welcome the other, carry their burdens and put up with their weaknesses without any distinction of external person, name, condition or anything else. THE CHURCH POSTIL (1540): SECOND SUNDAY IN ADVENT.[2]

LIKE JESUS, GENTILES SHOULD ESTEEM THE JEWS. THE ENGLISH ANNOTATIONS: Paul applies the example of Christ to the Jews, whom he vouchsafed this honor for the promises that were made to their fathers. They were never so unworthy; he executed the office of minister among them with marvelous patience. Therefore how much less should the Gentiles despise them for certain faults whom the Son of God so greatly esteemed! ANNOTATIONS ON ROMANS 15:8.[3]

CHRIST FULFILLS EVERY PROMISE. DAVID PAREUS: He understands that the promises were made to Abraham about the blessing of all nations through his seed; nay, rather they were made to our first parents about the seed of the woman. These promises had to be fulfilled for God to be truthful in his promises. Therefore, in order that God would make solid his reputation for truthfulness, Christ wanted to perform for the Jews whatever God had once promised to their fathers, that is, free blessing and salvation. Thus he teaches what Christ's ministry, preaching, suffering, resurrection and so on would be like. The confirmation and fulfillment of the old promises is what Christ saw in that ministry of his: to wit, first that he would confer salvation on the Jews, but finally that the glory of the truth would endure for God. This is what the apostle says in 2 Corinthians 1: "In Christ all the promises are Yes and Amen," that is to say,

the fulfillment and completion of them is found only in Christ. This statement is the basis for question 40 of our catechism: "Why was it necessary that Christ submit himself to death?" Thus the New Testament is rightly called the fulfillment of the Old, because Christ fulfilled the old promises made to the fathers in both word and type. He was the main promise behind circumcision: "I will be your God and the God of your offspring." COMMENTARY ON ROMANS 15:8.[4]

15:9b-12 New Covenant Proclamation of the Old Covenant

LITERALLY ABOUT THE MESSIAH. CARDINAL CAJETAN: And these are the words of David after he gave thanks to God for snatching him from all his enemies and for his vindication. Accordingly he concludes with a thanksgiving for the future benefits of the Messiah, already promised to him, so that to the benefits he has received he adds the reception of the greatest benefits. And so, according to the literal sense, this text is talking about the time of the Messiah. For David prophesies that he will acknowledge God through his Son the Messiah among the nations and sing the divine name. That, according to the literal sense, we see daily fulfilled, as long as David daily praises God and sings the divine name in every nation through his Psalms. That without a doubt the Messiah both has done and continues to do. COMMENTARY ON ROMANS 15:9.[5]

PAUL CORRECTS THE SEPTUAGINT HERE. THEODORE BEZA: This entire passage, Deuteronomy 32:43, is so corrupted in the Greek edition that is called by the name "Septuagint" that hardly any trace of the Hebrew truth appears. Now this is how the Hebrew reads: הרנינו גוים עמו (harnînû gōyîm 'ammōw). That is (as the Hebrew translators explain), "O nations, glorify his people." Paul,

---

[2]LW 75:87* (WA 10,1.2:89; E2 7:78-79).
[3]Downame, ed., *Annotations*, CCC2r*.

[4]Pareus, *In divinam Epistolam ad Romanos commentarius*, 1598; citing Gen 12:3; 22:18; 3:15; 2 Cor 1:20; Gen 17:7. See Heidelberg Catechism q. 40 (Creeds 3:320).
[5]Cajetan, *In Sacrae Scripturae Expositionem*, 5:79-80.

however, either supplemented the Hebrew עַ ('*im*), "with," so that it might read עַם עִמּוֹ ('*im 'ammōw*), "with his people," which is how the Syriac translation renders it, or he looked at the sentiment of the passage, not its words. Certainly the nations were not able to praise the people of God as happy and blessed from the bottom of their hearts unless they had come to know the same God and experienced his joy. ANNOTATIONS ON ROMANS 15:10.[6]

FULLY GOD AND FULLY MAN. CARDINAL CAJETAN: Both Christ's natures are prophesied. Indeed his human nature is prophesied by the phrase "root of Jesse," for Jesse was the father of David. And the Messiah is called "the root of Jesse," that is, from this root, from the generative power of Jesse, as far as according to his human nature, he originated. Now his divine nature is prophesied because it is said by the copulative phrase "and who will rise" from the dead to rule over the nations. And this is explained with what is added, "in him the nations will hope." And so Christ's incarnation, resurrection, kingdom and deity are indicated to the nations. COMMENTARY ON ROMANS 15:12.[7]

A WONDROUS AND CLEAR PROPHECY. JOHN CALVIN: This prophecy is the most illustrious of all. For in that passage, when things were nearly hopeless, the prophet consoles the tiny remnant of the faithful, that from the dried up and dead trunk of David's family a shoot will sprout and from that despised root a branch will blossom, who will restore the people of God to their former glory. This shoot is Christ, the Redeemer of the world—as is clear from the description in that passage. Then he adds that as a sign for the nations he will be raised up, so that he would be their salvation. These words indeed differ a bit from the actual Hebrew. Here where we read "who arises," the Hebrew has "to stand as a signal," which is the same—truly the form of the sign is preeminently visible. For the word *hope* the Hebrew has *seek*.

Still according to the most common usage in Scripture, to seek God is nothing other than to hope in him.

Moreover, twice in this prophecy the call of the Gentiles is confirmed: since it is said that Christ, who rules among the faithful alone, will be raised up as a sign, and that they will place their hope in Christ, which cannot happen without the preaching of the Word and the illumination of the Spirit. The Song of Simeon confirms these things. Also, hope in Christ is evidence of his divinity. COMMENTARY ON ROMANS 15:12.[8]

CHRIST IS THE ROOT OF JESSE. MARTIN LUTHER: The term "root" does not here refer to Jesse himself, but to Christ, on the basis of Isaiah 53. Otherwise he should have said: "the rod of Jesse" or "the flower of Jesse." . . . Therefore Christ according to the flesh has his root in David and the patriarchs from whom he has arisen, but according to the Spirit, he himself is the root from which the whole church has arisen. In the sense of the flesh, he is the flower [of his fathers], but, in the sense of the Spirit, they are his flower. SCHOLIA ON ROMANS 15:12.[9]

THE SURE HOPE OF CHRIST'S KINGDOM. PHILIPP MELANCHTHON: The reign of Christ will not be a worldly reign, but a heavenly one in which things are done in a heavenly way, and in which the will of God will be brought to us. Furthermore the meaning would be a sad one if it described a kingdom in which only threats of God's judgment against human beings were set before us. The kingdom of Christ is described very differently here. A very great comfort is set forth in the most pleasing manner in these words. "In him the Gentiles will hope." The reign of Christ will not be a reign of death and perdition, but a kingdom of hope and salvation. Christ came not in order to condemn, not to destroy, but that he might save and restore us already now before those damned and condemned to death.

---

[6]Beza, *Annotationes majores*, 2:146.
[7]Cajetan, *In Sacrae Scripturae Expositionem*, 5:80.
[8]CO 49:274 (cf. CTS 38:522-23); citing Is 11:10; Lk 2:29-32.
[9]LW 25:516-17* (WA 56:521); citing Is 53:2; 11:1; Rev 22:16.

This new kingdom has been established to be more powerful than the kingdom of sin and the law. Since the law had been given earlier, in which the wrath of God against sin had been shown, Christ did not come in order to bring a law in which he would again condemn us. He brings a promise and comfort against that condemnation. Although our sins terrify us, we should know that Christ has been given us in order that we should hope for salvation. Through this high priest we have a gracious God. This leader shields us against the devil, death and the savagery of the world. Therefore let us look to this verse in all afflictions: "In him the Gentiles will hope." Let us acknowledge that help and salvation must be sought and expected from Christ.

This phrase means the same thing: "He will stand as a sign to the peoples." This means he will reign, and people will look and flee to him as to the banner of a victor, and they will be defended by this leader and victor. This also indicates what the nature of the kingdom of Christ will be. When he says "they will hope," it signifies that we will be upheld by this hope. Meanwhile we are afflicted in this world and suffer harsh treatment. Nevertheless, we are defended and snatched out of our difficulties through Christ. But this tiny verse embraces so many things that it is difficult to enumerate them all; I am simply not confident that I could explain it.

Yet this explanation also must be added in the kingdom of Christ; the highest worship is to hope in him. This is an outstanding proclamation about faith. God wants to be worshiped chiefly by this hope and trust in mercy. It also contains great comfort; since it calls for this hope against wrath, it surely hates and forbids despair. Furthermore, this little verse ascribes to Christ divine power. It commands us to call on Christ, who is not reigning visibly. It commands us to hope in him. This certainly is ascribing to him divine power to hear prayer and work in us, although he does not dwell with us visibly and in the way mortals do. But I am not able to unwrap all the things that this passage in Isaiah contains. . . . This outstanding phrase . . . teaches us that the kingdom of Christ is not a kingdom of death and perdition, but a kingdom of hope and salvation. COMMENTARY ON ROMANS (1540).[10]

A PASSAGE TEEMING WITH GOSPEL. TILEMANN HESSHUS: This passage teems with a most fulsome teaching about the calling of the Gentiles, which the apostle has mentioned several times in this epistle. From it he has also sought out solid arguments and explained them as fully as possible. Therefore, when the apostle repeats this doctrine in this passage, let the reader recall these noteworthy main points:

1. The calling of the Gentiles attests that the kingdom of Christ belongs not only to the seed of Abraham but also to the Gentiles. For even if God punished the Gentiles for their blindness because of their contempt for the ministry and promise, he nonetheless did not ever deny them salvation if there were converted to God.

2. The calling of the Gentiles teaches that circumcision, sacrifices and the entire keeping of the law did not count as righteousness before God, but rather the Jews needed the mercy of God as much as the Gentiles did. For if circumcision had counted as righteousness, salvation could not have been promised to the Gentiles.

3. The calling of the Gentiles is a clear proof that we are justified freely apart from works of the law through the mercy of God for the sake of Jesus Christ through faith. For salvation was granted to the Gentiles, who did not have the law and could not present their works.

4. It also teaches that the promise is universal and pertains to all who are everywhere around the world and embrace the gospel with true faith.

5. In the calling of the Gentiles, who lived most wickedly, one manifestly sees that grace abounds more than sin, as Paul had said. For God forgave the Gentiles all their sins, which cannot be counted and cannot be set forth in a single

---

[10]Melanchthon, *Commentary on Romans*, 290-91* (MO 15:788-89); citing Is 11:10.

statement, and received the Gentiles into grace for the Redeemer's sake. Therefore nobody has grounds to despair of the grace of God.

6. The calling of the Gentiles attests that the church of the elect is not bound to a certain people, family, rank, station, place, persons, gifts or any similar sort of thing, but God selects a church for himself out of the entire human race amid all nations by the preaching of the gospel. And whoever seriously embraces the teaching of the apostles and has been grafted into Jesus Christ by faith is a citizen of the church. COMMENTARY ON ROMANS 15:7-12.[11]

15:13 The Holy Spirit's Joyful Ministry and Power

JOY AND PEACE, THE GOAL OF MINISTRY. TILEMANN HESSHUS: To his exhortation and evidence Paul adds this ardent prayer, that God himself through the Holy Spirit would will to be efficacious through his ministry and to speak efficacious consolation in the hearts of his hearers, so that they would believe this apostolic teaching and also through it experience joy and peace. For this is the goal of our ministry.

And surely on account of such great human weakness, even among the saints in the church, it is absolutely necessary that pastors ardently pray for their hearers, that Jesus Christ through the Holy Spirit would open their hearts. And in turn hearers should ask the Lord Jesus on behalf of their teachers and pastors, that they would clearly set forth sound doctrine and that their labors would be useful to the church and to their hearers. COMMENTARY ON ROMANS 15:13.[12]

DEPENDENCE ON THE HOLY SPIRIT. CARDINAL CAJETAN: Carrying others' weaknesses requires these two things in particular, namely, joy and peace, so that it would not be sorrowful to bear these, nor would it trouble the mind's tranquility. Also he adds

"in believing," so that he requires joy and peace to be founded on faith. . . . Notice that the goal for which he asks—peace and joy in believing, abundance of hope—does not depend on human strength; rather it depends on the Holy Spirit's strength. COMMENTARY ON ROMANS 15:13.[13]

DISTINCTION BETWEEN JOY OF THE WORLD AND JOY OF THE SPIRIT. TILEMANN HESSHUS: Paul gladly uses the word "fill," but I think that by this word he wanted to distinguish between the joy of the Spirit and the gladness of the world or flesh. The world laughs heartily and is glad, especially whenever it is dissolved in pleasures and riches. But it is an uncertain, brief joy, mixed with madness and petulance, and what often has to be repaid in grief. Excessive sardonic laughter is never sincere. For the world is always troubled by a guilty conscience. But the joy of the Spirit is full, that is, sincere, lasting, conquering death and all troubles, and lasting for all eternity, inasmuch as it originates in God. However, this joy and peace comes only from faith and is kindled by the Holy Spirit. COMMENTARY ON ROMANS 15:13.[14]

CHRISTIAN HOPE AND PATIENCE ARE DIFFERENT. RUDOLF GWALTHER: Paul here connects hope and patience. From this, then, we learn what true Christian patience is. It's also true that among the pagans some suffered great torment and torture with remarkable steadfastness, as we read of Gaius Mucius Scaevola, the gymnosophists in India and many others.[15] However, because such patience has no hope of eternal life, it's more of a temporary

---

[11]Hesshus, *Explicatio Epistolae Pauli ad Romanos*, 444v-445v*.
[12]Hesshus, *Explicatio Epistolae Pauli ad Romanos*, 445v.

[13]Cajetan, *In Sacrae Scripturae Expositionem*, 5:80.
[14]Hesshus, *Explicatio Epistolae Pauli ad Romanos*, 446r.
[15]Gaius Mucius was a famous example of Roman courage. He volunteered to assassinate an enemy king but was captured. Before the enemy could execute him, Mucius willingly burned his own right hand, saying, "Look, that you may see how cheap they hold their bodies whose eyes are fixed upon renown!" The enemy king released him since he "dared to harm yourself more than me." See Livy, *History of Rome* 2.12-13 (LCL 114:255-63, here p. 259). Greek philosophers attest that Indian Gymnosophists ("naked wise men") rejected human development and revered nature. They were likely Jain monks or Vedic Brachmanes, who both followed rigid ascetic lifestyles.

disposition and self-contrived passion, than a truly praiseworthy patience. And so it's absolutely unable to stand before God's judgment seat. But Christian patience flows out of faith in Jesus Christ, and trusts in the promise of God's grace and eternal life. And because it knows that God is true,

and that, as Paul says, he will not let us be tested beyond what we can bear, it does not let itself be conquered. And God is well-pleased on account of faith in Christ and the firm hope that we have in him. CONCERNING THE HOLY SCRIPTURES.[16]

---

[16]Gwalther, *Von der heiligen Gschrifft*, e6r; citing 1 Cor 10:13.

15:14-21 A MINISTER OF GOD'S GOSPEL

[14]*I myself am satisfied about you, my brothers,[a] that you yourselves are full of goodness, filled with all knowledge and able to instruct one another. [15]But on some points I have written to you very boldly by way of reminder, because of the grace given me by God [16]to be a minister of Christ Jesus to the Gentiles in the priestly service of the gospel of God, so that the offering of the Gentiles may be acceptable, sanctified by the Holy Spirit. [17]In Christ Jesus, then, I have reason to be proud of my work for God. [18]For I will not venture to speak of anything except what Christ has accom-plished through me to bring the Gentiles to obedience—by word and deed, [19]by the power of signs and wonders, by the power of the Spirit of God—so that from Jerusalem and all the way around to Illyricum I have fulfilled the ministry of the gospel of Christ; [20]and thus I make it my ambition to preach the gospel, not where Christ has already been named, lest I build on someone else's foundation, [21]but as it is written,*

*"Those who have never been told of him will see,
and those who have never heard will
understand."*

a Or *brothers and sisters*; also verse 30

OVERVIEW: The reformers reject the medieval theological axiom that faith needs to be formed by love to be true faith. Rather, they maintain that faith produces works of love like a good tree bears good fruit; rooted in anything else, such works are disordered, bad fruit. Nevertheless, knowledge without love is self-centered, puffs us up and does not help to instruct our neighbor.

With Paul, the reformers insist that there is one necessary sacrifice: the death and resurrection of Jesus Christ. What is pleasing to God as sacrifice is worship that includes preaching the gospel and celebrating with thanksgiving the sacraments not only in outward ceremonies but in spirit and truth. Thus Paul's ministry of offering the gospel is a kind of spiritual sacrifice to God.

Paul's comments on his own ministry provide the reformers with the opportunity to reflect on the pastoral office. The good news comes to human beings through the ministry of the pastor. The Word of God accomplishes what it promises in the forgiveness of sins and assurance of God's consolation for this life and the life to come. The grace of the gospel is communicated through the mouth of the pastor and heard through the ears of listeners, who are then comforted.

15:14 *Satisfied with Complete Knowledge and Love*

HUMBLE PAUL'S CUNNING. JOHN CALVIN: This is an *occupatio*[1] or a type of concession to appease the Romans, if by so many and so meticulous admonitions they feel offended and thus unjustly treated. And so he explains that he ventured to assume the role of teacher and exhorter to them: he says that he did this not because he was discouraged by their prudence or kindness or perseverance, but because he was compelled by his office. For in this way he allays all suspicion of temerity, which is most prominent when someone thrusts himself into another's office or handles matters that are inappropriate for him. By this the remarkable modesty of this holy man's heart is seen: nothing was more pleasing to him than to be considered nothing, if only the doctrine he preached held its authority.

The arrogance in the Romans was great. The name of their city even puffed up the lowest of the plebeians—they could hardly bear a foreign,

---

[1]A rhetorical device, more commonly known as apophasis, which implies an argument by denying that it will be addressed.

indeed a barbarian and Jewish teacher. Paul was not willing to quarrel with such scorn in his own private name. But nevertheless he conquered it by coddling it, as it were, since he testifies that he undertook these matters on account of his apostolic office. Commentary on Romans 15:14.[2]

The Distinguishable Yet Inseparable Relationship of Love and Knowledge.

Martin Luther: Note the careful order of his remarks: "full" first "of goodness," then "filled with all knowledge." For knowledge puffs up without love (which edifies). Nor can they "instruct one another" if they are not first filled with love or goodness. For knowledge, if it is all by itself, stays confined to itself and puffs up and does not deign to instruct another but only desires to be seen and despises others. But love overflows with knowledge and edifies. Neither does love without knowledge edify, however. To be sure, a holy simplicity that proceeds from a meritorious and exemplary life does edify, but an educated love does so both in itself and in its word, while knowledge both by example and by its message offends and does not instruct. Thus love in company with knowledge and knowledge by itself are totally contrary to one another. Knowledge by itself seeks its own, is pleased with itself and despises other people; thus it does not fear to cause offense by its example, and yet it refuses to give an account with a single word. But love by contrast teaches by its word and even refrains from any work that it will not be able to teach by a word that is offensive. Scholia on Romans 15:14.[3]

Love Confirms Faith.

Tilemann Hesshus: In order to confirm with an example the teaching that he handed down earlier, Paul shows that he thinks honorably about his hearers and does not pretend as if erudition and piety belong to him alone. For the Holy Spirit distributes his gifts in various ways and adorns each member of the body of the church in a notable manner. Ignatius is not equal to Paul in the preaching of the gospel and in the knowledge of the mysteries of God, but nonetheless an admirable constancy shines forth in him in his martyrdom. Therefore in this passage Paul attributes to the Romans kindness and knowledge, for a notable church was gathered in Rome at the time of the apostles by the ministry of the gospel and thereafter, as history teaches, but a short time later the Romans departed from both their kindness and their knowledge. For now Rome, as the seat of the Antichrist, excels in malice and blasphemies. Commentary on Romans 15:14.[4]

15:15-17 Ministers of the Gospel Wear Christ's Ministerial Mantle

For the Sake of the Ministry.

John Calvin: The excuse follows—in which he shows that he is more modest by way of concession. He says that he acted boldly, because he intervened in the same matter that they themselves were able to handle; but he adds that he assumed this audacity on account of his office's obligation, because he is a minister of the gospel among the Gentiles, and thus he was unable to neglect those who were among the number of the Gentiles. Nevertheless he humbles himself in this way to exalt the excellence of his office. For by holding up the grace of God that exalted him to that degree of honor, he indicates that on account of the apostolic office he will not permit his conduct to be despised. In addition he denies that he had assumed the teacher's role; rather he had assumed the exhorter's role, whose office is to remind people of those things that are otherwise unknown. Commentary on Romans 15:15.[5]

Stewards of the Mysteries of God.

Tilemann Hesshus: This is the second part of this chapter, in which Paul soothes and assuages the minds of his hearers so that they may not be

---

[2]CO 49:275 (cf. CTS 38:525-26).
[3]LW 25:518-19* (WA 56:523).

[4]Hesshus, *Explicatio Epistolae Pauli ad Romanos*, 446r-v.
[5]CO 49:276 (cf. CTS 38:526-27).

offended by his rather free reproof, instruction and exhortation. For there are many fierce, peevish and haughty natures that do not patiently put up with their character being scolded and their manner of living being prescribed to them. Therefore he explains by what authority and by what necessity he did so, that they may not look to the person of Paul but of God, who commanded Paul to teach all the nations and instruct them about the will of God. Therefore he makes mentions of his apostolic office and the fact he was equipped by the Holy Spirit with a unique gift of understanding the Scriptures and the mysteries of God and was appointed a minister and teacher of the Gentiles. Therefore it is right that they not only listen patiently and submissively to the apostle Paul's reproof but also obey his warnings and commandment, inasmuch as they originate from the Holy Spirit. What he means by "grace" he immediately explains: being a minister of Jesus Christ to the Gentiles. Therefore he understands the apostolic office and his ministry by the word "grace." COMMENTARY ON ROMANS 15:15-16.[6]

PASTORS SACRIFICE PARISHIONERS WITH THE GOSPEL. JOHN CALVIN: The gospel is like a sword by which the minister sacrifices humans as sacrifices to God. He adds that such sacrifices are acceptable to God. He does this to commend the ministry and to console especially those who surrender themselves to be consecrated. Now as the ancient sacrifices were dedicated to God by external consecration and washing, so also these sacrifices are consecrated to the Lord through the Spirit of holiness, by whose power—working within them—they are separated from this world. For though the soul's purity originates from faith in the Word, nevertheless, because the human voice is in itself ineffective and dead, the office of cleansing truly and properly belongs to the Spirit. COMMENTARY ON ROMANS 15:16.[7]

WE ARE THE SACRIFICIAL ANIMALS. TILEMANN HESSHUS: The Greeks call an administrator of a public office a *leitourgos*. Therefore Paul attests that he was legitimately called by God to be a public minister and teacher of the church, and indeed was appointed to call the Gentiles to the kingdom of Christ. "Offering the gospel as a sacrifice" is a metaphor taken from the rite of offerings and sacrifices in the law. The priests in the law sacrificed and offered the sacrificial offerings appointed by Moses, and God attested that he was honored and worshiped by this obedience, especially if the faith that looked for the Redeemer and Messiah would be present. But these sacrifices in the law were only types and figures that did not placate the wrath of God or remove sin and death, but only indicated that the Messiah would come as a sacrificial victim, who would expiate sins by his own blood. Therefore, if these things did not take place with a fervent faith, they were not true acts of worship to God, but only some empty spectacles.

In the New Testament we have another type of sacrifice, and that is twofold. There is first the *hilastikon* ["propitiatory"], the suffering and death of our Lord Jesus Christ, by which sole sacrifice God's wrath has been placated and the sin of the human race expiated. Another kind is the *eucharistikon* ["sacrifice of thanksgiving"], which does not consist of the slaughtering of animals or in external ceremonies or deeds, but in Spirit and truth, in the acknowledgment and honoring of the divine name, in faith and in calling on God, and in every form of godliness according to God's Word. For God affirms that these duties of ours produced in acknowledgment of and trust in the Redeemer are a pleasing sacrifice with which he is truly worshiped and honored. Therefore it is in this sense that Paul says that he offers the gospel as a sacrifice. That is to say, by preaching the gospel of Christ and spreading abroad the knowledge of God among people, he offers a spiritual sacrifice to God, that it may be acceptable to God the Father through Jesus Christ. And it is indeed much more pleasing to him than those Levitical sacrifices, the slaughtering of cattle, incense and things set ablaze.

[6]Hesshus, *Explicatio Epistolae Pauli ad Romanos*, 446v-447r.
[7]CO 49:276-77 (cf. CTS 38:527-28).

This is a noteworthy commendation of the labors that pious pastors and teachers endure in proclaiming the gospel. To be sure, the world thinks little of them and deems them unworthy of any pay. To the contrary, it judges them to be an obstacle to public peace. But the Spirit reckons that they are to be numbered among the most holy works and the sacrifices most pleasing to God. Therefore let us not linger over the warped judgment of the world, but let us prefer by far the testimonies of the Holy Spirit to the reproaches of the whole world, and let us with all due speed spread abroad the gospel of Christ in the world.

The very word *sacrifice* admonishes us not to flee dangers and the cross that are conjoined with the confession of Christ's doctrine. For we are like sacrificial animals destined to slaughter. "For your sake," he says, "we, the church, are slaughtered all day long," but in this way we are a pleasing aroma to God for Christ's sake.

In order that the offering of the Gentiles might be accepted and sanctified in the Holy Spirit, here he shows what fruit follows the labor of preaching the gospel, namely, the conversion of the Gentiles to God and their sanctification in the Holy Spirit. "For the gospel is the power of God to salvation to everyone who believes." This is how God gathers for himself a church by the ministry of the apostles, inclines human hearts to true repentance, makes them to partake in the benefits of the Redeemer and pours his Holy Spirit into them. It is in this way, moreover, that people, once they are converted to God through his Word and endowed with the knowledge of God and faith in the Redeemer, are made citizens of Christ's kingdom and sanctified by the Holy Spirit, just like an offering or spiritual sacrifice most pleasing to God. For Paul offers to God these fruits of his labors; and the Gentiles themselves, once they have been converted, no longer will sacrifice to idols but offer to God the sacrifices of righteousness, fear, love, faith, hope, patience, prayer, thanksgiving, confession and the proclamation of the divine name. This is a more pleasing sacrifice to God than a bull or a young bullock that bears horns and hooves (Psalm 69). COMMENTARY ON ROMANS 15:16.[8]

CHRIST MEDIATES HIS MINISTRY THROUGH PAUL. MARTIN LUTHER: By this expression the apostle is trying to say that it is not he himself who speaks or performs the things that he speaks or does "for the obedience of the Gentiles," but Christ. As in 2 Corinthians 13: "Do you want proof that Christ is speaking in me?" Thus he says that he does not dare to say anything except what Christ speaks in him. And he causes the word "to speak" to correspond with the word "he works," so as to express the idea both of word and work. For it is the same as if he were saying: "I do not dare to speak or to do anything except what Christ speaks and does through me," but in order to avoid wordiness, since in the first part he had discussed the matter of "speaking," it was not necessary to add the idea of "working," because he put this into the second part. And here it was not necessary to repeat "speaking," since he who works will thereby all the more speak of him, because it is even easier to speak than to do something. Moreover, since the "working" includes in itself both the speaking and the doing, he wanted to emphasize especially "what Christ has wrought through me" in order that he might express that not only his speaking but also everything he was doing was Christ's. SCHOLIA ON ROMANS 15:17.[9]

PRAISE FOR THE PASTORAL OFFICE. PHILIPP MELANCHTHON: Let us here observe the most honorable praises of the ministry of the Word. Preaching, explaining and discussing the gospel are the necessary sacrifices of the new testament. This ought to comfort both teachers and students of the gospel amid so many difficulties that must be endured by both. Teachers should know that this worship of God is necessary. They should know it must be rendered for the sake of the glory of God.

---

[8]Hesshus, *Explicatio Epistolae Pauli ad Romanos*, 447r-448v; citing Rom 8:36; 1:16; Ps 69:31.
[9]LW 25:519* (WA 56:523).

They should know that it pleases God, although some people hear the gospel negligently, others despise it and still others even persecute it. Also those who are learning the gospel should remember that zeal for learning the gospel is an act of worshiping God that God both demands and approves. For we see how earnestly God commands this when he says about the Son: "Hear him." Therefore it is necessary to offer to God this duty, this act of worship. COMMENTARY ON ROMANS (1540).[10]

15:18-21 Seeing and Understanding Come Through Christ's Word and Deed Alone

DIVINE MONERGISM. DAVID PAREUS: In the earlier part of the verse he explains how he is glorified in Christ, because he acknowledges that every fruit of his preaching is owed entirely to Christ as its author. Christ brought it about; I was only his instrument. This is an excellent praise of Christ by which God is shown to be true. For working through the ministry of the gospel, converting Gentiles and leading them to faith is clearly the work of God alone. But Christ *kateirgasato di' emou* ["worked through me"]. And he is the individual who still works today through the voice of the ministry, as is said: "The Father works until now, and I also work." Mark 16:20 says: "The apostles departed after the last commission and preached everywhere, as the Lord at the same time worked and confirmed his word through the signs that accompanied them." The same praise pertains to the honor of the evangelical ministry. For it is not a human work, but a divine one. The ministers do not speak or work, but Christ himself works efficaciously through his instruments in moving and converting the hearts of the elect. Therefore it is not a dead letter or voice, but the living voice of the gospel. It is the power of God to salvation to all who believe, the aroma of life to life for the elect.

Eis hypakoēn ethnōn ["for the obedience of the Gentiles"]. In another phrase he explains what Christ *kateirgasato* or accomplished through his ministry and by what means he did so. "I say, he was effective through me for the obedience of the Gentiles, that is, so that the Gentiles might obey the gospel by embracing it in faith and obedience." This was that "sacrifice acceptable to God," when the Gentiles offered themselves to God through the ministry of Paul. It is a purely divine work. For nobody can work faith and obedience in the hearts of hearers—and Gentiles, to boot, that is, the wickedest people; only the boundless power of God can do that. Thus he again avers that Christ is divine. COMMENTARY ON ROMANS 15:18.[11]

IN WORD AND DEED. DAVID PAREUS: He explains that phrase *di' emou*, "through me," namely, the two means through which Christ led the Gentiles to the obedience of faith: Christ did it through my word and through my work. He calls "the Word" his preaching of the word, that is, the gospel, including the public and private conversations and debates and the epistles that he wrote to the churches when he was absent. He calls "his work" first the labors, cares and troubles that he underwent with indefatigable zeal when he preached, about which one can read mainly throughout 2 Corinthians 11 and then the signs and wonders of miracles by which he proved the doctrine of the gospel, concerning which he adds the phrase *en dynamei sēmeiōn* ["in the power of signs"]. Furthermore, it will perhaps be very difficult to connect this phrase to the examples of life and character by which he sets himself forth as an example of his doctrine. Nonetheless, doubtlessly he includes also these things because here and there he requires them in a faithful preacher of the gospel. First Timothy 4:12 says: "Be an example for the faithfulness in your speech." Some join the phrase *ergō en dynamei sēmeiōn* ["by deed in the power of signs"] so that the prepositional phrase is an explanatory one; they understand "deed" to refer only to miracles because they have been the particular emblems of the apostolic office, while

---

[10]Melanchthon, *Commentary on Romans*, 293* (MO 15:791).

[11]Pareus, *In divinam Epistolam ad Romanos commentarius*, 1614; citing Jn 5:17; Mk 16:20; Rom 1:16; 2 Cor 2:17; Rom 12:1.

Paul had in common the other labors with all the faithful. But this fact does not keep us from linking the two. For Paul also had the preaching of the word in common with the other preachers, but he excelled all of them in his labors. First Corinthians 15:10: "I labored more than them all"; 2 Corinthians 11:19: "Who is afflicted and I am not afflicted?"

These are the two hallmarks of a faithful minister: *logō kai ergō,* "doctrine and work." He must be apt to teach and to convince his opponents, and he must be diligent in bearing the burdens of the ministry. In Timothy he designates the entire office of bishop with the one word *ergon* ["work"], calling it "a noble work." Those who neither are able nor willing to teach or to work and who pursue and make use of wealth or honors under the bishop's miter depart from this work. Commentary on Romans 15:18.[12]

The Twofold Power of God. The English Annotations: The word "power" in first part of the verse signifies the force and working of wonders; in the second part it signifies God's mighty power who is the worker of those wonders. In these words the apostle implies a dual action of God: outward in working wonders by the hands of St. Paul to the conversion of the Gentiles, and inward in which by the grace of his Spirit he wrought faith and repentance in them. Annotations on Romans 15:19.[13]

By the Power of the Holy Spirit. David Pareus: He calls signs and wonders the miracles of every kind, both great and small: healing of diseases, casting out demons, the resurrection of the dead, etc. It includes prophecies, tongues and oracles spoken through the apostles to confirm their heavenly doctrine. For their works were supernatural, and thus they were from the God who is Lord over nature. But God does not bear witness to a lie, but to the truth. He needed such

evidence in order to propagate his teaching; as Augustine says, "Now that this has been fully done, if someone were to seek a prodigy in order to believe, he himself will be a great prodigy, since the whole world now believes."

To be sure, also false omens and signs move people, as is taught in 2 Thess 2:10. Therefore, he adds, *en dynamei pneumatos theou,* "in the power of the Spirit of God." The apostolic signs move people by the power of the Spirit of God, but the false signs of the Antichrist and impostors move people . . . by satanic power. The former move people to faith in Christ, but the latter move people to deceptions. In Hebrews 2:4 one reads about the author and use of the miracles of the apostles: God offered the apostles his testimony by signs, wonders, various manifestations of power and distributions of the Holy Spirit, etc. In the last chapter of Mark the same power is ascribed to Christ. In this passage it is attributed to the Holy Spirit. When these are joined together, they offer an illuminating proof for both the divinity of Christ and the Holy Spirit and for the *homoousios* ["the same nature"] of the three (Father, Son and Holy Spirit). Commentary on Romans 15:19.[14]

The Inclusion of the Gentiles. Tilemann Hesshus: How Paul filled everywhere from Jerusalem to Illyria with the gospel of Christ can be sought out in the Acts of the Apostles. As to the fact that he says that he preached where Christ had not been mentioned, he states that he had undertaken the greatest labors for the gospel's sake. For it is an endeavor of the greatest labor to lay down the foundations of heavenly doctrine and to preach Christ there where a horrendous ignorance of God and madness for idols holds sway. But at the same time he now teaches that that time had come, which God had foretold in the prophets would come, when the Gentiles, who had heard nothing about Christ and did not know him,

---

[12]Pareus, *In divinam Epistolam ad Romanos commentarius,* 1614-15; citing 1 Tim 3:2; Tit 1:9.
[13]Downame, ed., *Annotations,* CCC2v*.
[14]Pareus, *In divinam Epistolam ad Romanos commentarius,* 1615-16; citing Augustine, *City of God* 22.8 (NPNF 2:484).

would believe in God and would be future allies of the church of the saints. COMMENTARY ON ROMANS 15:17-21.[15]

PAUL'S PREFERENCE. CARDINAL CAJETAN: Do not imagine by this that Paul refused to preach in places where Christ had already been proclaimed. For, as is clear in the Acts of the Apostles, he preached in Antioch, where Christ had already been proclaimed, as Acts 11 shows. Instead Paul preferred places where Christ had not been proclaimed to other places. Moreover, know that after he was separated from Barnabas, by the Holy Spirit, to preach to the Gentiles, perhaps on account of that he set down that phrase above, "[bring] the Gentiles into obedience." From that time he concentrated especially on this task: to lead the nations to the obedience of the gospel.

"Lest I build on another's foundation." These are not words of scorn but of preference. That is, not that he thinks it bad to build on another's foundation, but because he judged it better to preach where faith in Christ had not been established by others. And to this he directly and more fittingly joins the Scripture from Isaiah 52. COMMENTARY ON ROMANS 15:20.[16]

THE FOOLISH-WISE OFFICE OF THE WORD. MARTIN LUTHER: To preach the gospel was a despised and ignominious duty, just as it still is, void of all honor and glory, exposed to every kind of insult, reproach, persecution, etc., to such a degree that Christ says: "Whoever is ashamed of me before human beings, I will be ashamed of them before the angels of God." And Jeremiah confess that the Word of God "has become a reproach and a derision all the day long." . . . And also Christ confesses everywhere in the Psalms that he was despised and that "shame had covered his face." Likewise he says: "God, you know my folly

and my disrespect." And what happens to Christ, to the truth—for Christ is the truth—also happens to Christ's ministers, to the ministers of the truth. Like in 1 Corinthians 4: "I think that God has revealed us apostles as destined for death, because we have become a spectacle to the world and to angels and to human beings. We are fools for Christ, but you are wise in Christ. We are weak; you are strong." And a little later: "We have become, and are still, like the refuse of this world, like the scum of all things."

Therefore since preaching the gospel is not a matter of honor, with marvelous and apostolic love he regards what is its shame as being his glory, only in order that he may be of benefit to others. For to preach where Christ is known is not disgraceful, because there the first shame of the gospel is endured and overcome. But where he is not yet known, the disgrace poured on the gospel is still new and very great. . . .

But let us concede that because he was "set apart for the gospel of the uncircumcised," he strove with pious ambition to fulfill his office as if he alone wanted to bring the light to the Gentiles, a task in which he most strongly gave proof of his love. For the ambition to do good is truly rare and thoroughly apostolic. Moreover to preach the gospel is to bestow the greatest benefit, even if it is done through the greatest persecutions and enmities of the whole world. Therefore to strive as it were for this glory (and this is the strongest of all desires) of bringing the greatest benefit and blessing, and this as a free gift, and what a free gift it is, and to receive nothing but every kind of reproach for it—is this not something that is beyond humanity and truly apostolic, indeed a divine kind of ambition? How far from this lofty position, I ask you, is the person who is benevolent without receiving any return? Think about this. The gospel is an indescribable gift, which cannot be compared with any other riches, honors or pleasures. Furthermore, the one who gives good things, even to one's enemies and those who render that one evil in return, what is the benefit in comparison with the gospel? Yet the one who gives good things only to friends is less

---

[15]Hesshus, *Explicatio Epistolae Pauli ad Romanos*, 449r-v.
[16]Cajetan, *In Sacrae Scripturae Expositionem*, 5:81; citing Acts 15:35; 11:20; 15:36-41; Rom 15:18. In his commentary on Acts 15:39, Cajetan calls the division between Paul and Barnabas "not a severe sin"; see RCS NT 6:219.

than this person, who is really very rare; and lesser still is the person who lends goods; and below that one is the one who shares nothing; and worst of all is the one who even takes away these gifts either by thought (which nearly the whole human race is doing) or by deed, which a great many are doing. Therefore, when he boasts about his office, the apostle is merely commending the gospel. And what is more necessary for those who despise or attack the gospel than to hear it praised thus? So he does seek glory, but a glory that is the salvation of those among whom he seeks it. SCHOLIA ON ROMANS 15:20-21.[17]

DAILY CHRIST MUST BE PREACHED. JOHN CALVIN: By the prophecy of Isaiah he confirms what he had said about the seal of his apostolic office. For, while he's speaking about the kingdom of the Messiah, Isaiah predicts, among other things,

that the kingdom of the Messiah must expand over the whole globe. The knowledge of Christ himself must reach the Gentiles, among whom his name had never been heard. It was fitting that this happen through the apostle, to whom specifically that commission was given; therefore from that commission Paul's apostolic office becomes obvious, because this prophecy is fulfilled in him.

Incorrectly some will try to apply this passage to the pastoral office. For we know that in well-ordered churches where the gospel's truth has been accepted long ago, Christ's name must be preached constantly. Therefore read the passage this way: Paul was a herald among foreigners still ignorant of Christ, so that after his departure the same teaching should daily ring out through the mouth of pastors everywhere. For it is certain that the prophet discusses the origins of the kingdom of Christ. COMMENTARY ON ROMANS 15:21.[18]

---

[17]LW 25:521-22, 523-24 (WA 56:525-26, 527-28); citing Lk 9:26; Jer 20:8; Ps 14:6; 69:7, 5; 1 Cor 4:9-10, 13; Rom 1:1.

[18]CO 49:279 (cf. CTS 38:532); citing Is 52:10.

15:22-33 PAUL'S PERIPATETIC PLANS

²²This is the reason why I have so often been hindered from coming to you. ²³But now, since I no longer have any room for work in these regions, and since I have longed for many years to come to you, ²⁴I hope to see you in passing as I go to Spain, and to be helped on my journey there by you, once I have enjoyed your company for a while.²⁵At present, however, I am going to Jerusalem bringing aid to the saints. ²⁶For Macedonia and Achaia have been pleased to make some contribution for the poor among the saints at Jerusalem. ²⁷For they were pleased to do it, and indeed they owe it to them. For if the Gentiles have come to share in their spiritual blessings, they ought also to be of service to them in material blessings. ²⁸When therefore I have completed this and have delivered to them what has been collected,ᵃ I will leave for Spain by way of you. ²⁹I know that when I come to you I will come in the fullness of the blessingᵇ of Christ.

³⁰I appeal to you, brothers, by our Lord Jesus Christ and by the love of the Spirit, to strive together with me in your prayers to God on my behalf, ³¹that I may be delivered from the unbelievers in Judea, and that my service for Jerusalem may be acceptable to the saints, ³²so that by God's will I may come to you with joy and be refreshed in your company. ³³May the God of peace be with you all. Amen.

a Greek *sealed to them this fruit*   **b** Some manuscripts insert *of the gospel*

OVERVIEW: Paul outlines his plans to take the offering of the saints to the poor in Jerusalem and to visit Rome and ultimately Spain—the end of the western world. The planned trip to Spain would seem to achieve his goal to bring the gospel to the Gentiles, and it would make it possible for him to spread the gospel where no one else had laid the foundation for the church. The reformers— like the exegetical tradition—disagree whether Paul ever reached Spain: Jacques Lefèvre d'Étaples argues that he did go to Spain; Thomas Wilson argues that there is no support in Scripture for a journey to Spain; and Heinrich Bullinger argues that it does not matter. Whether Paul's plans were fulfilled during his lifetime, they seem to have had an eschatological aspiration.

Paul's collection for the saints in Jerusalem elicits economic and theological reflection from the reformers. First, Christians are siblings in Christ and are called to care for one another, spiritually and materially. The reformers knew from secular historians that a severe famine raged in the Roman Empire at the time Paul wrote to the Romans. It was especially drastic in the more arid region of Jerusalem. So, just as Paul asks the Gentiles to alleviate the hunger and poverty of those in Jerusalem, so also should Christians always seek to meet the material needs of the poor. Second, Christians are a people begotten through preaching and must support the ministry of the Word. In his wisdom God has called some to a full-time vocation of preaching and pastoring; how else will these preachers and pastors be able to nourish their bodies and families, unless those entrusted to their care voluntarily support them? Finally, these external, material gifts point to an internal reality of the people of God: their unity.

15:22-24 Thwarted Trips to Rome and the Spanish Mission

WHY PAUL HAD NOT YET VISITED ROME. HEINRICH BULLINGER: He discloses his plan, which observed, to the Romans: he preached to those foreign nations—surely so that he could place Christ right before their eyes—who still unschooled in Christian matters conducted themselves in impiety and idolatry. Now to this point he also treats Isaiah's prophecy from Isaiah 52. If you would consult this passage of the prophet, you will see that it fits the present matter very well. Moreover, when he says that he was unwilling to build on another's foundation, he does not reject the teaching of the other apostles. "For no one can lay another foundation than the one that has been laid, which is Christ." But he reveals his spirit's zeal, which was entirely in this: to expand farther the boundaries of the Christian religion. And the Greek words make this point very strongly. . . . *philotimoumenos* means "to exert oneself earnestly at something." Therefore he avoided with a sort of holy earnestness those places where in one way or another the foundations of the faith had already been built. Instead he raced to those places where Christ remained unknown, so that he would enlarge Christ's kingdom as broadly as possible. And this was the reason why he inserted this: as if he wanted to give a reason to those in Rome why he has not yet come to them. For the foundations of the faith had been established by the work of some other apostolic men [*virorum*]. Thus he adds, "For this reason I have often been prevented [from coming to you]." COMMENTARY ON ROMANS 15:20-21.[1]

HUMAN PURPOSES ARE CONTINGENT ON GOD'S PERFORMANCE. THOMAS WILSON: While Paul writes that he trusts to see them in his journey to Spain, we gather that this journey was not by special impulsion or motion of the Holy Spirit as sometimes occurred, but it was his human purpose. Therefore he says, "I trust," and indeed we do not read in sacred Scripture that he ever came to Spain. For this passage only mentions what he had in mind; it does not give certainty. He speaks only of his purpose, not of his performance. Paul undoubtedly meant it, yet with reverence to God's will, which overrules the events of human intentions, as in a special manner God governed the apostles in their administration.

Second, we learn that future things are contingent. We are to depend on God's goodwill and providence, without rash and peremptory presumption. We are obliged not only in the judgment and purpose of our soul to refer all to God's most wise and just disposition but also to signify the same with the words of our mouth, saying, "I trust to do this or that, I trust to have such a thing," etc. Third, it is a good fruit of love and reverence, which we owe to the ministers of Christ—who are true and faithful—to be their companions for their journey, to help them forward on their way, namely, when they travel through unknown and dangerous ways. If the people must lay down their necks, how much more should they take three or four steps for their ministers. A COMMENTARY ON ROMANS.[2]

UNIMPORTANT WHETHER PAUL WENT TO SPAIN. HEINRICH BULLINGER: Now he promises his coming. This event seemed quite likely to be capable to win over and unite the Romans. And Paul's words here are clearer than many of his words that need to be expounded. But if anyone seeks whether Paul truly went to Spain, or did not go, nothing sure can be answered from sacred Scripture. Nor does the Christian religion's hinge turn on this matter. For if he landed in Spain, it adds nothing to our religion; but if he did not land, it takes nothing away from true piety (that is, concerning the substance and main articles of piety). Jacques Lefèvre d'Étaples, a man of rare learning and piety, said this: "I truly believe that Paul arrived in Spain, for Sophronius, patriarch of Jerusalem, left behind written attestation of this. He writes that Italy, France and Spain were illuminated by the sojourn of most blessed Paul. In addition, it is said that Philotheus, ruler of Spain, devoted himself to Paul and became a confessor of Christ."[3] And of course if it is true, as all the ancients resolutely assert, that the apostle Paul died finally in the fourteenth year of Nero's reign, it

---

[1]Bullinger, *In sanctissimam Pauli ad Romanos Epistolam*, 174v-175r; citing 1 Cor 3:11.

[2]Wilson, *Commentarie upon Romanes*, 1226-27*; alluding to Acts 16:6-10 (cf. Acts 8:39-40).
[3]Lefèvre d'Étaples, *Epistola ad Rhomanos*, 98v; see below pp. 237-38.

would be credible that he lived many years before he was imprisoned in Jerusalem and eventually sent to Rome. Since in the second year of Nero's reign he came to Rome in chains; then for two years he remained in custody, unrestrained. That he was eventually freed from this imprisonment his epistles testify, especially 2 Timothy and Philemon. But to investigate these matters more thoroughly I leave to idle minds. I'll return to Paul now. COMMENTARY ON ROMANS 15:23-24.[4]

15:25-27 Collection for the Jerusalem Saints

GLOBAL FAMINE. PHILIPP MELANCHTHON: Under the emperor Claudius, during whose time this epistle of Paul was written, a great famine was endured in the whole world, most of all in the orient. At that time the Christians in Judea most of all needed foreign aid because they had been deprived of all their resources. COMMENTARY ON ROMANS (1540).[5]

ALLEVIATING THE POVERTY OF THE SAINTS IN JERUSALEM. JUAN DE VALDÉS: The service that St. Paul went to render the Christians in Jerusalem was to bring them the alms that had been given him in Macedonia and in Achaia. Because, as is gathered from the history of the apostles, the Christians at Jerusalem fell into great poverty, having sold their property so quickly after their conversion to the gospel, and because there was a famine at that time that overtook those parts.

Now I understand the poverty of the Jerusalem Christians to have been brought about by God. For it resulted from their satisfaction that the gospel should be preached to the Gentiles, as a remedy for their need. So the Jews, to whom the grace of the gospel came specially, admitted the Gentiles into it. While the Gentiles with their wealth supplied a remedy for the poverty of the Jews, they were thus mutually beneficial to each other.

I understand him to call alms a contribution [koinōnia; comunicacion], and from what follows, that the Gentiles were debtors to them to contribute "their carnal things," that is, their worldly goods, to the Jews, since the Jews contributed "their spiritual things," that is, the grace of the gospel and the gifts of the Holy Spirit conferred with it. COMMENTARY ON ROMANS 15:25-27.[6]

OBLIGATION ON ACCOUNT OF THE GOSPEL. JOHN CALVIN: Absolutely everyone sees that what is said here about obligation is said not so much for the Corinthians' sakes but for the Romans themselves. For in no way were the Corinthians or Macedonians more indebted to the Jews than the Romans. He adds the reason for this obligation: they had received the gospel from them. And he applies an argument from comparison of the lesser with the greater, which he also uses elsewhere: it should not seem an unjust or burdensome compensation to them; they are exchanging carnal things, which are of infinitely lesser value, for spiritual things. This also reveals the value of the gospel that he declares that they were obliged not only to their ministers but also to the entire nation, whence these ministers had come.

Also observe the word *leitourgēsai* for "to minister." It means to perform one's office for the state and to bear the burdens of one's calling—sometimes it's applied to sacred matters too. Nor do I doubt that Paul meant it to be a kind of sacrifice, when of their own initiative the faithful contribute to alleviate the poverty of their brethren. For in this way they execute the service of love that they owe, so that at the same time they offer to God a sacrifice with a pleasing aroma. However, in this passage he particularly considered that mutual duty of compensation. COMMENTARY ON ROMANS 15:27.[7]

---

[4]Bullinger, *In sanctissimam Pauli ad Romanos Epistolam*, 175r-v.
[5]Melanchthon, *Commentary on Romans*, 293-94* (MO 15:792); citing Acts 11:28. Both Suetonius and Josephus mention this famine. See Suetonius, *Lives of the Caesars* 5.18 (LCL 38:35-37); Josephus, *Antiquities* 15.9.1-2 (LCL 489:399-407); cf. RCS NT 6:157.
[6]Valdés, *Commentary upon Romans*, 282* (*Commentario de Romanos*, 323).
[7]CO 49:281 (cf. CTS 38:536); citing 1 Cor 9:11.

Sharing of Spiritual and Material Blessings. Tilemann Hesshus: By this example of his, Paul teaches godly and faithful pastors to apply themselves to this concern, namely, to take care of the poor, to admonish the rich frequently about contributing alms for the poor and to appoint faithful people in the church who can diligently distribute the alms. For kind treatment of others is especially befitting for the church. And because godly people are forced to risk all their wealth and even their life for the sake of confessing doctrine, it is most fair that he afflicts the wealthier with the troubles and poverty of their fellow citizens and members of the body of Christ.

Paul teaches, furthermore, that provisions and *didaktra* ["teacher's fee"] are owed to those by whose ministry we receive the saving doctrine of the gospel and are led to know Christ and his benefits. And we are obligated by divine law to be thankful to them and to share from our resources with which God has blessed us. "It pleased the saints," that is, they contributed with a spontaneous spirit and "were debtors," he says, for if the Gentiles were made partakers of the spiritual goods themselves, they ought in turn to share their carnal goods with them.

The spiritual goods are the heavenly doctrine, recognition of the true God, knowledge of the Redeemer and his kingdom, the remission of sins, righteousness, the giving of the Holy Spirit, peace in the conscience, joy and the inheritance of eternal life.

The carnal or physical goods are food, drink, clothing, lodging and whatever resources serve the needs of this life. Now there is no comparison of earthly honors with spiritual and eternal ones. Therefore it would be most wicked if those who receive spiritual and eternal goods were to refuse to repay their teachers in physical goods. For that reason our Lord too ordained that those who teach the gospel should live from the gospel (1 Cor 9). Paul also says: "You will not muzzle the mouth of an ox threshing grain"; and "Who serves in the military at his own cost?" (1 Cor 9). And again the Lord says (Mt 10): "The worker is worthy of his pay." Galatians 6: "Whoever is instructed by preaching should share every kind of good thing with him by whom he is taught." These words about thankfulness toward pastors and ministers by whom we are being taught in outstanding godliness pertain to the third commandment.

Therefore they are ungrateful, wicked and cruel people who will have no share in Christ's kingdom if they do not offer their pastors necessary provisions. But whoever snatches the goods of the church and divvies them up among themselves declares that they are open enemies of the truth.

When he says that he will come in fullness of blessing, he is speaking of his own ministry and the very rich fruit of the teaching of the gospel that he will bring to them. By "fullness of blessing" he means a very full blessing and a very abundant teaching that the Son of God out of his boundless kindness bestows on the world by Paul's ministry. For Paul was an excellent instrument of the Holy Spirit, and a marvelous light of doctrine gleamed in him. Paul instructed the whole world most copiously and earnestly about all the articles of faith. He calls this very rich doctrine and knowledge and acquaintance with Christ a "fullness of blessing." Commentary on Romans 15:25-29.[8]

Support the Ministry of the Word. Philipp Melanchthon: Since we are at presently living in a harsh age, in which those who teach and govern churches are treated most cruelly, I concluded that here readers should be admonished that they should consider what they owe to those who govern the churches. Let them learn likewise what grave punishments God has threatened to those who despise the priest and teachers of the church and do not aid them proportionally. . . . If we believe Christ, let us here show our faith and in this hope treat priests more humanely and generously, expecting that without doubt Christ will return thanks to us in greater measure. . . .

---

[8]Hesshus, *Explicatio Epistolae Pauli ad Romanos*, 451r-452r; citing 1 Cor 9:14, 9, 7; Mt 10:10; Gal 6:6.

But what is happening now? In some places priests are cut down with more than Scythian cruelty. In other places they are all but compelled to perish from hunger, together with their poor wives and little children. The people not only give nothing of their own to them but also shamefully rob them of the payments that were donated to the churches by the generosity of our ancestors for the support of teachers and students of Sacred Literature. In this matter there is a twofold evil: the present priests are killed by hunger, and because none are supported by the public to study Sacred Literature, there will be no one capable to teach the churches in the future. This threatens the destruction of the Christian religion everywhere. For how can religion be preserved without the study of Literature, without capable teachers? Those irreligious people are not only cruel toward present priests, but they also attempt to destroy the entire Christian religion as much as they can.

The laws of ancient rulers establish the most dreadful punishments for robbing temples. This is not, as the unlearned judge, because of some superstition, as though God wanted to be placated and worshiped with gold, but because the wisest rulers understood that the resources of the churches must be employed for preserving studies of Christian doctrine. It is good for the state not only that food be provided for the present priests but also so that Christian doctrine will be propagated to those who come after us. This can be done in no other way except if good intellects who are destined for the study of Sacred Literature are publicly supported so that there may be some left who are able to teach rightly for those who come after us. It is necessary that these should be publicly nourished like soldiers, because while they bestow their labor on this matter they are not able to learn other skills that bring in money. Paul says most earnestly both about those who teach and of those who learn, comparing this order with the military: "No one fights as a soldier at his own expense." For he shows that those who serve the church must be nourished at public expense.

But we shout these things in vain in these most miserable times, in which the Christian religion lies oppressed by manifold tyranny. However, the good are to be admonished all the more, lest they be led by these examples not to think reverently enough about priests. For we see how greatly these examples harm the common people. Therefore let us frequently remind ourselves of these things; let us inculcate them frequently in the people. We shall earn great rewards if we treat priests well. We will help them if we are concerned that the doctrine of Christ be faithfully propagated to those who come after us, and if we care that dreadful but just punishments will be given to those who are cruel to priests, who refuse to aid the study of Christian doctrine.

On the other hand, also let priests remember their duty to teach rightly, to heal wavering consciences and to adorn the gospel with fitting morals. Those Epicureans—who not only do not teach the gospel but also gleefully mock all religions and consider sacred things as a source of gain—do not deserve to be called priests. COMMENTARY ON ROMANS (1540).[9]

GOOD STEWARDS IN BUST AND BOOM. DIRK PHILIPS: Brotherly love is witnessed to by this.... We accept for ourselves the poverty of the saints giving richly according to our ability, yes, that it proceed among us just as happened in that literal Israel—those who gathered much heavenly bread had nothing left over; those who gathered little had no lack. Thus the rich also who have received much in temporal goods from the Lord shall minister to the poor with it and supply their needs, so that the poor in turn come to their aid if they need it. THE ENCHIRIDION: THE CONGREGATION OF GOD.[10]

15:28-29 The Mission to Spain

DID PAUL MAKE IT TO SPAIN? JACQUES LEFÈVRE D'ÉTAPLES: He knew that Spain was

---

[9]Melanchthon, *Commentary on Romans*, 294-95* (MO 15:792-94); citing Lk 10:7; Mt 10:42; 1 Cor 9:7.
[10]CRR 6:371* (BRN 10:401-2); citing Rom 12:13; Ex 16:18; 2 Cor 8:15; 2 Cor 8:9-10.

the western end of the world, that is, *tēs oikoumenēs*. And for that reason he was hoping partly to fulfill by himself this oracle: "Their voice went out into every land, and their words went to the ends of the earth." But you will say, "Did the apostle Paul ever set out to Spain?" I indeed believe so. Sophronius, patriarch of Jerusalem, left behind a written attestation to that fact.[11] For he writes that Italy, Gaul and Spain were illuminated by the most blessed sojourn of Paul. As he relates, when Paul had been welcomed as a guest in the home of a certain nobleman in Spain named Probus, and Xantippa, the wife of the same Probus, marveled at the modesty of the guest, even though she stared rather assiduously at him, it happened by divine will that while she was staring in this manner and was fixing her eyes on the face of the stranger, there appeared on Paul's forehead something written with golden letters, as it were: "The apostle Paul, preacher of Christ." Since she had heard many things about the apostle, because his fame preceded him, and she had long desired to be able to see the face of the apostle, she was undone equally by joy and by amazement and fell at the feet of Paul with tears. Once she had been taught the mysteries of Christ, she was reborn for Christ, along with her husband and family, since she had come upon the kingdom of eternal bliss. But it is also said that Philotheus, the ruler of that region, devoted himself to Paul, having become a confessor of Christ. O how fortunate are those who change an earthly kingdom for an eternal one!

But Paul also knew from the Holy Spirit that he would come to the Romans with an abundance of the blessing of preaching about Christ, provided that he would be freed from the Jews, the persecutors of Christ and the apostles and the disciples. For this reason he also indicates this thing to them: he also likewise implores the aid of their prayers so that would not be denied so great a good. Moreover, he asks that they pray that they

may be partakers of all the good things that were going to happen, in that offering that he was about to make for the saints, if God would accept both the offering and the one bringing it through prayers and if God would grant grace for him to set out to journey to them. For he offered all things to God, as someone who exists by God's entire providence over all things. Nonetheless we ought to dispose ourselves to receiving it as much as we can. ANNOTATIONS ON ROMANS 15:28.[12]

ALMS ARE FRUIT OF THE SPIRIT. THEODORE BEZA: *"This fruit,"* *ton karpon touton*, that is, this money collected for the benefit of the poor. This is certainly an elegant formula of speech, from which we should understand that true alms are fruits of faith and charity—whether you see them being given or received or both. ANNOTATIONS ON ROMANS 15:28.[13]

15:30-33 *Prayer and Peace*

PAUL'S HUMILITY. JOHN CALVIN: Slanderers had been so successful with their allegations that he was even worried that the offering would not be acceptable from his hands. Otherwise, during such a time of need, this offering would have been very opportune. Now from this his wonderful gentleness is apparent that he did not cease to labor for these people, although he doubted whether he would be acceptable to them. We should imitate this attitude, so that we do not cease to serve others, although we are uncertain of their gratitude. And we should also notice that he deems them worthy of the name "saints," although he feared he would be suspicious and unpleasing to them. Moreover, he knew saints could sometimes be led astray into unfavorable beliefs by false accusations. And although he knew that they treated him unjustly, nevertheless he did not cease speaking honorably of them. COMMENTARY ON ROMANS 15:31.[14]

---

[11]Sophronius of Jerusalem (c. 560–639), patriarch of Jerusalem, fought against monothelitism.

[12]Lefèvre d'Étaples, *Epistola ad Rhomanos*, 98v.
[13]Beza, *Annotationes majores*, 2:149.
[14]CO 49:283 (cf. CTS 38:540).

Our Dread Arms in Fight: Prayer. Tilemann Hesshus: This is truly the common condition of all godly teachers in the church: the more keenly they spread abroad the truth, fight for it, defend it and resist the efforts of the godless, the more dire hatreds and dangers they have to undergo. For the world hates the truth and strives to wipe it out with all its strength. And when Satan understands that there are faithful and eager pastors somewhere, who put the glory of God and the edification of the church before their own fortunes and life, he exerts all his strength to disgrace them with false accusations, terrify them with threats, surround them with dangers and thrust them out of the land of the living.

That is how he took hold of the fathers, the prophets, Christ, the apostles, the martyrs and the bishops. Paul too experienced this common condition of all godly teachers, as the history of Acts 13, 14, 16 and 21 attests. In these troubles and afflictions the apostle comforts himself with the Word of God and asks that the church of Christ would intercede for him before God. For these are our arms, by which we can and ought to defend ourselves, namely, the divine promises, patience, prayer, the hope of eternal life, the example of Christ and of the other saints.

But we ought to learn from this petition of the apostle what is the condition of those who faithfully serve the church of Christ, namely, that they are compelled to undergo tests of every kind, troubles, dangers and persecutions, just as Christ foretold in Luke 21: "And you will be hated by all people for my name's sake." Whoever refuses these troubles and difficulties is not fit for the ministry of the gospel. For that reason Paul teaches how much a godly person should value the prayer and intercession of the church with God.

The apostle Paul was a notable person, adorned with great gifts, carrying out the highest office in the church and dear to God. He had heard God himself in the third heaven, and the Son of God customarily replied to him in his prayers. Nonethe-

less, so great an apostle valued most highly the prayers and intercessions of the church on his behalf. For he knows that the promise of God is most certainly true: "Wherever two or three are gathered in my name, I am in their midst, and on whatever they agree and ask, it will be done for them by my heavenly Father." Therefore let us always value the prayers of the godly and at the same time take care not to hinder by our indifference or impiety the prayers poured out on our behalf. Commentary on Romans 15:30-33.[15]

Peace. Cyriacus Spangenberg: St. Paul concludes this chapter with this noble wish: "The God of peace be with you all." Here he himself does what he earlier commanded them to do: he longs that they would pray for one another. Here again he prays for them, that the Lord Jesus Christ, who is the true Prince of Peace and the one and only God of peace, would remain with and reign over them, and that he would not abandon them even for a moment. . . . Now he prays that God would create, cause and sustain harmony among them, so that they . . . would have satisfied hearts and unity of mind. As he also says in 2 Corinthians 13: "Have one mind, be satisfied, the God of love and peace will be with you." God has been ordained as Watchman and Defender according to his own Word and will; he desires to do this for those who trust him and love his Word.

Here Paul does not distinguish between the strong and the weak. Instead he wishes God's peace to all of them alike. Christian love in praying and wishing should not attend to the distinction of persons. And Paul closes with faith's dear word *Amen*, that is, "Yes, yes, it will be so." Dear God grant this to each of us too. Amen. Amen. Last Eight Chapters of Romans.[16]

---

[15]Hesshus, *Explicatio Epistolae Pauli ad Romanos*, 452v-453r; citing Lk 21:17; Mt 18:19-20.

[16]C. Spangenberg, *Außlegung der Letsten Acht Capitel der Episteln an die Römer*, 308v-309r; citing 2 Cor 13:11.

16:1-16 PERSONAL GREETINGS

I commend to you our sister Phoebe, a servant[a] of the church at Cenchreae, [2]that you may welcome her in the Lord in a way worthy of the saints, and help her in whatever she may need from you, for she has been a patron of many and of myself as well.

[3]Greet Prisca and Aquila, my fellow workers in Christ Jesus, [4]who risked their necks for my life, to whom not only I give thanks but all the churches of the Gentiles give thanks as well. [5]Greet also the church in their house. Greet my beloved Epaenetus, who was the first convert[b] to Christ in Asia. [6]Greet Mary, who has worked hard for you. [7]Greet Andronicus and Junia,[c] my kinsmen and my fellow prisoners. They are well known to the apostles,[d] and they were in Christ before me. [8]Greet Ampliatus, my beloved in the Lord. [9]Greet Urbanus, our fellow worker in Christ, and my beloved Stachys. [10]Greet Apelles, who is approved in Christ. Greet those who belong to the family of Aristobulus. [11]Greet my kinsman Herodion. Greet those in the Lord who belong to the family of Narcissus. [12]Greet those workers in the Lord, Tryphaena and Tryphosa. Greet the beloved Persis, who has worked hard in the Lord. [13]Greet Rufus, chosen in the Lord; also his mother, who has been a mother to me as well. [14]Greet Asyncritus, Phlegon, Hermes, Patrobas, Hermas, and the brothers[e] who are with them. [15]Greet Philologus, Julia, Nereus and his sister, and Olympas, and all the saints who are with them.[16]Greet one another with a holy kiss. All the churches of Christ greet you.

a Or deaconess   b Greek firstfruit   c Or Junias   d Or messengers   e Or brothers and sisters; also verse 17

OVERVIEW: Although the reformers acknowledge that this pericope is devoted to Paul's personal greetings, it is still Scripture, and as such it is the Word of God for the people of God. Those to whom Paul sends his greetings are chosen not for their status, rank or wealth, but for their faith in Christ and their work on behalf of the gospel. Thus, even simple personal greetings can point to the differences between what God values and what the world seeks. From these greetings the reformers get a picture of the earliest church and its assemblies as inclusive, charitable and organized. The congregation at Rome clearly included both men and women in a variety of leadership roles. For example, our commentators note the dignity that Paul ascribed to Phoebe, who would bear the letter to Rome and who from her wealth provided for Paul and the house church, the apostolic title that Paul grants to Junia and the fact that he names Prisca before Aquila, but they explain these things according to their understanding of the role of women at the time.[1] Finally, Paul greets the congregation at Rome with a "holy kiss," the kiss of peace that was shared in the churches as a symbol of communal

---

[1]In his study on Calvin's views of women, John Thompson summarizes the tradition's views on women and prophecy into four categories: passive, privately active, publicly active and ambiguous. See John L. Thompson, *John Calvin and the Daughters of Sarah: Women in Regular and Exceptional Roles in the Exegesis of Calvin, His Predecessors and His Contemporaries* (Geneva: Droz, 1992): 188-206; RCS NT 6:289-90, 292-94. Contemporary scholarship disagrees about how to understand *diakonos* when applied to Phoebe. Cranfield takes it as an obvious indication that Phoebe was indeed the deacon of Cenchreae. Fitzmyer observes that the term has generic and technical uses and leaves the matter undecided. Moo suggests that Phoebe held an official office in the church; however, he hedges, saying that the duties of deacons were still evolving. Thus he thinks it is speculative to say that Paul calls Phoebe *diakonos* in the same way he understands himself as *diakonos*. See C. E. B. Cranfield, *A Critical and Exegetical Commentary on the Epistle to the Romans*, International Critical Commentary (Edinburg: T&T Clark, 1985), 2:781; Joseph A. Fitzmyer, *Romans: A New Translation with Introduction and Commentary*, Anchor Bible 33 (New York: Doubleday, 1993), 729-30; Douglas J. Moo, *The Epistle to the Romans*, New International Commentary on the New Testament 38 (Grand Rapids: Eerdmans, 1996), 913-14.

love at the Eucharist. Although established in various cities, these congregations are united in Christ—in communion and fellowship.

Paul Greets Refugees from Jerusalem. Juan de Valdés: St. Paul devotes nearly this entire chapter to commendations. Most of which, I think, are for people who had either fled from Jerusalem to Rome or who had been driven there by the famine. Commentary on Romans 16.[2]

Do Not Ignore Paul's Greetings! Heinrich Bullinger: Chapter 16 at first glance seems to be simple and of little importance; however, underneath it holds more than what at first meets the eye. Even though the whole chapter seems to be devoted to straightforward greetings, nevertheless these greetings wonderfully place the duty of charity before our eyes. They relate friendliness and compassion, and teach us to show appropriate and due honor to each person. Now it is especially notable that Paul here praises no one on account of wealth or some other good fortune, but on account of faith, love, simplicity, hospitality and other virtues of this kind. In addition you see that there is no distinction here between believers, because of course the matter of faith and piety is concerned. Therefore they are listed in this catalog of saints and women. Commentary on Romans 16.[3]

Simple, Excellent and Honorable Greetings as Examples for Us. Johann Wild: This chapter has nearly nothing except for greetings. Nonetheless it is not useless. First, you have here the praises and titles with which Christians ought to be praised. For they are not praised by their riches, power or eloquence, but by their love, innocence, obedience, strength of faith, faithfulness of service, etc. Next you also see a marvelous simplicity in the titles adjoined to them, for some he calls "helpers in Christ," others "servants of the church," still others "excellent in Christ" and yet others people "who labor much." These are the titles of those who preside over the church. Finally, you see that women and servants are not excluded from Paul's greeting and ministry. For "there is neither male nor female," etc. Thus he calls Phoebe "sister," and then "a servant of the church." But how women may serve you can find in Titus 2. He adds in commending her that she had helped many others and also himself, for respect for others has the promise also of long life on earth. Thus Abraham and Lot attained the honor of hosting even angels as guests. And so, because Phoebe had helped others, she attained the honor of hosting the apostle. Exegesis of Romans 16:1.[4]

Let Us Commend Ourselves to One Another. David Pareus: Greetings follow, by which he greets the leading members of the Roman church by their names and adds praises to them one by one. Nor should one think that they are formulas or glad-handing done for the sake of charming the vulgar crowd, but they are testimonies of his true love and of the connection he has with members of the church. It teaches us that we ought to be concerned about the salvation of our fellow members, even those living very far away, for it is salutary to pray to God for the salvation of others as well as to show his benevolence to them. The apostle also endeavors that from these praises of those individuals who have been equipped with greater gifts and are able to be of more help they would have greater authority in the church, since indeed the gifts and diligence of people add authority to their office. Finally, he rouses them with warm praise so that they would diligently continue and make progress in their course of godliness. Commentary on Romans 16:1-16.[5]

Christ's Pathetic Flock Is United in His Spirit. Tilemann Hesshus: By these commendations and greetings we should learn what

---

[2]Valdés, *Commentary upon Romans*, 285* (*Commentario de Romanos*, 327).
[3]Bullinger, *In Romanos Epistolam*, 179r-v.

[4]Wild, *Exegesis in Epistolam ad Romanos*, 267r-v; citing Gal 3:28.
[5]Pareus, *In divinam Epistolam ad Romanos commentarius*, 1661.

sort of church the church of Christ is: without a doubt a very pathetic flock—scorned and despised before the world as poor without any protection, not enclosed within any certain kingdom but scattered throughout many kingdoms. Not many who are wise, noble, powerful, learned, leaders and kings are found in the church of Christ, for God chose the weak of the world to shame the wise and powerful. And Christ says, "I give thanks to you, O God, that you have hidden this from the wise and skillful, and you have revealed it to little children." In this catalog of saints the names of many powerful people are not found; instead Paul commends the saints with special titles.

Therefore when we seek the church we should not look for the courts of mighty leaders, for powerful, renowned people, for spacious empires; instead we should seek a community that embraces the teaching of the apostles and submits to the preaching of the faith, which Paul describes in this passage.

Next the apostle admonishes us by these greetings with what loving affection we should embrace and engage all who obey Christ through faith and who are going to be partakers of the same glory and salvation with us. Without a doubt we should embrace them wholly in brotherly love no differently than if they were offspring from the same parents as we. For the Holy Spirit—who rules all believers and adopts, nourishes and leads them as children of God, and unites them with God and one another—is a much tighter and firmer bond of friendship than a blood relation. Thus there is a purer relationship and more willing posture of service and more anchored love among the pious—who are lead by God's Spirit and who are one in Christ—than among brothers of the same womb. COMMENTARY ON ROMANS 16.[6]

WHAT ABOUT PETER? THEODORE BEZA: I beseech you, if Peter was in Rome—and indeed the "ecumenical bishop"—why then does Paul not only not greet Peter as such, but also pass over him unnamed? ANNOTATIONS ON ROMANS 16:1.[7]

16:1-2 *How Do Women Minister?*

WOMEN CAN TEACH YOUNG MEN. JOHANNES OECOLAMPADIUS: How can women minister? As you have in Titus 2: they teach younger men and serve others. ANNOTATIONS ON ROMANS 16:1.[8]

WOMEN CARE FOR THE POOR. PETER MARTYR VERMIGLI: She had been a minister in the church of Cenchreae—of course not by teaching publicly but by caring for the poor who were sustained by the church. It is fitting for widows to be entrusted with this task—either according to age or according to morals (as clearly written in the epistle to Timothy). COMMENTARY ON ROMANS 16:1.[9]

WOMEN AID OTHERS BY THEIR WEALTH OR WISDOM. HEINRICH BULLINGER: The first person mentioned is Phoebe through him—if the Greek text is trustworthy—this epistle was sent to Rome.... This Phoebe is not said to be a minister of the church, because in the early church women neither could teach or could hold other public offices of the church—for that had been forbidden in 1 Timothy 2—but that by the saints whom he here calls through *antonomasia*[10] the church she would have ministered either by her own abilities or other aids—again which Paul demands from women in 1 Timothy 5 and Titus 2. On the other hand they made her subject. "For she has been a help not only to many but also to me myself." So in this way she served the church. Now Paul depends on these wonderful arguments to convince the Romans to receive her and to make use of either her wealth or counsel. For

---

[6]Hesshus, *Explicatio Epistolae Pauli ad Romanos*, 454r-v; citing 1 Cor 1:26-27; Mt 11:25.

[7]Beza, *Annotationes majores*, 2:149.
[8]Oecolampadius, *In epistolam ad Rhomanos*, 106v. Zwingli gives the same gloss; see Zwingli, *In plerosque Novi Testamenti Libros*, 447.
[9]Vermigli, *A Commentarie upon the Epistle to the Romans*, 453v* (*In Epistolam ad Romanos*, 640); citing 1 Tim 2:11-12; 5:1-16.
[10]That is, substituting a title for a name.

to be a sister is to be a Christian. COMMENTARY ON ROMANS 16:1.[11]

WOMEN ARE HOSTESSES. THEODORE BEZA: *Prostatēs* generally indicates an overseer or a patron and defender. Many think that Phoebe is called *prostatin* here with that meaning because she had assisted many people and also Paul himself. But this name seems to be more authoritative than is fitting for a woman, if you should take it to have that meaning. Therefore one ought to know that the *prostatas* were called by a peculiar name, who were also called *proxenoi*, that is, those who were chosen by some city to welcome guests and travelers into their own home and into their own trust. This is what it means, as far as Eustathius is concerned: *proist-asthai tōn xenōn*, "to be in charge of the guests."[12] Therefore the apostle means that the home of this Phoebe, a servant of the church in Cenchreae, lay open to the brothers and travelers, as she served as public host of the saints. These are virtues Paul requires in a widow; 1 Timothy 5:10. The Syriac uses a more general word that means "to place someone into office." ANNOTATIONS ON ROMANS 16:2.[13]

WOMEN'S GODLY DUTIES. DAVID PAREUS: Phoebe herself, a holy woman, a benefactor and servant of the church, teaches that women also belong to Christ's kingdom, because in Christ there is neither male nor female, and women can offer useful help to the church. Even if women are not admitted into the teaching office, nonetheless they can help the church by their private instruction, benevolence and other godly duties, and they ought to do so, based on the example of this godly matron. But if women may

do these things, how much more may men and other Christians do them? COMMENTARY ON ROMANS 16:2.[14]

16:3-4 *Prisca and Aquila, Paul's Cosufferers*

COWORKERS IN CHRIST. DAVID PAREUS: He greets equally the couple Aquila and Priscilla, whom he calls his *synergous*, "helpers in Christ Jesus," that is, in spreading abroad the teaching of Christ. The reason for this commendation is found in Acts 18: They were *homotechnoi* ["people of the same trade"] as Paul. For they were tentmakers (Acts 18:4). Chrysostom calls them "furriers." Among *homotechnous* ["people of the same trade"] there is wont to be a connection. The apostle does not regard it, but rather praises them for the zeal of their piety, because they labored with him in equal zeal in spreading the teaching of Christ. An example of their zeal is mentioned in the same place: for they took Apollos, a learned and godly Jew, albeit still a catechumen, and they instructed him in the way of the Lord more accurately, for which they are commended not so much for their diligence as also for their unique skill. They are not said to have been presbyters, but rather laypeople, and yet they nonetheless were not kept from the duty of teaching others. But those sacerdotal papists, who for the sake of their holy orders arrogate to themselves alone the office of teaching—even though they for the most part are worthless at that task—despise all the laity, that is, everyone except for themselves. Moreover, that they were joined to Paul by a singular close connection is obvious, first, from the fact that he mentions them twice elsewhere in his greetings and, second, from the fact that when he was about to sail from Corinth in Acts 18:18, he made them his traveling companions. COMMENTARY ON ROMANS 16:3.[15]

[11]Bullinger, *In Romanos Epistolam*, 179v.
[12]See Eustathius of Thessalonica, *Commentarii ad Homeri Iliadem*, 4 vols. (Leipzig: J. A. G. Weigel, 1827–1830), 1:386; Eustathius (c. 1116–c. 1194), archbishop of Thessalonica, composed an account of the siege of Thessalonica (1185) and important commentaries on Homer's *Illiad* and *Odyssey*.
[13]Beza, *Annotationes majores*, 2:150.
[14]Pareus, *In divinam Epistolam ad Romanos commentarius*, 1660.
[15]Pareus, *In divinam Epistolam ad Romanos commentarius*, 1661-62; citing Acts 18:24-26.

PRISCILLA AND AQUILA. PETER MARTYR VERMIGLI: Why Paul places the woman before the man we do not know, but it is obvious that the love of each of them was notable, because for the sake of Paul they placed their own lives in danger. Therefore the apostle confesses that not only he himself is very much in their debt, but also all the churches of the Gentiles. It is evident that they provided a great benefit for all, in preferring their teacher and master over themselves. COMMENTARY ON ROMANS 16:3.[16]

PRISCILLA AND AQUILA RESCUED PAUL. DAVID PAREUS: He proclaims an example of singular constancy toward them and the reason for his goodwill toward them, because they had not hesitated for his sake to intervene immediately when his life was at stake. When and how they did so he does not mention. It is likely that it happened at Corinth when the Jews hauled Paul amid a mob to the tribunal of Gallio the proconsul. At that time they surely pled Paul's case with all courage and kept him safe—unless perhaps they did the same thing rather in the mob that broke out in Ephesus (Acts 19:22). On behalf of this act of kindness of theirs, he professes that he and all the churches of the Gentiles offer them their undying thanks. And not undeservedly, for through them the apostle had been saved so that the churches could be taught by him for a longer time. Thus the fruit of their courage redounded to the good of Paul and all the churches. COMMENTARY ON ROMANS 16:4.[17]

16:5a What Is a Church?

A TRUE CHURCH LIVES UNDER ONE ROOF. PETER WALPOT: That the community is not flung aside and torn to shreds by them is clearly and regularly proven. For Paul says that the congregation was in the house of Prisca and Aquila. Also the congregation at Laodicea in the house of Nymphas,[18] as Paul writes and greets them. Archippus, Paul's fellow soldier, also had a congregation living in his house. Now did they reside in these houses jointly? Indeed. They demonstrated in other matters that they held all things in common as in Jerusalem. They did not behave like the world or like today's falsely called "brothers," who without shame eat at a divided table—one better off, the other worse off. THE GREAT ARTICLE BOOK: ON PEACE AND JOINT PROPERTY.[19]

A BODY OF BELIEVERS. THEODORE BEZA: "The church," *ekklēsian*, that is, the assembly of the faithful. For there were those who were notable first for their piety and then for their erudition, as Luke and Paul himself attest, who numbers them among his colleagues. Nor is it astonishing that in so large a city that there were distinct gatherings of the faithful. Erasmus preferred to translate the word as "congregation," perhaps so that no one would surmise that the talk here was about some sacred building, as now that word is accustomed to be used, and many such things as that inept and ridiculous Abdias dared to babble on about in his *Lives of the Apostles*. But those words are adjoined to the third verse in the Codex Claromontanus, and perhaps more rightly so. ANNOTATIONS ON ROMANS 16:5.[20]

WHEREVER CHRIST IS. JUAN DE VALDÉS: In St. Paul's time, all the houses of Christians—where Christians were accustomed to hold their readings, their sermons, their prayers and discussions—were called churches. Their worship was Christian in Spirit and in truth. And here I understand, just as

---

[16]Vermigli, *A Commentarie upon the Epistle to the Romanes*, 454r* (*In Epistolam ad Romanos*, 640).

[17]Pareus, *In divinam Epistolam ad Romanos commentarius*, 1662-63; citing Acts 18:12-17.

[18]The Vulgate, following the Majority text, rendered this name and the corresponding possessive pronoun as masculine (Col 4:15). Most of the reformers accepted this; see, for example, Erasmus's discussion of the problem in *Annotations on Colossians* 4:15, LB 6:897 (cf. WADB 7:236-37).

[19]QGT 12:201; alluding to Rom 16:3-4; 1 Cor 16:19; Col 4:15; Philem 1:2.

[20]Beza, *Annotationes majores*, 2:150. Abdias was falsely attributed the author of a cycle of acts about the Twelve Apostles; today this author is called Pseudo-Abdias. See ANF 8:477-564.

Christ said, wherever two or three meet together in Christ's name, there Christ is too. Where Christ is, there is a church; where Christ is not, there is no church. COMMENTARY ON ROMANS 16:3-5.[21]

THOSE FAITHFUL WHO GATHER FOR INSTRUCTION AND WORSHIP. DAVID PAREUS: And this a notable praise of that couple, because the apostle praises them for having given their homes as a guest place for the church, since Christ, who is in the midst of the church, was dwelling with them. By "church" he either means their family that has been piously taught, which daily found time for holy reading and prayers amid their manual labors so that it was like a private church, or else he means the faithful who were accustomed to come together at that house for preaching and sacred matters. But where then were the basilicas of the Romans when the church was confined to the home of the one Aquila?

But let us note that the name "church" also applies to a few faithful people gathered in the name of Christ. Therefore all the privileges attributed to the church apply: namely, that it is the pillar and support of the truth, built on the rock, that it is led by the Holy Spirit into all truth according to the promise, "Where two or three are gathered in my name, I am in their midst." Nonetheless, nobody will conclude from that passage that some house church is simply infallible and cannot err or fail. Much less can these things be said about any particular larger church. Thus it is clear how ineptly the sophists try to squeeze out from those promises an absolute infallibility of the Roman Church, which they falsely call the Universal Church.

It also appears that the slander of the Jesuits is off base, namely, that there are a multitude of our churches that find fault with each other, even though in the creed we believe that there is only one church. They say, "You have a Wittenberg church, a Heidelberg church; you have as many churches as you have pastors. We believe in one Roman Catholic Church." They act as if not even the Scripture spoke of the Roman Church, the Corinthian Church, the Ephesian Church, etc. and distinguished those churches from the church catholic and designated by the name of the various churches certain particular assemblies (whether public or private, large or small) that are parts, as it were, of the one church—not the Roman Church, but the church catholic, which cannot be seen by the eyes but is embraced by faith. Moreover, by the same commendation the household of Aquila and Priscilla is praised in 1 Corinthians 16:9: "Aquila and Priscilla, along with the church that is in their home, greet you greatly in the Lord." From this passage there is an indication that they had changed residences and had earlier had a home in Ephesus, where Paul wrote that epistle sometime before this epistle to the Romans. Therefore they had migrated from Ephesus to Rome, whether for the sake of exercising their craft more readily there or for the sake of spreading the gospel. They seem not to have had a fixed abode. And yet, perhaps in a rented house, they wanted the church to dwell with them, first in Ephesus, then in Rome. Clearly it is an example of the rarest zeal, which faithful workers should imitate. But let the fathers of the household learn to rule the members of their household so that they may have a church in their home. In this way they will have Christ, God and a divine blessing in their home. COMMENTARY ON ROMANS 16:5.[22]

THE CHURCH IS A HOLY HOUSEHOLD. JOHANNES BRENZ: And here it should be observed that Paul calls these spouses' family a church. . . . By this example we learn that spouses do not hinder the church; no indeed, the true church is the domestic family. Accordingly we should acknowledge every pious family as a true church. Knowledge of this matter is useful for both faith and faith's fruit. For in any house where the family acknowledges Christ, there abides God the Father, Son and Holy Spirit, together with his angels,

[21]Valdés, *Commentary upon Romans*, 286* (*Commentario de Romanos*, 328); alluding to Jn 4:24; Mt 18:20.

[22]Pareus, *In divinam Epistolam ad Romanos commentarius*, 1663-65; citing Mt 18:20.

bringing every blessing and benefit. However, it should not be imagined that in such a family everything always is, according to external appearances, fortunate, but that everything whether in fortune or misfortune will tend toward good. According to that saying of Paul: "For those who love God all things work together for good, certainly they are called according to his purpose." The family of the patriarch Jacob was a church, in which God dwelled, but how great were their calamities and hardships! You see the same in David's family. But "all things work together for good." Knowledge of this matter stirs up in us zeal to do good works. For if the domestic family is a church, surely they should live most uprightly, not only in public but also at home. For in public a well-ordered church should not be reviled, should not gorge, should not be intoxicated, should not be characterized by any other abominable wicked deed. Thus also at home the church should perform no indecent act on account of the presence of God and his angels. COMMENTARY ON PAUL'S LETTER TO THE ROMANS.[23]

16:5b-15 *Various Greetings*

EPAENETUS, THE FIRSTFRUITS. DAVID PAREUS: That this man, whom he greets in the second place, was of great note is apparent from his attributes. For he calls him dear to himself. But nobody would be able to be so dear to so great an apostle unless he was adorned with a remarkable piety and virtue. He also calls him "the firstfruits of Achaea" (Origen reads "of Asia," as also does the Old Latin translation), either because he believed in Christ at an earlier time and preceded others in coming to faith, which was not a matter of mere modest praise, or because he surpassed the rest in his piety and zeal. Chrysostom combines the two meanings. So does Origen, who seeks a mystery in the latter explanation and says that the angels of God who help the church each offer one by one firstfruits from those who believe, but that the angels deem the firstfruits

to be not those who are first, temporally speaking, but those who excel in virtues and merits. He draws this opinion perhaps from that passage that is said in the Gospel: "Their angels constantly see the face of their Father in heaven." Again, "They rejoice over one sinner who repents," etc. But there is an allusion here to the ceremonies of the law, where the firstfruits are consecrated to God so that the remaining mass might be holy. Thus those who are the first to come to faith are rightly called the firstfruits, consecrated to God before the rest. Nonetheless this praise did not belong only to Epaenetus, for in 1 Corinthians 16:15 he also calls the household of Stephanas *aparchē achaias* ["the firstfruits of Achaea"]. Therefore perhaps a rather large number of people gave themselves to Christ in various regions of Achaea before others did. COMMENTARY ON ROMANS 16:5.[24]

MARY LIVED FOR OTHERS. DAVID PAREUS: In the third place, he greets and praises Mary, a holy woman, because she labored much on his behalf. How? Doubtlessly she furnished many things to the saints, things pertaining to hospitality, money for food and travel. But how had she labored for Paul, who had not seen her or been at Rome? Because she had helped other godly people, he praises her assistance to himself. And so he says, *eis hēmas*, not *eis eme*, "toward us" and not "toward me." For there was a fellowship of saints; either through letters or the retelling of other believers, he had learned who excelled beyond others in faith at Rome. And so he nonetheless knew by name and loved those whom he had not seen. COMMENTARY ON ROMANS 16:6.[25]

ANDRONICUS AND JUNIA. PETER MARTYR VERMIGLI: Blood relations alone would not have moved him. However, he remembers them rather cheerfully, because they suffered together with him. They came to Christ before Paul. They are called

---

[23]Brenz, *In Epistolam ad Romanos*, 376; citing Rom 8:28.

[24]Pareus, *In divinam Epistolam ad Romanos commentarius*, 1665-66; citing Mt 18:10; Lk 15:10.

[25]Pareus, *In divinam Epistolam ad Romanos commentarius*, 1666.

eminent among the apostles—not because they belonged to the company of the twelve apostles, but, as is more likely, because they had spread the gospel in many places and had raised up a fair number of churches. Origen believes that they could have belonged to the number of the seventy-two disciples.[26] I disagree, for they fell away from Christ. But in what sense does Paul attribute this to the wife? As if the apostolic office could be appropriate for her too? Perhaps they are said to be eminent among the apostles since they were, properly speaking, well-known to the apostles and not in the least undistinguished in the church of Christ. This sense does not displease me, if only because the very words do not oppose it. COMMENTARY ON ROMANS 16:7.[27]

COUNTED AS APOSTLES, EXCEPT JUNIA.

THEODORE BEZA: "Among the apostles," that is, their names are strong among the apostles. Or they are well-known to the apostles. For in this way now and again this name is taken in general for those who were emissaries of Christ's name, as in 2 Corinthians 8. But Junia—since you should most likely accept that name as female—Paul did not count among the apostles. ANNOTATIONS ON ROMANS 16:7.[28]

THE DIVINELY IMPLANTED LOVE OF FAMILY.

TILEMANN HESSHUS: Furthermore, in these greetings Paul shows that Christianity does not demand apatheian ["lack of feeling"], that is, that we remove all feelings of humanity and storgas ["love"]. For here Paul commends his own kinfolk and teaches by his example that those who are joined by blood should be accompanied with love and duty. For the Holy Spirit does not extinguish, but corrects nature. And God himself in his very creation has implanted in the hearts of spouses, parents, children and kinfolk sparks of natural benevolence and love so as to bind together as

tightly as possible the human race among itself by this bond. And if nature had remained uncorrupted, without sin, both an admirable wisdom and an admirable virtue would have shown in those very storgais ["tenderly affections"].

But now after humankind has fallen into sin, these affections have been foully contaminated, for the whole human nature has been disfigured. But nonetheless as much of natural benevolence is left from creation, it speaks a noteworthy testimony about God and is an item necessary for the conservation and propagation of the human race and agrees with the wisdom of the law. The Holy Spirit corrects the ataxiam ["disorder"] that was added to it from sin. Thereby he transforms us into the pristine image of God.

Therefore Christians who have been reborn through the Holy Spirit are not astorgoi ["heartless"]. They do not remove themselves from all humanity but embrace with true love those united by blood. Paul says, "If someone does not take care of especially his own family, they have denied the faith and are worse than an unbeliever."

They write about the anchorite Machetes that he threw into the fire a packet of unopened letters that he had received from his parents and friends, in order to show that he was not swayed by any desire for his parents and brothers.[29] This inhumanity and astorgia ["heartlessness"] is not a virtue pleasing to God or arising from the Holy Spirit, but instead is a gravely wicked deed that opposes the fourth commandment. COMMENTARY ON ROMANS 16:7-8.[30]

THE HOUSE OF NARCISSUS: GOD CREATED HOLINESS EX NIHILO.

TILEMANN HESSHUS: Exegetes think that the Narcissus whom Paul mentions was the Narcissus who is mentioned by Cornelius Tacitus and Suetonius in his Life of Claudius.[31] Since he was a freedman of Claudius, he was very thankful to the emperor and came to

---

[26]Origen, Commentary on Romans 10.21 (FC 104:293-94).

[27]Vermigli, In Epistolam ad Romanos, 640 (cf. A Commentarie upon the Epistle to the Romanes, 454r-v).

[28]Beza, Annotationes majores, 2:150; citing 2 Cor 8:23.

[29]See John Cassian, Institutes 5.32 (NPNF2 11:244-45).

[30]Hesshus, Explicatio Epistolae Pauli ad Romanos, 454v-455v.

[31]See Tacitus, Annals 11.29 (LCL 312:297–99); Suetonius, Lives of the Caesars 5.28 (LCL 38:57).

the very height of power, but a man contaminated by many disgraceful and shameful acts. The emperor permitted him to acquire and seize so much money that when he asked once about the low funds in the public treasury it was said that it would overflow with money if the two freedmen took it over as their common property.[32] Tacitus writes that Messalina was killed on the orders of this Narcissus.

But if this Narcissus is that Narcissus whom Paul mentions, we have a noteworthy example of the boundless mercy of God, because he nonetheless gathered a holy church for himself in the family of such a disgraceful and shameful person.

And let godly servants who are compelled to serve godless and disgraceful lords who fear neither God nor humans seek comfort here, because they have not been rejected by the Lord, but rather are cared for by him and loved by him. COMMENTARY ON ROMANS 16:11.[33]

MINISTRY LIKE PHOEBE'S. PETER MARTYR VERMIGLI: Perhaps he mentions these women, Tryphaena, Tryphosa, Persis and Mary, who worked because they had a ministry much like the one we said Phoebe had. COMMENTARY ON ROMANS 16:12.[34]

THE AUTHOR OF THE *SHEPHERD OF HERMAS*? THE ENGLISH ANNOTATIONS: Origen, a very learned and ancient writer, believed that this Hermas was the author of the book titled *Pastor*. Because the angel in it is said to appear in the likeness of a shepherd, Origen believed this book to be divinely inspired. But St. Jerome in his *Prologus Galeatus* counts it among the apocryphal books. And Eusebius in his third book of church history says that many in his time took exception against this book, even though many ascribed it to this Hermas whom St. Paul salutes. ANNOTATIONS ON THE EPISTLE OF PAUL TO THE ROMANS 16:14.[35]

16:16 *The Holy Kiss of the Church*

THIS SALUTATION IS CULTURALLY CONDITIONED. THE ENGLISH ANNOTATIONS: Paul calls that "a holy kiss" which proceeds from a heart that is full of holy love. Now this is to be referred to the custom of those days. ANNOTATIONS ON THE EPISTLE OF PAUL TO THE ROMANS 16:16.[36]

SYMBOL OF CHARITY. HULDRYCH ZWINGLI: Paul strongly alludes to the custom of his ancestors. It is as if he said, "As the people of this world receive one another with a kiss, so you in turn pursue them in charity." For a kiss is a symbol of sincere charity. ANNOTATIONS ON ROMANS 16:16.[37]

HARMONY, PEACE AND LOVE. DAVID PAREUS: Now by his own example he commends to them a mutual greeting, as the kiss was exchanged as a sign of peace and love among the Hebrews. He calls it a holy kiss, as opposed to a lascivious kiss. We explained the six kinds of kisses in our commentary on Genesis 29:11.[38] Thus Christians had a custom of kissing each other before Holy Communion, in order to attest their mutual love by that sign. Thus Origen says, "The apostle calls it a holy kiss, teaching first that the kisses that are given in the church are holy; next, that they are not feigned, as was the kiss of Judas, who kissed with his lips and yet pondered treason in his heart. But first let the faithful kiss be chaste; then it will have peace and genuineness in a love that is not pretend."[39] It is not a universal commandment, obliging all to

[32]Pallas was the other greedy freedman.
[33]Hesshus, *Explicatio Epistolae Pauli ad Romanos*, 456r-v.
[34]Vermigli, *A Commentarie upon the Epistle to the Romanes*, 454v* (*In Epistolam ad Romanos*, 640).
[35]Downame, ed., *Annotations*, CCC2v*; citing Origen, Commen-

tary on Romans 10.31 (FC 104:296-97); Jerome, "Preface to the Books of Samuel and Kings" (NPNF2 6:490); Eusebius, *Church History* 3.3 (NPNF2 1:135).
[36]Downame, ed., *Annotations*, CCC2v*; alluding to 1 Cor 16:20; 2 Cor 13:12; 1 Pet 5:14.
[37]Zwingli, *In plerosque Novi Testamenti Libros*, 447.
[38]The six categories of kisses, identified by holy and profane writers alike, are unchaste, chaste, friendly greeting, "exploratory" (e.g., some Roman husbands would kiss their wives to find out if they had been drinking), betrayal and holy. See David Pareus, *In Genesin Mosis commentarius* (Frankfurt am Main: Johann Rhodius, 1609), 1620.
[39]Origen, *Commentary on Romans* 10.33 (FC 104:297).

keep this rite, but rather commanding all to keep the substance itself signified by the kiss, that is, harmony, peace and love. COMMENTARY ON ROMANS 16:16.[40]

WE ARE ONE BODY. HEINRICH BULLINGER: There is only one catholic church of Christ, which acquires various names connected to various places. Now it is called Antiochene, then Alexandrine, later Jerusalemite, but also Roman. All of them are one body. They have one head, Christ. And they listen to the voice of their one and only shepherd. COMMENTARY ON ROMANS 16:16.[41]

---

[40]Pareus, *In divinam Epistolam ad Romanos commentarius*, 1671-72.

[41]Bullinger, *In Epistolam ad Romanos*, 182r; alluding to Jn 10:1-18.

16:17-24 FINAL INSTRUCTIONS AND GREETINGS

[17]I appeal to you, brothers, to watch out for those who cause divisions and create obstacles contrary to the doctrine that you have been taught; avoid them. [18]For such persons do not serve our Lord Christ, but their own appetites,[a] and by smooth talk and flattery they deceive the hearts of the naive. [19]For your obedience is known to all, so that I rejoice over you, but I want you to be wise as to what is good and innocent as to what is evil. [20]The God of peace will soon crush Satan under your feet. The grace of our Lord Jesus Christ be with you.

[21]Timothy, my fellow worker, greets you; so do Lucius and Jason and Sosipater, my kinsmen.

[22]I Tertius, who wrote this letter, greet you in the Lord.

[23]Gaius, who is host to me and to the whole church, greets you. Erastus, the city treasurer, and our brother Quartus, greet you.[b]

a Greek *their own belly*   b Some manuscripts insert verse 24: *The grace of our Lord Jesus Christ be with you all. Amen.*

OVERVIEW: Paul exhorts his readers to guard against any gospel different from the gospel he proclaimed, namely, that by grace through faith the cross and resurrection of Jesus Christ are for our justification and sanctification. He is most concerned as are the reformers that those who wanted to reinstate the ceremonial and dietary laws would unwind the freedom for which Christ had set his followers free. The commentators are aware that before the Last Day theological arguments and disagreements always exist in the church, as they did at the time of the Reformation.

In that light, they warn that wherever Christ builds his church the devil builds a cathedral beside it, and one must always be on guard against those who are divisive and destructive of the Christian community. When Paul did not succeed in convincing his colleagues, he often advised that they go separate ways, as the cause of the gospel mission is greater than human egos. Both Paul and our commentators see that the unity of the church is both a present reality but also a hope for the future. By his Holy Spirit Christ thwarts the wiles of the devil; the gospel is the power of God for the salvation of all who believe.

PREEMPTIVE PRECAUTIONS AGAINST THE DIVISIVE. DAVID PAREUS: Paul had begun to greet them by the churches' name. And then at verse 21 he adds greetings to other private individuals. Why, I ask, does he interrupt these greetings here? Because the same concern comes to his mind as among the Corinthians, Galatians and everywhere else: perhaps troublemakers in the Roman churches are rending their unity. Accordingly as a parenthetical aside he inserts an admonition that they take precautions against such troublemakers. COMMENTARY ON ROMANS 16:17.[1]

16:17-19 *United and Innocent in Christ*

THE ESSENCE OF PAUL'S TEACHING. JOHANNES OECOLAMPADIUS: The apostle rightly commends his teaching to them, lest they be lead astray by pseudo-apostles. And this is the summary of Paul's teaching: to be saved by faith in Christ, not by works. But pseudo-apostles commended Jewish ceremonies and enticed them away from faith to works. ANNOTATIONS ON ROMANS 16:17.[2]

BE NOT DISTURBED BY DISSENSION. DAVID PAREUS: It does not seem doubtful that he is censuring the Jews who, although professing the Christian faith, mix the keeping of the ceremonies

---

[1]Pareus, *In divinam Epistolam ad Romanos commentarius*, 1673.
[2]Oecolampadius, *In epistolam ad Rhomanos*, 107v.

of the law with the gospel and so distort the teaching of Christ and thereby throw the church into confusion by their causes of offense. Paul complains about such people now and then (Phil 3; 1 Tim 4; 2 Tim 3; Titus 1), calling them teachers of the law, evildoers, who overthrow entire households by teaching what is not right for the sake of filthy gain. But those were not the only ones. In later times there were many more such people, and today there are those who similarly distort the doctrine and disturb the peace of the church. Therefore the apostle warns that these people have to be watched and avoided, that is, excluded from the fellowship of the church, as Titus 3 says: "After one or two admonitions, avoid a heretical person." There Chrysostom, scolding the tyranny of a Roman, says quite clearly, "He did not say, 'Attack them and settle the matter with fists, fighting hand to hand,' but rather 'avoid them.'"

First, let us learn not to be offended at the present disputes about religion, since Satan already in apostolic times disturbed the church in various ways with schismatics and heretics. Even if disagreements are the work of Satan, nonetheless it does not follow thereupon that where there are disagreements or dissension about the faith, there the church does not exist, since Satan always stirs up disagreements not outside but inside the church. Next, let us remember that the authors of quarrels ought to be earnestly avoided. The best reason for avoiding them is that, if we are following precisely the rule and agreement of apostolic teaching, we will also not allow ourselves to be led away from it even one finger's width. But lest we come into danger here, let us observe the norm of the holy Scriptures as uniquely our North Star. Origen writes in a memorable sentence that by this means alone danger can largely be avoided at this time. He says, "See how near to dangers those people are who neglect to be trained in the divine Scriptures, from which ALONE discernment for this kind of examination is learned." Therefore Origen recognizes that the HOLY SCRIPTURES are not only a norm, but also the ONLY norm for contro-

versies of the faith—a point in opposition to the blasphemous dogma of the Jesuits that the Scripture is not a norm or at least it is not the only norm or the full norm, but only a partial norm of dogmas that must be completed by the traditions of the church. Incidentally, teaching something besides the doctrine of the Scripture is teaching something contrary to the Scripture when it comes to those things that pertain to the faith. COMMENTARY ON ROMANS 16:17.[3]

FOLLOWERS OF THE TRUE GOD OR OF FALSE GODS. JOHANNES OECOLAMPADIUS: Paul teaches to distinguish between true and false apostles. True apostles seek the glory of Christ, whom they serve with all ministers of God; false apostles do not make great the glory of Christ. True apostles seek what is profitable for others; pseudo-apostles are slaves to their own bellies. True apostles teach the Word of God; false apostles, however, smooth talk and flattery, not at all concerned with the Word of God, which they are not afraid to distort. ANNOTATIONS ON ROMANS 16:18.[4]

DECEITFUL APPEARANCES AND WORDS. THEODORE BEZA: "Through flattery," *dia tēs chrēstologias.* Since this word is made up of two words, it has thus a double force, which you are not able to express in Latin except by a long circumlocution. For first a *chrēstologos* is one who promises much with their words, but offers nothing in reality. Second, it is an individual who (if you should happen to hear them talk) you would say was more concerned about you and your advantage than about themselves. An example of this vice is the temptation of Satan by which he deceived Eve, although we do not have to go so far away to see very many and very clear examples of this. Thus Capitolinus says that the emperor Pertinax was commonly said to have been *chrēstologon,* because he spoke well but behaved badly or rather (as

---

[3]Pareus, *In divinam Epistolam ad Romanos commentarius,* 1674-76; citing Phil 3:2; 1 Tim 4:1-5; 2 Tim 3:6-8; Tit 1:7-16; 3:10. [4]Oecolampadius, *In epistolam ad Rhomanos,* 107v.

Aurelius Victor elegantly expressed it) because he was flattering rather than kind. ANNOTATIONS ON ROMANS 16:18.[5]

A WARNING FOR CHRISTIANS OF ALL TIMES AND PLACES. JUAN DE VALDÉS: What St. Paul urges here is necessary at all times. There are always tares among the wheat; there is no greater or more pernicious enemy than a domestic one. It is true that everything pestilent to Christian piety sprouts from false Christians, and not merely those who feign to be Christians, but even from those who convince themselves that they are Christians—indeed, these are the most pernicious. The mark that St. Paul gives by which false Christians are to be recognized is that they are always seditious, causing scandal—something very foreign to Christians. Sure, Christians cause scandal, but they do so as Christ did (and as Paul did). The difference between the scandal true Christians cause and false Christians I understand to be what St. Paul here states: False Christians scandalize true Christians by being opposed to the doctrine that St. Paul has established in this epistle.

By "doctrine" he does not mean the gospel—as he did in chapter 6, where he called it a form of doctrine. Instead he calls doctrine the Christian instruction that is needed after having faith, infused by the gift of God by which the gospel is received. . . .

Christians need the wisdom of the serpent in order not to be deceived in Christian matters by worldly human beings. Likewise, I understand that Christians need the simplicity of the dove, in order to pass nimbly by the things of this present life as things that do not concern them, yes, as things that are entirely foreign to them. COMMENTARY ON ROMANS 16:17-19.[6]

EXCOMMUNICATION IS FOR THE HEALTH OF THE CHURCH AND ITS PEOPLE. DIRK PHILIPS: Without evangelical separation God's congregation may not exist. For if the unfruitful branches of the vine are not cut, they injure the good and fruitful branches. If one does not expel that kind of member, then the whole body must perish; that is, if one does not exclude public sinners, trespassers and unlawful ones, the entire congregation will become impure. And if one retains the false brothers, one becomes a participant in their sins, and in this regard we have many examples and testimonies in the Scripture. . . . Out of such and similar histories and examples of holy Scripture, it is well to notice and understand how no congregation may exist before God when they do not use the ban or separation in an orderly and humble manner according to the command of Christ, the teaching and example of the apostles. But the common saying applies exactly here, that a little leaven sours the whole dough and a scabby sheep makes the whole flock unclean. Yes, just as the priest or prophet is, so also are the people.

The separation must also be used in order that those who have sinned, being chastised in the flesh and made ashamed, may amend themselves and remain redeemed in the day of Jesus, which is the highest love, and the best of all healing stuff or medicine for their sick soul. . . . Necessity requires such also, that one shall separate the fallen or evil one, so that the name of God, the gospel of Jesus Christ and the congregation of the Lord shall not be defamed on account of it. . . . What the congregation of the Lord thus judges with his Word is judged before God. THE ENCHIRIDION: THE CONGREGATION OF GOD.[7]

THE IMPORTANCE OF OBEDIENCE AND SIMPLICITY FOR PIETY. DESIDERIUS ERASMUS: The first step toward piety is obedience. And yet you must constantly keep in mind whom to obey.

---

[5]Beza, *Annotationes majores*, 2:151. The son of a freed slave, Pertinax (126–193) was Roman emperor for three months; the Praetorian guard executed him in response to his attempts to reform their discipline.
[6]Valdés, *Commentary upon Romans*, 288, 289* (*Commentario de Romanos*, 331, 332); alluding to Mt 13:24-30, 36-43; 10:16.

[7]CRR 6:368, 369* (BRN 10:399-400); citing Jn 15:5; Mt 5:30; 18:17; 1 Cor 5:10; 1 Thess 5:14; 2 Jn 11; 1 Cor 5:6; Hos 6:9; 1 Cor 5:3-5; Ps 50:21; Ezek 36:20; Rom 2:24.

Simplicity ought to be praised; and yet since it does not know how to be suspicious, it is often subject to deception. Consequently I want you to be simple in such a way that while you do not harm or deceive anyone, you are nevertheless wise and keep your eyes open to pursue what is good and avoid things that corrupt the integrity of piety. PARAPHRASE ON ROMANS 16:19.[8]

16:20 Trample Satan

GOD'S VICTORY OVER SATAN. JOHANN WILD: Satan means "adversary"; by this name we understand either the devil or false teachers or even persecutors. But even the words themselves bear an emphasis. First, he makes God—not the saints or any creature—the author of peace. Second, he says, "God himself will crush Satan." For the devil is too strong to be crushed by our strength. Third, "under the feet," where he promises Christians perfect dominion and victory over all evils. Fourth, he adds, "Under your feet," for he subjects the devil to godly people, but rouses Satan against the ungodly so that they may learn how big a difference there is between serving God and serving the devil. Fifth, he adds, "Quickly." Their destruction does not sleep. And the psalmist says: "Like grass they will quickly dry up," etc. Hence Jeremiah sees a branch standing watch and hastening. For the judgment of God always comes on those not expecting it. EXEGESIS OF ROMANS 16:20.[9]

ALL CHRIST'S ENEMIES WILL SUFFER THE SAME FATE. HEINRICH BULLINGER: By "Satan" he means every force opposed to Christ and his gospel, whether they are false apostles or tyrants. This sentence of consolation is added because of their circumstances, lest on account of the false prophet's fraud they are grieved excessively. COMMENTARY ON ROMANS 16:20.[10]

THE SAFETY OF THE CHURCH. TILEMANN HESSHUS: He adds a noteworthy comfort to the admonition: God will keep in check the plots, the cunning and tricks of Satan, and our labor in teaching and preaching will not be in vain. Indeed, we are too unknown to be able to avoid and wipe away all the tricks and snares of the devil. But God says that he will be present with us with his Spirit, and he himself will crush Satan underneath our feet, reveal his deceptions, keep his power in check, throw his plans into confusion and impede his attempts. But he will console the church, comfort the godly with his Spirit, watch over them and will not allow the ministry "to be tested beyond your strength," but at last will grant glorious victory to the godly so that with great joy they may rule over sin, death, Satan and hell. For Christ overcame the world, and the prince of this world has been cast out. Now Paul took this phrase from Genesis 3, where it is said, "The seed of the woman will crush the head of the serpent." For when Christ crushed and destroyed all of Satan's power, all who are grafted into Christ by faith are in this way victors over Satan and they admirably conquer his astuteness and power. Even boys and girls in their confession of the faith have indeed conquered every cruelty of his. Therefore let not pious minds grow despondent in such great struggles, and let them not be disturbed either by their own weakness or Satan's power, but let them always be mindful of this divine promise. As in the beginning of the epistle, so here at the end he desires at Rome the grace of our Lord Jesus Christ, that is, all the benefits of the Redeemer. This is to show that his entire heart beats for nothing other than the safety of the church. COMMENTARY ON ROMANS 16:20.[11]

PAUL'S SIGNATURE BENEDICTION. DAVID PAREUS: He closes the exhortation with a prayer as he implores the grace of our Lord Jesus Christ on each and every one of them, by which alone they may be able to fulfill what he has commanded: to

---

[8]CWE 42:89.
[9]Wild, Exegesis in Epistolam ad Romanos, 269r-v; citing Ps 37:2; Jer 1:11-12.
[10]Bullinger, In Epistolam ad Romanos, 183r.

[11]Hesshus, Explicatio Epistolae Pauli ad Romanos, 458v-459r; citing 1 Cor 10:13; Gen 3:15.

despise and avoid impostors, to discern wisely good things from evil, and finally to evade and overcome the stratagems of Satan. With this prayer he began the epistle in chapter 1, verse 7; now he closes it with the same prayer. There he joined "grace and peace," and implored it from the Father as much as from the Son, which we saw was his argument for the equal power and goodness of the Father and the Son. Here he recalls only the grace of Christ, since he encompasses everything under it and deems that he has sufficiently shown that Christ is the only dispenser of every grace.

Furthermore, from 2 Thessalonians [3]:17 it is certain that this prayer is the genuine signature of all the genuine letters of Paul. He says, "This is the seal in every epistle; so I write: the grace of our Lord Jesus Christ be with you all. Amen." Thus we have a clear argument that this epistle is truly apostolic and Paul's. Even if the rest of the epistle were written through the agency of an amanuensis, Paul appends this prayer with his own hand, whereby its author could be clearly recognized. The same phrase is repeated in verse 24. Also Chrysostom has that phrase here and there, but Origen and Ambrose have it only in this passage. The Syriac has it in this verse and repeats it at the end after the *doxologian* ["doxology"]. The variation has arisen perhaps from the fact that this entire epilogue was formerly interpolated by Marcion from chapter 15 to be at the end, as Origen attests.[12] More about that later. COMMENTARY ON ROMANS 16:20.[13]

16:21-23 Paul's Team: Timothy, Tertius and Gaius

FOUR ADDITIONAL SIGNERS. DAVID PAREUS: With the parenthesis completed, he continues others' greetings to the Romans, partly so that the letter may foster a connection between brothers situated far apart, and partly so that the epistle, confirmed by so many signers, as it were, may have greater weight with the Romans. For even if the

authority of Paul did not need anyone else's testimony, nonetheless the harmony of the godly was doing not just a little to strengthen the Romans. Nor do we reject or despise the orthodox concord of the church, as the papists slander, but we greatly value it, require it and commend it, because from it not just a little strength is added to our faith, because we have been persuaded that not just we alone, but rather many people, indeed all godly people, have always believed in this way about God, Christ and the way of salvation.

He joins four witnesses here. The first of them is Timothy; one can find in the history of Acts 16 about his circumcision and adoption into the family and discipline of Paul. He was at that time a colleague of Paul's in Corinth. He calls the three remaining individuals his relatives. Origen suggests that Lucius is Luke the Evangelist, whom Paul in three other passages (Col 4:14; 2 Tim 4:11; Philemon 24) attests was a dear and inseparable person like his Achates.[14] I think rather that Lucius of Cyrene is to be understood, who was numbered along with Saul among the prophets of the church in Antioch in Acts 13:1. Jason doubtlessly is the person whose hospitality, courage and prudence is praised in Acts [17]:5. For he received Paul and his friends in his home at Thessalonica, and when a riot had been stirred because of it and the Jews had invaded his home, he endured the violence of the crowd and calmed the madness of the Jews with a prudent defense. Origen thinks that Sosipater was that Sopater from Berea, who (along with Timothy and Gaius from Derbe) is said in Acts 20:4 to have led Paul as he was sailing to Syria. COMMENTARY ON ROMANS 16:21.[15]

WHICH GAIUS? THEODORE BEZA: Three men named Gaius are mentioned in the apostolic record: one at Derbe, who accompanied Paul (Acts 20:4); another in Macedonia, who also was himself one of Paul's followers (Acts 19:29); and a third at

---

[12]Origen, *Commentary on Romans* 10.43.2 (FC 104:307-8).
[13]Pareus, *In divinam Epistolam ad Romanos commentarius*, 1679-80.

[14]Achates was a faithful friend of Aeneas and a model for friendship in the Roman world.
[15]Pareus, *In divinam Epistolam ad Romanos commentarius*, 1681-82. See Origen, *Commentary on Romans* 10.39.1 (FC 104:304).

Corinth, whom Paul himself baptized (1 Cor 1:14), who is probably the one mentioned here. And thus I agree with those who think that this letter was written at Corinth when the apostle came there, as he himself indicated in 2 Corinthians 12:14, namely, on that last journey into Greece, which is described at the beginning of Acts 20. When he had departed from there and come to Jerusalem, he was captured there and transported at last from there to Rome. ANNOTATIONS ON ROMANS 16:23.[16]

ERASTUS, CORINTH'S TREASURER. DAVID PAREUS: Graec. *oikonomos tēs poleōs* ["the city treasurer"]. Origen and the Old Latin translation renders it "treasurer," while others translate it "treasurer of the city," namely, of Corinth, where he was writing these things. About him Paul says in 2 Timothy 4:20, "Erastus remained at Corinth, namely, devoting his time to the public office of the state"; nonetheless, here he is said to have given his assent to the departure and ministry of Paul and to have been sent by him with Timothy to Macedonia. He was a political man, with a splendid reputation, inasmuch as he was put in charge of the city's treasurer. Nonetheless, he was a godly man and diligent toward the apostle and Christian brothers.

Because the apostle mentioned his office, he showed by that very fact that neither the riches nor the worries of preeminence nor any other of these things is an impediment for him who had given himself to Christ. Origen makes him an allegorical treasury, that is, a dispenser of that city whose architect and builder is God, that is, of the church, and so he says, "Paul did not mention the name of which city he was treasurer."[17] Nonetheless, he leaves it unresolved whether it ought to be understood allegorically or literally. Let the literal sense be retained. COMMENTARY ON ROMANS 16:23.[18]

16:24 *Our Lord's Grace and Blessing*

DISAGREEMENTS ABOUT VERSE 24. THEODORE BEZA: Because these same things have been placed shortly before, namely, in verse 20, they are not repeated here in Ambrose and Origen or in the very ancient Constantinopolitan Codex. In Chrysostom they are not added in the previous location but only here, and then after the *doxologian* ["the doxology"], that is to say, so that they close out the letter. Erasmus agrees. ANNOTATIONS ON ROMANS 16:24.[19]

---

[16]Beza, *Annotationes majores*, 2:151-52.

[17]Origen, *Commentary on Romans* 10.42 (FC 104:307).
[18]Pareus, *In divinam Epistolam ad Romanos commentarius*, 1683-84.
[19]Beza, *Annotationes majores*, 2:152.

16:25-27 DOXOLOGY

²⁵Now to him who is able to strengthen you according to my gospel and the preaching of Jesus Christ, according to the revelation of the mystery that was kept secret for long ages ²⁶but has now been disclosed and through the prophetic writings has been made known to all nations, according to the command of the eternal God, to bring about the obedience of faith— ²⁷to the only wise God be glory forevermore through Jesus Christ! Amen.

OVERVIEW: Paul ends his letter with a benediction that witnesses to the grace of Christ and appeals to his apostolic office in order to lend authority to this epistle. Our commentators note that Paul skillfully weaves together doctrine and praise, exalting the mystery of God revealed in Christ for all people. The good news that has been revealed in Jesus Christ led both Paul and the reformers to declare the glory and wonders of God.

TEXT-CRITICAL NOTES ABOUT THE DOXOLOGY. DAVID PAREUS: Origen noted that this *doxologian* ["doxology"] was once removed by Marcion, but in other manuscripts that were not defiled by Marcion it was found to have been placed in various places. For in some it was added in chapter 14 after the words, "Whatever is not of faith is sin." And thus Chrysostom expounded on it there, not here. But other codices have placed it here, as we now have it. Therefore, leaving it here, we judge (and not without very good reasons) that the apostle wanted to close this most noble epistle with such a praise of God. COMMENTARY ON ROMANS 16:25.[1]

A CONFUSING BUT IMPORTANT SUMMARY OF THE LETTER. JUAN DE VALDÉS: The order of the text in the Greek itself is confused—the sentences run one into another. Still they are all of great importance, since the intention of the whole epistle is condensed into them. COMMENTARY ON ROMANS 16:25-27.[2]

ROMANS IS ABOUT JUSTIFICATION BY FAITH ALONE. JOHANN WILD: He does two things in these words. First, he concludes briefly what he wanted to teach in this epistle when he says, "according to my gospel," etc. "in manifestation of the mystery," as if he were to say, "By this epistle I desired nothing else than to manifest that mystery which was once silent, namely, that we are justified by faith alone in Christ and not by any of our merits. Therefore I wanted to teach and persuade the obedience of faith, not based on myself, but on the commandment of God. And so this is what I wanted to teach in the whole epistle," etc. Second, the epistle ends with a thanksgiving, "for we were created for these things." Hence "Whatever you do, do it for the glory of God." EXEGESIS OF ROMANS 16:25-27.[3]

DOCTRINE AND PRAISE INTERTWINED. HEINRICH BULLINGER: Now Paul concludes his epistle with a wonderful epilogue, simultaneously weaving together the sum of the gospel and singing the praise of God. Concerning the sum of the gospel enough has been said in the inscription of this epistle, please consider conferring the commentary there. This one thing remains to be expounded: how the gospel was passed over in silence from eternity, until at last it was revealed in the time of the apostles. Therefore it had been satisfactorily known among the Jews, but hidden to the Gentiles; why this is the case stands in

---

[1]Pareus, *In divinam Epistolam ad Romanos commentarius*, 1685; citing Rom 14:23.
[2]Valdés, *Commentary upon Romans*, 292* (*Commentario de Romanos*, 336).

[3]Wild, *Exegesis in Epistolam ad Romanos*, 270r; citing Is 43:7; 1 Cor 10:31. That Wild is a Catholic makes this comment all the more remarkable.

Ephesians chapters 2 and 4. COMMENTARY ON ROMANS 16:25-27.[4]

GIVE THANKS TO GOD. TILEMANN HESSHUS: In this final passage, Paul thanks God for the very rich doctrine of this epistle and the revelation of the gospel. And just as he set forth a splendid definition of the gospel already in the introduction to the epistle, so he repeats it here at the end, so that its reader might remember it. He also repeats the chief points of doctrine, namely, that the gospel of Christ is a secret mystery unknown to reason and to the human race but has been revealed through Jesus Christ. Paul also leads us back to the Scripture of the prophets, by which we ought to seek the true knowledge and solid foundations of this mystery. He also shows the goal for which the entire ministry was established, namely, so that obedience may be rendered to the faith. Finally, he repeats the doctrine of the calling of the Gentiles and of the universal promise.

Therefore we together with the apostle Paul give thanks to the eternal and almighty God with all our heart and with true sighs, both for all his countless and boundless benefits and for the marvelous revelation of the gospel concerning our Lord Jesus Christ, through which he has also called us into fellowship with his church and offers us freely the forgiveness of sins, righteousness, life, and eternal and heavenly glory. We also give thanks to the Son of God for this incomparable treasure, because he by Paul's ministry has explained with such perspicuity the benefits of his kingdom in this letter. Let the same be done through the Holy Spirit that we may persist continually in this salvific doctrine and exalt him in all eternity with all the elect. Amen. *Theō doxa* ["to God be the glory"]. COMMENTARY ON ROMANS 16:25-27.[5]

16:25 Strength in the Mystery of the Gospel

IN, THROUGH AND WITH GOD ALONE. JUAN DE VALDÉS: By saying "to him who is able to

strengthen you" St. Paul means God who in his might is able to strengthen you and to confirm his election and his vocation in you. It is as if he should say, "You could not do it yourselves unless God works it in you." COMMENTARY ON ROMANS 16:25-27.[6]

NO OTHER FOUNDATION. DAVID PAREUS: He teaches that our faith and consolation have been established on the gospel alone, not on the law or philosophy. COMMENTARY ON ROMANS 16:25.[7]

PAUL'S GOSPEL IS JESUS' GOSPEL. JUAN DE VALDÉS: By saying "according to my gospel" I understand St. Paul to mean, "God is able to strengthen you in concord with what is preached and affirmed in the gospel that I preach." The expressions "the preaching of Jesus Christ" and "my gospel" are synonymous. COMMENTARY ON ROMANS 16:25-27.[8]

THE GOSPEL IS SALVATION THROUGH CHRIST IN FAITH. HULDRYCH ZWINGLI: He defines what his gospel is. For the gospel is the revelation of what is hidden and mysterious—what was unknown to past generations and many ages— announced and proclaimed through the apostles. And this was the mystery: all people are saved through Christ in faith and not by their own works. ANNOTATIONS ON ROMANS 16:25.[9]

THE GOSPEL IS ETERNAL. JUAN DE VALDÉS: When St. Paul says, "it was kept secret," he means that there was indeed a gospel, but that it had not been promulgated to all human beings, although revealed to some. It is as if a prince would declare an indulgence or general pardon to all the criminals in his kingdom, but for a time he does not choose to promulgate it, but let a

---

[4]Bullinger, *In Romanos Epistolam*, 183v-184r; citing 2 Thess 3:17.
[5]Hesshus, *Explicatio Epistolae Pauli ad Romanos*, 460r-v.

[6]Valdés, *Commentary upon Romans*, 292* (*Commentario de Romanos*, 336).
[7]Pareus, *In divinam Epistolam ad Romanos commentarius*, 1687.
[8]Valdés, *Commentary upon Romans*, 292* (*Commentario de Romanos*, 336).
[9]Zwingli, *In plerosque Novi Testamenti Libros*, 448. Beza agrees; see *Annotationes majores*, 2:152.

chosen few discover it privately. COMMENTARY ON ROMANS 16:25-27.[10]

MYSTERY OF THE INCARNATE WORD AND OUR STRENGTH. CARDINAL CAJETAN: Whether by the term "mystery" in this passage the mystery of the Word incarnate or the mystery of Christians' strength should be understood is not easy to distinguish. According to the literal sense, nevertheless, it seems to indicate the mystery of the Word incarnate, not only in himself but also in his fruit. And so both are included: indeed Christians' strength is according to the revelation of the mystery of the incarnate Word. COMMENTARY ON ROMANS 16:25.[11]

16:26 Full Revelation of the Hebrew Scripture's Essence

PROPHETIC AND APOSTOLIC AGES. CARDINAL CAJETAN: The mystery of the Word incarnate was passed over in silence from eternity past, known by God alone. But now it has been revealed in the coming of the Messiah through the writings of the prophets. He indicates two ages. One of the prophets who preached this mystery, but it was not yet revealed at that time, because the prophets wrote about it under a veil. The other is the age of the apostles, beginning with Christ. And this proved by saying "now revealed" by the testimony also of the prophet's writings. COMMENTARY ON ROMANS 16:26.[12]

NO NEW DOCTRINE. PETER MARTYR VERMIGLI: By this assertion he answers their thinking, which suspected the gospel to be a new doctrine. "It is not," says he, "for it was before the world began, but it was hidden with silence and kept secret a long time." But why God even from the beginning revealed unto some of the fathers, although indeed to a very few, so great a secret, namely, that all humankind

should by so wonderful a means be renewed and saved by Christ, and why he revealed this to the people of the Jews only, and that not otherwise than in shadows and prophecies, we cannot attain to by our own conjectures or understanding. For God according to his most high liberty and wisdom showed this secret both when, and to whom and in what sort he himself wanted. COMMENTARY ON ROMANS 16:25-27.[13]

THE ETERNALITY OF THE GOSPEL. JOHN CALVIN: The other things are mentioned to commend the power and dignity of the gospel. Paul calls the gospel "the preaching of Jesus Christ" inasmuch as the whole sum and substance of it is no doubt included in the knowledge of Christ. Its doctrine is "the revelation of the mystery," and this its character ought not only to make us more attentive to hear it but also to impress on our minds the highest veneration for it. And he intimates how sublime a secret it is by adding that it was hidden for many ages, from the beginning of the world.

It does not indeed contain a turgid and proud wisdom, such as the children of this world—by whom it is held on this account in contempt—seek, but it unfolds the ineffable treasures of celestial wisdom, much higher than all human learning. Since the very angels regard them with wonder, surely none of us can sufficiently admire them. But this wisdom ought not to be less esteemed because it is conveyed in a humble, plain and simple style. Thus it has pleased the Lord to bring down the arrogance of the flesh.

And as it might have created some doubt how this mystery, concealed for so many ages, could have so suddenly emerged, he teaches us that this has not happened through the hasty actions of human beings or through chance but through the eternal ordination of God. Here also he closes the door against all those curious questions that the waywardness of the human mind is wont to raise. For whatever happens suddenly and unexpectedly,

[10]Valdés, *Commentary upon Romans*, 293* (*Commentario de Romanos*, 336).
[11]Cajetan, *In Sacrae Scripturae Expositionem*, 5:83.
[12]Cajetan, *In Sacrae Scripturae Expositionem*, 5:83.
[13]Vermigli, *A Commentarie upon the Epistle to the Romanes*, 456v* (*In Epistolam ad Romanos*, 643).

they think, happens at random, and hence they absurdly conclude that the works of God are unreasonable—or at least they entangle themselves in many perplexing doubts. Paul therefore reminds us that what appeared then suddenly had been decreed by God before the foundation of the world.

But that no one might raise a dispute on the subject, and charge the gospel with being a new thing, and thus defame it, he refers to the prophetic Scriptures, in which we now see that what is fulfilled had been foretold. For all the prophets have rendered to the gospel so clear a testimony that it can in no other way be so fully confirmed. And in this way God duly prepared the mind of his people, so that the newness of these unfamiliar matters would not upset them too much.

If anyone objects and says that there is an inconsistency in the words of Paul because he says that the mystery, of which God had testified by his prophets, was hidden throughout all the ages, the solution of this knot is plainly given by Peter. The prophets, when they sedulously inquired of the salvation made known to us, ministered, not to themselves, but to us. God then was at that time silent, though he spoke; for he held in suspense the revelation of those things concerning which he designed that his servants should prophesy.

In what sense he calls the gospel a hidden mystery—used here as well as in Ephesians 3 and Colossians 1—scholars do not completely agree. Certainly the idea that it refers to the calling of the Gentiles, which he states explicitly in Colossians, has more solidity. Now, though I allow this to be one reason, I yet cannot be brought to believe that it is the only reason. It seems to me more probable that Paul had also a regard to some other differences between the Old and the New Testament. For though the prophets formerly taught all those things that have been explained by Christ and his apostles, yet they taught them with so much obscurity that in comparison with the clear brightness of gospel light, it is no wonder that those things are said to have been hidden that are now made manifest. Nor was it indeed to no purpose that Malachi declared that the Sun of righteousness

would arise or that Isaiah had beforehand so highly eulogized the embassy of the Messiah. And lastly, it is not without reason that the gospel is called the kingdom of God. But we may conclude from the event itself that only then were the treasures of celestial wisdom opened, when God appeared to his ancient people through his only-begotten Son, as it were face to face, all shadows having been done away with. He again refers to the purpose (mentioned at the beginning of the first chapter) for which the gospel is to be preached: that God may lead all nations to "the obedience of faith." Commentary on Romans 16:25-27.[14]

16:27 The Only Wise God of Our Lord Jesus

Jesus Christ Is the Wisdom and Power of God. David Pareus: But the apostle calls us back to praising the power and wisdom of God because when both virtues shine forth in all matters, it is nonetheless especially resplendent in the gospel. For this doctrine surpasses the understanding of all creatures. By this doctrine God is preached as reconciled to human beings through and for the sake of the *lytron* ["atonement"] of his Son, so that he grants eternal life to those who believe in him. Besides this wisdom, all the wisdom of the world is folly. To God alone. Chrysostom rightly observes that the Son is not excluded, because he is the eternal Wisdom of the Father; rather "God" is here the opposite of "all creatures." Through Jesus Christ. It is not that God is wise through Christ, but that he revealed his wisdom to the world through him. Or the phrase refers to the following phrase: *hē doxa*, "may glory be" through Jesus Christ to God who alone is wise. Origen correctly says, "The glory is brought back to God 'through Jesus Christ,' who shows that God alone is so wise that he himself begat Wisdom, Jesus Christ, who is the Power of God and the Wisdom of God." Commentary on Romans 16:27.[15]

---

[14]CTS 38:553-56* (CO 49:290-92); citing 1 Pet 1:12; Eph 3:9; Col 1:26; Mal 4:2.

[15]Pareus, *In divinam Epistolam ad Romanos commentarius*, 1689-90.

A Trinitarian Benediction. Johann Wild: Nothing is full without Christ, because all things are through him. When he is recognized, God the Father is given praise through him, because God is known through him by his wisdom in which he saves those who believe in him. Therefore glory to the Father through the Son, that is, to both be glory in the Holy Spirit because each is united in one glory. The glory of our Lord Jesus Christ be with you all. AMEN. Exegesis of Romans 16:25-27.[16]

Additional Information. Cardinal Cajetan: Finally these additional words are found in the Greek: "To the Romans, sent from Corinth through Phoebe, minister of the church of Cenchreae." From this inscription it clearly indicates the place in which this epistle was written, agreeing with what was said above. And that it was sent through this woman named Phoebe who was the minister of the church of Cenchreae. It was not disgraceful for Paul to employ the kindness of a distinguished woman to deliver the letter—and according to her status in the world, going to Rome was not beneath her. For she was chosen as the safest and surest bearer of the epistle, on account of the customary reverence shown by this kind of woman and the certainty that she would not wander or be diverted to another place to be assaulted by men. Commentary on Romans 16:27.[17]

Daily Bread. Martin Luther: This epistle is really the chief part of the New Testament and the purest gospel, which is worthy not only that every Christian should know it word for word, by heart, but also that he should occupy himself with it every day, as the daily bread of the soul. It can never be read or contemplated too much and too well. And the more it's dealt with, the more precious it becomes and the better it tastes. Preface to Paul's Letter to the Romans (1546).[18]

Go and Live Accordingly. William Tyndale: Now reader, go and do according to the command of Paul's writing. First behold yourself diligently in the law of God and in it see your just damnation. Second, turn your eyes to Christ and see in him the exceeding mercy of your most kind and loving Father. Third, remember that Christ did not bring about this atonement for you to anger God again. Neither did Christ die for your sins, so that you should still live in them. Nor did he cleanse you, so that you should like a swine return to your old mud puddle again. But you are to be a new creature and live a new life according to the will of God and not according to the flesh. And be diligent, lest through your own negligence and unthankfulness you lose this favor and mercy again. Prologue on Romans.[19]

Prayer for God's Grace by His Spirit and Word. Philipp Melanchthon: May God govern our hearts with his Holy Spirit for the sake of our Lord Jesus Christ, that we may hold fast the gospel taught from heaven and go forward in knowledge and trust in Christ. May we adorn the glory of the gospel with all godly duties, and may God again grant a godly and lasting concord to the church. Amen. Thanks be to God! Commentary on Romans (1540).[20]

---

[16]Wild, *Exegesis in Epistolam ad Romanos*, 271v.
[17]Cajetan, *In Sacrae Scripturae Expositionem*, 5:84.
[18]LW 35:365* (WADB 7:3).
[19]Tyndale, *The Work of William Tyndale*, 144*.
[20]Melanchthon, *Commentary on Romans*, 297 (CO 15:796).

Map of Europe at the Time of the Reformation

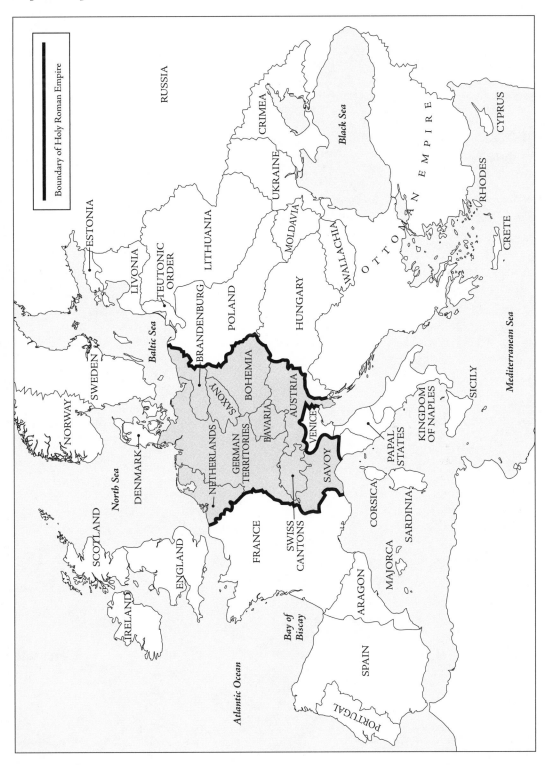

Boundary of Holy Roman Empire

RUSSIA

CRIMEA

Black Sea

CYPRUS

OTTOMAN EMPIRE

RHODES

CRETE

ESTONIA

UKRAINE

LIVONIA

LITHUANIA

MOLDAVIA

WALLACHIA

TEUTONIC ORDER

BRANDENBURG

POLAND

HUNGARY

Baltic Sea

SWEDEN

NORWAY

SAXONY

BOHEMIA

AUSTRIA

Mediterranean Sea

SICILY

NETHERLANDS

GERMAN TERRITORIES

BAVARIA

VENICE

KINGDOM OF NAPLES

North Sea

DENMARK

SAVOY

PAPAL STATES

SCOTLAND

FRANCE

SWISS CANTONS

CORSICA

SARDINIA

ENGLAND

MAJORCA

IRELAND

Bay of Biscay

ARAGON

SPAIN

Atlantic Ocean

PORTUGAL

Timeline of the Reformation

	German Territories	France	Spain	Italy	Switzerland	Netherlands	British Isles
1337–1453		d. Nicholas of Lyra Hundred Years' War	b. Paul of Burgos (Solomon ha-Levi)(d. 1435) Alonso Tostado (1400–1455)				Hundred Years' War
1378–1415		Western Schism (Avignon Papacy)		Western Schism			
1384							d. John Wycliffe
1414–1418					Council of Basel (1431–1437)		
1415				Council of Constance; d. Jan Hus; Martin V (r. 1417–1431); Council of Florence (1438–1445)			
1450	Invention of printing press						
1452				b. Leonardo da Vinci (d. 1519)			
1453				Fall of Constantinople			
1455–1485	b. Johannes Reuchlin (d. 1522)						War of Roses; rise of House of Tudor
1456	Gutenberg Bible						
1460				*Execrabilis*			
1466		b. Jacques Lefèvres d'Étaples (d. 1536)					
1467						b. Desiderius Erasmus (d. 1536)	b. John Colet (d. 1519)
1469	b. Antoius Broickwy von Königstein (d. 541)						
1470				b. Santes Pagninus (d. 1541)			b. John (Mair) Major (d. 1550)
1475				b. Michelangelo (d. 1564)			
1478	b. Wolfgang Capito (d. 1541)		Ferdinand and Isabella	b. Jacopo Sadoleto (d. 1547)			b. Thomas More (d. 1535)

	German Territories	France	Spain	Italy	Switzerland	Netherlands	British Isles
1480	b. Balthasar Hubmaier (d. 1528); b. Andreas Bodenstein von Karlstadt (d. 1541)						
1481–1530			Spanish Inquisition				
1482					b. Johannes Oecolampadius (d. 1531)		
1483	b. Martin Luther (d. 1546)						
1484	b. Johann Spangenberg (d. 1550)				b. Huldrych Zwingli (d. 1531)		
1485	b. Johannes Bugenhagen (d. 1554)						b. Hugh Latimer (d. 1555)
1486	r. Frederick the Wise, Elector (d. 1525); b. Johann Eck (d. 1543)						
1488	b. Otto Brunfels (d. 1534)						b. Miles Coverdale (d. 1568)
1489	b. Thomas Müntzer (d. 1525); b. Kaspar von Schwenckfeld (d. 1561)						b. Thomas Cranmer (d. 1556)
1491	b. Martin Bucer (d. 1551)		b. Ignatius Loyola (d. 1556)				
1492			Defeat of Moors in Grenada; Columbus discovers America; expulsion of Jews from Spain	Alexander VI (r. 1492–1503)			
1493	b. Justus Jonas (d. 1555)						
1494							b. William Tyndale (d. 1536)
1496	b. Andreas Osiander (d. 1552)					b. Menno Simons (d. 1561)	
1497	b. Philipp Melanchthon (d. 1560); b. Wolfgang Musculus (d. 1563); b. Johannes (Ferus) Wild (d. 1554)						
1498				d. Girolamo Savonarola	b. Conrad Grebel (d. 1526)		

	German Territories	France	Spain	Italy	Switzerland	Netherlands	British Isles
1499	b. Johannes Brenz (d. 1570) b. Justus Menius (d. 1558)			b. Peter Martyr Vermigli (d. 1562)			
1500			b. Charles V (–1558)				
1501	b. Erasmus Sarcerius (d. 1559)						
1502	Founding of University of Wittenberg			Julius II (r. 1503–1513)		b. Frans Titelmans (d. 1537)	
1504					b. Heinrich Bullinger (d. 1575)		
1505	Luther joins Augustinian Order			b. Benedict Aretius (d. 1574)			
1506		b. Augustin Marlorat (d. 1562)		Restoration to St. Peter's begins			
1507				Sale of indulgences approved to fund building			
1508	b. Lucas Lossius (d. 1582)						
1509		b. John Calvin (d. 1564)					r. Henry VIII (–1547)
1510	Luther moves to Rome			b. Immanuel Tremellius (d. 1580)			b. Nicholas Ridley (d. 1555)
1511	Luther moves to Wittenberg						
1512				Sistene Chapel completed			
1512–1517				Fifth Lateran Council; rejection of conciliarism			
1513	Luther lectures on Psalms			r. Pope Leo X (–1521)			b. John Knox (d. 1572)
1515	Luther lectures on Romans	r. Francis I (–1547); b. Peter Ramus (d. 1572)					
1516		Est. French National Church (via Concordat of Bologna)		Concordat of Bologna		Publication of Erasmus's Greek New Testament	
1517	Tetzel sells indulgences in Saxony; Luther's Ninety-five Theses						
1518	Heidelberg Disputation; Luther examined by Eck at Diet of Augsburg			Diet of Augsburg			

	German Territories	France	Spain	Italy	Switzerland	Netherlands	British Isles
1519	Leipzig Disputation	b. Theodore Beza (d. 1605)	Cortés conquers Aztecs; Portuguese sailor Magellan circumnavigates the globe		Zwingli appointed pastor of Grossmünster in Zurich; b. Rudolf Gwalther (d. 1586)		
1520	Publication of Luther's "Three Treatises"; burning of papal bull in Wittenberg		Coronation of Charles V	Papal Bull v. Luther: *Exsurge Domine*			
1521	Luther excommunicated; Diet/Edict of Worms—Luther condemned; Luther in hiding; Melanchthon's *Loci communes*	French-Spanish War (–1526)	French-Spanish War; Loyola converts	Papal excommunication of Luther			Henry VIII publishes *Affirmation of the Seven Sacraments* against Luther; awarded title "Defender of the Faith" by Pope
1521–1522	Disorder in Wittenberg; Luther translates New Testament						
1521–1525		First and Second Habsburg–Valois War					
1522	Luther returns to Wittenberg; Luther's NT published; criticizes Zwickau prophets; b. Martin Chemnitz (d. 1586)		Publication of Complutensian Polyglot Bible under Cisneros		Sausage Affair and reform begins in Zurich under Zwingli		
1523	Knight's Revolt	Bucer begins ministry in Strasbourg	Loyola writes Spiritual Exercises	r. Pope Clement VII (–1534)	Iconoclasm in Zurich		
1524	Luther criticizes peasants; d. Johann von Staupitz					Erasmus's disputation on free will	
1524–1526	Peasants' War						
1525	Luther marries; execution of Thomas Müntzer				Abolition of mass in Zurich; disputation on baptism; first believers' baptism performed in Zurich		
1526					Zurich council mandates capital punishment of Anabaptists	Publication of Tyndale's English translation of NT	

	German Territories	France	Spain	Italy	Switzerland	Netherlands	British Isles
1527	d. Hans Denck (b. c. 1500) d. Hans Hut (b. 1490) b. Tilemann Hesshus (d. 1588)			Sack of Rome by mutinous troops of Charles V	First Anabaptist executed in Zurich; drafting of Schleitheim Confession		
1528	Execution of Hubmaier						
1529	Second Diet of Speyer; evangelical "protest"; publication of Luther's catechisms; Marburg Colloquy; siege of Vienna by Turkish forces	Abolition of mass in Strasbourg			d. Georg Blaurock (b. 1492)		Thomas More appointed chancellor to Henry VIII
1530	Diet of Augsburg; Confession of Augsburg	d. Francois Lambert (Lambert of Avignon) (b. 1487)	Charles V crowned Holy Roman Emperor				
1531	Formation of Schmalkaldic League				d. H. Zwingli; succeeded by H. Bullinger		
1532		Publication of Calvin's commentary on Seneca; conversion of Calvin	b. Francisco de Toledo (d. 1596)				
1533	b. Valentein Weigel (d. 1588)	Nicholas Cop addresses University of Paris; Cop and Calvin implicated as "Lutheran" sympathizers	b. Juan de Maldonado (d. 1583)				Thomas Cranmer appointed as Archbishop of Canterbury; Henry VIII divorces
1534	First edition of Luther's Bible published	Affair of the Placards; Calvin flees d. Guillame Briçonnet (b. 1470)		Jesuits founded; d. Cardinal Cajetan (Thomas de Vio) (b. 1469)			Act of Supremacy; English church breaks with Rome
1535	Bohemian Confession of 1535; Anabaptist theocracy at Münster collapses after eighteen months				b. Lambert Daneau (d. 1595)		d. Thomas More; d. John Fisher

	German Territories	France	Spain	Italy	Switzerland	Netherlands	British Isles
1536	Wittenberg Concord; b. Kaspar Olevianus (d. 1587)				First edition of Calvin's *Institutes* published; Calvin arrives in Geneva (–1538); First Helvetic Confession	Publication of Tyndale's translation of NT; d. W. Tyndale	d. A. Boleyn; Henry VIII dissolves monasteries (–1541)
1537					Calvin presents ecclesiastical ordinances to Genevan Council		
1538					Calvin exiled from Geneva; arrives in Strasbourg (–1541)		
1539		Calvin publishes second edition of *Institutes* in Strasbourg		d. Felix Pratensis			Statute of Six Articles; publication of Coverdale's Wheat Bible
1540				Papal approval of Jesuit order			d. Thomas Cromwell
1541	Colloquy of Regensberg	French translation of Calvin's *Institutes* published	d. Juan de Valdés (b. 1500/1510)		d. A. Karlstadt; Calvin returns to Geneva (–1564)		
1542	d. Sebastian Franck (b. 1499)			Institution of Roman Inquisition			War between England and Scotland; James V of Scotland defeated; Ireland declared sovereign kingdom
1543	Copernicus publishes *On the Revolutions of the Heavenly Spheres*; d. Johann Eck (Johann Maier of Eck) (b. 1486)						
1545–1547	Schmalkaldic Wars; d. Martin Luther			First session of Council of Trent			b. Richard Bancroft (d. 1610)
1546	b. Johannes Piscator (d. 1625)						
1547	Defeat of Protestants at Mühlberg	d. Francis I; r. Henri II (–1559)					d. Henry VIII; r. Edward VI (–1553)
1548	Augsburg Interim (–1552) d. Caspar Cruciger (b. 1504) b. David Pareus (d. 1622)						

	German Territories	France	Spain	Italy	Switzerland	Netherlands	British Isles
1549	d. Paul Fagius (b. 1504)	d. Marguerite d'Angoulême (b. 1492)			Consensus Tigurinus between Calvin and Bullinger		First Book of Common Prayer published
1550	b. Aegidius Hunnius (d. 1603)						
1551–1552				Second session of Council of Trent			Cranmer's Forty-Two Articles
1552	d. Sebastian Münster (b. 1488) d. Friedrich Nausea (b. c. 1496)						
1553	d. Johannes Aepinus (b. 1449)						Book of Common Prayer revised; d. Edward VI; r. Mary I (1558)
1554							Richard Hooker (d. 1600)
1555	Diet of Augsburg; Peace of Augsburg establishes legal territorial existence of Lutheranism and Catholicism b. Johann Arndt (d. 1621)	First mission of French pastors trained in Geneva				b. Sibbrandus Lubbertus (d. 1625)	b. Lancelot Andrewes (d. 1626) b. Robert Rollock (d. 1599); d. Hugh Latimer; d. Nicholas Ridley d. John Hooper
1556	d. Pilgram Marpeck (b. 1495) d. Konrad Pellikan (b. 1478) d. Peter Riedemann (b. 1506)		Charles V resigns			d. David Joris (b. c. 1501)	d. Thomas Cranmer
1557					Michael Servetus executed in Geneva		Alliance with Spain in war against France
1558			d. Charles V				b. William Perkins (d. 1602); d. Mary I; r. Elizabeth I (–1603)
1559		d. Henry II; r. Francis II (–1560); first national synod of French reformed churches (1559) in Paris; Gallic Confession		First index of prohibited books issued	Final edition of Calvin's *Institutes*; founding of Genevan Academy	b. Jacobus Arminius (d. 1609)	Elizabethan Settlement

	German Territories	France	Spain	Italy	Switzerland	Netherlands	British Isles
1560	d. P. Melanchthon	d. Francis II; r. Charles IX (1574); Edict of Toleration created peace with Huguenots	d. Domingo de Soto (b. 1494)		Geneva Bible		Kirk of Scotland established; Scottish Confession
1561-1563				Third session of Council of Trent			
1561						Belgic Confession	
1562	d. Katharina Schütz Zell (b. 1497/98)	Massacre of Huguenots begins French Wars of Religion (–1598)					The Articles of Religion—in Elizabethan "final" form (1562/71)
1563	Heidelberg Catechism						
1564				b. Galileo (d. 1642)	d. J. Calvin		b. William Shakespeare (d. 1616)
1566	d. Johann Agricola (b. 1494)			Roman Catechism	Second Helvetic Confession		
1567						Spanish occupation	Abdication of Scottish throne by Mary Stuart; r. James VI (1603–1625)
1568						d. Dirk Phillips (b. 1504) Dutch movement for liberation (–1645)	Bishops' Bible
1570		d. Johannes Mercerus (Jean Mercier)		Papal Bull Regnans in Excelsis excommunicates Elizabeth I			Elizabeth I excommunicated
1571	b. Johannes Kepler (d. 1630)		Spain defeats Ottoman navy at Battle of Lepanto				b. John Downame (d. 1652)
1572		Massacre of Huguenots on St. Bartholomew's Day		r. Pope Gregory XIII (1583–1585)		William of Orange invades	b. John Donne (d. 1631)
1574		d. Charles IX; r. Henri III (d. 1589)					
1575	d. Georg Major (b. 1502); Bohemian Confession of 1575						
1576		Declaration of Toleration; formation of Catholic League		b. Giovanni Diodati (d. 1649)		Sack of Antwerp; Pacification of Ghent	

	German Territories	France	Spain	Italy	Switzerland	Netherlands	British Isles
1577	Lutheran Formula of Concord						England allies with Netherlands against Spain
1578	Swiss Brethren Confession of Hesse d. Peter Walpot		Truce with Ottomans				Sir Francis Drake circumnavigates the globe
1579			Expeditions to Ireland			Division of Dutch provinces	
1580	Lutheran Book of Concord						
1581			d. Teresa of Avila				Anti-Catholic statutes passed
1582				Gregorian Reform of calendar			
1583							b. David Dickson (d. 1663)
1584		Treaty of Joinville with Spain	Treaty of Joinville; Spain inducted into Catholic League; defeats Dutch at Antwerp			Fall of Antwerp; d. William of Orange	
1585	d. Josua Opitz (b. c. 1542)	Henri of Navarre excommunicated		r. Pope Sixtus V (–1590)			
1586							Sir Francis Drake's expedition to West Indies; Sir Walter Raleigh in Roanoke
1587	d. Johann Wigand (b. 1523)	Henri of Navarre defeats royal army					d. Mary Stuart of Scotland
1588		Henri of Navarre drives Henri III from Paris; assassination of Catholic League Leaders	Armada destroyed				English Mary defeats Spanish Armada
1589		d. Henri III; r. Henri (of Navarre) IV (–1610)	Victory over England at Lisbon				Defeated by Spain in Lisbon
1590		Henri IV's siege of Paris		d. Girolamo Zanchi (b. 1516)			Alliance with Henri IV
1592	d. Nikolaus Selnecker (b. 1530)						
1593		Henri IV converts to Catholicism					
1594		Henri grants toleration to Huguenots					

	German Territories	France	Spain	Italy	Switzerland	Netherlands	British Isles
1595		Henri IV declares war on Spain; received into Catholic Church		Pope Sixtus accepts Henri IV into Church			Alliance with France
1596		b. René Descartes (d. 1650) b. Moïse Amyraut (d. 1664)					
1598		Edict of Nantes; toleration of Huguenots; peace with Spain	Treaty of Vervins; peace with France				
1600	d. David Chytraeus (b. 1531)						
1601							b. John Trapp (d. 1669)
1602					d. Daniel Toussain (b. 1541)		
1603							d. Elizabeth I; r. James I (James VI of Scotland) (–1625)
1604	d. Cyriacus Spangenberg (b. 1528)						d. John Whitgift (b. 1530)
1605						b. Rembrandt (d. 1669)	Guy Fawkes and gunpowder plot
1606							Jamestown Settlement
1607							b. John Milton (d. 1674)
1608							
1610		d. Henri IV; r. Louis XIII (–1643)	d. Benedict Pererius (b. 1535)			The Remonstrance; Short Confession	
1611							Publication of Authorized English Translation of Bible (AV/KJV)
1612							b. Richard Crashaw (d. 1649)
1616							b. John Owen (d. 1683)
1617							b. Ralph Cudworth (d. 1689)
1618–1619						Synod of Dordrecht	
1618–1648	Thirty Years' War						
1620							English Puritans land in Massachusetts

	German Territories	France	Spain	Italy	Switzerland	Netherlands	British Isles
1621							d. Andrew Willet (b. 1562)
1633	d. Christoph Pelargus (b. 1565)						Laud becomes Archbishop of Canterbury
1637	d. Johann Gerhard (b. 1582)					*Statenvertaling*	
1638							d. Joseph Mede (b. 1638)
1640				Diodati's Italian translation of Bible published			
1642–1649							English civil wars; d. Charles I; r. Oliver Cromwell (1660)
1643		d. Louis XIII; r. Louis XIV (–1715)					
1643–1649							Westminster Assembly
1645							d. William Laud (b. 1573)
1648		Treaty of Westphalia ends Thirty Years' War					
1656	d. Georg Calixtus (b. 1586)						
1660							English Restoration; d. Oliver Cromwell; r. Charles II (–1685)
1662							Act of Uniformity
1664						d. Thieleman Jans van Braght (b. 1625)	d. John Mayer (b. 1583)
1671							d. William Greenhill (b. 1591)
1677							d. Thomas Manton (b. 1620)
1678						d. Anna Maria von Schurman (b. 1607)	
1688							Glorious Revolution; r. William and Mary (-1702); d. John Bunyan (b. 1628)
1691							d. Richard Baxter (b. 1615)

BIOGRAPHICAL SKETCHES OF
REFORMATION-ERA FIGURES AND WORKS

For works consulted, see "Sources for Biographical Sketches," p. 314.

Thomas Adams (1583–1653). English Puritan pastor in Buckinghamshire and London. A popular and eloquent Calvinist preacher, many of his sermons were published during his lifetime; his sermons were collected into three volumes after his death.

Johannes Aepinus (1499–1553). German Lutheran preacher and theologian. Aepinus studied under Martin Luther,* Philipp Melanchthon* and Johannes Bugenhagen* in Wittenberg. Because of his Lutheran beliefs, Aepinus lost his first teaching position in Brandenburg. He fled north to Stralsund and became a preacher and superintendent at Saint Peter's Church in Hamburg. In 1534, he made a diplomatic visit to England but could not convince Henry VIII to embrace the Augsburg Confession.* His works include sermons and theological writings. Aepinus became best known as leader of the Infernalists, who believed that Christ underwent torment in hell after his crucifixion.

Johann Agricola (c. 1494–1566). German Lutheran pastor and theologian. An early student of Martin Luther,* Agricola eventually began a controversy over the role of the law, first with Melanchthon* and then with Luther himself. Agricola claimed to defend Luther's true position, asserting that only the gospel of the crucified Christ calls Christians to truly good works, not the fear of the law. After this first controversy, Agricola seems to have radicalized his views to the

point that he eliminated Luther's *simul iustus et peccator* ("at the same time righteous and sinful") paradox of the Christian life, emphasizing instead that believers have no need for the law once they are united with Christ through faith. Luther responded by writing anonymous pamphlets against antinomianism. Agricola later published a recantation of his views, hoping to assuage relations with Luther, although they were never personally reconciled. He published a commentary on Luke, a series of sermons on Colossians, and a massive collection of German proverbs.

Henry Ainsworth (1571–1622/1623). English Puritan Hebraist. In 1593, under threat of persecution, Ainsworth relocated to Amsterdam, where he served as a teacher in an English congregation. He composed a confession of faith for the community and a number of polemical and exegetical works, including annotations on the Pentateuch, the Psalms and Song of Songs.

Henry Airay (c. 1560–1616). English Puritan professor and pastor. He was especially noted for his preaching, a blend of hostility toward Catholicism and articulate exposition of English Calvinism. He was promoted to provost of Queen's College Oxford (1598) and then to vice chancellor of the university in 1606. He disputed with William Laud* concerning Laud's putative Catholicization of the Church of England, particularly over the practice of genuflection, which Airay vehemently opposed. He also opposed fellow Puritans who wished to separate from the Church of England. His lectures on Philippians were his only work published during his lifetime.

Alexander (Ales) Alesius (1500–1565). Scottish Lutheran theologian. Following the martyrdom of his theological adversary Patrick Hamilton (c. 1504–1528), Alesius converted to the Reformation and fled to Germany. In 1535 Martin Luther* and Philip Melanchthon* sent him as an emissary to Henry VIII and Thomas Cranmer.* He taught briefly at Cambridge, but after the Act of Six Articles reasserted Catholic sacramental theology he returned to Germany, where he lectured at Frankfurt an der Oder and Leipzig. Alesius composed many exegetical, theological and polemical works, including commentaries on John, Romans, 1–2 Timothy, Titus and the Psalms.

Moïse Amyraut (1596–1664). French Reformed pastor and professor. Originally intending to be a lawyer, Amyraut turned to theology after an encounter with several Huguenot pastors and having read Calvin's* *Institutes*. After a brief stint as a parish pastor, Amyraut spent the majority of his career at the Saumur Academy. He was well known for his irenicism and ecumenicism (for example, in advocating intercommunion with Lutherans). Certain aspects of his writings on justification, faith, the covenants and especially predestination proved controversial among the Reformed. His doctrine of election is often called hypothetical universalism or Amyraldianism, stating that Christ's atoning work was intended by God for all human beings indiscriminately, although its effectiveness for salvation depends on faith, which is a free gift of God given only to those whom God has chosen from eternity. Amyraut was charged with grave doctrinal error three times before the National Synod but was acquitted each time. Aside from his theological treatises, Amyraut published paraphrases of almost the entire New Testament and the Psalms, as well as many sermons.

Jakob Andreae (1528–1590). German Lutheran theologian. Andreae studied at the University of Tübingen before being called to the diaconate in

Stuttgart in 1546. He was appointed ecclesiastical superintendent of Göppingen in 1553 and supported Johannes Brenz's* proposal to place the church under civil administrative control. An ecclesial diplomat for the duke of Württemberg, Andreae debated eucharistic theology, the use of images and predestination with Theodore Beza* at the Colloquy of Montbéliard (1586) to determine whether French Reformed exiles would be required to submit to the Formula of Concord.* Andreae coauthored the Formula of Concord. He and his wife had eighteen children.

Lancelot Andrewes (1555–1626). Anglican bishop. A scholar, pastor and preacher, Andrews prominently shaped a distinctly Anglican identity between the poles of Puritanism and Catholicism. He oversaw the translation of Genesis to 2 Kings for the Authorized Version.* His eight-volume collected works—primarily devotional tracts and sermons—are marked by his fluency in Scripture, the Christian tradition and classical literature.

Benedict Aretius (d. 1574). Swiss Reformed professor. Trained at the universities of Bern, Strasbourg and Marburg, Aretius taught logic and philosophy as well as the biblical languages and theology. He advocated for stronger unity and peace between the Lutheran and Reformed churches. Aretius joined others in denouncing the antitrinitarian Giovanni Valentino Gentile (d. 1566). He published commentaries on the New Testament, as well as various works on astronomy, botany and medicine.

Jacobus Arminius (1559–1609). Dutch Remonstrant pastor and theologian. Arminius was a vocal critic of high Calvinist scholasticism, whose views were repudiated by the Synod of Dordrecht. Arminius was a student of Theodore Beza* at the academy of Geneva. He served as a pastor in Amsterdam and later joined the faculty of theology at the university in Leiden, where his lectures on predestination were popular and controversial. Predestination, as Arminius understood it, was the decree of God determined on the basis of divine foreknowledge of faith or rejection by humans who are the recipients of prevenient, but resistible, grace.

Johann Arndt (1555–1621). German Lutheran pastor and theologian. After a brief time teaching, Arndt pastored in Badeborn (Anhalt) until 1590, when Prince Johann Georg von Anhalt (1567–1618) began introducing Reformed ecclesial policies. Arndt ministered in Quedlinberg, Brunswick, Eisleben and Celle. Heavily influenced by medieval mysticism, Arndt centered his theology on Christ's mystical union with the believer, out of which flows love of God and neighbor. He is best known for his *True Christianity* (1605–1609), which greatly influenced Philipp Jakob Spener (1635–1705) and later Pietists.

John Arrowsmith (1602–1659). English Puritan theologian. Arrowsmith participated in the Westminster Assembly, and later taught at Cambridge. His works, all published posthumously, include three sermons preached to Parliament and an unfinished catechism.

Articles of Religion (1562; revised 1571). The Articles underwent a long editorial process that drew from the influence of Continental confessions in England, resulting in a uniquely Anglican blend of Protestantism and Catholicism. In their final form, they were reduced from Thomas Cranmer's* Forty-two Articles (1539) to the Elizabethan Thirty-Nine Articles (1571), excising polemical articles against the Anabaptists and Millenarians as well as adding articles on the Holy Spirit, good works and Communion. Originating in a 1535 meeting with Lutherans, the Articles retained a minor influence from the Augsburg Confession* and Württemberg Confession (1552), but showed significant revision in accordance with Genevan theology, as well as the Second Helvetic Confession.*

Anne Askew (1521–1546). English Protestant martyr. Askew was forced to marry her deceased sister's intended husband, who later expelled Askew from his house—after the birth of two children—on account of her religious views. After unsuccessfully seeking a divorce in Lincoln, Askew moved to London, where she met other Protestants and began to preach. In 1546, she was arrested, imprisoned and convicted of heresy for denying the doctrine of transubstantiation. Under torture in the Tower of London she refused to name any other Protestants. On July 16, 1546, she was burned at the stake. Askew is best known through her accounts of her arrests and examinations. John Bale (1495–1563), a bishop, historian and playwright, published these manuscripts. Later John Foxe (1516–1587) included them in his *Acts and Monuments*, presenting her as a role model for other pious Protestant women.

Augsburg Confession (1530). In the wake of Luther's* stand against ecclesial authorities at the Diet of Worms (1521), the Holy Roman Empire splintered along theological lines. Emperor Charles V sought to ameliorate this—while also hoping to secure a united European front against Turkish invasion—by calling together another imperial diet in Augsburg in 1530. The Evangelical party was cast in a strongly heretical light at the diet by Johann Eck.* For this reason, Philipp Melanchthon* and Justus Jonas* thought it best to strike a conciliatory tone (Luther, as an official outlaw, did not attend), submitting a confession rather than a defense. The resulting Augsburg Confession was approved by many of the rulers of the northeastern Empire; however, due to differences in eucharistic theology, Martin Bucer* and the representatives of Strasbourg, Constance, Lindau and Memmingen drafted a separate confession (the Tetrapolitan Confession). Charles V accepted neither confession, demanding that the Evangelicals accept the Catholic rebuttal instead. In 1531, along with the publication of the Augsburg Confession itself, Melanchthon released a defense of the confession that responded to the Catholic confutation and expanded on the original articles. Most subsequent Protestant confessions followed the general structure of the Augsburg Confession.

Authorized Version (1611). In 1604 King James I* commissioned this new translation—popularly remembered as the King James Version—for uniform use in the public worship of the Church of England. The Bible and the Apocrypha was divided into six portions and assigned to six companies of nine scholars—both Anglicans and Puritans—centered at Cambridge, Oxford and Westminster.

Richard Bancroft, the general editor of the Authorized Version, composed fifteen rules to guide the translators and to guard against overly partisan decisions. Rather than offer an entirely fresh English translation, the companies were to follow the Bishops' Bible* as closely as possible. "Truly (good Christian Reader)," the preface states, "we neuer thought from the beginning that we should need to make a new Translation, nor yet to make of a bad one a good one . . . but make a good one better, or out of many good ones, one principall good one, not iustly to be excepted against: that hath bene our endeauour, that our mark." Other rules standardized spelling, dictated traditional ecclesial terms (e.g., *church*, *baptize* and *bishop*), and allowed only for linguistic marginal notes and cross-references. Each book of the Bible went through a rigorous revision process: first, each person in a company made an initial draft, then the company put together a composite draft, then a supercommittee composed of representatives from each company reviewed these drafts, and finally two bishops and Bancroft scrutinized the final edits. The text and translation process of the Authorized Version have widely influenced biblical translations ever since.

Robert Bagnall (b. 1559 or 1560). English Protestant minister. Bagnall authored *The Steward's Last Account* (1622), a collection of five sermons on Luke 16.

John Ball (1585–1640). English Puritan theologian. Ball was a respected educator. He briefly held a church office until he was removed on account of his Puritanism. He composed popular catechisms and tracts on faith, the church and the covenant of grace.

Thomas Bastard (c. 1565–1618). English Protestant minister and poet. Educated at Winchester and New College, Oxford, Bastard published numerous works, including collections of poems and sermons; his most famous title is *Chrestoleros* (1598), a collection of epigrams. Bastard was alleged to be the author of an anonymous work, *An Admonition to the City of Oxford*, which revealed the carnal vices of many clergy and scholars in Oxford; despite denying authorship, he was dismissed from

Oxford in 1591. Bastard was recognized as a skilled classical scholar and preacher. He died impoverished in a debtor's prison in Dorchester.

Jeremias Bastingius (1551–1595). Dutch Reformed theologian. Educated in Heidelberg and Geneva, Bastingius pastored the Reformed church in Antwerp for nearly a decade until the Spanish overran the city in 1585; he later settled in Dordrecht. He spent the last few years of his life in Leiden on the university's board of regents. He wrote an influential commentary on the Heidelberg Catechism that was translated into English, Dutch, German and Flemish.

Johann (Pomarius) Baumgart (1514–1578). Lutheran pastor and amateur playwright. Baumgart studied under Georg Major,* Martin Luther* and Philipp Melanchthon* at the University of Wittenberg. Before becoming pastor of the Church of the Holy Spirit in 1540, Baumgart taught secondary school. He authored catechetical and polemical works, a postil for the Gospel readings throughout the church year, numerous hymns and a didactic play (*Juditium Salomonis*).

Richard Baxter (1615–1691). English Puritan minister. Baxter was a leading Puritan pastor, evangelist and theologian, known throughout England for his landmark ministry in Kidderminster and a prodigious literary output, producing 135 books in just over forty years. Baxter came to faith through reading William Perkins,* Richard Sibbes* and other early Puritan writers and was the first cleric to decline the terms of ministry in the national English church imposed by the 1662 Act of Uniformity; Baxter wrote on behalf of the more than 1700 who shared ejection from the national church. He hoped for restoration to national church ministry, or toleration, that would allow lawful preaching and pastoring. Baxter sought unity in theological, ecclesiastical, sociopolitical and personal terms and is regarded as a forerunner of Noncomformist ecumenicity, though he was defeated in his efforts at the 1661 Savoy Conference to take seriously Puritan objections to the revision of the 1604 Prayer Book. Baxter's views on church ministry were considerably hybrid: he was a paedo-baptist, Nonconformist minister who approved of synodical Episcopal government and fixed liturgy. He is most known for his classic writings on the Christian life, such as *The Saints' Everlasting Rest* and *A Christian Directory*, and pastoral ministry, such as *The Reformed Pastor*. He also produced *Catholick Theology*, a large volume squaring current Reformed, Lutheran, Arminian and Roman Catholic systems with each other.

Thomas Becon (1511/1512–1567). English Puritan preacher. Becon was a friend of Hugh Latimer,* and for several years chaplain to Archbishop Thomas Cranmer.* Becon was sent to the Tower of London by Mary I and then exiled for his controversial preaching at the English royal court. He returned to England upon Elizabeth I's accession. Becon was one of the most widely read popular preachers in England during the Reformation. He published many of his sermons, including a postil, or collection of sermon helps for undertrained or inexperienced preachers.

Belgic Confession (1561). Written by Guy de Brès (1523–1567), this statement of Dutch Reformed faith was heavily reliant on the Gallic Confession,* although more detailed, especially in how strongly it distances the Reformed from Roman Catholics and Anabaptists. The Confession first appeared in French in 1561 and was translated to Dutch in 1562. It was presented to Philip II (1527–1598) in the hope that he would grant toleration to the Reformed, to no avail. At the Synod of Dordrecht* the Confession was revised, clarifying and strengthening the article on election as well as sharpening the distinctives of Reformed theology against the Anabaptists, thus situating the Dutch Reformed more closely to the international Calvinist movement. The Belgic Confession in conjunction with the Heidelberg Catechism* and the Canons of Dordrecht were granted official status as the confessional standards (the Three Forms of Unity) of the Dutch Reformed Church.

Theodore Beza (1519–1605). French pastor and professor. Beza was compatriot and successor to John Calvin* as moderator of the Company of Pastors in Geneva during the second half of the sixteenth century. He was a noteworthy New Testament scholar whose *Codex Bezae* formed the basis of the New Testament section of later English translations. A leader in the academy and the church, Beza served as professor of Greek at the Lausanne Academy until 1558, at which time he moved to Geneva to become the rector of the newly founded Genevan Academy. He enjoyed an international reputation through his correspondence with key European leaders. Beza developed and extended Calvin's doctrinal thought on several important themes such as the nature of predestination and the real spiritual presence of Christ in the Eucharist.

Hugh Binning (1627–1653). Scottish Presbyterian theologian. At the age of eighteen, Binning became a professor of philosophy at the University of Glasgow. In his early twenties he left this post for parish ministry, and died of consumption a few years later. His commentary on the Westminster Confession and a selection of his sermons were published after his death.

Bishops' Bible (1568). Anglicans were polarized by the two most recent English translations of the Bible: the Great Bible (1539) relied too heavily on the Vulgate* and was thus perceived as too Catholic, while the Geneva Bible's* marginal notes were too Calvinist for many Anglicans. So Archbishop Matthew Parker (1504–1575) commissioned a new translation of Scripture from the original languages with marginal annotations (many of which, ironically, were from the Geneva Bible). Published under royal warrant, the Bishops' Bible became the official translation for the Church of England. The 1602 edition provided the basis for the King James Bible (1611).

Georg Blaurock (1492–1529). Swiss Anabaptist. Blaurock (a nickname meaning "blue coat," because of his preference for this garment) was one of the first leaders of Switzerland's radical reform movement. In the first public disputations on baptism in Zurich, he argued for believer's baptism and was the first person to receive adult believers' baptism there, having been baptized by Conrad Grebel* in 1525. Blaurock was arrested several times for performing mass adult baptisms and engaging in social disobedience by disrupting worship services. He was eventually expelled from Zurich but continued preaching and baptizing in various Swiss cantons until his execution.

Bohemian Confession (1535). Bohemian Christianity was subdivided between traditional Catholics, Utraquists (who demanded Communion in both kinds) and the *Unitas Fratrum*, who were not Protestants but whose theology bore strong affinities to the Waldensians and the Reformed. The 1535 Latin edition of this confession—an earlier Czech edition had already been drafted—was an attempt to clarify and redefine the beliefs of the *Unitas Fratrum*. This confession purged all earlier openness to rebaptism and inched toward Luther's* eucharistic theology. Jan Augusta (c. 1500–1572) and Jan Roh (also Johannes Horn; c. 1490–1547) presented the confession to King Ferdinand I (1503–1564) in Vienna, but the king would not print it. The *Unitas Fratrum* sought, and with slight amendments eventually obtained, Luther's advocacy of the confession. It generally follows the structure of the Augsburg Confession.*

Bohemian Confession (1575). This confession was an attempt to shield Bohemian Christian minorities—the Utraquists and the *Unitas Fratrum*—from the Counter-Reformation and Habsburg insistence on uniformity. The hope was that this umbrella consensus would ensure peace in the midst of Christian diversity; anyone who affirmed the 1575 Confession, passed by the Bohemian legislature, would be tolerated. This confession, like the Bohemian Confession of 1535, patterned after the Augsburg Confession.* It emphasizes both justification by faith alone and good works as the fruit of salvation. Baptism and the Eucharist are the focus of the sacramental section, although the five traditional Catholic sacraments are also listed for the Utraquists. Though it was eventually accepted in 1609 by Rudolf II (1552–1612), the Thirty Years' War (1618–1648) rendered the confession moot.

Book of Common Prayer (1549; 1552). After the Church of England's break with Rome, it needed a liturgical manual to distinguish its theology and practice from that of Catholicism. Thomas Cranmer* drafted the Book of Common Prayer based on the medieval Roman Missal, under the dual influence of the revised Lutheran Mass and the reforms of the Spanish Cardinal Quiñones. This manual details the eucharistic service, as well as services for rites such as baptism, confirmation, marriage and funerals. It includes a matrix of the epistle and Gospel readings and the appropriate collect for each Sunday and feast day of the church year. The 1548 Act of Uniformity established the Book of Common Prayer as *the* authoritative liturgical manual for the Church of England, to be implemented everywhere by Pentecost 1549. After its 1552 revision, Queen Mary I banned it; Elizabeth reestablished it in 1559, although it was rejected by Puritans and Catholics alike.

The Book of Homilies (1547; 1563; 1570). This collection of approved sermons, published in three parts during the reigns of Edward VI and Elizabeth I, was intended to inculcate Anglican theological distinctives and mitigate the problems raised by the lack of educated preachers. Addressing doctrinal and practical topics, Thomas Cranmer* likely wrote the majority of the first twelve sermons, published in 1547; John Jewel* added another twenty sermons in 1563. A final sermon, *A Homily Against Disobedience*, was appended to the canon in 1570. Reprinted regularly, the *Book of Homilies* was an important resource in Anglican preaching until at least the end of the seventeenth century.

Martin (Cellarius) Borrhaus (1499–1564). German Reformed theologian. After a dispute with his mentor Johann Eck,* Borrhaus settled in Wittenberg, where he was influenced by the radical Zwickau Prophets. He travelled extensively, and finally settled in Basel to teach philosophy and Old Testament. Despite his objections, many accused Borrhaus of Anabaptism; he argued that baptism was a matter of conscience. On account of his association with Sebastian Castellio (1515–1563) and Michael Servetus (1511–1553), some scholars posit that Borrhaus was an antitrinitarian. His writings include a treatise on the Trinity and commentaries on the Torah, historical books, Ecclesiastes and Isaiah.

John Boys (1571–1625). Anglican priest and theologian. Before doctoral work at Cambridge, Boys pastored several parishes in Kent; after completing his studies he was appointed to more prominent positions, culminating in his 1619 appointment as the Dean of Canterbury by James I. Boys published a popular four-volume postil of the Gospel and epistle readings for the church year, as well as a companion volume for the Psalms.

Thieleman Jans van Braght (1625–1664). Dutch Radical preacher. After demonstrating great ability with languages, this cloth merchant was made preacher in his hometown of Dordrecht in 1648. He served in this office for the next sixteen years, until his death. This celebrated preacher had a reputation for engaging in debate wherever an opportunity presented itself, particularly concerning infant baptism. The publication of his book of martyrs, *Het Bloedigh Tooneel of Martel-aersspiegel* (1660; *Martyrs' Mirror*), proved to be his lasting contribution to the Mennonite tradition. *Martyrs' Mirror* is heavily indebted to the earlier martyr book *Offer des Heeren* (1562), to which Braght added many early church martyrs who rejected infant baptism, as well as over 800 contemporary martyrs.

Johannes Brenz (1499–1570). German Lutheran theologian and pastor. Brenz was converted to the reformation cause after hearing Martin Luther* speak; later, Brenz became a student of Johannes Oecolampadius.* His central achievement lay in his talent for organization. As city preacher in Schwäbisch-Hall and afterward in Württemberg and Tübingen, he oversaw the introduction of reform measures and doctrines and new governing structures for ecclesial and educational communities. Brenz also helped establish Lutheran orthodoxy through treatises, commentaries and catechisms. He defended Luther's position on eucharistic presence against Huldrych Zwingli* and opposed the death penalty for religious dissenters.

Guillaume Briçonnet (1470–1534). French Catholic abbot and bishop. Briçonnet created a short-lived circle of reformist-minded humanists in his diocese under the sponsorship of Marguerite d'Angoulême. His desire for ecclesial reform developed throughout his prestigious career (including positions as royal chaplain to the queen, abbot at Saint-Germain-des-Prés and bishop of Meaux), influenced by Jacques Lefèvre d'Étaples.* Briçonnet encouraged reform through ministerial visitation, Scripture and preaching in the vernacular and active study of the Bible. When this triggered the ire of the theology faculty at the Sorbonne in Paris, Briçonnet quelled the activity and departed, envisioning an ecclesial reform that proceeded hierarchically.

Thomas Brightman (1562–1607). English Puritan pastor and exegete. Under alleged divine inspiration, Brightman wrote a well known commentary on Revelation, influenced by Joachim of Fiore (d. 1202). In contrast to the putatively true churches of Geneva and Scotland, he depicted the Church of England as a type of the lukewarm Laodicean church. He believed that the Reformation would result in the defeat of the Vatican and the Ottoman Empire and that all humanity would be regenerated through the spread of the gospel before Christ's final return and judgment.

Otto Brunfels (c. 1488–1534). German Lutheran botanist, teacher and physician. Brunfels joined the Carthusian order, where he developed interests in the natural sciences and became involved with a humanist circle associated with Ulrich von Hutten and Wolfgang Capito.* In 1521, after coming into contact with Luther's* teaching, Brunfels abandoned the monastic life, traveling and spending time in botanical research and pastoral care. He received a medical degree in Basel and was appointed city physician of Bern in 1534. Brunfels penned defenses of Luther and Hutten, devotional biographies of biblical figures, a prayer book, and annotations on the Gospels and the Acts of the Apostles. His most influential contribution, however, is as a Renaissance botanist.

Martin Bucer (1491–1551). German Reformed theologian and pastor. A Dominican friar, Bucer was influenced by Desiderius Erasmus* during his doctoral studies at the University of Heidelberg, where he began corresponding with Martin Luther.* After advocating reform in Alsace, Bucer was excommunicated and fled to Strasbourg, where he became a leader in the city's Reformed ecclesial and educational communities. Bucer sought concord between Lutherans and Zwinglians and Protestants and Catholics. He emigrated to England, becoming a professor at Cambridge. Bucer's greatest theological concern was the centrality of Christ's sacrificial death, which achieved justification and sanctification and orients Christian community.

Johannes Bugenhagen (1485–1558). German Lutheran pastor and professor. Bugenhagen, a priest and lecturer at a Premonstratensian monastery, became a city preacher in Wittenberg during the reform efforts of Martin Luther* and Philipp Melanchthon.* Initially influenced by his reading of Desiderius Erasmus,* Bugenhagen grew in evangelical orientation through Luther's works; later, he studied under Melanchthon at the University of Wittenberg, eventually serving as rector and faculty member there. Bugenhagen was a versatile commentator, exegete and lecturer on Scripture. Through these roles and his development of lectionary and devotional material, Bugenhagen facilitated rapid establishment of church order throughout many German provinces.

Heinrich Bullinger (1504–1575). Swiss Reformed pastor and theologian. Bullinger succeeded Huldrych Zwingli* as minister and leader in Zurich. The primary author of the First and Second Helvetic Confessions,* Bullinger was drawn toward reform through the works of Martin Luther* and Philipp Melanchthon.* After Zwingli died, Bullinger was vital in maintaining adherence to the cause of reform; he oversaw the expansion of the Zurich synodal system while preaching, teaching and writing extensively. One of Bullinger's lasting legacies was the development of a federal view of the divine covenant with humanity, making baptism and the Eucharist covenantal signs.

John Bunyan (1628–1688). English Puritan preacher and writer. His *Pilgrim's Progress* is one of the best-selling English-language titles in history. Born to a working-class family, Bunyan was largely unschooled, gaining literacy (and entering the faith) through reading the Bible and such early Puritan devotional works as *The Plain Man's Pathway to Heaven* and *The Practice of Piety*. Following a short stint in Oliver Cromwell's parliamentary army, in which Bunyan narrowly escaped death in combat, he turned to a preaching ministry, succeeding John Gifford as pastor at the Congregational church in Bedford. A noted preacher, Bunyan drew large crowds in itinerant appearances and it was in the sermonic form that Bunyan developed his theological outlook, which was an Augustinian-inflected Calvinism. Bunyan's opposition to the Book of Common Prayer and refusal of official ecclesiastical licensure led to multiple imprisonments, where he wrote many of his famous allegorical works, including *Pilgrim's Progress*, *The Holy City*, *Prison Meditations* and *Holy War*.

Jeremiah Burroughs (c. 1600–1646). English Puritan pastor and delegate to the Westminster Assembly. Burroughs left Cambridge, as well as a rectorate in Norfolk, because of his nonconformity. After returning to England from pastoring an English congregation in Rotterdam for several years (1637–1641), he became one of only a few dissenters from the official presbyterianism of the Assembly in favor of a congregationalist polity. Nevertheless, he was well known and respected by presbyterian colleagues such as Richard Baxter* for his irenic tone and conciliatory manner. The vast majority of Burroughs's corpus was published posthumously, although during his lifetime he published annotations on Hosea and several polemical works.

Cardinal Cajetan (Thomas de Vio) (1469–1534). Italian Catholic cardinal, professor, theologian and biblical exegete. This Dominican monk was the leading Thomist theologian and one of the most important Catholic exegetes of the sixteenth century. Cajetan is best-known for his interview with Martin Luther* at the Diet of Augsburg (1518). Among his many works are polemical treatises, extensive biblical commentaries and most importantly a four-volume commentary (1508–1523) on the *Summa Theologiae* of Thomas Aquinas.

Georg Calixtus (1586–1656). German Lutheran theologian. Calixtus studied at the University of Helmstedt where he developed regard for Philipp Melanchthon.* Between his time as a student and later as a professor at Helmstedt, Calixtus traveled through Europe seeking a way to unite and reconcile Lutherans, Calvinists and Catholics. He attempted to fuse these denominations through use of the Scriptures, the Apostles' Creed, and the first five centuries, interpreted by the Vincentian canon. Calixtus's position was stamped as syncretist and yielded further debate even after his death.

John Calvin (1509–1564). French Reformed pastor and theologian. In his *Institutes of the Christian Religion*, Calvin provided a theological dogmatics for the Reformed churches. Calvin's gradual conversion to the cause of reform occurred through his study with chief humanist scholars in Paris, but he spent most of his career in Geneva (excepting a three-year exile in Strasbourg with Martin Bucer*). In Geneva, Calvin reorganized the structure and governance of the church and established an academy that became an international center for theological education. He was a tireless writer, producing his *Institutes*, theological treatises and Scripture commentaries.

Wolfgang Capito (1478?–1541). German Reformed humanist and theologian. Capito, a Hebrew scholar, produced a Hebrew grammar and published several Latin commentaries on books of the Hebrew Scriptures. He corresponded with Desiderius Erasmus* and fellow humanists. Capito translated Martin Luther's* early works into Latin for the printer Johann Froben. On meeting Luther, Capito was converted to Luther's vision, left Mainz and settled in Strasbourg, where he lectured on Luther's theology to the city clergy. With Martin Bucer,* Capito reformed liturgy, ecclesial life and teachings, education, welfare and government. Capito worked for the theological unification of the Swiss cantons with Strasbourg.

Thomas Cartwright (1535–1606). English Puritan preacher and professor. Cartwright was educated at St. John's College, Cambridge, although as an influential leader of the Presbyterian party in the Church of England he was continually at odds with the Anglican party, especially John Whitgift.* Cartwright spent some time as an exile in Geneva and Heidelberg as well as in Antwerp, where he pastored an English church. In 1585, Cartwright was arrested and eventually jailed for trying to return to England despite Elizabeth I's refusal of his request. Many acknowledged him to be learned but also quite cantankerous. His publications include commentaries on Colossians, Ecclesiastes, Proverbs and the Gospels, as well as a dispute against Whitgift on church discipline.

Mathew Caylie (unknown). English Protestant minister. Caylie authored *The Cleansing of the Ten Lepers* (1623), an exposition of Luke 17:14-18.

John Chardon (d. 1601). Irish Anglican bishop. Chardon was educated at Oxford. He advocated Reformed doctrine in his preaching, yet opposed those Puritans who rejected Anglican church order. He published several sermons.

Martin Chemnitz (1522–1586). German Lutheran theologian. A leading figure in establishing Lutheran orthodoxy, Chemnitz studied theology and patristics at the University of Wittenburg, later becoming a defender of Philipp Melanchthon's* interpretation of the doctrine of justification. Chemnitz drafted a compendium of doctrine and reorganized the structure of the church in Wolfenbüttel; later, he led efforts to reconcile divisions within Lutheranism, culminating in the Formula of Concord*. One of his chief theological accomplishments was a modification of the christological doctrine of the *communicatio idiomatium*, which provided a Lutheran platform for understanding the sacramental presence of Christ's humanity in the Eucharist.

David Chytraeus (1531–1600). German Lutheran professor, theologian and biblical exegete. At the age of eight Chytraeus was admitted to the University of Tübingen. There he studied law, philology, philosophy, and theology, finally receiving his master's degree in 1546. Chytraeus befriended Philipp Melanchthon* while sojourning in Wittenberg, where he taught the *Loci communes*. While teaching exegesis at the University of Rostock Chytraeus became acquainted with Tilemann Heshusius,* who strongly influenced Chytraeus away from Philippist theology. As a defender of Gnesio-Lutheran theology Chytraeus helped organize churches throughout Austria in accordance with the Augsburg Confession.* Chytraeus coauthored the Formula of Concord* with Martin Chemnitz,* Andreas Musculus (1514–1581), Nikolaus Selnecker* and Jakob Andreae.* He wrote commentaries on most of the Bible, as well as a devotional work titled *Regula vitae* (1555) that described the Christian virtues.

David Clarkson (1622–1686). English Puritan theologian. After his dismissal from the pastorate on account of the Act of Uniformity (1662), little is known about Clarkson. At the end of his life he ministered with John Owen* in London.

John Colet (1467–1519). English Catholic priest, preacher and educator. Colet, appointed dean of Saint Paul's Cathedral by Henry VII, was a friend of Desiderius Erasmus,* on whose classical ideals Colet reconstructed the curriculum of Saint Paul's school. Colet was convinced that the foundation of moral reform lay in the education of children. Though an ardent advocate of reform, Colet, like Erasmus, remained loyal to the Catholic Church throughout his life. Colet's agenda of reform was oriented around spiritual and ethical themes, demonstrated in his commentaries on select books of the New Testament and the writings of Pseudo-Dionysius the Areopagite.

Gasparo Contarini (1483–1542). Italian states-man, theologian and reform-minded cardinal. Contarini was an able negotiator and graceful compromiser. Charles V requested Contarini as the papal legate for the Colloquy of Regensburg (1541), where Contarini reached agreement with Melanchthon* on the doctrine of justification (although neither the pope nor Luther* ratified the agreement). He had come to a similar belief in

the priority of faith in the work of Christ rather than works as the basis for Christian life in 1511, though unlike Luther, he never left the papal church over the issue; instead he remainied within it to try to seek gentle reform, and he adhered to papal sacramental teaching. Contarini was an important voice for reform within the Catholic Church, always seeking reconciliation rather than confrontation with Protestant reformers. He wrote many works, including a treatise detailing the ideal bishop, a manual for lay church leaders, a political text on right governance and brief commentaries on the Pauline letters.

John Cosin (1594–1672). Anglican preacher and bishop. Early in his career Cosin was the vice chancellor of Cambridge and canon at the Durham cathedral. But as a friend of William Laud* and an advocate for "Laudian" changes, he was suspected of being a crypto-Catholic. In 1640 during the Long Parliament a Puritan lodged a complaint with the House of Commons concerning Cosin's "popish innovations." Cosin was promptly removed from office. During the turmoil of the English Civil Wars, Cosin sojourned in Paris among English nobility but struggled financially. Cosin returned to England after the Restoration in 1660 to be consecrated as the bishop of Durham. He pub-lished annotations on the Book of Common Prayer* and a history of the canon.

Council of Constance (1414–1418). Convened to resolve the Western Schism, root out heresy and reform the church in head and members, the council asserted in *Sacrosancta* (1415) the immedi-ate authority of ecumenical councils assembled in the Holy Spirit under Christ—even over the pope. Martin V was elected pope in 1417 after the three papal claimants were deposed; thus, the council ended the schism. The council condemned Jan Hus,* Jerome of Prague (c. 1365–1416) and, posthumously, John Wycliffe. Hus and Jerome, despite letters of safe conduct, were burned at the stake. Their deaths ignited the Hussite Wars, which ended as a result of the Council of Basel's concessions to the Bohemian church. The council fathers sought to reform the church through the regular convocation of councils (*Frequens*; 1417). Martin V begrudgingly complied by calling the required councils, then immediately disbanding them. Pius II (r. 1458–1464) reasserted papal dominance through *Execrabilis* (1460), which condemned any appeal to a future council apart from the pope's authority.

Miles Coverdale (1488–1568). Anglican bishop. Coverdale is known for his translations of the Bible into English, completing William Tyndale's* efforts and later producing the Great Bible commissioned by Henry VIII (1539). A former friar, Coverdale was among the Cambridge scholars who met at the White Horse Tavern to discuss Martin Luther's* ideas. During Coverdale's three terms of exile in Europe, he undertook various translations, including the Geneva Bible*. He was appointed bishop of Exeter by Thomas Cranmer* and served as chaplain to Edward VI. Coverdale contributed to Cranmer's first edition of the Book of Common Prayer.*

William Cowper (Couper) (1568–1619). Scottish Puritan bishop. After graduating from the University of St. Andrews, Cowper worked in parish ministry for twenty-five years before becoming bishop. As a zealous Puritan and advocate of regular preaching and rigorous discipline, Cowper championed Presbyterian polity and lay participation in church government. Cowper published devotional works, sermon collections and a commentary on Revelation.

Thomas Cranmer (1489–1556). Anglican archbishop and theologian. Cranmer supervised church reform and produced the first two editions of the Book of Common Prayer.* As a doctoral student at Cambridge, he was involved in the discussions at the White Horse Tavern. Cranmer contributed to a religious defense of Henry VIII's divorce; Henry then appointed him Archbishop of Canterbury. Cranmer cautiously steered the course of reform, accelerating under Edward VI. After supporting the attempted coup to prevent Mary's assuming the throne, Cranmer was convicted of treason and burned at the stake. Cranmer's legacy is the splendid English of his liturgy and prayer books.

Richard Crashaw (1612–1649). English Catholic poet. Educated at Cambridge, Crashaw was fluent in Hebrew, Greek and Latin. His first volume of poetry was *Epigrammatum sacrorum liber* (1634). Despite being born into a Puritan family, Crashaw was attracted to Catholicism, finally converting in 1644 after he was forced to resign his fellowship for not signing the Solemn League and Covenant (1643). In 1649, he was made a subcanon of Our Lady of Loretto by Cardinal Palotta.

Herbert Croft (1603–1691). Anglican bishop. As a boy Croft converted to Catholicism; he returned to the Church of England during his studies at Oxford. Before the English Civil Wars, he served as chaplain to Charles I. After the Restoration, Charles II appointed him as bishop. Croft ardently opposed Catholicism in his later years.

John Crompe (d. 1661). Anglican priest. Educated at Cambridge, Crompe published a commentary on the Apostles' Creed, a sermon on Psalm 21:3 and an exposition of Christ's passion.

Caspar Cruciger (1504–1548). German Lutheran theologian. Recognized for his alignment with the theological views of Philipp Melanchthon,* Cruciger was a scholar respected among both Protestants and Catholics. In 1521, Cruciger came Wittenberg to study Hebrew and remained there most of his life. He became a valuable partner for Martin Luther* in translating the Old Testament and served as teacher, delegate to major theological colloquies and rector. Cruciger was an agent of reform in his birthplace of Leipzig, where at the age of fifteen he had observed the disputation between Luther and Johann Eck.*

Marguerite d'Angoulême (1492–1549). French Catholic noblewoman. The elder sister of King Francis I of France, Marguerite was the Queen of Navarre and Duchess of Alençon and Berry. She was a poet and author of the French Renaissance. She composed *The Mirror of a Sinful Soul* (1531)—condemned by the theologians of the Sorbonne for containing Lutheran ideas—and an unfinished collection of short stories, the *Heptaméron* (1558). A leading figure in the French Reformation, Marguerite was at the center of a network of reform-minded individuals that included Guillame Briçonnet,* Jacques Lefèvre d'Etaples,* Gérard Roussel (1500–1550) and Guillame Farel (1489–1565).

Jakob Dachser (1486–1567). German Anabaptist theologian and hymnist. Dachser served as a Catholic priest in Vienna until he was imprisoned and then exiled for defending the Lutheran understanding of the Mass and fasting. Hans Hut* rebaptized him in Augsburg, where Dachser was appointed as a leader of the Anabaptist congregation. Lutheran authorities imprisoned him for nearly four years. In 1531 he recanted his Radical beliefs and began to catechize children with the permission of the city council. Dachser was expelled from Augsburg as a possible insurrectionist in 1552 and relocated to Pfalz-Neuberg. He published a number of poems, hymns and mystical works, and he versified several psalms.

Jean Daillé (1594–1670). French Reformed pastor. Born into a devout Reformed family, Daillé studied theology and philosophy at Saumur under the most influential contemporary lay leader in French Protestantism, Philippe Duplessis-Mornay (1549–1623). Daillé held to Amyraldianism—the belief that Christ died for all humanity inclusively, not particularly for the elect who would inherit salvation (though only the elect are in fact saved). He wrote a controversial treatise on the church fathers that aggravated many Catholic and Anglican scholars because of Daillé's apparent demotion of patristic authority in matters of faith.

Lambert Daneau (1535–1595). French Reformed pastor and theologian. After a decade of pastoring in France, following the St. Bartholomew's Day Massacre, Daneau fled to Geneva to teach theology at the Academy. He later taught in the Low Countries, finishing his career in southern France. Daneau's diverse works include tracts on science, ethics and morality as well as numerous theological and exegetical works.

John Davenant (1576–1641). Anglican bishop and professor. Davenant attended Queen's College, Cambridge, where he received his doctorate and was appointed professor of divinity. During the Remonstrant controversy, James I sent Davenant as one of the four representatives for the Church of England to the Synod of Dordrecht.* Following James's instructions, Davenant advocated a *via media* between the Calvinists and the Remonstrants, although in later years he defended against the rise of Arminianism in England. In 1621, Davenant was promoted to the bishopric of Salisbury, where he was generally receptive to Laudian reforms. Davenant's lectures on Colossians are his best-known work.

Defense of the Augsburg Confession (1531). See *Augsburg Confession*.

Hans Denck (c. 1500–1527). German Radical theologian. Denck, a crucial early figure of the German Anabaptist movement, combined medieval German mysticism with the radical sacramental theology of Andreas Bodenstein von Karlstadt* and Thomas Müntzer.* Denck argued that the exterior forms of Scripture and sacrament are symbolic witnesses secondary to the internally revealed truth of the Sprit in the human soul. This view led to his expulsion from Nuremberg in 1525; he spent the next two years in various centers of reform in the German territories. At the time of his death, violent persecution against Anabaptists was on the rise throughout northern Europe.

Stephen Denison (unknown). English Puritan pastor. Denison received the post of curate at St. Katherine Cree in London sometime in the 1610s, where he ministered until his ejection from office in 1635. During his career at St. Katherine Cree, Denison waded into controversy with both Puritans (over the doctrine of predestination) and Anglicans (over concerns about liturgical ceremonies). He approached both altercations with rancor and rigidity, although he seems to have been quite popular and beloved by most of his congregation. In 1631, William Laud* consecrated the newly renovated St. Katherine Cree, and as part of the festivities Denison offered a sermon on Luke 19:27 in which he publicly rebuked Laud for fashioning the Lord's house into a "den of robbers." Aside from the record of his quarrels, very little is known about Denison. In addition to *The White*

Wolf (a 1627 sermon against another opponent), he published a catechism for children (1621), a treatise on the sacraments (1621) and a commentary on 2 Peter 1 (1622).

Marie Dentière (1495–1561). Belgian Reformed theologian. Dentière relinquished her monastic vows and married Simon Robert (d.1533), a former priest, in Strasbourg. After Robert died, she married Antoine Froment (1508–1581), a reformer in Geneva, and became involved in the reform of that city. Her best-known writings are a tract addressed to Marguerite d'Angoulême,* the *Very Useful Epistle* (1539), in which she espoused the evangelical faith and the right of women to interpret and teach scripture, and a preface to Calvin's sermon on 1 Timothy 2:8-12. Dentière is the only woman to have her name inscribed on the International Monument to the Reformation in Geneva.

David Dickson (1583?–1663). Scottish Reformed pastor, preacher, professor and theologian. Dickson defended the Presbyterian form of ecclesial reformation in Scotland and was recognized for his iteration of Calvinist federal theology and expository biblical commentaries. Dickson served for over twenty years as professor of philosophy at the University of Glasgow before being appointed professor of divinity. He opposed the imposition of Episcopalian measures on the church in Scotland and was active in political and ecclesial venues to protest and prohibit such influences. Dickson was removed from his academic post following his refusal of the oath of supremacy during the Restoration era.

Veit Dietrich (1506–1549). German Lutheran preacher and theologian. Dietrich intended to study medicine at the University of Wittenberg, but Martin Luther* and Philipp Melanchthon* convinced him to study theology instead. Dietrich developed a strong relationship with Luther, accompanying him to the Marburg Colloquy (1529) and to Coburg Castle during the Diet of Augsburg (1530). After graduating, Dietrich taught on the arts faculty, eventually becoming dean. In 1535 he returned to his hometown, Nuremberg, to pastor.

Later in life, Dietrich worked with Melanchthon to reform the church in Regensburg. In 1547, when Charles V arrived in Nuremberg, Dietrich was suspended from the pastorate; he resisted the imposition of the Augsburg Interim to no avail. In addition to transcribing some of Luther's lectures, portions of the Table Talk and the very popular *Hauspostille* (1544), Dietrich published his own sermons for children, a manual for pastors and a summary of the Bible.

Giovanni Diodati (1576–1649). Italian Reformed theologian. Diodati was from an Italian banking family who fled for religious reasons to Geneva. There he trained under Theodore Beza;* on completion of his doctoral degree, Diodati became professor of Hebrew at the academy. He was an ecclesiastical representative of the church in Geneva (for whom he was a delegate at the Synod of Dordrecht*) and an advocate for reform in Venice. Diodati's chief contribution to the Italian reform movement was a translation of the Bible into Italian (1640–1641), which remains the standard translation in Italian Protestantism.

John Dod (c. 1549–1645). English Puritan pastor. Over the course of his lengthy pastoral career (spanning roughly sixty years), Dod was twice suspended for nonconformity and twice reinstated. A popular preacher, he published many sermons as well as commentaries on the Ten Commandments and the Lord's Prayer; collections of his sayings and anecdotes were compiled after his death.

John Donne (1572–1631). Anglican poet and preacher. Donne was born into a strong Catholic family. However, sometime between his brother's death from the plague while in prison in 1593 and the publication of his *Pseudo-Martyr* in 1610, Donne joined the Church of England. Ordained to the Anglican priesthood in 1615 and already widely recognized for his verse, Donne quickly rose to prominence as a preacher—some have deemed him the best of his era. His textual corpus is an amalgam of erotic *and* divine poetry (e.g., "Batter My Heart"), as well as a great number of sermons.

Dordrecht Confession (1632). Dutch Mennonite confession. Adriaan Cornelisz (1581–1632) wrote the Dordrecht Confession to unify Dutch Mennonites. This basic statement of Mennonite belief and practice affirms distinctive doctrines such as nonresistance, shunning, footwashing and the refusal to swear oaths. Most continental Mennonites subscribed to this confession during the second half of the seventeenth century.

John Downame (c. 1571–1652). English Puritan pastor and theologian. See *English Annotations*.

Charles Drelincourt (1595–1669). French Reformed pastor, theologian and controversialist. After studying at Saumur Academy, Drelincourt pastored the Reformed Church in Paris for nearly fifty years. He was well known for his ministry to the sick. In addition to polemical works against Catholicism, he published numerous pastoral resources: catechisms, three volumes of sermons and a five-volume series on consolation for the suffering.

The Dutch Annotations (1657). See *Statenvertaling*.

Daniel Dyke (d. 1614). English Puritan preacher. Born of nonconformist stock, Dyke championed a more thorough reformation of church practice in England. After the promulgation of John Whitgift's* articles in 1583, Dyke refused to accept what he saw as remnants of Catholicism, bringing him into conflict with the bishop of London. Despite the petitions of his congregation and some politicians, the bishop of London suspended Dyke from his ministry for refusing priestly ordination and conformity to the Book of Common Prayer.* All of his work was published posthumously; it is mostly focused on biblical interpretation.

Johann Eck (Johann Maier of Eck) (1486–1543). German Catholic theologian. Though Eck was not an antagonist of Martin Luther* until the dispute over indulgences, Luther's Ninety-five Theses (1517) sealed the two as adversaries. After their debate at the Leipzig Disputation (1519), Eck participated in the writing of the papal bull that led to Luther's excommunication. Much of Eck's work was written to oppose Protestantism or to defend Catholic doctrine and the papacy; his *Enchiridion* was a manual written to counter Protestant doctrine. However, Eck was also deeply invested in the status of parish preaching, publishing a five-volume set of postils. He participated in the assemblies at Regensburg and Augsburg and led the Catholics in their rejection of the Augsburg Confession.

English Annotations (1645; 1651; 1657). Under a commission from the Westminster Assembly, the editors of the English Annotations—John Downame* along with unnamed colleagues—translated, collated and digested in a compact and accessible format several significant Continental biblical resources, including Calvin's* commentaries, Beza's* *Annotationes majores* and Diodati's* *Annotations*.

Desiderius Erasmus (1466–1536). Dutch Catholic humanist and pedagogue. Erasmus, a celebrated humanist scholar, was recognized for translations of ancient texts, reform of education according to classical studies, moral and spiritual writings and the first printed edition of the Greek New Testament. A former Augustinian who never left the Catholic Church, Erasmus addressed deficiencies he saw in the church and society, challenging numerous prevailing doctrines but advocating reform. He envisioned a simple, spiritual Christian life shaped by the teachings of Jesus and ancient wisdom. He was often accused of collusion with Martin Luther* on account of some resonance of their ideas but hotly debated Luther on human will.

Paul Fagius (1504–1549). German Reformed Hebraist and pastor. After studying at the University of Heidelberg, Fagius went to Strasbourg where he perfected his Hebrew under Wolfgang Capito.* In Isny im Allgäu (Baden-Württemberg) he met the great Jewish grammarian Elias Levita (1469–1549), with whom he established a Hebrew printing press. In 1544 Fagius returned to Strasbourg, succeeding Capito as preacher and Old Testament lecturer. During the Augsburg Interim, Fagius (with Martin Bucer*) accepted Thomas Cranmer's* invitation to translate and interpret the Bible at Cambridge. However, Fagius died before he could begin any of the work. Fagius wrote commentaries on the first four chapters of Genesis and the deuterocanonical books of Sirach and Tobit.

John Fary (unknown). English Puritan pastor. Fary authored *God's Severity on Man's Sterility* (1645), a sermon on the fruitless fig tree in Luke 13:6-9.

William Fenner (1600–1640). English Puritan pastor. After studying at Cambridge and Oxford, Fenner ministered at Sedgley and Rochford. Fenner's extant writings, which primarily deal with practical and devotional topics, demonstrate a zealous Puritan piety and a keen interest in Scripture and theology.

First Helvetic Confession (1536). Anticipating the planned church council at Mantua (1537, but delayed until 1545 at Trent), Reformed theologians of the Swiss cantons drafted a confession to distinguish themselves from both Catholics and the churches of the Augsburg Confession.* Heinrich Bullinger* led the discussion and wrote the confession itself; Leo Jud, Oswald Myconius, Simon Grynaeus and others were part of the assembly. Martin Bucer* and Wolfgang Capito* had desired to draw the Lutheran and Reformed communions closer together through this document, but Luther* proved unwilling after Bullinger refused to accept the Wittenberg Concord (1536). This confession was largely eclipsed by Bullinger's Second Helvetic Confession.*

John Fisher (1469–1535). English Catholic bishop and theologian. This reputed preacher defended Catholic orthodoxy and strove to reform abuses in the church. In 1521 Henry VIII honored Fisher with the title *Fidei Defensor* ("defender of the faith"). Nevertheless, Fisher opposed the king's divorce of Catherine of Aragon (1485–1536) and the independent establishment of the Church of England; he was convicted for treason and executed. Most of Fisher's works are polemical and occasional (e.g., on transubstantiation, against Martin Luther*); however, he also published a series of sermons on the seven penitential psalms. In addition to his episcopal duties, Fisher was the chancellor of Cambridge from 1504 until his death.

John Flavel (c. 1630–1691). English Puritan pastor. Trained at Oxford, Flavel ministered in southwest England from 1650 until the Act of Uniformity in 1662, which reaffirmed the compulsory use of the Book of Common Prayer. Flavel preached unofficially for many years, until his congregation was eventually allowed to build a meeting place in 1687. His works were numerous, varied and popular.

Giovanni Battista Folengo (1490–1559). Italian Catholic exegete. In 1528 Folengo left the Benedictine order, questioning the validity of monastic vows; he returned to the monastic life in 1534. During this hiatus Folengo came into contact with the Neapolitan reform-minded circle founded by Juan de Valdés.* Folengo published commentaries on the Psalms, John, 1–2 Peter and James. Augustin Marlorat* included Folengo's comment in his anthology of exegesis on the Psalms. In 1580 Folengo's Psalms commentary was added to the Index of Prohibited Books.

Formula of Concord (1577). After Luther's* death, intra-Lutheran controversies between the Gnesio-Lutherans (partisans of Luther) and the Philippists (partisans of Melanchthon*) threatened to cause a split among those who had subscribed to the Augsburg Confession.* In 1576, Jakob Andreae,* Martin Chemnitz,* Nikolaus Selnecker,* David Chytraeus* and Andreas Musculus (1514–1581) met with the intent of resolving the controversies, which mainly regarded the relationship between good works and salvation, the third use of the law, and the role of the human will in accepting God's grace. In 1580, celebrating the fiftieth anniversary of the presentation of the Augsburg Confession to Charles V (1500–1558), the *Book of Concord* was printed as the authoritative interpretation of the Augsburg Confession; it included the three ancient creeds, the Augsburg Confession, its Apology (1531), the Schmalkald Articles,* Luther's *Treatise on the Power and Primacy of the Pope* (1537) and both his Small and Large Catechisms (1529).

Sebastian Franck (1499–1542). German Radical theologian. Franck became a Lutheran in 1525, but by 1529 he began to develop ideas that distanced him from Protestants and Catholics.

Expelled from Strasbourg and later Ulm due to his controversial writings, Franck spent the end of his life in Basel. Franck emphasized God's word as a divine internal spark that cannot be adequately expressed in outward forms. Thus he criticized religious institutions and dogmas. His work consists mostly of commentaries, compilations and translations. In his sweeping historical *Chronica* (1531), Franck supported numerous heretics condemned by the Catholic Church and criticized political and church authorities.

Leonhard Frick (d. 1528). Austrian Radical martyr. See *Kunstbuch*.

Gallic Confession (1559). This confession was accepted at the first National Synod of the Reformed Churches of France (1559). It was intended to be a touchstone of Reformed faith but also to show to the people of France that the Huguenots—who faced persecution—were not seditious. The French Reformed Church presented this confession to Francis II (1544–1560) in 1560, and to his successor, Charles IX (1550–1574), in 1561. The later Genevan draft, likely written by Calvin,* Beza* and Pierre Viret (1511–1571), was received as the true Reformed confession at the seventh National Synod in La Rochelle (1571).

Geneva Bible (originally printed 1560). During Mary I's reign many English Protestants sought safety abroad in Reformed territories of the Empire and the Swiss Cantons, especially in Calvin's* Geneva. A team of English exiles in Geneva led by William Whittingham (c. 1524–1579) brought this complete translation to press in the course of two years. Notable for several innovations—Roman type, verse numbers, italics indicating English idiom and not literal phrasing of the original languages, even variant readings in the Gospels and Acts—this translation is most well known for its marginal notes, which reflect a strongly Calvinist theology. The notes explained Scripture in an accessible way for the laity, also giving unlearned clergy a new sermon resource. Although controversial because of its implicit critique of royal power, this translation was wildly popular; even after the publication of the Authorized Version (1611) and

James I's 1616 ban on its printing, the Geneva Bible continued to be the most popular English translation until after the English Civil Wars.

Johann Gerhard (1582–1637). German Lutheran theologian, professor and superintendent. Gerhard is considered one of the most eminent Lutheran theologians, after Martin Luther* and Martin Chemnitz.* After studying patristics and Hebrew at Wittenberg, Jena and Marburg, Gerhard was appointed superintendent at the age of twenty-four. In 1616 he was appointed to a post at the University of Jena, where he reintroduced Aristotelian metaphysics to theology and gained widespread fame. His most important work was the nine-volume *Loci Theologici* (1610–1625). He also expanded Chemnitz's harmony of the Gospels (*Harmonia Evangelicae*), which was finally published by Polykarp Leyser (1552–1610) in 1593. Gerhard was well-known for an irenic spirit and an ability to communicate clearly.

George Gifford (c. 1548–1600). English Puritan pastor. Gifford was suspended for nonconformity in 1584. With private support, however, he was able to continue his ministry. Through his published works he wanted to help develop lay piety and biblical literacy.

Anthony Gilby (c. 1510–1585). English Puritan translator. During Mary I's reign, Gilby fled to Geneva, where he assisted William Whittingham (c. 1524–1579) with the Geneva Bible.* He returned to England to pastor after Elizabeth I's accession. In addition to translating numerous continental Reformed works into English—especially those of John Calvin* and Theodore Beza*—Gilby also wrote commentaries on Micah and Malachi.

Bernard Gilpin (1517–1583). Anglican theologian and priest. In public disputations, Gilpin defended Roman Catholic theology against John Hooper (c. 1495-1555) and Peter Martyr Vermigli.* These debates caused Gilpin to reexamine his faith. Upon Mary I's accession, Gilpin resigned his benefice. He sojourned in Belgium and France, returning to pastoral ministry in England in 1556. Gilpin dedicated himself to a preaching circuit in northern England, thus earning the moniker "the Apostle to the North." His zealous preaching and almsgiving roused royal opposition and a warrant for his arrest. On his way to the queen's commission, Gilpin fractured his leg, delaying his arrival in London until after Mary's death and thus likely saving his life. His only extant writing is a sermon on Luke 2 confronting clerical abuses.

Glossa ordinaria. This standard collection of biblical commentaries consists of interlinear and marginal notes drawn from patristic and Carolingian exegesis appended to the Vulgate*; later editions also include Nicholas of Lyra's* *Postilla*. The *Glossa ordinaria* and the Sentences of Peter Lombard (c. 1100–1160) were essential resources for all late medieval and early modern commentators.

Conrad Grebel (c. 1498–1526). Swiss Radical theologian. Grebel, considered the father of the Anabaptist movement, was one of the first defenders and performers of believers' baptism, for which he was eventually imprisoned in Zurich. One of Huldrych Zwingli's* early compatriots, Grebel advocated rapid, radical reform, clashing publicly with the civil authorities and Zwingli. Grebel's views, particularly on baptism, were influenced by Andreas Bodenstein von Karlstadt* and Thomas Müntzer.* Grebel advocated elimination of magisterial involvement in governing the church; instead, he envisioned the church as lay Christians determining their own affairs with strict adherence to the biblical text, and unified in volitional baptism.

William Greenhill (1591–1671). English Puritan pastor. Greenhill attended and worked at Magdalen College. He ministered in the diocese of Norwich but soon left for London, where he preached at Stepney. Greenhill was a member of the Westminster Assembly of Divines and was appointed the parliament chaplain by the children of Charles I. Oliver Cromwell included him among the preachers who helped draw up the Savoy Declaration. Greenhill was evicted from his post following the Restoration, after which he pastored independently. Among Greenhill's most significant contributions to church history was his *Exposition of the Prophet of Ezekiel*.

Catharina Regina von Greiffenberg (1633–1694). Austrian Lutheran poet. Upon her adulthood her guardian (and half uncle) sought to marry her; despite her protests of their consanguinity and her desire to remain celibate, she relented in 1664. After the deaths of her mother and husband, Greiffenberg abandoned her home to debtors and joined her friends Susanne Popp (d. 1683) and Sigmund von Birken (1626–1681) in Nuremberg. During her final years she dedicated herself to studying the biblical languages and to writing meditations on Jesus' death and resurrection, which she never completed. One of the most important and learned Austrian poets of the Baroque period, Greiffenberg published a collection of sonnets, songs and poems (1662) as well as three sets of mystical meditations on Jesus' life, suffering and death (1672; 1683; 1693). She participated in a society of poets called the Ister Gesellschaft.

Rudolf Gwalther (1519–1586). Swiss Reformed preacher. Gwalther was a consummate servant of the Reformed church in Zurich, its chief religious officer and preacher, a responsibility fulfilled previously by Huldrych Zwingli* and Heinrich Bullinger.* Gwalther provided sermons and commentaries and translated the works of Zwingli into Latin. He worked for many years alongside Bullinger in structuring and governing the church in Zurich. Gwalther also strove to strengthen the connections to the Reformed churches on the Continent and England: he was a participant in the Colloquy of Regensburg (1541) and an opponent of the Formula of Concord.*

Hans Has von Hallstatt (d. 1527). Austrian Reformed pastor. See *Kunstbuch*.

Henry Hammond (1605–1660). Anglican priest. After completing his studies at Oxford, Hammond was ordained in 1629. A Royalist, Hammond helped recruit soldiers for the king; he was chaplain to Charles I. During the king's captivity, Hammond was imprisoned for not submitting to Parliament. Later he was allowed to pastor again, until his death. Hammond published a catechism, numerous polemical sermons and treatises as well as his *Paraphrase and Annotations on the New Testament* (1653).

Peter Hausted (d. 1645). Anglican priest and playwright. Educated at Cambridge and Oxford, Hausted ministered in a number of parishes and preached adamantly and vehemently against Puritanism. He is best known for his play *The Rival Friends*, which is filled with invective against the Puritans; during a performance before the king and queen, a riot nearly broke out. Haustead died during the siege of Banbury Castle.

Heidelberg Catechism (1563). This German Reformed catechism was commissioned by the elector of the Palatinate, Frederick III (1515–1576) for pastors and teachers in his territories to use in instructing children and new believers in the faith. It was written by theologian Zacharias Ursinus (1534–1583) in consultation with Frederick's court preacher Kaspar Olevianus* and the entire theology faculty at the University of Heidelberg. The Heidelberg Catechism was accepted as one of the Dutch Reformed Church's Three Forms of Unity— along with the Belgic Confession* and the Canons of Dordrecht—at the Synod of Dordrecht,* and became widely popular among other Reformed confessional traditions throughout Europe.

Niels Hemmingsen (1513–1600). Danish Lutheran theologian. Hemmingsen studied at the University of Wittenberg, where he befriended Philipp Melanchthon.* In 1542, Hemmingsen returned to Denmark to pastor and to teach Greek, dialectics and theology at the University of Copenhagen. Foremost of the Danish theologians, Hemmingsen oversaw the preparation and publication of the first Danish Bible (1550). Later in his career he became embroiled in controversies because of his Philippist theology, especially regarding the Eucharist. Due to rising tensions with Lutheran nobles outside of Denmark, King Frederick II (1534–1588) dismissed Hemmingsen from his university post in 1579, transferring him to a prominent but less internationally visible Cathedral outside of Copenhagen. Hemmingsen was a prolific author, writing commentaries on the New Testament and Psalms, sermon collections and several methodological, theological and pastoral handbooks.

Tilemann Hesshus (1527–1588). German Lutheran theologian and pastor. Hesshus studied under Philipp Melanchthon* but was a staunch Gnesio-Lutheran. With great hesitation—and later regret—he affirmed the Formula of Concord.* Heshuss ardently advocated for church discipline, considering obedience a mark of the church. Unwilling to compromise his strong convictions, especially regarding matters of discipline, Hesshus was regularly embroiled in controversy. He was expelled or pressed to leave Goslar, Rostock, Heidelberg, Bremen, Magdeburg, Wesel, Königsberg and Samland before settling in Helmstedt, where he remained until his death. He wrote numerous polemical tracts concerning ecclesiology, justification, the sacraments and original sin, as well as commentaries on Psalms, Romans, 1–2 Corinthians, Galatians, Colossians and 1–2 Timothy, and a postil collection.

Christopher Hooke (unknown). English Puritan physician and pastor. Hooke published a treatise promoting the joys and blessings of childbirth (1590) and a sermon on Hebrews 12:11-12. To support the poor, Hooke proposed a bank funded by voluntary investment of wealthy households.

Richard Hooker (c. 1553–1600). Anglican priest. Shortly after graduating from Corpus Christi College Oxford, Hooker took holy orders as a priest in 1581. After his marriage, he struggled to find work and temporarily tended sheep until Archbishop John Whitgift* appointed him to the Temple Church in London. Hooker's primary work is *The Laws of Ecclesiastical Polity* (1593), in which he sought to establish a philosophical and logical foundation for the highly controversial Elizabethan Religious Settlement (1559). The Elizabethan Settlement, through the Act of Supremacy, reasserted the Church of England's independence from the Church of Rome, and, through the Act of Uniformity, constructed a common church structure based on the reinstitution of the Book of Common Prayer.* Hooker's argumentation strongly emphasizes natural law and anticipates the social contract theory of John Locke (1632–1704).

John Hooper (d. 1555). English Protestant bishop and martyr. Impressed by the works of Huldrych Zwingli* and Heinrich Bullinger,* Hooper joined the Protestant movement in England. However, after the Act of Six Articles was passed, he fled to Zurich, where he spent ten years. He returned to England in 1549 and was appointed as a bishop. He stoutly advocated a Zwinglian reform agenda, arguing against the use of vestments and for a less "popish" Book of Common Prayer.* Condemned as a heretic for denying transubstantiation, Hooper was burned at the stake during Mary I's reign.

Rudolf Hospinian (Wirth) (1547–1626). Swiss Reformed theologian and minister. After studying theology at Marburg and Heidelberg, Hospinian pastored in rural parishes around Zurich and taught secondary school. In 1588, he transferred to Zurich, ministering at Grossmünster and Frau-münster. A keen student of church history, Hospinian wanted to show the differences between early church doctrine and contemporary Catholic teaching, particularly with regard to sacramental theology. He also criticized Lutheran dogma and the Formula of Concord*. Most of Hospinian's corpus consists of polemical treatises; he also published a series of sermons on the Magnificat.

Caspar Huberinus (1500–1553). German Lutheran theologian and pastor. After studying theology at Wittenberg, Huberinus moved to Augsburg to serve as Urbanus Rhegius's* assistant. Huberinus represented Augsburg at the Bern Disputation (1528) on the Eucharist and images. In 1551, along with the nobility, Huberinus supported the Augsburg Interim, so long as communion of both kinds and regular preaching were allowed. Nevertheless the people viewed him as a traitor because of his official participation in the Interim, nicknaming him "Buberinus" (i.e., scoundrel). He wrote a number of popular devotional works as well as tracts defending Lutheran eucharistic theology against Zwinglian and Anabaptist detractions.

Balthasar Hubmaier (1480/5–1528). German Radical theologian. Hubmaier, a former priest who studied under Johann Eck,* is identified with his leadership in the peasants' uprising at Waldshut. Hubmaier served as the cathedral preacher in Regensberg, where he became involved in a series of anti-Semitic attacks. He was drawn to reform through the early works of Martin Luther*; his contact with Huldrych Zwingli* made Hubmaier a defender of more radical reform, including believers' baptism and a memorialist account of the Eucharist. His involvement in the Peasants' War led to his extradition and execution by the Austrians.

Aegidius Hunnius (1550–1603). German Lutheran theologian and preacher. Educated at Tübingen by Jakob Andreae (1528–1590) and Johannes Brenz,* Hunnius bolstered and advanced early Lutheran orthodoxy. After his crusade to root out all "crypto-Calvinism" divided Hesse into Lutheran and Reformed regions, Hunnius joined the Wittenberg theological faculty, where with Polykarp Leyser (1552–1610) he helped shape the university into an orthodox stronghold. Passionately confessional, Hunnius developed and nuanced the orthodox doctrines of predestination, Scripture, the church and Christology (more explicitly Chalcedonian), reflecting their codification in the Formula of Concord.* He was unafraid to engage in confessional polemics from the pulpit. In addition to his many treatises (most notably *De persona Christi*, in which he defended Christ's ubiquity), Hunnius published commentaries on Matthew, John, Ephesians and Colossians; his notes on Galatians, Philemon and 1 Corinthians were published posthumously.

Jan Hus (d. 1415). Bohemian reformer and martyr. This popular preacher strove for reform in the church, moral improvement in society, and an end to clerical abuses and popular religious superstition. He was branded a heretic for his alleged affinity for John Wycliffe's writings; however, while he agreed that a priest in mortal sin rendered the sacraments inefficacious, he affirmed the doctrine of transubstantiation. The Council of Constance* convicted Hus of heresy, banned his books and teaching, and, despite a letter of safe conduct, burned him at the stake.

Hans Hut (1490–1527). German Radical leader. Hut was an early leader of a mystical, apocalyptic strand of Anabaptist radical reform. His theological views were shaped by Andreas Bodenstein von Karlstadt,* Thomas Müntzer* and Hans Denck,* by whom Hut had been baptized. Hut rejected society and the established church and heralded the imminent end of days, which he perceived in the Peasants' War. Eventually arrested for practicing believers' baptism and participating in the Peasants' War, Hut was tortured and died accidentally in a fire in the Augsburg prison. The next day, the authorities sentenced his corpse to death and burned him.

George Hutcheson (1615–1674). Scottish Puritan pastor. Hutcheson, a pastor in Edinburgh, published commentaries on Job, John and the Minor Prophets, as well as sermons on Psalm 130.

Roger Hutchinson (d. 1555). English reformer. Little is known about Hutchinson except for his controversies. He disputed against the Mass while at Cambridge and debated with Joan Bocher (d. 1550), who affirmed the doctrine of the celestial flesh. During the Marian Restoration he was deprived of his fellowship at Eton because he was married.

Abraham Ibn Ezra (1089–c. 1167). Spanish Jewish rabbi, exegete and poet. In 1140 Ibn Ezra fled his native Spain to escape persecution by the Almohad Caliphate. He spent the rest of his life as an exile, traveling through Europe, North Africa and the Middle East. His corpus consists of works on poetry, exegesis, grammar, philosophy, mathematics and astrology. In his commentaries on the Old Testament, Ibn Ezra restricts himself to *peshat* (see *quadriga*).

Valentin Ickelshamer (c. 1500–1547). German Radical teacher. After time at Erfurt, he studied under Luther,* Melanchthon,* Bugenhagen* and Karlstadt* in Wittenberg. He sided with Karlstadt against Luther, writing a treatise in Karlstadt's defense. Ickelshamer also represented the Wittenberg guilds in opposition to the city council. This guild committee allied with the peasants in 1525, leading to Ickelshamer's eventual exile. His poem in the Marpeck Circle's *Kunstbuch** is an expansion of a similar poem by Sebastian Franck.*

Thomas Jackson (1579–1640). Anglican theologian and priest. Before serving as the president of Corpus Christi College at Oxford for the final decade of his life, Jackson was a parish priest and chaplain to the king. His best known work is a twelve-volume commentary on the Apostles' Creed.

King James I of England (VI of Scotland) (1566–1625). English monarch. The son of Mary, Queen of Scots, James ascended to the Scottish throne in 1567 following his mother's abdication. In the Union of the Crowns (1603), he took the English and Irish thrones after the death of his cousin, Elizabeth I. James's reign was tumultuous and tense: Parliament and the nobility often opposed him, church factions squabbled over worship forms and ecclesiology, climaxing in the Gunpowder Plot. James wrote treatises on the divine right of kings, law, the evils of smoking tobacco and demonology. His religious writings include a versification of the Psalms, a paraphrase of Revelation and meditations on the Lord's Prayer and passages from Chronicles, Matthew and Revelation. He also sponsored the translation of the Authorized Version*—popularly remembered as the King James Version.

John Jewel (1522–1571). Anglican theologian and bishop. Jewel studied at Oxford where he met Peter Martyr Vermigli.* After graduating in 1552, Jewel was appointed to his first vicarage and became the orator for the university. Upon Mary I's accession, Jewel lost his post as orator because of his Protestant views. After the trials of Thomas Cranmer* and Nicholas Ridley,* Jewel affirmed Catholic teaching to avoid their fate. Still he had to flee to the continent. Confronted by John Knox,* Jewel publicly repented of his cowardice before the English congregation in Frankfurt, then reunited with Vermigli in Strasbourg. After Mary I's death, Jewel returned to England and was consecrated bishop in 1560. He advocated low-church ecclesiology, but supported the Elizabethan Settlement against Catholics and

Puritans. In response to the Council of Trent, he published the *Apoligia ecclesiae Anglicanae* (1562), which established him as the apostle for Anglicanism and incited numerous controversies.

Justus Jonas (1493–1555). German Lutheran theologian, pastor and administrator. Jonas studied law at Erfurt, where he befriended the poet Eobanus Hessus (1488–1540), whom Luther* dubbed "king of the poets"; later, under the influence of the humanist Konrad Muth, Jonas focused on theology. In 1516 he was ordained as a priest, and in 1518 he became a doctor of theology and law. After witnessing the Leipzig Disputation, Jonas was converted to Luther's* cause. While traveling with Luther to the Diet of Worms, Jonas was appointed professor of canon law at Wittenberg. Later he became its dean of theology, lecturing on Romans, Acts and the Psalms. Jonas was also instrumental for reform in Halle. He preached Luther's funeral sermon but had a falling-out with Melanchthon* over the Leipzig Interim. Jonas's most influential contribution was translating Luther's *The Bondage of the Will* and Melanchthon's *Loci communes* into German.

David Joris (c. 1501–1556). Dutch Radical pastor and hymnist. This former glass painter was one of the leading Dutch Anabaptist leaders after the fall of Münster (1535), although due to his increasingly radical ideas his influence waned in the early 1540s. Joris came to see himself as a "third David," a Spirit-anointed prophet ordained to proclaim the coming third kingdom of God, which would be established in the Netherlands with Dutch as its *lingua franca*. Joris's interpretation of Scripture, with his heavy emphasis on personal mystical experience, led to a very public dispute with Menno Simons* whom Joris considered a teacher of the "dead letter." In 1544 Joris and about one hundred followers moved to Basel, conforming outwardly to the teaching of the Reformed church there. Today 240 of Joris's books are extant, the most important of which is his *Twonder Boek* (1542/43).

Andreas Bodenstein von Karlstadt (Carlstadt) (1486–1541). German Radical theologian. Karlstadt, an early associate of Martin Luther* and Philipp Melanchthon* at the University of Wittenberg, participated alongside Luther in the dispute at Leipzig with Johann Eck.* He also influenced the configuration of the Old Testament canon in Protestantism. During Luther's captivity in Wartburg Castle in Eisenach, Karlstadt oversaw reform in Wittenberg. His acceleration of the pace of reform brought conflict with Luther, so Karlstadt left Wittenberg, eventually settling at the University of Basel as professor of Old Testament (after a sojourn in Zurich with Huldrych Zwingli*). During his time in Switzerland, Karlstadt opposed infant baptism and repudiated Luther's doctrine of Christ's real presence in the Eucharist.

Edward Kellett (d. 1641). Anglican theologian and priest. Kellett published a sermon concerning the reconversion of an Englishman from Islam, a tract on the soul and a discourse on the Lord's Supper in connection with Passover.

David Kimchi (Radak) (1160–1235). French Jewish rabbi, exegete and philosopher. Kimchi wrote an important Hebrew grammar and dictionary, as well as commentaries on Genesis, 1–2 Chronicles, the Psalms and the Prophets. He focused on *peshat* (see *quadriga*). In his Psalms commentary he attacks Christian interpretation as forced, irrational and inadmissible. While Sebastian Münster* censors and condemns these arguments in his *Miqdaš YHWH* (1534–1535), he and many other Christian commentators valued Kimchi's work as a grammatical resource.

Moses Kimchi (Remak) (1127–1190). French Jewish rabbi and exegete. He was David Kimchi's* brother. He wrote commentaries on Proverbs and Ezra-Nehemiah. Sebastian Münster* translated Kimchi's concise Hebrew grammar into Latin; many sixteenth-century Christian exegetes used this resource.

John Knox (1513–1572). Scottish Reformed preacher. Knox, a fiery preacher to monarchs and zealous defender of high Calvinism, was a leading figure of reform in Scotland. Following imprisonment in the French galleys, Knox went to England, where he became a royal chaplain to Edward VI. At the accession of Mary, Knox fled to Geneva, studying under John Calvin* and serving as a pastor. Knox returned to Scotland after Mary's death and became a chief architect of the reform of the Scottish church (Presbyterian), serving as one of the authors of the Book of Discipline and writing many pamphlets and sermons.

Antonius Broickwy von Königstein (1470–1541). German Catholic preacher. Very little is known about this important cathedral preacher in Cologne. Strongly opposed to evangelicals, he sought to develop robust resources for Catholic homilies. His postils were bestsellers, and his biblical concordance helped Catholic preachers to construct doctrinal loci from Scripture itself.

Kunstbuch. In 1956, two German students rediscovered this unique collection of Anabaptist works. Four hundred years earlier, a friend of the recently deceased Pilgram Marpeck*—the painter Jörg Probst—had entrusted this collection of letters, tracts and poetry to a Zurich bindery; today only half of it remains. Probst's redaction arranges various compositions from the Marpeck Circle into a devotional anthology focused on the theme of the church as Christ incarnate (cf. Gal 2:20).

Osmund Lake (c. 1543–1621). English Pastor who ministered at Ringwood in Hampshire.

François Lambert (Lambert of Avignon) (1487–1530). French Reformed theologian. In 1522, after becoming drawn to the writings of Martin Luther* and meeting Huldrych Zwingli,* Lambert left the Franciscan order. He spent time in Wittenberg, Strasbourg, and Hesse, where Lambert took a leading role at the Homberg Synod (1526) and in creating a biblically based plan for church reform. He served as professor of theology at Marburg University from 1527 to his death. After the Marburg Colloquy (1529), Lambert accepted Zwingli's symbolic view of the Eucharist. Lambert produced nineteen books, mostly biblical commentaries that favored spiritual interpretations; his unfinished work of comprehensive theology was published posthumously.

Hugh Latimer (c. 1485–1555). Anglican bishop and preacher. Latimer was celebrated for his sermons critiquing the idolatrous nature of Catholic practices and the social injustices visited on the underclass by the aristocracy and the individualism of Protestant government. After his support for Henry's petition of divorce he served as a court preacher under Henry VIII and Edward VI. Latimer became a proponent of reform following his education at Cambridge University and received license as a preacher. Following Edward's death, Latimer was tried for heresy, perishing at the stake with Nicholas Ridley* and Thomas Cranmer.*

William Laud (1573–1645). Anglican archbishop, one of the most pivotal and controversial figures in Anglican church history. Early in his career, Laud offended many with his highly traditional, anti-Puritan approach to ecclesial policies. After his election as Archbishop of Canterbury in 1633, Laud continued to strive against the Puritans, demanding the eastward placement of the Communion altar (affirming the religious centrality of the Eucharist), the use of clerical garments, the reintroduction of stained-glass windows, and the uniform use of the Book of Common Prayer.* Laud was accused of being a crypto-Catholic—an ominous accusation during the protracted threat of invasion by the Spanish Armada. In 1640 the Long Parliament met, quickly impeached Laud on charges of treason, and placed him in jail for several years before his execution.

Ludwig Lavater (1527–1586). Swiss Reformed pastor and theologian. Under his father-in-law Heinrich Bullinger,* Lavater became an archdeacon in Zurich. In 1585 he succeeded Rudolf Gwalther* as the city's Antistes. He authored a widely disseminated book on demonology, commentaries on Chronicles, Proverbs, Ecclesiastes, Nehemiah and Ezekiel, theological works, and biographies of Bullinger and Konrad Pellikan.*

John Lawson (unknown). Seventeenth-century English Puritan. Lawson wrote *Gleanings and Expositions of Some of Scripture* (1646) and a treatise on the sabbath in the New Testament.

Jacques Lefèvre d'Étaples (Faber Stapulensis) (1460?–1536). French Catholic humanist, publisher and translator. Lefèvre d'Étaples studied classical literature and philosophy, as well as patristic and medieval mysticism. He advocated the principle of *ad fontes*, issuing a full-scale annotation on the corpus of Aristotle, publishing the writings of key Christian mystics, and contributing to efforts at biblical translation and commentary. Although he never broke with the Catholic Church, his views prefigured those of Martin Luther,* for which he was condemned by the University of Sorbonne in Paris. He then found refuge in the court of Marguerite d'Angoulême, where he met John Calvin* and Martin Bucer.*

Edward Leigh (1602–1671). English Puritan biblical critic, historian and politician. Educated at Oxford, Leigh's public career included appointments as a Justice of the Peace, an officer in the parliamentary army during the English Civil Wars and a member of Parliament. Although never ordained, Leigh devoted himself to the study of theology and Scripture; he participated in the Westminster Assembly. Leigh published a diverse corpus, including lexicons of Greek, Hebrew and juristic terms, and histories of Roman, Greek and English rulers. His most important theological work is *A Systeme or Body of Divinity* (1662).

John Lightfoot (1602–1675). Anglican priest and biblical scholar. After graduating from Cambridge, Lightfoot was ordained and pastored at several small parishes. He continued to study classics under the support of the politician Rowland Cotton (1581–1634). Siding with the Parliamentarians during the English Civil Wars, Lightfoot relocated to London in 1643. He was one of the original members of the Westminster Assembly, where he defended a moderate Presbyterianism. His best-known work is the six-volume *Horae Hebraicae et Talmudicae* (1658–1677), a verse-by-verse commentary illumined by Hebrew customs, language and the Jewish interpretive tradition.

Lucas Lossius (1508–1582). German Lutheran teacher and musician. While a student at Leipzig and Wittenberg, Lossius was deeply influenced by Melanchthon* and Luther,* who found work for him as Urbanus Rhegius's* secretary. Soon after going to work for Rhegius, Lossius began teaching at a local gymnasium (or secondary school), *Das Johanneum*, eventually becoming its headmaster. Lossius remained at *Das Johanneum* until his death, even turning down appointments to university professorships. A man of varied interests, he wrote on dialectics, music and church history, as well as publishing a postil and a five-volume set of annotations on the New Testament.

Sibrandus Lubbertus (c. 1555–1625). Dutch Reformed theologian. Lubbertis, a key figure in the establishment of orthodox Calvinism in Frisia, studied theology at Wittenburg and Geneva (under Theodore Beza*) before his appointment as professor of theology at the University of Franeker. Throughout his career, Lubbertis advocated for high Calvinist theology, defending it in disputes with representatives of Socinianism, Arminianism and Roman Catholicism. Lubbertis criticized the Catholic theologian Robert Bellarmine and fellow Dutch reformer Jacobus Arminius*; the views of the latter he opposed as a prominent participant in the Synod of Dordrecht.*

Martin Luther (1483–1546). German Lutheran priest, professor and theologian. While a professor in Wittenberg, Luther reinterpreted the doctrine of justification. Convinced that righteousness comes only from God's grace, he disputed the sale of indulgences with the Ninety-five Theses. Luther's positions brought conflict with Rome; his denial of papal authority led to excommunication. He also challenged the Mass, transubstantiation and communion under one kind. Though Luther was condemned by the Diet of Worms, the Elector of Saxony provided him safe haven. Luther returned to Wittenberg with public order collapsing under Andreas Bodenstein von Karlstadt;* Luther steered a more cautious path of reform. His rendering of the Bible and liturgy in the vernacular, as well as his hymns and sermons, proved extensively influential.

Georg Major (1502–1574). German Lutheran theologian. Major was on the theological faculty of the University of Wittenberg, succeeding as dean Johannes Bugenhagen* and Philipp Melanchthon.* One of the chief editors on the Wittenberg edition of Luther's works, Major is most identified with the controversy bearing his name, in which he stated that good works are necessary to salvation. Major qualified his statement, which was in reference to the totality of the Christian life. The Formula of Concord* rejected the statement, ending the controversy. As a theologian, Major further refined Lutheran views of the inspiration of Scripture and the doctrine of the Trinity.

John (Mair) Major (1467–1550). Scottish Catholic philosopher. Major taught logic and theology at the universities of Paris (his alma mater), Glasgow and St Andrews. His broad interests and impressive work drew students from all over Europe. While disapproving of evangelicals (though he did teach John Knox*), Major advocated reform programs for Rome. He supported collegial episcopacy and even challenged the curia's teaching on sexuality. Still he was a nominalist who was critical of humanist approaches to biblical exegesis. His best-known publication is *A History of Greater Britain, Both England and Scotland* (1521), which promoted the union of the kingdoms. He also published a commentary on Peter Lombard's *Sentences* and the Gospel of John.

Juan de Maldonado (1533–1583). Spanish Catholic biblical scholar. A student of Francisco de Toledo,* Maldonado taught philosophy and theology at the universities of Paris and Salamanca. Ordained to the priesthood in Rome, he revised the Septuagint under papal appointment. While Maldonado vehemently criticized Protestants, he asserted that Reformed baptism was valid and that mixed confessional marriages were acceptable. His views on Mary's immaculate conception proved controversial among many Catholics who conflated his statement that it was not an article of faith with its denial. He was intrigued by demonology (blaming demonic influence for the Reformation). All his work was published posthumously; his Gospel commentaries were highly valued and important.

Thomas Manton (1620–1677). English Puritan minister. Manton, educated at Oxford, served for a time as lecturer at Westminster Abbey and rector of St. Paul's, Covent Garden, and was a strong advocate of Presbyterianism. He was known as a rigorous evangelical Calvinist who preached long expository sermons. At different times in his ecclesial career he worked side-by-side with Richard Baxter* and John Owen.* In his later life, Manton's Nonconformist position led to his ejection as a clergyman from the Church of England (1662) and eventual imprisonment (1670). Although a voluminous writer, Manton was best known for his preaching. At his funeral in 1677, he was dubbed "the king of preachers."

Augustin Marlorat (c. 1506–1562). French Reformed pastor. Committed by his family to a monastery at the age of eight, Marlorat was also ordained into the priesthood at an early age in 1524. He fled to Geneva in 1535, where he pastored until the Genevan Company of Pastors sent him to France to shepherd the nascent evangelical congregations. His petition to the young Charles IX (1550–1574) for the right to public evangelical worship was denied. In response to a massacre of evangelicals in Vassy (over sixty dead, many more wounded), Marlorat's congregation planned to overtake Rouen. After the crown captured Rouen, Marlorat was arrested and executed three days later for treason. His principle published work was an anthology of New Testament comment modeled after Thomas Aquinas's *Catena aurea in quatuor Evangelia*. Marlorat harmonized Reformed and Lutheran comment with the church fathers, interspersed with his own brief comments. He also wrote such anthologies for Genesis, Job, the Psalms, Song of Songs and Isaiah.

Pilgram Marpeck (c. 1495–1556). Austrian Radical elder and theologian. During a brief sojourn in Strasbourg, Marpeck debated with Martin Bucer* before the city council; Bucer was declared the winner, and Marpeck was asked to leave Strasbourg for his views concerning paedo-baptism (which he compared to a sacrifice to Moloch). After his time in Strasbourg, Marpeck traveled throughout southern Germany and western Austria, planting Anabaptist congregations. Marpeck criticized the strict use of the ban, however, particularly among the Swiss brethren. He also engaged in a christological controversy with Kaspar von Schwenckfeld.*

Johannes Mathesius (1504–1565). German Lutheran theologian and pastor. After reading Martin Luther's* *On Good Works*, Mathesius left his teaching post in Ingolstadt and traveled to Wittenberg to study theology. Mathesius was an important agent of reform in the Bohemian town of Jáchymov, where he pastored, preached and taught. Over one thousand of Mathesius's sermons are extant, including numerous wedding and funeral sermons as well as a series on Luther's life. Mathesius also transcribed portions of Luther's Table Talk.

John Mayer (1583–1664). Anglican priest and biblical exegete. Mayer dedicated much of his life to biblical exegesis, writing a seven-volume commentary on the entire Bible (1627–1653). Styled after Philipp Melanchthon's* *locus* method, Mayer's work avoided running commentary, focusing instead on textual and theological problems. He was a parish priest for fifty-five years. In the office of priest Mayer also wrote a popular catechism, *The English Catechisme, or a Commentarie on the Short Catechisme* (1621), which went through twelve editions in his lifetime.

Joseph Mede (1586–1638). Anglican biblical scholar, Hebraist and Greek lecturer. A man of encyclopedic knowledge, Mede was interested in numerous fields, varying from philology and history to mathematics and physics, although millennial thought and apocalyptic prophesy were clearly his chief interests. Mede's most important work was his *Clavis Apocalyptica* (1627, later translated into English as *The Key of the Revelation*). This work examined the structure of Revelation as the key to its interpretation. Mede saw the visions as a connected and chronological sequence hinging around Revelation 17:18. He is remembered as an important figure in the history of millenarian theology. He was respected as a mild-mannered and generous scholar who avoided controversy and debate, but who had many original thoughts.

Philipp Melanchthon (1497–1560). German Lutheran educator, reformer and theologian. Melanchthon is known as the partner and successor to Martin Luther* in reform in Germany and for his pioneering *Loci communes*, which served as a theological textbook. Melanchthon participated with Luther in the Leipzig disputation, helped implement reform in Wittenberg and was a chief architect of the Augsburg Confession.* Later, Melanchthon and Martin Bucer* worked for union between the reformed and Catholic churches. On account of Melanchthon's more ecumenical disposition and his modification of several of Luther's doctrines, he was held in suspicion by some.

Justus Menius (1499–1558). German Lutheran pastor and theologian. Menius was a prominent reformer in Thuringia. He participated in the Marburg Colloquy and, with others, helped Martin Luther* compose the Schmalkald Articles.* Throughout his career Menius entered into numerous controversies with Anabaptists and even fellow Lutherans. He rejected Andreas Osiander's (d. 1552) doctrine of justification—that the indwelling of Christ's divine nature justifies, rather than the imputed alien righteousness of Christ's person, declared through God's mercy. Against Nikolaus von Amsdorf (1483–1565) and Matthias Flacius (1520–1575), Menius agreed with Georg Major* that good works are necessary to salvation. Osiander's view of justification was censored in Article 3 of the Formula of Concord*; Menius's understanding of the relationship between good works and salvation was rejected in Article 4. Menius translated many of Luther's Latin works into German. He also composed a handbook for Christian households and an influential commentary on 1 Samuel.

Johannes Mercerus (Jean Mercier) (d. 1570). French Hebraist. Mercerus studied under the first

Hebrew chair at the Collège Royal de Paris, François Vatable (d. 1547), whom he succeeded in 1546. John Calvin* tried to recruit Mercerus to the Genevan Academy as professor of Hebrew, once in 1558 and again in 1563; he refused both times. During his lifetime Mercerus published grammatical helps for Hebrew and Chaldean, an aid to the Masoretic symbols in the Hebrew text, and translated the commentaries and grammars of several medieval rabbis. He himself wrote commentaries on Genesis, the wisdom books, and most of the Minor Prophets. These commentaries—most of them only published after his death—were philologically focused and interacted with the work of Jerome, Nicholas of Lyra,* notable rabbis and Johannes Oecolampadius.*

Ambrose Moibanus (1494–1554). German Lutheran bishop and theologian. Moibanus helped reform the church of Breslau (modern Wroclaw, Poland). He revised the Mass, bolstered pastoral care and welfare for the poor, and wrote a new evangelical catechism.

Thomas More (1478–1535). English Catholic lawyer, politician, humanist and martyr. More briefly studied at Oxford, but completed his legal studies in London. After contemplating the priesthood for four years, he opted for politics and was elected a member of Parliament in 1504. A devout Catholic, More worked with church leaders in England to root out heresy while he also confronted Lutheran teachings in writing. After four years as Lord Chancellor, More resigned due to heightened tensions with Henry VIII over papal supremacy (which More supported and Henry did not). Tensions did not abate. More's steadfast refusal to accept the Act of Supremacy (1534)—which declared the King of England to be the supreme ecclesial primate not the pope—resulted in his arrest and trial for high treason. He was found guilty and beheaded with John Fisher (1469–1535). Friends with John Colet* and Desiderius Erasmus,* More was a widely respected humanist in England as well as on the continent. Well-known for his novel *Utopia* (1516), More also penned several religious treatises on Christ's passion and suffering during his imprisonment in the Tower of London, which were published posthumously.

Sebastian Münster (1488–1552). German Reformed Hebraist, exegete, printer, and geographer. After converting to the Reformation in 1524, Münster taught Hebrew at the universities of Heidelberg and Basel. During his lengthy tenure in Basel he published more than seventy books, including Hebrew dictionaries and rabbinic commentaries. He also produced an evangelistic work for Jews titled *Vikuach* (1539). Münster's *Torat ha-Maschiach* (1537), the Gospel of Matthew, was the first published Hebrew translation of any portion of the New Testament. Despite his massive contribution to contemporary understanding of the Hebrew language, Münster was criticized by many of the reformers as a Judaizer.

Thomas Müntzer (c. 1489–1525). German Radical preacher. As a preacher in the town of Zwickau, Müntzer was influenced by German mysticism and, growing convinced that Martin Luther* had not carried through reform properly, sought to restore the pure apostolic church of the New Testament. Müntzer's radical ideas led to expulsions from various cities; he developed a highly apocalyptic theology, in which he heralded the last days that would establish the pure community out of suffering, prompting Müntzer's proactive role in the Peasants' War, which he perceived as a crucial apocalyptic event. Six thousand of Müntzer's followers were annihilated by magisterial troops; Müntzer was executed.

John Murcot (1625–1654). English Puritan pastor. After completing his bachelor's at Oxford in 1647, Murcot was ordained as a pastor, transferring to several parishes until in 1651 he moved to Dublin. All his works were published posthumously.

Simon Musaeus (1521–1582). German Lutheran theologian. After studying at the universities of Frankfurt an der Oder and Wittenberg, Musaeus began teaching Greek at the Cathedral school in Nuremberg and was ordained. Having returned to Wittenberg to complete a doctoral degree, Musaeus spent the rest of his career in numerous ecclesial and academic administrative posts. He opposed Matthias Flacius's (1505–1575) view of original sin—that the formal essence of human beings is marred by original sin—even calling the pro-Flacian faculty at Wittenberg "the devil's latrine." Musaeus published a disputation on original sin and a postil.

Wolfgang Musculus (1497–1563). German Reformed pastor and theologian. Musculus produced translations, biblical commentaries and an influential theological text, *Loci communes Sacrae Theologiae* (*Commonplaces of Sacred Theology*), outlining a Zwinglian theology. Musculus began to study theology while at a Benedictine monastery; he departed in 1527 and became secretary to Martin Bucer* in Strasbourg. He was later installed as a pastor in Augsburg, eventually performing the first evangelical liturgy in the city's cathedral. Displaced by the Augsburg Interim, Musculus ended his career as professor of theology at Bern. Though Musculus was active in the pursuit of the reform agenda, he was also concerned for ecumenism, participating in the Wittenberg Concord (1536) and discussions between Lutherans and Catholics.

Friedrich Nausea (c. 1496–1552). German Catholic bishop and preacher. After completing his studies at Leipzig, this famed preacher was appointed priest in Frankfurt but was run out of town by his congregants during his first sermon. He transferred to Mainz as cathedral preacher. Nausea was well connected through the German papal hierarchy and traveled widely to preach to influential ecclesial and secular courts. Court preacher for Ferdinand I (1503–1564), his reform tendencies fit well with royal Austrian theological leanings, and he was enthroned as the bishop of Vienna. Nausea thought that rather than endless colloquies only a council could settle reform. Unfortunately he could not participate in the first session of Trent due to insufficient funding, but he arrived for the second session. Nausea defended the laity's reception of the cup and stressed the importance of promulgating official Catholic teaching in the vernacular.

Melchior Neukirch (1540–1597). German Lutheran pastor and playwright. Neukirch's pastoral career spanned more than thirty years in several northern German parishes. Neukirch published a history of the Braunschweig church since the Reformation and a dramatization of Acts 4–7. He died of the plague.

Nicholas of Lyra (1270–1349). French Catholic biblical exegete. Very little is known about this influential medieval theologian of the Sorbonne aside from the works he published, particularly the *Postilla litteralis super totam Bibliam* (1322–1333). With the advent of the printing press this work was regularly published alongside the Latin Vulgate and the *Glossa ordinaria*. In this running commentary on the Bible Nicholas promoted literal interpretation as the basis for theology. Despite his preference for literal interpretation, Nicholas also published a companion volume, the *Postilla moralis super totam Bibliam* (1339), a commentary on the spiritual meaning of the biblical text. Nicholas was a major conversation partner for many reformers though many of them rejected his exegesis as too literal and too "Jewish" (not concerned enough with the Bible's fulfillment in Jesus Christ).

Johannes Oecolampadius (Johannes Huszgen) (1482–1531). Swiss-German Reformed humanist, reformer and theologian. Oecolampadius (an assumed name meaning "house light") assisted with Desiderius Erasmus's* Greek New Testament, lectured on biblical languages and exegesis and completed an influential Greek grammar. After joining the evangelical cause through studying patristics and the work of Martin Luther,* Oecolampadius went to Basel, where he lectured on biblical exegesis and participated in ecclesial reform. On account of Oecolampadius's effort, the city council passed legislation restricting preaching to the gospel and releasing the city from compulsory Mass. Oecolampadius was a chief ally of Huldrych Zwingli,* whom he supported at the Marburg Colloquy (1529).

Kaspar Olevianus (1536–1587). German Reformed theologian. Olevianus is celebrated for composing the Heidelberg Catechism and producing a critical edition of Calvin's *Institutes* in German. Olevianus studied theology with many, including John Calvin,* Theodore Beza,* Heinrich Bullinger* and Peter Martyr Vermigli.* As an advocate of Reformed doctrine, Olevianus oversaw the shift from Lutheranism to Calvinism throughout Heidelberg, organizing the city's churches after Calvin's Geneva. The Calvinist ecclesial vision of Olevianus entangled him in a dispute with another Heidelberg reformer over the rights of ecclesiastical discipline, which Olevianus felt belonged to the council of clergy and elders rather than civil magistrates.

Josua Opitz (c. 1542–1585). German Lutheran pastor. After a brief stint as superintendent in Regensburg, Opitz, a longtime preacher, was dismissed for his support of Matthias Flacius's (1520–1575) view of original sin. (Using Aristotelian categories, Flacius argued that the formal essence of human beings is marred by original sin, forming sinners into the image of Satan; his views were officially rejected in Article 1 of the Formula of Concord.*) Hans Wilhelm Roggendorf (1533–1591) invited Opitz to lower Austria as part of his Lutheranizing program. Unfortunately Roggendorf and Opitz never succeed in getting Lutheranism legal recognition, perhaps in large part due to Opitz's staunch criticism of Catholics, which resulted in his exile. He died of plague.

Lucas Osiander (1534–1604). German Lutheran pastor. For three decades, Osiander— son of the controversial Nuremberg reformer Andreas Osiander (d. 1552)—served as pastor and court preacher in Stuttgart, until he fell out of favor with the duke in 1598. Osiander produced numerous theological and exegetical works, as well as an influential hymnal.

John Owen (1616–1683). English Puritan theologian. Owen trained at Oxford University, where he was later appointed dean of Christ Church and vice chancellor of the university, following his service as chaplain to Oliver Cromwell. Although Owen began his career as a Presbyterian minister, he eventually departed to the party of Independents.

Owen composed many sermons, biblical commentaries (including seven volumes on the book of Hebrews), theological treatises and controversial monographs (including disputations with Arminians, Anglicans, Catholics and Socinians).

Santes Pagninus (c. 1470–1541). Italian Catholic biblical scholar. Pagninus studied under Girolamo Savonarola* and later taught in Rome, Avignon and Lyons. He translated the Old Testament into Latin according to a tight, almost wooden, adherence to the Hebrew. This translation and his Hebrew lexicon *Thesaurus linguae sanctae* (1529) were important resources for translators and commentators.

David (Wängler) Pareus (1548–1622). German Reformed pastor and theologian. Born at Frankenstein in Lower Silesia, Pareus studied theology at Heidelberg under Zacharias Ursinus (1534–1583), the principal author of the Heidelberg Catechism.* After reforming several churches, Pareus returned to Heidelberg to teach at the Reformed seminary. He then joined the theological faculty at the University of Heidelberg, first as a professor of Old Testament and later as a professor of New Testament. Pareus edited the *Neustadter Bibel* (1587), a publication of Martin Luther's* German translation with Reformed annotations—which was strongly denounced by Lutherans, especially Jakob Andreae* and Johann Georg Sigwart (1554–1618). In an extended debate, Pareus defended the orthodoxy of Calvin's exegesis against Aegidius Hunnius,* who accused Calvin of "judaizing" by rejecting many traditional Christological interpretations of Old Testament passages. Towards the end of his career, Pareus wrote commentaries on Genesis, Hosea, Matthew, Romans, 1 Corinthians, Galatians, Hebrews and Revelation.

Paul of Burgos (Solomon ha-Levi) (c. 1351–1435). Spanish Catholic archbishop. In 1391 Solomon ha-Levi, a rabbi and Talmudic scholar, converted to Christianity, receiving baptism with his entire family (except for his wife). He changed his name to Paul de Santa Maria. Some have suggested that he converted to avoid persecution; he himself stated that Thomas Aquinas's (1225–

1274) work persuaded him of the truth of Christian faith. After studying theology in Paris, he was ordained bishop in 1403. He actively and ardently persecuted Jews, trying to compel them to convert. In order to convince Jews that Christians correctly interpret the Hebrew Scriptures, Paul wrote *Dialogus Pauli et Sauli contra Judaeos, sive Scrutinium Scripturarum* (1434), a book filled with vile language toward the Jews. He also wrote a series of controversial marginal notes and comments on Nicholas of Lyra's* *Postilla*, many of which criticized Nicholas's use of Jewish scholarship.

Christoph Pelargus (1565–1633). German Lutheran pastor, theologian, professor and superintendent. Pelargus studied philosophy and theology at the University of Frankfurt an der Oder, in Brandenburg. This irenic Philippist was appointed as the superintendent of Brandenburg and later became a pastor in Frankfurt, although the local authorities first required him to condemn Calvinist theology, because several years earlier he had been called before the consistory in Berlin under suspicion of being a crypto-Calvinist. Among his most important works were a four-volume commentary on *De orthodoxa fide* by John of Damascus (d. 749), a treatise defending the breaking of the bread during communion, and a volume of funeral sermons. He also published commentaries on the Pentateuch, the Psalms, Matthew, John and Acts.

Konrad Pellikan (1478–1556). German Reformed Hebraist and theologian. Pellikan attended the University of Heidelberg, where he mastered Hebrew under Johannes Reuchlin. In 1504 Pellikan published one of the first Hebrew grammars that was not merely a translation of the work of medieval rabbis. While living in Basel, Pellikan assisted the printer Johannes Amerbach, with whom he published some of Luther's* early writings. He also worked with Sebastian Münster* and Wolfgang Capito* on a Hebrew Psalter (1516). In 1526, after teaching theology for three years at the University of Basel, Huldrych Zwingli* brought Pellikan to Zurich to chair the faculty of Old Testament. Pellikan's magnum opus is a seven-volume commentary on the entire Bible (except Revelation) and the Apocrypha; it is often heavily dependent upon the work of others (esp. Desiderius Erasmus* and Johannes Oecolampadius*).

Benedict Pererius (1535–1610). Spanish Catholic theologian, philosopher and exegete. Pererius entered the Society of Jesus in 1552. He taught philosophy, theology, and exegesis at the Roman College of the Jesuits. Early in his career he warned against neo-Platonism and astrology in his *De principiis* (1576). Pererius wrote a lengthy commentary on Daniel, and five volumes of exegetical theses on Exodus, Romans, Revelation and part of the Gospel of John (chs. 1–14). His four-volume commentary on Genesis (1591–1599) was lauded by Protestants and Catholics alike.

William Perkins (1558–1602). English Puritan preacher and theologian. Perkins was a highly regarded Puritan Presbyterian preacher and biblical commentator in the Elizabethan era. He studied at Cambridge University and later became a fellow of Christ's Church college as a preacher and professor, receiving acclaim for his sermons and lectures. Even more, Perkins gained an esteemed reputation for his ardent exposition of Calvinist reformed doctrine in the style of Petrus Ramus,* becoming one of the first English reformed theologians to achieve international recognition. Perkins influenced the federal Calvinist shape of Puritan theology and the vision of logical, practical expository preaching.

François Perrault (1577–1657). French Reformed pastor for over fifty years. His book on demonology was prominent, perhaps because of the intrigue at his home in 1612. According to his account, a poltergeist made a commotion and argued points of theology; a few months later Perrault's parishioners slew a large snake slithering out of his house.

Dirk Philips (1504–1568). Dutch Radical elder and theologian. This former Franciscan monk, known for being severe and obstinate, was a leading theologian of the sixteenth-century Anabaptist movement. Despite the fame of Menno Simons* and his own older brother Obbe, Philips wielded great influence over Anabaptists in the Netherlands and northern Germany where he ministered. As a result of Philips's understanding of the apostolic church as radically separated from the children of the world, he advocated a very strict interpretation of the ban, including formal shunning. His writings were collected and published near the end of his life as *Enchiridion oft Hantboecxken van de Christelijcke Leere* (1564).

Johannes Piscator (1546–1625). German Reformed theologian. Educated at Tübingen (though he wanted to study at Wittenberg), Piscator taught at the universities of Strasbourg and Heidelberg, as well as academies in Neustadt and Herborn. His commentaries on both the Old and New Testaments involve a tripartite analysis of a given passage's argument, of scholia on the text and of doctrinal loci. Some consider Piscator's method to be a full flowering of Beza's* "logical" scriptural analysis, focused on the text's meaning and its relationship to the pericopes around it.

Felix Pratensis (d. 1539). Italian Catholic Hebraist. Pratensis, the son of a rabbi, converted to Christianity and entered the Augustinian Hermits around the turn of the sixteenth century. In 1515, with papal permission, Pratensis published a new translation of the Psalms based on the Hebrew text. His *Biblia Rabbinica* (1517–1518), printed in Jewish and Christian editions, included text-critical notes in the margins as well as the Targum and rabbinic commentaries on each book (e.g., Rashi* on the Pentateuch and David Kimchi* on the Prophets). Many of the reformers consulted this valuable resource as they labored on their own translations and expositions of the Old Testament.

Quadriga. The *quadriga*, or four senses of Scripture, grew out of the exegetical legacy of Paul's dichotomy of letter and spirit (2 Cor 3:6), as well as church fathers like Origen (c. 185–254), Jerome (c. 347–420) and Augustine (354–430). Advocates for this method—the primary framework for biblical exegesis during the medieval era—assumed the necessity of the gift of faith under the guidance of the Holy Spirit. The literal-historical meaning of the text served as the foundation for the fuller perception of Scripture's meaning in the three spiritual senses, accessible only through faith: the allegorical sense taught what should be believed, the tropological or moral sense taught what should be done, and the anagogical or eschatological sense taught what should be hoped for. Medieval Jewish exegesis also had a fourfold interpretive method—not necessarily related to the *quadriga*—called *pardes* ("grove"): *peshat*, the simple, literal sense of the text according to grammar; *remez*, the allegorical sense; *derash*, the moral sense; and *sod*, the mystic sense related to Kabbalah. Scholars hotly dispute the precise use and meaning of these terms.

Petrus Ramus (1515–1572). French Reformed humanist philosopher. Ramus was an influential professor of philosophy and logic at the French royal college in Paris; he converted to Protestantism and left France for Germany, where he came under the influence of Calvinist thought. Ramus was a trenchant critic of Aristotle and noted for his method of classification based on a deductive movement from universals to particulars, the latter becoming branching divisions that provided a visual chart of the parts to the whole. His system profoundly influenced Puritan theology and preaching. After returning to Paris, Ramus died in the Saint Bartholomew's Day Massacre.

Rashi (**Shlomo Yitzchaki**) (1040–1105). French Jewish rabbi and exegete. After completing his studies, Rashi founded a yeshiva in Troyes. He composed the first comprehensive commentary on the Talmud, as well as commentaries on the entire Old Testament except for 1–2 Chronicles. These works remain influential within orthodox Judaism. Late medieval and early modern Christian scholars valued his exegesis, characterized by his preference for peshat (see quadriga).

Remonstrance (1610). See *Synod of Dordrecht.*

Johannes Reuchlin (1455–1522). German Catholic lawyer, humanist and Hebraist. Reuchlin held judicial appointments for the dukes of Württemberg, the Supreme Court in Speyer and the imperial court of the Swabian League. He pioneered the study of Hebrew among Christians in Germany, standing against those who, like Johannes Pfefferkorn (1469–1523), wanted to destroy Jewish literature. Among his many works he published a Latin dictionary, an introductory Greek grammar, the most important early modern Hebrew grammar and dictionary (*De rudimentis hebraicis*; 1506), and a commentary on the penitential psalms.

Edward Reynolds (1599–1676). Anglican bishop. Reynolds succeeded John Donne* as the preacher at Lincoln's Inn before entering parish ministry in Northamptonshire. During the English Civil Wars, he supported the Puritans because of his sympathy toward their simplicity and piety—despite believing that Scripture demanded no particular form of government; later he refused to support the abolition of the monarchy. Until the Restoration he ministered in London; afterward he became the bishop of Norwich. He wrote the general thanksgiving prayer which is part of the morning office in the *Book of Common Prayer.**

Urbanus Rhegius (1489–1541). German Lutheran pastor. Rhegius, who was likely the son of a priest, studied under the humanists at Freiburg and Ingolstadt. After a brief stint as a foot soldier, he received ordination in 1519 and was made cathedral preacher in Augsburg. During his time in Augsburg he closely read Luther's* works, becoming an enthusiastic follower. Despite his close friendship with Zwingli* and Oecolampadius,* Rhegius supported Luther in the eucharistic debates, later playing a major role in the Wittenberg Concord (1536). He advocated for peace during the Peasants' War and had extended interactions with the Anabaptists in Augsburg. Later in his career he concerned himself with the training of pastors, writing a pastoral guide and two catechisms. About one hundred of his writings were published posthumously.

Lancelot Ridley (d. 1576). Anglican preacher. Ridley was the first cousin of Nicholas Ridley,* the bishop of London who was martyred during the Marian persecutions. By Cranmer's* recom-

mendation, Ridley became one of the six Canterbury Cathedral preachers. Upon Mary I's accession in 1553, Ridley was defrocked (as a married priest). Ridley returned to Canterbury Cathedral after Mary's death. He wrote commentaries on Jude, Ephesians, Philippians and Colossians.

Nicholas Ridley (c. 1502–1555). Anglican bishop. Ridley was a student and fellow at Cambridge University who was appointed chaplain to Archbishop Thomas Cranmer* and is thought to be partially responsible for Cranmer's shift to a symbolic view of the Eucharist. Cranmer promoted Ridley twice: as bishop of Rochester, where he openly advocated Reformed theological views, and, later, as bishop of London. Ridley assisted Cranmer in the revisions of the Book of Common Prayer.* Ridley's support of Lady Jane Grey against the claims of Mary to the throne led to his arrest; he was tried for heresy and burned at the stake with Hugh Latimer.*

Peter Riedemann (1506–1556). German Radical elder, theologian and hymnist. While traveling as a Silesian cobbler, Riedemann came into contact with Anabaptist teachings and joined a congregation in Linz. In 1529 he was called to be a minister, only to be imprisoned soon after as part of Archduke Ferdinand's efforts to suppress heterodoxy in his realm. Once he was released, he moved to Moravia in 1532 where he was elected as a minister and missionary of the Hutterite community there. His *Account of Our Religion, Doctrine and Faith* (1542), with its more than two thousand biblical references, is Riedemann's most important work and is still used by Hutterites today.

John Robinson (1576–1625). English Puritan pastor. After his suspension for nonconformity, Robinson fled to the Netherlands with his congregation, eventually settling in Leiden in 1609. Robinson entered into controversies over Arminianism, separation and congregationalism. Most of his healthy congregants immigrated to Plymouth in 1620; Robinson remained in Leiden with those unable to travel.

Nehemiah Rogers (1593–1660). Anglican priest. After studying at Cambridge, Rogers ministered at numerous parishes during his more than forty-year career. In 1643, he seems to have been forced out of a parish on account of being a Royalist and friend of William Laud.* Rogers published a number of sermons and tracts, including a series of expositions on Jesus' parables in the Gospels.

Robert Rollock (c. 1555–1599). Scottish Reformed pastor, educator and theologian. Rollock was deeply influenced by Petrus Ramus's* system of logic, which he implemented as a tutor and (later) principal of Edinburgh University and in his expositions of the Bible. Rollock, as a divinity professor and theologian, was instrumental in diffusing a federalist Calvinism in the Scottish church; he lectured on theology using the texts of Theodore Beza* and articulated a highly covenantal interpretation of the biblical narratives. He was a prolific writer of sermons, expositions, commentaries, lectures and occasional treatises.

Jacopo Sadoleto (1477–1547). Italian Catholic Cardinal. Sadoleto, attaché to Leo X's court, was appointed bishop in 1517, cardinal in 1536. He participated in the reform commission led by Gasparo Contarini.* However, he tried to reconcile with Protestants apart from the commission, sending several letters to Protestant leaders in addition to his famous letter to the city of Geneva, which John Calvin* pointedly answered. Sadoleto published a commentary on Romans that was censored as semi-Pelagian. His insufficient treatment of prevenient grace left him vulnerable to this charge. Sadoleto emphasized grammar as the rule and norm of exegesis.

Heinrich Salmuth (1522–1576). German Lutheran theologian. After earning his doctorate from the University of Leipzig, Salmuth served in several coterminous pastoral and academic positions. He was integral to the reorganization of the University of Jena. Except for a few disputations, all of Salmuth's works—mostly sermons—were published posthumously by his son.

Robert Sanderson (1587–1663). Anglican bishop and philosopher. Before his appointment as professor of divinity at Oxford in 1642, Sanderson pastored in several parishes. Because of his loyalty to the Crown during the English Civil Wars, the Parliamentarians stripped Sanderson of his post at Oxford. After the Restoration he was reinstated at Oxford and consecrated bishop. He wrote an influential textbook on logic.

Edwin Sandys (1519–1588). Anglican bishop. During his doctoral studies at Cambridge, Sandys befriended Martin Bucer.* Having supported the Protestant Lady Jane Grey's claim to the throne, Sandys resigned his post at Cambridge upon Mary I's accession. He was then arrested and imprisoned in the Tower of London. Released in 1554, he sojourned on the continent until Mary's death. On his return to England he was appointed to revise the liturgy and was consecrated bishop. Many of his sermons were published, but his most significant literary legacy is his work as a translator of the Bishop's Bible (1568), which served as the foundational English text for the translators of the King James Bible (1611).

Erasmus Sarcerius (1501–1559). German Lutheran superintendent, educator and pastor. Sarcerius served as educational superintendent, court preacher and pastor in Nassau and, later, in Leipzig. The hallmark of Sarcerius's reputation was his ethical emphasis as exercised through ecclesial oversight and family structure; he also drafted disciplinary codes for regional churches in Germany. Sarcerius served with Philipp Melanchthon* as Protestant delegates at the Council of Trent, though both withdrew prior to the dismissal of the session; he eventually became an opponent of Melanchthon, contesting the latter's understanding of the Eucharist at a colloquy in Worms in 1557.

Michael Sattler (c. 1490–1527). Swiss Radical leader. Sattler was a Benedictine monk who abandoned the monastic life during the upheavals of the Peasants' War. He took up the trade of weaving under the guidance of an outspoken Anabaptist. It seems that Sattler did not openly join the Anabaptist movement until after the suppression of the Peasants' War in 1526. Sattler interceded with Martin Bucer* and Wolfgang Capito* for imprisoned Anabaptists in Strasbourg.

Shortly before he was convicted of heresy and executed, he wrote the definitive expression of Anabaptist theology, the Schleitheim Articles.*

Girolamo Savonarola (1452–1498). Italian Catholic preacher and martyr. Outraged by clerical corruption and the neglect of the poor, Savonarola traveled to preach against these abuses and to prophesy impending judgment—a mighty king would scourge and reform the church. Savonarola thought that the French invasion of Italy in 1494 confirmed his apocalyptic visions. Thus he pressed to purge Florence of vice and institute public welfare, in order to usher in a new age of Christianity. Florence's refusal to join papal resistance against the French enraged Alexander VI (r. 1492–1503). He blamed Savonarola, promptly excommunicating him and threatening Florence with an interdict. After an ordeal by fire turned into a riot, Savonarola was arrested. Under torture he admitted to charges of conspiracy and false prophecy; he was hanged and burned. In addition to numerous sermons and letters, he wrote meditations on Psalms 31 and 51 as well as *The Triumph of the Cross* (1497).

Leupold Scharnschlager (d. 1563). Austrian Radical elder. See *Kunstbuch*.

Leonhard Schiemer (d. 1528). Austrian Radical martyr. See *Kunstbuch*.

Hans Schlaffer (c. 1490–1528). Austrian Radical martyr. See *Kunstbuch*.

Schleitheim Articles (1527). After the death of Conrad Grebel* in 1526 and the execution of Felix Manz (born c. 1498) in early 1527, the young Swiss Anabaptist movement was in need of unity and direction. A synod convened at Schleitheim under the chairmanship of Michael Sattler,* which passed seven articles of Anabaptist distinctives—likely defined against both magisterial reformers and other Anabaptists with less orthodox and more militant views (e.g., Balthasar Hubmaier*). Unlike most confessions, these articles do not explicitly address traditional creedal interests; they explicate instead the Anabaptist view of the sacraments, church discipline, separatism, the role of ministers, pacifism and oaths. Throughout the document there is a resolute focus on Christ's

example. The Schleitheim Articles are considered the definitive statement of Anabaptist theology, particularly regarding separatism.

Schmalkald Articles (1537). In response to Pope Paul III's (1468–1549) 1536 decree ordering a general church council to solve the Protestant crisis, Elector John Frederick (1503–1554) commissioned Martin Luther* to draft the sum of his teaching. Intended by Luther as a last will and testament—and composed with advice from well-known colleagues Justus Jonas,* Johann Bugenhagen,* Caspar Cruciger,* Nikolaus von Amsdorf (1483–1565), Georg Spalatin (1484–1545), Philipp Melanchthon* and Johann Agricola*—these articles provide perhaps the briefest and most systematic summary of Luther's teaching. The document was not adopted formally by the Lutheran Schmalkald League, as was hoped, and the general church council was postponed for several years (until convening at Trent in 1545). Only in 1580 were the articles officially received, by being incorporated into the *Book of Concord* defining orthodox Lutheranism.

Anna Maria van Schurman (1607–1678). Dutch Reformed polymath. Van Schurman cultivated talents in art, poetry, botany, linguistics and theology. She mastered most contemporary European languages, in addition to Latin, Greek, Hebrew, Arabic, Farsi and Ethiopian. With the encouragement of leading Reformed theologian Gisbertus Voetius (1589–1676), van Schurman attended lectures at the University of Utrecht—although she was required to sit behind a wooden screen so that the male students could not see her. In 1638 van Schurman published her famous treatise advocating female scholarship, *Amica dissertatio . . . de capacitate ingenii muliebris ad scientias*. In addition to these more polemical works, van Schurman also wrote hymns and poems, including a paraphrase of Genesis 1–3. Later in life she became a devotee of Jean de Labadie (1610–1674), a former Jesuit who was also expelled from the Reformed church for his separatist leanings. Her *Eucleria* (1673) is the most well known defense of Labadie's theology.

Kaspar von Schwenckfeld (1489–1561). German Radical reformer. Schwenckfeld was a Silesian nobleman who encountered Luther's* works in 1521. He traveled to Wittenberg twice: first to meet Luther and Karlstadt,* and a second time to convince Luther of his doctrine of the "internal word"—emphasizing inner revelation so strongly that he did not see church meetings or the sacraments as necessary—after which Luther considered him heterodox. Schwenckfeld won his native territory to the Reformation in 1524 and later lived in Strasbourg for five years until Bucer* sought to purify the city of less traditional theologies. Schwenckfeld wrote numerous polemical and exegetical tracts.

Scots Confession (1560). In 1560, the Scottish Parliament undertook to reform the Church of Scotland and to commission a Reformed confession of faith. In the course of four days, a committee—which included John Knox*—wrote this confession, largely based on Calvin's* work, the Confession of the English Congregation in Geneva (1556) and the Gallic Confession.* The articles were not ratified until 1567 and were displaced by the Westminster Confession (1646), adopted by the Scottish in 1647.

Second Helvetic Confession (1566). Believing he would soon die, Heinrich Bullinger* penned a personal statement of his Reformed faith in 1561 as a theological will. In 1563, Bullinger sent a copy of this confession, which blended Zwingli's and Calvin's theology, to the elector of the Palatinate, Frederick III (1515–1576), who had asked for a complete explication of the Reformed faith in order to defend himself against aggressive Lutheran attacks after printing the Heidelberg Confession.* Although not published until 1566, the Second Helvetic Confession became the definitive sixteenth-century Reformed statement of faith. Theodore Beza* used it as the organizing confession for his *Harmonia Confessionum* (1581), which sought to emphasize the unity of the Reformed churches. Bullinger's personal confession was adopted by the Reformed churches of Scotland (1566), Hungary (1567), France (1571) and Poland (1571).

Obadiah Sedgwick (c. 1600–1658). English Puritan minister. Educated at Oxford, Sedgwick pastored in London and participated in the Westminster Assembly. An ardent Puritan, Sedgwick was appointed by Oliver Cromwell (1599–1658) to examine clerical candidates. Sedgwick published a catechism, several sermons and a treatise on how to deal with doubt.

Nikolaus Selnecker (1530–1592). German Lutheran theologian, preacher, pastor and hymnist. Selnecker taught in Wittenberg, Jena and Leipzig, preached in Dresden and Wolfenbüttel, and pastored in Leipzig. He was forced out of his post at Jena because of suspicions that he was a crypto-Calvinist. He sought refuge in Wolfenbüttel, where he met Martin Chemnitz* and Jakob Andreae.* Under their influence Selnecker was drawn away from Philippist theology. Selnecker's shift in theology can be seen in his *Institutio religionis christianae* (1573). Selnecker coauthored the Formula of Concord* with Chemnitz, Andreae, Andreas Musculus (1514–1581), and David Chytraeus.* Selnecker also published lectures on Genesis, the Psalms, and the New Testament epistles, as well as composing over a hundred hymn tunes and texts.

Short Confession (1610). In response to some of William Laud's* reforms in the Church of England—particularly a law stating that ministers who refused to comply with the Book of Common Prayer* would lose their ordination—a group of English Puritans immigrated to the Netherlands in protest, where they eventually embraced the practice of believer's baptism. The resulting Short Confession was an attempt at union between these Puritans and local Dutch Anabaptists ("Waterlanders"). The document highlights the importance of love in the church and reflects optimism regarding the freedom of the will while explicitly rejecting double predestination.

Richard Sibbes (1577–1635). English Puritan preacher. Sibbes was educated at St. John's College, Cambridge, where he was converted to reforming views and became a popular preacher. As a moderate Puritan emphasizing interior piety and brotherly love, Sibbes always remained within the established Church of England, though opposed to some of its liturgical ceremonies. His collected sermons constitute his main literary legacy.

Menno Simons (c. 1496–1561). Dutch Radical leader. Simons led a separatist Anabaptist group in the Netherlands that would later be called Mennonites, known for nonviolence and renunciation of the world. A former priest, Simons rejected Catholicism through the influence of Anabaptist disciples of Melchior Hoffmann and based on his study of Scripture, in which he found no support for transubstantiation or infant baptism. Following the sack of Anabaptists at Münster, Simons committed to a nonviolent way of life. Simons proclaimed a message of radical discipleship of obedience and inner purity, marked by voluntary adult baptism and communal discipline.

Henry Smith (c. 1550–1591). English Puritan minister. Smith stridently opposed the Book of Common Prayer* and refused to subscribe to the Articles of Religion,* thus limiting his pastoral opportunities. Nevertheless he gained a reputation as an eloquent preacher in London. He published sermon collections as well as several treatises.

Domingo de Soto (1494–1560). Spanish Catholic theologian. Soto taught philosophy for four years at the University in Alcalá before entering the Dominican order. In 1532 he became chair of theology at the University of Salamanca; Soto sought to reintroduce Aristotle in the curriculum. He served as confessor and spiritual advisor to Charles V, who enlisted Soto as imperial theologian for the Council of Trent. Alongside commentaries on the works of Aristotle and Peter Lombard (c. 1100–1160), Soto commented on Romans and wrote an influential treatise on nature and grace.

Cyriacus Spangenberg (1528–1604). German Lutheran pastor, preacher and theologian. Spangenberg was a staunch, often acerbic, Gnesio-Lutheran. He rejected the Formula of Concord* because of concerns about the princely control of the church, as well as its rejection of

Flacian language of original sin (as constituting the "substance" of human nature after the fall). He published many commentaries and sermons, most famously seventy wedding sermons (*Ehespiegel* [1561]), his sermons on Luther* (*Theander Luther* [1562–1571]) and Luther's hymns (*Cithara Lutheri* [1569–1570]). He also published an analysis of the Old Testament (though he only got as far as Job), based on a methodology that anticipated the logical bifurcations of Peter Ramus.*

Johann Spangenberg (1484–1550). German Lutheran pastor and catechist. Spangenberg studied at the University of Erfurt, where he was welcomed into a group of humanists associated with Konrad Muth (1470–1526). There he met the reformer Justus Jonas,* and Eobanus Hessius (1488–1540), whom Luther* dubbed "king of the poets." Spangenberg served at parishes in Stolberg (1520–1524), Nordhausen (1524–1546) and, by Luther's recommendation, Eisleben (1546–1550). Spangenberg published one of the best-selling postils of the sixteenth century, the *Postilla Teütsch*, a six-volume work meant to prepare children to understand the lectionary readings. It borrowed the question-answer form of Luther's *Small Catechism* and was so popular that a monk, Johannes Craendonch, purged overt anti-Catholic statements from it and republished it under his own name. Among Spangenberg's other pastoral works are *ars moriendi* ("the art of dying") booklets, a postil for the Acts of the Apostles and a question-answer version of Luther's *Large Catechism*. In addition to preaching and pastoring, Spangenberg wrote pamphlets on controversial topics such as purgatory, as well as textbooks on music, mathematics and grammar.

Georg Spindler (1525–1605). German Reformed theologian and pastor. After studying theology under Caspar Cruciger* and Philipp Melanchthon,* Spindler accepted a pastorate in Bohemia. A well-respected preacher, Spindler published postils in 1576 which some of his peers viewed as crypto-Calvinist. To investigate this allegation Spindler read John Calvin's* *Institutes*, and subsequently converted to the Reformed faith. After years of travel, he settled in the Palatinate and pastored there until his death. In addition to his Lutheran postils, Spindler also published Reformed postils in 1594 as well as several treatises on the Lord's Supper and predestination.

Statenvertaling (1637). The Synod of Dordrecht* commissioned this new Dutch translation of the Bible ("State's Translation"). The six theologians who undertook this translation also wrote prefaces for each biblical book, annotated obscure words and difficult passages, and provided cross-references; they even explained certain significant translation decisions. At the request of the Westminster Assembly, Theodore Haak (1605–1690) translated the *Statenvertaling* into English as *The Dutch Annotations Upon the Whole Bible* (1657).

Johann von Staupitz (d. 1524). German Catholic theologian, professor and preacher. Frederick the Wise summoned this Augustinian monk to serve as professor of Bible and first dean of the theology faculty at the University of Wittenberg. As Vicar-General of the Reformed Augustinian Hermits in Germany, Staupitz sought to reform the order and attempted unsuccessfully to reunite with the conventional Augustinians. While in Wittenberg, Staupitz was Martin Luther's* teacher, confessor and spiritual father. He supported Luther in the early controversies over indulgences, but after releasing Luther from his monastic vows (to protect him), he distanced himself from the conflict. He relocated to Salzburg, where he was court preacher to Cardinal Matthäus Lang von Wellenburg (d. 1540) and abbot of the Benedictine monastery. Staupitz wrote treatises on predestination, faith and the love of God. Many of his sermons were collected and published during his lifetime.

Michael Stifel (1486–1567). German Lutheran mathematician, theologian and pastor. An Augustinian monk, Stifel's interest in mysticism, apocalypticism and numerology led him to identify Pope Leo X as the antichrist. Stifel soon joined the reform movement, writing a 1522 pamphlet in support of Martin Luther's* theology. After Luther quelled the fallout of Stifel's failed prediction of the Apocalypse—October 19, 1533 at 8 a.m.—Stifel focused more on mathematics and his pastoral duties. He was the first professor of mathematics at the University of Jena. He published several numerological interpretations of texts from the Gospels, Daniel and Revelation. However, Stifel's most important work is his *Arithmetica Integra* (1544), in which he standardized the approach to quadratic equations. He also developed notations for exponents and radicals.

Viktorin Strigel (1524–1569). German Lutheran theologian. Strigel taught at Wittenberg, Erfurt, Jena, Leipzig and Heidelberg. During his time in Jena he disputed with Matthias Flacius (1520–1575) over the human will's autonomy. Following Philipp Melanchthon,* Strigel asserted that in conversion the human will obediently cooperates with the divine will through the Holy Spirit and the Word of God. In the Weimar Disputation (1560), Strigel elicited Flacius's opinion that sin is a substance that mars the formal essence of human beings. Flacius's views were officially rejected in Article 1 of the Formula of Concord*; Strigel's, in Article 2. In 1567 the University of Leipzig suspended Strigel from teaching on account of suspicions that he affirmed Reformed Eucharistic theology; he acknowledged that he did and joined the Reformed confession on the faculty of the University of Heidelberg. In addition to controversial tracts, Strigel published commentaries on the entire Bible (except Lamentations) and the Apocrypha.

Johann Sutell (1504–1575). German Lutheran pastor. After studying at the University of Wittenberg, Sutell received a call to a pastorate in Göttingen, where he eventually became superintendent. He wrote new church orders for Göttingen (1531) and Schweinfurt (1543), and expanded two sermons for publication, *The Dreadful Destruction of Jerusalem* (1539) and *History of Lazarus* (1543).

Swiss Brethren Confession of Hesse (1578). Anabaptist leader Hans Pauly Kuchenbecker penned this confession after a 1577 interrogation by Lutheran authorities. This confession was unusually amenable to Lutheran views—there is no mention of pacifism or rejection of oath taking.

Synod of Dordrecht (1618–1619). This large Dutch Reformed Church council—also attended by English, German and Swiss delegates—met to settle the theological issues raised by the followers of Jacobus Arminius.* Arminius's theological disagreements with mainstream Reformed teaching erupted into open conflict with the publication of the *Remonstrance* (1610). This "protest" was based on five points: that election is based on foreseen faith or unbelief; that Christ died indiscriminately for all people (although only believers receive salvation); that people are thoroughly sinful by nature apart from the prevenient grace of God that enables their free will to embrace or reject the gospel; that humans are able to resist the working of God's grace; and that it is possible for true believers to fall away from faith completely. The Synod ruled in favor of the Contra-Remonstrants, its Canons often remembered with a TULIP acrostic—total depravity, unconditional election, limited atonement, irresistible grace, perseverance of the saints—each letter countering one of the five Remonstrant articles. The Synod also officially accepted the Belgic Confession,* Heidelberg Catechism* and the Canons of Dordrecht as standards of the Dutch Reformed Church.

Arcangela Tarabotti (1604–1652). Italian Catholic nun. At the age of eleven, Tarabotti entered a Benedictine convent as a student-boarder; three years later her father forced her to take monastic vows. The dignity of women and their treatment in the male-controlled institutions of early modern Venice concerned Tarabotti deeply. She protested forced cloistering, the denial of education to women, the exclusion of women from public life and the double standards by which men and women were judged. Tarbotti authored numerous polemical works and an extensive correspondence.

Richard Taverner (1505–1575). English Puritan humanist and translator. After graduating from Oxford, Taverner briefly studied abroad. When he returned to England, he joined Thomas Cromwell's (1485–1540) circle. After Cromwell's beheading, Taverner escaped severe punishment and retired from public life during Mary I's reign. Under Elizabeth I, Taverner served as justice of the peace, sheriff and a licensed lay preacher. Taverner translated many important continental Reformation works into English, most notably the Augsburg Confession* and several of Desiderius Erasmus's* works. Some of these translations—John Calvin's* 1536 catechism, Wolfgang Capito's* work on the Psalms and probably Erasmus Sarcerius's* postils— he presented as his own work. Underwritten by Cromwell, Taverner also published an edited version of the Matthew Bible (1537).

Thomas Thorowgood (1595–1669). English Puritan pastor. Thorowgood was a Puritan minister in Norfolk and the chief financier of John Eliot (1604–1690), a Puritan missionary among the Native American tribes in Massachusetts. In 1650, under the title *Jews in America, or, Probabilities that Americans be of that Race*, Thorowgood became one of the first to put forward the thesis that Native Americans were actually the ten lost tribes of Israel.

Frans Titelmans (1502–1537). Belgian Catholic philosopher. Titelmans studied at the University of Leuven, where he was influenced by Petrus Ramus.* After first joining a Franciscan monastery, Titelmans realigned with the stricter Capuchins and moved to Italy. He is best known for his advocacy for the Vulgate and his debates with Desiderius Erasmus* over Pauline theology (1527–1530)—he was deeply suspicious of the fruits of humanism, especially regarding biblical studies. His work was published posthumously by his brother, Pieter Titelmans (1501–1572).

Francisco de Toledo (1532–1596). Spanish Catholic theologian. This important Jesuit taught philosophy at the universities of Salamanca and Rome. He published works on Aristotelian philosophy and a commentary on Thomas Aquinas's work, as well as biblical commentaries on John, Romans and the first half of Luke. He was also the general editor for the Clementine Vulgate (1598).

Alonso Tostado (1400–1455). Spanish Catholic bishop and exegete. Tostado lectured on theology, law and philosophy at the University of Salamanca, in addition to ministering in a local parish. Tostado entered into disputes over papal supremacy and the date of Christ's birth. Tostado's thirteen-volume collected works include commentaries on the historical books of the Old Testament and the Gospel of Matthew.

Daniel Toussain (1541–1602). Swiss Reformed pastor and professor. Toussain became pastor at Orléans after attending college in Basel. After the third War of Religion, Toussain was exiled, eventually returning to Montbéliard, his birthplace. In 1571, he faced opposition there from the strict Lutheran rulers and was eventually exiled due to his influence over the clergy. He returned to Orléans but fled following the Saint Bartholomew's Day Massacre (1572), eventually becoming pastor in Basel. He relocated to Heidelberg in 1583 as pastor to the new regent, becoming professor of theology at the university, and he remained there until his death.

John Trapp (1601–1669). Anglican biblical exegete. After studying at Oxford, Trapp entered the pastorate in 1636. During the English Civil Wars he sided with Parliament, which later made it difficult for him to collect tithes from a congregation whose royalist pastor had been evicted. Trapp published commentaries on all the books of the Bible from 1646 to 1656.

Immanuel Tremellius (1510–1580). Italian Reformed Hebraist. Around 1540, Tremellius received baptism by Cardinal Reginald Pole (1500–1558) and converted from Judaism to Christianity; he affiliated with evangelicals the next year. On account of the political and religious upheaval, Tremellius relocated often, teaching Hebrew in Lucca; Strasbourg, fleeing the Inquisition; Cambridge, displaced by the Schmalkaldic War; Heidelberg, escaping Mary I's persecutions; and Sedan, expelled by the new Lutheran Elector of the Palatine. Many considered Tremellius's translation of the Old Testa-

ment as the most accurate available. He also published a Hebrew grammar and translated John Calvin's* catechism into Hebrew.

William Tyndale (Hychyns) (1494–1536). English reformer, theologian and translator. Tyndale was educated at Oxford University, where he was influenced by the writings of humanist thinkers. Believing that piety is fostered through personal encounter with the Bible, he asked to translate the Bible into English; denied permission, Tyndale left for the Continent to complete the task. His New Testament was the equivalent of a modern-day bestseller in England but was banned and ordered burned. Tyndale's theology was oriented around justification, the authority of Scripture and Christian obedience; Tyndale emphasized the ethical as a concomitant reality of justification. He was martyred in Brussels before completing his English translation of the Old Testament, which Miles Coverdale* finished.

Juan de Valdés (1500/10–1541). Spanish Catholic theologian and writer. Although Valdés adopted an evangelical doctrine, had Erasmian affiliations and published works that were listed on the Index of Prohibited Books, Valdés rebuked the reformers for creating disunity and never left the Catholic Church. His writings included translations of the Hebrew Psalter and various biblical books, a work on the Spanish language and several commentaries. Valdés fled to Rome in 1531 to escape the Spanish Inquisition and worked in the court of Clement VII in Bologna until the pope's death in 1534. Valdés subsequently returned to Naples, where he led the reform- and revival-minded Valdesian circle.

Peter Martyr Vermigli (1499–1562). Italian Reformed humanist and theologian. Vermigli was one of the most influential theologians of the era, held in common regard with such figures as Martin Luther* and John Calvin.* In Italy, Vermigli was a distinguished theologian, preacher and advocate for moral reform; however, during the reinstitution of the Roman Inquisition Vermigli fled to Protestant regions in northern Europe. He was eventually appointed professor of divinity at

Oxford University, where Vermigli delivered acclaimed disputations on the Eucharist. Vermigli was widely noted for his deeply integrated biblical commentaries and theological treatises.

Vulgate. In 382 Pope Damasus I (c. 300–384) commissioned Jerome (c. 347–420) to translate the four Gospels into Latin based on Old Latin and Greek manuscripts. Jerome completed the translation of the Gospels and the Old Testament around 405. It is widely debated how much of the rest of the New Testament was translated by Jerome. During the Middle Ages, the Vulgate became the Catholic Church's standard Latin translation. The Council of Trent recognized it as the official text of Scripture.

Peter Walpot (d. 1578). Moravian Radical pastor and bishop. Walpot was a bishop of the Hutterite community after Jakob Hutter, Peter Riedemann* and Leonhard Lanzenstiel. Riedemann's *Confession of Faith* (1545; 1565) became a vital authority for Hutterite exegesis, theology and morals. Walpot added his own *Great Article Book* (1577), which collates primary biblical passages on baptism, communion, the community of goods, the sword and divorce. In keeping with Hutterite theology, Walpot defended the community of goods as a mark of the true church.

Valentin Weigel (1533–1588). German Lutheran pastor. Weigel studied at Leipzig and Wittenberg, entering the pastorate in 1567. Despite a strong anti-institutional bias, he was recognized by the church hierarchy as a talented preacher and compassionate minister of mercy to the poor. Although he signed the Formula of Concord,* Weigel's orthodoxy was questioned so openly that he had to publish a defense. He appears to have tried to synthesize several medieval mystics with the ideas of Sebastian Franck,* Thomas Müntzer* and others. His posthumously published works have led some recent scholars to suggest that Weigel's works may have deeply influenced later Pietism.

Hieronymus Weller von Molsdorf (1499–1572). German Lutheran theologian. Originally intending to study law, Weller devoted himself to theology after hearing one of Martin Luther's* sermons on the catechism. He boarded with Luther and tutored Luther's son. In 1539 he moved to Freiburg, where he lectured on the Bible and held theological disputations at the Latin school. In addition to hymns, works of practical theology and a postil set, Weller published commentaries on Genesis, 1–2 Samuel, 1–2 Kings, Job, the Psalms, Christ's passion, Ephesians, Philippians, 1–2 Thessalonians and 1–2 Peter.

John Whitgift (1530–1604). Anglican archbishop. Though Whitgift shared much theological common ground with Puritans, after his election as Archbishop of Canterbury (1583) he moved decisively to squelch the political and ecclesiastical threat they posed during Elizabeth's reign. Whitgift enforced strict compliance to the Book of Common Prayer,* the Act of Uniformity (1559) and the Articles of Religion.* Whitgift's policies led to a large migration of Puritans to Holland. The bulk of Whitgift's published corpus is the fruit of a lengthy public disputation with Thomas Cartwright,* in which Whitgift defines Anglican doctrine against Cartwright's staunch Puritanism.

Johann Wigand (1523–1587). German Lutheran theologian. Wigand is most noted as one of the compilers of the *Magdeburg Centuries*, a German ecclesiastical history of the first thirteen centuries of the church. He was a student of Philipp Melanchthon* at the University of Wittenburg and became a significant figure in the controversies dividing Lutheranism. Strongly opposed to Roman Catholicism, Wigand lobbied against innovations in Lutheran theology that appeared sympathetic to Catholic thought. In the later debates, Wigand's support for Gnesio-Lutheranism established his role in the development of confessional Lutheranism. Wigand was appointed bishop of Pomerania after serving academic posts at the universities in Jena and Königsburg.

Thomas Wilcox (c. 1549–1608). English Puritan theologian. In 1572, Wilcox objected to Parliament against the episcopacy and the Book of Common Prayer,* advocating for presbyterian church governance. He was imprisoned for sedition. After his release, he preached itinerantly. He was brought before the courts twice more for his continued protest against the Church of England's episcopal structure. He translated some of Theodore Beza* and John Calvin's* sermons into English, and he wrote polemical and occasional works as well as commentaries on the Psalms and Song of Songs.

Johann (Ferus) Wild (1495–1554). German Catholic pastor. After studying at Heidelberg and teaching at Tübingen, this Franciscan was appointed as lector in the Mainz cathedral, eventually being promoted to cathedral preacher—a post for which he became widely popular but also controversial. Wild strongly identified as Catholic but was not unwilling to criticize the curia. Known for an irenic spirit—criticized in fact as *too* kind—he was troubled by the polemics between all parties of the Reformation. He preached with great lucidity, integrating the liturgy, Scripture and doctrine to exposit Catholic worship and teaching for common people. His sermons on John were pirated for publication without his knowledge; the Sorbonne banned them as heretical. Despite his popularity among clergy, the majority of his works were on the Roman Index until 1900.

Andrew Willet (1562–1621). Anglican priest, professor, and biblical expositor. Willet was a gifted biblical expositor and powerful preacher. He walked away from a promising university career in 1588 when he was ordained a priest in the Church of England. For the next thirty-three years he served as a parish priest. Willet's commentaries summarized the present state of discussion while also offering practical applications for preachers. They have been cited as some of the most technical commentaries of the early seventeenth century. His most important publication was *Synopsis Papismi, or a General View of Papistrie* (1594), in which he responded to many of Robert Bellarmine's critiques. After years of royal favor, Willet was imprisoned in 1618 for a month after presenting to King James I his opposition to the "Spanish Match" of Prince Charles to the Infanta Maria. While serving as a parish priest, he wrote forty-two works, most of which were either commentaries on books of the Bible or controversial works against Catholics.

Thomas Wilson (d. 1586). English Anglican priest. A fellow of St John's, Cambridge, Wilson fled to Frankfurt to escape the Marian Persecution. After his return to England, he served as a canon and Dean of Worcester.

John Woolton (c. 1535–1594). Anglican bishop. After graduating from Oxford, Woolton lived in Germany until the accession of Elizabeth I. He was ordained as a priest in 1560 and as a bishop in 1578. Woolton published many theological, devotional and practical works, including a treatise on the immortality of the soul, a discourse on conscience and a manual for Christian living.

Girolamo Zanchi (1516–1590). Italian Reformed theologian and pastor. Zanchi joined an Augustinian monastery at the age of fifteen, where he studied Greek and Latin, the church fathers and the works of Aristotle and Thomas Aquinas. Under the influence of his prior, Peter Martyr Vermigli,* Zanchi also imbibed the writings of the Swiss and German reformers. To avoid the Inquisition, Zanchi fled to Geneva where he was strongly attracted to the preaching and teaching of John Calvin.* Zanchi taught biblical theology and the *locus* method at academies in Strasbourg, Heidelberg, and Neustadt. He also served as pastor of an Italian refugee congregation. Zanchi's theological works, *De tribus Elohim* (1572) and *De natura Dei* (1577), have received more attention than his commentaries. His commentaries comprise about a quarter of his literary output, however, and display a strong typological and christological interpretation in conversation with the church fathers, medieval exegetes, and other reformers.

Katharina Schütz Zell (1497/98–1562). German Reformed writer. Zell became infamous in Strasbourg and the Empire when in 1523 she married the priest Matthias Zell, and then published an apology defending her husband against charges of impiety and libertinism. Longing for a united church, she called for toleration of Catholics and Anabaptists, famously writing to Martin Luther* after the failed Marburg Colloquy of 1529 to exhort him to check his hostility and to be ruled instead by Christian charity. Much to the chagrin of her contemporaries, Zell published diverse works, ranging from polemical treatises on marriage to letters of consolation, as well as editing a hymnal and penning an exposition of Psalm 51.

Huldrych Zwingli (1484–1531). Swiss Reformed humanist, preacher and theologian. Zwingli, a parish priest, was influenced by the writings of Desiderius Erasmus* and taught himself Greek.

While a preacher to the city cathedral in Zurich, Zwingli enacted reform through sermons, public disputations and conciliation with the town council, abolishing the Mass and images in the church. Zwingli broke with the lectionary preaching tradition, instead preaching serial expository biblical sermons. He later was embroiled in controversy with Anabaptists over infant baptism and with Martin Luther* at the Marburg Colloquy (1529) over their differing views of the Eucharist. Zwingli, serving as chaplain to Zurich's military, was killed in battle.

SOURCES FOR
BIOGRAPHICAL SKETCHES

General Reference Works

Allgemeine Deutsche Biographie. 56 vols. Leipzig: Duncker & Humblot, 1875–1912; reprint, 1967–1971. Accessible online via deutsche -biographie.de/index.html.

Baskin, Judith R., ed. *The Cambridge Dictionary of Judaism and Jewish Culture.* New York: Cambridge University Press, 2011.

Bettenson, Henry and Chris Maunder, eds. *Documents of the Christian Church.* 3rd ed. Oxford: Oxford University Press, 1999.

Betz, Hans Dieter, Don Browning, Bernd Janowski and Eberhard Jüngel, eds. *Religion Past & Present: Encyclopedia of Theology and Relgion.* 13 vols. Leiden: Brill, 2007–2013.

Bremer, Francis J. and Tom Webster, eds. *Puritans and Puritanism in Europe and America: A Comprehensive Encyclopedia.* 2 vols. Santa Barbara, CA: ABC-CLIO, 2006.

Haag, Eugene and Émile Haag. *La France protestante ou vies des protestants français.* 2nd ed. 6 vols. Paris: Sandoz & Fischbacher, 1877–1888.

Hillerbrand, Hans J., ed. *Oxford Encyclopedia of the Reformation.* 4 vols. New York: Oxford University Press, 1996.

Kolb, Robert, and Timothy J. Wengert, eds. *The Book of Concord: The Confessions of the Evangelical Lutheran Church.* Translated by Charles Arand et al. Minneapolis: Fortress, 2000.

McKim, Donald K., ed. *Dictionary of Major Biblical Interpreters.* Downers Grove, IL: InterVarsity Press, 2007.

Müller, Gerhard, et al., ed. *Theologische Realenzyklopädie.* Berlin: Walter de Gruyter, 1994.

Neue Deutsche Biographie. 28 vols. projected. Berlin: Duncker & Humblot, 1953–. Accessible online via deutsche-biographie.de/index.html.

New Catholic Encyclopedia. 15 vols. New York: McGraw-Hill, 1967; 2nd ed., Detroit: Thomson-Gale, 2002.

Oxford Dictionary of National Biography. 60 vols. Oxford: Oxford University Press, 2004.

Pelikan, Jaroslav. *The Christian Tradition.* 5 vols. Chicago: University of Chicago Press, 1971–1989.

Stephen, Leslie, and Sidney Lee, eds. *Dictionary of National Biography.* 63 vols. London: Smith, Elder and Co., 1885–1900.

Terry, Michael, ed. *Reader's Guide to Judaism.* New York: Routledge, 2000.

Wordsworth, Christopher, ed. *Lives of Eminent Men connected with the History of Religion in England.* 4 vols. London: J. G. & F. Rivington, 1839.

Additional Works for Individual Sketches

Akin, Daniel L. "An Expositional Analysis of the Schleitheim Confession." *Criswell Theological Review* 2 (1988): 345-70.

Bald, R. C. *John Donne: A Life.* Oxford: Oxford University Press, 1970.

Burke, David G. "The Enduring Significance of the KJV." *Word and World* 31, no. 3 (2011): 229-44.

Campbell, Gordon. *Bible: The Story of the King James Version, 1611–2011.* Oxford: Oxford University Press, 2010.

Doornkaat Koolman, J ten. "The First Edition of Peter Riedemann's 'Rechenschaft.'" *Mennonite Quarterly Review* 36, no. 2 (1962): 169-70.

Fischlin, Daniel and Mark Fortier, eds. *Royal Subjects: Essays on the Writings of James VI and I.* Detroit: Wayne State University Press, 2002.

Fishbane, Michael A. "Teacher and the Hermeneutical Task: A Reinterpretation of Medieval Exegesis." *Journal of the American Academy of Religion* 43, no. 4 (1975): 709-21.

Friedmann, Robert. "Second Generation Anabaptism as Illustrated by the Walpot Era of the Hutterites." *Mennonite Quarterly* 44, no. 4 (1970): 390-93.

Frymire, John M. *The Primacy of the Postils: Catholics, Protestants, and the Dissemination of Ideas in Early Modern Germany.* Leiden: Brill, 2010.

Furcha, Edward J. "Key Concepts in Caspar von Schwenckfeld's Thought, Regeneration and the

New Life." *Church History* 37, no. 2 (1968): 160-73.

Greaves, Richard L. *Society and Religion in Elizabethan England.* Minneapolis: University of Minnesota, 1981.

Greiffenberg, Catharina Regina von. *Meditations on the Incarnation, Passion and Death of Jesus Christ.* Edited and translated by Lynne Tatlock. The Other Voice in Early Modern Europe. Chicago: University of Chicago Press, 2009.

Grendler, Paul. "Italian biblical humanism and the papacy, 1515-1535." In *Biblical Humanism and Scholasticism in the Age of Erasmus.* Edited by Erika Rummel, 225-76. Leiden: Brill, 2008.

Heiden, Albert van der. "Pardes: Methodological Reflections on the Theory of the Four Senses." *Journal of Jewish Studies* 34, no. 2 (1983): 147-59.

Hendrix, Scott H., ed. and trans. *Early Protestant Spirituality.* New York: Paulist Press, 2009.

Hvolbek, Russell H. "Being and Knowing: Spiritualist Epistelmology and Anthropology from Schwenckfeld to Böhme." *Sixteenth Century Journal* 22, no. 1 (1991): 97-110.

Kahle, Paul. "Felix Pratensis—a Prato, Felix. Der Herausgeber der Ersten Rabbinerbibel, Venedig 1516/7." *Die Welt des Orients* 1, no. 1 (1947): 32-36.

Kelly, Joseph Francis. *The Ecumenical Councils of the Catholic Church: A History.* Collegeville, MN: Liturgical Press, 2009.

Lake, Peter. *The Boxmaker's Revenge: "Orthodoxy", "Heterodox" and the Politics of the Parish in Early Stuart London.* Stanford, CA: Stanford University Press, 2001.

Lockhart, Paul Douglas. *Frederick II and the Protestant Cause: Denmark's Role in the Wars of Religion, 1559–1596.* Leiden: Brill, 2004.

Lubac, Henri de. *Medieval Exegesis: The Four Senses of Scripture.* 3 vols. Translated by Mark Sebanc and E. M. Macierowski. Grand Rapids: Eerdmans, 1998–2009.

McKinley, Mary B. "Volume Editor's Introduction." In *Epistle to Marguerite of Navarre and Preface to a Sermon by John Calvin,* edited and translated by Mary B. McKiney. Chicago: University of Chicago Press, 2004.

Norton, David. *A Textual History of the King James Bible.* New York: Cambridge University Press, 2005

Packull, Werner O. "The Origins of Peter Riedemann's Account of Our Faith." *Sixteenth Century Journal* 30, no. 1 (1999): 61-69.

Papazian, Mary Arshagouni, ed. *John Donne and the Protestant Reformation: New Perspectives.* Detroit: Wayne State University Press, 2003.

Paulicelli, Eugenia. "Sister Arcangela Tarabotti: Hair, Wigs and Other Vices." In *Writing Fashion in Early Modern Italy: From Sprezzatura to Satire,* by idem, 177-204. Farnham, Surrey, UK: Ashgate, 2014.

Pragman, James H. "The Augsburg Confession in the English Reformation: Richard Taverner's Contribution." *Sixteenth Century Journal* 11, no. 3 (1980): 75-85.

Rashi. *Rashi's Commentary on Psalms.* Translated by Mayer I. Gruber. Atlanta: Scholars Press, 1998.

Reid, Jonathan A. *King's Sister—Queen of Dissent: Marguerite of Navarre (1492–1549) and her Evangelical Network.* Leiden: Brill, 2009.

Spinka, Matthew. *John Hus: A Biography.* Princeton, NJ: Princeton University Press, 1968.

———. *John Hus at the Council of Constance.* New York: Columbia University Press, 1968.

———. *John Hus and the Czech Reform.* Hamden, CT: Archon Books, 1966.

Steinmetz, David C. *Reformers in the Wings: From Geiler von Kayserberg to Theodore Beza.* Oxford: Oxford University Press, 2000.

———. "The Superiority of Pre-Critical Exegesis." *Theology Today* 37, no. 1 (1980): 27-38.

Synder, C. Arnold. "The Confession of the Swiss Brethren in Hesse, 1578." In *Anabaptism Revisited: Essays on Anabaptist/Mennonite Studies in Honor of C. J. Dyck.* Edited by Walter Klaassen, 29-49. Waterloo, ON; Scottdale, PA: Herald Press, 1992.

———. "The Schleitheim Articles in Light of the Revolution of the Common Man: Continuation or Departure?" *Sixteenth Century Journal* 16, no. 4 (1985): 419-30.

Todd, Margo. "Bishops in the Kirk: William Cowper of Galloway and the Puritan Episcopacy of Scotland." *Scottish Journal of Theology,* 57 (2004): 300-312.

Van Liere, Frans. *An Introduction to the Medieval Bible.* New York: Cambridge University Press, 2014.

Voogt, Gerrit. "Remonstrant-Counter-Remonstrant Debates: Crafting a Principled Defense of Toleration after the Synod of Dordrecht (1619–1650)." *Church History and Religious Culture* 89, no. 4

(2009): 489-524.

Wallace, Dewey D. Jr. "George Gifford, Puritan Propaganda and Popular Religion in Elizabethan England." *Sixteenth Century Journal* 9, no. 1 (1978): 27-49.

Wengert, Timothy J. "'Fear and Love' in the Ten Commandments." *Concordia Journal* 21, no. 1 (1995): 14-27.

———. "Philip Melanchthon and John Calvin against Andreas Osiander: Coming to Terms with Forensic Justification." In *Calvin and Luther: The Continuing Relationship*, edited by R. Ward Holder, 63-87. Göttingen: Vandenhoeck & Ruprecht, 2013.

Wilkinson, Robert J. *Tetragrammaton: Western Christians and the Hebrew Name of God.* Leiden: Brill, 2015.

BIBLIOGRAPHY

Primary Sources and Translations Used in the Volume

Arminius, Jacobus. *The Works of James Arminius.* 3 vols. Translated by James Nichols and W. R. Bagnall. Auburn, NY: Derby, Miller and Orton, 1853. Digital copy online at archive.org.

Beza, Theodore. *Theodori Bezae Annotationes majores in Novum Dn. Nostri Jesu Christi Testamentum.* 2 vols. Geneva: Jeremie des Planches, 1594. Digital copy online at www.e-rara.ch.

Brenz, Johannes. *Erklerung der Epistel S. Pauls an die Römer.* Translated by Jakob Gretter. Frankfurt am Main: Peter Braubach, 1566. Digital copy online at books.google.com.

———. *Godly Magistrates and Church Order: Johannes Brenz and the Establishment of the Lutheran Territorial Church in Germany (1524–1559).* Translated and edited by James M. Estes. Toronto: Centre for Reformation and Renaissance Studies, 2001.

———. *Kurtze Ausslegung der Epistel, so nach altem Brauch auff einen jeden Sontag in der Kirchen für gelesen werden.* Translated by Jacobus Gretter. Frankfurt am Main: Peter Braubach, 1560. Digital copy online at www.gateway-bayern.de.

———. *Werke: Eine Studienausgabe.* 3 vols. Edited by Martin Brecht and Gerhard Schäfer. Tübingen: Mohr Siebeck, 1970–1986.

Bucer, Martin. *Common Places of Martin Bucer.* Translated by David F. Wright. Appleford, UK: Sutton Courtenay Press, 1972.

———. *Loci communes in usus Sacrae Theologiae.* Basel: Johann Herwagen, 1560.

———. *Metaphrasis et Enarratio in Epistolam D. Pauli Apostoli ad Romanos.* Basel: Peter Perna, 1562. Digital copy online at www.gateway-bayern.de.

Bugenhagen, Johannes. *In epistolam Pauli ad Romanos interpretatio.* Edited by Ambrose Moibanus. Hagenau: Johannes Setzer, 1527.

Bullinger, Heinrich. *In Sanctissimam Pauli ad Rhomanos Epistolam.* Zurich: Christoph Froschauer, 1533. Digital copy online at www.e-rara.ch.

Cajetan, Cardinal (Thomas de Vio). *Opera omnia qvotqvot in Sacrae Scripturae expositionem reperiuntur.* 5 vols. Lyons: Jean and Pierre Prost, 1639. Digital copy online at books.google.com.

Calvin, John. *Commentaries on the Epistle of Paul the Apostle to the Romans.* Translated and edited by John Owen. CTS 38. Edinburgh: Calvin Translation Society, 1849.

———. *Institutes of the Christian Religion (1559).* Edited by John T. McNeill. Translated by Ford Lewis Battles. LCC 20–21. Philadelphia: Westminster, 1960. Latin text available in CO 2 (1864).

———. *Ioannis Calvini Opera quae supersunt omnia.* 59 vols. Corpus Reformatorum 29–88. Edited by G. Baum, E. Cunitz and E. Reuss. Brunswick and Berlin: C. A. Schwetschke, 1863–1900. Digital copy online at archive-ouverte.unige.ch/unige:650.

———. *Supplementa Calviniana: Sermon inédits.* 11 vols. planned. Neukirchen-Vluyn: Neukirchener Verlag; Geneva: Droz, 1961–.

Colet, John. *An Exposition of St. Paul's Epistle to the Romans (1497).* Edited by J. H. Lupton. London: Bell & Daldy, 1873.

Denck, Hans. *Selected Writings of Hans Denck 1500–1527*. Edited and translated by E. J. Furcha. Lewiston, NY: Edwin Mellen Press, 1989.

Dentière, Marie. *Epistle to Marguerite de Navarre; and, Preface to a Sermon by John Calvin*. Edited and translated by Mary B. McKinley. Chicago: University of Chicago Press, 2004.

Donne, John. *The Works of John Donne*. 6 vols. Edited by Henry Alford. London: John Parker, 1839. Digital copy online at books.google.com.

Downame, John, ed. *Annotations upon all the Books of the Old and New Testament*. London: Evan Tyler, 1657. Digital copy online at EEBO.

Eck, Johann. *Christenliche Predigen*. 5 vols. Ingolstadt: Apian, 1530–1539. Digital copy online at www.gateway-bayern.de.

Erasmus, Desiderius. *Annotations on Romans*. Edited by Robert D. Sider. Translated by John B. Payne et al. CWE 56. Toronto: University of Toronto Press, 1994.

———. *Paraphrases on Romans and Galatians*. Edited by Robert D. Sider. Translated by John B. Payne, Albert Rabil Jr. and Warren S. Smith Jr. CWE 42. Toronto: University of Toronto Press, 1984.

Erasmus, Desiderius, and Martin Luther. *Luther and Erasmus: Free Will and Salvation*. Edited and translated by Gordon E. Rupp and Philip S. Watson. LCC 17. Philadelphia: Westminster, 1969.

Friedmann, Robert, ed. *Glaubenszeugnisse oberdeutscher Taufgesinnter II*. QGT 12. Gütersloh: Gerd Mohn, 1967.

Gwalther, Rudolf. *In D. Pauli Apostoli Epistolam ad Romanos homiliae*. Zurich: Christoph Froschauer, 1580. Digital copy online at www.gateway-bayern.de.

———. *Von der heiligen Gschrifft und irem ursprung, desglychen in was wirde und ansähens die selbig sye und zuo was nutzes sy uns menschen dienen solle, etc.* Zurich: Christoph Froschauer, 1553. Digital copy online at books.google.com

Hesshus, Tilemann. *Explicatio Epistolae Pauli ad Romanos*. Jena: Gunther Huttich, 1571. Digital copy online at www.gateway-bayern.de.

Hooper, John. *Certain and Most Necessary Annotations upon the Thirteenth Chapter of Romans*. Somerset: Rupert Waldegrave, 1583. Digital copy online at EEBO.

Hubmaier, Balthasar. *Balthasar Hubmaier: Theologian of Anabaptism*. Translated and edited by H. Wayne Pipkin and John H. Yoder. CRR 5. Scottdale, PA: Herald Press, 1989.

———. *Schriften*. Edited by Gunnar Westin and Torsten Bergsten. QGT 9. Gütersloh: Gerd Mohn, 1962.

Joris, David. *The Anabaptist Writings of David Joris, 1535–1543*. Edited and translated by Gary K. Waite. CRR 7. Scottdale, PA: Herald Press, 1993.

Kolb, Robert, and Timothy J. Wengert, eds. *The Book of Concord: The Confessions of the Evangelical Lutheran Church*. Translated by Charles Arand et al. Minneapolis: Fortress, 2000.

Koop, Karl, ed. *Confessions of Faith in the Anabaptist Tradition 1527–1660*. Translated by Cornelius J. Dyck et al. CRR 11. Kitchener, ON: Pandora Press, 2006.

Lefèvre d'Etaples, Jacques. *Epistola ad Rhomanos*. Paris: H. Stephanus, 1512. Digital copy online at www.gateway-bayern.de.

Luther, Martin. *D. Martin Luthers Werke, Kritische Gesamtausgabe: Deutsche Bibel*. 12 vols. Weimar: Böhlaus Nachfolger, 1906–1961. Digitial copy online at archive.org.

———. *D. Martin Luthers Werke, Kritische Gesamtausgabe: [Schriften]*. 73 vols. Weimar: Hermann Böhlaus Nachfolger, 1883–2009. Digital copy online at archive.org.

———. *D. Martin Luthers Werke, Kritische Gesamtausgabe: Tischreden*. 6 vols. Weimar: Hermann Böhlaus Nachfolger, 1912–1921. Digital copy online at archive.org.

———. *Luther's Works*. American ed. 82 vols. planned. St. Louis: Concordia; Philadelphia: Fortress, 1955–1986; 2009–.

Marguerite de Navarre. *Selected Writings*. Translated by Rouben Cholakian and Mary Skemp. Chicago: University of Chicago Press, 2008.

Melanchthon, Philipp. *Commentary on Romans*. Translated by Fred Kramer. St. Louis: Concordia, 1992.

———. *Philippi Melanthonis Opera quae supersunt omnia*. 28 vols. Corpus Reformatorum 1–28. Edited by C. G. Bretschneider. Halle: C. A. Schwetschke, 1834–1860. Digital copies online at archive.org and books.google.com.

———. *Verlegung etlicher unchristlicher Artikel: Welche die Widerteuffer furgeben*. Wittenberg: Georg Rhau, 1534. Digital copy online at www.gateway-bayern.de.

Müntzer, Thomas. *Schriften und Briefe: Kritische Gesamtausgabe*. Edited by Paul Kirn and Günther Franz. Gütersloh: Gerd Mohn, 1968.

Musculus, Wolfgang. *In epistolam Apostoli Pauli ad Romanos commentarii*. Basel: Johannes Herwagen, 1562. Digital copy online at www.gateway-bayern.de.

Oecolampadius, Johannes. *In epistolam B. Pauli Apostoli ad Rhomanos adnotationes*. Basel: Andreas Cratander, 1525. Digital copy online at www.e-rara-ch.

Pareus, David. *In divinam ad Romanos S. Pauli apostoli Epistolam commentarius*. Frankfurt am Main: Johann Rhodius, 1608. Digital copy online at www.gateway-bayern.de.

Philips, Dirk. *The Writings of Dirk Philips 1504–1568*. Edited by Cornelius J. Dyck, William E. Keeney and Alvin J. Beachy. CRR 6. Scottdale, PA: Herald Press, 1992.

Rempel, John D., ed. *Jörg Maler's Kunstbuch: Writings of the Pilgram Marpeck Circle*. CRR 12. Kitchener, ON: Pandora Press, 2010.

Riedemann, Peter. *Peter Riedemann's Hutterite Confession of Faith: Translation of the 1565 German Edition of Confession of Our Religion, Teaching and Faith by the Brothers Who Are Known as the Hutterites*. Edited and translated by John J. Friesen. CRR 9. Scottdale, PA: Herald Press, 1999.

Sattler, Michael. *The Legacy of Michael Sattler*. Translated and edited by John H. Yoder. CRR 1. Scottdale, PA: Herald Press, 1973.

Schaff, Philip. *The Creeds of Christendom: With a Critical History and Notes*. 3 vols. New York: Harper & Row, 1877. Reprint, Grand Rapids: Baker, 1977. Accessible online at ccel.org.

Simons, Menno. *The Complete Writings of Menno Simons*. Edited by John Christian Wenger. Scottdale, PA: Herald Press, 1956.

Snyder, C. Arnold. *Sources of South German/Austrian Anabaptism*. Translated by Walter Klaassen, Frank Friesen and Werner O. Packull. CRR 10. Kitchener, ON: Pandora Press, 2001.

Soto, Domingo de. *In Epistolam divi Pauli ad Romanos commentarii*. Antwerp: Steelsius, 1550. Digital copy online at www.gateway-bayern.de.

Spangenberg, Cyriacus. *Aüßlegung der Letsten Acht Capitel der Episteln S. Pauli an die Römer*. Strasbourg: Emmel, 1569. Digital copy online at www.gateway-bayern.de.

Spangenberg, Johann. [*Postilla Teüsch:*] *Austegung der Episteln, so auff die Sonntage vom Advent biß auff Ostern in der Kirchen gelesen werden*. Postilla Teüsch 4. Magdeburg: Michael Lotter, 1544. Digital copy online at www.gateway-bayern.de.

Spangenberg, Johann and Johannes Craendonch. *Wintertheil. Der Postillen oder ausslegurg Sontagischer Episteln and Evalgelien, auch der fürnemsten Festen . . . Churfürstlichestad Meyntz* (Electoral City of Mainz): Frantz Behem, 1567.

Staupitz, Johann von. *Libellus de Executione eterne predestinationis*. Nuremberg: Federicus Peypus, 1517. Digital copy online at www.gateway-bayern.de.

Tyndale, William. *The Work of William Tyndale*. Edited by G. E. Duffield. Philadelphia: Fortress, 1965.

Valdes, Juan de. *Commentario, o declarcion breve, y compediosa sobre la Epistola de S. Paulo Apostol a los Romanos*. Venice: Juan Philadelpho, 1556. Digital copy online at books.google.com.

———. *Juan de Valdes' Commentary upon St. Paul's Epistle to the Romans*. Translated by John T. Betts. London: Trübner, 1883. Digital copy online at archive.org.

———. *Valdés' Two Catechisms: The Dialogue on Christian Doctrine and the Christian Instruction for Children*. Translated by William B. and Carol D. Jones. Edited by José C. Nieto. Lawrence, KS: Coronado Press, 1981.

Vermigli, Peter Martyr. *In epistolam S. Pauli Apostoli ad Romanos*. Basel: Pietro Perna, 1558. Digital copy online at www.e-rara.ch.

———. *Most Learned and Fruitfull Commentaries of D. Peter Martir Vermilius . . . upon the Epistle of S. Paul to the Romanes*. Translated by Henry Billingsley. London: John Daye, 1568. Digital copy online at EEBO.

Wild, Johann. *Exegesis in Epistolam Pauli ad Romanos*. Mainz: Franciscus Behem, 1558. Digital copy online at www.gateway-bayern.de.

Williams, George H., and Angel M. Mergal, eds. *Spiritual and Anabaptist Writers*. LCC 25. Philadelphia: Westminster, 1957.

Wilson, Thomas. *A Commentarie upon the Most Divine Epistle of S. Paul to the Romanes*. London: W. Iaggard, 1614.

Zwingli, Huldrych. *In plerosque Novi Testamenti Libros*. Zurich: Christoph Froschauer, 1581. Digital copy online at books.google.com.

Zwingli, Huldrych, and Heinrich Bullinger. *Zwingli and Bullinger*. Translated and edited by Geoffrey W. Bromiley. LCC 24. Philadelphia: Westminster, 1953.

Other Works Consulted

Allen, Michael, and Jonathan A. Linebaugh, eds. *Reformation Readings of Paul: Explorations in History and Exegesis*. Downers Grove, IL: IVP Academic, 2015.

Althaus, Paul. *The Ethics of Martin Luther*. Translated by Robert C. Schultz. Philadelphia: Fortress, 1972.

———. *The Theology of Martin Luther*. Translated by Robert C. Schultz. Philadelphia: Fortress, 1963.

Beckwith, Carl L, ed. *Ezekiel, Daniel*. RCS OT 12. Downers Grove, IL: IVP Academic, 2012.

Bettenson, Henry, and Chris Maunder, eds. *Documents of the Christian Church*. 3rd ed. Oxford: Oxford University Press, 1999.

Bray, Gerald L., ed. *Galatians, Ephesians*. RCS NT 10. Downers Grove, IL: IVP Academic, 2011.

———. ed. *Romans*. ACCS NT 6. Downers Grove, IL: InterVarsity Press, 1998.

Britz, Dolf. "Politics and Social Life." In *The Calvin Handbook*, edited by Herman J. Selderhuis, 435-48. Grand Rapids: Eerdmans, 2009.

Brown, Peter. *Augustine of Hippo: A Biography*. Berkeley: University of California Press, 1967.

Bullinger, Heinrich. *In divinum Iesu Christi Domini nostri Euangelium secundum Ioannem, Commentariorum libri X*. Zurich: Froschauer, 1543. Digital copy online at www.e-rara.ch.

Calvin, John. "Apology of John Calvin to Messrs. the Nicodemites upon the Complaint That They Make of His Too Great Rigour (1544)." Translated by Eric Kayayan. *Calvin Theological Journal* 29, no. 2 (1994): 346-63.

———. *Commentaries on the Epistles of Paul the Apostle to the Corinthians*. 2 vols. Translated and edited by John Pringle. CTS 39–40. Edinburgh: Calvin Translation Society, 1848–1849. Digital copy online at archive.org.

Cooper, Derek, and Martin J. Lohrmann, eds. *1–2 Samuel, 1–2 Kings, 1–2 Chronicles*. RCS OT 5. Downers Grove, IL: IVP Academic, 2016.

Chung-Kim, Esther, and Todd R. Hains, eds. *Acts*. RCS NT 6. Downers Grove, IL: IVP Academic, 2014.

Cranfield, C. E. B. *A Critical and Exegetical Commentary on the Epistle to the Romans*. 2 vols. International Critical Commentary. Edinburg: T&T Clark, 1985.

———. *Romans: A Shorter Commentary*. Grand Rapids: Eerdmans, 1985.

Donaldson, Amy M. "Explicit References to New Testament Variant Readings Among Greek and Latin Church Fathers." PhD diss., University of Notre Dame, 2009. Digital copy online at curate.nd.edu.

Eustathius of Thessalonica. *Commentarii ad Homeri Iliadem*. 4 vols. Leipzig: J. A. G. Weigel, 1827–1830. Digital copy online at babel.hathitrust.org.

Farmer, Craig S., ed. *John 1–12*. RCS NT 4. Downers Grove, IL: IVP Academic, 2014.

Ferrero, Anna Maria. "Lost and Fragmentary Works." In *Brill's Companion to Seneca: Philosopher and Dramatist*, edited by Gregor Damschen and Andreas Heil, 207-12. Leiden: Brill, 2013.

Finger, Thomas N. *A Contemporary Anabaptist Theology: Biblical, Historical, Constructive*. Downers Grove, IL: InterVarsity Press, 2004.

Fitzmyer, Joseph A. *First Corinthians: A New Translation with Introduction and Commentary*. Anchor Bible 32. New Haven, CT: Yale University Press, 2008.

———. *Romans: A New Translation with Introduction and Commentary*. Anchor Bible 33. New York: Doubleday, 1993.

Gerrish, Brian A. "Piety, Theology and the Lutheran Dogma: Erasmus's Book on Free Will." In *The Old Protestantism and the New: Essays on the Reformation Heritage*, 11-26. Chicago: University of Chicago Press, 1982.

Goldingay, John. *Psalms*. 3 vols. *Baker Commentary on the Old Testament Wisdom and Psalms*. Grand Rapids: Baker Academic, 2006.

Gordon, Bruce. *Calvin*. New Haven, CT: Yale University Press, 2009.

Green, Lowell C. "The 'Third Use of the Law' and Elert's Position." *Logia* 22, no. 2 (2013): 27-33.

Gritsch, Eric. *Martin Luther's Anti-Semitism: Against His Better Judgment*. Grand Rapids: Eerdmans, 2012.

Haile, H. G. *Luther: An Experiment in Biography*. New York: Doubleday, 1980.

Heine, Ronald E., trans. and ed. *The Commentaries of Origen and Jerome on St. Paul's Epistles to the Ephesians*. Oxford: Oxford University Press, 2002.

Hesshus, Tilemann. *Commentarius in libros Psalmorum*. Helmstadt: Lucius, 1586. Digital copy online at www.gateway-bayern.de.

Hobbs, R. Gerald. "Conrad Pellican and the Psalms: The Ambivalent Legacy of a Pioneer Hebraist." *Reformation & Renaissance Review* 1, no. 1 (1999): 72-99.

Holder, R. Ward. "Introduction—Paul in the Sixteenth Century: Invitation and a Challenge." In *A Companion to Paul in the Reformation*, edited by R. Ward Holder, 1-12. Leiden: Brill, 2009.

Josephus. *Jewish Antiquities, Volume 6: Books 14–15*. Translated by Ralph Marcus and Allen Wikgren. LCL 489. Cambridge, MA: Harvard University Press, 1943.

Kolb, Robert. "God's Select Vessel and Chosen Instrument: The Interpretation of Paul in Late Reformation Lutheran Theologians." In *A Companion to Paul in the Reformation*, edited by R. Ward Holder, 187-211. Leiden: Brill, 2009.

Kraus, Hans-Joachim. *Psalms 1–59: A Commentary*. Continental Commentaries. Translated by Hilton C. Oswald. Minneapolis: Augsburg, 1988.

Kreitzer, Beth, ed. *Luke*. RCS NT 3. Downers Grove, IL: IVP Academic, 2015.

Krey, Philip D. W. and Peter D. S. Krey, eds. *Luther's Spirituality*. New York: Paulist Press, 2007.

Lefèvre d'Étaples, Jacques. *Commentarii initiatorii in quatuor Evangelia*. Basel: Andreas Cratander, 1523. Digital copy online at www.e-rara.ch.

Levering, Matthew. *Predestination: Biblical and Theological Paths*. Oxford: Oxford University Press, 2011.

———. *The Theology of Augustine: An Introductory Guide to His Most Important Works*. Grand Rapids: Baker Academic, 2013.

Livy. *History of Rome: Books 1–2*. Translated by B. O. Foster. LCL 114. Cambridge, MA: Harvard University Press, 1919.

Luy, David J. *Dominus Mortus: Martin Luther on the Incorruptibility of God in Christ*. Minneapolis: Fortress, 2014.

Manetsch, Scott M., ed. *1 Corinthians*. RCS NT 9a. Downers Grove, IL: IVP Academic, forthcoming, 2017.

Mannermaa, Tuomo. *Two Kinds of Love: Martin Luther's Religious World*. Translated and edited by Kirsi Stjerna. Minneapolis: Fortress, 2010.

McGrath, Alister E. *Reformation Thought: An Introduction*, 4th ed. Oxford: Wiley-Blackwell, 2012.

Metzger, Bruce M. *A Textual Commentary on the Greek New Testament*. 2nd ed. Stuttgart: Deutsche Bibelgesellschaft, 1994.

Moo, Douglas J. *The Epistle to the Romans*. New International Commentary on the New Testament 38. Grand Rapids: Eerdmans, 1996.

Muller, Richard A. *Christ and the Decree: Christology and Predestination in Reformed Theology from Calvin to Perkins*. Grand Rapids: Baker Academic, 1986; reprint, 2008.

———. *Dictionary of Latin and Greek Theological Terms: Drawn Principally from Protestant Scholastic Theology*. Grand Rapids: Baker Academic, 1985.

Murray, Scott R. *Law, Life, and the Living God: The Third Use of the Law in Modern American Lutheranism*. St. Louis: Concordia, 2001.

Myers, Jason A. "Laws, Lies and Letter Writing: An Analysis of Jerome and Augustine on the Antioch Incident (Galatians 2:11-14)." *Scottish Journal of Theology* 66, no. 2 (2013): 127-39.

Oberman, Heiko A. *The Harvest of Medieval Theology: Gabriel Biel and Late Medieval Nominalism*. Grand Rapids: Baker Academic, 2000.

———. *The Roots of Anti-Semitism: In the Age of Renaissance and Reformation*. Translated by James I. Porter. Philadelphia: Fortress, 1984.

Oecumenius. *Commentary on the Apocalypse*. Translated by John N. Suggit. FC 112. Washington, DC: Catholic University of America Press, 2006.

Olson, Roger E. *Arminian Theology: Myths and Realities*. Downers Grove, IL: IVP Academic, 2006.

Origen. *Commentary on the Epistle to the Romans, Books 6–10*. Translated by Thomas P. Scheck. FC 104. Washington, DC: Catholic University of America Press, 2002.

Pareus, David. *In Genesin Mosis commentarius*. Frankfurt am Main: Johann Rhodius, 1609. Digital copy online at www.gateway-bayern.de.

Parker, T. H. L. *Commentaries on the Epistle to the Romans (1532–1542)*. Edinburgh: T&T Clark, 1986.

Pelikan, Jaroslav. *The Christian Tradition*. 5 vols. Chicago: University of Chicago Press, 1971–1989.

Plass, Ewald, ed. *What Luther Says: An Anthology*. 3 vols. St. Louis: Concordia, 1959.

Sallust. *The War with Catiline*. Edited by John T. Ramsey. Translated by J. C. Rolfe. LCL 116. Cambridge, MA: Harvard University Press, 2013.

Selderhuis, Herman J., ed. *Psalms 1–72*. RCS OT 7. Downers Grove, IL: IVP Academic, 2015.

Soto, Domingo de. *De natura et gratia*. Paris: Foucher, 1549. Digital copy online at www.gateway -bayern.de.

Spangenberg, Cyriacus. *Außlegung der Ersten Acht Capitel der Episteln S. Pauli an die Römer*. Strasbourg: Samuel Emmel, 1566. Digital copy online at books.google.com.

Spring, Carl P. E. *Luther's Aesop*. Kirksville, MO: Truman State University Press, 2011.

Stanglin, Keith D., and Thomas H. McCall. *Jacob Arminius: Theologian of Grace*. Oxford: Oxford University Press, 2012.

Steinmetz, David C. *Luther in Context*. 2nd ed. Grand Rapids: Baker Academic, 1995.

Suetonius. *Lives of the Caesars, Volume II: Claudius; Nero; Galba; Otho; Vitellius. Vespasian. Titus, Domitian. Lives of Illustrious Men: Grammarians and Rhetoricians. Poets. Lives of Pliny the Elder and Passienus Crispus*. Edited and translated by J. C. Rolfe. LCL 38. Cambridge, MA: Harvard University Press, 1914.

Tacitus. *Annals: Books 4–6, 11–12*. Translated by John Jackson. LCL 312. Cambridge, MA: Harvard University Press, 1937.

Thompson, John L., ed. *Genesis 1–11*. RCS OT 1. Downers Grove, IL: IVP Academic, 2012.

———.*John Calvin and the Daughters of Sarah: Women in Regular and Exceptional Roles in the Exegesis of Calvin, His Predecessors and His Contemporaries*. Geneva: Droz, 1992.

Tomlin, Graham, ed. *Philippians, Colossians*. RCS NT 11. Downers Grove, IL: IVP Academic, 2013.

Trapè, A. "Augustine of Hippo." In *Encyclopedia of Ancient Christianity*. 3 vols. Edited by Angelo Di Berardino, 1:292-99. Downers Grove, IL: IVP Academic, 2014.

Veen, Mirjam G. K. van. "Calvin and His Opponents." In *The Calvin Handbook*, edited by Herman J. Selderhuis, 156-64. Grand Rapids: Eerdmans, 2009.

Venema, Cornelius P. *Heinrich Bullinger and the Doctrine of Predestination: Author of "The Other Reformed Tradition"?* Grand Rapids: Eerdmans, 2002.

Vermigli, Peter Martyr. *In Selectissimam S. Pauli Apostoli Priorem ad Corinth. Epistolam . . . Commentarii doctissimi*. Zurich: Christoph Froschauer, 1551. Digital copy online at www.e-rara.ch.

Weinrich, William C., ed. *Revelation*. ACCS NT 12. Downers Grove, IL: InterVarsity Press, 2005.

Westerholm, Stephen. *Perspectives Old and New on Paul: The "Lutheran" Paul and His Critics*. Grand Rapids: Eerdmans, 2004.

Whitford, David M. "Robbing Paul to Pay Peter: The Reception of Paul in Sixteenth Century Political Theology." In *A Companion to Paul in the Reformation*, edited by R. Ward Holder, 573-606. Leiden: Brill, 2009.

Williams, George H. *The Radical Reformation*. 3rd ed. Kirksville, MO: Sixteenth Century Journal Publishers, 1992.

Author and Writings Index

Subject Index

Scripture Index